THE DEBATE BETWEEN SARTRE AND MERLEAU-PONTY

Northwestern University
Studies in Phenomenology
and
Existential Philosophy

THE DEBATE BETWEEN SARTRE AND MERLEAU-PONTY

Edited by
Jon Stewart

Northwestern University Press
Evanston, Illinois

Northwestern University Press
Evanston, Illinois 60208–4210

Printed in the United States of America

ISBN 0–8101-1531-X (cloth)
ISBN 0–8101-1532–8 (paper)

Library of Congress Cataloging-in-Publication Data

The debate between Sartre and Merleau-Ponty / edited by Jon Stewart.
p. cm. — (Northwestern University studies in phenomenology and existential philosophy)
Includes bibliographical references (p.).
ISBN 0–8101-1531-X (cloth). — ISBN 0–8101-1532–8 (pbk.)
1. Sartre, Jean Paul, 1905– . 2. Merleau-Ponty, Maurice, 1908–1961. I. Stewart, Jon (Jon Bartley) II. Series: Northwestern University studies in phenomenology & existential philosophy.
B2430.S34D36 1998
194—dc21 98–24673
CIP

The paper used in this publication meets the minimum requirements of the American National Standard for Information Sciences—Permanence of Paper for Printed Library Materials, ANSI Z39.48–1984.

Contents

Acknowledgments

This collection would not have been possible if it were not for the generosity of the following journals and publishing houses in granting the reprint rights for the essays included here: Colorado Associated University Press, George Borchardt Agency, *Dialogue,* Duquesne University Press, *French Studies, Human Inquiries,* Humanities Press International, *International Studies in Philosophy, Journal of Phenomenological Psychology, Journal of Philosophy, Journal of the British Society for Phenomenology,* Open Court, *Philosophical Forum, Philosophical Studies, Philosophy and Phenomenological Research, Philosophy Research Archives,* and *Philosophy Today.* I would like to thank the Belgian American Educational Foundation for a generous research grant in the 1993–94 academic year, which enabled me to do much of the work for this collection at the Université Libre de Bruxelles and the Katholieke Universiteit in Louvain, Belgium.

I am deeply grateful to Professor Marc Richir of the Université Libre and the Collège International de Philosophie in Paris for his invaluable supervision of my work on Sartre and Merleau-Ponty. The project also owes much to Professor Rudolf Bernet from the Katholieke Universiteit in Louvain and Professor Jacques Taminiaux from the Centre d'Études Phénoménologiques at Louvain-la-Neuve, both of whom I thank for their interest and support. In addition, I would like to thank Professors Robert B. Pippin and Frederick A. Olafson for their active encouragement of the project. I am also grateful to the contributors for their willing participation, positive feedback, and suggestions on the various aspects of this collection. A special thanks is in order for Niels Jørgen Cappelørn, Director of the Søren Kierkegaard Research Centre, for his unwavering support of this and countless other projects.

I would also like to thank Stacey Ake for her useful suggestions and help with the proofreading. The project would not have been possible, were it not for the computer expertise of Karsten Kynde, whom I thank for his infinite patience with me. Finally, I would like to thank my brother, Loy Stewart, for his constant support and encouragement of all of my academic endeavors.

Introduction

Jon Stewart

The thought and biographical relation between Jean-Paul Sartre and Maurice Merleau-Ponty has been a complex one which has not always attracted the attention that it is due in Anglophone philosophy, despite the importance and status of the two men in French intellectual life in this century. They were both acquainted with and worked alongside the leading intellectual figures in the French-speaking world and elsewhere during an extremely rich period in the history of French letters. Moreover, they lived during one of the most volatile epochs in European history, which included the Russian and Chinese Revolutions, the two World Wars as well as the Korean, Vietnam, and Algerian conflicts. An understanding of the development of their relationship is important in any attempt to come to terms with their respective philosophies. The present collection attempts to illuminate various aspects of this relationship. Articles from leading scholars of French phenomenology and existentialism have been assembled and ordered according to theme. In addition, a number of primary texts from Sartre, Merleau-Ponty, and Simone de Beauvoir have been reprinted here due to their relevance for the debate. By way of introduction, I would like to sketch briefly the biographical points of contact between the two men. This will allow us to situate their texts in the appropriate historical context and to indicate how the essays featured here treat these points of overlap.

I. Biographical Overview of the Relation between Sartre and Merleau-Ponty

The relationship between Sartre and Merleau-Ponty can, for the sake of convenience, be divided into three distinct periods. First, there was an extended period of friendship and collaboration which began with their initial contact as students in Paris at the École Normale Supérieure in 1927 and which ended in 1953 with an open break between the two men marked by Merleau-Ponty's resignation as coeditor of the famous political and literary review, *Les Temps modernes*. Second, there was the period of open enmity in which Merleau-Ponty's most virulent attack on Sartre appears in his *Adventures of the Dialectic* in 1955. Finally, there ensued a period of rapprochement which began in 1956 when Sartre and Merleau-Ponty saw each other for virtually the first time since Merleau-Ponty's resignation from the journal and effected a partial reconciliation which lasted until Merleau-Ponty's sudden death in 1961.

Without a doubt, the most important source of information for the biographical development of the relation between the two men is Sartre's longish essay, entitled "Merleau-Ponty vivant," which was written for *Les Temps modernes* as a sort of eulogy shortly after Merleau-Ponty's death.[1] There, Sartre canvasses the entire history of their association and goes into some detail about their personal and political differences. This essay is invaluable for an understanding of the relation of the two men and thus has been included in the present collection. Although Sartre insists that his reminiscences are sincere, thereby implying that his account contains some measure of objectivity, nonetheless he is naturally limited to telling the story from his own perspective, and it is regrettable that we do not have a similar account from Merleau-Ponty's hand to balance the interpretation given by Sartre. This is particularly unfortunate given the fact that there is right from the start considerably less biographical information on Merleau-Ponty than on Sartre. Nonetheless we are fortunate to have at our disposal a wealth of recently published material on or by Sartre, which includes biographies,[2] interviews,[3] notebooks,[4] and letters,[5] that help us to fill out the biographical information provided in his own published account.

A. Friendship and Collaboration (1927–53)

Acquaintance at the École Normale Supérieure

The friendship between Sartre and Merleau-Ponty goes back to their days as students at the famous École Normale Supérieure in Paris in 1927. Sartre at the age of nineteen entered the École in 1924 and Merleau-Ponty three years later in 1927. At this elite Parisian school, in addition to Sartre and Merleau-Ponty, there were a number of other gifted young students who would later take their place as the next generation of

French intellectuals: Simone de Beauvoir, Claude Lévi-Strauss, Simone Weil, Raymond Aron, Jean Hyppolite, and others. In an essay written in 1947 and reprinted in *Sense and Non-Sense,*[6] Merleau-Ponty anecdotally describes his first encounter with Sartre: "I met him one day twenty years ago when the École Normale unleashed its fury against one of my classmates and myself for having hissed the traditional songs too vulgar to suit us. He slipped between us and our persecutors and contrived a way for us to get out of our heroic and ridiculous situation without concessions or damages."[7] This first encounter began a relationship that would last long beyond Sartre's departure from the École in 1929 after his *agrégation.*

In February 1929, Husserl gave lectures in German at the Sorbonne on transcendental phenomenology which Merleau-Ponty attended.[8] Although he hardly knew German at the time, this encounter seems to have been important in inspiring him to study Husserl's work more carefully in the years to come. In addition to attending Husserl's lectures, Merleau-Ponty was also present at Gurvitch's courses on German philosophy from 1928–30, which included treatments of Husserl and Heidegger. The growing influence of Husserl's philosophy in France received an additional stimulus when the German philosopher's lectures were published in a French translation in 1931.[9] Sartre, who had already left the École, became interested in Husserl only later when Raymond Aron introduced him to the basic concepts of phenomenology and urged him to apply for a fellowship to pursue research in Germany.[10]

One interesting personal event took place during this period, which seems to have escaped the notice of many commentators, and which Sartre fails to mention in "Merleau-Ponty vivant." Nevertheless the episode in question appears to have been significant in many ways for the later relationship between the two men. Simone de Beauvoir recounts the melancholy story in her *Memories of a Dutiful Daughter,* in which she portrays the young Merleau-Ponty under the anonym "Jean Pradelle."[11] It was de Beauvoir who around 1929 introduced Merleau-Ponty to her best friend from infancy, Elizabeth Mabille, whom she refers to affectionately as "Zaza." A courtship quickly ensued, but when the deeply religious and conservative Madame Mabille got wind of Merleau-Ponty's advances, she enjoined him *per* letter to renounce his relation with her daughter and to desist from pursuing any further contact with her. When Merleau-Ponty docilely ceded to this demand, both Sartre and Simone de Beauvoir were shocked and deeply disappointed at what they perceived as a grave lack of character on his part. Years after the fact, in an interview with his official biographer, Sartre describes a certain hostility toward Merleau-Ponty originating from this event, a hostility which is not entirely consonant with his generally positive written account presented in "Merleau-Ponty vivant." In the interview in question, Sartre says, "True, we [sc. Simone de Beauvoir and himself] didn't like him [sc. Merleau-Ponty] very much. I thought he was too haughty, too arrogant. But we shared some philosophical positions and, during the war and early postwar periods, we had similar political positions. But influenced by what I knew of his disgusting cowardice towards Zaza, I remained aloof."[12] The most important thing that this event reveals is that there were personal conflicts and differences in temperament and character even before the highly charged philosophical and political disputes that would arise in the years to come and which Sartre discusses at length in "Merleau-Ponty vivant."

This initial period seems to have been marked more by common experiences and interests than by any genuinely warm friendship. In most comparative studies it is customary to allude to the friendship that reigned between Sartre and Merleau-Ponty during their carefree school days, with Merleau-Ponty's anecdote cited as evidence; however, the term "friendship" evokes a greater degree of familiarity than was ever actually the case. In fact, Sartre says directly, "At the École Normale, we knew each other without being friends."[13] In Sartre's unpublished account, he says in a similar fashion that their relationship at the École was not a warm one: "During our stay at the École Normale, we ignored each other. He was a day student, I was a boarder; he was delicate, I was coarse. And then above all, around this time, he was the one who believed in Heaven and I was he who did not believe."[14] Although Sartre and Merleau-Ponty were acquaintances at this early age, they, despite the anecdote recounted by Merleau-Ponty, do not seem to have been on particularly amicable terms, and it is easy to overestimate their friendship at this early stage based on their cooperative work at later periods. The most generous characterization that Sartre ever gave of his relation to Merleau-Ponty at this time was to say that it was a "vague friendship."[15]

Departure from the École

After their studies, the two men went their separate ways for a time. Sartre performed his obligatory eighteen-month military service from 1929 to 1930 at Saint-Cyr near Tours.[16] Then, in 1931, he began his teaching career at a *lycée* in Le Havre where he wrote what would later become the celebrated novel *Nausea*. He spent the academic year 1933–34 on a research grant in Berlin where he studied the works of Edmund Husserl.[17] It was this passion for Husserl which would later form a common bond between him and Merleau-Ponty.[18] He returned to Le Havre in 1934 where he resumed his post at the *lycée* and continued to digest the works of Husserl. In his article "The Transcendence of the Ego" from 1937, he took issue with Husserl's conception of a pure transcendental ego which stands behind consciousness, seeing in this doctrine a betrayal of Husserl's own phenomenological method. From this early period as well date his treatises *The Imagination* (1936) and *Sketch of a Theory of Emotions* (1939), both of which did much to pave the way for some of the key doctrines of *Being and Nothingness.* After spending the academic year 1936–37 as a teacher in Laon, Sartre took up a much more congenial position in Paris at the Lycée Pasteur de Neuilly. He would remain there until the mobilization in 1939 when he would be made a soldier once again.

Merleau-Ponty in his turn graduated in 1931 and pursued much the same course as Sartre. He completed his military service from 1930 to 1931 and began his teaching career at Lycée de Beauvais, where he remained until 1933. It was during this period that he began his study of Gestalt psychology and behaviorism. Lacking the leisure and the library resources necessary for undertaking a serious study of recent developments in experimental psychology, Merleau-Ponty applied for and received a research grant that carried a stipend of one year from the Caisse Nationale de la Recherche Scientifique.[19] At the completion of his fellowship, he resumed his teaching career in 1934 at the Lycée de Chartres, where he remained until 1935. It was during this period (1935–36) that Merleau-Ponty experienced a crisis of faith which led him to renounce the Christian beliefs of his youth. Sartre later recalls Merleau-Ponty's famous words in this context, "We believe that we believe, but we don't believe."[20] Merleau-Ponty's crisis was occasioned by the violence and conservatism of the Christian Socialists in Austria who seem to have alienated him considerably.[21] In 1935 he returned to Paris to his and Sartre's *alma mater,* the École Normale Supérieure. In 1936, Merleau-Ponty, in one of his first publications,[22] wrote a generally approving review of Sartre's *The Imagination.*[23] Merleau-Ponty's return to Paris afforded him the opportunity to attend the celebrated lectures on Hegel's *Phenomenology of Spirit* delivered by the Russian emigré Alexandre Kojève.[24] This also not coincidentally marks the period of Merleau-Ponty's first serious study of Marx. Merleau-Ponty taught at his post at the École Normale until his mobilization in 1939.

Of the separation after their school days Sartre would write,

> We lost sight of each other. He had a teaching post at Beauvais, I think, while I taught in Le Havre. Each of us, nevertheless, was preparing himself, without knowing it, for an encounter with the other. Each of us was trying to understand the world insofar as he could, and with the means at his disposal. And we had the same means—then called Husserl and Heidegger—since we were similarly disposed.[25]

Merleau-Ponty was primarily interested in Husserl's later unpublished works. In 1938 he was attracted by a special edition of the journal *Revue internationale de philosophie* which was dedicated to Husserl on the occasion of the death of the philosopher in that year.[26] In 1939 he went to Louvain in Belgium to consult unpublished manuscripts at the recently established Husserl Archives and was active through the years of the war, the Occupation, and later into the postwar period in establishing a Husserl Research Center in Paris at the Sorbonne and the library at the University of Paris in cooperation with the authorities at Louvain.[27]

The Onset of the War

In 1939, with the general mobilization, Sartre and Merleau-Ponty were called from their teaching posts and made soldiers. Sartre, after training at Nancy, was sent to the front in the southeast of France where he was occupied as a meteorological specialist. What this amounted to was launching weather balloons in order to test the strength and direction of the wind, information that would then be used by the officers for various ballistic purposes.[28] He remained aloof to his situation and, until the Germans attacked, spent much of his time writing during this period which he refers to as the *drôle de guerre*. On 21 June 1940, Sartre was taken prisoner[29] and sent to a prisoner of war camp in Trier in the west of Germany near the French border. Sartre's eight-month period as a prisoner of war is an interesting one. He came out of his isolation and intellectualism and seems to have thrived in the solidarity of the life of a prisoner.[30] Moreover, he fraternized with the priests in the camp, who were the only other intellectuals and the only other bachelors.[31] With them he read Heidegger's *Being and Time* daily.[32] It was in this context that Sartre began work on *Being and Nothingness*. According to one biographer, he wrote the first hundred pages in draft form at Trier.[33] Life in the camp furnished Sartre with a model for freedom and responsibility that he developed in this and later works.[34]

For Christmas 1940 while still in captivity, he wrote, directed and even acted in a stage drama called *Bariona*[35] which, although purportedly a simple Christmas play, contained hidden references to engagement and resistance.[36] He would say later,

> The important thing for me in that experience was that I was going to speak as a prisoner to other prisoners and bring up our common problems. The play was full of allusions to the situation we were in, and each one of us understood them perfectly well. In our minds, the Roman envoy to Jerusalem was the German. Our captors saw him as the Englishman in his colonies![37]

It was here that his interest in drama was awakened and that he first came upon the idea of a theater of resistance that he would later develop fully in *The Flies*.[38] He describes his realization as follows: "on this occasion, as I addressed my comrades across the footlights, speaking to them of their state as prisoners . . . I suddenly saw them so remarkably silent and attentive, I realized what theater ought to be—a great collective, religious phenomenon."[39] This realization would stamp his character in an important way, as is evinced by the fact that he campaigned for a *littérature engagée* after his departure from the camp, during the Occupation and the postwar years, and indeed for the rest of his life. Sartre remained in captivity until March of 1941, when he was released by virtue of a forged medical certificate which declared that he suffered from periods of partial blindness in the right eye purportedly resulting in disorientation.[40]

Merleau-Ponty's experiences during this crucial period differed from Sartre's in certain key respects. Called from his teaching post at the École Normale Supérieure, he was mobilized in August of 1939 and made a part of the 5th infantry regiment and later the 59th light infantry division. Unlike Sartre, Merleau-Ponty became an officer, a lieutenant in the infantry. Also unlike Sartre, Merleau-Ponty was never in a prisoner of war camp. He served until September of 1940 when he was demobilized following the French defeat. Nevertheless, as one writer puts it, "the experience of the war left indelible traces on his thinking."[41] He returned to Paris immediately while Sartre was still in the camp at Trier.

Occupation and Resistance

Sartre returned to an occupied Paris in spring of 1941 and, somewhat to the horror of Simone de Beauvoir, immediately sought to organize a group of intellectuals for the Resistance.[42] It was in this capacity that he was once again brought into contact with Merleau-Ponty, who had resumed his teaching career at the Lycée Carnot after his return to Paris in September of 1940. By this time Merleau-Ponty had already begun work in a resistance group called "Sous la botte." Along with Simone de Beauvoir and a number of other intellectuals and students, the two founded a short-lived resistance group called "Socialism and Liberty."[43] The guiding ideas of the organization were (1) to forge a third alternative for resistance between, on the one hand, the communists and, on the other hand, the Gaullists; and (2) to create a political future for France, organized along socialist lines, which would be installed after the liberation. During this time, Merleau-Ponty was a convinced Marxist, whereas Sartre remained rather noncommittal or at least unaffiliated, rejecting communism as such.

The budding group sought the support of internationally known French writers such as Gidé and Malraux, both of whom were living comfortably in the nonoccupied south of France. Being rebuffed by both of these figures, the group began to lose its impetus. Plagued in addition by internal tensions, the group discontinued its activities and ultimately dissolved in 1942. Many years later, Sartre dispassionately described the life and death of "Socialism and Liberty" as follows:

> In 1941, intellectuals, more or less throughout the country, formed groups which claimed to be resisting the conquering enemy. I belonged to one of these groups, "Socialism and Liberty." Merleau joined us. This encounter was not the result of chance. Each of us had come from a *petit bourgeois* background. Our tastes, our tradition and our professional conscience moved both of us to defend freedom of the pen. Through this freedom we discovered all the others. But aside from that, we were simpletons. Born of enthusiasm, our little group caught a fever and died a year later, of not knowing what to do.[44]

Although this group proved to be ineffective, dissolving after only one year, it was nevertheless important insofar as it served the function of bringing Sartre and Merleau-Ponty together again and of showing them their common philosophical interests and social concerns.

Far from being emotionally crushed by the failure of "Socialism and Liberty," both Sartre and Merleau-Ponty began a very productive period following the demise of the resistance group. In 1942 Sartre completed two major works, his play, *The Flies,* and his philosophical masterpiece, *Being and Nothingness.* Merleau-Ponty helped Sartre get *The Flies* produced by finding financial backing for the piece, which was by no means easy during the Occupation.[45] In addition, he wrote a review of Sartre's play in which he rebuked critics for failing to see in it the explicit message and theme of human freedom.[46] *The Flies* was first performed in 1943, and in it Sartre developed an analogy for occupied France, urging resistance and authenticity in the face of oppression.[47] During the trying circumstances of the Occupation, Sartre in 1943 published *Being and Nothingness: An Essay on Phenomenological Ontology.* This work, although receiving little immediate attention,[48] soon became a classic in French philosophy in the twentieth century with its controversial account of human relations characterized by "the look," with its dualistic ontology of being-in-itself and being-for-itself, and, perhaps best known, with its theory of so-called "radical freedom." This book clearly established Sartre as the most important French philosopher of the day.

Merleau-Ponty was likewise extremely productive during this period, publishing his first major work, *The Structure of Behavior* in 1942, which had apparently been completed some years earlier,[49] and setting to work on *Phenomenology of Perception* directly thereafter. During this period Merleau-Ponty was active in negotiations with the Husserl Archives in Louvain in Belgium to set up a Center for Husserl Studies in Paris with copies of the original manuscripts. This perhaps otherwise unnoteworthy episode throws a positive light on Merleau-Ponty's moral character since he was running a great risk during the Occupation in his attempts to disseminate the unpublished writings of the Jewish philosopher, which had been smuggled out of Germany at great peril. The slightest indiscretion might well have resulted in arrest and in the irretrievable loss of Husserl's *Nachlaß*.[50] It is conceivable that for Merleau-Ponty these negotiations in many ways took the place of the aborted resistance group. It was also during this time in 1943 that Sartre joined a group of communist writers in the Resistance called the "Comité National des Ecrivains" which doubtless served as his *Ersatz* for the failure of "Socialism and Liberty." This group, which included Camus, was known for its publication of the clandestine journal *Les Lettres françaises*.[51]

The Liberation and the Foundation of Les Temps Modernes

The year 1945 proved to be an important one not merely from the perspective of world history but also from the perspective of the individual lives of Sartre and Merleau-Ponty. It was in this year that Sartre delivered his controversial lecture "Existentialism Is a Humanism,"[52] in which he attempted to present the fundamental theses of *Being and Nothingness* in a more accessible fashion. That year also saw the publication of Merleau-Ponty's undisputed *magnum opus*, the *Phenomenology of Perception*. This work proved to be profoundly influential in its criticism of classical psychology and its positing of an alternative to Sartre's phenomenology. There Merleau-Ponty tacitly takes issue with a number of theories espoused in *Being and Nothingness*, such as Sartre's dualism, his account of time, his view of the transparency of human consciousness and, in a celebrated final chapter, his theory of radical freedom. The profundity of this work would not be fully realized until years later. In the same year, Merleau-Ponty was appointed to a lectureship at the University of Lyon where he would receive a professorship three years later in 1948. Unlike, Sartre, who reveled in ridiculing university scholars, Merleau-Ponty followed a more or less purely academic career,[53] later receiving the distinguished Chair for Psychology and Pedagogy at the Sorbonne in 1949, where he remained until 1952.

In the same year as the publication of *Phenomenology of Perception,* Sartre and Merleau-Ponty began the most productive period of cooperative work that their relationship was to know. During the period of the Occupation and their work in the Resistance, they conceived of the idea of publishing a literary and philosophical journal,[54] and then in 1945 after the war, they were able to realize their plan.[55] In October of that year the first number of the celebrated review *Les Temps modernes* made its appearance with Sartre and Merleau-Ponty as coeditors. The journal had a decided political tone, and this eventually proved to be the undoing of the amicable and collaborative relationship between the two men. The political idea guiding the journal was to provide a middle ground between the communists and the Christians,[56] a goal which was consonant with that of "Socialism and Liberty" which, as we have seen, tried to provide an alternative between Gaullism and communism. The political bent of the journal might have been relatively harmless in itself, had not Merleau-Ponty been in charge of editing the articles concerned with political themes. In some of the first numbers of the journal, Merleau-Ponty published two laudatory essays on Sartre's philosophy: "The Battle over Existentialism"[57] and "A Scandalous Author"[58] are strong testimony that the relationship between the two during this time was at least reasonably strong.

During the immediate *post bellum* period and at the onset of the Cold War, the political views of the two men do not seem to have been in any fundamental doctrinal conflict. In fact in 1948, upon being solicited, they both played a more or less public role in the newly grounded political party, the Rassemblement Démocratique Révolutionnaire.[59] Merleau-Ponty's enthusiasm seems to have been only lukewarm in comparison to Sartre's, even though both of them were founding members of the original governing board. The goal of the new party was once again to provide a third option, as Sartre explains:

> Its [sc. the R.D.R.'s] immediate objective is to preserve the revolutionary ideal and to work to establish the conditions for an authentic socialism. It does not want reforms but a revolution. . . . This revolution, which must be carried out on a European scale, should allow Europe to become an intervening force between the U.S.S.R. and the U.S.A.[60]

In less than eighteen months the party faded away, much to the relief of both Sartre and Merleau-Ponty, and shortly thereafter their respective political views began to diverge.

Merleau-Ponty had for some time associated himself with communism in a fashion no less ardent than Sartre would later. In *Humanism and Terror,* published in 1947, he gave a sort of *apologia* for the Soviet Union on the occasion of the Moscow trials. Similarly, in 1950, when it became known that there were concentration camps in the Soviet Union, Merleau-Ponty wrote with Sartre's approbation an article, translated as "The U.S.S.R. and the Camps,"[61] which, while criticizing Soviet policy, continued to emphasize the historical mission of the proletariat. Using a sort of *tu quoque* argument, Merleau-Ponty reproached the United States and other countries for underwriting similar forms of injustice but without any deeper historical mission or vision. Despite its apologetic rhetoric, this article effectively alienated the intellectuals of the French Communist Party from the editorial staff of *Les Temps modernes.*[62] By this time both Sartre and Merleau-Ponty were becoming uneasy about the historical evolution of Marxism and when the crisis came, they reacted entirely differently, moving, in fact, in diametrically opposed directions. Sartre says, "as for us, a gale knocked our heads together, and a moment later, it tossed each of us at opposite poles of the other."[63]

The outbreak of the Korean War with the invasion of South Korea in 1950 caused a crisis in faith for Merleau-Ponty.[64] He regarded the Soviet Union quite straightforwardly as the aggressor and as the cause of the war. Sartre writes,

> For Merleau-Ponty, as for many others, 1950 was the crucial year. Then he believed he had seen the Stalinist doctrine without its mask. . . . Either the U.S.S.R. was not the country of socialism, in which case socialism didn't exist anywhere and doubtless wasn't even possible; or else, socialism was *that,* this abominable monster, this police state, the power of beasts of prey.[65]

Merleau-Ponty saw the Soviet Union as an imperialist power in the Korean conflict; however, he was understandably reluctant to take a stand on the issue publicly in *Les Temps modernes,* and it was this which caused him to resign from his post as political editor (to stay on as editor-in-chief).[66] He tried to withdraw from politics, and in practice, much to Sartre's discomfiture, imposed a silence on the journal, insisting that the political themes of *Les Temps modernes* be limited or eliminated entirely.[67] Cut adrift of its past political orientation, the review became "a vessel without a captain,"[68] and the silence would last from 1950 to 1952, when it could no longer be maintained. Merleau-Ponty drifted further and further away from the communism of the party and of the East Block. Although Soviet involvement in Korea disturbed Sartre somewhat, he still perceived American interests and provocation to be at the heart of the conflict.[69] In contrast to Merleau-Ponty's crisis of faith, Sartre underwent what he called a "conversion," in which his once lukewarm allegiance to communism became ever more convinced and radical.

The break or "conversion" for Sartre came in 1952. When General Ridgway arrived as the replacement for General Eisenhower as the commander of the N.A.T.O. forces in Europe, the French communists under Jacques Duclos organized a demonstration to voice their disapproval of the pro-American French policy.[70] A riot erupted at the demonstration that saw violent clashes between the police and the demonstrators. On the strength of the most circumstantial of evidence, Duclos was arrested on the trumped-up charge of having organized a conspiracy. It was this unrestrained action on the part of the government which pushed Sartre beyond the point of no return. He describes his "conversion" to communism, which took place upon his learning of these events during his vacation in Italy in June of 1952:

> I learned from the Italian papers of Duclos' arrest. . . . These sordid childish tricks turned my stomach. There may have been more ignoble ones, but none more revelatory. An anticommunist is a rat. I couldn't see any way out of that one, and I never will. . . . I swore to the bourgeoisie a hatred which would only die with me. When I precipitously returned to Paris, I had to write or suffocate. Day and night, I wrote the first part of *The Communists and Peace.*[71]

Sartre thus became an outspoken, uncompromising communist. He expressed this position in a series of articles entitled *The Communists and Peace,* written for *Les Temps modernes* between 1952 and 1954. This was the occasion of an impassioned debate between Sartre and Claude Lefort, another colleague from the journal and the future editor of Merleau-Ponty's posthumous works.[72] Merleau-Ponty tried to mediate these debates where he could, although he himself was by this time thoroughly estranged from Marxism in its Soviet incarnation.

The Break

The ground for the break had already been prepared for a long time with the diverging political views of the two men, and there was already much tension in the air at *Les Temps modernes.* It seemed that all that was needed was an occasion to set the conflict loose. The decisive dispute between Sartre and Merleau-Ponty came after Sartre's political turnabout in 1952 when Merleau-Ponty resigned from his position as coeditor of the journal. His resignation was occasioned by Sartre's ignoring his editorial instructions about an article which an unnamed Marxist acquaintance[73] had written about the contradictions of capitalism.[74] The essay was originally proposed to Sartre, who was in agreement with its political tone and stance. In Sartre's absence, Merleau-Ponty, in his role as editor-in-chief, felt uncomfortable about the article and prefaced it with a somewhat apologetic note to the readers. He further allowed himself a criticism of the article for failing to examine the contradictions of socialism after discussing the problems of consistency in capitalism. When Sartre saw the change that Merleau-Ponty had effected, he was somewhat insulted by the effrontery and heavy-handedness of the preface, which he then proceeded to remove, allowing the article to appear without comment as originally planned. Merleau-Ponty, who was at the time away from Paris, knew nothing of this until he saw the proofs for the number of the journal. It was this event that triggered his immediate resignation, which he effected with an extended telephone call to Sartre.[75]

We must observe that the friendship with Merleau-Ponty was not the only one that fell victim to Sartre's political conversion. Simone de Beauvoir recalls that during this period many friends and acquaintances were anxious to distance themselves from him,[76] and many colleagues at *Les Temps modernes* were uneasy about the effects his views might have on the direction of the journal.[77] In fact, Sartre's new change in orientation set off a series of personal conflicts. Slightly before Sartre's political turnabout came the bitter break with Albert Camus, which was the result of a negative review featured in *Les Temps modernes* of Camus's philosophical work, *The Rebel*. Camus, deeply offended, held Sartre as editor personally responsible and directed a venomous letter to him in his capacity as director of the journal. Sartre, who had not authored the review, nonetheless felt himself obliged to reply in like tone,[78] with the result that the personal conflict became all the uglier for its publicity.[79] There followed a conflict with a colleague on the editorial staff of *Les Temps modernes* whom Sartre fired in the most hostile of terms for the latter's lumping together of communists and fascists.[80] Then came the aforementioned debate in the journal itself with Claude Lefort, who was in turn soon estranged.[81] Finally, Merleau-Ponty was the last in this line of broken friendships, all apparently triggered by Sartre's new political views or at least by his new dogmatism with respect to politics.

Thus ended the long period of friendship and collaboration between two of France's foremost intellectual figures. What is interesting about this first period seen as a whole is that the two men were able to bear patiently a number of significant differences in opinion concerning themes in metaphysics and epistemology found in *Being and Nothingness* and *Phenomenology of Perception*. Only at the beginning of the 1950s when the differences became political did the situation explode. In 1943, in his review of Sartre's play *The Flies,* Merleau-Ponty rebukes Sartre's critics for not having understood Sartre's theory of freedom—precisely the theory of freedom which he himself would criticize in the *Phenomenology of Perception* two years later. In the two aforementioned articles in 1945 and 1947, Merleau-Ponty defended Sartre's literary and philosophical works once again against mud-slinging critics, and even went so far as to laud his moral character.[82] Even in 1952, when the relationship was already showing evidence of stress, Merleau-Ponty dedicated to Sartre the article, "Indirect Language and the Voices of Silence."[83] There thus seems to have been a sort of productive difference of opinion between the two men for a long period of time. Although they differed on fundamental issues, these differences were apparently not considered threatening, and there was a genuine effort made to minimize them and to highlight the commonalities. Although the *Phenomenology of Perception* can be seen as a critical dialogue with *Being and Nothingness,* Merleau-Ponty mentions the latter directly only a few times.[84] Although it is clear, for example, that the final chapter of *Phenomenology of Perception* is a direct criticism of Sartre's theory of freedom, it mentions Sartre by name only once.[85] Thus, with respect to metaphysics or ontology, the differences were not perceived as any particular cause for alarm; however, when the theme turned to politics, everything changed. The differences came to be perceived as much more acute and menacing. Although both men demonstrated admirable self-restraint and only later aired out their grievances in print, nevertheless the responsibility for the public forum of *Les Temps modernes* doubtless contributed to the potential acuity of the problem, as Sartre acknowledges: "Without *Les Temps modernes,* the events of 1950 would not have had that much influence on our friendship. We would simply have fought over politics more often, or taken greater care never to discuss them."[86] The differences in opinion now in the tense context of the Cold War seemed to be not mere issues of an academic nature but ones which affected the very lives of individuals in France and abroad. It was in this area where neither Sartre nor Merleau-Ponty was able to distance himself personally from the dispute. And thus it was the political differences which ultimately led to the break between the two.

B. The Period of Separation (1953–56)

During the untoward period from 1953 to 1956, Sartre and Merleau-Ponty rarely saw one another and the political dispute between them reached its zenith. The years of the break between the two men correspond, whether by accident or design, to the years of Sartre's quasi-official affiliation with the French Communist Party and *ipso facto* with the communism of the

Soviet Union. After Sartre's trip to the U.S.S.R. in 1954, he returned enthusiastic, offering an unqualified *encomium* of Soviet life and politics in a series of articles for *Libération,* the journal of the French Communist Party.[87] His literary production during these years amounted to little more than the propagation of communist party doctrine and ideology, as is evinced by his play *Nekrassov* from 1953 and his screenplay *Les Sorcières de Salem* from 1956, the latter representing a sort of thinly veiled parable for McCarthyism in the United States.[88] For his part, Merleau-Ponty received a distinguished professorship at the Collège de France in 1952. He held his famous inaugural lecture there on 15 January 1953, which was later published under the title "In Praise of Philosophy." He would remain at this post until his death in 1961.

This strained period is best characterized by the open political debate between the two men. If in times past they had taken pains to minimize their differences in opinion and had shown great restraint and discretion in keeping their conflict a private one, now the dispute became public with no holds barred, and its tone turned needlessly abrasive. Sartre completed his articles, *The Communists and Peace,* in 1954. Shortly after the publication of these essays, Merleau-Ponty in 1955 published his critical response in the form of his book, *Adventures of the Dialectic.* There, in a long chapter entitled "Sartre and Ultrabolshevism," Merleau-Ponty criticizes Sartre's political views, often in a somewhat biting fashion. Sartre, not acknowledging the criticisms in *Phenomenology of Perception,*[89] says that this was the only occasion when they argued in print.

Although Sartre himself never replied personally to the criticisms of Merleau-Ponty, he was not wanting for political allies. The debate was hotly rejoined by Marxists eager to take up the cause on his behalf.[90] Moreover, Sartre's lifelong companion Simone de Beauvoir also offered a riposte to Merleau-Ponty's criticism in the form of a no less virulent article, "Merleau-Ponty and Pseudo-Sartreanism,"[91] the title of which plays on the title of Merleau-Ponty's chapter "Sartre and Ultrabolshevism." She accuses Merleau-Ponty of willfully misrepresenting Sartre's position and of attributing to him views which he in fact never held; thus, instead of attacking Sartre himself, Merleau Ponty was attacking a strawman or a "pseudo-Sartreanism." An English translation of this rich essay along with Merleau-Ponty's chapter "Sartre and Ultrabolshevism" have been included in the present collection.

This three-year period of separation is not one that Sartre says much about in "Merleau-Ponty vivant." In fact, he tries to interpret Merleau-Ponty's reticence during this time in psychologistic terms, seeing the withdrawn behavior of his friend largely as a result of the death of Merleau-Ponty's mother in 1952.[92] The tendency toward this sort of psychologistic reduction has irritated some commentators who would see genuine philosophical and political issues and differences at the heart of the dispute.[93] This criticism of Sartre seems to be at least in part justified in view of the fact that it was Sartre's changing political orientation—and not the death of Merleau-Ponty's mother—which originally precipitated the changes in the relationship. Certainly, Merleau-Ponty's bereavement could have conceivably aggravated the problem, but it is highly improbable that it was its original source.

C. Rapprochement (1956–61)

Sartre recounts that he saw Merleau-Ponty again for the first time in a long while in 1956 in Venice at a conference of La Société Européenne de Culture.[94] Here they effected a partial rapprochement, and although not the friends they had once been, they began to see each other anew. By this time, however, their intellectual commitments were developing in different directions, and it was this which precluded a complete rapprochement or any new cooperative projects. Sartre's rapprochement with Merleau-Ponty was doubtlessly strengthened considerably when he officially broke with the Communist Party some months later. The occasion of this new "conversion" was the Soviet invasion of Hungary in 1956.[95] Sartre, fully disillusioned with the Soviet Union, writes in *L'Express,* in November of 1956, "I condemn the Russian aggression completely and unreservedly. Without holding the Russian people responsible for it, I repeat that their present government has committed a crime."[96] This new change in political orientation is significant for Sartre's relation to Merleau-Ponty, who was by this time clearly a persona non grata in the eyes of the French Communist Party.

From this final period, we gain three more important sources for Merleau-Ponty's criticism of Sartre's philosophy. In a colloquium given in 1959 under the title "The Philosophy of Existence," Merleau-Ponty gives a useful account of the heroic years of existentialism, beginning with the period just before the war.[97] He dedicates the second half of that account to an overview of Sartre's early philosophy. This work, which is included in the present collection, contains much useful historical information about the intellectual context in which French existentialism was born, as well as personal information about the two men. It is the closest thing that we have from Merleau-Ponty's hand to a "Sartre vivant."

In addition, in the second half of the introduction to *Signs* from 1960,[98] also included here, Merleau-Ponty comments on Sartre's long preface to the work *Aden Arabie,*[99] authored by their long since deceased friend of youth, Paul Nizan. An inseparable friend and former roommate and classmate of Sartre at the École Normale, Nizan turned to communism at an early age and thus became politicized long before either Sartre or Merleau-Ponty. With the signing of the Nazi-Soviet Pact in 1939, Nizan broke with the party and was killed during the war shortly thereafter at the age of thirty-five.[100] In his preface, Sartre reproaches himself for never having been the rebellious youth that Nizan had been and for never truly understanding Nizan until years after the fact. In *Signs,* Merleau-Ponty likewise reflects on Nizan's political alignment and tries to show that Sartre's self-reproach is misplaced. Although the tone of Merleau-Ponty's comments is hardly polemical but more one of reminiscence, nonetheless Sartre took Merleau-Ponty's comments there somewhat amiss.[101]

Merleau-Ponty died unexpectedly of a heart attack on May 3, 1961. A work-in-progress entitled *The Visible and the Invisible,* dating from March 1959, was found among his papers. The manuscript was subsequently edited and published by Claude Lefort in 1964 to the great benefit of students of the philosophy of Merleau-Ponty. The second major part of this work, entitled "Interrogation and Dialectic," takes up once again a criticism of Sartre's early philosophy in *Being and Nothingness.* This important chapter has been included in the present collection. The extended discussion there complements in important ways the criticisms of Sartre that Merleau-Ponty published in his own lifetime.

How are we to understand the complex relation between Sartre and Merleau-Ponty as a whole? This question is extremely difficult to answer in a few words, not because their relation had so many different phases and aspects or because it was so convoluted, but rather because it was contradictory in itself. Sartre characterizes his relationship with Merleau-Ponty in different and often perplexing and inconsistent ways: sometimes there is a note of measured amicability or fondness, and at other times a strain of hostility and estrangement. However, it seems fairly safe to say that the emotional extremes of love and hate were never present. On the one hand, years after Merleau-Ponty's death, Sartre confirms that Merleau-Ponty was never in the intimate circle of his friends. He was seen rather as someone, a scholar, philosopher, or colleague, for whom one had a degree of deference but nothing more.[102] But then, on the other hand, even at the point when their alienation reached its apex following Merleau-Ponty's resignation from the review, they still remained cordial and polite, occasionally seeing each other, even if only *par hasard.* Their relationship operated between the poles of love and hate and, although avoiding these extremes, seems to have gone back and forth between a number of other contradictory terms. There was a confused aggregate of conflicting factors—personal feelings, common experiences, professional interests, political commitments, and philosophical theories—all of which were constantly in movement in their relationship.

These various contradictions seem to issue from the fact that Sartre and Merleau-Ponty were stamped with two fundamentally different dispositions. Sartre characterizes himself as more polemical than Merleau-Ponty: "On small issues, then, it seemed to me that I ought to relinquish my points of view if I hadn't been able to convince my interlocutor to relinquish his. Merleau-Ponty, on the contrary, found his security in a multiplicity of perspectives, seeing in them the different facets of being."[103] Likewise, Sartre discerned a strain of dialectical thinking in Merleau-Ponty which was somewhat foreign to his own frequent juxtaposition of uncompromising either-or alternatives: "I was the more dogmatic, he the more subtle, but this was a matter of temperament, or, as we said, of character."[104] Finally, in reflecting on their lives as a whole, Sartre characterizes their differences by saying that their lives were simply "out-of-step" with one another.[105] Simone de Beauvoir writes of her early encounters with Merleau-Ponty, "I saw quickly that in spite of our affinities there was a good deal of distance between Pradelle [sc. Merleau-Ponty] and I. In his purely cerebral inquietude, I did not recognize my inner anguishing." She writes quoting from her own journal, "I judged him to be 'without complication, without mystery, a good schoolboy.' "[106] Sartre and Simone de Beauvoir had known an alienation from their families and their place in the bourgeois social order, and this awareness led to a hint of the anguished conscience of youth which, according to their account, was absent in Merleau-Ponty. Thus, despite many common interests and experiences, there were many differences in temperament that separated the two men. For these reasons, it would be a distortion simply to say that Sartre and Merleau-Ponty were friends and to leave it at that as many commentators have done. Friends, colleagues, classmates—all of these terms are too impoverished to capture the complexity of the relation between them. In a sense, we could do worse than to leave the matter where Sartre left it after Merleau-Ponty's death when he wrote, "Absent, we shall always be for one another what we have always been. Strangers."[107] The enigma of their personal relationship is in many ways paralleled by the complexity of their philosophical positions. It is the latter which the present collection tries to address.

II. The Present Collection

The bulk of the essays contained in the first four parts of this anthology treat the doctrines expounded above all in *Being and Nothingness* and

Phenomenology of Perception. These two works contain numerous points of contact which have only just begun to be explored adequately. In the present anthology these points of contact have been ordered under the headings, "Ontology," "Subjectivity and Intersubjectivity," "The Body," and "Freedom."

In the first part, the collection presents four essays which explore the different aspects of the fundamental ontological positions of Sartre and Merleau-Ponty in their respective philosophical masterpieces. Leo Rauch's article explores the differing interpretations of Husserl that are offered by Sartre and Merleau-Ponty and indicates the way in which both thinkers see themselves as continuing Husserl's project of phenomenological ontology. Rauch examines Sartre's characterization of consciousness and human subjectivity as something negative and Merleau-Ponty's criticism of this conception *via* his account of perception. John M. Moreland analyzes Merleau-Ponty's chapter, "The Cogito," from *Phenomenology of Perception,* and highlights its criticisms of Sartre's dualistic ontology. This article also complements Rauch's account of the fundamental differences between the two men on the issue of subjectivity and the prereflective *cogito.* Colin Smith's essay treats, among other things, the ontological presuppositions of Sartre's theory of the subject's relation to objects and human action. He presents Merleau-Ponty's theory of perception and contextual knowledge as a more plausible view. James F. Sheridan goes back to the ontological theories of the early Sartre, which so forcefully shaped Sartre's later political views. He then uses this to shed light on Merleau-Ponty's criticism of Sartre's political views in "Sartre and Ultrabolshevism" as well as on the rejoinder by Simone de Beauvoir. In her article, Margaret Whitford explores Merleau-Ponty's criticisms of Sartre's ontological dualism and rationalism. She tries to indicate that the criticisms are only partially successful by demonstrating that they are based on misinterpretations of Sartre's position.

The second part deals with theories of the *cogito* or the phenomenological subject and the relations between subjects. The essay "Phenomenology, Consciousness, and Freedom" by C.M.T. Hanley examines Sartre's ontological theory of the human subject as a prereflective consciousness, and Merleau-Ponty's criticisms of this doctrine and its corollaries in *Phenomenology of Perception.* Hanley argues that, while Merleau-Ponty's proposal of a prepersonal self does largely overcome the shortcomings of Sartre's prereflective ego, it cannot ultimately be successful without abandoning a phenomenological approach entirely. François H. Lapointe's article examines the account of the phenomenological subject's problematic relation to other subjects, or what is known as the problem of the other or of intersubjectivity. He traces the differing accounts of the other in Sartre and Merleau-Ponty back to their respective ontological presuppositions. Monika Langer's article begins with the political discussion and tries to show that Merleau-Ponty's criticism of Sartre's political views is mistaken since there is in fact a notion of an "interworld" in Sartre. She then sketches in some detail Sartre's notion of human relations, intersubjectivity, and the body, drawing on texts such as *Being and Nothingness* and *The Transcendence of the Ego.*

The celebrated accounts of the human body found in *Being and Nothingness* and *Phenomenology of Perception* are treated directly by three articles which constitute part 3. First Martin C. Dillon's essay, "Sartre on the Phenomenal Body and Merleau-Ponty's Critique," provides a useful overview of the issue of the body as a philosophical problem as well as the phenomenological treatments of it by Sartre and Merleau-Ponty. He argues that Sartre's view is ultimately too dualistic to overcome the problems of immanence and transcendence, whereas Merleau-Ponty's more integrated approach is more promising. The essay by Glen A. Mazis examines the sexual aspect of the body as understood by Sartre and Merleau-Ponty. He treats the account of tactile contact and the caress in *Being and Nothingness* as an example of Sartre's theory of sexuality, and offers a criticism of it which is suggested by Merleau-Ponty's analysis of the fundamental difference between touch and vision. In his essay, Joseph S. Catalano defends Sartre's theory of the body in *Being and Nothingness* against Merleau-Ponty's charges. He claims that though Sartre's discussion of the body comes at the end of the work, this does not imply that it is unimportant for him; on the contrary, its placement at the end reflects Sartre's own phenomenological methodology. Catalano thus argues that the body plays a central role in *Being and Nothingness* which has been heretofore overlooked.

Sartre's famous account of human freedom in *Being and Nothingness* and Merleau-Ponty's criticism of it in the final chapter of *Phenomenology of Perception* is treated by three essays in part 4. First, John J. Compton's essay, "Sartre, Merleau-Ponty, and Human Freedom," explores various aspects of the account of freedom given by the two thinkers, and traces the differences in their views back to their fundamental ontological commitments about human motivation, natural limitation, the nature of the subject's relation to the world, etc. The following essay, by Ronald L. Hall, argues that ultimately Merleau-Ponty's account is more satisfying as an attempt to overcome the Cartesian picture of the self and the will, since Merleau-Ponty sees the individual in a concrete situation which both gives and receives meaning, whereas Sartre's view tends to isolate the subject and to see it alone as the sole source of action and meaning. The final essay on this topic, entitled "Merleau-Ponty's Criticisms of Sartre's Theory of Freedom," isolates and explores three different criticisms of Sartre's theory from the chapter "Freedom" of *Phenomenology of Perception*. The author offers a defense of Sartre's position and argues that ultimately it is in many regards compatible with Merleau-Ponty's account of situated freedom.

The political differences between the two men that characterize the period of open hostility are treated by four different essays in part 5. "Sartre and Merleau-Ponty: An Existentialist Quarrel," by Graham Daniels, provides a useful overview of the development of the political debate up to the period of *Adventures of the Dialectic*. Daniels reconstructs key differences in the ontologies of Sartre and Merleau-Ponty from their earlier works, which set the context for the later political dispute. Ronald Aronson's article traces in a detailed fashion the political debate between the two men starting at this period and working through Sartre's posthumous second tome of *Critique of Dialectical Reason*, first published in 1985. He offers an extensive analysis of that work, which shows how it brings together much of Sartre's political thought. Thomas R. Flynn offers an interpretation of Sartre's *Critique of Dialectical Reason* as a response to Merleau-Ponty's criticisms in "Sartre and Ultrabolshevism." He argues that Sartre's late work modifies some of his earlier positions and is a generally successful response to Merleau-Ponty's criticisms. Mikel Dufrenne's essay claims that Sartre's views in the *Critique* are not necessarily incompatible with those of Merleau-Ponty. Instead, the two are concerned with two different spheres: Sartre with the social and Merleau-Ponty with the natural. The author argues that Sartre succeeds in sketching a theory of history and social life in accordance with his earlier phenomenological principles and without appealing to abstract metaphysics.

Part 6 is dedicated to the views on aesthetics in Sartre and Merleau-Ponty. Marjorie Grene's essay, "The Aesthetic Dialogue of Sartre and Merleau-Ponty," treats four of the most important themes from *Being and Nothingness*—being-in-the-world, the body, communication, and freedom—from the perspective of art. She uses a variety of other texts besides *Being and Nothingness* and *Phenomenology of Perception* for her comparison of the aesthetic views of the two philosophers. She portrays Sartre as fixated on the written word, in contrast to Merleau-Ponty who was more the philosopher of "vision." In John O'Neill's essay, "Situation and Temporality," the author argues that Sartre's phenomenological account of time in *Being and Nothingness* is crucial for an understanding of his later views of art and literature, and discusses Sartre's evaluation of various contemporary writers according to his artistic criteria. He tries to argue on the basis of this analysis that Merleau-Ponty's charge against Sartre's "lucidity" is unjust.

As has been indicated above, a number of primary texts from Sartre, Merleau-Ponty, and Simone de Beauvoir have been included in the final part. These texts have been chosen for their relevance for the various points of debate between the two men. Part 7 begins with three hitherto untranslated letters that passed between Sartre and Merleau-Ponty in 1953 at the time of their falling out. Merleau-Ponty's chapter, "Sartre and Ultrabolshevism," from *Adventures of the Dialectic,* has been included along with Simone de Beauvoir's critical response, "Merleau-Ponty and Pseudo-Sartreanism." Following this is the text from Merleau-Ponty's colloquium, entitled "The Philosophy of Existence," which surveys the origins and development of French existentialism. Also included is the second half of Merleau-Ponty's introduction to *Signs,* in which he discusses Sartre's political views and his relation to Nizan. The chapter "Interrogation and Dialectic" from Merleau-Ponty's posthumous work, *The Visible and the Invisible,* has also been included. Finally, Sartre's long eulogy of Merleau-Ponty constitutes the last article.

The goal of the present collection in bringing together for the first time important articles that examine the various points of contact between Sartre and Merleau-Ponty as well as the most relevant primary texts is twofold: first it is hoped that this anthology will serve the function of introducing English-speaking students and educated persons in general to the rich yet somewhat neglected tradition of French phenomenology and existentialism. Moreover, it is hoped that this collection of essays along with the included primary texts and bibliography will be of use to professional scholars and specialists in the work of Sartre and Merleau-Ponty in their attempt to come to terms with the complex relation between the two men. This will then in turn serve the cause of increasing an appreciation for the achievements of the tradition of French phenomenology in the world of Anglo-American philosophy, where it has been so poorly understood for so long now.

Notes

1. Jean-Paul Sartre, "Merleau-Ponty vivant," *Les Temps modernes* 17, nos. 184–85 (1961) (hereafter *TM*). In English as "Merleau-Ponty." In *Situations,* trans. Benita Eisler (New York: Braziller, 1965) (hereafter *Sits*). An early unpublished draft of this essay provides other useful information: Jean-Paul Sartre, "Merleau-Ponty," trans. William S. Hamrick, *Journal of the British Society for Phenomenology* 15 (special issue, *Sartre on Merleau-Ponty*) (1984), 128–54. Original French version, "Merleau-Ponty," *Revue internationale de philosophie* 39 (1985), 3–29. See Michel Contat and Michel Rybalka, *Les Écrits de Sartre: Chronologie, bibliographie commentée*

(Paris: Gallimard, 1970), 61/365. In English as *The Writings of Jean-Paul Sartre*, 2 vols. (vol. 1: *A Bibliographical Life*), trans. Richard McCleary (Evanston: Northwestern University Press, 1974). Cited by entry number and not by page number so as to facilitate reference to both the French and English editions. (Hereafter cited as Contat-Rybalka.)

2. Most notably, Annie Cohen-Solal, *Sartre: 1905–1980* (Paris: Gallimard, 1985) (hereafter Cohen-Solal); John Gerassi, *Jean-Paul Sartre: Hated Conscience of His Century*, vol. 1 (Chicago: University of Chicago Press, 1989).

3. Simone de Beauvoir, *La Cérémonie des adieux* (Paris: Gallimard, 1981).

4. *Les Carnets de la drôle de guerre* (Paris: Gallimard, 1983). In English as *The War Diaries of Jean-Paul Sartre*, trans. Quintin Hoare (New York: Pantheon Books, 1984). *Cahiers pour une morale* (Paris: Gallimard, 1983). In English as *Notebooks for an Ethics*, trans. David Pellauer (Chicago: University of Chicago Press, 1992).

5. Simone de Beauvoir, *Lettres au Castor* (Paris: Gallimard, 1983). In English as *Witness to My Life: The Letters of Jean-Paul Sartre to Simone de Beauvoir, 1926–1939*, ed. Simone de Beauvoir, trans. Lee Fahnestock and Norman McAfee (New York: Macmillan, 1992).

6. Originally, "Jean-Paul Sartre, ou un auteur scandaleux," *Le Figaro littéraire* 2, no. 85 (December 1947). Reprinted as "Un auteur scandaleux," in *Sens et non-sens* (Paris: Nagel, 1948), 73–84 (hereafter *Sens*). In English as "A Scandalous Author," in *Sense and Non-Sense*, trans. Hubert L. Dreyfus and Patricia Allen Dreyfus (Evanston: Northwestern University Press, 1964), 41–47 (hereafter *SNS*).

7. *Sens*, 73; *SNS* 41. Sartre recounts this anecdote as well: de Beauvoir, *La Cérémonie des adieux*, 366. See Simone de Beauvoir, *Mémoires d'une jeune fille rangée* (Paris: Gallimard, 1958), 341: "He [sc. Merleau-Ponty] disapproved of the coarse manners of his comrades, the obscene songs, the dirty jokes, the violence, the debauchery, the dissipation of the heart and the senses."

8. Reported in Theodore F. Geraets, *Vers une nouvelle philosophie transcendentale: La genèse de la philosophie de Maurice Merleau-Ponty jusqu'à la "Phénoménologie de la perception"* (The Hague: Martinus Nijhoff, 1971), 7.

9. Edmund Husserl, *Méditations cartésiennes: Introduction à la phénoménologie*, trans. Gabrielle Peiffer and Emmanuel Levinas (Paris: Colin, 1931).

10. Simone de Beauvoir, *La Force de l'âge* (Paris: Gallimard, 1960), 156.

11. Cf. Gerassi, *Jean-Paul Sartre*, 102.

12. Ibid., 105.

13. *TM*, 304; *Sits*, 156; reprinted below 565.

14. Sartre, "Merleau-Ponty," 4; cf. also 5, 15. English trans., 129; cf. also 130, 138. Cf. de Beauvoir, *La Cérémonie des adieux*, 329.

15. De Beauvoir, *La Cérémonie des adieux*, 571.

16. Cf. ibid.

17. Cf. ibid., 226–27, 246ff. Cf. Sartre's account of his encounters with the works of Husserl and Heidegger in *Les Carnets*, 224ff.

18. Cf. Sartre, "Merleau-Ponty," 5, 15. English trans., 129–30, 138. Cf. "Merleau-Ponty vivant," *TM*, 304–5; *Sits*. 156–57; below 565–66. For their respective relations to Husserl, see Herbert Spiegelberg, *The Phenomenological Movement*,

vol. 2 (The Hague: Martinus Nijhoff, 1965), 517, 522ff. Cf. Margaret Whitford, *Merleau-Ponty's Critique of Sartre's Philosophy* (Lexington: French Forum Publishers, 1982), 13ff.

19. Cf. Geraets, *Vers une nouvelle philosophie,* 8.

20. *TM,* 315; *Sits,* 167; below 574.

21. Cf. his autobiographical account in the essay "Faith and Good Faith" from *SNS:* "There was once a young Catholic who was led 'to the Left' by the demands of his faith. This was the time when Dollfuss inaugurated Europe's first Christian Socialist government by shelling the working-class sections of Vienna. A magazine inspired by Christians protested to President Miklas, and the protest was said to be surported by the most progressive of our great religious orders. The young man was welcomed at the table of some monks belonging to this order. In the middle of lunch he was astonished to hear that, after all, the Dollfuss government was the established power, that it had the right to a police force since it was the proper government, and that Catholics, as Catholics, had nothing against it, although as citizens they were free to censure it." (*Sens,* 305–6; *SNS,* 172)

22. For the others, Geraets, *Vers une nouvelle philosophie,* 13ff.

23. Maurice Merleau-Ponty, "Jean-Paul Sartre: L'Imagination," *Journal de psychologie normale et pathologique* 33, nos. 9–10 (November–December, 1936), 756–61.

24. Later collected and published as Alexandre Kojève, *Introduction à la lecture de Hegel* (Paris: Gallimard, 1947). In English as *An Introduction to the Reading of Hegel,* ed. Alan Bloom, trans. J. H. Nichols (Ithaca: Cornell University Press, 1969).

25. *TM,* 304–5; *Sits,* 156–57; below 565.

26. *Revue internationale de philosophie* 1, no. 2 (15 January 1939).

27. Cf. H. L. Van Breda, "Maurice Merleau-Ponty et les Archives-Husserl à Louvain," *Revue de métaphysique et de morale* 67 (1962), 410–30. In English as "Merleau-Ponty and the Husserl Archives at Louvain," trans. Stephen Michelman, in *Texts and Dialogues: Maurice Merleau-Ponty,* ed. Hugh J. Silverman and James Barry, Jr. (Atlantic Highlands: Humanities Press, 1992), 150–61.

28. See de Beauvoir, *La Force de l'âge,* 489–90; *La Cérémonie des adieux,* 503.

29. Cf. his own account in de Beauvoir, *La Cérémonie des adieux,* 547ff.

30. Merleau-Ponty comments on the solidarity in the resistance in *Sens,* 266; *SNS,* 151. Simone de Beauvoir comments on the solidarity of the prisoner of war camps in *La Force des choses,* vol. 1 (Paris: Gallimard, 1963), 16–17.

31. Merleau-Ponty comments on this in "A Scandalous Author," *Sens,* 73; *SNS,* 41. Cf. de Beauvoir, *La Cérémonie des adieux,* 376, 614. Cf. Marius Perris, *Avec Sartre au Stalag XIID* (Paris: Jean-Pierre Delarge, 1980).

32. De Beauvoir, *La Cérémonie des adieux,* 246ff.

33. Gerassi, *Jean-Paul Sartre,* 157. Cf. also de Beauvoir, *La Cérémonie des adieux,* 505.

34. See de Beauvoir, *La Force de l'âge* (Paris: Gallimard, 1960), 549–50.

35. Published in Contat and Rybalka, *Les Écrits de Sartre,* 565–633. *The*

Writings of Jean-Paul Sartre, vol. 2: *Selected Prose,* 72–136. See de Beauvoir, *La Force des choses,* vol. 1, 17.

36. De Beauvoir, *La Cérémonie des adieux,* 263–64.

37. Contat-Rybalka, 62/368.

38. De Beauvoir, *La Force des choses,* vol. 1, 64.

39. Contat-Rybalka, 62/368.

40. Cohen-Solal, 289.

41. Spiegelberg, *The Phenomenological Movement,* vol. 2, 530. For an exemplary essay in regard to the lesson of the war for Merleau-Ponty, see his "The War Has Taken Place," in *Sens,* 245–70; *SNS,* 139–52.

42. De Beauvoir, *La Cérémonie des adieux,* 550–51ff.

43. See de Beauvoir, *La Force de l'âge,* 552ff.

44. *TM,* 306–7; *Sits,* 158–59; below 567.

45. See de Beauvoir, *La Force de l'âge,* 590.

46. Maurice Merleau-Ponty, "*Les Mouches* par Jean-Paul Sartre," *Confluences* 3, no. 25 (September–October 1943), 514–16.

47. Gerassi, *Jean-Paul Sartre,* 182. Cohen-Solal, 325ff.

48. Merleau-Ponty speculates on the reasons for this in "The Battle over Existentialism," in *Sens,* 123ff; *SNS,* 71ff. See de Beauvoir, *La Force de l'âge,* 636.

49. Cf. Geraets, *Vers une nouvelle philosophie,* 28–29. Cf. also Xavier Tilliette, "Maurice Merleau-Ponty (1908–1961) ou la mesure de l'homme," *Archives de philosophie* 24 (1961), 400.

50. Cf. Van Breda, "Maurice Merleau-Ponty," 418.

51. See de Beauvoir, *La Force de l'âge,* 613–14, 637. Cf. *La Cérémonie des adieux,* 380–81, 554.

52. De Beauvoir, *La Force des choses,* vol. 1, 61.

53. Sartre would say later, "Merleau-Ponty . . . considered philosophy somewhat from the inside of the professorial system; moreover, I don't know why. His books were not particularly academic books but nevertheless there was between us, I think, the difference that he accepted the university from the very beginning as a means of doing philosophy and I did not" (de Beauvoir, *La Cérémonie des adieux,* 360). For his *hortatio* for an engaged literature in contrast to a purely academic life, see Sartre's "Présentation des Temps Modernes," *Les Temps modernes* 1 (October 1945), 1–21. Reprinted in *Situations,* II (Paris: Gallimard, 1948), 1–30. In English as "The Case for Responsible Literature," trans. Natalia Galitzine, *Horizon* 9, no. 65 (May 1945), 307–12.

54. See Cohen-Solal, 440. See *TM,* 316; *Sits,* 168; below 575. See de Beauvoir, *La Force de l'âge,* 644; *La Cérémonie des adieux,* 510ff.

55. See de Beauvoir, *La Force des choses,* vol. 1, op. cit., 27ff., 72ff.

56. For Sartre's own account of the agenda of *Les Temps modernes,* see de Beauvoir, *La Cérémonie des adieux,* 511.

57. Merleau-Ponty, "La Querelle de l'Existentialisme," *Les Temps modernes* 1, no. 2 (November 1945), 344–56. Reprinted in *Sens,* 123–43; *SNS,* 71–82.

58. See *Sens,* 73–84; *SNS,* 41–47.

59. Cf. Cohen-Solal, 506ff. Cf. *TM,* 328ff.; *Sits,* 180ff; below 585ff.

60. Contat-Rybalka, 48/171.

61. Reprinted in *Signes* (Paris: Gallimard, 1960), 330–43 (hereafter *Signes*), *Signs,* trans. Richard C. McCleary (Evanston: Northwestern University Press, 1964), 263–73 (hereafter *Signs*). See Sartre's discussion of it in *TM,* 330ff.; *Sits,* 182ff; below 587ff. Cf. de Beauvoir, *La Cérémonie des adieux,* 558. See de Beauvoir, *La Force des choses,* vol. 1, 279–80.

62. *TM,* 336; *Sits,* 186; below 591.

63. *TM,* 304; *Sits,* 156; below 565.

64. See his discussion in *Aventures de la dialectique* (Paris: Gallimard, 1955), 229ff.; *Adventures of the Dialectic,* trans. Joseph Bien (Evanston: Northwestern University Press, 1973), 185ff.

65. *TM,* 338–39; *Sits,* 190; below 594.

66. *TM,* 351; *Sits,* 202; below 604.

67. De Beauvoir, *La Force des choses,* vol. 1, 317, 344; see Sartre's account in *TM,* 338, 344; *Sits,* 189, 195; below 593, 599.

68. *TM,* 345; *Sits,* 196; below 600.

69. De Beauvoir, *La Force des choses,* vol. 1, 319ff. Sartre writes, "In this whole miserable business, the real war-mongers were the feudalists of the South [sc. of Korea] and the American imperialists" (*TM,* 340; *Sits,* 191; below 595).

70. De Beauvoir, *La Force des choses,* vol. 1, 356–57.

71. *TM,* 347–48; *Sits,* 198; below 601. See also his account in de Beauvoir, *La Cérémonie des adieux,* 514.

72. Claude Lefort, "Le Marxisme et Sartre," *Les Temps modernes,* no. 89 (April 1953), 1541–70; Sartre, "Réponse à Claude Lefort," ibid., 1571–1629.

73. Apparently one Pierre Naville, the loquacious questioner in *L'Existentialisme est un humanisme* (Paris: Nagel, 1961), 105–41; *Existentialism and Humanism,* trans. Philip Mairet (London: Methuen, 1948), 59–70. The essay in question was Naville's "États-Unis et contradictions capitalistes," *Les Temps modernes,* no. 86 (December 1953), 899–914. Cf. John F. Bannan, "Merleau-Ponty and Sartre," in his *The Philosophy of Merleau-Ponty* (New York: Harcourt, Brace and World, 1967), 238.

74. Cf. *TM,* 355; *Sits,* 205; below 607; Rabil in his account has this wrong, mistakenly taking Sartre as the author. Cf. Albert Rabil, "Merleau-Ponty and Sartrian Existentialism—Political and Philosophical," in his *Merleau-Ponty: Existentialist of the Social World* (New York: Columbia University Press, 1967), 121.

75. Cf. Merleau-Ponty, "La Philosophie de l'existence," *Dialogue* 5 (1966–67), 321; in English as "The Philosophy of Existence," trans. Allen S. Weiss, in *Texts and Dialogues,* ed. Silverman and Barry, 138; below 501.

76. De Beauvoir, *La Force des choses,* vol. 2, 2.

77. Cf. *TM,* 351–52; *Sits,* 201–2; below 604–5.

78. Sartre, "Réponse à Albert Camus," *Les Temps modernes,* no. 82 (August 1952), 334–53. Reprinted in *Situations,* IV (Paris: Gallimard, 1964), 90–125.

79. Cf. de Beauvoir, *La Cérémonie des adieux,* 382ff. Useful brief overviews of this conflict include the following: Cohen-Solal, 561ff.; Raymond Aron, *L'Opium des intellectuels* (Paris: Calmann-Lévy); de Beauvoir, *La Force des choses,* vol. 1,

151ff., 353ff.; Francis Jeanson, "Note sur l'affaire Camus," in his *Sartre dans sa vie* (Paris: Seuil, 1974), 183–89. More detailed accounts of Sartre's relation to Camus include Germaine Brée's classic *Camus and Sartre: Crises and Commitment* (New York: Delta Books, 1972); and Peter Royle, *The Sartre-Camus Controversy: A Literary and Philosophical Critique* (Ottawa: University of Ottawa Press, 1982).

80. Cohen-Solal, 578.

81. De Beauvoir, *La Force des choses,* vol. 2, 23.

82. See Merleau-Ponty, *Sens,* 73–84, 123–43; *SNS,* 41–47, 71–82.

83. Merleau-Ponty, "Le langage indirect et les voix du silence, (I)," *Les Temps modernes* 7, no. 80 (1951–52), 2113–44; and II, ibid. 8, no. 81 (1952–53), 70–94. Reprinted in *Signes,* 49–104; in English as "Indirect Language and the Voices of Silence," *Signs,* 39–83.

84. See Kwant, who takes this as a sign of politeness on the part of Merleau-Ponty, who wanted to give the appearance of agreement and harmony for the sake of the friendship. Rémy C. Kwant,"Merleau-Ponty and Sartre," in his *The Phenomenological Philosophy of Merleau-Ponty* (Pittsburgh: Duquesne University Press, 1963), 203–4. Spiegelberg agrees: "Some of this restraint has to be seen against the background of the history of their personal relationship" (Spiegelberg, *The Phenomenological Movement,* vol. 2, 519).

85. Maurice Merleau-Ponty, *Phénoménologie de la perception* (Paris: Gallimard, 1945), 500; *Phenomenology of Perception,* trans. Colin Smith (London: Routledge and Kegan Paul, 1962), 438.

86. *TM,* 356; *Sits,* 206; below 608.

87. "Les impressions de Jean-Paul Sartre sur son voyage en U.R.S.S." Cf. Contat-Rybalka, 54/260.

88. Cf. Contat-Rybalka, 56/287.

89. *TM,* 370; *Sits,* 220; below 619.

90. Roger Garaudy, *et al.,* eds., *Mésaventures de l'antimarxisme: Les Malheurs de Maurice Merleau-Ponty* (Paris: Éditions Sociales, 1956).

91. *Les Temps modernes* 10, nos. 114–15 (July 1955), 2072–2122. Reprinted in *Privilèges* (Paris: Gallimard, 1955), 203–72; in English as "Merleau-Ponty and Pseudo-Sartreanism," trans. Veronique Zaytzeff, *International Studies in Philosophy* 21 (1989), 3–48. See de Beauvoir, *La Force des choses,* vol. 2, 61–62.

92. *TM,* 357–58; *Sits,* 208–9; below 609–10.

93. Kwant, "Merleau-Ponty and Sartre," 219ff.

94. Cf. *TM,* 370; *Sits,* 220; below 619. See their discussion at the conference in part reprinted in Contat-Rybalka, 56/288.

95. De Beauvoir, *La Force des choses,* vol. 2, 110ff.

96. Contat-Rybalka, 56/289. Cf. Cohen-Solal, 605–6.

97. Merleau-Ponty, "La Philosophie de l'existence," 307–22; "The Philosophy of Existence," 129–39.

98. *Signes,* 31–47; *Signs,* 22–35.

99. Paul Nizan, *Aden Arabie* (Paris: François Maspéro, 1960), 9–62. See Contat-Rybalka, 60/333.

100. Cf. de Beauvoir, *La Force de l'âge,* 535ff.

101. Cf. *TM,* 314–15; *Sits,* 166–67; below 574.

102. Cf. de Beauvoir, *La Cérémonie des adieux,* 384.

103. *TM,* 308; *Sits,* 159–60; below 568.

104. *TM,* 316; *Sits,* 168; below 575.

105. *TM,* 375; *Sits,* 225; below 624. Cf. David Archard's discussion in his *Marxism and Existentialism: The Political Philosophy of Sartre and Merleau-Ponty* (Belfast: Blackstaff Press, 1980), xiff.

106. De Beauvoir, *Mémoires d'une jeune fille rangée,* 342.

107. *TM,* 372; *Sits,* 222; below 621.

Biographical Overview

	Jean-Paul Sartre		Maurice Merleau-Ponty
1905	Born at Paris	1908	Born at Rochefort-sur-mer
1906–15	Infancy, Paris		
1915–17	Student, Paris, Lycée Henri IV		
1917–20	Student, La Rochelle		Student, Lycée Le Havre
1920–22	Student, Paris, Lycée, Henri IV		Student, Lycée Janson de Sailly
1922–24	Student, Paris, Lycée Louis-le-Grand	1924–26	Student, Paris, Lycée Louis-le-Grand
1924–29	Student, Paris, École Normale Supérieure	1926–30	Student, Paris, École Normale Supérieure
1929	Agrégation		
1929–30	Military service, Saint-Cyr and Saint-Symphorien	1930–31	Military service
1931–33	Teacher, Le Havre	1931–33	Teacher, Lycée de Beauvais
1933–34	Research grant, Berlin	1933–34	Grant holder, Caisse Nationale de la Recherche Scientifique
1934–36	Teacher, Le Havre	1934–35	Teacher, Lycée de Chartres
1936–37	Teacher, Laon		
1936	*The Imagination: A Psychological Critique*		
1937	*The Transcendence of the Ego*		
1937–39	Teacher, Paris, Lycée Pasteur de Neuilly	1935–39	Teacher, Paris, École Normale Supérieure
1938	*Nausea*		

	Jean-Paul Sartre		Maurice Merleau-Ponty
1939	*Sketch for a Theory of the Emotions* *The Wall*		
1939–40	Soldier, Essey-lès-Nancy, Brumath and Morsbronn	1939–40	Soldier
1940	*The Psychology of the Imagination*		
1940–41	Prisoner of war, Trier	1940–44	Teacher, Lycée Carnot; work in Resistance
1941	Teacher, Paris, Lycée Pasteur de Neuilly		
1941–44	Teacher, Paris, Lycée Condorcet; Resistance	1942	*The Structure of Behavior*
1943	*Being and Nothingness* *The Flies*	1944	Teacher, Lycée Condorcet
		1945	*Phenomenology of Perception*
1944	*No Exit* (performed)		
1945	Retires from teaching Trip to the United States Public Lecture: "Existentialism Is a Humanism" *The Age of Reason* *The Reprieve* First issues of *Les Temps modernes*	1945–49	Professor, University of Lyon Coeditor, *Les Temps modernes*
1946	Second trip to the United States *The Victors* *Anti-Semite and Jew* *The Respectable Prostitute*		
1947	*What Is Literature?* *The Chips Are Down* *Baudelaire* *Situations,* I	1947	*Humanism and Terror* "The Primacy of Perception"
1948	Trip to Mexico and Guatemala	1948	*Sense and Non-Sense*

	Jean-Paul Sartre		Maurice Merleau-Ponty
	Foundation of the Political Party "Rassemblement Démocratique Révolutionnaire"		
	Dirty Hands		
	In the Mesh		
	Situations, II		
1949	*Situations,* III	1949–52	Chair of Psychology and Pedagogy, Sorbonne
	Troubled Sleep		
1951	*The Devil and the Good Lord*		
1952	"Conversion" to Communism	1952–61	Professor, Paris, Collège de France
	The Communists and Peace (1952–54)	1952	"Indirect Language and the Voices of Silence"
	Participation in Communist Congress in Vienna		
	Saint Genet: Actor and Martyr		
		1953	*In Praise of Philosophy* (inaugural lecture at the Collège de France)
1954	Trip to the Soviet Union		Resignation from *Les Temps modernes*
	Kean or Disorder and Genius		
1955	*Nekrassov*	1955	*Adventures of the Dialectic*
1957	*Search for a Method*		
1959	*The Condemned of Altona*		
1960	*Critique of Dialectical Reason,* volume 1	1960	*Signs*
			"The Eye and Mind"
		1961	†
1963	*The Words*		
1964	Refusal of the Nobel Prize for Literature	1964	*The Visible and the Invisible* (posthumous)
	Situations, IV		
	Situations, V		
	Situations, VI		
1965	*Situations,* VII		

	Jean-Paul Sartre		Maurice Merleau-Ponty
	The Trojan Women		
		1969	*The Prose of the World* (posthumous)
1970	Editor of Maoist journal *La Cause du peuple*		
1971	*The Family Idiot. Gustav Flaubert,* I and II		
1972	*The Family Idiot. Gustav Flaubert,* III *Situations,* VIII *Situations,* IX		
1973	Blindness		
1976	*Situations,* X		
1980	†		
1983	*Quiet Moments in a War* (posthumous) *Notebooks for an Ethics* (posthumous)		
1985	*Critique of Dialectical Reason,* volume 2 (posthumous)		

Original Sources of the Essays

1. Leo Rauch, "Sartre, Merleau-Ponty and the 'Hole in Being,'" *Philosophical Studies* 18 (1969), 119–32. Reprinted with kind permission from Kluwer Academic Publishers.
2. John M. Moreland, "For-itself and In-itself in Sartre and Merleau-Ponty," *Philosophy Today* 17 (1973), 311–18.
3. Colin Smith, "Sartre and Merleau Ponty: The Case for a Modified Essentialism," *Journal of the British Society for Phenomenology* 1 (1970), 73–79.
4. James F. Sheridan, "On Ontology and Politics: A Polemic," *Dialogue* 7 (1968), 449–60.
5. Margaret Whitford, "Merleau-Ponty's Critique of Sartre's Philosophy: An Interpretative Account," *French Studies* 33 (1979), 305–18.
6. C. M. T. Hanly, "Phenomenology, Consciousness and Freedom," *Dialogue* 5 (1996), 323–45.
7. François H. Lapointe, "The Existence of Alter Egos: Jean-Paul Sartre and Maurice Merleau-Ponty," *Journal of Phenomenological Psychology* 6 (1976), 209–16.
8. Monika Langer, "Sartre and Merleau-Ponty: A Reappraisal," in *The Philosophy of Jean-Paul Sartre,* ed. Paul Arthur Schlipp (La Salle: Open Court, 1981), 300–325. Reprinted by permission of Open Court Publishing Company, a division of Carus Publishing.
9. Martin C. Dillon, "Sartre on the Phenomenal Body and Merleau-Ponty's Critique," *Journal of the British Society for Phenomenology* 5 (1974), 144–58.
10. Glen A. Mazis, "Touch and Vision: Rethinking with Merleau-Ponty Sartre on the Caress," *Philosophy Today* 23 (1979), 321–28.
11. Joseph S. Catalano, "The Body and the Book: Reading *Being and Nothingness,*" published for the first time in this collection.
12. John J. Compton, "Sartre, Merleau-Ponty, and Human Freedom," *Journal of Philosophy* 79 (1982), 577–88. Reprinted by permission of John J. Compton and the *Journal of Philosophy.*

13. Ronald L. Hall, "Freedom: Merleau-Ponty's Critique of Sartre," *Philosophy Research Archives* 6 (1980), 360–70.
14. Jon Stewart, "Merleau-Ponty's Criticisms of Sartre's Theory of Freedom," *Philosophy Today* 39 (1995), 311–24.
15. Graham Daniels, "Sartre and Merleau-Ponty: An Existentialist Quarrel," *French Studies* 24 (1970), 379–92.
16. Ronald Aronson, "Vicissitudes of the Dialectic: From Merleau-Ponty's *Les Aventures de la Dialectique* to Sartre's *Second Critique*," *Philosophical Forum* 18 (1987), 358–91.
17. Thomas R. Flynn, "Merleau-Ponty and the *Critique of Dialectical Reason*," in *Hypatia*, ed. William M. Calder III, Ulrich K. Goldsmith, and Phyllis B. Kenevan (Boulder: Colorado Associated University Press, 1985), 241–50.
18. Mikel Dufrenne, "Sartre and Merleau-Ponty," in *Jean-Paul Sartre: Contemporary Approaches to His Philosophy*, ed. Hugh J. Silverman (Pittsburgh: Duquesne University Press, 1980), 209–18.
19. Marjorie Grene, "The Aesthetic Dialogue of Sartre and Merleau-Ponty," *Journal of the British Society for Phenomenology* 1 (1970), 59–70.
20. John O'Neill, "Situation and Temporality," *Philosophy and Phenomenological Research* 28 (1968), 413–22.
21. "Philosophy and Political Engagement: Letters from the Quarrel Between Sartre and Merleau-Ponty," trans. and ed. Jon Stewart. This translation appears here for the first time. A translation of "Sartre, Merleau-Ponty: les lettres d'une rupture," *Magazine liltéraire*, no. 320 (April 1994), 67–85.
22. Maurice Merleau-Ponty, "Sartre and Ultrabolshevism," in *Adventures of the Dialectic*, trans. Joseph Bien (Evanston: Northwestern University Press, 1973), 95–201.
23. Simone de Beauvoir, "Merleau-Ponty and Pseudo-Sartreanism," trans. Veronique Zaytzeff, *International Studies in Philosophy* 21 (1989), 3–48. Originally in *Les Temps modernes* 10, nos. 114–15 (July 1955), 2072–2122. Reprinted in *Privilèges* (Paris: Gallimard, 1955), 203–72.
24. Maurice Merleau-Ponty, "The Philosophy of Existence," trans. Allen S. Weiss, in *Texts and Dialogues: Merleau-Ponty*, ed. Hugh J. Silverman and James Barry, Jr. (Atlantic Highlands: Humanities Press International, Inc., 1992), 129–39. This piece was first presented on 17 November 1959 as part of a Canadian radio program entitled "Conference." A transcript (from which this text is taken) was published in 1966 in *Dialogue* 5, no. 3.
25. Maurice Merleau-Ponty, "Introduction," in *Signs*, trans. Richard C. McCleary (Evanston: Northwestern University Press, 1964), 3–35.
26. Maurice Merleau-Ponty, "Interrogation and Dialectic," in *The Visible*

and the Invisible, trans. Alphonso Lingis (Evanston: Northwestern University Press, 1968), 50–104.

27. Jean-Paul Sartre, "Merleau-Ponty," trans. Benita Eisler, in *Situations IV* (New York: Braziller, Inc., 1966), 156–226. Copyright © 1964 by Éditions Gallimard; reprinted by permission of Georges Borchardt, Inc. Originally "Merleau-Ponty vivant," *Les Temps modernes,* 17, nos. 184–85 (1961).

PART 1

ONTOLOGY

1

Sartre, Merleau-Ponty, and the "Hole in Being"

Leo Rauch

Jean-Paul Sartre and Maurice Merleau-Ponty share the composite position of acknowledging the influence of Husserl on their work and of claiming to fulfill Husserl's intentions, yet of criticizing Husserl for having failed to live up to his own intentions. This is the outer form of their explicit criticism of Husserl. Their work itself constitutes an implicit criticism of Husserl, while it gives us some indication of the direction that Husserl's continued researches might have taken.

Especially remarkable is the fact that Sartre and Merleau-Ponty share these explicit and implicit standpoints while going in diametrically opposed directions: Sartre emphasizes the Cartesian standpoint which he says he shares with Husserl—leading him to differ with Husserl; Merleau-Ponty emphasizes his rejection of Husserl's Cartesian standpoint—leading him (paradoxically, in his own view) closer to the position and to the fulfillment of Husserl's aims.

What first strikes the Husserl reader upon contact with Sartre and Merleau-Ponty is that their spheres of inquiry differ so sharply from Husserl's. They seem to be concerned not so much with discussion of the nature of phenomenology and its relation to the other sciences (as is so often the case with Husserl), nor with formal preparatory analyses, but rather with the content which is to fill out those formal preparatory analyses. Only rarely did Husserl get around to such content. He was always stressing the point that his analyses were devoted mainly to the noetic side of experience (the side concerned with the *acts* of knowing) and that these analyses of his would some day have to be complemented by noematic analyses (analyses of the object-referents of noetic acts). This direction (away from the noetic, the formal side, and toward the noematic, the contextual side) is one which Husserl might have taken.

Sartre gives us noetic analyses of the emotions and of the imagination, as well as noematic analyses of, for example, the "other" and of the "thing." Moreover, he has developed an "existential psychoanalysis" (nontherapeutic in purpose) with which to achieve noematic analyses of certain aspects of experience such as the "viscosity" of objects. This is to such an extent an analysis of objects as known rather than of knowing acts that it amounts to an "existential psychoanalysis" of objects themselves. He believes that he has gone beyond Husserl in closing the gap between the "I can" and the "I think" (in effect, the *cogito* is seen entirely in terms of *possum* and *facio*). This is part of his analysis of consciousness in terms of its absolute autonomy, its translucency, its freedom from all determination as an object, its "nothingness."

Merleau-Ponty gives us analyses of perception which purport to overcome the subject-object distinction altogether. Whether this amounts to a violation of Husserl's noesis-noema distinction, and whether Husserl himself would ultimately have taken such a position cannot be argued here. The fact is that Merleau-Ponty seems to have sidestepped Husserl's problem of how consciousness constitutes its world. (The problem, for Husserl, is how consciousness constitutes the world of *its* experience as somehow independent of its experience. Thus, Husserl retains the distinction between consciousness and world, between the knowing act and the object known. But how can the distinction be retained, Husserl asks himself, if the world is experienced only in acts of "internal" consciousness, and if all metaphysical questions as to whether the world "really" is there "outside" consciousness must be put aside?) Merleau-Ponty sidesteps the problem by refusing to isolate consciousness from its world: he sees consciousness as already *in* its world. For example, he is not so much concerned with the role of his body in experience as he is with his experience of the body itself. He is not concerned with the interrelation of an *ego* and its *tu,* but with a nonegological view of experience in its broader historical setting. He expresses the claim that he is being guided by the Husserl of the later period, and that he is following lines implicit in Husserl, even if this leads him into conflict with Husserl's explicit views—all the more reason for seeing in Merleau-Ponty's work some provocative suggestions of the direction in which Husserl might have (or ought to have) gone.

Sartre

Let us begin with the explicit criticism of Husserl by Sartre. He accuses Husserl of the following:[1] (1) infidelity to his original conception of phenomenology (the infidelity of yielding to a Berkeleyan idealism rendering Being and transcendent objects unreal); (2) "pure immanentism"; (3) failure to escape the "thing-illusion" (by introducing into his picture of consciousness a passive *hyle* as well as his doctrine of sensation); (4) remaining on the level of a "functional description" of appearances, a level which bars him from "existential dialectics"; (5) being a phenomenalist rather than a phenomenologist; (6) failure to describe adequately how we transcend consciousness and get into the world, and how we transcend the immediate present and arrive at a knowledge of past and future; (7) failure to escape solipsism (as much as Kant fails), particularly by introducing the useless hypothesis of a transcendental subject; (8) failure to observe the obstructive elements embedded in our immediate experience; (9) failure to identify freedom with consciousness and with the human essence, and mistakenly thinking that an eidetic phenomenology of essences can grasp freedom; and (10) on the whole, attempting to describe the essential structure of consciousness without raising the ontological question of the being of consciousness.

How justifiable these criticisms are is not our problem. It is enough to point out that Husserl expressly brackets all questions of "reality" (putting the word "reality" in quotation marks) in order to penetrate to the constituting consciousness itself. Indeed, for Husserl such bracketing of all metaphysical issues (e.g. bracketing the questions of the "reality" of the world when it is not impinging on our consciousness; bracketing the question of how an "objective" world affects our "subjective" consciousness) is the first indispensable step in approaching the process of the constituting consciousness. Only by turning away from all such questions regarding "externals" are we led to the "internal" acts by which consciousness projects its objects as "external." We get "to the things themselves" by turning inward. It is useless, therefore, to fault Husserl for having failed to resolve problems of transcendence and ontology when he explicitly refuses to undertake their solution and tells us repeatedly why he must refuse. He refuses on the grounds that he must regard things only in terms of their status as phenomena for consciousness ("*Was die Dinge sind . . . das sind sie als Dinge der Erfahrung*").[2]

There is in Sartre's work the attempt to bridge an ontological gap which Husserl was content to leave a gap: "Between consciousness and reality there yawns a veritable abyss of sense" ("*Zwischen Bewußtsein und*

Realität gähnt ein wahrer Abgrund des Sinnes").[3] This is not a metaphysical dualism but a dualism of the subject-object relation whereby "reality" is grasped and consciousness does the grasping: i.e., Husserl proposes to regard "reality" only as a phenomenon *for* consciousness, and consciousness as a consciousness *of* reality. It is the interplay and the separation of these two senses (for and of) that characterizes the intentional relation. To reduce one term of the relation to the other term is to abandon phenomenology for natural science or metaphysics, neither of which are Husserl's proper concern as phenomenologist. Rather, it is Husserl's aim to describe phenomena as the correlates of the intentional acts of consciousness. The reduction of subject to object or of object to subject, then, does not destroy phenomenology but merely ignores its pervasive theme: the characteristic of consciousness as intentional, as "pointing," the characteristic by which the subject grasps its object as something other than itself.

For Husserl, it is of fundamental importance to keep before us this difference between reality and consciousness, between object and subject, between *for* and *of*. It is Sartre's aim, however, "to reconcile the object and the subject."[4] Although Husserl would hold that this reconciliation is no aim belonging properly to phenomenology (since the intentional relation is inescapably a relation *between* subject and object as polar terms), it is nevertheless seen by Sartre as a genuine problem of phenomenology. For Sartre, the object becomes a "thing" involved in human existence, and its chief role as "thing" is that of thwarting human freedom: on the most elementary level, it is a physical obstruction to human purposes; on a higher level, it is the paradigm of the inertness and inertia to which human consciousness itself tends. Thus, the dualism of subject and object becomes a metaphysical dualism of freedom *versus* the thing, of nothing and being, of *pour-soi* and *en-soi*—and as such, it may be said to present more of a continuum than a polar duality.

The expression of human freedom is the choice in favor of being a subject rather than an object or thing. The subject must, therefore, be free of all objective determination, so that if to be a thing is to be real, then to be a free subject is to be "nothing." It is only because the *cogito* can think anything, and thus "become" anything, that it "is" nothing. Sartre feels that Husserl has in some way reified the ego, and it is for this reason that he must oppose Husserl, namely to free the ego of all determination as object, even of the determination as "object" of reflection. (The equivocation of the two senses of the word "object" is obvious. The former is metaphysical; the latter is intentional.)

The identification of consciousness with freedom (in every sense of the term, e.g., freedom from physiological or Freudian causality, freedom in creativity) becomes the main theme for Sartre. It is a theme which is not inimical to Husserl, since Husserl emphasizes the need for bracketing all considerations of physiological causation, and since he places almost as great an emphasis on the role of the "I can" as he does on the "I think." It is possible to imagine, therefore, that Husserl would have attempted to work toward a closer identification of consciousness and freedom, albeit not necessarily along Sartre's metaphysical lines.

For Sartre, the primary contrast is in the fact that consciousness is translucent and free while the reified ego is opaque and fixed; the ego is therefore an impediment to consciousness, is even "the death of consciousness."[5] Accordingly, it is not Husserl's transcendental subjectivity that Sartre attacks but the possible reification involved in the notion of a transcendental ego. He seems ignorant of Husserl's repeated warnings along these lines, namely, that the ego is not an object—whether as thing or as object of consciousness. (Had Husserl been content to regard the ego as another object of consciousness, and to say with Descartes "I know myself better than I know anything," he would hardly have had the problems he did have. But Husserl cannot accede to so facile a blindness. His problems arise from the fact that his phenomenology requires the ego as one pole of the intentional relationship of consciousness to its object, while he always remains painfully aware that such an ego can *never* be an object of experience.) Sartre is wrong, therefore, to connect the notion of a reified ego with Husserl, since Husserl had emphatically rejected such a reification long before Sartre. In any case, the transcendental consciousness (not ego) becomes for Sartre an impersonal spontaneity, uncaused (whether by the self or by any extraneous causes) and at each instant a creation *ex nihilo.*[6]

In these respects, Sartre's notion of transcendental subjectivity differs little from Husserl's—except that Sartre has a new answer to the problem of solipsism: in such impersonal subjectivity, no subject is given preeminence over any other, so that there is no problem of how to get out of *this* subject which I may or may not know as *my* "ego." The only question remaining is whether Husserl would have gone from the "transcendental ego" to a "transcendental consciousness"—if these can at all be said to be distinct for him. If they are distinct for him, then there is good ground for the view that he could make this step easily—since the "transcendental ego" is no entity at all, but merely the subjective correlate of "the universe of possible sense" ("*das Universum möglichen Sinnes*").[7] Consider the totality of meaning, all the meaning there is, and consider that any particular piece of meaning is a subjective product, and you already have the notion of transcendental subjectivity as the basis of that all-inclusive totality. Transcendental subjectivity is no one's identity, but subjectivity considered as such, and in association with all sense possible. (So much for the reputed abstruseness of the notion.)

As for the pure ego, the ego grasped in reflection, Sartre's discussion of the reflective and prereflective levels of consciousness is not altogether novel. Husserl discusses them.[8] The problem connected with reflection as a mode of consciousness is that reflection reverses the usual outward-direction of the intentional consciousness; since reflection is directed inward at consciousness itself, there is a problem in achieving a scrutiny of consciousness without disturbing that consciousness. The problem is raised even by Brentano, Husserl's teacher, and it can be expressed thus: if the fundamental characteristic of consciousness is its intentionality, its directedness to an object other than itself in its knowing-act (as when, in the quite ordinary way, I am conscious of the piece of paper before me rather than being conscious of my act of perceiving it)—then by what extraordinary mode is a consciousness *of* consciousness itself achieved? Far from being at one with itself, it would seem that in self-consciousness we have a consciousness that is disunited. Sartre feels that the unity of consciousness is achieved not in reflection but in its unity with the objects of its experience. Thus, consciousness "unifies itself by escaping itself."[9] Here he admits to following Husserl.

What is new in Sartre's discussion is the characterization of consciousness as negation. It was William James[10] who pointed out that consciousness is a nonentity. But Sartre goes farther by saying that the function of this nonentity is that of negation, i.e., knowing is negating or (as Desan translates Sartre's *néantisation)* knowing is a "nihilation."

For Sartre, it is the characteristic of consciousness as negation that makes possible the reconciliation of object and subject. It is difficult to see how he achieves this, if indeed he does. The trouble with the introduction of any metaphysical dualism with subjectivity as one of its terms is that the element of subjectivity tilts the balance to its weaker side: the emphasis is on subjectivity as unreal, rather than on reality as unintelligible. Subjectivity is "the hole in Being" (as Sartre puts it). The result is no resolution at all, but at best a lessening of the ambivalence arising in the process of defining subject and object in terms of each other.

As a negation of Being, it may be possible to regard consciousness as the dialectical counterpoise to Being.[11] And this may suggest a metaphysical (and perhaps also a metaphorical) resolution: Being is without sense, consciousness is without Being. Yet Husserl's nonmetaphysical contrast between the *sense* of consciousness and the *sense* of reality is here retained by Sartre, despite his efforts to reconcile the subject and object in these altogether different metaphysical senses. Sartre states that by attempting to bestow sense on Being, consciousness seeks to fashion a "world." As a project, this attempt at reconciliation is thoroughly Cartesian and Husserlian. For Sartre, however, this project is as impossible to achieve in actuality as is an attempt to combine the in-itself with the for-itself, to combine (or to try to reconcile) some inert thing with a free mind as though the two could have some common denominator. How can we combine rocks and meaning, when they are in two utterly different "worlds"? To say that meaning is somehow bestowed on rocks, as though it were painted on, is to commit the gravest category-mistake. But what makes the attempted reconciliation impossible is not merely a metaphysical polarity but rather an indissoluble polarity of two senses. From Sartre's metaphysical standpoint, we might ask: How can unconscious Being be absorbed in unreal consciousness? From a Kantian standpoint, we might ask: What category of understanding could possibly include both? But from a phenomenological standpoint, we might ask: How can an object (as something intended by consciousness) be combined with the intending consciousness?—and suddenly we are made aware that what is metaphysically irreconcilable is phenomenologically reconcilable, simply because no metaphysical problem exists if everything is reduced to the status of phenomenon for consciousness. Thus, Sartre's attempt is futile, as long as it is a metaphysical attempt and not a phenomenological attempt.

The error (of regarding Being as supposedly identical with consciousness) has been committed many times before, under various guises: it is the error implicit in the ontological argument. It is the error in saying "*Cogito, ergo sum.*" Worse, it is like the human attempt to become God, an undertaking doomed to failure because it is self-contradictory. This is self-contradictory because consciousness must remain free of *all* determination, even free of the fixating determination which Being would lend to it. When Sartre characterizes consciousness as "that which is what it is not, and is not what it is" he intends to suggest that consciousness is free of all ties to its past, creating itself as it creates its future. This means that a transcendental consciousness (which Sartre never rejected, since it is only the transcendental subject he rejects) is still lurking behind any sense "bestowed" on an otherwise blind universe—even if such a transcendental consciousness is beset with *hybris* and inevitable failure.

The source of failure is not only in the self-contradiction implicit in any metaphysical attempt to combine the in-itself with the for-itself. The failure arises also in the negating function of consciousness itself. (If this negating is what consciousness—in its freedom— is all about, then a unification of Being and consciousness would result in a nonbeing Being.) The best example of such negating is in the act of imagining, which posits its intended object as not existing. When we imagine the unicorn, the very act of imagining is itself a contribution to the unicorn's nonexistence, since we are aware throughout the act that we are merely imagining him. This very act of consciousness, then, drains the object's Being from it. Sartre extends this negative aspect to all other phases of consciousness: since consciousness in one way or another negates its objects, consciousness is therefore a standing off from reality. Negation comes into the world only with consciousness; nature itself has no privations, no absences. Any and all determination by consciousness is, for Sartre, a determination in the scholastic sense in which *omnis determinatio est negatio.*

For Husserl, on the other hand, the act of consciousness is not a negating act; the "I can" is a positive, creative function. Nor does consciousness "stand off" from the world (except in some way in reflection). Consciousness does not grasp its objects as transcending consciousness (for then it could not grasp them at all), but grasps them as transcending only the immanent stream of consciousness. (This point is, again, not at all metaphysical but intentional, phenomenological.) For Sartre, however, the object does transcend consciousness—and he faults Husserl for failing to see this: the object is *intended* as being independent of consciousness altogether, since the Being of an object is opposed to the non-Being of consciousness. (Although Sartre speaks of "intending," here, his point is clearly metaphysical, not phenomenological.) Not only is it the transcendent object that is independent of consciousness for Sartre, but consciousness as it is grasped in reflection is independent of consciousness as well (since it unifies itself only by escaping itself). For Husserl, there is such a function as a nonreflective consciousness, as there is for Sartre. But that it should be by nature independent of all possible reflection is unimaginable.

In any case, the consideration of transcendent objects apart from consciousness is bracketed by Husserl: a transphenomenal thing is conceivable, although it is as otiose a conception as Kant's *Ding an sich;* a transphenomenal phenomenon is a logical absurdity.

Merleau-Ponty

We saw that for Husserl it is vital that the tension of his characteristic dualism be maintained. In ordinary language (the "ordinary" loaded with the metaphysical presuppositions which Husserl seeks to circumvent), we would express this dualism by saying that the external world is grasped by an internal consciousness. And the history of philosophy has shown us what enormous problems are occasioned by expressing the dualism in such terms. But in the more circumspect language of phenomenology, in which such metaphysical references to the "external" and the "internal" status of world and consciousness are put in quotation marks (set aside, put out of play), we would state the dualism in the following way: although the experienced world is constituted in immanent consciousness, that world is experienced as transcending the immanence of consciousness (not, that is, transcending consciousness itself but transcending its immanent stream). All metaphysics aside, transcendence is experienced as different from immanence: the difference being between (1) the sense of the object as experienced and (2) the nature of the act of experience.

Now, from the standpoint of Sartre and Merleau-Ponty, we may ask: If such a dualism is so basic to phenomenology, can there be a phenomenology without it? Further, can such a nondualistic phenomenology claim to preserve and fulfill Husserl's aims?

For Sartre, the attempted reconciliation of object and subject leads to a self-contradiction when that reconciliation is framed in terms of the in-itself and the for-itself. (Merleau-Ponty regards Sartre's distinction between the in-itself and the for-itself as excessively dualistic and not phenomenological.) Further, Sartre says, the attempt to bestow a sense on the blind world is doomed to futility because the world was, is, and will continue as blind, intractable Being—a fabric in which the presence of consciousness "makes a hole."

For Merleau-Ponty, the reconciliation is not only possible, it is constant, ubiquitous, and by no means futile as an aim. The bestowal of sense is not an enterprise which is alien to the Being of the world; only the Cartesian dualism of Husserl and Sartre can lead to such a view, even if Husserl never held such a view. Merleau-Ponty's feeling is that Husserl's ultimate standpoint would have been non-Cartesian, and that he (Merleau-Ponty) is fulfilling that unexpressed aim in finding a reconciliation.

Another reconciliation which Merleau-Ponty proposes to achieve is that between the objective sciences and the excessively subjective Cartesianism of philosophy. Husserl gave his reasons for holding that such a reconciliation is impossible: from the point of view of phenomenology—the genuinely "strict" science—the natural sciences share a common error: they posit a world as external and real, while they ignore that act of metaphysical positing and then attempt to refer the meaning of our experience of the world to that posited world itself. Thus, the sciences never rise above what Husserl calls the "natural attitude" or the "natural standpoint." We could even borrow the phrase of G. E. Moore and say that they commit a "naturalistic fallacy."

In this respect all natural science is naive, since it pays no heed to its own presuppositions. Such naïveté leads to all sorts of systematic weaknesses, perhaps the most serious of which is the error of psychologism: the attempted reduction of logic to psychology, as well as the unquestioning accommodation of that psychology to naturalism and relativism. It is an error we are warned against by Mach and Bradley, among others, although their argument lacks a systematic justification on the order of Husserl's. It is the error made by Mill, of trying to validate certain purely formal concepts in terms of the psychological processes in which they are engendered. In effect, it is the error of reducing "relations of ideas" to "matters of fact." What Husserl is after, then, is a "presuppositionless," non-naturalistic (and therefore nonmetaphysical) study—"a science of consciousness that is not psychology."

Phenomenology is really a process of stripping away as many presuppositions as one possibly can, and thus going back to what is primary: the intentional acts in which we constitute our experience. Such a concern must keep the object and subject separated. A reconciliation of the two (or a reduction of the one to the other) is therefore not possible; that would be to repeat the multifarious errors of metaphysics and natural science.

Merleau-Ponty too, however, goes back to what is primary[12] and, on the basis of this, gives us his grounds for believing in the possibility of such a reconciliation. The world as perceived is to be the basis for science as well as for philosophy—a familiar and innocent-looking proposal, except for what that "world" includes and excludes. He speaks of "re-achieving a direct and primitive contact with the world" (always avoiding, of course, that which we have called the "naturalistic fallacy" of the sciences); he speaks also of "reawakening the basic experience of the world of which science is the second-order expression."[13] Thus, the world of our experience is not the product of intellectual syntheses. Rather, the world is there, prior to any and all analysis—and it is to this prereflective, prepredicative experience he asks us to return.

This takes us back to one of the earliest ways of characterizing phenomenology: pure description. And it asks us to avoid that of which so much bad description is guilty: "construction." This is one of the many meanings Husserl loaded onto his motto: "To the things themselves." When Merleau-Ponty tells us that "The real has to be described not constructed," he is going farther than Husserl and saying that our primary relation to the world is that of direct perception, not synthesis or judgment. But this is not to be taken to mean that a consciousness is first of all distinct and that it then relates itself to the world; rather, its relation to the world is already part of its conscious acts. (The ambiguity arises in the word "act" and the phrase "act of consciousness," since "act" suggests an autonomous "agent." But no, consciousness is not something self-contained, prior to experience. Rather, consciousness is inextricably a consciousness "of," and so much so that no autonomous "act" is implied: "Perception is not a science of the world it is not even act, a deliberate taking up of a position; it is the background from which all acts stand out and is presupposed by them.")

What he is aiming at is a view of man that would avoid all suggestion of man's separability from the world—whether that separability were to be suggested by explicit theory, by implied analogy, or by mere equivocation. What this amounts to, then, is a new form of Sartre's attempt at reconciliation: the sciences present a study of "objectivity" and philosophy a study of "subjectivity," and it is the special task of phenomenology "to understand the relations between consciousness and nature."[14] This is taken by Merleau-Ponty in the sense of that relation as it is manifested in the *Lebenswelt*—except that Merleau-Ponty does not take this back to the acts of a subject, as Husserl does, but emphasizes the aim of viewing the world as there (*là*) and of viewing man *in* that world. This would seem to conflict with Husserl's bracketing of the *là* and with his words at the end of *Cartesian Meditations,* urging us to turn inward where truth resides.[15] Except for these serious reservations, Merleau-Ponty's aim is consistent with Husserl's ultimate aim of getting around to noematic analyses.

Merleau-Ponty is concerned to show the primacy of the given.[16] In this light, in which nothing is to be presupposed, the perceived world is not to be regarded as a sum of objects. Nor, in our role as perceiver, is our relation to the world that of a thinker to an object of thought. Nor is the unity of the perceived thing, in being perceived by several consciousnesses, in any way comparable to the unity of a proposition as understood by several thinkers (as it is for Husserl). What Merleau-Ponty is denying in all this is the continuity whereby an object of perception passes easily into an object of thought, the continuity whereby the act of perception is amalgamated with the act of thinking.

On the basis of this proposed discontinuity, Merleau-Ponty holds that we cannot apply the form-matter distinction to perception (as we might apply it to thought). Nor can we speak of the perceiving subject as performing acts which approximate the act of thinking. Thus, we must not speak of the perceiver as "interpreting," "deciphering," or "ordering" a sensible matter, as though the object is grasped without its sense before its sense is bestowed or as though its "matter" (Husserl's "*hyle*") precedes its "form." The perceived object is already in a *world* of sense; matter is already pregnant with its form—which would seem to indicate that for Merleau-Ponty intentionality no longer serves (as it does for Husserl) as the "form" to sensory "matter."

This perceived world—shall we call it a "world of sense as given"?—is the implicit foundation of all rationality, all value, all existence.[17] This foundation is a nondiscursive, noninferential foundation. It is a foundation in immediacy. Let us contrast this with the cultivated rationality of Brentano, for whom even the psychical phenomena known as feelings are invariably based on judgments. There is a similar continuity between mere presentations *(Vorstellungen)* and judgments, lending to presentations a quasi-judgmental character. This intellectualism—even if it is expressed in the empiricism of a Locke, the skepticism of a Hume, or the matter-form doctrine of a Husserl—is what Merleau-Ponty is attacking.

For Descartes and Kant, consciousness is the condition of there being anything at all. In this way, they manage to detach the subject from the world. Merleau-Ponty wants to reconnect it. The point of Merleau-Ponty's argument is that it is in the act of thinking, not in perception, that we experience the most apparent division between subject and object. In perception, the subject is already "at the world" (*au monde*). Accordingly, the first step in overcoming the subject-object dichotomy is to remove from our explanation of perception any element relating it to thinking.

For example, in perceiving a cube, I cannot say that I *represent* to myself the unseen sides. To represent something to oneself is to grasp it quasi-intellectually as not actually existing. But the unseen sides are grasped not as being imaginary, only hidden. Nor can I say that I anticipate seeing the unseen sides (if I were to turn the cube), thereby identifying the grasp of the unseen (in perception) with the intellectual process of anticipation. What is given in the perception of a cube is not a discursive formula such as "If a cube is turned . . ." Perception does not give propositional truths, but presences. I grasp the unseen sides as present—not as the objects of a possible perception, nor as a conclusion following an intellectual synthesis, but as a practical synthesis: the other sides *are* accessible to my touch. (Again this is a way of replacing the *cogito,* as the basic act of consciousness, with *possum* and *facio.)*

This means that the synthesis "constituting" (we must take care to avoid the quasi-intellectual connotations of this word) the unity of a perceived object is not an intellectual synthesis. The object is not given as a collection of sense-data intellectually synthesized into transcendent qualities, which qualities are then intellectually synthesized into objects. (This is Husserl's view of the act of constitution.) Rather, the whole (with its sense) is prior to its parts. Merleau-Ponty admits that he is reiterating

Husserl's notion of *passive* synthesis, except that there is an increased emphasis on the tension between the perspectival aspect and the sense which draws us beyond it: we never have more than a partial perspective, yet always with a sense of the whole: in perceiving the cube, we grasp it as having more than the (at most) three faces we see of it; the sense of any object we perceive is always a sense transcending the limited perspective we happen to be having of it. "Perception is thus paradoxical. The perceived thing itself is paradoxical."[18] The paradox consists in the fact that although the psychologically constituted object is not foreign to the consciousness of the perceiver, yet the object always contains more than what is given in perception. It is a tension between immanence and transcendence, but with this difference: for Husserl, the problem is how the immanent experience grasps its object as transcending that immanence; for Merleau-Ponty, the problem is how a sense grasped immanently can refer (in a noninferential, nonsymbolic manner) to a *sense* transcending that immanence, in such a way that there is in every perception both a presence and an absence, i.e., sides seen, and sides "seen" as unseen.

What Merleau-Ponty seeks to accomplish in his emphasis on the primacy of perception is the circumvention of the intellectual reductionism whereby (to take one example) the world is seen as composed of nothing but sense-data and its composites. If this were possible—i.e., if it were possible to isolate the sensory "matter" of experience from its animating sense—then Sartre's senseless Being would be conceivable as a notion. Sartre feels that he can derive such an isolation from Husserl's schema. Merleau-Ponty, however, feels that Husserl's emphasis on the given obviates the possibility of such an isolation. The aforementioned sense of paradox supports this.

In Merleau-Ponty's sense of paradox, Sartre's distinction between a senseless reality and an unreal consciousness is overcome: there is no experience of Being which is an experience without sense. Since no such an instance of Being is ever given, there is no sense in hypostatizing it—and, in doing so, Sartre shows himself to be indulging in the same nonexistential intellectualism as is Husserl. If all we experience is a world already there *(déjà là)*, a world of sense, then how can we speak of a "matter" being animated by sense (a sense-datum, that is, animated by a "meaning"), let alone of a Being opposed to sense?

This analysis of Merleau-Ponty's launches a direct attack upon Husserl's excessively intellectualistic view of perception as expressed in the first volume of *Ideen*. Yet Merleau-Ponty considers himself to be doing nothing more than returning to the *Lebenswelt*, as the later Husserl urged.[19] In this way, Merleau-Ponty is retreating from a study of essences and approaching a study of what he considers are existing facts—another path in which he claims to be following the implicit Husserl.[20] In this way, moreover, he believes himself to be consistent with Husserl's view of the underlying rationality of the world.[21] For Merleau-Ponty, this can be shown only in the synthesis of the idea "world" with the idea "rationality." Such a synthesis has been achieved by Husserl, Merleau-Ponty feels. Not only is it the most important achievement of phenomenology, it is made possible only by combining extreme subjectivism with extreme objectivism. Thus, the apparent drift of the later phenomenology of Husserl would, perhaps, have been toward an even more dialectical form of analysis and resolution, together with, and perhaps even identical with, a still more intensive return "to the things themselves" ("*zu den Sachen selbst!*").

Notes

1. See Herbert Spiegelberg, *The Phenomenological Movement* (The Hague, 1960), 451f. Spiegelberg distilled this list from Sartre's *Being and Nothingness.* I have condensed and modified Spiegelberg's list.

2. Edmund Husserl, *Ideen zu einer reinen Phänomenologie und phänomenologischen Philosophie,* vol. 1 (The Hague, 1950), 111.

3. Ibid., 117.

4. Quoted by Spiegelberg, *The Phenomenological Movement,* 455, from Sartre's *Saint Genet.*

5. Jean-Paul Sartre, *The Transcendence of the Ego* (New York, 1957), 40.

6. Ibid., 98f.

7. Edmund Husserl, *Cartesianische Meditationen* (The Hague, 1963), 117.

8. See Husserl, *Ideen,* 177f.

9. Sartre, *Transcendence,* 177f.

10. See W. Desan, *The Tragic Finale* (New York, 1960), 145f.

11. See Spiegelberg, *The Phenomenological Movement,* 470f.

12. Maurice Merleau-Ponty, "The Primacy of Perception and its Philosophical Consequences," in *Readings in Existential Phenomenology,* ed. N. Lawrence and D. O'Connor (Englewood Cliffs, N.J., 1967).

13. Maurice Merleau-Ponty, *Phenomenology of Perception* (New York, 1962), viif.

14. Quoted by Spiegelberg, *The Phenomenological Movement,* 528, from Merleau-Ponty's *La Structure du comportement.*

15. Husserl, *Cartesianische Meditationen,* 183.

16. Merleau-Ponty, "The Primacy of Perception," 31f.

17. Ibid., 32.

18. Ibid., 34.

19. Edmund Husserl, *Die Krisis der europäischen Wissenschaften und die transzendentale Phänomenologie* (The Hague, 1954), 157.

20. See Spiegelberg, *The Phenomenological Movement,* 535.

21. Husserl, *Ideen,* 313.

2

For-Itself and In-Itself in Sartre and Merleau-Ponty

John M. Moreland

Sartre maintains that consciousness is "transparent" to itself. Merleau-Ponty maintains that it is not. In the chapter of the *Phenomenology of Perception* entitled "The Cogito," Merleau-Ponty displays some of the reasons for this difference of views. I will attempt to make clear just what some of these reasons are. In doing this, this paper will become more an attempt to state the criticisms of Sartre implicit in Merleau-Ponty rather than an attempt to justify Merleau-Ponty's position itself.

In *Being and Nothingness* it is difficult to understand the relationship between the in-itself and the for-itself. The *ontological* distinction, as Sartre draws it, between the in-itself and the for-itself makes the nature of their interaction problematic. In this regard it is helpful to note a criticism made by de Waelhens. After noting that in Sartre the for-itself and the in-itself are radically separated—the for-itself is pure Nothingness and the in-itself is pure Being—de Waelhens has this to say in criticism: "Once the for-itself and the in-itself are radically separated, once consciousness becomes a spectator without consistency in its own right, the die is cast: such a consciousness will know or not know, but it cannot know in several ways or be related to the in-itself in an ambiguous fashion. As soon as it knows, it pierces through; as soon as it speaks, everything is said at once."[1] There is a striking similarity between this argument and Hume's argument to the conclusion that there is only one act of the mind. Hume's argument, briefly, is that since consciousness just *is* the occurrence of impressions and ideas, all purported acts of the mind are reducible to one: conception, the act of having an impression or idea. De Waelhens's point is just that from an ontological point of view, there is only one kind of consciousness, the for-itself in contact with the in-itself, a consequence even Sartre could not accept on the phenomenological level. For on the phenomenological level, there clearly are different acts of the mind, different ways in which the for-itself is related to the in-itself: one knows, doubts, perceives, imagines, etc. But if the for-itself is ontologically distinct from the in-itself in an absolute sense, this is incomprehensible. Either the for-itself reaches the in-itself or it does not: if it does, then all is given, all is known; if it does not, there is nothing, there is not even consciousness, for the for-itself removed from the in-itself is pure nothingness.

It would be a mistake, I think, to say that Sartre defines for-itself and in-itself as ontological contraries and thus makes it impossible for there to be *any* interaction between the two.[2] Given the strong criticism Sartre makes of the Cartesian position, to interpret him as advocating a dualism which equals in radicalism that of Descartes is to be grossly unfair to Sartre. The criticism to be considered here is less radical. It is assumed there is no lack of coherency in the notion of distinct ontological categories interacting. The problem is rather what sorts of interactions are possible given the descriptions Sartre gives of the ontological categories. Sartre gives a phenomenological description of human experience that is in many places insightful and, I think, correct. But much of Sartre that one would wish to accept on the phenomenological level seems to be without foundation in view of the description of for-itself and in-itself with which he begins *Being and Nothingness.*

I take it that this is the general problem that Merleau-Ponty is dealing with in "The Cogito."[3] It is necessary to have a clear grasp of the relation of the for-itself to the in-itself to be able to understand the various functionings of consciousness—doubting, affirming, perceiving, etc. In both Sartre and Merleau-Ponty, an individual conscious act (e.g., a perceiving) involves a particular relation between the for-itself and the in-itself. Presumably, in a perceiving, this relation is different than in the case of an imagining, etc. Thus, to understand the structure of these various mental acts, one must understand the various possible ways in which the for-itself and the in-itself can be related.

According to Merleau-Ponty, it is important not only to *understand* the possible relations of for-itself and in-itself, but to have some *experience* of their relations. For example, the other is present first of all as an object among objects. In the gaze is found the experience of the other as a transcendence. But, Merleau-Ponty contends, "Unless I learn within myself to recognize the junction of the *for itself* and the *in itself,* none of those mechanisms called other bodies will ever be able to come to life; unless I have an exterior others have no interior" (*PP,* 373). In the experience of the other, one experiences for-itself as supported in in-itself; one experiences in-itself as for-itself. If one has in oneself no experience of this junction of for-itself and in-itself, the experience of it in others is impossible. According to Merleau-Ponty, it is in the *cogito* that one experiences this junction of the for-itself and in-itself.

There is much in Sartre's account of the *cogito* that Merleau-Ponty can accept. In particular, he can accept Sartre's critique of the Cartesian *cogito* as being reflective and thus unable to give one knowledge of a *thinking* self. The self which is the object of all acts of reflection is the empirical ego, a transcendent object which falls in the *epoché.* The self which thinks is a nothingness and can never be an object of consciousness.

But Merleau-Ponty's disagreements with Sartre are more important than his agreements. Regarding the Cartesian *cogito,* for example, Merleau-Ponty claims there is no certain knowledge which comes in this act. Sartre, on the other hand, would allow one to be certain when reflecting on momentary acts of consciousness.[4] This disagreement points to a fundamental difference in the views of consciousness held by these two men. For Sartre, consciousness is "transparent" to itself. This seems to mean that, at least in certain cases, reflection leads to certain knowledge of my consciousness. It need not be thought, however, that the transparency of consciousness *must* involve claims of the indubitability of reflective knowledge. Indubitability seems to arise for Sartre when one considers a reflective act which takes as its object *present* consciousness (e.g., the present appearance of this chair). If I say that there is a consciousness of a chair, I cannot be mistaken if the claim is not taken to mean there is a chair of which I am conscious and which would appear again in various prescribed situations. Indubitability is possible so long as one attends in reflection to the present consciousness. But when I transcend this consciousness to the objects, states, actions, etc. to which it points, I open the possibility of error. So Sartre says, "Reflection has limits, both limits of validity and limits in fact. It is consciousness which posits a consciousness. Everything that it affirms regarding this consciousness is certain and adequate. But if other objects appear to it through this consciousness, there is no reason that these objects should participate in the characteristics of consciousness."[5] Thus, if the sight of Peter arouses in me a profound convulsion of repugnance and anger, "I cannot be mistaken when I say: I feel at this moment a violent repugnance for Peter."[6] But if I go on to say I hate Peter, I might well be mistaken, for this implies that a certain structure applies to consciousness that is no longer or not yet present and, thus, about which I can have no certain knowledge.

There is a way of reading Sartre in which the notion of indubitability sinks into vacuity. This reading pays especially close attention to the early pages of the introduction of *Being and Nothingness.* If the present content of consciousness is an appearance and if in order to say what it is an appearance of, one must transcend the appearance to the infinite series of possible appearances it indicates, then to the extent to which I have indubitable knowledge of the appearance, this knowledge is inarticulate. For suppose there is an appearance, and I say it is an appearance of a chair. This is to transcend the appearance toward the series of possible appearances of the chair, and I can have no indubitable knowledge of this series.

It is not clear to me that this is a misreading of Sartre. He says that essence is revealed through the appearance but that the essence "is the manifest law which presides over the succession of its appearances, it is the principle of the series" (*BN,* xlvi). Thus essence, say that it is a *chair*-appearance, arises only at the level of transcendence and this is clearly beyond the realm of the indubitable. On the other hand, the essence is itself an appearance which, due to the transparency of consciousness, reflection can presumably reach indubitably. It is clear that Sartre thinks that reflection yields knowledge that is both indubitable and articulate. I have quoted passages above that are incontestable on this point and will mention one or two more below.

Suppose I imagine a chair. Then, reflecting on this present consciousness, I gain the certain knowledge that I am in fact imagining a chair. Sartre distinguishes between imagining and perceiving in the following way: "Whether I see or imagine that chair, the object of my perception and that of my image are identical: it is that chair of straw on which I am seated. Only consciousness *is related* in two different ways to the same chair."[7] And this is precisely just what Sartre *must* say: "consciousness is *related* in two different ways to the same chair." For in perception my hold on the chair is tenuous. I might make mistakes concerning it, because I see it from only one side at a time. But in the imagination I have the chair in its totality. I can make no mistakes concerning it because, unlike in the case of perception, the image (of the chair) "is complete at the very moment of its appearance."[8] It is this facet of Sartre's phenomenology which provides the occasion for de Waelhens's criticism. De Waelhens's criticism, reduced to this case, amounts to saying that, given Sartre's metaphysical position, this way of distinguishing between imagination and perception is incoherent. Perception must yield knowledge as certain as that yielded by the imagination.

One might attempt to distinguish between the various acts of consciousness by distinguishing between their objects (*BN,* liii). So perceiving and imagining differ in that they have different sorts of objects. The objects of perceivings are ambiguous in ways the objects of imaginings are not, so one can err in perceiving in ways one cannot in imagining. One is led in this view to the notion of an "intentional object." Different intentional acts require different intentional objects. So when I see the chair, the object of my seeing is one thing (an intentional object appropriate to seeing), and when I remember the chair, the object of my remembering is another thing (an intentional object appropriate to remembering). This view makes incoherent much that one wishes to say about one's conscious acts. It is *impossible* to remember the chair I saw this morning; nor can I imagine it, doubt its existence, etc. For each of these acts demands not only a different object, but a different *kind* of object. It need only be added that neither Merleau-Ponty nor Sartre subscribes to such a view. Not only do different acts of consciousness *not* demand different *kinds* of objects, they may have the *same* object. So in the quotation above, Sartre claims one can both perceive and imagine the same chair.

Merleau-Ponty contends that every act of consciousness is in some sense perceptual and is thus open to much of the possibility of error that perception is. The greatest portion of the chapter on the *cogito* is taken up with Merleau-Ponty's arguments for the opacity of consciousness. I will return to this difference between Sartre and Merleau-Ponty in a moment.

A further point of disagreement involves the notion of a prereflective *cogito.* The Cartesian *cogito,* being reflective, does not reveal a *thinking* self. As was stated above, it reveals only the empirical ego, an object in the world. If, then, the Kantian claim is correct that it must be possible to attach an "I think" to every act of consciousness, there are only two possibilities: first, one might make the mistake of thinking that every act of consciousness is at least implicitly reflective. This is the appeal to the notion of an unconscious; it is to put in consciousness all that will ever be found there. The second possibility, chosen by Sartre, is to posit a prereflective, nonpositional awareness of consciousness. In that, according to Sartre, every act of consciousness is positional; this nonpositional, prereflective act is somehow carried along with or conjoined with every positional act of consciousness. Sartre gives the following example: suppose I am counting the cigarettes in a pack. I have the awareness of uncovering an objective property of the collection of cigarettes: "they are a dozen." At the same time, I may have no positional awareness of counting them: I do not know myself as counting. But should someone ask me what I was doing, I could reply immediately that I was counting. Since I can relate each consciousness to a self (my own) which was not present in the act itself, there must have been a nonpositional awareness of that consciousness (*BN,* liii).

Merleau-Ponty must reject, or significantly modify, Sartre's account of the prereflective *cogito* because it purports to be a direct awareness of consciousness, pure for-itself. In the first place, such an awareness seems impossible even on Sartrean grounds. Consciousness is a nothingness, and what can it mean to be aware of a nothingness other than, for example, as an expectation unfulfilled? Further, Merleau-Ponty is interested in making clear the relationship between the for-itself and the in-itself. A *cogito* which reaches directly to consciousness, i.e., pure for-itself, even if it were possible, is no more help in this regard than a *cogito* which reaches only the empirical ego. Neither of these acts reveals a lived experience, and it is the lived experience which is the basis for all our knowledge.

The *cogito* with which Merleau-Ponty is concerned, which he calls the "silent" or "tacit" *cogito,* is neither the reflective *cogito* of Descartes nor the prereflective *cogito* of Sartre. It is prereflective (though Merleau-Ponty never calls it this), but it is not a direct awareness of consciousness. Rather, the *cogito* reveals my *self* as the core of a *situation* in the world. The world comes to us as the "field of our experience." Our experience does not teach us that we are locked inside our own perceptions and unable to share our experiences. I am in a world which is the same world that others are in. But I am aware of myself as a "living cohesion" in that I am aware of a particular *experience* of the world. I am a single experience, and it is an experience of the world. Because the world is the field of my experience and not the totality of my experience, that is, because the world is distinct from my experience of it, I can be aware of myself as distinct from the world. I an aware of my *self* in that I am aware of the world as the *field* of my experience. And in the awareness of my *self* as distinct from the world and as in a situation, I am aware of my self as a body: "In so far as, when I reflect on the essence of subjectivity, I find it bound up with that of the body and that of the world, this is because my existence as subjectivity is merely one with my existence as a body and with the existence of the world, and because the subject that I am, when taken concretely, is inseparable from this body and this world"(*PP,* 408).

In short, the point is this: Sartre made the mistake of denying structure to the pure in-itself. The world became the structure imposed upon the in-itself by the for-itself. This made it difficult to explain the fact that we all have a common experience. Merleau-Ponty makes the following point: "Paul and I 'together' see this landscape, we are jointly present in it, it is the same for both of us, not only as an intelligible significance, but as a certain accent of the world's style down to its very thisness" (*PP,* 406). For Sartre, this is difficult to understand in that we each have a different world. In addition, Sartre's denial of structure to the in-itself makes it impossible to understand the existence of various kinds of mental acts, as has already been noted. Merleau-Ponty avoids these problems by identifying the world with the in-itself. My world is your world. The world is the field of our experience, that out of which we create situations. The tacit *cogito* is an awareness of the world given in a *situation,* that is, of the world as distinct from my experience of it, as the field of my experience.[9] I am given as the body at the core of this situation, as *this experience of the world,* as this meeting of the for-itself with the in-itself. This, in turn, makes the experience of the other understandable. To say that I am the body at the center of *this* situation, the body which creates *this* situation in the world, is to allow the possibility of there being situations created by other bodies, by other for-itselves.

This difference in the nature of the world makes it possible to understand why Sartre maintained that consciousness was completely transparent and why Merleau-Ponty maintained that it was opaque. For Sartre, the world is just the meeting of the for-itself and the in-itself. That which is present to consciousness is just the world. How is it that one could be mistaken concerning that of which one is conscious? One could be mistaken only if that which was present to consciousness was not the whole of the object of consciousness, if there was some part of the object of consciousness which was not revealed to consciousness. Sartre is willing to admit that there are certain objects of consciousness concerning which one cannot make mistakes; for example, imaginary objects and momentary consciousness, such as anger. What is impossible with Sartre is to understand how one could be mistaken concerning *any* object of consciousness. In perception, for example, error presumably arises from the fact that in no perceptual act is the totality of the perceptual object given. But this cannot be for Sartre. To say this would be to suggest that the in-itself, apart from any contact with the for-itself, contains a structure of which the perceptual judgment is only partially cognizant. And Sartre claims that the in-itself has *no* structure; it is pure, undifferentiated Being.

Merleau-Ponty, on the other hand, maintains that the world is merely the field of our experience. My action, my being in the world, does not define the world as such, but merely a situation in the world. It is clear that perception cannot be indubitable. That which is in the world is revealed only partially in each of my perceptual judgments. Further, there is no part of my consciousness of which I can have certain knowledge. Suppose, for example, that I am at this moment angry. Sartre would admit that I can be certain, so long as this anger is a momentary consciousness, that I am in fact angry. But Merleau-Ponty points out that the very understanding of this anger, the very conceptual framework through which I make the judgment that I am angry, is the product of a history which is mine and a culture which is mine. And neither this history nor this culture do I understand fully; neither this history nor this culture is fully revealed to me in any act of consciousness. Since every consciousness involves this history and this culture, consciousness is irrevocably opaque.

I add one further point. "For-itself" and "in-itself" are meant in Sartre as terms descriptive of our experience. They are most naturally used and can be plausibly thought to arise in the description of the body. Sartre was led, following Heidegger, to turn the terms of phenomenological description into ontological categories. He began by describing for-itself and in-itself in the abstract and then attempted to show how the precise structures of our experiences were generated by these notions. Merleau-Ponty, on the other hand, was content to leave "for-itself" and "in-itself" as descriptive terms to be used attributively. They do not denote different kinds of beings; rather, they are different attributes beings can have.

The first thing that can be said here derives from Merleau-Ponty's characterization of phenomenology: Phenomenology "is a matter of describing, not of explaining or analyzing" (*PP,* viii). For-itself and in-itself cease to become merely descriptive terms in Sartre. When they become ontological categories, they are no longer just terms appropriate for the *description* of one's experience. Rather, they are the terms through which one's experience is to be understood or *explained*. Second, Merleau-Ponty begins with a description of the body, that in terms of which the for-itself and in-itself gain significance, while Sartre was led by his beginning to delay consideration of the body until the structures of for-itself and in-itself were nearly fully developed.[10]

Merleau-Ponty's and Sartre's disagreement over the transparency and opacity of consciousness can be seen to find its foundation in their beginnings. Merleau-Ponty began with the body and allowed the notions of for-itself and in-itself to evolve from the description of the body. The notions that thus evolved prompted him to think consciousness is opaque. Sartre began with the notions of for-itself and in-itself in the abstract and was led through argument quite removed from experience to the conclusion that consciousness is transparent.[11] It may be that phenomenology and ontology are not incompatible, but it is clear that making ontological categories of phenomenologically descriptive terms in turn reflects on the phenomenological description of experience one finally accepts.

Notes

This a somewhat enlarged version of a paper I read at the Pacific Division meeting of the American Philosophical Association in 1973. There I profited from the criticisms of Professor Gary Overvold, though I still disagree with him on many substantive issues.

1. Alphonso de Waelhens, "A Philosophy of the Ambiguous," foreword to Maurice Merleau-Ponty, *The Structure of Behavior,* trans. Alden L. Fisher (Boston: Beacon Press, 1967), xxi.

2. Sartre easily admits such an interpretation, however. In considering the for-itself and the in-itelf and what account can be given of their interaction, Sartre asks the following question: "If idealism and realism both fail to explain the relations which *in fact* unite these regions which *in theory* are without communication, what other solution can we find for this problem?" *Being and Nothingness,* trans. Hazel E. Barnes (New York: Philosophical Library, 1956), lxvii. Hereafter *BN.* It seems plausible to reject any theory which has consequences counter to fact.

3. Maurice Merleau-Ponty, "The Cogito," in *Phenomenology of Perception,* trans. Colin Smith (New York: The Humanities Press, 1962), 369–409. Hereafter *PP.*

4. Jean-Paul Sartre, *The Transcendence of the Ego: An Existentialist Theory of Consciousness,* trans. Forrest Williams and Robert Kirkpatrick (New York: Farrar, Straus and Giroux, 1957), 62.

5. Ibid., 61–62.

6. Ibid., 62. This is not quite right. All Sartre can allow is that I can be certain when I say: "There is at this moment a violent repugnance for Peter." The "I" refers to the empirical ego about which I can have no certain knowledge. See ibid., 53–54.

7. Jean-Paul Sartre, *The Psychology of the Imagination,* trans. Bernard Frechtman (New York: Washington Square Press, 1966), 7.

8. Ibid., 10.

9. Much that Merleau-Ponty says is clearly Sartrean. The important point, of course, is that given the ontological premise with which Sartre begins, much of the phenomenology which follows in *Being and Nothingness* seems incoherent.

10. One should not think, however, that the account of the body and perception in the *Phenomenology of Perception* is pure phenomenological description and not theory-laden. I wish merely to contrast the respective beginnings of Sartre and Merleau-Ponty.

11. It is no doubt historically more accurate to say that Sartre began with a commitment to the transparency of consciousness and was led by this to his analysis of the for-itself and the in-itself. But in either case it is clear that Sartre's analysis of the structure of consciousness is less firmly grounded phenomenologically than is Merleau-Ponty's.

3

Sartre and Merleau-Ponty: The Case for a Modified Essentialism

Colin Smith

It is now a quarter of a century since the first appearance of Sartre's *Being and Nothingness*, and it is natural that after that lapse of time one should be beginning to take a jaundiced view of much of it. Authors and their works inevitably go through a period of eclipse, when people wonder what they ever found there to interest them. My own reactions over a period of twenty years or so to *Being and Nothingness* was, first, incomprehension, and sympathy with someone whom I heard describe it as unreadable, then the feeling that it was not at all difficult if one simply ploughed on, and allowed oneself to be enlightened by dint of sheer repetition. Finally, and increasingly in very recent years, a feeling that one has been taken in, and that the book represents very little said at great length.

What Sartre seems to be doing in this phenomenological ontology, as he calls it, is ignoring, consistently with phenomenological principles, the Humean distinction between the "is" and the "ought," and offering an analysis of experience and a set of precepts in one amalgam. Is either acceptable? I am tempted to answer "No."

Consciousness, for Sartre, is such that we are aware now of things to be done in order to make good the deficiencies we perceive in our given situation. There is a void to be filled in some way, a lack to be made good. Our freedom is expressed in the transaction to be completed between the situation and our project. The project is a sort of free destiny (wildly paradoxical expressions are always appropriate in an existentialist context). It is a kind of inner necessity which has to contend with the adversity factor offered by everything which we feel to be outside our autonomy. We see possibilities ahead which we choose in the service of our project.

Now taking this as the general structure of consciousness, I want to consider how Sartre appears to see its detail, and to criticize it, because I think that it is here that his description and prescription fail. Gabriel Marcel complains that Sartre sees freedom as a kind of *compulsive* making good of a lack. "For him, we are *condemned* to be free, freedom is our fate, our servitude rather than our triumph. This is because in reality it is conceived in relation to a lack, not a fullness, and one is sometimes tempted to wonder whether it is not a defect, whether it is not our imperfection made manifest" *(Homo Viator).*

Sartre sharply distinguishes between "being for oneself" and "being for others." But Sartre's being for oneself appears spurious, if one understands thereby finding free self-expression. Being for oneself, on his terms, is intermediate between a real self-expressiveness and being for others. It is rather being for a kind of *alter ego,* which acts as a kind of censor. Sartre professes fear of the gaze of the other, but he seems to be even more fearful of his own gaze. The freedom which is the dynamic force of being for oneself is not really freedom at all. Or at least it is no more than a kind of lateral elbow room, which we enjoy to a limited extent while we are carried forward, willy nilly, in time. I want to suggest that it is a misapprehension of our relationship to time that causes Sartre to falsify human reality. I have said that Sartre leaves only lateral freedom. Since most Sartrean philosophy, and therefore most criticism of it, is expressed in metaphorical terms, one may say that we are comparable to a motorist driving a car with no brakes but efficient steering, so that when we come to a fork we can take either road, but we cannot stop. Sartre argues that time marches on, it waits for no man, and that it is filled with whatever we do or don't do. To choose not to choose is still to choose. This has an air of necessary truth about it. But insofar as it is a statement of fact, it is trivially true, and insofar as it has prescriptive overtones, its implications are morally good only in a rigidly puritanical way.

When he discusses intentionality, which is the force which in general and in detail governs the working out of the "project," Sartre gives the example of writing a book, in which no manual act is ever *totally* immersed in the formation of a letter, or the spelling of a word, or the construction of a sentence. These operations are always conducted in and toward the still nonexistent context of the chapter and ultimately the book. This is intelligible enough, but it carries with it the implication that all experience is so articulated that it faces us instant by instant with a new exigency, which has to be met before we can pass on, and where any misgiving or hesitation runs the risk of betraying the whole project.

"Bad faith" consists in evading these successive and reiterated challenges in some way. It consists in freezing time and suspending action; or filling time on the cheap, so to speak, by a repetition of prefabricated actions. Or perhaps undertaking to act in a certain way at an appropriate time in the future. This may amount to enjoying the fruits of an act in advance of its performance, and may take the form of assuming the attribute, or "essence" of, for example, heroism, on the mere promise of future action. I have in mind Garcin, in *No Exit.*

Sartre's examples of these types of moral or existential failure given in *Being and Nothingness* are: the woman invited out to dinner, or the example of suspended action, secondly the waiter, or the example of the ready-made performance. One may add Garcin, the would-be hero of *No Exit,* who proves unequal in action to the essence he has given himself: that of the man of principle. Now it seems that there is a good deal more to be said in defense of all these people, allegedly in bad faith, than Sartre is prepared to concede.

In the case of the woman, whose behavior Sartre shows, quite cleverly, to be bereft of intentionality, one wants to ask what she should have done. How *could* her behavior have been different? There may be a certain socially unmentionable element in it, but it is surely normal, intelligible, and inevitable.

It is clear that choice or commitment in Sartre is something which finds expression in overt action. And such overt action is always *required,* anything short of it being a manifestation of moral inadequacy. The question arises how far this idea of existence as empirically verifiable effect is valid, or, if it is a recommendation, how far it is commendable. The woman is clearly called upon to do something, and not merely have her hand held. But what? In evading the implications of the situation the woman is refusing to take up the irrevocable position (or risk taking up such a position) that verbal expression commits one to. It is interesting that the consequences of *naming* things are discussed in a different context in *What Is Literature?* when Sartre discusses the relative roles of prose and poetry. Poetry provides us with an aesthetic object; our attention is absorbed in that object without transcending it. Prose *names* things and situations, and brings them into existence in such a way that they have to be reckoned with. Sartre there follows Brice Parain by instancing the jealousy of Mosca in *La Chartreuse de Parme.* He sees the feelings of Fabrice and Sanseverina for each other, and hopes only that the word love will not pass between them, for if it does, all will be lost because all will be irremediable. In the same way the woman Sartre describes refuses to bring an irreversible situation into existence by recognizing it and referring to it. But this refusal of commitment is entirely understandable. It would scarcely occur to anybody but Sartre to suggest that it is in any way exceptionable. We are quite entitled to suspend judgment, and it would be a very uncomfortable world in which no judgment were ever suspended. To suspend judgment is not a sign of irresolution, it is to recognize that time unfolds situations rather than springing them upon us. Sartre seems to want an explicit response to situations which are not response-provoking. He tacitly envisages experience as atomistic, each instant calling for an action, describable in principle by a verb.

A world in which each instant (an abstraction) does not bring absolute novelty fills him with fear. The idea of repetition or stylization fills him with the fear of being caught in a trap or on a treadmill. Take the case of the *waiter.* He *is* a waiter primarily in order to be able to stop being one, and do something else, when he goes off duty. *Being* a waiter, i.e., having a waiter-essence, may be seen as an economy device. We shall see that Merleau-Ponty takes a view similar to this. Sartre, in the chapter devoted to bad faith, mentions also the *beau-parleur,* the good talker. It is true that the *beau-parleur* is not an exponent of "authentic" language. What he has is a ready-made behavior that saves him the trouble of finding his words. He has available *appropriate* behavior; appropriate behavior is always a *form* of behavior. A form of behavior follows a flexible pattern, and is not completely extemporized instant by instant. Sartre sees authentic behavior as constantly extemporized; but creation is intermittent, not unremitting.

So far then we can say that Sartre wants every situation to be an occasion for action, and every action to be a novelty. Under these circumstances one might expect that he would allow a certain latitude for misapprehension, miscalculation, and general ignorance of the world and the self. But he piles on the agony, and demands a sort of infallibility as a final hurdle.

This is seen in his attitude to the future, which is in a sense the recipient of commitment. He wants the future to be open and undetermined and yet in a sense able to be relied on. The possibility of a cruel irony in future events haunts him, as in *The Victors.* Here a carefully foreseen future backfires on us. And yet a rigidly programmed future is equally a failure. As in *Dirty Hands,* where Hugo elects to *be* a communist down to the last detail, and receives a lesson in existential opportunism from Hoederer. Sartre wants an indeterminate future which yet fulfills our present intentions without *either* moral backsliding on our part *or* utter contingency in the course of events. He wants to have his cake and eat it.

To make fine Kierkegaardian leaps into indeterminacy, and land safely on his feet.

Garcin, in *No Exit,* tries to maintain that he was what he chose to be over a period of many years, i.e., a man of principle, and that his failure of nerve, when it came to the test, was a momentary weakness which should not count in the balance. Inès tells him that a man is what he does, that is, if you have an essence on credit you must ultimately pay for it. An act of will is nothing without the visible behavior which ratifies it. Garcin's private resolution has no value for Sartre, because it is not equal to the crucial *instant* when it is called upon to stand the test. Now I think that what is implied here is a very unrealistic kind of quasi morality. There is an example of a not dissimilar kind, and a true one, in Crozier's *A Brass Hat in No Man's Land,* written from the point of view of a high-ranking officer in the First World War. Crozier at one stage commanded a brigade of the Ulster Rifles, and tells of the terrible experience of having to have a man shot for desertion from the front line. When one of his fellow-officers returns to Belfast on leave, some businessmen in a club, who are doing pretty well out of the war, express concern that the local regiment has been disgraced in this way. To which the reply was: this man volunteered to serve his country in the field; you have not done even that yet. He went through the trials of a truly terrible winter in the trenches. He endured bombardment, mud, exposure, cold, frost, trench feet, sleepless nights and daily drudgery under conditions in which man was never intended to play a part (he had to play a part the whole time to keep going at all). This quite unnatural test broke his spirit. His brain was probably affected. In despair he quit the line. Why don't you and your other slacking and profiteering friends join up and have a shot at doing better than this unhappy comrade of ours? If you can't stand the test and are executed because you are not endowed with the steel-like qualities which make for war efficiency, I shall think better of you than I do now.

The Christian says: judge not that thou be not judged. Sartre says: judge and be judged. There is a certain exhilarating ferocity about this, but, apart from the demands of charity and compassion, is there not something else to be said against this?

In holding that you never really intended what you did not do, Sartre seems to be confusing decision and prediction. A decision is a prediction only in a very special and limited sense. It says, as Stuart Hampshire points out in *Thought and Action,* "I will try." This has a certainty about it not contained in "He will try," or "I will succeed." The last two are predictions, and assess the adversity factor, as Bachelard calls it, of reality in a way that "I will try" makes no attempt to do. My subsequent failure does not abolish my decision, any more than the fact that one side loses a game of football abolishes the game. Furthermore, the fact that in a sense Garcin's failure is a failure of nerve (an inner failure) doesn't alter the case, because I want to suggest—following in a way the behaviorist line of argument—that the dualism of the private, inner, ghostly life, on the one hand, that of private resolve, and of the empirically verifiable, public, one on the other, is only a very approximate distinction. Sartre wants to say that Garcin's original decision was never taken because he subsequently ran away. Would he say that the Ulster rifleman never volunteered because *he* subsequently ran away? It seems to me that the two cases are identical, and that it is untrue to say that Garcin's resolution was nonexistent because it didn't involve a publicly observable event, like going to a recruiting office. They both do two things, make a decision and fail to stand by it. Garcin and the riflemen are better than the businessmen, and not so good as the man who wins a V.C. It may be objected that the rifleman *tries* in a sense in which Garcin does not. It is true that he does more things, and suffers more hardships, in the service of his resolve (to fight). If man is what he does, then quantitatively speaking the rifleman is more of a man. But "man is what he does," and "you are the sum of your acts" means surely that a man is the sum of the resolves that he carries to fulfillment, not that he is what happens to him. On this interpretation the two men are, in the last resort, equally cowardly. It is because we feel that something important is being left out of the Sartrean assessment that I hold Sartre's view to imply a truncated deficient morality.

What I am really saying is that everything is behavior, and that there is no behavior which offers a guarantee of the future. To try to make it do so is, as I see it, to *discourage* commitment in the first place. There must be room for failure, including moral failure. So, to sum up again, Sartre wants us to meet every situation with immediate action, and with action which is "authentic," and not "everyday" or habitual; and he wants us to have complete autonomy over our mental states so that every commitment into which we enter is binding. Though we are not determined by the external world, we *are* determined, he seems to say, by our private, mental goings-on. Sartre is obsessed with the treachery of *things,* and with what he calls in the *Critique of Dialectical Reason, antipraxis* and the *pratico-inerte.* To compensate for this external uncertainty, he seems to suggest that the will is exempt from contingency. In order to circumvent the manifest falsity of this contention, he holds that we cannot have willed what we don't achieve. If this is anything, it is an unsatisfactory moral precept put in the form of a supposed psychological fact, which is not so much unsatisfactory as untrue. The truth is that "I will try" is only a limited prediction, and in the last resort the self is just as unreliable as the world in which it operates. It may in fact not be a prediction at all, but only grammatically related to the future. In any case there is an adversity factor in ourselves no less than in things.

It is true, of course, that Sartre is aware of a certain need for variability of means in the pursuit of an end, and Hoederer gives Hugo a lesson in political opportunism in *Dirty Hands.* But my concern is with Sartre's view of ends themselves, and the way they are chosen. His philosophy seems to imply that we are under a *moral obligation* to make a "costing" choice (to use James's expression) *impulsively* and adhere blindly to a commitment on pain of being considered no better than the man who from the start took the line of least resistance. I suggest that the mentality which would result from following such a general precept would be one of neurotic restlessness, or, equally probably, one of neurasthenic irresolution. In case we are misled into taking Sartre for a moralist of results, a left-wing pragmatist, we should recall that Hugo, in *Dirty Hands,* is driven to his death by the dilemma of trying to determine which motive to choose for what he *has already done.* In contrast, of course, Orestes in *The Flies,* alone in the play, remains faithful to a resolve, and shows himself entirely *rücksichtslos* (it is Gabriel Marcel, in another context, who finds the German word particularly appropriate, with its meaning of "not looking back"). But how much less human is Orestes than Electra, who falters and finally falls a prey to guilt! What one objects to in general is the alien character of the Sartrean ideal—alien to normal human psychology, and alien to normal human morality.

I suggest that the whole problem of the self with its consistencies and inconsistencies is better treated in Merleau-Ponty's *Phenomenology of Perception,* where the difficulties of certainty, reliability, and consistency are dealt with in a more relaxed and rational way. For Merleau-Ponty experience could be described as contextual and exploratory. Contextual, in that we perceive things not in isolation, but as figures on a ground. He talks about the "point-horizon" structure of perception. Now the context is not just spatial: it is also temporal. We bring the dimension of our past and future into our awareness and assessment of the world. We are aware in general of intentions, and our consciousness is selective and is given direction by these. We live and have our being in the total context of our world.

So much for our belonging to the world as essentially contextual. How is our experience exploratory? Well, we can all be victims of illusion. But if we are "in the world" we can correct it, not by some additional resource of the mind (by "attention," for example), but through the natural, *temporal* unfolding of the situation which makes further and more searching demands on us. We can never be sure of our perception. We simply elect to believe provisionally in a world. Perception is provisional because we can verify and identify its content now, but without ever being sure that we have definitively constituted it. The present never guarantees the future, and truth is never more than a precarious hold on reality. The world is always open to further exploration, because being in a situation always stands in the way of our perceiving simultaneously every aspect of an object. The result is that we always apprehend *some* meaning, and never *no* meaning, but also never final and total meaning. We never definitively understand.

But Merleau-Ponty goes on to ask, though this is the unstable nature of our transactions with the world, do we not enjoy autonomy in our own mental states? He invokes, as contemporary French philosophers are accustomed to do, the Cartesian *cogito*. Can I not be certain that when I think I love or exert my will, I really do? Surely everything is indubitable within consciousness, and we can never be deluded other than with regard to an external object. But we *can* be mistaken about being in love. How? Merleau-Ponty calls in the notion of an involvement of the whole person. In mistaken love, only one accidental aspect of the person is involved: "the man of forty" in late love, "the traveler" in the case of exotic appeal, "the child" where the mother is recalled. Only afterwards, and in retrospect, can I discover my "true" feeling (and I may still be wrong). So the inner life too is "open," and its experiences never fully predictable and secure.

Everything is historical, says Merleau-Ponty, and nothing eternal. Just as this goes for the world of moral values, so it may equally be applicable to the world of what we regard as necessary truths. Euclidean geometry is seen to have a limited validity in space, and this has been shown to be so in the course of *time*. Following up the statement that "there are truths just as there are perceptions" and "all consciousness is, in some measure, perceptual consciousness," he goes on to assert that *certainty is doubt*, showing himself thus to be capable of playing the Franco-German philosophical game of paradox, and contradiction-as-truth. But he doesn't leave us without explaining this. He says that it is of the essence of certainty to be established only with reservations, whether it be a certainty of perception of absolute values which are intellectual commitments, or of our affective states which lead to emotional commitments. There is a sort of relativism and pragmatism underlying this thinking, but it is a relativism of meaning and not of instrumentality.

What I want to emphasize in contrasting Sartre and Merleau-Ponty is that, as it seems to me, Sartre sees man as a traveler in an express-train bound for a destination chosen by him, and stopping nowhere. For Merleau-Ponty, the traveler is, to use the expression of another philosopher, *homo viator,* and he occasionally spends the night somewhere, and can sometimes change trains if he changes his mind about where he wants to go.

It is possible that Sartre's cult of melodramatic and unswerving commitment may be an antidote to his basically atomistic conception of experience. "In the world in which I commit myself," he says, "my acts put up values like partridges." This view of value as waiting upon action, and being startled out of the undergrowth like a hunted bird, is a measure of the extent to which Sartre wants to prevent norms and values from being governing forces. He sees them as following the act and as brought into being by it. The choice of a value, therefore, or a cause, would seem to be the adoption of a stabilizing factor for consciousness, and the attempt to stabilize consciousness is "bad faith." Merleau-Ponty raises the question in the following terms:

> But are there any absolute commitments? Is it not of the essence of commitment to leave unimpaired the autonomy of the person who commits himself, in the sense that it is never complete, and does it not therefore follow that we have no longer any means of describing certain feelings as authentic? To define the subject in terms of existence, that is to say in terms of a process in which he transcends himself, is surely by that very act to condemn him to illusion, since he will never be able to *be* anything. Through refraining, in consciousness, from defining reality in terms of appearance, have we not severed the links binding us to ourselves? . . . Are we not faced with the dilemma of an absolute consciousness on the one hand and endless doubt on the other? And have we not by our rejection of the first solution, made the *cogito* impossible?[1]

Applying this to Sartre, one might say that in order to achieve a certainty which eludes him, he commits himself to an "absolute consciousness" in order to *be* something. In despair at the prospect of "defining the subject in terms of existence, and self-transcendence" he assumes an essence. In effect Merleau-Ponty says, this is all right, but it is a purely provisional essence, and none the worse for that. In fact it is necessarily so. And my own contention is that this kind of modified essentialism, or modified existentialism, is alone consistent with sanity.

Sartre is exercised by identity, in fact A. R. Manser describes most of his dramatic characters as being in search of an identity, which, one might suggest, is being in search of a meaningful continuity through change. But the notion of freedom within the context of a directing intention is not well illustrated by Sartre. I think it *is* well illustrated by Merleau-Ponty, from a variety of fields of experience. He sees the body itself, the most obvious manifestation of our identity, as what he calls an *inborn complex,* a set of behavior patterns relegated to automatic availability. This prepersonal cleaving to the general form of the world releases us from the need to be perpetually rediscovering our responses. He tells us that the elaboration of these responses, instead of occurring at the center of our existence, must take place on the periphery, and must be outlined once and for all in their generality. Thus, by giving up part of our spontaneity, by becoming involved in the world through stable organs and preestablished circuits, we can acquire the mental and practical space which will theoretically free us from our environment and allow us to *see* it (*PP,* 87).

In other words we perceive and realize novelty only by way of an habitual body and acquired patterns of behavior. The habitual body provides sets of "preestablished circuits," but in characteristically human action these cannot remain at the level of being "preestablished," or if they do, they indicate some illness. Thus Gelb and Goldstein's patient Schneider, who has suffered brain injury, cannot perform "abstract" movements, i.e., movements for no purpose and performed to order. But he *can* do his work as a leather worker which belongs to the category of a preestablished circuit. The normal person's acquired movements can go beyond their own set patterns, and be generalized and adapted to realize what is merely possible or imaginary. Schneider and Sartre's waiter are both caught in "closed" behavior, but for different reasons. Schneider because he is handicapped, the waiter because he is reserving his spontaneity for his nonfunctional life, i.e., for his friends and his leisure time. Our failure to be permanently creative is not a manifestation of "bad faith." It is merely a sign that our habitual being is the reservoir of our spontaneity. And the new forms thrown up by our freedom are of strictly limited validity and duration. Neither the world nor myself is exempt from the collapse of their structures. Commitment probably arises more frequently from such collapse or rearrangement than from deliberate choice. Sartre will not have this because he rejects any unconscious motivation. But whether we recognize "the unconscious" or not, we are obliged to reject his dualism of an autonomous self and a contingent world. We "belong to the world" (*nous sommes au monde*) and we partake of its contingency. It is not a question of being "thrown into the world," or of our lives being "for nothing" or "useless passions." It is a case of our transaction with the world being such that the equilibrium that we establish between ourselves and it is permanently unstable. We enjoy periods of harmony but discord inevitably sets in, and it is then up to us to find fresh resolving chords. It is for this that we have to be *disponibles.* The alternation of stable, habitual thinking with radical reassessment, corresponding either to an open morality or to an open rationalism, is similar to "conversion" as described by William James in his *Varieties of Religious Experience.* It is to be noticed that there is here even an anticipation of Merleau-Ponty's insistence on the interchangeability of point and horizon, of focus and background. James talks about "the habitual center of a man's personal energy" and adds:

> It makes a great difference to a man whether one set of his ideas, or another, be the center of his energy; and it makes a great difference, as regards any set of ideas which he may possess, whether they become central or remain peripheral in him. To say that a man is "converted" means, in these terms, that religious ideas, previously peripheral in his consciousness, now take a central place, and that religious aims form the habitual center of his energy.

Sartre seems torn between a sort of psychological randomness and an extreme, quasi-Protestant notion of moral autonomy and predestination. The atomistic conception of consciousness implied in the analysis of *Being and Nothingness* (we "put up" values like partridges) compels Sartre, in spite of himself, to go in search of "projects," which are slices of experience. Without these intentional structures, consciousness is random and passive, as it is for the extreme sensationalist. But Sartre does not fully realize that intentions are as precarious and "absurd" as the world in which they operate. Sartre is a kind of idealist. Merleau-Ponty, on the other hand, posits an interaction and mutual dependence between the self and its world. Each infects the other with its instability. But this instability does not exclude provisional equilibrium, and such equilibrium is seen in truths, values, hypotheses, identities, and decisions, which persist for as long as they serve our being-in-the-world, and our belonging-to-the-world. Merleau-Ponty presents consciousness as shaped and structured in accordance with our actions and our tasks; his phenomenology is, as the etymology of the term requires, an account of the itinerary of consciousness through a world of appearances.

Notes

1. Maurice Merleau-Ponty, *Phenomenology of Perception,* trans. Colin Smith (London: Routledge and Kegan Paul 1962), 382. Hereafter *PP.*

4

On Ontology and Politics: A Polemic

James F. Sheridan

There are those who say that the changes in the position of Jean-Paul Sartre from the publication of *Being and Nothingness* to the appearance of *Critique of Dialectical Reason* constitute a "radical conversion."[1] Some attribute this conversion to the influence of Maurice Merleau-Ponty. Sartre has given support to this claim by acknowledging that Merleau-Ponty taught him politics and in doing so helped to move Sartre from the fierce individualism of his early period to the position which culminated in *Critique of Dialectical Reason,* a position informed by a much greater appreciation for social entanglement.[2] But what is not clear is that Merleau-Ponty's influence upon Sartre extended to Sartre's fundamental convictions, particularly to his fundamental ontological theses. Kwant tells us that Merleau-Ponty's objections to Sartre in the last days of his life indicate that he believed that Sartre had not altered his ontological views.[3] Sartre has not commented upon that issue. It is of vital interest because Merleau-Ponty explicitly claimed in *Adventures of the Dialectic* that Sartre's mistaken political views were a consequence of his mistaken ontological principles.[4] Were this true, and were it true that Sartre had not made significant alterations in his ontology, one would expect that Merleau-Ponty would have to have said that Sartre's political views in *Critique of Dialectical Reason* were similarly mistaken. We know that he did make some comments to that effect but, since Merleau-Ponty's tragic death prevented the full articulation of his latest opinions, we cannot be certain. And what of Sartre? What had he to say on this question? Very little, indeed. His longest comment upon Merleau-Ponty took the form of a eulogy and little can be inferred from that.

Are we then in the position of being unable to assess Merleau-Ponty's role in Sartre's move from "existentialism" to "Marxism," from, to quote Sartre, a "phenomenological ontology" to an "ideology"? No complete assessment is possible for the reasons cited above, but a partial appreciation is possible, which can also serve as a ground for extrapolation. In a piece called "Sartre and Ultrabolshevism," Merleau-Ponty launched an extended and vitriolic attack upon Sartre in which he detailed the view mentioned above that Sartre's politics were mistaken *because* his ontological views were mistaken.[5] Thus we have a full statement of Merleau-Ponty's opinions not too long before his death. While we do not have Sartre's reply, we do have something better than silence in Simone de Beauvoir's reply to Merleau-Ponty, a reply which was endorsed by Sartre when he spoke of that piece as the first and only time that he and Merleau-Ponty quarreled in public.[6] But given Sartre's reluctance to contend with Merleau-Ponty publicly and Sartre's statement of his fondness for Merleau-Ponty, one wonders if Sartre could have endorsed de Beauvoir's tone. She replied to Merleau-Ponty in kind and presented a view so radically opposed to his that she asserts that Merleau-Ponty is not only in error but also deliberately misrepresented Sartre. Knowing that Sartre had set himself a limited task in the article which Merleau-Ponty directly attacked, *The Communists and Peace,* Merleau-Ponty deliberately sought for what such a restricted effort could not contain, a complete and definitive philosophy of history. Failing to find it, Merleau-Ponty suggested that its absence was a matter of philosophical consequence and took it upon himself to construct what Sartre *must* say given what Sartre had said in *Being and Nothingness,* that is, in his ontology (*TM,* 2072).

What Merleau-Ponty did, according to de Beauvoir, was to construct a "pseudo-Sartreanism" which bore so little resemblance to Sartre's position that one cannot neglect the possibility that Merleau-Ponty deliberately misrepresented Sartre's views. Here is de Beauvoir's summary statement of "pseudo-Sartreanism," that is, of Sartre according to Merleau-Ponty:

> *Le pseudo-Sartisme est une philosophie du sujet; celui-ci se confond avec la conscience, qui est pure translucidité et coextensive au monde; à sa transparence s'oppose l'opacité de l'être en soi qui ne possède aucune signification; le sens est imposé aux choses par un décret de la conscience se motivant ex nihilo. L'existence de l'Autre ne brise pas ce tête-à-tête car l'Autre n'apparaît jamais que sous la figure d'un autre sujet; le rapport de Je et l'Autre se réduit au regard; chacun demeure seul au coeur de son propre univers sur lequel il règne en souverain: il n'y a pas d'intermonde.* (*TM,* 2073)

> Pseudo-Sartreanism is a philosophy of the subject; the subject merges with consciousness which is pure translucence and is coextensive with the world; its transparency is opposed to the opacity of the being-in-itself which possesses no significant [*signification*]; meaning [*sens*] is imposed on things by a decree of consciousness which is motivated *ex nihilo*. The existence of the other does not break the *tête-à-tête* since the other never appears except under the figure of another subject. The relationship between the I [*Je*] and the other is reduced to the look; each subject lives alone at the heart of that subject's own universe, a universe of which that subject is the sole sovereign: there is no interworld. ("Merleau-Ponty and Pseudo-Sartreanism," p. 449 below)

One's first response to this summary is that it is not obvious that these are the views of a "pseudo" Sartre. A passing acquaintance with those who have written about Sartre would clearly show that Merleau-Ponty was not alone in reading Sartre in this manner. But that is part of the reason for de Beauvoir's fury. Merleau-Ponty, she believed, knew better and thus did worse. For instance, Merleau-Ponty knew very well that Sartre had never had a philosophy of the subject. Sartre seldom uses the term "subject" or "self" and when he does it is always in a way which is compatible with his claim that the ego is "in" the world and not "in" consciousness. Even before *Being and Nothingness,* in the work called *The Transcendence of the Ego,* Sartre had mounted a massive polemic against Husserl's egological conception of consciousness. To suggest or to assert an identification of consciousness with mind or self or ego or subject is either travesty or comedy in de Beauvoir's eyes. One sympathizes with her, but at the same time, one wonders. Could a man of Merleau-Ponty's intellectual powers have made such an obvious error?

De Beauvoir does not wonder. Merleau-Ponty certainly had claimed that, for Sartre, consciousness was the source of meaning through the pure act of the pure affirmation. With many others, Merleau-Ponty took Sartre to have *said* that neither physical assault nor psychic influence could *directly* affect human consciousness or coerce that singularization of consciousness, the free human being. But de Beauvoir points out that this was not *all Sartre* had said:

> *Fidèle sur ce point à la thèse heideggerienne selon laquelle la réalité humaine se fait annoncer ce qu'elle est à partir du monde, Sartre a toujours insisté sur le conditionnement réciproque du monde et du moi. "Sans le monde, pas d'ipséité, pas de personne: sans l'ipséité, sans la personne, pas de monde."* (*TM,* 2074)

> Faithful on this point to the Heideggerian thesis that human reality announces what it is based on the world, Sartre has always insisted on the reciprocal conditioning of the world and that of Ego [*Moi*]: "Without the world, there is no selfness, no person; without the person, there is no world." ("Merleau-Ponty and Pseudo-Sartreanism," p. 450 below)

But must this mean that the "conditioning" is *a direct* mutual influence? Sartre had certainly held that the human reality externalizes itself in order to obtain purchase in the material world and *thus* make itself available for material manipulation. Sartre had indeed held that consciousness was intentional and thus was *nothing* apart from that of which it was the negation. True, consciousness was not the "self" but, as such, it was related to the self and to the world as well as "coextensive" with the world. But man is his freedom. If de Beauvoir means to say that man is *also* freedom in a situation, that is all well and good. But one wonders if she has forgotten freedom in emphasizing situation. To hold that the self and the world are necessary conditions of each other is not to hold that either is a sufficient condition. To hold that consciousness is incarnate is not to hold that it is therefore of a piece with the world, or, better, an aspect thereof. One would rather say with Sartre that the human reality as consciousness incarnate is a "distance within proximity." But de Beauvoir will have no such equivocation:

> *Ma conscience ne peut dépasser le monde qu'en s'y engageant, c'est-à-dire en se condamnant à le saisir dans une perspective univoque et finie, donc à être infiniment et sans recours débordé par lui: et c'est pourquoi il n'y a de conscience qu'incarnée.* (*TM,* 2074–75)

> My consciousness can only go beyond the world by engaging itself in it that is by condemning itself to grasp the world in a univocal and finite perspective, and therefore to be perpetually overwhelmed by it: this is why there can be only an embodied consciousness. ("Merleau-Ponty and Pseudo-Sartreanism," p. 450 below)

If one did not know the source, the last line could have been written by Merleau-Ponty; indeed, he almost did write it in his essay "The Battle over Existentialism."[7] Thus we have the apparent paradox of de Beauvoir writing Merleau-Ponty's lines as an explication of Sartre's position. The point is striking. If de Beauvoir is right, Merleau-Ponty was objecting to views which he and Sartre explicitly shared. At the close of her response, de Beauvoir does suggest that Merleau-Ponty did have difficulty in distinguishing his views from those of the "real" Sartre and that this in part accounts for his invention of the pseudo-Sartre (*TM,* 2121–22). She underscores this curious circumstance with the following passage:

> *Il faut que je me perde dans le monde pour que le monde existe et que je puisse le transcender. Dépasser le monde c'est précisément ne pas le survoler, c'est s'engager en lui pour en émerger, c'est nécessairement se faire cette perspective de dépassement. En ce sens la finitude est condition nécessaire du projet originel du Pour-soi.* (*TM,* 2075)

> I must *lose myself* in the world for the world to exist and for me to be able to transcend it. To surpass the world is precisely not to survey it but to be engaged in it in order to emerge from it; it is always necessary that a *particular* perspective of surpassing be effected. In this sense *finitude* is the necessary condition of the original project of the for-itself. ("Merleau-Ponty and Pseudo-Sartreanism," p. 451 below)

The lines are de Beauvoir's, paraphrasing Sartre, but they could just as well be Merleau-Ponty reporting his own views.

This strange conglomeration requires comment. What one is tempted to say is that de Beauvoir understood Sartre as Merleau-Ponty understood Sartre in the early days of their relationship, but she would not have been hesitant to accept Sartre as Merleau-Ponty was even then. Merleau-Ponty had said in 1945 that when *pour-soi* and *en-soi* were regarded as being as antithetical as Sartre conceived them to be, it was hard to see how *any* relationship between them was possible, much less the kind of contact in which one transcended one's situation by becoming immersed in it. Merleau-Ponty apparently believed that what Sartre had done was to extend and emphasize his "antitheses" so that Merleau-Ponty's reservations had become violent objections. De Beauvoir obviously thought that Sartre had never been that "rigid" and certainly was not in 1955. But the reader has a very uneasy feeling that de Beauvoir and Merleau-Ponty operate at two quite different levels. It is as though de Beauvoir were taking Sartre's claims about the human reality as a *worldly* being as the point of departure and interpreting his ontological claims from that focus. Her frequent reference to Sartre's *current* work, his "political" writing, is one sign of that focus. Perhaps that is congruent with her claim that there was neither a complete philosophy of history nor an ontology in *The Communists and Peace.* Merleau-Ponty, in contrast, deals with ontological issues as ontological and then shows how that effort "applies" to the political sphere. Thus one has the impression that one is faced with two juxtaposed monologues rather than with dialogue. One thinks of the kind of situation in which two people fail to communicate because they simply cannot entertain the notion that the other could be so "blind." In this case, of course, it is de Beauvoir alone of whom we can speak since she replied and Merleau-Ponty did not counter. In brief, she found it *incomprehensible* that Merleau-Ponty should have offered the reading of Sartre which he did. If we assume good faith on the part of both de Beauvoir and Merleau-Ponty, Sartre's early work admits of startlingly different renderings even to one who is accustomed to the freedom of interpretation which professional philosophers allow themselves. De Beauvoir presents solid evidence from chapter and verse. Merleau-Ponty also does close textual exegesis and, in addition, provides insightful interpretation. At this point, one is tempted to say that there are at least two men named Sartre, and they are very different men.

There is no question, however, that de Beauvoir would say that the assumption we made that Merleau-Ponty was in good faith is unwarranted. She not only accuses Merleau-Ponty of using tactics but of using them unfairly. She calls the construction of the position of the pseudo-Sartre an instance of a tactical move called "*le coup du paradoxe*," thus furthering her claim that Merleau-Ponty's misreading of Sartre is deliberate. Another such tactic is "*le coup de la sursignification; isolant de son contexte une phrase qui, prise en soi, n'est qu'un lieu commun banal, il la charge d'un sens singulier et en fait une clé de la pensée de Sartre*" (*TM* , 2076) ("'the ruse of oversignification.' He takes a sentence out of context, which by itself is nothing but a trite commonplace, assigns it a singular meaning and makes that a key to Sartre's thought" ["Merleau-Ponty and Pseudo-Sartreanism," p. 452 below]). For instance, Sartre had used the expression, "*Il y a des hommes, des bêtes, et des choses*" ("There are men, animals, and things"),[8] to suggest that the issues with which he was centrally concerned were those of this world. Merleau-Ponty "understands" the phrase to mean that what is may only be fitted into one or the other of these mutually exclusive categories and thus to infer that any effect of an element of one upon an element of the other is miraculous. But to do this is to try to show that Sartre does not have and cannot have any notion of an *intermonde*, that, as Merleau-Ponty in fact says, Sartre has subjectivity but not intersubjectivity. The claim infuriates de Beauvoir since, as early as *Being and Nothingness*, Sartre explicitly refuses such a reading. For instance, against the notion of a creative consciousness, he says:

> *Dans mon monde il existe des significations objectives qui se donnent aussitôt à moi comme n'ayant pas été mises au jour par moi. Moi par qui les significations viennent aux choses je me trouve engagé dans un monde déjà signifiant qui me réfléchit des significations que je n'y ai pas mises.* (*EN*, 592)[9]

> [In my world] there exist objective meanings which are given to me as not having been brought to light by me. I, by whom meanings come to things, I find myself engaged in an already meaningful world which reflects to me meanings which I have not put into it. (*BN*, 510)

It is easy for de Beauvoir to find additional citations both from *Being and Nothingness* and from Sartre's later works:

> *Le pour soi surgit dans un monde qui est monde pour d'autres pour soi. Tel est le donné. Et par lá même, nous l'avons vu, le sens du monde lui est aliéné. Cela veut dire justement qu'il se trouve en présence de sens qui ne viennent pas au monde par lui.* (*EN*, 602)[10]
>
> It means that the for-itself arises in a world which is a world for other for-itselfs. Such is the *given*. And thereby, as we have seen, the meaning of the world is *alien* to the for-itself. This means simply that each man finds himself in the presence of meanings which do not come into the world through him. (*BN*, 520)

The citations from the later work, in this instance from *Saint Genet* (542) are even more direct:

> *Contre l'interprétation de Merleau-Ponty, je citerai encore—entre tant d'autres textes—celui-ci qui est particulièrement décisif: "Nous ne saurions être tous objets que ce ne soit pour un sujet transcendant, ni tous sujets que nous n'entreprenions d'abord l'impossible liquidation de l'objectivité; quant à la réciprocité absolue, elle est masquée par les conditions historiques de race, et de classe. . . . Ainsi vivons-nous à l'ordinaire dans une sorte d'indistinction familière et irréfléchie . . . nous ne sommes ni tout à fait objets ni sujets tout à fait. L'Autre, c'est cet instrument qui obéit à la voix, qui règle, répartit, distribue, et c'est en même temps cette chaude atmosphère diffuse qui nous enveloppe.* (*TM*, 2084)
>
> To counter Merleau-Ponty's interpretation, I shall also quote the following passage—one of many possible texts—which is particularly conclusive: "We cannot all be objects unless it be for a transcendent subject, *nor can we all be unless we first undertake the impossible liquidation of all objectivity;* as for absolute reciprocity, it is concealed by the historical conditions of race and class. . . . Thus, we usually live in a state of familiar and unthinking vagueness . . . we are not quite objects and are not quite subjects. The Other is that instrument which obeys the voice, which regulates, divides, distributes, and it is, at the same time, that warm, diffused atmosphere which envelops us." ("Merleau-Ponty and Pseudo-Sartreanism," p. 458 below)

To ignore such clear texts would indeed be simply to misrepresent. For de Beauvoir, Sartre holds clearly and forcefully that the revelation of the world occurs within the region of intersubjectivity and reveals realities which resist consciousness and are governed by their own laws. As Sartre had said as early as "Materialism and Revolution," freedom *requires partial* causal linkages for the world of action in which its intelligibility arises.

Thus far we have exhibited some of the main themes in de Beauvoir's response to Merleau-Ponty's construction of Sartre's ontology, a construction which is to explain Sartre's erroneous political views. We have noted that de Beauvoir openly finds Merleau-Ponty guilty of a misrepresentation so extreme that no man of his intelligence could produce it except with deliberate malice and intent to deceive. Her fury at Merleau-Ponty's account of Sartre's political views is no less intense. For instance, Merleau-Ponty had claimed that Sartre abhorred a world which admitted of knowledge that was probable at best and had said this in a manner which suggested that this was a "psychological" distaste, an aversion. De Beauvoir points out that Merleau-Ponty acknowledges that Sartre had *said* precisely the opposite. She cites several examples of Sartre's insistence that we find ourselves in an ambiguous world. Each fact, *taken by itself,* is equivocal and obscure. But he adds that it is possible to clarify each fact through other facts over time. De Beauvoir's best citation to this effect is as follows:

> *Le vrai Sartre avait précisément parlé d'un déchiffrement qui réclame du temps et s'opère à plusieurs; il adhère à l'idée marxiste d'une genèse de la vérité, puisqu'il écrit que "tout sera clair"; cette vérité devenue n'a rien à faire avec la vérité voulue du pseudo-Sartre dont Merleau-Ponty dit qu'elle "autorise à avancer contre les apparences, elle est par elle-même folie." On est en droit de se demander si les paradoxes de Sartre et sa folie ne s'expliqueraient pas en fait par l'incompréhension de son commentateur.* (*TM,* 2087)

> The real Sartre had spoken clearly about a deciphering which requires time and several hands to decipher it. He adheres to the Marxist idea of a genesis of truth, since he had written "everything *will be* clear." This having-become truth [*vérité devenue*] has nothing to do with pseudo-Sartre's willed truth [*vérité voulue*] of which Merleau-Ponty says "it authorizes one to go ahead against all appearances; in itself is madness." One has the right to ask whether Sartre's paradoxes and madness could be, in fact, explained by this commentator's lack of comprehension. ("Merleau-Ponty and Pseudo-Sartreanism," p. 461 below)

This ambiguity which is not chaos because it has structures is nowhere better seen than in history. On Merleau-Ponty's account, there is no such thing as history for Sartre, in the sense that meaning comes to be in and through history. For the pseudo-Sartre, meaning stems from the pure act of an acosmic consciousness. For the pseudo-Sartre, meaning is bestowed, not revealed. On this point, de Beauvoir's response is powerful and well documented, as the following passage from *Being and Nothingness* illustrates:

> *Ainsi faudrait-il une histoire humaine finie pour que tel événement, par exemple la prise de la Bastille, reçût un sens définitif. . . . Celui qui voudrait en décider aujourd'hui oublierait que l'historien est lui-même historique, c'est-à-dire qu'il s'historialise en éclairant l'histoire de ses projets et de ceux de sa société. . . . Ainsi faut-il dire que le sens du passé est perpétuellement en sursis.* (*EN,* 582)[11]

> Thus human history would have to be *finished* before a particular event, for example the taking of the Bastille, could receive a definitive *meaning*. . . . He who would like to decide the question today forgets that the historian is himself *historical;* that is, that he historicizes himself by illuminating "history" in the light of his projects and of those of his society. Thus it is necessary to say that the meaning of the social past is perpetually "in suspense." (*BN,* 501)

If what a man *says* is a significant clue to discerning what he means, this citation is decisive.

De Beauvoir is equally forceful in her emphasis upon the fact that Sartre has always been insistent that our actions, verbal or other, always begin from and are projected into a realm in which they have adventures quite independent of our intentions. In short, there is and there has always been alienation in Sartre's world. It would be astounding if there were not for a writer, for few know better than those who try to write how their intentions become strangers when filtered through the regard of another. In addition, Sartre's frequent use of the notion of the "objective" meaning of an event or action is not merely a parroting of the Marxist attitude but is wholly compatible with the *ontology* exhibited in *Being and Nothingness.* Similarly, his view of temporality as elaborated in *Being and Nothingness* simply forbids the notion of an *instant* in which a pure act might take place (*TM,* 2088). The immediate consequence of these observations is that Merleau-Ponty's claim that Sartre had never taken dialectic seriously and had now abandoned it *because* his ontology forbids it simply cannot be accepted. If Sartre had abandoned dialectic, it is not for this reason.

One could go on almost indefinitely with the detail of de Beauvoir's response to Merleau-Ponty, but nothing of great additional consequence would be added by doing so. Although our earlier comments indicated that we were troubled about de Beauvoir's response to Merleau-Ponty, the development of our remarks indicates that we concur with her belief that Merleau-Ponty either did not or would not understand Sartre. But her "explanation" of Merleau-Ponty's failure still gives us pause. For instance, she makes the suggestion that Merleau-Ponty talks like those well-known guardians of the middle class, the idealists. She implies that Merleau-Ponty is entranced with the idea of the proletariat rather than with the proletarians. But her cruelest gambit is the charge that Merleau-Ponty was simply a man looking for a replacement for the religious heritage of his youth. He was led, she says, to believe that the revolution would free him of the world in which he found himself, a world in which he was never at home. It would free him of a world in which only judgments of probability were available, that is, against Merleau-Ponty, she makes the very charge he makes against Sartre. The revolution was to be the object of a sacred commitment which would be the result of a solicitation. But most importantly, the revolution would come soon. Its failure to do so is what de Beauvoir emphasizes as the deepest source of Merleau-Ponty's distress and the motive for his rancor against Sartre. It was Sartre who had claimed that one must act in terms of the future—but from the present and if the present did not admit of final or even of decisive action, one must nevertheless "act without hope." Sartre, then, was the exemplar of the man who did not find his current world entirely habitable but who also refused to abandon it. But this very failure to abandon indicated to Merleau-Ponty that Sartre failed *to appreciate* the holy character of the "cause" since to pursue it in such niggling circumstances was to demean it. Thus Merleau-Ponty attacks Sartre as a persistent, unrepentant sinner.

We said that we hesitated to accept this "explanation," and it is easy to see why. Even if one is accustomed to the European determination to refuse sharp separation between the "philosophical" and the "personal," this accounting by de Beauvoir smacks altogether too much of the invalid use of *argumentum ad hominem.*[12] But that is not all. De Beauvoir does cite forceful passages from *Being and Nothingness* in support of her objections. But it is also true that her most *persuasive* citations are from works of Sartre's "middle" period, works like *Saint Genet* and the preface to *Aden Arabie.* Does this suggest that Sartre was moving toward an importantly different view, a view which finally culminated in *Critique of Dialectical Reason?* Can we suppose that de Beauvoir here alludes to intimations of what some have called Sartre's "radical conversion"? Consider, for instance, a passage on this point from her concluding remarks

> *En admettant que la conciliation de l'ontologie et de la phénoménologie de Sartre soulève des difficultés, on n'a pas le droit de lui arracher des mains un "des deux bouts de la chaîne," pour parler comme Merleau-Ponty; et cette violence est encore*

> *plus scandaleuse aujourd'hui qu'il y a dix ans, car à travers le développement de son oeuvre Sartre a insisté de plus en plus sur le caractère engagé de la liberté, sur la facticité du monde, l'incarnation de la conscience, la continuité du temps vécu, le caractère totalitaire de toute vie.* (*TM,* 2121–22)
>
> Even if the conciliation of Sartre's ontology with his phenomenology raises difficulties, one does not have the right to grab from his hands one "of the two ends of the chain," to use Merleau-Ponty's words. Such violence is even more scandalous today than ten years ago, because throughout the development of his work Sartre had insisted more and more on the engaged character of freedom, the facticity of the world, the embodiment of consciousness, the continuity of lived experience, the totalitarian character of the entire life. ("Merleau-Ponty and Pseudo-Sartreanism," p. 489 below)

One notes that de Beauvoir says that Sartre insisted "*de plus en plus,*" which intimates that he merely amplified views which he had always held. But if amplification is required, Sartre's earlier views were not so determinate as to prevent misinterpretation even by Sartre. Why not, then, Merleau-Ponty?

I suggest that the view which best reconciles these snarls is the one mentioned twice above. If it were true—and it is—that Sartre's *total* stance as including but not as limited to *Being and Nothingness* was not wholly formed, one might well find shifts in emphasis, even major shifts. With this reading, one could allow both de Beauvoir's claim that Merleau-Ponty selected themes to the point of falsification and her acknowledgment that Sartre was progressively moving toward a more "worldly" view of freedom. In short, both Sartre and Merleau-Ponty were interpreting Sartre's early work differently. To talk in this way is certainly to talk with Merleau-Ponty, since much of his polemic against Sartre was based upon the claim that one should treat any complex enterprise like Sartre's position by disengaging themes both implicit and hidden in that enterprise. If Merleau-Ponty invented instead of disengaging in his own treatment of Sartre's self-interpretation, perhaps that is for some of the reasons cited in de Beauvoir's grim accounting. But it is also to talk as Sartre could talk and has talked in other contexts. One might well say that *Being and Nothingness* was the externalization of Sartre's internalization of phenomenology and the impelling events of his time. To have thus externalized was indeed to have surpassed, surpassed in a sense which is structurally parallel to the claim that to be in a situation is to be beyond it. One must, then, commend de Beauvoir for taking Sartre at his word that the human reality is not what it is without denying the sedimentation called *Being and Nothingness.*

One must say that the "consistency" which de Beauvoir asserted with respect to Sartre's position is not incompatible with the belief that the differences in his later stance are as important as the similarities, so that the themes of *Being and Nothingness* should not be treated as univocal signs of the one in the many. To the extent that Merleau-Ponty treats Sartre's early work as a schema which was merely fleshed out by his later work, both de Beauvoir's treatment of Merleau-Ponty and our discussion of their confrontation show that Merleau-Ponty did not do justice to Sartre. Perhaps this is why Sartre's own response to him was silence—and then eulogy.

Notes

1. Jean-Paul Sartre, *L'Être et le néant* (Paris: Gallimard). Hereafter referred to as *EN*. *Critique de la raison dialectique* (Paris: Gallimard). Hereafter referred to as *CRD*.

2. Jean-Paul Sartre, "Merleau-Ponty vivant," in *Situations* (New York: Braziller), 174; below 580–81.

3. Rémy C. Kwant, *From Phenomenology to Metaphysics* (Pittsburgh: Duquesne University Press), 131–32.

4. Maurice Merleau-Ponty, *Aventures de la dialectique* (Paris: Gallimard), 134–37.

5. Ibid., 131–271.

6. Simone de Beauvoir, "Merleau-Ponty et le pseudo-Sartrisme," *Les Temps modernes* (1955), 2072–2122. Hereafter *TM*.

7. Maurice Merleau-Ponty, "The Battle over Existentialism," in *Sense and Non-Sense* (Evanston: Northwestern University Press), 72.

8. Jean-Paul Sartre, *The Communists and Peace,* trans. Martha H. Fletcher (New York: G. Braziller, 1968), 82; "Les Communistes et la paix," *Situations,* vi (Paris: Gallimard, 1964), 197.

9. *TM,* 2077; below 453.

10. *TM,* 2080; below 455.

11. *TM,* 2088; below 462.

12. For this distinction, see Henry W. Johnstone, Jr., *Philosophy and Argument* (State College: Pennsylvania State University Press), 57–92.

5

Merleau-Ponty's Critique of Sartre's Philosophy: An Interpretative Account

Margaret Whitford

Sartre's philosophy has been more or less continuously under attack since *Being and Nothingness* was first published in 1943. Apart from broadsides from Marxist or Christian opponents who attacked him on ideological or theological grounds, most of his critics have been content to pick holes in his arguments, point out logical flaws or denounce him for having a pessimistic or unrealistic view of human experience. Merleau-Ponty's critique is of a rather different order in that he is not just concerned with pointing out internal inconsistencies in Sartre's system, or even suggesting that Sartre's conceptual framework is inadequate, though he does both of these things. He also wants to say that Sartre has not taken into account the implications of the phenomenological standpoint, and to propose an alternative account of a phenomenological philosophy.

In the present article I wish to outline briefly the scope of Merleau-Ponty's critique of Sartre's philosophy. I shall begin by isolating what I consider to be the two fundamental tendencies in Sartre's philosophy, suggesting that Merleau-Ponty's version of Sartre substantially takes account of only one of them. I shall then summarize Merleau-Ponty's account of phenomenology and the grounds for his critique of Sartre. I shall go on to argue that Merleau-Ponty's critique is limited as an overall assessment of Sartre.[1]

The influence of Husserl's phenomenology[2] has been particularly significant in reorientating philosophical speculation in France in this century.[3] Husserl's work became more widely known in the thirties and was to be influential in the immediate postwar years, though in the last couple of decades it has been subject to fundamental criticism. Both Merleau-Ponty and Sartre were dissatisfied with the pervasive rationalist spirit in French philosophy;[4] they felt that phenomenology with its slogan "Back to things themselves" offered a chance to bring philosophy back to earth and relate it to the world of "lived" experience. In the *Phenomenology of Perception,*[5] Merleau-Ponty comments: "*En lisant Husserl ou Heidegger, plusieurs de nos contemporains ont eu le sentiment bien moins de rencontrer une philosophie nouvelle que de reconnaître ce qu'ils attendaient*" (*Pp,* ii) (". . . a number of present-day readers [have had] the impression, on reading Husserl or Heidegger, not so much of encountering a new philosophy as of recognizing what they had been waiting for" [*PP,* viii]). Sartre hails Husserl's *Ideen* as the "*grand événement de la philosophie d'avant-guerre*" ("great event of pre–World War I philosophy").[6]

However, the evidence of their philosophical writings shows that they were looking to phenomenology for rather different things. Whereas Merleau-Ponty's primary concern was with the prereflective, preconceptual areas of experience, Sartre's thought is dominated by the problem of human freedom and its implications. Although they were both concerned to elucidate the relationship between consciousness and its world, in Merleau-Ponty's case it was in order to define the nature and limits of our *understanding* of the world, whereas Sartre wants to provide the basis for a philosophy of *action.* Their subsequent political development reflects these basic trends:[7] Sartre has tried to work out a synthesis between Marxism and existentialism, politics and philosophy, while Merleau-Ponty came to the conclusion that Marx is no longer a living reality but a classic[8] and advocated a return to

> *une philosophie d'autant moins liée par les responsabilités politiques qu'elle a les siennes . . . qu'elle ne joue pas aux passions, à la politique, à la vie, qu'elle ne les refait pas dans l'imaginaire, mais dévoile précisément l'Être que nous habitons.*"[9]

> a philosophy which is all the less tied down by political responsibilities to the extent it has its own . . . it . . . (does not play at passions, politics, and life, or reconstruct them in imagination) but discloses exactly the Being we inhabit. (*Signs* 13)

Merleau-Ponty's critique[10] derives much of its effectiveness from the fact that he was himself trying to get to grips with some of the philosophical problems approached in Sartre's philosophy. On the other hand, his critique of Sartre is an assessment undertaken by someone who is interested in Sartre only to the extent that the latter's philosophy can help or hinder his own attempts to work out a coherent philosophy. This makes it both valuable and misleading to the less specialized reader. Merleau-Ponty is in a better position than the average critic to evaluate the shortcomings of Sartre's conceptual structure, but at the same time his own preoccupations lead him to do less than justice to the more positive aspects of Sartre's philosophy because he tends to discard all those elements which he cannot make use of for his own purposes.[11] It is a feature of Merleau-Ponty's work that he defines himself in relation to his predecessors: Sartre figures in his work as an interlocutor, but of a particular kind: the embodiment of philosophical tendencies which Merleau-Ponty considers fundamentally misconceived. As a result, areas of divergence are dwelt on; points of convergence get little more than a mention.

It was not until 1955 that Merleau-Ponty made his first public attack on Sartre in his book *Adventures of the Dialectic.*[12] It drew an immediate response from Simone de Beauvoir in *Les Temps modernes,* where she accused Merleau-Ponty of intellectual dishonesty, deliberate misrepresentation, *mauvaise foi,* and delirium,[13] among other things. The burden of her article was that on all the major themes of Sartre's philosophy, the theory of consciousness, the theory of freedom, the theory of temporality, and so on, Merleau-Ponty had got it wrong. The dispute is on first impression puzzling: both the participants seem to have a case. Simone de Beauvoir herself points to what I think is the source of the clash when she writes that "*la conciliation de l'ontologie et de la phénoménologie de Sartre soulève des difficultés*"[14] ("the conciliation of Sartre's ontology with his phenomenology raises difficulties" ["Merleau-Ponty and Pseudo-Sartreanism," p. 489 below]). But whereas she mentions this problem only in passing, I would consider that it lies at the heart of Sartre's philosophy.

Sartre's philosophy divides Being, or reality, into two categories, the *pour-soi* and the *en-soi*—in very broad terms, consciousness and the world. What is the status of these categories? Is Sartre proposing a model of Being, that is, is he suggesting that reality can be reduced to an exhaustive set of categories proposed by human consciousness, or is he offering a conceptual framework designed to make sense of experience and which is therefore open to revision in the light of experience? Certainly he intends the latter; in practice, however, because of the interpretative function of such a framework, the concepts become reified, so that what starts off as a heuristic framework rapidly becomes identified with the structures of reality itself. Is Sartre, in other words, primarily a rationalist or a phenomenologist? Simone de Beauvoir considers him to be primarily a phenomenologist; Merleau-Ponty considers that his rationalism is more fundamental.

Rationalism would make consciousness the measure of Being, reducing Being to the categories proposed by consciousness. Phenomenology on the other hand recognizes that the creation of order through conceptual patterning is limited by the very structures of consciousness, in particular the necessity for consciousness to be situated and to be limited by its perspective.

Phenomenology, then, is defined as the perspective of what appears to consciousness. Sartre states clearly that reality overflows its appearances, being the *condition* of all appearance. So that whereas in his phenomenology he would state that concepts are approximations of a reality which eludes total or definitive conceptualization, in his ontology he proposes a model of Being as a whole which suggests the reverse, which seems to suggest that Being *can* be reduced to a set of categories. As a consequence, the interpretation of Sartre presents a difficulty in that the concepts of *pour-soi* and *en-soi* do not precisely coincide with those of *consciousness* and *world*—statements about the *pour-soi* cannot always be translated directly into statements about consciousness, and Merleau-Ponty is quite right to object that Sartre's *en-soi/pour-soi* framework does not fit particularly well with the experience it purports to describe.

It should be noted that the tension between these two positions, between the rationalist and phenomenological tendencies, is never resolved in Sartre's philosophy, and, far from being a peripheral problem, is a central one, accounting for the many contradictions in Sartre and also for the many conflicting interpretations of his philosophy.

According to his own account, it seems that Merleau-Ponty did initially look to Sartre the phenomenologist: "*nous nous sommes . . . demandés si une philosophie du négatif ne nous restituerait pas l'être brut de l'irréfléchi sans compromettre notre pouvoir de réflexion.*"[15] ("We have therefore asked ourselves if a philosophy of the negative would not restore to us the brute being of the unreflected without compromising our power of reflection" [*Visible and Invisible,* 74; reprinted below p. 538].) However, he rapidly concludes that as far as he is concerned, Sartre's philosophy is another, insidious, form of rationalism.

The underlying themes of Merleau-Ponty's own philosophy are defined in relation to his criticism of psychological rationalism (*intellectualisme*) and of *la pensée objective* (which corresponds to a crude form of empiricism). The first, *intellectualisme,* finds in the world only meanings which it has put there itself. Objecting to *intellectualisme,* Merleau-Ponty considers that the recognition that total reflective grasp of things is impossible is sufficient to discredit the intellectualist perspective. His analysis of perception is designed to show that vision is always richer than we can anticipate and that the constituting mind is always dependent on what is already given to supply it with categories, so it is always partly constituted as well as constituent. The second attitude, *la pensée objective,* makes the contrary mistake: it does not give the mind enough to do. The mind, from this point of view, is merely there to register sense-data, and the role of the mind in organizing the perceptual field is ignored.[16] Both attitudes are guilty of the *pensée de survol:*

> *L'un et l'autre prennent pour objet d'analyse le monde objectif qui n'est premier ni selon le temps ni selon son sens, l'un et l'autre sont incapables d'exprimer la manière particulière dont la conscience perceptive constitue son objet. Tous deux gardent leur distance à l'égard de la perception au lieu d'y adhérer.* (*Pp,* 34)

> Both take the objective world as the object of their analysis, when this comes first neither in time nor in virtue of its meaning; and both are incapable of expressing the peculiar way in which perceptual consciousness constitutes its object. Both keep their distance in relation to perception, instead of sticking closely to it. (*PP,* 26)

Merleau-Ponty hoped that phenomenology would steer a middle course between *intellectualisme* and *la pensée objective.* He stresses the necessity for a philosophical approach which would begin with *l'être au monde* (existence in the world), taking as its explicit theme the world as it is lived and experienced before conceptualization. The central philosophical problem for him is that of the constitution of meaning, the relationship between perception and concept (*Pp,* 77).

In the *Phenomenology of Perception,* Merleau-Ponty criticizes traditional explanations of the phenomenon of perception by showing that they obscure rather than clarify the phenomenon they purport to explain. He identifies two misconceptions in particular of which, he suggests, both *intellectualisme* and *la pensée objective* are in their different ways guilty. One is what he designates the attitude of the outside or impartial spectator (*le spectateur étranger*). This attitude sees the mind as outside the scene which it observes, viewing it impartially. The other misconception, which is another version of the first, consists in considering the body, which is my point of view on the world, as just another object in the world, whereas in fact the body mediates the world to consciousness, in ways which require elucidation. In both cases what is forgotten or ignored is the fact that all our knowledge of the world is limited by our perspective. Merleau-Ponty points out that conceptualization, which is the proper function of objective thought, is preceded by perception. All the objective thinking of science, for example, is based on the primary experience of the lived world. Reflection depends upon an unreflective immersion in the world, and Merleau-Ponty comments that "*rien n'est plus difficile que de savoir au juste ce que nous voyons*" (*Pp,* 71) ("nothing is more difficult than to know precisely *what we see*" [*PP,* 58]). So it is the task of philosophy to investigate the relation of consciousness to its world, to bring to reflective awareness the nature of unreflective experience, though Merleau-Ponty emphasizes the impossibility of ever completing this task, since "*nous ne sommes jamais comme sujet méditant le sujet irréfléchi que nous cherchons à connaître*" (*Pp,* 76) ("as a thinking subject we are never the unreflective subject that we seek to know" [*PP,* 62]). This impossibility is a feature of our existence in the world and in time.

He considers that the real epistemological problem is that of the constitution of knowledge from perceptual experience at the unreflective or "lived" level. He argues that the only things of which we can be certain (in the philosophical sense) are that we perceive, in general, and that we perceive something, and in the *Phenomenology of Perception* he settles for a kind of provisional certainty; we accept the validity of perceptions for a time until further perceptual evidence disproves them: "*Je ne révoque en doute telle perception qu'au nom d'une perception plus vraie qui la corrigerait*" (*Pp,* 413) ("I call such and such a perception into question only in the name of a truer one capable of correcting it" [*PP,* 360]).

The evidence seems to suggest that his objection to Sartre's philosophy is less to Sartre's phenomenological position (about which he has little to say) than to the ontology of *en-soi* and *pour-soi* which, by defining the *pour-soi* and *en-soi* as mutually exclusive and thereby, as Merleau-Ponty sees it, cutting off consciousness from its world, perpetuates the misconceptions of the *spectateur étranger* versions of philosophy. For Merleau-Ponty, then, Sartre's *en-soi/pour-soi* dichotomy is a form of the "outside spectator" approach.

Merleau-Ponty's critique presents the following difficulty: his polemical procedure is somewhat indirect and his presentation of his opponent already shaped and even distorted by the objections which he is about to formulate. Though he nowhere makes his procedure explicit, his critique of Sartre employs what is in effect a kind of *reductio ad absurdum* argument. It takes as its point of departure Sartre's fundamental ambiguity: the difficulty of translating statements about the *pour-soi* and *en-soi* directly into statements about experience (see above). His argument explores the consequences (and inevitable contradictions) of identifying the *pour-soi* rigorously with *consciousness* and treating statements about either as completely interchangeable. So for the purposes of his argument, he starts with the assumption that consciousness *is* identical with *pour-soi* (that consciousness, in other words, is nothing but *néant* or *néantisation*). He then makes a further assumption (again never stated explicitly but which he considers a consequence of the first) that Sartre's translucid *consciousness* is in fact the translucid *subject* of idealism. Having made these fundamental assumptions, it is then a straightforward matter to show that Sartre's account of experience is unsatisfactory.

What are the consequences of these two assumptions for Merleau-Ponty's interpretation of Sartre's philosophy?

Sartre's philosophy hinges on the theory of intentionality,[17] that is, the theory that "*toute conscience . . . est conscience de quelque chose*"[18] ("all consciousness . . . is consciousness *of* something" [*BN*, li]), or, in other words, that consciousness is translucid and is given thickness or substance only by its objects. The theory constitutes an attempt to solve the problems posed by Cartesian dualism which, by positing minds and things as separate *substances,* could not within its own terms account for their interaction. Intentionality makes consciousness dependent for its very existence on the existence of its objects—without an object, consciousness would not exist. As Sartre puts it vividly in "*Une Idée fondamentale de Husserl*":

> *si, par impossible, vous entriez "dans" une conscience, vous seriez saisi par un tourbillon et rejeté au dehors, près de l'arbre, en pleine poussière, car la conscience n'a pas de "dedans"; elle n'est rien que le dehors d'elle-même et c'est cette fuite absolue, ce refus d'être substance qui la constituent comme conscience.*[19]

> if you could do the impossible and get "inside" anyone's consciousness, you would be caught up in a whirlwind and thrown out, next to the tree, down in the dust, for consciousness has no "inside," it is nothing apart from its exterior, and it is this absolute flight, this refusal to be substance, which constitutes consciousness as such.

Further, the theory of intentionality is a theory of consciousness and not a theory of knowledge. "*La conscience que nous prenons des choses ne se limite point à leur connaissance*"[20] ("The consciousness which we have of things is not limited to our knowledge of them"). Knowledge is logically a secondary activity since it presupposes consciousness. The theory of intentionality enables Sartre to make his vital distinction between "*conscience de soi*" and "*connaissance de soi.*" If these two are not distinct, and if "*conscience de soi*" is equivalent to "*connaissance de soi,*" the result is an idealist philosophy of the kind Sartre and Merleau-Ponty are both endeavoring to avoid. Merleau-Ponty's critique derives considerable force from the fact that Sartre, despite an intention of differentiating between *conscience* and *connaissance*, has difficulty in establishing the distinction in terms of the *en-soi* and *pour-soi*.[21]

On the basis of intentionality, Sartre makes a further distinction between *consciousness* and *subject*. Sartre's theory of the ego is well known; he writes: "*C'est en tant qu'Ego que nous sommes sujets*" (*EN*, 209) ("It is as the Ego that we are subjects in fact" [*BN*, 162]). And he maintains throughout that the ego is an *object* for consciousness. Since consciousness is translucid or empty, it cannot in any sense "contain" the ego as pole or source of conscious feelings. It follows that everything which can be described under the heading of ego—states of mind, qualities of character, emotions—is an intentional object of consciousness.

Now, if the ego is an object of consciousness, and if consciousness and knowledge are not identical, one can distinguish between the ego as an object of consciousness whose existence is *certain* and the ego as an object of knowledge about which we can make mistakes. In other words, this theory should account for the fact that we are not transparent to ourselves. If it is the subject, as distinct from consciousness, which is translucid, on the other hand, it follows that there is no distinction, and the consequence would be that we cannot make mistakes about ourselves, we cannot be unsure of our feelings, unaware of our motives and so on. This is so patently at variance with experience that it cannot be long maintained. Nevertheless it is clearly in these terms that Merleau-Ponty interprets Sartre. Sartre's theory, he says, allows for deliberate self-deception and malice; it does not allow for stupidity, ignorance, and folly.[22]

Merleau-Ponty offers a reason for his interpretation: that the relationship between consciousness and world has to be mediated, and it is this mediation which he claims to be lacking between the *en-soi* and the *pour-soi*. The fundamental aim of philosophy, Merleau-Ponty suggested in the *Phenomenology of Perception*, is to uncover and bring to light the nature of unreflective experience. The difficulty with an ontology that divides Being into *en-soi* and *pour-soi* is, as he puts it in *The Structure of Behavior*, that "*on veut . . . égaler la conscience à l'expérience entière, recueillir dans la conscience pour soi toute la vie de la conscience en soi*" ("on the contrary, we want to make consciousness equal with the whole of experience, to gather into consciousness for-itself all the life of consciousness in-itself").[23] Because the *pour-soi* is defined as translucid, there is no distance between it and the world; there can be no opacity in unreflective experience which resists our grasp. Sartrean consciousness is "*un être dont toute l'essence est de se savoir, c'est-à-dire . . . une conscience*" ("a being whose whole essence is to know itself, that is to say . . . a consciousness").[24] (Note Merleau-Ponty's equation here of consciousness with knowledge in accordance with the procedure I have outlined above). In Sartre's philosophy, he claims, the relationship between the *pour-soi* and its world is totally unmediated: the *pour-soi* is pure presence to itself and to the world (*EN*, 120). The subject's self-knowledge, however, should require mediation. But in Sartre there are no mediations; there is no distance within the self to be mediated because such a distance has been defined out of existence; there is therefore no distance between the being of the *pour-soi* and the being of the consciousness of the *subject*. And if the relation of the *pour-soi* as *subject* to the world is unmediated, the conclusion is unavoidable: the experience of obscurity or ignorance is ruled out.

All the other objections really follow from these first two. I will confine myself here to indicating three of them.

Firstly, Merleau-Ponty suggests that with only two mutually exclusive categories at our disposal, we cannot adequately conceptualize those apparently intermediate categories such as would be represented by the body, by behavior, or by language—to name the examples to which Merleau-Ponty gives the most attention.

To consider the body as an *en-soi* is to commit the error of the *pensée objective* which sees the body as just another object in the world without recognizing that it is also one's point of view on the world. To consider the body as *pour-soi*—as Sartre is forced to do, some of the time, to avoid these consequences—is to undermine the definition of *pour-soi* as *néant*, and by extension to undermine the vital concept of intentionality. The precise relationship between the body and consciousness, the body and the world, of course remains to be elucidated. But Merleau-Ponty points out that the body preempts some of the functions of consciousness, taking over when consciousness itself is absent or engaged elsewhere. He instances the case of a patient (Schneider) who, as a result of brain injuries, was unable to perform abstract actions, that is to say, actions in a context other than that in which they were learnt or in the absence of any specific context, though he could perform habitual actions, even quite complicated ones, such as the movements of his trade which had become automatic through long practice. For example, when asked by the doctor to indicate a part of his body, Schneider finds he cannot—the act of pointing to something involves the capacity for abstraction which he has lost. But when bitten by a mosquito, he immediately slaps the spot concerned.[25] In a sense, then, he clearly does know where the parts of his body are, even though he cannot point to them. Merleau-Ponty concludes that actions which are habitual can be carried out when the more sophisticated functions of the mind have been affected by illness or disease. He suggests that the categories of *en-soi* and *pour-soi* are not adequate to describe the complex role of the body. His own preference is for less exact concepts, particularly when we are describing something whose exact mechanism we do not fully understand. In the *Phenomenology of Perception* he describes the body as a *pivot,* the "*véhicule de l'être au monde*" (*Pp,* 97) ("the vehicle of being in the world" [*PP,* 82]).[26]

Secondly, Merleau-Ponty points out that the absence of mediation between the *pour-soi* and the *en-soi* means that the *pour-soi* cannot be affected by the *en-soi:* they have no apparent means of having any effect on each other. This has a number of consequences, the most important of which is the implication that the *pour-soi,* as the active element of the pair, must be totally constituent (whereas the phenomenological position taken by Merleau-Ponty would claim that consciousness is neither totally constituent nor totally constituted.) Now if each *pour-soi* is constituent, if each *pour-soi* structures the world according to its own project, there is no guarantee that these projects will meet or overlap. Sartre's ontology, says Merleau-Ponty, accounts for the possibility of a plurality of subjects, but not for an intersubjective world in which these projects might meet and coexist. He sees Sartre's arguments for the existence of other people as an argument showing at the most that the existence of one consciousness is not incompatible with that of others. He does not go as far as some critics have done in accusing Sartre of solipsism, but he points out that in Sartre's ontology, there is no foundation for the common world of experience that he calls the *intermonde.* There seems, in Sartre's account, to be no intrinsic link between consciousnesses arising out of their common participation in the same world.

Thirdly, Merleau-Ponty's reference to Sartre's "*maudite lucidité*" ("cursed lucidity" [*Signs,* p. 505 below)[27] is another aspect of his critique of rationalism. Sartre, claims Merleau-Ponty, refuses to recognize indeterminate categories, such as the probable or the ambiguous. Merleau-Ponty points out in his analysis of perception that perception as a mode of being-in-the-world is very often nonthematic and forms the background against which positing acts stand out. The boundaries of the visual field are blurred, and different areas within our field of vision become sharper or vaguer depending on what we are focusing on at any given moment. This means that there are areas of the perceptual field which, although present, are not at the center of attention. These indeterminate areas interest Merleau-Ponty as much as the more determinate perceptions, because of the implications for conceptualization. Especially in his later philosophy, Merleau-Ponty will show a preference for concepts which do not have an exact meaning. He believes there is a limit to what can be expressed in clear concepts. Or rather, he is suspicious of anything too systematic in that it may mislead us into thinking we have a total understanding. Concepts should be considered as at best provisional.

Once the claim is made that one's philosophy is an adequate expression of reality, then it has become a misrepresentation. (Hence Merleau-Ponty's suspicion of any form of orthodoxy and one of the grounds for his objections to Marxism.) He makes an attempt to do philosophy with unfamiliar notions and suggests: "*Remplacer les notions de concept, idée, esprit, représentation par les notions de dimensions, articulation, niveau, charnières, pivot, configuration.*"[28] ("Replace the notions of concept, idea, mind, representation with the notions of dimensions, articulation, level, hinges, pivots, configuration" [*VI,* 224].) The use of familiar notions means that we come to philosophy with preconceived ideas which may prevent us from taking up the genuine philosophical attitude of "*étonnement devant le monde.*" One could see this attitude as a partial explanation for the obscurities of Merleau-Ponty's own style.

There is a danger that this approach could lead to a radical skepticism. Merleau-Ponty's thought here can be shown more clearly with reference to the account of perception in the *Phenomenology of Perception.* Every perception is potentially an illusion, but it can be seen to be such only in the light of another perception which reveals the first to be illusory. But although I can call into question any individual perception, I cannot doubt that Being in general, the source of perception, exists. I have to admit that "*il y a quelque chose en général*" (*Pp,* 414) ("there is something in general" [*PP,* 360]). Similarly, "*il y a des vérités comme il y a des perceptions*" (*Pp,* 452) ("there are truths just as there are perceptions" [*PP,* 395]). So we can say that there is truth, in general, but that it is always becoming, it is a progressive revelation.

Merleau-Ponty's view that philosophy and literature have essentially similar aims is in line with his general position. Both are concerned with translating experience into language:

> *La tâche de la littérature et celle de la philosophie ne peuvent plus être séparées. Quand il s'agit de faire parler l'expérience du monde et de montrer comment la conscience s'échappe dans le monde, on ne peut plus se flatter de parvenir à une transparence parfaite de l'expression. L'expression philosophique assume les mêmes ambiguïtés que l'expression littéraire, si le monde est fait de telle sorte qu'il ne puisse être exprimé que dans des "histoires" et comme montré du doigt.*[29]

> From now on the tasks of literature and philosophy can no longer be separated. When one is concerned with giving voice to the experience of the world and showing how consciousness escapes into the world, one can no longer credit oneself with attaining a perfect transparence of expression. Philosophical expression assumes the same ambiguities

> as literary expression, if the world is such that it cannot be expressed in "stories" and, as it were, pointed at.

Merleau-Ponty speculates that the language of philosophy will have to become more expressive through indirect means in order to attain its ends. Quoting Husserl, Merleau-Ponty defines the aim of philosophy as "*l'expérience . . . muette encore qu'il s'agit d'amener à l'expression pure de son propre sens*" (*Pp,* 253–54), "the still mute experience which it is a question of bringing to the pure expression of its own significance" (*PP,* 219), and suggests that the means to this expression lie in a direction contrary to the normal philosophical tendency to reduce ambiguity as far as possible:

> *C'est donc une question de savoir si la philosophie comme reconquête de l'être brut ou sauvage peut s'accomplir par les moyens du langage éloquent, ou s'il ne lui faudrait pas en faire un usage qui lui ôte sa puissance de signification immédiate ou directe pour l'égaler à ce qu'elle veut tout de même dire.* (*Vi,* 139)

> Hence it is a question whether philosophy as reconquest of brute or wild being can be accomplished by the resources of the eloquent language, or whether it would not be necessary for philosophy to use language in a way that takes from it its power of immediate or direct significance in order to equal it with what it wishes all the same to say. (*Visible and the Invisible,* 102–3, reprinted below p. 561)

Almost inevitably, then, Merleau-Ponty becomes convinced that Sartre's "*esprit de système*" can only predetermine the outcome of investigation.

Merleau-Ponty's critique of Sartre is subordinated to his more central attack on the *spectateur étranger* tradition in philosophy of which Sartre is seen as a prominent example. This choice of focus is particularly illuminating: it shows the extent to which Sartre was unable to free himself entirely from the rationalism of the tradition he was opposing; by placing Sartre in a framework which relates him to other philosophers, it enables the reader to evaluate him more adequately; it highlights the tension between phenomenology and ontology in *Being and Nothingness* and brings out the difficulties of interpretation which this work presents. As an overall assessment of Sartre, however, it does have certain weaknesses. I will confine myself here to indicating two.

Firstly, the leap from the specific objections to Sartre which I have outlined above to the more general criticism of *maudite lucidité* would require substantial justification. The requirements of clarity are not necessarily at cross-purposes with the aims of phenomenology. To say, as Merleau-Ponty does, that one cannot achieve "*une transparence parfaite de l'expression*" has become a commonplace since Wittgenstein, but is hardly an excuse for being obscure or confused. The advantage of clarity is that mistakes or misconceptions can be more readily identified; it is not evident that the substitution of an ambiguous or indeterminate concept for a clear and distinct one is automatically an advantage. Critics have already pointed out that Merleau-Ponty's own "lack of academic rigor constitutes an obstacle to understanding."[30] Clarity and ambiguity undoubtedly each have their place; the case for a "*philosophie de l'ambiguïté*" is not strengthened if the philosopher's statements are themselves ambiguous.

Secondly, Sartre is well known to most readers of his work, particularly those who are familiar with his novels and plays, as a philosopher of the concrete, concerned with existence in the world, the problems of freedom, contingency, and problematical relations with other people, problems that are quite specifically phenomenological in Merleau-Ponty's sense, in that they are issues of the relationship between consciousness and world and the ways in which we confer meaning on our experience. By limiting his focus so exclusively, and by avoiding any systematic or sustained discussion of the phenomenological perspective of Sartre's thought, Merleau-Ponty weakens his overall case against Sartre. His critique gives us only one side of the story, losing sight of the tension between rationalist and phenomenologist which Sartre's work embodies, and simplifying Sartre's complexity.

Notes

I should like to thank Professor M. M. Bowie and Mrs. R. E. Goldthorpe for their help in the preparation of this article. An earlier version of this article was presented as a paper at the University of Wales conference center, Gregynog, December 1977. I should like to thank all those who took part in the discussion which followed.

1. I hope to complete the argument in a subsequent article by giving an account of some of the ways in which Sartre could reply to Merleau-Ponty.

2. For an introductory account of Husserl's philosophy, see Herbert Spiegelberg, *The Phenomenological Movement: A Historical Introduction,* 2 vols. (The Hague: Nijhoff, 1960); Marvin Farber, *The Aims of Phenomenology: The Motives, Methods and Impact of Husserl's Thought* (New York: Harper and Row, 1966); and Quentin Lauer, *Phenomenology: Its Genesis and Prospect* (New York: Harper and Row, 1965).

3. See Ian W. Alexander, "The Phenomenological Philosophy in France: An Analysis of Its Themes, Significance and Implications," in *Currents of Thought in French Literature: Essays in Memory of G. T. Clapton* (Oxford: Basil Blackwell, 1965), 325–51.

4. For Sartre's account of their dissatisfaction with the philosophy they had been taught at university, see his article "Merleau-Ponty vivant" in *Les Temps modernes,* nos. 184–185 (October 1961), 304–76; reprinted in *Situations,* IV (Paris: Gallimard, 1964), 189–287, under the title "Merleau-Ponty."

5. Maurice Merleau-Ponty, *Phénoménologie de la perception* (Paris: Gallimard, 1945). I shall refer to this work by the abbreviation *Pp.*

6. Jean-Paul Sartre, *L'Imagination,* 2d ed. (Paris: PUF, 1949), 139 (first published in 1936); *Imagination: A Psychological Critique,* trans. Forrest Williams (Ann Arbor: University of Michigan Press, 1962).

7. The relationship between politics and philosophy in Sartre and Merleau-Ponty is very clearly presented in Graham Daniels's article "Sartre and Merleau-Ponty: An Existentialist Quarrel," *French Studies* 24 (1970), 379–92. For a succinct account of the relations between Merleau-Ponty and Sartre, see Michel Contat and Michel Rybalka, *Les Écrits de Sartre: Chronologie, bibliographie commentée* (Paris: Gallimard, 1970), 368–70.

8. Maurice Merleau-Ponty, *Signes* (Paris: Gallimard, 1960), 17.

9. Ibid., 20.

10. For the principal statements of Merleau-Ponty's views on Sartre, see: *La Structure du comportement* (Paris: PUF, 1942), which contains a guarded response to Sartre's *La Transcendance de l'ego* in the final chapter; *Phénoménologie de la perception* (particularly the last three chapters); *Aventures de la dialectique* (Paris: Gallimard, 1955), chap. 5, "Sartre et l'ultra-bolchévisme"; *Le Visible et l'invisible* (Paris: Gallimard, 1964), in particular the chapter entitled "Interrogation et dialectique"; a review of *Les Mouches* in *Confluences* 25, no. 3 (September–October 1943), 514–16; a review of *L'Imagination* in *Journal de Psychologie normale et pathologique* 33, nos. 9–10 (November–December 1936), 756–61; "Jean-Paul Sartre ou un auteur scandaleux," in *Le Figaro littéraire* (6 December 1947), reprinted in *Sens et non-sens* (Paris: Nagel, 1948) under the title "Un Auteur scandaleux"; "La Querelle de l'existentialisme," *Les Temps modernes* 1 (October 1945), 344–56, reprinted in *Sens et non-sens;* a reply to Sartre's *Qu'est-ce que la littérature?* in the form of (a) an article: "Le Langage indirect et les voix du silence" (*Les Temps modernes* 7 [June 1952], 2113–44, and 8 [July 1952], 70–94, reprinted in *Signes*) and (b) a book: *La Prose du monde* (Paris: Gallimard, 1969); a discussion of Sartre's portrait of Paul Nizan in *Signes,* 31–47. References to Sartre can also be found in Merleau-Ponty's lecture courses at the *École Normale Supérieure* (see *L'Union de l'âme et du corps chez Malebranche, Biran et Bergson* [Vrin, 1968]), at the Sorbonne (see "Maurice Merleau-Ponty à la Sorbonne, résumé de ses cours," *Bulletin de psychologie* 18, no. 236 [November 1964]), and *Les Sciences de l'homme et la phénoménologie* (Centre de Documentation Universitaire, 1952); and at the Collège de France (see *Résumés de cours* [Paris: Gallimard, 1968]).

11. There has been a tendency on the part of critics to accept rather uncritically Merleau-Ponty's assessment of Sartre's philosophy. See for example Rémy C. Kwant, *The Phenomenological Philosophy of Merleau-Ponty* (Pittsburgh: Duquesne University Press, 1963), 203–23; and Rémy C. Kwant, *From Phenomenology to Metaphysics: An Inquiry into the Last Period of Merleau-Ponty's Philosophical Life* (Pittsburgh:

Duquesne University Press, 1966), 130–56. Cf. also Albert Rabil, Jr., *Merleau-Ponty: Existentialist of the Social World* (New York: Columbia University Press, 1967), 29–31, 69–75, 115–40; and John F. Bannan, *The Philosophy of Merleau-Ponty* (New York: Harcourt, Brace and World, 1967), 133–38, 229–43, where Merleau-Ponty's views are presented without any critical comment.

12. Maurice Merleau-Ponty, *Aventures de la dialectique* (Paris: Gallimard, 1955).

13. Simone de Beauvoir, "Merleau-Ponty et le pseudo-sartrisme," *Les Temps modernes,* nos. 114–15 (June–July 1955), 2072–2122; reprinted in *Privilèges* (Paris: Gallimard, 1955). References are to *Privilèges,* 203, 205, 205, and 271 respectively.

14. De Beauvoir, *Privilèges,* 271.

15. Merleau-Ponty, *Le Visible et l'invisible,* 104. I shall refer to this work by the abbreviation *Vi.*

16. For a fuller account of Merleau-Ponty's attitude to *intellectualisme* and *la pensée objective,* see Colin Smith, "The Notion of Object in the Phenomenology of Merleau-Ponty," *Philosophy* 39, no. 148 (April 1964), 110–19; and Colin Smith, *Contemporary French Philosophy* (London: Methuen, 1964), 114–36.

17. For a history of the concept of intentionality, see Spiegelberg, *The Phenomenological Movement,* especially vol. 1.

18. Jean-Paul Sartre, *L'Être et le néant* (Paris: Gallimard, 1943), 17. I shall refer to this work by the abbreviation *EN.*

19. Jean-Paul Sartre, *Situations,* I (Paris: Gallimard, 1947), 33.

20. Ibid., 34.

21. For example, the following definitions of *pour-soi,* consciousness, and knowledge would seem to make them indistinguishable: *Pour-soi:* "*La loi d'être du pour-soi, comme fondement ontologique de la conscience, c'est d'être lui-même sous la forme de présence à soi*" (*EN,* 119). Consciousness: "*L'être de la conscience, en tant que conscience, c'est d'exister à distance de soi comme présence à soi et cette distance nulle que l'être porte dans son être, c'est le Néant*" (*EN,* 120). Knowledge: "*Le connaître . . . est l'être même du pour-soi en tant qu'il est présence à . . . c'est-à-dire en tant qu'il a à être son être en se faisant ne pas être un certain être à qui il est présent*" (*EN,* 222–23).

22. See *Pp,* 145–46, and *Aventures de la dialectique,* 213.

23. Merleau-Ponty, *La Structure du comportement,* 303 (2d. ed., 1949, 240); *The Structure of Behavior,* trans. Alden L. Fisher (Boston: Beacon Press, 1967), 223.

24. Merleau-Ponty, *Aventures de la dialectique,* 268; *Adventures of the Dialectic,* trans. Joseph Bien (Evanston: Northwestern University Press, 1973), 199, reprinted below p. 436.

25. For Merleau-Ponty's analysis of Schneider, see *Pp,* part 1, chap. 3.

26. Language is another example. To consider language as *en-soi* is to leave out of account the *parole* or the possibility of the generation of meaning. To consider language as *pour-soi,* however, would imply the recreation of language by each individual speaker. For Merleau-Ponty's discussion of language in *Pp,* see part 1, chap. 6.

27. Merleau-Ponty, *Signes,* 33.

28. *Vi,* 277; cf. also *Vi,* 209, 289, 307, 324.

29. Maurice Merleau-Ponty, *Sens et non-sens,* 2d ed. (Paris: Nagel, 1958), 48–49; "Metaphysics and the Novel," in *Sense and Non-Sense,* trans. Hubert L. Dreyfus (Evanston: Northwestern University Press, 1964), 28.

30. Mary Warnock, *Existentialism* (London: Oxford University Press, 1970), 72.

PART 2

SUBJECTIVITY AND INTERSUBJECTIVITY

6

Phenomenology, Consciousness, and Freedom

C. M. T. Hanly

The phenomenological theory of motivation was first extensively developed by Sartre in his early *Sketch of a Theory of Emotions* and then in *The Transcendence of the Ego, Being and Nothingness,* and *Critique of Dialectical Reason.* Sartre's theory presents three difficulties which were recognized by Merleau-Ponty, whose position, as formulated in *Phenomenology of Perception,* is, in part, an attempt to resolve them. The point of view of this paper is that Merleau-Ponty has not satisfactorily resolved the difficulties and that, moreover, no adaptations of the theory could resolve them short of abandoning phenomenology as such by going beyond it.

Three Flaws in the Existentialist Theory of Motivation

Sartre bases his theory on the idea that consciousness is pure spontaneity. This means that all forms of mental energy are, in their initial phase of formation, pure psychically unqualified intentions toward the world. The initial upsurges of consciousness (prereflective consciousness) that originate projects and situations exist first without as yet having a nature. Viewed from the perspective of human behavior, objects and artifacts, customs, institutions, legal and moral laws, as well as instincts, desires, and aversions are so many abstract schema representing possibilities for action until they are freely endowed by prereflective consciousness with motive force. Therefore, consciousness cannot stand in a passive relation to anything else which might determine its nature and manner of acting. To be sure, impure reflective consciousness fabricates a phantom self which *appears* to be subject to causal influences. But such a self is a flight from the anxiety associated with the spontaneity of unreflective consciousness, and it is a form of inauthentic existence or bad faith.

This concept of consciousness is at odds with traditional thought which appears to be unanimously opposed to it. The plight of Leontius (which Plato uses to demonstrate the existence of the spirit function in the soul)[1] implies a concept of a consciousness which passively attests to the triumph of a perverse lust over moral scruples for mastery over the sense of sight. The Hobbesian conception of volition as the last desire or aversion in a sequence of desires and aversions implies that consciousness is simply a witness of the internal process that precedes behavior.[2] Correspondingly, the common assumption of both the Platonic and Hobbesian conceptions is that emotional life moves forward under its own steam rather than on a spontaneity "borrowed" from consciousness. The same assumptions about consciousness and emotions are adopted by Kant despite obvious differences between his concept of volition and that of Hobbes.

Secondly, Sartre's theory logically requires an unconscious. For he takes the view that

> psychological determinism, before being a theoretical conception, is . . . the basis of all attitudes of excuse. It is reflective conduct with respect to anguish; it asserts that there are within us antagonistic forces whose type of existence is comparable to that of things. . . . It provides us with a *nature* productive of our acts. . . . Psychological determinism denies that transcendence of human reality which makes it emerge in anguish beyond its own essence.[3]

Let us suppose that what Sartre says about psychological determinism is, in fact, true. Sartre must then build into the logic of his theory some way of explaining how it is that persons using normal self-awareness and empirical psychologists can be so mistaken about human reality, especially when they are themselves examples of that reality and, in the latter case, trained observers of it. After all, what is at issue is not some accidental characteristic that varies from individual to individual.

Sartre's difficulty is not diminished by his adoption of the assumption that consciousness is the existence of the self. "Self-consciousness . . . [is] *the only mode of existence which is possible for a consciousness of something.*

Just as an extended object is compelled to exist according to three dimensions, so an intention, a pleasure, a grief can exist only as immediate self-consciousness" (*BN,* liv). How then can Sartre account for being in bad faith? What his theory requires is more than the "knowing without knowing that one knows" of Plato's *Meno,* because that state of self-ignorance is compatible with a simple absence of knowing; whereas what bad faith requires is a positive state of self-deception. The psychoanalytic theory would appear to provide just the explanation his theory requires. But following Stekel, Sartre rejects the psychoanalytic concept of the unconscious which, according to Sartre, establishes bad faith in bad faith because it explains self-deception as the product of an involuntary and unconscious mental process. Sartre also found the psychoanalytic theory of the instincts untenable: a position logically entailed by his concept of consciousness as pure spontaneity. "Shall I uncover in myself 'drives,' even though it be to affirm them in shame? But is this not deliberately to forget that these drives are realized with my consent, that they are not forces of nature but that I lend them their efficacy by a perpetually renewed decision concerning their value?" (*BN,* 63). The resulting logical predicament is crucial. If deterministic thinking is a flight from the anguish of freedom, it must be conscious of being so. But how then can it fail to acknowledge its own falsification of human reality? As Sartre says, "I flee in order not to know, but I cannot avoid knowing that I am fleeing. . . . Thus anguish can be neither hidden nor avoided" (*BN,* 43). Therefore, in order to give an account of the "river of Lethe effect" on which bad faith is based, Sartre is obliged to attribute to consciousness a nihilating power by means of which it can be anguish in the form of not-being it. (Superficially, existential nihilation is similar to what psychiatry refers to as the mechanism of denial[4] or what psychoanalysis refers to as repression.[5] The effect of inner deception is the same. But otherwise they are completely different conceptions.) Sartre does not explain just how the individual's ability to "decenter himself" in relation to what he is and his ability to "dispose of a nihilating power at the heart of anguish itself" (*BN,* 44) can actually create all the effects he attributes to it. Elsewhere Sartre likens putting oneself in bad faith to going to sleep. But the point of the metaphor would appear to be a suggested similarity between segments of waking life and the state of unconsciousness induced in us by reduced levels of brain activity. Sartre's sense of reality appears to be sounder than his conceptual formulations, and he found a way to smuggle the unconscious back into his theory. But the problem remains: we are confronted either by a major inconsistency or by an ontological category—nothingness—which, if it is meaningful at all, has no more than a contextual meaning within existentialist philosophy itself—and probably by both.

Finally, once consciousness has been defined as pure spontaneity and endowed with a nihilating power which it cannot but use, selfhood must be understood as perpetual disengagement. This disengagement has several forms, but a consideration of one will suffice. Insofar as a self is related to his past, that relation must take the form of a consciousness of being what he was in the past. But the consciousness which knows the past is already not the past which it knows. Nihilation effects the conversion of present into past and in so doing liberates a new unqualified consciousness in the present. This means for Sartre that what one has done, and consequently been, cannot get a grip on the new formation of consciousness that arises out of the disengagement of the self from its last project. There is no way in which being a loyal husband for many years can absolve one of the necessity of reestablishing that commitment each morning. This does not mean that Sartre denies that people preserve the natures they have gradually accumulated or that they do not find motives, in their past, for present undertakings; but rather that past motives must be incorporated into the present by a free act of renewal.[6] Therefore, past experiences cannot in and by themselves determine behavior. Consequently, the facticity of the past, combined with fresh possibilities for action in the present, defines the total range of possibilities from which consciousness can choose. But these possibilities *and* their negations are *equipossible*. The extent to which Sartre generalizes this concept is shown by the statement that consciousness "can be limited only by itself." The metaphysical ancestor of Sartrean consciousness is Spinoza's God. The result is a harvest of paradoxes. The schizophrenic woman who pushed a complete stranger into the path of a subway train in response to "voices" must have elected to credit them and adopt them as the motive for a gratuitous homicide. The discipline of the ascetic by which he seeks mastery over his animal nature is repeatedly undone unknown to him from within himself. Or, looking at the ascetic's life from another perspective, the mastery he seeks now over his instincts is already vouchsafed him because they too are no more than permanent possibilities for action.

These difficulties in the existentialist theory have long been recognized. I state them here because they provide a useful perspective on Merleau-Ponty's thought which can be construed as an attempt at modifying the phenomenological theory of motivation with a view to resolving them. But before examining some of these modifications, it should be made perfectly clear that Merleau-Ponty shares Sartre's philosophical purposes, as the following quotation will make amply clear:

> Whether we are concerned with my body, the natural world, the past, birth or death, the question is always how I can be open to phenomena which transcend me, and which nevertheless exist only to the extent that I take them up and live them; *how the presence to myself which establishes my own limits and conditions every alien presence is at the same time de-presentation and throws me outside myself.* Both idealism and realism, the former by making the external world immanent in me, the latter by subjecting me to a causal action, falsify the motivational relations existing between the external and internal worlds, and make this relationship unintelligible.[7]

Merleau-Ponty's Attempt to Remedy the Flaws

In *Phenomenology of Perception,* Merleau-Ponty replaces the concept of prereflective consciousness with the idea of a prepersonal self. The prepersonal self is an anonymous project toward the world "in which there are so far no 'states of consciousness,' nor, *a fortiori,* qualifications of any sort." Consequently, Merleau-Ponty shares with Sartre (and Russell) the view that the veridical content of the Cartesian *cogito* is not "I think," which presupposes an ego, but "there is thinking." In other respects, however, his conception is different.

The anonymous self is not pure consciousness. It can be poetically described as a mute conversation of man's living body with the world. But a more precise conceptual clarification is possible by means of a phenomenological description of a psychological error. If the appropriateness of this selection of an explanatory example is not apparent, it should be remembered that Merleau-Ponty considered Freud to be one of the great phenomenologists.

A woman was driving north on an expressway deep in conversation with a new acquaintance about a matter of great personal importance to her. Her intention was to drive home, which involved making an exit from the expressway via a cloverleaf which would take her under the expressway and so toward her home in a westerly direction. What she in fact did was to drive the car back on to the expressway by proceeding under the bridge, then up the ramp, and so back on to the expressway. She had driven almost a mile back along it before she discovered her predicament: for a dizzy moment the "world" seemed to revolve through a ninety-degree arc around the axis of her body and come to rest again in reality.

The psychological error reveals and is made possible by an existential structure that permits a discontinuity and ambiguity in spatial orientation. The spatial orientation of the situation formed by the driver's intention to drive home came to be out of phase with the spatial orientation anonymously established by her body and which enabled her *in fact* to execute safely the erroneous driving maneuver despite her belief that nothing was amiss and that she was heading home. Furthermore, it was this anonymous spatial orientation that provided the polarities for her reorientation.

Therefore, the anonymous self cannot be understood as a pure upsurge of consciousness. For the life of the prepersonal self preserves in existence, among other things, a projection of spatial directions onto the world. It also establishes prepersonal evaluations of things, actions, and persons. A person who is "wrapped up" in grief, and withdrawn from society into himself, as the result of a death will, nevertheless, begin to experience a disintegration of the grief to which his personal life is committed through the reabsorption of his life back into the world of objects and persons that can again engage his interest and desire. It is a prepersonal self that performs the work of reabsorption and establishes the absolute impersonal value of life and the world. Consequently, personal existence does not rest, as Sartre assumes, upon a pure spontaneous upsurge of consciousness, but rather on an "initial foundation of acquired and stabilized existence."

The concept of the prepersonal self provides phenomenology with two important theoretical assets: (1) It can provide an object for a witnessing and attesting self-awareness which is neither itself the originator of what it witnesses, like a playwright at the performance of his own play (Sartre's pure reflection), nor committed necessarily to a falsifying *Gestalt* of the self (Sartre's impure reflection). (2) It provides for a concept of the unconscious and an account of self-deception that is consistent with the philosophical goals and commitments of phenomenology, i.e., to give an account of human experience independently of causal and "objective" (scientific) categories of thought and to preserve for consciousness a nuclear role in mental life—something that the phenomenological method itself requires.

Merleau-Ponty rejects both Sartre's concept of a pure spontaneous consciousness which is transparent to itself and the psychoanalytic concept of the unconscious for essentially the same reason: both involve the same "retrospective illusion" (*PP,* 381). For they locate in the person as an explicit object everything that is slowly going to dawn upon him about himself. Thus, if being in love or being a political activist is the consequence of a constantly renewed self-transparent choice, how can it come about that the awareness of being in love or being keenly committed to political goals occurs only at the end of a period in which they have been in process of formation? Neither, according to Merleau-Ponty, can the love be a thing already constituted but hidden in my unconscious to be gradually converted into consciousness. These conceptions, each in their own way, radically diminish the reality of becoming. Merleau-Ponty, then, recognizes both a passive, attesting self-awareness and a self-ignorance that is not a form of deliberate dissimulation. "We are not perpetually in possession of ourselves in our whole reality, and we are justified in speaking of an inner perception . . . working from us to ourselves which ceaselessly goes some, but not all, the way in providing knowledge of our life and our being" (*PP,* 380).

The phenomenological account of self-ignorance constitutes a non-mechanistic theory of the unconscious. One of the most striking forms of self-ignorance is the dream experience—an experience sufficiently impenetrable to consciousness that ancient peoples, for example, experienced dreaming as a form of perception revealing a world unavailable to the waking senses but forming part of a complete system of reality. Freud conceptualized this fact about dreaming by distinguishing the *manifest* from the *latent* content of a dream. The manifest content is the distorted conscious surface of the dream of which the dreamer is aware. The latent content is the memories from which the manifest dream images are drawn, as well as the desires and emotions which animate them, of which the dreamer is not aware. The manifest dream images stand for, or symbolize, the unconscious memories and wishes. Now, phenomenology can accept (given the modifications involved in the concepts of prepersonal self and passive consciousness) the *fact about* dreaming indicated by the psychoanalytic distinction between manifest and latent content. What it cannot accept is the psychoanalytic *causal explanation* of this fact.

Merleau-Ponty's account turns on (1) the differentiation he finds within the human being between the personal self and the prepersonal self; and (2) his view that the correlate of this differentiation in a field of awareness is its organization into a figure on a background. Thus the formation of an explicit perception takes place on the basis of a preperceptual detachment of an object from its background (*PP,* 3–12, 52–53). To take a specific case, the bricklayer who inspects a batch of mortar for consistency is exploiting an organization of his field of awareness into object-for-inspection with everything else held-in-suspense. His inspection of the mortar, which is an expression of his personal life as a worker, is able to cooperate with an anonymous prepersonal life to call into existence a "workman's world." In contrast, an inexperienced person who visits a construction site will often find that objects in his perceptual field will undergo a minor spatial distortion in that they appear "flattened" into a single plane or in a weird disarray; he will find the experience itself mildly upsetting and will feel relieved to return to a work environment in which he can "feel at home." This is because such a person cannot manipulate any of the machinery, tools, and materials on the site. His body is "closed" to them and, consequently, their links with the masses of earth, concrete, steel, and wire that form the unfinished building are not exhibited in his visual field. The result is a "collapse" within the visual field. The significance of that "collapse" is that objects acquire an unreality and begin to look like one-dimensional cardboard figures.

Employing these ideas, phenomenology is able to render an account of the self-ignorance peculiar to dream experience. In sleep, the personal self is absent through a retreat back into the anonymity of the prepersonal self. Consequently, cooperation in the formation of a field of awareness cannot occur between the personal and prepersonal self. Therefore, when one dreams the entire field of awareness is uniformly dominated by sexuality. This very saturation of the images of the manifest dream-content terminates in a dream world in which sexual meanings cannot stand out because there are no nonsexual elements to form a background against which they can emerge (*PP,* 154ff., 381). Accordingly, the prepersonal spatializing function organizes a world in which to fall through the air or scale a ladder has a sexual significance. But this meaning, even while being lived by the dreamer, cannot be recognized by him because there can occur no falling or climbing actions that are asexual and merely mechanical within "the dream world"—hence the inability of the dreamer to be conscious of the sexual nature of his dream or to comprehend its meaning, and hence the presence within the person of an unacknowledged life of his person.

Merleau-Ponty's account of the self-ignorance involved in dreaming is a specific application of a more generic concept. The dreamer is not caused to remain unaware of the meaning of his dream because of the specific and forbidding nature of the impulses that produce it; he remains unaware of its meaning because of the uniformity with which sexuality pervades it. (The idea is similar to the ancient Pythagorean idea that the motions of astronomical bodies produce a music that we cannot hear because it always and everywhere uniformly permeates our hearing.) Similarly, a person cannot form an explicit thought about his own death as he can about the deaths of other persons. What we can explicitly conceptualize is rather the negation of our own death, as when we form the thought that we are the creatures through whom creation becomes known and who should, for that reason, outlast nature. But one's own death as an existential significance pervades the horizon of one's fields of awareness. It is neither an explicit object of consciousness nor a fear bound to an explicit representation of "my" death which has been repressed. My death is the lived personal sense that contingency has for me.

As a result, Merleau-Ponty can provide for an opacity within consciousness that lays down the theoretical foundation necessary for understanding how the intellectual errors involved in mechanistic anthropology could arise. Illusion is possible because consciousness can cease to know what it is doing. Otherwise, it would be conscious of having formed the illusion and could not treat it as anything other than what it is—in which case, it would not *be* an illusion. Thus the coincidence of oneself with oneself through self-awareness is never a real coincidence, "but merely an intentional and presumptive one" (*PP,* 344). The phenomenological interpretation of the unconscious, combined with the concept of the anonymity of the prepersonal self, provides the logical basis needed for understanding mechanistic anthropology as intellectual error rather than intellectual perversity. Merleau-Ponty has been able to disengage the phenomenological critique of the empirical sciences of man from the moral connotations implicit in Sartre's categories of authentic and inauthentic existence, and at the same time avoid the inconsistency implicit in existentialism.

Has Merleau-Ponty been as successful in dealing with the problems involved in the concepts of disengagement, transcendence, nihilation, and choice? Has Merleau-Ponty discovered a way of avoiding the paradoxes of the equipossibility of motives and actions with the unwanted consequence of appearing to reduce the human lot to the dilemma that destroyed Buridan's ass?

Sartre's theory is committed to the existence of nothingness as the real separation between past and present, instinct and instinctive behavior. At the same time the direction of force is always from a spontaneous consciousness which readopts past motives and aims or chooses new ones. Consequently, for existentialism the individual's decision latitude is infinite.

Merleau-Ponty has introduced an important clarification and modification in the phenomenological categories of disengagement and transcendence. It is agreed that the person can at any time interrupt his projects. Having given one's support to one political party, it is always possible to withdraw that support and give it to another. But the disengagement involved has an inevitable structure such that (1) one cannot choose oneself continually from "a starting point of nothing at all"; (2) one can only disengage oneself from one project by becoming engaged in another: "I may defy all accepted form, and spurn everything, for there is no case in which I am utterly committed: but in this case I do not withdraw into my freedom, I commit myself elsewhere" (*PP,* 452). And (3) the self is dependent on a social and natural environment that offers "invitations" to act and these "invitations" enter into the formation of the behavior that takes them up. If men are able to choose themselves as workers or capitalists with an absolute initiative, neither personal history nor national history could have the stable structure or direction over time which, in fact, it does have. Furthermore, persons are always located in a specific social environment, endowed with the powers of a specific body, and have already lived a certain kind of life. Therefore, even though one can commit oneself elsewhere, one cannot transform oneself instantaneously into what one decides to be. A teacher can go into business, but it takes time to be a businessman, i.e., to assume the style of life that makes the difference between being a teacher and a businessman. The result is a concept of disengagement that provides the theoretical basis for a rejection of determinism without a logical commitment to the existence of nothingness. Merleau-Ponty has freed phenomenology from the necessity of treating nothingness as itself a kind of existent. The concept of nothingness or nonexistence is limited by him to two meanings: first, as a description of the ontological status of things and states of affairs which once were or which are yet to be, second, as a reference to the absence of any causal mechanisms that fixate a person's actions and motives.

By extending this "naturalization" of existential categories to time, Merleau-Ponty is able both to provide a diagnosis of a major source of Sartre's philosophical difficulties and to lay the groundwork for a more plausible phenomenology of motivational stability and uniformity in human beings.

Time cannot be deduced as Sartre attempts to deduce it from the spontaneity of consciousness. To be sure, it is through subjectivity that time appears. But the time through which we unfold our personal lives is itself grounded in the natural time of our bodies. The anonymous organic rhythms of the bodily functions, respiration, pulse, and the cyclical fluctuations of the appetites adumbrate a continuous passage from cessation or quiescence, action in process of development, fulfillment, a return to quiescence, and so on, as the pattern repeats itself. Hence there is a natural ground in the living body itself for a *subjectivity that is constantly in process of making itself without ever having to be fixed once and for all in what it has already made of itself.* This ground does not depend on consciousness for its being. Like the other functions of the prepersonal self, it rests upon itself. It incorporates man's life in the passage of time of the natural world.

If, on the other hand, as Sartre supposed, temporality is originated by the spontaneity of consciousness, then the movement which carries existence into the future and transfers the present into the past must be sustained by an act. Consequently, not only must conscious acts move our personal lives forward, they must also generate such things as the respiratory reflex. Therefore, Sartre's understanding of humanity involves the notion that the decision to go to work in the morning which organizes and dedicates our personal life for the day also brings in train with it all the vital functions of our bodies. One motivates oneself to breathe just as one motivates oneself to go to work. It is this conception of temporality that gives Sartre's notion of anxiety its pathological dimensions. For if the existential concept of temporality were sound, then every act of authentic awareness would reveal that the choice to go on living could be just as easily reversed at any time. But human existence is not, in fact, intrinsically that precarious. Suicide, either physical or moral, is not an option for most people most of the time.

Merleau-Ponty is able to derive the more plausible conclusion that "a consciousness for which the world 'can be taken for granted,' which finds it 'already constituted' and present even in consciousness itself, does not *absolutely* choose either its being or its manner of being" (*PP*, 453). Persons do not choose to be alive. Neither do we choose to want to be alive. A prepersonal yearning after life may be either taken up and confirmed in the style of our personal lives or neglected, but it is there in the way in which our bodies are there.

Merleau-Ponty's phenomenology of human temporality has a specific theoretical utility denied to both existentialism and its theoretical antithesis, physiological determinism. Merleau-Ponty's conception allows for a dissonance between the prepersonal temporality of the body and the temporality of personal life that parallels the possibility of ambiguity in spatial organization described above. The phenomena of arrestment and regression uncovered by psychoanalysis imply just such a dissonance in human temporality. The personal life of the individual as defined by the experiences of satisfaction he seeks can either take up and utilize the matured sexual powers of the body or it can adopt a form of refusal, such as a perversion or a character formation that combines moral fastidiousness with political or religious fanaticism.

Binswanger, who has contributed most to the creation of existential psychiatry, has made his contribution, in part, by importing these phenomenological concepts of spatiality and temporality into psychiatry, where he has put them to work providing new explanations of the formation of neurosis. Thus in his famous case study of Ellen West[8] the disturbances of the subject's adult life terminating in suicide are understood in terms of an extreme case of dissonance in the temporal structure of her existence, resulting from her having lived out her entire personal history in childhood through a phantasy adult life, leaving her adult body life without a subjectivity to live it. Suicide was the only way she had of reuniting her body life with her personal life and thus unifying the temporal structures of her existence. To quote Binswanger:

> The life-meaning of this *Dasein* had already been fulfilled "in early years," in accordance with the stormy life-tempo and the circular life-movement of this existence, in which the *Dasein* had soon "run idle." Existential aging had hurried ahead of biological aging, just as existential death, the "being-a-corpse among people" had hurried ahead of the biological end of life. The suicide is the necessary-voluntary consequence of this existential state of things.[9]

More generally, Minkowski assumes that the way in which an individual temporalizes his existence is a fundamental determinant of his entire mental life. Existential psychiatry precisely reverses the classical picture of the relationship between a person's affectivity and his sense of time. Classical psychiatry would explain a disorder in a subject's sense of the future, such as the depressing paranoid feeling that the future exists for others but not for him as the effect, say, of a delusional belief that he is to be executed. Existential psychiatry assumes, on the contrary, that "the more basic disorder is the distorted attitude toward the future," the delusion of execution being only one of its manifestations.[10]

Merleau-Ponty uses these modified existential categories to formulate a theory of motivation that is rather closer to traditional concepts than to Sartre, except for one crucial agreement with Sartre. Freedom cannot be located in an act of will. The individual who has already elected to guarantee his own safety by not attempting a rescue, when confronted by a situation in which someone is drowning, may have recourse to an act of will to force himself into the water. Or again, the individual who is bent on adultery may impose a joyless fidelity on himself. But in each case the real decision is to secure one's own life or to enjoy a mistress. These decisions are not made by the will; neither are they *ipso facto* revoked by the will even when it determines what we actually do. The more fundamental decisions to which the will has no access can undermine willed behavior from within and leave it hollow. The aim of willed behavior is to demonstrate our powerlessness rather than express our autonomy. Consequently, it is an error to interpret the meaning of transcendence in phenomenology in terms of the power of the will to impose duties on an amoral affectivity. Merleau-Ponty agrees with Sartre in rejecting the classical concept of freedom as a deliberately willed act. "The classical conception of deliberation is relevant only to a freedom 'in bad faith' which secretly harbors antagonistic motives without being prepared to act on them, and so itself manufactures the alleged proofs of its impotence" (*PP,* 438). But if Merleau-Ponty rejected the view that human freedom can be understood in terms of a self-determining will, he also refused to understand it in terms of the nihilating power of consciousness.

Freedom can never be understood simply as an attitude of intellectual reserve expressed by the words, "I could always do and be otherwise." Freedom is the activity of bringing things about. Consequently, social, economic, political, and natural realities can get at it to reduce or to increase its scope. But, more importantly, freedom is always engaged in a situation. This means that freedom must find its motives in things. It cannot find in itself a motivational self-sufficiency. The politician who is fed up with injustices and is getting ready to launch an attack on government policies will ground his discontent and his attack in the facts of the situation as he sees them. Thus a Fulbright will be motivated by events in Vietnam. Similarly, the individual who engages in an act of personal heroism will enlist his friendship for the endangered person, a hatred of suffering, or an identification with the victim as a motive for his act. Freedom must find a bulwark for its existence and stabilize itself in things, states, and conditions. Consequently, psychological and environmental determinism are not understood adequately by means of the existential category "attitudes of excuse," for their explanations contain a truth.

Nevertheless, events, desires, states of affairs, and things cannot *in* and *by themselves* get a grip on behavior so as to act as its cause. There is no way in which the events of the war in Vietnam, their descriptions in communications media, or their domestic consequences could, of themselves, bring it about that this or that American politician will become a government critic. Events can make the time ripe for an action but they cannot of themselves produce the agent or his action. Events and their consequences need the compliance of persons in order to be converted into human actions of political protest. Consequently, as Merleau-Ponty puts it in a crucial statement, "Our freedom does not destroy our situation, but gears itself to it: as long as we are alive, our situation is open, which implies both that it calls up specially favoured modes of resolution, and also that it is powerless to bring one into being by itself" (*PP* 442).

As a result Merleau-Ponty is able to assign sense and significance to probable predictions about human behavior and events. Freedom is dependent in its existence on situations. Situations, in turn, make their own demands for modes of resolution. They yield success to some actions and doom others to futility. Similarly, there is a "sedimentation" of repeated personal decisions and undertakings into the general forms of existence of the prepersonal self. Consequently, it makes sense to say of the banker who has taken satisfaction in the confidence placed in him by the clients of his bank over the years that it is most unlikely that he would commit larceny. With this conception, the existential paradoxes would appear to have been removed from phenomenology. Merleau-Ponty has found a phenomenological basis for probabilistic and statistical thinking about human behavior.

Merleau-Ponty's work, having abandoned the intuitionism of existentialism, appears to justify amply Binswanger's distinction between two types of empirical scientific knowledge: *discursive-inductive* knowledge in the sense of describing, explaining, and controlling natural events; and *phenomenological-empirical* knowledge in the sense of a methodical, critical interpretation of phenomenal contents.[11] Phenomenology, then, has yielded up to philosophical thought a domain of fresh philosophical data which can claim to have provided a basis in fact for bypassing the old dichotomies of subject-object, freedom and determinism, mind and matter, and to have restored philosophy to the status of a substantive enquiry.

Inherent Limitations of Phenomenology

But the problem is not that simple. To be sure, Merleau-Ponty has managed to conceptualize the significance of Sartre's own phenomenological descriptions more adequately and realistically than Sartre himself. But difficulties remain. These difficulties are intrinsic to *any* consistent phenomenology. They stem methodologically from the complete abandonment of analysis and *explanation* in favor of *description;* they stem philosophically from an overestimation of consciousness, an underestimation of causality, and a misunderstanding of the nature of freedom. These inadequacies intersect at a number of points, one of which I shall now examine: the phenomenological account of self-ignorance in dreaming.

Analysis shows that the phenomenological account of dreaming cannot be true. For if the sexual nature of dream experience cannot be recognized because of the uniform saturation of dream images with sexual affect, then how can the sexual nature of dream experience ever be known? The dreamer *ex hypothesi* cannot recognize it. The awakened dreamer must do the recognizing. Now the waking state, according to phenomenology, is the return of the activities of personal life out of the anonymity of the sleeper; this change brings in train a reengagement of life with the spatiality and objectivity of the world. Waking experience, therefore, acts immediately as a background against which the sexual significance of the dream experience can stand out and, thereby, attain the clarity of an explicit consciousness. Therefore, the integration of the remembered dream experience with renewed waking experience should bring its meaning to light. But the phenomena run counter to this expectation. It is natural for people who are able to recall their dreams and recount them and recognize their disparity with reality, to remain ignorant of their meaning.

Phenomenology can adopt either of two strategies to meet the difficulty: (1) it can assign additional weight to the opacity of duration and to the intentional and presumptive nature of a person's self-awareness, or (2) it can invoke the principle of *Gestalt* indeterminacy that characterizes our perceptions of intrinsically ambiguous images. But the first strategy works altogether too well. It would make it impossible to explain how phenomenology got to know that the meaning of dreams actually is sexual rather than religious, for example, and that dreams are not just senseless, random combinations of images as the prepsychoanalytic medical theory supposed. The second strategy does not work well enough. Although it might account for the fact that some persons (those who do not use their waking experience as a ground against which to throw into perspective their dream experience) do not become aware of the meaning of their dreams, it cannot account at all for those who do discover the strangeness of the dream experience by setting it over against waking experience but who remain, nevertheless, entirely unable to grasp the significance of this strangeness. Therefore, a logical analysis of the phenomenological account of dreaming shows that it cannot do the work of describing the phenomena it was designed to do.

The phenomenological hypothesis is not helped by the fact that not all dreams have a sexual significance, whereas those that do often also contain images whose meanings are both connected with sexuality and also differentiated from it, such as jealousy, ambition, and environmentally generated frustration, fear, and anger. But the phenomenological account cannot accommodate these facts. For if some of the images of a dream are sexual and some are nonsexual in meaning, then the conditions are present within the manifest content of the dream itself to provide the ground against which the meaning of the images could be apprised, in which case the dream has lost its opacity and strangeness. Analysis shows that Merleau-Ponty has not found a way to avoid the absolute transparency of consciousness of existentialism.

What is required to understand the phenomena is just what phenomenology rejects: memory experiences strongly charged with emotion from which the dream images are detached and reassembled by a distorting process, and a force within the mental life of the person which frustrates his efforts to decipher the dream. That is to say, what is required is (1) an unconscious in the sense of memories that cannot be voluntarily recovered and which cannot become preconscious memory associations reactivated by perceptions, but which can, nevertheless, decisively influence the formation of experience and behavior; and (2) the operation of involuntary causal forces within the personality in the form of unconscious desire, anger, jealousy, and fear, which produce their effects independently of the conscious wishes of the individual and before ego wishes can intervene. Without these it is impossible to account for the way in which circuits of behavior that are potentially open and available to individuals remain rigidly closed, or the way in which individuals become fixed in circuits of behavior from which they cannot detach themselves despite maladaptation and personal suffering. But it is precisely these factors that phenomenology systematically rejects along with its rejection of inferential thinking and scientific techniques of observation (in this case free association) for the sake of an overestimation of the epistemic value and practical efficacy of consciousness.

The flaws uncovered in the modified phenomenological concept of the unconscious in connection with dream experience lead directly to similar difficulties in the phenomenological theory of motivation.

Merleau-Ponty's description of the structures of subjective temporality represent a substantial improvement on existentialism. But it is still not adequate to the phenomena. When the concept of prepersonal temporality is defined precisely, an ambiguity emerges at a crucial point. According to the phenomenological account, the rhythms of the involuntary psychophysical processes, such as the appetites, provide an anonymous prepersonal ground for a commitment of renewal or innovation in the personal behavior patterns they energize. Consequently, there must be a phase in the periodicity of an appetite during which it is open to a deviation into another form. In fact, one essential use of the term "existence" in phenomenology is precisely as a reference to this "openness" or "intrinsic adaptability." It is reasonable to suppose that the phase involved is that of quiescence or cessation.

Therefore, it is no merely verbal matter whether we refer to a quiescent phase of a continuing appetite or an actual interval of cessation in which the continuity of the individual's existence is sustained, not by the appetite itself, but by the synthesis of consciousness. If the latter, then phenomenology wins the day, but if the former is the true description of the phenomena, then phenomenology as such must be abandoned.

Crucial situations indicate continuity of the appetite. Crucial situations, in this context, are those in which a transformation of behavior patterns sustained by an appetite is needed and sought.[12] For example, a child may be fixated in the pursuit of oral satisfaction as a source of inner content and comfort even after the acquisitive instinct has already abandoned the sucking reflex as a means of satisfying itself. Now, the child can want to abandon the habit out of a real acceptance of obedience to parental wishes; parents for their part can provide a range of motives in the nature of threats and special inducements. But nothing will happen until either the child has developed, at a later stage, the character formation necessary for the repression of the desire energizing the behavior patterns involved, or adults in his environment find a way back into the child's confidence so that he can find comfort and security through his relations with them and begin to mature emotionally.

Similarly, an adult sexual perversion may have the periodicity of the normal appetite. But this does not mean that a person who suffers it is offered a periodic opportunity either to cooperate with the demands of his desires or gradually to deflect them into heterosexuality. The tragic histories of men who have actively committed themselves to find grounds for heterosexuality "in the world" through allegiance to a church, self-dedication to its moral ideals, marriage and parenthood, on the mistaken assumption that engagement of their lives and bodies in the personal and social forms of heterosexuality would induce in them the passion itself, present phenomena that demand causal interpretation. For they refer us to forces operating psychophysical structures that have their influence on conscious life and behavior independently of its preferences. These crucial situations shed an especially clear light on the inadequacies of the phenomenological theory of motivation. But it would be a serious error to suppose, as some have, that healthy appetites function any differently.[13] Heterosexual desire is equally the cause of the behavior associated with it. Only the impact of powerful frustrations can produce a regression in it that will break down the behavior patterns it stabilizes and cause it to reactivate psychophysical formations that had been abandoned by the growth process.

Therefore, despite Merleau-Ponty's modifications in existentialist categories and principles, phenomenology still subscribes to two ideas that are inconsistent with the facts. "In relation to what we are by reason of our acquisitions and this pre-existent world, we have a power of placing in abeyance, and that suffices to ensure our freedom from determinism" (*PP*, 395). The corollary of this principle is that neither environmental conditions, bodily states, a neurosis, character formation, instinct, nor desire is sufficient in itself to move a person to act in a determinate manner apart from an act of compliance on his part. Consequently, Merleau-Ponty can affirm that "Since freedom does not tolerate any motive in its path, my habitual being in the world is at each moment equally precarious, and the complexes which I have allowed to develop over the years always remain equally soothing, and the free act can with no difficulty blow them sky-high" (*PP,* 441). But it is a serious distortion of the facts to say that an individual allows an inferiority complex to develop by taking a pleasure in feelings of inadequacy and submission, although it is perfectly true that he does in fact receive a kind of pleasure from so acting. Consider a specific case. A student at the university suffers from a pervasive feeling of futility and worthlessness. He feels that he is an incompetent impostor. He suffers profound fits of depression lasting for days at a time, during which he cannot work. Nevertheless, he applies himself with great success to his studies and achieves high standing both in essay and examination work, demonstrating genuine abilities in his field of study. His abilities are acknowledged by peers and teachers, in some cases enthusiastically. Now if freedom, as phenomenology claims, can find a bulwark for itself in things, without bondage to the past, then there could hardly be a better motivational foundation on which to base a gradual self-transformation into a happy, confident person than real achievement actually recognized. But in fact the student cannot do so. His achievements do not "rub off" on his life, despite the fact that he is perfectly conscious of them and try as he might to take courage from them. Thus we encounter in the phenomena of human life the work of causal forces producing unwanted and even frightening effects in consciousness and behavior. They act, with or without an invitation, to produce a range of involuntary effects the existence of which phenomenology cannot in principle comprehend because they require causal explanation and not phenomenological description.

Alternative concepts of consciousness and freedom emerge from this examination of phenomenology. Consciousness is a quality of some but not all mental activities, structures, and processes. It is a category-mistake to treat consciousness as a substantive, as phenomenology is logically committed to doing. Similarly, freedom is a quality of some but not all human actions. Motives are those causes, of which we happen to be aware, that determine us to act. However, the fact that we happen to be aware of them does not alter their causal nature. Thus the question of human freedom or enslavement is decided not by the presence or absence of causes compelling us to act, but by the *nature* of the causes that move us. Our character is our *daimon.*

Notes

1. Plato, *The Republic,* book IV, 439–40.

2. Thomas Hobbes, *Leviathan,* part 1, chap. 6.

3. Jean-Paul Sartre, *Being and Nothingness,* trans. Hazel E. Barnes (New York: Philosophical Library, 1956), 40. Hereafter *BN.*

4. See J. Frank, "Breaking through the Thought Barriers," *Psychiatry: Journal for the Study of Interpersonal Processes* 23, no. 3.

5. Sigmund Freud, *The Interpretation of Dreams* (New York, 1961), 598–610.

6. Cf. Descartes's cosmological concept that preservation takes as much energy as creation.

7. Maurice Merleau-Ponty, *Phenomenology of Perception,* trans. Colin Smith (London: Routledge and Kegan Paul, 1962), 363–64. Hereafter *PP.*

8. L. Binswanger, "The Case of Ellen West," in *Existence: A New Dimension in Psychiatry and Psychology,* ed. R. May, et al. (New York, 1958).

9. Ibid., 295.

10. E. Minkowski, "A Case of Schizophrenic Depression," in *Existence.*

11. L. Binswanger, "The Existential Analysis School of Thought," in *Existence.*

12. See *Phenomenology of Perception,* 438–39. Merleau-Ponty would agree that such situations are crucial for understanding the nature of freedom.

13. John Hospers makes a similar point in "Meaning and Free Will," *Philosophy and Phenomenological Research* 10 (1950), 316–30. His position in that paper is in agreement with the conclusions advanced here.

7

The Existence of Alter Egos: Jean-Paul Sartre and Maurice Merleau-Ponty

François H. Lapointe

From the critical viewpoint, the existence of alter egos is the fundamental problem facing a phenomenological psychology. It is difficult to see how a philosophy grounded totally in experience could avoid eventuating in a position of solipsism or pure subjectivism. That this is a real and constant risk, amounting virtually to a tendency within phenomenology, is evidenced in recurring interpretations like that of Quentin Lauer.[1] In this respect, intersubjectivity becomes a crucial distinguishing theme and a foundation-block for a phenomenological psychology. The main purpose of this investigation is to clarify the question of how we come to know another person according to Sartre and Merleau-Ponty. We will attempt to follow the analyses which led each of them to the revelation of other human existents as such.

For Sartre the problem amounts to the conversion into a subject of what might just as well, at first glance, be an object among other objects. He answers this question quite simply by stating that "It is not only conjectural but *probable* that this voice which I hear is that of a man and not a song on a phonograph. . . . Without going beyond the limits of probability and indeed because of this very probability, my apprehension of the Other as an object essentially refers me to a fundamental apprehension of the Other in which he will not be revealed to me as an object but as a 'presence in person.' "[2]

Sartre has previously established that the perceptive field refers to me as its center; but as soon as I apprehend the other, I experience a spatiality which is not mine. The objects of my experience flee from me and arrange themselves around that "privileged object" which, however, nevertheless remains an object for me (*BN,* 313). But if I am able to see the other as an object, then it follows that the subjectivity of the other is announced in the act whereby he sees me as an object. "My apprehension of the other in the world as *probably being* a man refers to my permanent possibility of being-seen-by-him; that is, to the permanent possibility that a subject who sees me may be substituted for the object seen by me" (*BN,* 315). But the other, in looking at me and in fact by nature of this very activity on his part, fixes me in the world as an object, an *en-soi.* The look finds me "at the heart of my situation and grasps me only in irresolvable relations with instruments" (*BN,* 323). The other is able to transcend my transcendence and in so doing alienate my world and even to alienate my own possibilities. Even my look as it fixes on other people and makes them into objects loses its power; I cannot make these other people into objects for the other because they are already objects for him (*BN,* 326).

In the look, then, the other becomes that which can never be an object; on the contrary, his look transforms me into an object, and is apprehended by me as transcendent to both me and my world. Thus at the same time as I experience my own objectness, I experience the other's absolute freedom. The other, in other words, is always present to me in my always being-for-the-other. My first experience of the other, then, is not at all bodily but rather takes place within the ontological system of the *en-soi* and the *pour-soi,* the subject-object dichotomy in which I first of all and in the most primordial experience of the other exist as an object for the other as subject: "To be an object-for-others or to-be-a-body are two ontological modalities which are strictly equivalent expressions of the being-for-others on the part of the for-itself" (*BN,* 424). Again Sartre affirms a chasm between the body (identical to an object for the other) and the consciousness which views it: "I feel myself touched by the Other in my factual existence; it is my being-there-for-others for which I am responsible. This *being-there* is precisely the body" (*BN,* 431).

Merleau-Ponty, on the other hand, finds no necessity in relating the experience of other people to the subject-object distinction; for him this original experience already takes place at the personal level, the level of "intersubjectivity." The other is, in fact, equiprimordial with the world and the body: "To be a consciousness or rather to be an *experience* is to hold inner communication with the world, the body and other people, to be with them instead of being beside them."[3]

Merleau-Ponty criticizes the Sartrean "*en-soi/pour-soi*" dichotomy as it is related to the look. Merleau-Ponty states in several places that there is already contained in the first moment of the look its implicit resolution. In an article entitled "Hegel's Existentialism" in *Sense and Non-Sense* he discusses the look in connection with an experience of death. (Sartre construes it as the death of my possibilities.) While admitting the danger inherent in my encounter with the other's look, Merleau-Ponty passes immediately beyond this problem:

> We cannot be aware of the conflict unless we are aware of our reciprocal relationship and our common humanity. We do not deny each other except by mutual recognition of our consciousness. That negation of everything and of others which I am is completed only by reduplicating itself through another's negation of it. And just as my consciousness of myself as death and nothingness is deceitful and contains an affirmation of my being and my life, so my consciousness of another as an enemy comprises an affirmation of him as an equal. If I am negation, then by following the implication of this universal negation to its ultimate conclusion, I will witness the self-denial of that very negation and its transformation into coexistence. By myself I cannot be free, nor can I be a consciousness or a man; and that other whom I first saw as my rival is a rival only because he is myself. I discover myself in the other, just as I discover consciousness of death, because I am from the start this mixture of life and death, solitude and communication, which is heading toward its resolution.[4]

The result of this resolution of the two looks is that there are no longer two conflicting consciousnesses but two mutually unfolding glances seeking a fulfillment which will be the same for both.[5]

My actions, then, and my very existence are not observed by the other as though he were a pure thinking subject and I a pure bodily object; my actions are rather taken up and understood by him, and his by me. The look of a total stranger is felt to be antagonistic only because it takes the place of possible communication; yet even this refusal to communicate is itself a communication (*PP*, 361). It is because I recognize within myself the junction of the *en-soi* and the *pour-soi* that others can come to life for me as men: "Unless I have an exterior, others have no interior. The plurality of consciousness is impossible if I have an absolute consciousness of myself" (*PP*, 373).

In this way the structures Sartre designates as my body-for-others must already be dimensions of my body-for-me. An experience of the other-as-object is as impossible as one of myself as absolute subjectivity.

I must "apprehend around my absolute individuality a kind of halo of generality or a kind of atmosphere of 'sociality' " (*PP,* 448). And centered in this atmosphere as I am, I must admit a meaning of my life and my actions which I do not constitute. There must be an intersubjectivity in which I, as a situated being, am anonymous both as absolutely individual and as absolutely general. It is thus that Merleau-Ponty says that "the solitude from which we emerge into intersubjective life is not that of the monad. It is only the haze of an anonymous life that separates us from being; and the barrier between us and others is impalpable. If there is a break, it is not between me and the other person; it is between a primordial generality we are intermingled in and the precise system, myself-the others" (*Signs,* 174).

From the beginning, then, Merleau-Ponty asserts that man is involved inextricably in the world with others. It is for this reason that he sees all man's actions as ambiguous; other people, as "permanent coordinates of our lives," may see our actions as meaningful in various ways. As soon as I become aware of the existence of others, I must allow myself to be what they think I am (*SNS,* 37). It has already become apparent that Merleau-Ponty finds no necessity to attempt to "prove" the existence of others; they are permanently and self-evidently there from the first moment of my awareness. Consequently the other must begin to exist for me on a level below that of thought; that level at which the existence of the other first becomes possible is precisely that of perception (*Signs,* 170).

I realize at the heart of my most personal and solitary experience a contradiction whereby that experience is placed in the visual field of others and submitted to their regard. Once again Merleau-Ponty affirms the ambiguous coexistence in me of the absolutely individual and the absolutely general. "Just as I grasp time through my present and by being present, I perceive others through my individual life, in the tension of an experience which transcends itself" (*PP,* 357). Indeed, the experience of others is a precondition for my being able to speak of solitude at all. Just as my reflection is given only as an assumption of the unreflected, so also my experience is given as a tension toward another whose existence on the horizon of my life cannot be doubted, even if it is only vaguely conceptualized (*PP,* 359). I experience around me not only the natural world of earth, air, and water but also a world of objects molded to my human actions: roads, churches, villages, implements. The civilization of which I am a part is self-evident because of these various "cultural objects" which, although ambiguous, are nevertheless present. "In the cultural objects, I feel the close presence of others beneath a veil of anonymity"(*PP,* 348).

But Merleau-Ponty takes his analysis a step further: the body of the other person, "as the vehicle of a form of behavior," is itself a cultural object, the first of all and the one by which the others exist. The question which now must be asked is "how an object in space can become the eloquent relic of an existence; how, conversely, an intention, a thought or a project can detach themselves from the personal subject and become visible outside him in the shape of his body, and in the environment which he builds for himself" (*PP,* 348–49). The real task of Merleau-Ponty, then, is to discover not *whether* other people exist for me (which is unnecessary) but rather *how,* as subjectivities, they can manifest themselves to me.

To answer this question Merleau-Ponty returns to his conclusions in regard to the "*corps propre,*" the body-subject. To begin with, my body and the world are not related as objects spread out before my absolute and constituting consciousness; I *have* the world through my body because my body is a movement toward the world as a potentiality of the world. And this is not all: "At the same time as the body withdraws from the objective world, and forms between the pure subject and the object a third genus of being, the subject loses its purity and its transparency" (*PP,* 350). This being the case, I have not an all-embracing view of the world but a *point of view* (which is my body); and my perception, similarly, is not a constitution of the object but an inherence in things. If then, I experience this inhering of my consciousness in my body and my world, my perception of other people is no longer a problem; for there is no reason why the bodies I see should not be inhabited by consciousnesses just as mine is. "Through phenomenal reflection I discover vision . . . as a gaze at grips with a visible world, and that is why for me there can be another's gaze; that expressive instrument called a face can carry an existence, as my own existence is carried by my body, that knowledge-acquiring apparatus" (*PP,* 351).

There can be other people for me because I am not transparent to myself and because "my subjectivity draws its body in its wake" (*PP,* 352). I thus know myself to be a subjectivity situated in the world by means of my body, and this knowledge prevents me from ever positing myself as object for the subjectivity of the other; instead, we see each other's bodies as manifestations of behavior. We find that our perceptions "slip into each other and are brought together finally in the thing. In the same way we must learn to find the communication between one consciousness and another in one and the same world" (*PP,* 353).

The things before me in my perceived world by their very existence for me exhibit "a kind of demand that what I see be seen by [the other] also. And at the same time this communication is required by the very thing which I am looking at. . . . The thing imposes itself not as true for every intellect, but as real for every subject who is standing where I am."[6] I thus perceive the other as another "myself" open to the same truths as I am and thus conferring on the objects of my perception a dimension of intersubjective being, i.e., of objectivity. His is an open life, like mine; he projects himself into his environment, as I do, by means of cultural objects.

It is not surprising that Merleau-Ponty, in considering communication as the basis of interpersonal experience, should assign such prominence to language in his descriptions. Dialogue places between the other and me a common ground and institutes between us a shared operation of which neither of us is the creator. We become coexistent in a common world. The contradiction inherent in a solipsist philosophy becomes obvious in Merleau-Ponty's analysis: in adopting such a position, I am addressing my thoughts to an audience of other men who hear and understand those thoughts. Not even thought is possible without speech; the existence of others and my communication with them become, therefore, a necessary precondition to and coefficient of my emergence as a human being. Thought and speech anticipate one another; they derive from and finally return to each other. "Operative language makes us think, and living thought magically finds its words. There is not *thought* and *language;* upon examination each of the two orders splits in two and puts out a branch into the other. There is sensible speech, which is called thought, and abortive thought, which is called language" (*Signs,* 18).

Language, further, by virtue of its communicative and thus intersubjective nature initiates a thought which is not individual but universal. This is not to say that there are "pure" concepts which every mind would have identically; language is the "call" of a situated thought to others and their response as other situated thoughts. And not only our language but all our actions and all our creations are, for the same reason, intersubjective: "Our life is essentially universal" (*PrP,* 10). Each aspect of each culture at each moment in its history thus becomes meaningful to all others and to its successors; such a possibility exists because of "the permanent, harmonious thought of this plurality of beings who recognize one another as 'semblables' " (*PrP,* 10).

Because we are in the world with others, then, there is not a word, not a gesture which is not meaningful; I and the others are caught up in history in a single drama in which it is impossible to do or say anything which is not historically significant. "History is other people," and (because for them every word and gesture of ours must be significant) "we are condemned to meaning."

Sartre too gives language priority in his descriptions of human relations. For him language, far from being a secondary addition to man's being-for-others, *is* that very being. Furthermore, because my activities are open to the inspection of others, I *am* language (*BN,* 455). Nevertheless, this phenomenon too is inserted into the basic Sartrean ontology: language as externalized here becomes a condition of my being as looked-at, i.e., as an object for the other-as-subject. In conclusion, we see how both Merleau-Ponty and Sartre evolve their respective discussions of interhuman relationships from their original philosophical premises: the body-subject on the one hand, and the *en-soi/pour-soi* distinction on the other.

Notes

1. Quentin Lauer, *The Triumph of Subjectivity* (New York: Fordham University Press, 1958).

2. Jean-Paul Sartre, *Being and Nothingness,* trans. Hazel E. Barnes (New York: Washington Square Press, 1966), 310. Hereafter *BN.*

3. Maurice Merleau-Ponty, *Phenomenology of Perception,* trans. Colin Smith (New York: Humanities Press, 1962), 96. Hereafter *PP.*

4. Maurice Merleau-Ponty, *Sense and Non-Sense,* trans. Hubert L. Dreyfus (Evanston: Northwestern University Press, 1964), 68. Hereafter *SNS.*

5. Maurice Merleau-Ponty, *Signs,* trans. Richard C. McCleary (Evanston: Northwestern University Press, 1964), 17. Hereafter *Signs.*

6. Maurice Merleau-Ponty, *The Primacy of Perception,* ed., trans. James M. Edie (Evanston: Northwestern University Press, 1964), 17. Hereafter *PrP.*

8

Sartre and Merleau-Ponty: A Reappraisal

Monika Langer

One of Sartre's finest articles is that written on the occasion of Merleau-Ponty's death in 1961. Reminiscing about their long and sometimes rather painful friendship, Sartre acknowledged that it was Merleau-Ponty who had "converted" him to a genuine appreciation of history as the universal setting of human action. Although three years Sartre's junior, Merleau-Ponty was nevertheless Sartre's guide, and the profound respect the elder accorded the younger never waned. During the turbulent postwar years the two collaborated in the editing of *Les Temps modernes:* "Merleau had no other boss but himself," observed Sartre. "He was much better oriented than I in the ambiguous world of politics. I knew this. And it would be an understatement to say that I had faith in him. It seemed to me, reading him, that he revealed my own thoughts to me."[1]

Simone de Beauvoir, Sartre's lifelong associate, nevertheless has argued that Merleau-Ponty failed to understand Sartre.[2] Such failure to comprehend need not rest on fundamental philosophical differences: de Beauvoir in fact suggests that the ideas the two men shared led Merleau-Ponty, in the interests of proclaiming his own originality, to invent a "pseudo-Sartreanism" that served as a "counter–Merleau-Pontyism" (*TM,* 2122; below 489). Although I would question the ascription of such motives to Merleau-Ponty, it seems to me that there is indeed a fundamental accord between his position and that of Sartre. Further, I am in agreement with de Beauvoir's contention that the Sartreanism which Merleau-Ponty submitted to such scathing criticism in *Adventures of the Dialectic* is a "pseudo-Sartreanism."

I would maintain that, aside from any inherent interest their long association might hold for us, there is a very real philosophical gain to be made from reappraising the relationship between Sartre and Merleau-Ponty. Of Sartre's innumerable critics, Merleau-Ponty was without question the one best versed in both phenomenological ontology and Marxism. Sartre observed that they were not only friends but equals (*Sits,* 156; below 565). Merleau-Ponty's "pseudo-Sartreanism" is by no means unique. Other critics have adopted a very similar interpretation of Sartre's position. In fact, it seems to me that such a reading constitutes the most widespread interpretation.[3] Moreover, de Beauvoir points out that the public, aware both of Merleau-Ponty's philosophical prestige and his long acquaintance with Sartre, has largely assumed that he knew Sartre's thought (*TM,* 2072; below 448). It is of no little importance, therefore, to establish whether this was in fact the case. An investigation of Merleau-Ponty's "pseudo-Sartreanism" will, I think, bring "genuine Sartreanism" into focus and help to discredit previous misinterpretations.

It is impossible within the confines of an article to examine all aspects of the relationship between Sartre and Merleau-Ponty. I shall therefore confine my discussion to some of the most important features. Further, I shall argue that the *leitmotif* of Merleau-Ponty's whole philosophy provides the key to an understanding of Sartre's own position. In order to appreciate the full significance of Merleau-Ponty's criticisms, the context of the immediate object of his attack, *The Communists and Peace,* must be indicated. It is therefore essential to begin with a brief sketch of the sociopolitical environment shared by the two philosophers.[4]

Like many French intellectuals, Sartre and Merleau-Ponty experienced an awakening of political consciousness during World War II. Although initially "to the right of Merleau-Ponty," Sartre gradually aligned himself more closely with the P.C.F. (Parti Communiste Francais. It should be noted, however, that neither Sartre nor Merleau-Ponty ever became a party member.) Merleau-Ponty, on the other hand, became increasingly disillusioned not only with communism as practiced in the Soviet Union but also with Marxism itself. As early as 1945 he was sharply critical of some aspects of Marx's thought, although at that time he still considered Marxism to be "the only universal and human politics."[5] He was growing increasingly pessimistic about the possibility of a proletarian revolution, but he continued to advise his readers to follow the policy of the communist party. Information about the Stalinist camps led him to conclude that both communism and Marxism were in need of reevaluation. And when the Korean War broke out he decided that sympathy without adhesion was no longer warranted because, in his eyes, the U.S.S.R. had shown itself to be imperialistic; it therefore no longer deserved any privileged status. Merleau-Ponty now opted for silence, gave up his post as political director of *Les Temps modernes,* and eventually resigned altogether.

Sartre, on the other hand, thought that the alliance of the bourgeoisie and the French socialist leaders left "no other alternative but to stay as close to the Communist Party as possible." Although the chances of a leftist regrouping seemed remote, he felt it imperative "to keep its possibility alive from day to day by concluding alliances with the Party on a local basis" (*Sits,* 203; below 606). Thus while Sartre was convinced he was being faithful to Merleau-Ponty's thought of 1945, Merleau-Ponty was abandoning his former emphasis on a united left and at the same time thinking that he was remaining true to himself and Sartre was betraying him (*Sits,* 202; below 604–5). Sartre's contempt for the bourgeoisie, which had long been accumulating, finally burst out in *The Communists and Peace:* "I had to write or suffocate" (*Sits,* 198; below 601). Although he did not mention the Korean conflict, he was to realize in retrospect that he wrote "heedlessly" and "tactlessly," and that, contrary to his own intentions, it seemed as though he had planned a systematic refutation of Merleau-Ponty (*Sits,* 199; below 601–2). Understandably, therefore, Merleau-Ponty was stung, and he replied sharply, albeit a few years later. If the exchange between the two had been merely a matter of "verbal warfare" it would hardly merit investigation. There was, however, considerably more at stake. Merleau-Ponty thought that beneath the immediate political differences he detected a profound *philosophical* incompatibility between his own position and that of Sartre. *The Communists and Peace* aroused him to elaborate these supposed differences. In order to evaluate Merleau-Ponty's interpretation of Sartre's philosophy, it is therefore necessary to examine, if only briefly, the stand taken by Sartre in *The Communists and Peace.* After suggesting and developing an interpretation of Sartre that runs directly contrary to that adopted by Merleau-Ponty, I shall, toward the end of this paper, outline a reinterpretation of *The Communists and Peace.* Since, as Merleau-Ponty himself claimed, Sartre's political stance is directly related to his philosophical position, a reinterpretation of the latter must involve a concomitant reevaluation of the former. It is with this in mind that I propose now to undertake a short investigation of *The Communists and Peace.*

This work first appeared in *Les Temps modernes* in several installments beginning in July 1952. It was devoted mainly to a criticism of the moderate left, an analysis of the significance of the May 28th demonstration and the June 4th strike, and a discussion of the advantages of an alliance between the proletariat and the Communist Party. Sartre outlined the "four inevitable stages" through which many on the left were passing from disillusionment with the Communist Party to alignment with the United States. Opposing the construction of "the true socialism, international, democratic, and reformist" which these people sought, Sartre attempted to demonstrate "to what extent the C.P. is the *necessary* expression of the working class, and to what extent it is the *exact* expression."[6] In the course of his discussion, Sartre drew attention to the essential ambiguity of democratic centralization and tried to explain that "the revolutionary who lives in our epoch, and whose task is to prepare for the Revolution with the means at hand and in his historical situation . . . must indissolubly associate the Soviet cause with that of the proletariat" (*CP,* 10, 12). Unlike the United States, whose "show of force" served to break the will of the colonized peoples by terror, the Soviet Union, according to Sartre, proved daily that it wanted peace. Along these lines, Sartre declared that the May 25th demonstration "was a supreme effort toward peace" and "was acting out the deep-seated pacifism of the masses." He asked that the recourse to violence during that demonstration be understood in the perspective of the "climate of pessimism" (*CP,* 15, 23, 24). Sartre took pains to point out that reformism, in confining itself to elementary demands, necessarily involves a *de facto* rejection of the revolution and the betrayal of the working class. He also drew attention to the impotence of the communists in the Assembly and to the hidden violence in bourgeois legality. Sartre went on to discuss the relationships between "interiorized" and "exteriorized" violence, and stressed that the violence exercised by the worker was in fact humanism: "From the point of view of a future society which will be born thanks to his efforts, his violence is a positive humanism. . . . Not a means of achieving humanism. Not even a necessary condition. But the humanism itself, insofar as it asserts itself against 'reification' " (*CP,* 55).

According to Sartre, "on June 4th . . . there *wasn't* any working class" (*CP,* 67). He maintained that the proletariat was not synonymous with a great number of individuals, or even with "the great majority of the workers." The proletarian, Sartre contended, no longer shows the relationship between his immediate struggles and "the destiny of the proletariat." He recalled Marx's claim that "the proletariat can act as a class only by shaping itself into a distinct political party," and concluded that "if the working class wants to detach itself from the Party, it has only one means at its disposal: to crumble into dust" (*CP,* 76, 87, 88). In his view, an opposition between the working class and the party was "not even conceivable." The *unity* of the workers characterized the class, and in the absence of the party this unity was not possible. Sartre argued that "the class makes and remakes itself continuously": "The proletariat forms itself by its day-to-day action. It exists only by acting. It is action. If it ceases to act, it decomposes" (*CP*, 89, 97). He depicted class as "a system in motion" that prevents the individual from reverting to inertia and isolation (*CP*, 98). In keeping with this view, he declared the proletariat to be utterly impotent unless unified by the party, and emphasized the need for obedience to party authority.

Merleau-Ponty was particularly disturbed by this view of the relationship between the proletariat and the party. In *Adventures of the Dialectic* (1955), he bitterly accused Sartre of "ultrabolshevism." Merleau-Ponty himself was by this time questioning the very idea of revolution and coming to the conclusion that revolutions inevitably fail. Ultimately, he felt, they could not tolerate opposition, and therefore they invariably substituted equivocation for dialectic. To concentrate all negativity and all sense of history in the proletariat constituted, in Merleau-Ponty's view, a grave error and involved a failure to appreciate both the ambiguity of power and the inertia of history. Convinced that revolutions could accomplish only relative progress, Merleau-Ponty finally found himself incapable of believing any longer in the revolution of the proletariat. The Korean War, by reminding him of the identity of theory and practice, brought him to the realization that Marxism could not be considered both true as critique or negation and false as positive action. Merleau-Ponty now advocated a reexamination of Marxism, in the belief that the failures of its action must be foreshadowed within its critique. Although he remained convinced that a politics based on anticommunism was a politics of aggression, he now contended that there were many fruitful ways of being noncommunist. Merleau-Ponty therefore felt compelled to replace the idea of revolution with that of responsible reform, and to support a parliamentary democracy insofar as it alone guaranteed at least a minimum of opposition and truths.[7]

These views, of course, were diametrically opposed to those expounded by Sartre in *The Communists and Peace.* As already indicated, Merleau-Ponty was convinced that the differences between Sartre and himself went far beyond an immediate political divergence—that, indeed, their differences were ultimately philosophical.[8] Merleau-Ponty's entire philosophical thought is based on the notion of an "interworld." It seems to me that all his criticisms of Sartre resolve themselves ultimately into the question of the presence or absence of this "interworld" in the latter's philosophy. I shall argue that there is indeed such a "third term" for Sartre, and that it is, moreover, the key to "genuine Sartreanism."

According to Merleau-Ponty, the "interworld" is incarnation, carnality, the "flesh of the world." Its vehicle is the living human body—not as physiological system but as embodied, situated subjectivity. The "interworld" is there where "subjective" and "objective" intersect (*inter secare*), merge, and are transformed. In this realm, natural facts become cultural acquisitions, temporal *ekstases* flow into one another, and history is born. This is the world of lived ambiguity, of expression, of dialogue. Here, the centrifugal is also centripetal;[9] meanings are not imposed, but elicited; events do not coerce, but solicit response. This is the sphere "in between" inertia and pure spontaneity; between contingency and necessity, transparency and opacity. It is the locus of praxis, of dialectic. In such an "interworld," the living, expressing human body is the "third term" mediating between the self and others. Embodied subjects open onto a common world, a world "in between" them—in short, an *intersubjectivity* where subjects *interact*, perspectives merge, and truth comes-to-be.

The "interworld," then, is neither lifeless matter nor abstract *Geist*. It is truly *flesh*. As I have already pointed out, Merleau-Ponty's entire "pseudo-Sartreanism" is ultimately reducible to the charge that such "flesh" is nonexistent in Sartre's philosophy. In *Adventures of the Dialectic*, Merleau-Ponty argued that Sartre's whole theory of the Communist Party and the proletariat was derived from his philosophy of fact, of consciousness, and of time. He claimed that Sartre's subject is a translucent consciousness coextensive with the world. In his criticism of idealism in *Phenomenology of Perception* (1945), Merleau-Ponty had already explained at length that it is impossible to be simultaneously coextensive with, and situated in, the world. The Sartrean subject, therefore, is a "spectator consciousness" possessing absolute knowledge. Merleau-Ponty contended that, for Sartre, meaning does not come from the world but is imposed on it by the constituting consciousness. There are, thus, no meanings that are operative before being known. Subject and world, meaning and being, are irreconcilably opposed.

In short, Sartrean philosophy is, in Merleau-Ponty's eyes, a Cartesian dualism which confronts absolute lucidity, pure consciousness (*pour-soi*) with impenetrably opaque matter (*en-soi*), and categorically denies any "in-between." Because consciousness is solely centrifugal, there is a fundamental closure of meaning. In his chapter "Other People and the Human World" in the *Phenomenology of Perception*, Merleau-Ponty had already argued that a philosophy in which the subject enjoys absolute lucidity is necessarily solipsistic. If consciousness is coextensive with, and wholly constitutive of the world, the other consciousnesses are inevitably incorporated into that world as objects:

> In so far as I constitute the world, I cannot conceive another consciousness, for it too would have to constitute the world and, at least as regards this other view of the world, I should not be the constituting agent. Even if I succeeded in thinking of it as constituting the world, it would be I who

> would be constituting the consciousness as such, and once more I should be the sole constituting agent. (*PP*, 350)

Merleau-Ponty therefore replaced idealism with a philosophy of incarnate subjectivity. In place of an absolute consciousness, he put a subjectivity that "draws its body in its wake." Such a body "forms between the pure subject and the object a third genus of being" (*PP*, 352, 350). In Merleau-Ponty's philosophy, "the subject loses its purity and its transparency," and an "internal relation" is established not only "between my consciousness and my body as I experience it," but also "between this phenomenal body of mine and that of another as I see it from the outside." The other, here, appears as "the completion of the system" (*PP*, 352).

On the other hand, if subjectivity is "transcendence through and through," if all meaning proceeds from the individual, then there is no "in-between," no room for meaning which arises elsewhere, whether from others or from the natural world. The only alternative such idealism offers is plurality—a plurality of worlds, each constituted entirely by its own single sovereign consciousness. Intersubjectivity, however, is completely ruled out, precisely because there is no "interworld," no realm in which subjects can participate in something which "lies between" them, which is *shared*. There is a radical separation between the self and the other. Each lives exclusively in his own world. If such plurality is rejected, rivalry and "false fraternity" are all that remain. In short, if a universe of monads is replaced by a single world, consciousnesses will fight for sovereignty, for the satisfaction of constituting meaning rather than the degradation of being constituted as an element of another's world.

The paradigm of possible relations between consciousnesses in "pseudo-Sartreanism" is that of the look, in which subjectivity can remain subjectivity, pure transcendence, only on condition that it objectify the other. Thus, the subject either objectifies the other or is himself objectified. There is no "in-between." I am either subject or object, either sovereign or slave. There is no "interworld." The other, therefore, is a rival, an intruder in *my* world. He alone threatens my sovereign subjectivity, my absolute transcendence. He alone can, by his gaze, decenter my freedom. The Sartrean subject lacks any "hinge," any anchorage in the world. Consequently, his action must be impingement, imposition, intervention in being. Since there is no "hold" on being, there can be no acquisition, no continuity. Action is not "true" or "substantial," but utterly "pure": it is continual rupture, continual creation *ex nihilo*. The subject is pure spontaneity confronting opaque, inert "matter." Antidialectic has replaced dialectic. There is no revolutionary "ebb and flow." Action is reduced to absolute, rootless initiative, to pure trickery which confronts the force of being. There is no *praxis,* no adjustment of action to the situation, no deciphering of events, no "historical matter." Instead, there are merely continual creations *ex nihilo* on the part of a nonsituated, or "spectator," consciousness. In the absence of a shared "field" of experience there can be no mutual projects, but only individual encounters, traps, and tasks. Mere "cinders of consciousness" lie "between men and things" (*AD,* 99ff., 124ff., 138ff., 165). Time is atomized—there is no "temporal thickness" separating volition from action. To will is to do; action is the immediate result of volition. The Sartrean subject is, therefore, radically free. Anything and everything is equally possible at any instant. The subject makes himself to be whatever he wishes. In the absence of any "common ground," any "interworld" between consciousness and being, the law of "all or nothing" takes over. There is no sphere of becoming, no genesis of meaning, no evolution of truth, no process, no dialectic, no social realm, no history (*AD,* 111ff., 124ff., 132, 162, 199ff.).

The nature of Sartre's political thought is easily understood, argued Merleau-Ponty, when viewed against this background. Since "facts" belong to the impenetrable realm of the *en-soi,* they are absolutely equivocal. Their meaning is external to them; it is imposed by the *pour-soi.* Political life is thus reduced to the level of judgment. Since, in the absence of an "interworld," intersubjectivity is ruled out, the relation between the party and the proletariat can be no other than that of subject to object, sovereign to slave. There can be no participation, no interaction, no discussion, no deliberation. The party, therefore, wields absolute authority and demands unquestioning obedience. Revolution becomes the exclusive concern of party leaders; history is reduced to personal volitions, to "a pact of wills." In its role as subject, the party enjoys complete lucidity, absolute knowledge. There is no possibility of error. The facts themselves are utterly devoid of significance. Since they bear no meaning of their own, they can be interpreted at will. The party consequently is not subjected to any controls but is entirely free to impose any meaning on the facts, to make history in whatever way it deems fit. It is the sole agent of history. The party thus has a "blank check" for terrorism. In keeping with the law of "all or nothing," whoever is not for the party is against it. Since there is no mixture of fact and meaning, no "interworld," truth is a *willed* truth, a dogmatism that authorizes one to go ahead against all appearances. Truth is imposed on the world by the political judgments of the communist party. Sartre's political philosophy, therefore, lacks a humanist perspective. It is an "ultrabolshevism," a communism that no longer justifies itself by truth, by a philosophy of history, or by the dialectic. Merleau-Ponty conceded that Sartre perhaps intended to follow his essays in *The Communists and Peace* with a critical expose of the party.

However, he contended that any such appraisal had already been ruled out by Sartre's desperate justification of a communism that did not admit of restriction (*AD,* 99ff; below 357ff.).

In her article "Merleau-Ponty and Pseudo-Sartreanism," Simone de Beauvoir declared that Merleau-Ponty had falsified Sartre's ontology and made a travesty of his political thought (*TM,* 2074; below 449). Through a systematic juxtaposition of Merleau-Ponty's criticisms with carefully selected passages from Sartre's own works, she sought to counter Merleau-Ponty's attack point by point. For example, she accused Merleau-Ponty of having neglected Sartre's theory of facticity and of having overlooked his description of the other as presented in *Saint Genet.* She reminded him of the "Reply to Albert Camus," in which Sartre had insisted on the insertion of consciousness and action in history. She called Merleau-Ponty's attention to Sartre's stress on the "weight" and ambiguity of history, as presented, for example, in his criticisms of the Trotskyites and Lefort. In the course of her counterattack, de Beauvoir acknowledged that Sartre's philosophy presented difficulties. She hastened to add, however, that these would be remedied in a book which Sartre was then in the process of writing. Since Merleau-Ponty, however, had no access to this new work (*Critique of Dialectical Reason*), I shall try to meet his objections without reference to it.

According to de Beauvoir, Merleau-Ponty not only had fallen victim to traditional idealism, but also had demonstrated bad faith in deliberately misreading Sartre in using phrases out of context, in constructing artificial antinomies, paradoxes, equivocations, and so on (*TM,* 2077; below 453). It seems to me, however, that there *are* genuine grounds for Merleau-Ponty's (mis-)interpretation of Sartre. As already pointed out, the notion of "interworld" is central to Merleau-Ponty's own work. His whole emphasis is on intersubjectivity, on community, on dialogue, on participation. Yet Sartre's philosophy indeed seems to deny these outright. The very title *Being and Nothingness,* for example, smacks of dualism and seems to indicate that becoming is at best unimportant and, at worst, nonexistent. In *Being and Nothingness,* Sartre does say quite clearly that "the essence of relations between consciousnesses is not *Mitsein*": it is "conflict"; "conflict is the original meaning of being-for-others."[10] Dialectic and intersubjectivity seem to be denied in Sartre's analysis of concrete relations with others, for he insists that such relations constitute a circle in which we are "ceaselessly tossed from being-a-look to being-looked-at" (*BN,* 499). According to Sartre,

> We are indefinitely referred from the Other-as-object to the Other-as-subject and vice versa. The movement is never arrested and this movement

> with its abrupt reversals of direction constitutes our relation with the Other. At whatever moment a person is considered, he is in one or the other of these attitudes. . . . we shall never place ourselves concretely on the plane of equality: that is, on the plane where the recognition of the Other's freedom would involve the Other's recognition of our freedom. (*BN,* 499)

Sartre concludes that "respect for the Other's freedom is an empty word" (*BN,* 501). There is no dialectic for my relations toward the Other but rather a circle"; and this circle is unbreakable because, "at the very root of my being," I am "the project of assimilating and making an object of the Other" (*BN,* 444).

One could find many additional passages like the above in Sartre's works. These will suffice, however, to show that Sartre's own work would seem to support the tenor of Merleau-Ponty's interpretation as presented in *Adventures of the Dialectic.* I shall now attempt to show why, despite the apparent viability of such all interpretation, I nevertheless feel compelled to reject it in favor of another.

There are several approaches one could adopt regarding Sartre's philosophy. One might argue, for example, as Merleau-Ponty does, that Sartre presents a thoroughly negative view of human relationships, that he succumbs to a Cartesian dualism, and that his phenomenological ontology therefore discounts any "third term" or "interworld." Instead, one might contend that Sartre's philosophy as presented in *Being and Nothingness* is not really a phenomenological ontology at all, but rather a descriptive analysis of human experience within a certain historical framework— namely, the framework of alienation, or "prehistory," in the Marxian sense. In this view, human relationships are negative, are relationships of conflict, and will continue to be so until a proletarian revolution ushers in a genuinely human society. When this occurs, conflict will be replaced by dialogue, bourgeois individualism by genuine intersubjectivity, and the circle by a dialectical spiral.

Neither of the foregoing approaches strikes me as acceptable. Against the second, I contend that *Being and Nothingness* does present a genuine phenomenological ontology depicting human experience as such and is, therefore, a transhistorical description rather than a depiction of human relationships within the confines of capitalist society. Against the first, I would maintain that Sartre's philosophy does indeed leave room for an "interworld"—that, in fact, the notion of "interworld" lies at the very heart of "authentic Sartreanism." Further, I would argue that Sartre's view of human relationships is not necessarily negative, although both his terminology and his choice of examples easily lead one to believe that this is the case. I shall not present in this article my reasons for thinking that *Being and Nothingness* is indeed, as its subtitle indicates, an essay in phenomenological ontology. Rather, I propose to address myself to the claim shared by the positions outlined above: that in Sartre's philosophy (at least, in *Being and Nothingness* and in other "early" works) the "interworld" is absent and human relationships are presented as negative. To counter such interpretations, it is not sufficient that one simply present various quotations from Sartre's works. I propose, therefore, to pick up the thread of Simone de Beauvoir's defense and to pursue it a little further.

In her attack on *Adventures of the Dialectic,* de Beauvoir accuses Merleau-Ponty of confounding the notion of consciousness with that of the subject in Sartre's philosophy (*TM,* 2074; below 449). It seems to me not only that this criticism is valid, but also that it strikes at the very root of Merleau-Ponty's "pseudo-Sartreanism." I shall therefore pursue it beyond the few quotations offered in its defense by de Beauvoir.

In *The Transcendence of the Ego,* Sartre takes great care to insist on the distinction between consciousness and subject. Following Husserl, he declares that all consciousness is intentional. In its primary mode (that is, as prereflective consciousness), consciousness is absolute, nonpersonal spontaneity; it is nonpositional self-consciousness, immediate presence, *lived* interiority. The subject, or ego, on the contrary, is an object constituted and apprehended by reflective, or secondary, consciousness. The ego is *opaque;* it gives itself to reflection as an interiority closed upon itself. As the ideal unity of states and actions, the ego tends to mask from consciousness its very spontaneity—a spontaneity which is beyond freedom. Since consciousness is pure spontaneity, "all lightness, all translucence," pure power to nihilate, it possesses no "inner life," no contents of its own.[11] It is not inhabited by a self, as is commonly supposed. The ego is not a structure of consciousness. It "is neither formally nor materially in consciousness: it is outside, *in the world,*" and it "participates in all the vicissitudes of the world" (*TE,* 31, 104). As there is nothing "in" consciousness, the philosopher must turn his attention to the world if he wishes to describe the being of the human reality. Thus any attempt to study consciousness while "bracketing" the world is doomed to failure. Sartre declares that, contrary to idealism, his phenomenology "plunges" the human being back into the world (*TE,* 105). The "me," as the ideal unity of qualities and states, draws its entire content from the world. The ego neither creates nor is created by the world. Rather, consciousness, as the "absolute source of existence," constitutes not only being "as a world," but also its own activities as an ego, and establishes their interdependence (*TE,* 106; *BN,* xiv).

In *The Transcendence of the Ego,* Sartre states that "consciousness is defined by intentionality," and that, by intentionality, "consciousness transcends itself" (*TE,* 38). Consequently, there is always a "gap" between the clarity and lucidity of consciousness and the characteristic opacity of its objects (*TE,* 40). Although involvement in the work is inevitable, coincidence with that world is impossible. It is ridiculous, however, to deplore this permanent *écart,* since its disappearance would necessarily spell the death of consciousness. It is equally senseless to suppose that the constituting of the ego as an object by, and for, consciousness, connotes rivalry, hostility, or hatred on the part of consciousness. Nor does *écart* indicate dualism. Since consciousness's "pure ecstatic presence to the world," its link with that which it transcends is inextricable. Although the ego, as an opaque object of consciousness, belongs to the order of *en-soi,* "the relation between the for-itself and the in-itself is not one of juxtaposition or indifferent exteriority. Its relation with the in-itself, which is the foundation of all relations, is the internal negation" (*BN,* 193, 225). In fact, it is "the for-itself relation" (*BN,* 442).

While it is always already beyond itself, the for-itself is "a unitary structure of being." Consequently, reflection involves a "separating nothingness" but not "an addition of being." Instead of a completely new consciousness directed on the unreflective for-itself, there is here

> all intrastructural modification; which the for-itself realizes in itself; in a word, it is the for-itself which makes itself exist in the mode reflective-reflected-on. . . . The one who is reflecting on me is not some sort of non-temporal regard but myself, myself who am enduring engaged in the circuit of my selfness, in danger in the world, with my historicity. This historicity and this being-in-the-world, and this circuit of selfness—these the for-itself which I am lives in the mode of reflective dissociation [*dédoublement*]. (*BN,* 185)

Inasmuch as for-itself and world are *internally* related, they cannot be two closed entities standing in opposition. The for-itself is not some sort of "free-floating" consciousness hovering over the world, but rather human reality engaged "at the heart of the world" (*BN,* 377). As Sartre points out, "for human reality, to be is to-be-there," and "to-be-there" is to exist its body. Consciousness is always incarnate: "The body is nothing other than the for-itself," inasmuch as the for-itself necessarily exists "as an engaged, contingent being among other contingent beings" (*BN,* 377, 379). Sartre points out: "As such, the body is not distinct from the *situation* of the for-itself, since for the for-itself, to exist and to be situated are one and the same; on the other hand the body is identified with the whole world inasmuch as the world is the total situation of the for-itself and the measure of its existence" (*BN,* 378–79). The for-itself is at one and the same time wholly body and wholly consciousness; it is neither a consciousness *united with* a body, nor a psyche *behind* a body. There is no question here of a "contingent bringing together of two substances radically distinct." Sartre points out that "on the contrary, the very nature of the for-itself demands that it be a body; that is, that its nihilating escape from being should be made in the form of an engagement in the world" (*BN,* 379).

Since consciousness is not an *entity* located *within* the body, "the body is not a screen between things and ourselves" (*BN,* 399). Rather, "the body is the totality of meaningful relations to the world" (*BN,* 422). As pure power of transcendence, consciousness is always already beyond the situation which, as body, it lives. Consequently, "in one sense the body is what I immediately am. In another sense I am separated from it by the infinite density of the world" (*BN,* 399). It is only in virtue of being a body that consciousness can exist at all; yet its existence *as* body spells an inevitable and eradicable alienation insofar as it engages consciousness in a world which it continually surpasses, and confers on it an eternally elusive "being-for-others."

The relationship between one consciousness and another, like that between consciousness and the ego, involves negation and, correlatively, objectification. Consciousness *of* its *self* implies that consciousness is already *beyond* that self and, consequently, is *not* that self. Therefore, as already explained, there is an internal negation here on the part of consciousness. Similarly, consciousness of an other involves a consciousness of not being that other. This "withdrawal" on the part of consciousness institutes a "gap" between it and the other. Although a nothingness is thus interposed between consciousness and the other, it is no more (and no less) a "barrier" than that which surges up between nonpersonal spontaneity and the ego. As Sartre maintains, the ego "is a being of the world, like the ego of another" (*TE,* 31). Contrary to common belief, my emotions and states, my ego itself, are not my exclusive property. I have no privileged access to my own states; far from being absolute, the "I," though more intimate, is no more certain for consciousness than the "I" of others (*TE,* 94, 104). Another's "I" is accessible to my intuition as well as to his own; consequently, there is nothing "impenetrable" about the other except his very consciousness. Refractory to both intuition and thought, "his consciousness is *radically* impenetrable"; but then, as Sartre points out, Rimbaud was correct in stating that even "I is *an other*" (*TE,* 97). Since the ego is object, rather than owner, of consciousness, "we never have a direct intuition of the spontaneity of an instantaneous consciousness as produced by the ego" (*TE,* 97). The reason for this is simply that transcendental consciousness does not emanate from the "I," but is an impersonal spontaneity which ceaselessly creates itself *ex nihilo* and surpasses the "me" (*TE,* 97ff.).

Both ego and other, then, are objects for consciousness. However, the other is not originally given to me as an object but as a "presence in person," as a subject who reveals to me my "being-for-others." In virtue of its body, consciousness has an "exterior," and can experience the other's look. This look simultaneously reveals the other as subject and makes me aware of a facet of my own being which, on principle, will always elude me.

Simone de Beauvoir criticized Merleau-Ponty for attempting to reduce all Sartre's relationships between the self and the other to the look (*TM,* 2109). Yet Sartre *does* say clearly that the look is the "fundamental connection which must form the basis of any theory concerning the Other" and that "being-in-the-act-of-looking and . . . being-looked-at . . . constitute the fundamental relations of the for-itself with the Other" (*BN,* 315, 507). The problem, therefore, it would seem to me, lies not in reducing relationships to the look, but rather in deciding how to interpret it.

By looking at me, the other invariably freezes my freedom, circumscribes my possibilities, confers an "exterior" on me. I shall never know how the other sees me; yet, I *am* this being which he apprehends. The other therefore simultaneously "steals" my being from me and "causes 'there to be' a being which is my being" (*BN,* 445). In distinguishing himself from me, the other "nihilates" me, objectifies me, surpasses my ends toward his own. On the other hand, insofar as I apprehend the other as *not* being me, I in turn distance myself from him and constitute his "otherness." Nevertheless, in objectifying the other, I cannot wrench from him the "secret" of my being—that is, my own being-for-others. It should be noted that the other's body is not synonymous with his objectivity. The latter "is his transcendence as transcended. The body is the facticity of this transcendence. But the other's corporeality and objectivity are strictly inseparable" (*BN,* 430).

My body is at one and the same time the body which I live and the body which is an object for the other. "The other's look fashions my body . . . causes it to be born, sculptures it, produces it as it *is,* sees it as I shall never see it" (*BN,* 445). Since my being-for-others is a fundamental structure of my being, "I *need* the Other in order to realize fully all the structures of my being" (*BN,* 273). My original relation to the other is an internal negation, such that the being of each is distinguished from, and determined through, that of the other (*BN,* 285).

The permanent "gap" created by this surpassing of each by the other rules out any *coinciding* of incarnate consciousnesses. "Distance," or lack of coincidence, however, need not indicate hostility. Instead of a *stare,* the look may be a *caress.* In both cases, of course, consciousness draws a distinction between itself and the other whom it encounters by virtue of its body. Nonetheless, such an *écart* can be the source of mutual enrichment. Internal negation is a mediation effected in and through the body. Just as consciousness requires the body-in-situation in order to *be* a subject, so consciousness requires the other in order to appreciate its own facticity, to become aware of its anchorage in the world. Consciousness exists its body sexually; consequently, it is fundamentally characterized by affective intentionality. As incarnate, consciousness experiences desire—indeed, it *exists* that desire. Sexuality is the "skeleton" upon which all human relationships are constructed. Sartre insists that sexuality is not "a contingent accident bound to our physiological nature," but rather, that "the for-itself is sexual in its very upsurge in the fact of the Other" (*BN,* 469, 497).

In desire, I "call" to the other (*BN,* 480). As object *of* desire the other never coincides with the desiring consciousness. Yet, I reach the other in his body and cause him to be born as *flesh,* as "unutilizable facticity," not only for him, but also for me. In the caress, a "double reciprocal incarnation" occurs, such that we both experience our fundamental anchorage in the world and in each other. Flesh is neither pure spontaneity nor inert "matter." Rather, it is the "pure contingency of presence" (*BN,* 494, 476). As presence, the for-itself is not at rest in itself but is intentionally directed outside itself upon that being to which it is present. "And it must adhere to being as closely as is possible without identification" (*BN,* 146, 148).

I would argue that the key to genuine or "authentic," Sartreanism, lies in this notion of flesh. In desire, the for-itself exists its body in a particular way, thereby placing itself "on a particular level of existence." Consciousness becomes "clogged" by facticity; it "is engulfed in a body which is engulfed in the world" (*BN,* 473ff., 479ff.). Daily activities break down, normal involvement in the world is suspended. At such times, the for-itself ceases to *live* its situation, to be actively engaged in the pursuit of its projects. Lived space becomes transformed, denying it that distance required for the maintenance of perspective. Desire compromises the human being to such an extent that he may " 'suffocate' with desire, and experience the world as suffocating," while discovering his body "as the fascinating revelation of facticity, that is, as flesh" (*BN,* 480, 176).

Desire expresses itself in the *caress,* which seeks to transform the other's body from a body-in-situation into "the pure contingency of presence"; that is, into flesh. While the other transcends his body toward his goals, and while I grasp his body-in-situation, that body does not exist explicitly as flesh for either of us. The birth of flesh occurs through the caress, which "strips" the body of its action and severs it from its surrounding possibilities. In "shaping" the other's body, my caress reveals his flesh by uncovering "the web of inertia" which lies beneath, and sustains, his actions (*BN,* 477). However, the revelation of the other's flesh can he made only through my own flesh: "In desire and in the caress which expresses desire, I incarnate myself in order to realize the incarnation of the Other. The caress, by *realizing* the Other's incarnation, reveals to me my own incarnation . . . my caresses cause my flesh to be born for me in so far as it is for the Other flesh causing her to be born as flesh" (*BN,* 478). Incarnation, in short, can only be *reciprocal.* Desire cannot be held at a distance; in desire, the for-itself "experiences the vertigo of its own body" (*BN,* 475). The desiring consciousness "chooses to exist its facticity on another plane"; it becomes opaque to itself, "heavy." In making itself flesh, the for-itself "tastes" its own contingency, which is "the very texture of consciousness" (*BN,* 474ff., 406).

Sexual desire brings about a radical transformation of both for-itself and world. As soon as the body begins to be lived as flesh, the world comes into being for the for-itself "in a new way." The world "ensnares" my body (*BN,* 479). In a world of desire, objects cease to be apprehended as instrumental complexes, and become instead "the transcendent ensemble which reveals my incarnation to me." I become sensitive to their *matter.* To the extent that I make myself passive, I experience their contact as a caress. Sartre points out that "in my desiring perception I discover something like a *flesh* of objects" (*BN,* 479). In a world constituted by desire, objects are present to me "without distance"; they "reveal my flesh by means of their flesh." Desire, thus, is a "lived project" which "destructures" the world (*BN,* 479, 483).

In choosing to live my body as flesh, I renounce being the one who establishes references and unfolds distances. Desire aims, fundamentally, at the appropriation of the other's freedom. However, since the other can be grasped only in his objective facticity, desire attempts "to ensnare his freedom within this facticity" (*BN,* 484, 481). To this end, the situation lived by the other must be dissolved. However, "I can neither wish nor even conceive of the incarnation of the Other except in and by means of my own incarnation" (*BN,* 483). Consequently, to the extent that I make the Other's facticity emerge by "corroding" his relations in the world, I bring about the disintegration of my own situation. Nonetheless, this suspension of my own situation is not to be understood negatively. My flesh, in finding the way to that of the other, achieves a mutually *enriching* "communion of desire." As Sartre says: "Each consciousness, by incarnating itself, has realized the incarnation of the other . . . and is thereby so much enriched" (*BN,* 484).

Sexual relationships, as already noted, form the basis of our concrete relations with others. However, they visually "remain implicit inside more complex conduct," "just as a skeleton is veiled by the flesh which surrounds it" (*BN,* 497). Although "there are thousands of other ways . . . to exist our contingency" (*BN,* 414), sexual desire constitutes a very special experience for the for-itself. In the experience of fear, for example, I do not relinquish my hold on the environment. Rather, my project of flight induces instrumental-object configurations to emerge into the foreground. I surpass my body in "nihilating" noxious elements of the situation: a vase becomes not an ornament but a weapon for shielding myself from the other's wrath; my legs become vehicles of flight; a nothingness surges up between my present frightening situation and that haven toward which I flee. I apprehend the other as a center of reference, as one who blocks my possibilities in transcending them toward his own ends. I experience my contingency in this precarious position insofar as the other threatens me and I am vulnerable. Nevertheless, since I am intent on transcending this frightening situation, I do not really *taste* my anchorage in being, my *texture* as flesh, my basic *reciprocity* with the other. In the case of pain—especially that experienced at the hands of the sadist—I may indeed consent to become passive, to submerge consciousness in my body; but again, that fundamental reciprocity is missing.

In the language of the caress, on the other hand, the environment is made to retreat; my body and that of the other are stripped of their customary actions and are reduced to flesh. In the (double) reciprocity of incarnation, each of us *tastes* his pure *presence,* the weight of facticity, the interdependence of incarnate consciousness. Since daily projects are temporarily arrested, the full weight of consciousness's inherence in the body can be genuinely appreciated. The prereflective, *bodily cogito,* usually overlooked, is here experienced. The body alone "knows" how to reach the other in his flesh. The world reveals itself as flesh to my flesh, and through my flesh I become aware of the world's texture. Objects, stripped of their form and function, reveal their matter, their inertia, to our flesh. Through the destructuring of the everyday environment, we come to grasp the textural harmony of world and incarnate consciousness. We apprehend that we are not only *in* the world but *of* the world in the truest sense.

Consciousness cannot remain indefinitely fascinated by flesh. The vertigo of its own body gradually gives way to the natural momentum of spontaneity and the concomitant resumption of arrested projects. Desire carries the seeds of its failure within itself, insofar as it reaches out for an impossible goal, namely, "to possess the Other's transcendence as pure transcendence and at the same time as body" (*BN,* 482); to apprehend simultaneously the other's freedom and his objectivity (*BN,* 499). As long as he is alive, the other's consciousness continues to hover on the horizon of his body; consequently, I can never reduce him entirely to an object. Moreover, satiation breaks the spell of reciprocal incarnation. One of the incarnate consciousnesses may become so submerged in its bodily being that it ceases to aim at the other's incarnation through its own, and seeks instead to strip itself of all transcendence—that is, to become a mere object in the other's world. The permanent danger of such degeneration into masochism is accompanied by the constant threat of sadism. In the latter case, consciousness begins to focus exclusively on appropriation as *taking,* or grasping. Thereby, it transforms the other from flesh into mere instrument, hence destroying the reciprocity of incarnation. Thus, despite the fact that sexuality, for Sartre, constitutes the cornerstone of human relationships in general, its radical modification of for-itself and world cannot be permanent. Nevertheless, I would argue that the transience, the inherent instability of (sexual) desire, does not detract from the importance of this experience. Caught up in our daily projects, we are seldom explicitly aware of our fundamental facticity, our basic inherence in the work and in one another. We require that relationship which is initiated by desire to remind us of our moorings and to exhibit the fallacies of taking ourselves to be nonsituated, abstract consciousnesses. It should be noted that the reciprocity of incarnation, though central, is not primary. As Sartre says:

> the body is not that which first manifests the Other to me. In fact if the fundamental relation of my being to that of the Other were reduced to the relation of my body to the Other's body it would be a purely external relation. But my connection with the Other is inconceivable if it is not an internal negation. I must apprehend the Other first as the one for whom I exist as an object. (*BN,* 415)

Again: "The appearance of the Other's body is not therefore the primary encounter; on the contrary . . . the Other exists for me first, and I apprehend him in his body *subsequently.* The Other's body is for me a secondary structure" (*BN,* 416).

In desire, incarnate consciousness projects itself toward a concrete *human individual,* rather than toward a lifeless thing. Thus, reciprocal incarnation presupposes an awareness of the "humanness" and the "otherness" of the object of desire. The other, in sum, must be given to me originally not as *object,* but as inapprehensible *subjectivity.* The prereflective *cogito* reveals the other to me in this way through the look: "In my own inmost depths I find the Other himself as not being me" (*BN,* 308). Therefore, the awareness of textural accord between my flesh and that of the other, as well as that of the world, is based on a primary comprehension of our similarity, insofar as the other and I are both freedoms, or subjects. We are linked through our bodies with one another and the world; yet there always remains a "gap," an "ontological separation" (*BN,* 298), insofar as each of us is *distinct* or *unique.* Ontological separation, however, need not imply hostility. It simply means that the other's subjectivity is ultimately inapprehensible and that he and I can never coincide. Any striving for such coincidence is inevitably thwarted. There can be no unity, if by *unity* we mean *identity.* It is in this sense that "the separation and conflict of consciousnesses" will remain "so long as consciousnesses exist" (*BN,* 299). What we have here is no raging battle, but an assertion of the fact that consciousness necessarily *individualizes* itself.

I have argued that the notion of flesh, as the vehicle of an "interworld," is the key to genuine Sartreanism. It is with a view to the existence of such an interworld in Sartre's philosophy that one must approach his discussion of action, freedom, knowledge, meaning, truth, history, the social world, and dialectic. "Flesh" has been shown to be neither lifeless object nor translucent consciousness, but a "third term" lying "in-between." Furthermore, sexuality has emerged as a fundamental structure of the very being of human reality. Consciousness, in realizing itself as desire, has proven its own carnality as well as its need for, and its reciprocity with, other embodied consciousnesses. In making itself flesh, consciousness has revealed its fundamental inherence in the world, thereby bringing to light the interworld. Any charge of dualism has thus been dispelled.

If human reality is *situated* in the world, and if there is "something like a flesh of objects," then *meaning* cannot be the sole creation of a consciousness; neither can it be imposed on facts which are themselves devoid of significance. On the contrary, the existence of an interworld rules out a radical separation of facts from meanings. Insofar as the human being is not only *in* the world, but truly *of* the world—i.e., insofar as there is a common *texture*—there is not only a *creation* but also a *sedimentation* of significances. The human being finds himself in an already meaningful world, in a world already possessing a cultural heritage. Since consciousnesses are anchored in the world and are mediated through the body, there is a genuine intersubjectivity. If consciousness is incarnate, action ceases to be intervention, imposition from without. Instead of a "spectator" consciousness surveying a world of inert objects, we now have a *pour-soi* actively engaged within the world. Desire, in revealing both *pour-soi* and world as flesh, has shown these to have "weight," and to be "of a piece." The "web of inertia" subtending not only the *pour-soi* but also the things of the world, ensures that freedom both encounters obstacles and leaves acquisitions. It prevents the immediate coincidence of volition and action, by interposing the "thickness" of facticity. As a result, action ceases to be "pure"; freedom ceases to be "rootless"; knowledge ceases to be absolute; truth ceases to be arbitrary. The social world replaces the isolated individual; history stops being absolute creation.

At the beginning of this article I stated that Sartre's thought was in fundamental accord with that of Merleau-Ponty, and that the latter's criticisms constituted a pseudo-Sartreanism. Having established the existence of flesh as vehicle of an interworld in Sartre's philosophy, I now propose to return briefly to Merleau-Ponty's accusations in order to explicate the basic harmony between the two philosophies.

Merleau-Ponty, it will be recalled, had accused Sartre of having "a plurality of subjects but no intersubjectivity" (*AD,* 205). It has emerged that Sartre does indeed have a plurality, in the sense that there is a "gap," an ontological separation between the for-itself and the other. However, plurality in *this* sense is, in fact, intersubjectivity. It has been shown that Sartrean subjects are fundamentally interdependent while retaining their individuality and that, for Sartre, intersubjectivity is a carnal reciprocity which rules out equally a unity of identity or coincidence, on the one hand, and an external negation, on the other. It will be recalled that incarnation *does* make for an inevitable alienation. Sartre states that alienation "is an essential characteristic of all situations in general . . . [and we] cannot escape this alienation since it would be absurd even to think of existing otherwise than in situation" (*BN,* 643). Merleau-Ponty's *own* philosophy, however, also admits an eradicable aspect of alienation in all human relationships. Like Sartre, Merleau-Ponty holds that the primordial encounter of incarnate consciousnesses occurs at the level of the prereflective *cogito,* and is an experience involving a permanent *écart:* I am necessarily destined never to experience the presence of another person to himself. And yet each person does exist for me as an unchallengeable style or setting of coexistence, and my life has a social atmosphere (*PP,* 364–65). For Merleau-Ponty, there is a violence which is an inevitable element of the human situation. I have argued at length elsewhere (*VMP,* 112ff.) that, according to Merleau-Ponty, human beings, as incarnate subjects, inevitably encroach upon one another; that there is already at the level of perception an unavoidable type of "invasion." I have shown there that, although Merleau-Ponty stresses the "internal relationship," the lived presence of incarnate beings to each other, nevertheless his description of incarnate subjectivity as "the junction of the *for-itself* and the in-itself" provides an ontological basis for his contention that the very fact of intersubjectivity makes encroachment inevitable. For Merleau-Ponty, then, there is already an element of alienation at the most fundamental level of human coexistence.

In his attack on Sartre, Merleau-Ponty further accused him of reducing knowledge to an abstraction and attaching human beings mentally to history (*AD*, 158; below 401–2). Merleau-Ponty's *own* philosophy emphasized that the incarnate subject is characterized by "historical density." It ruled out any abstract knowledge or absolute standpoint, and stated that knowledge is always perspectival, incomplete, "situated" (*PP*, viii, 61). However, I would contend that for Sartre, *just as* for Merleau-Ponty, the realm of interworld prohibits idealism and ensures the fundamental inseparability of knowledge and action. Like Merleau-Ponty, Sartre was aware that if, through abstract thought, "I place myself in a state of simple surveying" and "escape from the senses which I am," then "I cut my bonds with the world" (*BN*, 391) and adopt a contradictory position:

> The point of view of pure knowledge is contradictory; there is only the point of view of engaged knowledge. This amounts to saying that knowledge and action are only two abstract aspects of an original, concrete relation. . . . A pure knowledge in fact would be a knowledge without a point of view; therefore a knowledge of the world but on principle located outside the world. But this makes no sense; . . . thus knowledge can be only an engaged upsurge in a determined point of view which one *is*. (*BN*, 377)

Another of Merleau-Ponty's criticisms concerned the status of freedom in Sartre's philosophy. I noted earlier that Merleau-Ponty dismissed Sartre's conception of freedom as an abstraction. In its place, he wished to put a freedom which "gears itself" to the situation, which is not a matter of instantaneous transformations or intellectual projects (*PP*, 442). In line with this, Merleau-Ponty declared that, "in reality, the intellectual project and the positing of ends are merely the bringing to completion of an existential project" (*PP*, 447). Merleau-Ponty's subject finds himself already situated within a social world and a prepersonal tradition. His existence therefore bears "an atmosphere of ambiguity," which endows his choices and actions with a certain opacity and inertia. Already in his *Phenomenology of Perception* Merleau-Ponty had warned against placing the for-itself and in-itself in opposition without mediation. He argued that there is "never determinism and never absolute choice . . . I am never a thing and never bare consciousness"; that the choice which I make of my life is always based on a certain givenness (*PP*, 453, 455).

Despite Merleau-Ponty's statements to the contrary, his philosophy is in fact in agreement with "genuine Sartreanism." Sartre, too, insists that freedom is not a matter of caprice; that it does not denote the ability to do "anything whatsoever," that it involves a fundamental "lived" project. "Genuine Sartreanism" insists on "the coefficient of adversity of things" and the dialectical relationship between intention and action (*BN*, 554, 587, 589, 592). Like Merleau-Ponty, Sartre emphasizes that there is a continual *inter*change between the human reality and the situation within which it finds itself: "[T]here is freedom only in a *situation*, and there is a situation only through freedom. Human-reality everywhere encounters resistances and obstacles which it has not created, but these resistances and obstacles have meaning only in and through the free choice which human-reality is" (*BN*, 599). Sartre, like Merleau-Ponty, recognizes that freedom does not mean incessant rupture, that even "the most radical decisions" are made in reference to the past, and that "that past is immensely important as a backdrop and a point of view" (*BN*, 607). Sartre even cautions his readers lest they forget that "action requires time to be accomplished"; that "it has articulations," "moments" (*TE*, 69). The past which gives birth to a particular action does not act deterministically; yet it definitely has "weight." As Sartre says, "We choose our past in the light of a certain end, but from then on it imposes itself upon us and devours us" (*BN*, 615).

In *Adventures of the Dialectic*, Merleau-Ponty attacked Sartre's conception of meaning and truth, arguing, in supposed opposition to Sartre's position, that meaning is neither imposed nor undergone, but "taken up and carried forward" by the incarnate subject (*AD*, 144, 159, 200; *PP*, 450). Merleau-Ponty insisted that the subject's life has a significance which he himself does not constitute; and that history likewise has "at least a fragmentary meaning" of its own which it "puts forward"; that, briefly, meaning comes into being through the complex interplay of the subjective and the objective (*PP*, xix, xxi, 448–49). Merleau-Ponty argued that, because consciousness is incarnate, its historical inherence is "the point of origin of all truth."[12] Consequently, truth always retains "its coefficient of facticity" and is never final or completed (*PP*, 394, 395). For Merleau-Ponty, truth is always truth in genesis, and demands a continual effort of creative expression on the part of the human being. The human being is already in primordial contact with truth by the mere fact of existing as incarnate subjectivity. It is now evident that contrary to Merleau-Ponty's contention, Sartre's conception of truth and meaning is in harmony with this view (*BN*, 617, 625). More generally, it can now be seen that the fundamentals of "authentic Sartreanism" harmonize with those of Merleau-Ponty. The latter, notwithstanding, failed to appreciate that the notion of *flesh,* which lies at the core of his own philosophy, is central also to Sartre's thought. It will be easier to understand why Merleau-Ponty overlooked the positive significance of flesh in Sartre's philosophy if it is kept in mind that Sartre did not focus *explicitly* on the sociohistorical world in *Being and Nothingness.* Nevertheless, in establishing the interworld in that important treatise, Sartre did create the necessary condition for action and intersubjectivity. In so doing, he laid the foundation for the intensive social-political study later undertaken in *Critique of Dialectical Reason.* Already in *Being and Nothingness,* Sartre indicated the direction which such a treatment would take (see *BN,* 617, 625); and it is within this framework that a reinterpretation of *The Communists and Peace* must be sought.

It was, as I noted earlier, *The Communists and Peace* which sparked Merleau-Ponty's anger and caused him to elaborate what he considered to be basic philosophical differences between Sartre and himself. Consequently, it is necessary to provide, if only in outline, a reinterpretation of this work in light of the approach to Sartre suggested in this article; unfortunately, space limitations for the present prevent a more exhaustive treatment. It will be recalled that Merleau-Ponty accused Sartre of reducing political life to the level of judgment. I would argue, however, that Sartre, in analyzing the failure of the communist-led demonstrations of 1952, makes it amply clear that, for the proletariat at least, political life is not an intellectual, but rather an existential project. Given the interworld, it is clear that the relation of party to proletariat cannot be that of sovereign to slave. In view of the "thickness" of the world, history can never be reduced to "a pact of wills," to "personal decisions." Meanings are visible in history. Even if the relationship of party to proletariat were reducible to a subject-object relationship, this would not imply absolute knowledge on the part of the party. The reason for this is that the subject as such has been shown to be *embodied.* Insofar as consciousness is incarnate, it cannot, on principle, take a "spectator's" view. Consequently, the party cannot be omniscient. Facts bear a significance of their own and therefore will not allow of purely arbitrary interpretations. Since the subject is incarnate, it cannot enjoy complete lucidity. In keeping with this, the party is not free to make history simply in any way whatsoever, to impose any meaning on the facts. If there is an interworld, then there can be genuine dialogue between proletariat and party; revolution ceases to be reduced to personal volitions. The party, therefore, is not the sole historical agent. I have shown earlier that the relationship between two subjects is inherently unstable, and therefore calls for controls. Since absolute knowledge, utter lucidity, is ruled out, truth ceases to be a dogmatism that is imposed. Therefore, the party cannot become dictatorial or terroristic. It follows from this that Sartre's philosophy does not lack a humanist perspective, despite Merleau-Ponty's claims to the contrary.

The above reappraisal is admittedly sketchy; however, it serves to indicate the sort of reappraisal of Sartreanism that can emerge once the interworld is reclaimed for Sartre. In this article I have made it my task to establish the existence of an interworld in Sartre's philosophy to show that the notion of *flesh,* which is central to Merleau-Ponty's thought, also provides the key to "authentic Sartreanism." To this end, I submitted Merleau-Ponty's criticism of Sartre to a reexamination. It should be noted that Merleau-Ponty's comments regarding Sartre's philosophy did not end with his *Adventures of the Dialectic.* At the time of his death in 1961, Merleau-Ponty was in fact working on a book that was to provide the ontological foundation for his previous works. In this book Merleau-Ponty intended to develop theories of intersubjectivity and truth, and more generally, to take up again, deepen, and rectify his earlier philosophizing.[13] Unfortunately, this work never progressed beyond some working notes and a manuscript containing the first part of the projected book. In this material, Merleau-Ponty returned again to the consideration of Sartre's philosophy. Although his treatment here was concerned directly with the philosophical foundations of Sartre's thought, it reaffirmed the interpretation which had already emerged in his earlier *Adventures of the Dialectic.*[14] Merleau-Ponty, in this unfinished manuscript, returned to the very core of his own philosophy in stressing "that every being presents itself at a distance, which does not prevent us from knowing it, which is on the contrary the guarantee for knowing it . . . [that] the presence of the world is precisely the presence of its flesh to my flesh, that I 'am of the world' and that I am not it . . . [that] there is this thickness of flesh between us and the 'hard core' of Being" (*VI,* 127). Is not this precisely what "*genuine* Sartreanism" itself claims?

Notes

1. Jean-Paul Sartre, *Situations,* trans. Benita Eisler (New York: Fawcett World Library, 1966), 174; below 580. Hereafter *Sits.*

2. Simone de Beauvoir, "Merleau-Ponty et le Pseudo-Sartrisme," *Les Temps modernes* 10, no. 2 (1955), 2121; below 488. Hereafter *TM.*

3. See, e.g., Ronald Aronson, "Interpreting Husserl and Heidegger: The Root of Sartre's Thought," *Telos* 13 (Fall 1972), 47–67; Ronald Aronson, "Sartre's Individualist Social Theory," *Telos* 16 (Summer 1973), 68–91; Colin Smith, "Sartre and Merleau-Ponty: The Case for a Modified Essentialism," *Journal of the British Society for Phenomenology* 1 (May 1970), 73–79; M. de Tollenaere, Jr., "Intersubjectivity

in Jean-Paul Sartre," *International Philosophical Quarterly* 5 (May 1965), 203–20; and Mary Warnock, *The Philosophy of Sartre* (New York: Barnes and Noble, 1965). On the other hand, James F. Sheridan, *Sartre: The Radical Conversion* (Athens: Ohio University Press, 1969) presents a very different interpretation.

4. For a more detailed account of the social and political events that took place during the years of their friendship, I refer the reader to such works as: David Caute, *Communism and the French Intellectuals 1914–1960;* George Lichtheim *Marxism in Modern France;* Michel-Antoine Burnier, *Choice of Action: The French Existentialists on the Political Front Line;* and Sartre's essay, "Merleau-Ponty" in *Sits.* See also Monika Langer, *Violence in the Philosophy of Merleau-Ponty* (thesis 1973). Hereafter *VMP.*

5. Maurice Merleau-Ponty, *Sense and Non-Sense,* trans. Hubert Dreyfus and Patricia Dreyfus (Evanston: Northwestern University Press, 1964), 122. Hereafter *SNS.*

6. Jean-Paul Sartre, *The Communists and Peace,* trans. Martha H. Fletcher (New York: G. Braziller, 1968), 4, 9. Hereafter *CP.*

7. Maurice Merleau-Ponty, *Adventures of the Dialectic,* trans. Joseph Bien (Evanston: Northwestern University Press, 1973), 207–32. Hereafter *AD.*

8. *AD,* 188; below 427; in my thesis *VMP,* I have argued that Merleau-Ponty's position regarding political issues occupies a crucial place in the framework of his philosophy.

9. Maurice Merleau-Ponty, *Phénoménologie de la perception* (Paris: Gallimard, 1945); *Phenomenology of Perception,* trans. Colin Smith (New York: The Humanities Press, 1962), 439, 450. Hereafter *PP.*

10. Jean-Paul Sartre, *L'Être et le néant* (Paris: Gallimard, 1943); *Being and Nothingness,* trans. Hazel E. Barnes (New York: Washington Square Press, 1966), 525, 445. Hereafter *BN.*

11. Jean-Paul Sartre, *La Transcendence de l'ego* (Paris: Bonvin, 1936); *The Transcendence of the Ego,* trans. Forrest Williams and Robert Kirkpatrick (New York: The Noonday Press, 1957), 80ff., 100, 42. Hereafter *TE.*

12. Maurice Merleau-Ponty, *Signs,* trans. Richard C. McCleary (Evanston: Northwestern University Press, 1964), 109.

13. Maurice Merleau-Ponty, *Le Visible et l'invisible* (Paris: Gallimard, 1964); *The Visible and the Invisible,* trans. Alphonso Lingis (Evanston: Northwestern University Press, 1968), 183. Hereafter *VI.*

14. See, e.g., *VI,* 50, 258, 272; see also Albert Rabil, *Merleau-Ponty: Existentialist of the Social World* (New York: Columbia University Press, 1967).

PART 3

THE BODY

9

Sartre on the Phenomenal Body and Merleau-Ponty's Critique

Martin C. Dillon

I. The Phenomenal Body and the Problem of Immanence and Transcendence

There is a mind-body problem because we think of minds and bodies in such a way that what is largely admitted to be a factual reality—a conscious body—almost inevitably turns out to be a theoretical impossibility. If consciousness is conceived as sheer immanence, the absolute and transparent presence to itself of thought, and the body is regarded as completely transcendent, an organism composed entirely of fleshly matter, then the problem of explaining their conjunction appears insurmountable. The principal reason for this lies in the fact that, within our Cartesian tradition, the categories of immanence and transcendence have acquired the significance of demarcating two disparate and mutually exclusive ontological spheres: the being of consciousness or being-for-itself has been set over against being outside of consciousness (i.e., being which is not consciousness) or being-in-itself. If the being of minds (*res cogitans,* the ontological sphere of immanence) is so conceived as to exclude the being of bodies (*res extensa,* the ontological sphere of transcendence) and if their incommensurability is taken as inherently definitive of both minds and bodies, then the notion of incarnate spirit involves a contradiction in terms, i.e., the conjunction of incompossibles. Since spirit *is* incarnate, however, something must be wrong with the traditional way of thinking about minds and bodies.

Phenomenology purports to offer an alternative to the Cartesian tradition. Sartre and Merleau-Ponty, as phenomenologists, attempt to overthrow dualistic modes of thought in which the spheres of immanence and transcendence are seen as radically disjunct and replace them with standpoints based on the thesis of the ontological primacy of phenomena. In short, this thesis contends (1) that phenomena are the primary reality and (2) that they incorporate aspects of both immanence and transcendence. Suspending judgment, if we may, about the general merits of this phenomenological approach, at least this much is clear: in an ontology where the spheres of immanence and transcendence can coincide without contradiction, resolution of the mind-body problem is not logically precluded from the outset—as it is for all forms of Cartesian dualism.

The claim that phenomena are the primary reality needs a more extended explication and defense than could be set forth within the parameters of this essay.[1] Accordingly, we shall confine ourselves, for the most part, to the question of the compatibility of immanence and transcendence within a phenomenological ontology. More specifically, we shall be concerned with the problem of immanence and transcendence as it applies to the phenomenal body. The phenomenon of the body, or the phenomenal body, is described by Sartre and Merleau-Ponty as incorporating aspects of both immanence and transcendence. The validity of their descriptions rests on the extent to which they succeed in reconciling the traditionally exclusive categories—but without losing sight, in the process, of the legitimate grounds for regarding the immanent aspects of embodiment as different from, if not opposed to, the transcendent.

Insofar as one's own body is manifest to oneself, insofar as it is revealed, meaningful, available, it may be regarded as immanent, as known. Correlatively, the body is transcendent to the extent that it eludes knowledge, remains opaque, concealed, puzzling, beyond full comprehension.

The various forms of realism or physicalism derive credibility from the transcendence of the body: precisely insofar as the body does tend to surprise us, disappoint us, defy our attempts to control, subdue and plaster it, we leave grounds for regarding our own bodies as responsive to laws that we neither drafted nor ratified. Camus makes this point forcefully in a passage on the living contradiction of a man who is convinced that suicide is the only appropriate response to this absurd existence, but who continues to go on living. "The body's judgment is as good as the mind's," Camus writes, "and the body shrinks from annihilation."[2] Be it as good as the mind's or not, the body's judgment, as attested here, is certainly different from the mind's and as strong, if not stronger. Instances where the body refuses to do as it is bid by the mind are not hard to find: the inability to swing a golf club or tennis racquet in accordance with a form one understands perfectly well, the inability to stop oneself from flinching when shooting skeet or trap, the sheer impossibility of not scratching when one itches, and so on. The body lived as transcendent is the body conceived as alien. To the adolescent whose body, of its own accord and frequently without his desire or even consent, begins to manifest sexual characteristics that are often as intrusive and repugnant as they are compelling and exciting, the body he inhabits is something of mystery, dark portent and ominous uncertainty. In its transcendent aspects, the body is something we live with in the colloquial sense that someone "lives with" a situation which intimately affects him but which he cannot significantly alter. As such, the body invites objectification and reification. It becomes a thing.

Just as the transcendence of the body abets the reification of realism's reductionist understanding, so does its immanence support the kind of objectification involved in the idealist's form of reductionism. My experience of my body is manifestly my own, and it is my own in the paradigmatic sense that it cannot be shared with others. My bodily sensations, including pleasures, pains, and kinesthetic sensations together with the data of the sense organs, are held to be private and incorrigible: they withhold nothing from me and everything from others. The body I live is the consciousness I have of my corporeality; the phenomenal body is the body as experienced by consciousness. What others experience as my body is an object for them which is utterly different from my body as the subject of my experience. The privacy and incorrigibility of the experiences which comprise my living of my body place it entirely within the realm of immanence: the phenomenal body is the body I am conscious of, the distinction between living through it and being conscious of it is obscured because both are conceived in terms of the privacy and incorrigibility characteristic of immanence (i.e., immanence as regarded from the standpoint of dualism).

Although idealism overstates the case, the immanent aspect of the body is evident in the full range of experience. Others do not suffer my pain as I do; they do not feel my hunger or fatigue, they do not taste what I eat, and they will survive my death. My limbs respond to my volitions alone. Ultimately, I am the only one who knows whether my gestures and expressions are designed to convey or conceal my thoughts and emotions. Try as I may to share the experiences through which I live my body, all such attempts are merely approximations which finally fail: only I can live my body.

Although neither of these reductionist accounts can be considered adequate, both must be taken seriously: any truly adequate description of the body will have to accommodate both the transcendent aspects stressed by the realist and the immanent aspects stressed by the idealist. Yet, the two accounts cannot simply be conjoined because as they have been set forth, they are incompatible. How could the body be both immanent and transcendent? If it is immanent, it is known fully only to me, responsive only to my volitions, etc. If it is transcendent, it is not known fully to me, defiant of my volitions, etc. How can it be both when the two appear so irreconcilable? As Merleau-Ponty points out (*PP*, 95),[3] even if one accepts the *de facto* union of soul and body, immanence and transcendence, there still remains the need to explain the *de jure* possibility of that union.[4]

We noted earlier that phenomenology purports to provide a means of reconciliation by approaching the body as a phenomenon and by regarding phenomena as intrinsically both immanent and transcendent. The success of this endeavor depends upon whether the phenomenologist can account for the theoretical compossibility of immanence and transcendence within the sphere of phenomena. Essentially, there are two ways in which one can attempt to establish this theoretical compossibility. The first of these to be considered here is that taken by Sartre.

II. Sartre's Account of the Phenomenal Body

Sartre belongs among those who have tried to resolve the conflict between the body as immanent and the body as transcendent by distinguishing within the notion of the phenomenal body that which grounds its transcendent aspect (e.g., its physical component) from that which grounds its immanent aspect (e.g., its psychical component). We shall argue that this sort of approach merely postpones the problem: the ground of the transcendent aspect will be as incompatible with the ground of the immanent aspect as immanence and transcendence are with each other. Thus, attempts at resolution of this kind remain within the parameters of Cartesian thought and are heir to its difficulties. Either one is left with an unresolved dualism within the phenomenal body, or one of the poles constituting the dualism is reduced to the other, thus distorting the reduced pole and undercutting its ability to ground the aspect of the body initially associated with it.

Sartre's ambivalent "phenomenological Cartesianism" is the result of trying to incorporate the traditional categories of immanence and transcendence—without significant alteration—within the standpoint of an ontology based on the primacy of phenomena. Insofar as Sartre explicitly refuses to posit a noumenal reality underlying phenomena, his ontology is phenomenological; but, insofar as his attempt to ground the immanent and transcendent aspects of phenomena in the spheres of being-for-itself and being-in-itself constitutes an implicit reversion to dualistic thought, his ontology is Cartesian.[5] Although Sartre seeks to avoid such a reversion by defining being-for-itself and being-in-itself as "transphenomenal phenomena" (*BN,* l–lxviii),[6] hoping thereby to circumvent the attribution of noumenal status to these two ontological categories, his use of the categories belies his terminology and undermines his intent. Being-for-itself is functionally identical to the traditional sphere of immanence, and being-in-itself is equivalent to transcendence. Although, as transphenomenal phenomena, they are supposed to manifest themselves in every phenomenon, still, in the context of Sartre's ontology, this coincidence within a unitary realm involves a basic contradiction.

In order to substantiate these critical claims, we turn now to the specifics of Sartre's account of the phenomenal body. We shall try to show that Sartre's description of the immanent aspect of the body renders it effectively equivalent to consciousness (or being-for-itself), that his description of the transcendent aspect places it utterly beyond consciousness (hence makes it akin, if not identical to, being-in-itself), and that his attempt to reconcile the two brings him up against a contradiction which reveals the mutually exclusive nature of the categories.

What Sartre says about a part of the body (the eyes in particular and the sense organs in general) holds true for his view of the body as such: "Either it is a thing among other things, or else it is that by which things are revealed to me. But it cannot be both at the same time" (*BN,* 304). His point is that sense organs admit of two diverse kinds of experience: I can sense them as I sense other objects (e.g., I can touch my eyes as I touch this pencil), or I can use them to sense the other things (e.g., my eyes are that by which I see/sense the pencil). I cannot, however, sense the sensing or see the seeing. The eyes I see in the mirror are objects for me; I cannot see them in their seeing or as they see. Hence, to say that I can use my senses to sense other things is apt to be misleading, insofar as it allows us to think of our senses as instruments akin to other worldly objects which serve our purposes. Our senses are indeed means and may be regarded as instrumental in that sense, but Sartre is adamant on the point that they differ from all other instruments in that they cannot be apprehended (sensed) as they are being used. To use a term Sartre takes from Husserl, I can know or intend my senses as instruments, but only *emptily* (*BN,* 324): i.e., in the absence of the concrete and fulfilling evidence one would have were one (*per impossible*) to sense his sense sensing. "The body is, in fact, the point of view on which I can take no point of view, the instrument which I cannot utilize in the way I utilize any other instrument" (*BN*, 340). Sartre's claim here is that worldly instruments are objects for me, even when I am using them, but in sensing, my body is not an object for me.[7] The mode of my awareness (of)[8] my body and sensing is nonthetic; in this mode, "I exist my body" (*BN*, 351), I do not posit it as an object. Of course I can, in a thetic mode, posit my body as an object or my senses as instruments, but what I positionally experience as object/instrument is not the body I exist in sensing. I can take no point of view on the body I exist because it is the point from which I view every other object. Sartre contends that, corresponding to these two essentially different modes (i.e., nonthetic and thetic) of awareness of the body, there are differences in what is being experienced: here he says, "we are dealing with two essentially different orders of reality" (*BN*, 304).

In fact, Sartre's analysis of the body results in not two, but three distinct "orders of reality" or "dimensions of being." The first "ontological dimension" of the body is "the body as being-for-itself"; the second is "the body-for-others"; and the third we might describe as the body-for-itself-for-others.[9] We shall consider them in the order indicated, but first it would be well to examine the lines along which the distinctions are drawn.

As the terms he has chosen indicate, Sartre is claiming that what is experienced in the case of the body is not one univocal "dimension of being," but three: Sartre's ontological dimensions of the body, taken literally, distinguish the "what" of body experience into three "orders of reality." Nevertheless, we have seen that *what* is experienced is closely tied to *how* it is experienced (i.e., the mode of consciousness involved). Furthermore, as we shall see, what is experienced and how it is experienced are also related to the nature of the encounter between the for-itself (or consciousness) and the other. The determinations constituting Sartre's threefold distinction are, thus, also three in number: (1) the being experienced, (2) the mode of experience (including the prereflective/reflective modal distinction as well as the nonthetic/thetic distinction mentioned above), and (3) the situation of the experience (specifically, the "attitude" governing the nature of the concrete-for-itself-other relationship involved in the experience). As will become apparent, the complexities introduced by this multiplicity of determinations tend to give rise to confusion and contradiction in Sartre's characterization of the three ontological dimensions.

A. The body as being-for-itself

The first ontological dimension of the body is that (described earlier) of the body as sensing or experiencing; it is the body I exist. In simple (but perhaps alien) terms, it is the body as subject of its experience. The mode of consciousness is prereflective, and consciousness (of) the body is nonthetic. There is positional consciousness of an object, but that intentional object is not the body. However, this is not to say that consciousness is totally unaware of the body: rather, there is nonthetic consciousness (of) the body as experiencing. The for-itself is engaged in being consciousness of the objects of the world, and the body is neglected save for the residual nonthetic consciousness (of) the body as the facticity which is the for-itself's point of entry into the world and which the for-itself surpasses in its immersion in its worldly projects. Finally, Sartre defines the body-for-itself without explicit reference to the other. The first ontological dimension of the body is the body nonthetically experienced prior to the upheaval occasioned by the encounter with the other.

Two difficulties arise out of this description which should be noted before going on. First, although Sartre characterizes the body-for-itself as the for-itself's consciousness (of) its embodiment in a world undisturbed by the intrusion of the other, still, as Zaner has shown, "everything in Sartre's theory of the Other and that of the body seems to indicate that even the body's 'being-for-itself' does not emerge until *after* the encounter with the Other.' "[10]

The second difficulty concerns the relationship between the body as being-for-itself and consciousness as being-for-itself. Sartre describes the being of the for-itself as grounded in the prereflective *cogito,* i.e., in the nonthetic consciousness (of) itself which consciousness *is.* He also says, "the body . . . belongs to the structures of the nonthetic self-consciousness" (*BN,* 330). From an ontological standpoint, then, consciousness as being-for-itself and the body as being-for-itself are structurally identical, insofar as the being of each is grounded in the relation to itself (i.e., its nonthetic awareness [of] itself) which it *is.* Yet, Sartre explicitly states that it is impossible to identify the body-for-itself with nonthetic self-consciousness (i.e., the prereflective *cogito*)—although three sentences later he says, "the body is what this consciousness [i.e., nonthetic self-consciousness] *is*" (*BN,* 330).

The difficulty at hand lies in the fact that Sartre must have it both ways. What the body for-itself is as an "ontological dimension," as a distinct "order of reality," can be nothing other than consciousness (of) itself on the part of the body. In order to maintain his thesis that the body-for-itself involves no positional consciousness of the body (which, in turn, must be maintained if he is to retain the radical distinction between the body as sensing and the body as sensed), Sartre must void the first ontological dimension of the body of all content and rigorously limit its definition to the categories of relation and modality. Indeed, for the most part, Sartre does just that and treats the body-for-itself as sheer immanence (i.e., as nothing more or less than the unmediated presence to itself of nonthetic self-consciousness). The introduction of a determination that would suffice to distinguish the body-for-itself from nonthetic self-consciousness (or consciousness-for-itself) would constitute an objective qualification; that is, it would transform the body as sensing into the body as something sensed (i.e., an object which, in itself, is determined in some way). In short, the being of the body-for-itself must be described in terms of a mode of self-relatedness which excludes all positive content. Attribution of a determination sufficient to distinguish it from the nonthetic self-consciousness of the prereflective *cogito* would necessarily change the ontological dimension from the body as being-for-itself to the body as being-in-itself-for-itself.

On the other hand, Sartre must maintain a distinction between consciousness-for-itself and the body-for-itself in order for the facticity of the latter to function as the ground of the situatedness of the former. If the body-for-itself were not distinct from consciousness-for-itself, then consciousness would have no point of entry into the world. Having grounded the being of consciousness in sheer interiority (i.e., in the prereflective *cogito*), Sartre needs something other than consciousness to serve as the ground of its inherence in a world, to give it an exterior, as it were, and to bring it into contact with being-in-itself. This is a structural necessity for Sartre and he attempts to fulfill it by means of the body.

The implications of Sartre's equivocal position with regard to the body-for-itself will be developed later on. At this stage we need only note the following. The first ontological dimension of the body is the body defined both as for-itself and as facticity. To function as that in which consciousness can become incarnate, the body must be defined in both ways, yet the ontological categories involved are themselves independently defined as mutually exclusive.

B. The body for others

The second ontological dimension of the body is characterized both in terms of modality of conscious reference and in terms of the encounter of the for-itself and the other. The mode of consciousness operative here is still prereflective, but the nonthetic mode of the body-for-itself has changed to the thetic mode of the body-for-other.

When I apprehend another's body (or when the other apprehends my body), it appears as an instrument which can be utilized. I apprehend the other's body as an object; my consciousness of his body is, thus, thetic. Correlatively, he apprehends my body in the same way; it is an object for him. When—through the phenomenon of "the look" (*BN,* 252–302)—I become aware of my body as the object of another's consciousness, when I feel his objectifying gaze upon my body, my experience is one of being objectified. This is a prereflective experience: that is, initially I do not reflectively posit my body as the object of the other's consciousness (this does not take place until the third ontological dimension (of the body); it is, rather, that I have the experience of being looked at and regarded as an object.

In his discussion of the second ontological dimension of the body, Sartre equates "the body for-others" with "the Other's body." "To study the way in which *my* body appears to the Other or the way in which the Other's body appears to me *amounts to the same thing*" (*BN,* 33; emphasis added). Then "for the sake of convenience" he focuses his treatment on the other's body (i.e., my experience of the other's body) rather than on the body-for-*others.*[11]

The other's body "appears to me originally as a point of view on which I can take a point of view, an instrument which I can utilize with other instruments" (*BN,* 340). Insofar as the other's body includes his senses, I can apprehend them as sensing or knowing.

The senses of the other are "*senses known as knowing*" (*BN,* 341). As noted above, however, my knowledge of the other's senses as instruments for knowing "remains empty in [the] sense that I shall never know *the act of knowing*" (*BN,* 341). By virtue of the fact that the act of knowing/sensing the other performs by means of his senses is an act I shall never be able to experience (in the way that I can experience my own acts of sensing in the nonthetic mode at the level of the first ontological dimension of the body), the other's body transcends me. Yet, by virtue of the fact that my apprehension of the other's body makes it an object and gives it a significance for me which he cannot experience, I transcend the other. "In the fundamental phenomenon of making an object of the Other, he appears to me as a transcendence-transcended" (*BN,* 339). Regarding the second ontological dimension of the body, only one difficulty need be recorded for future reference. The difficulty arises from the fact that Sartre defines the body-for-others both in terms of the for-itself–other relation and in terms of conscious modality. It is clear that the other's body (which Sartre has implied is ontologically equivalent to the body-for-others) appears as an object to me; hence my consciousness of it is thetic or positional. Equally evident is the fact that the other's body must appear to my consciousness in a nonreflective mode; since reflection is a relation of consciousness to itself, this relation to a transcendent entity could hardly be regarded as reflective. However, things are not quite so clear when we examine the conscious modes involved in the apprehension of the body-for-others.

Granting that the other's look presents my body as an object of his consciousness, and allowing also the less obvious point that the other's look transforms my own apprehension of my body into that of the body as object, there is nonetheless something paradoxical in the contention that the body-for-others is lived unreflectively. The other's look is an anxiety provoking upheaval because it refers consciousness back to its incarnation in a point of view upon the world. Thus, it would seem that the response of consciousness to the other's look involves some kind of relation of consciousness to itself. If the look were the occasion of nothing more than the reference of consciousness to an object like any other, then why should this reference provoke anxiety and upheaval? If the experience of being looked at is to have an existential impact involving shame, the sense of one's freedom being drained off, and so on, then there must be some complicity (if not identification) between consciousness and the body-for-others. And this complicity would then seem to put consciousness into a mode of self-relatedness that fits the definition of reflection.

At stake in this issue of the conscious modality constitutive of the body-for-others are several questions about immediacy and distance. If the body-for-others is posited as an object, then there must be a certain distance between consciousness and the body: according to Sartre, every thetic act which posits an object is accompanied by nonthetic consciousness (of) not being that object. On the other hand, if the body-for-others is experienced prereflectively (or unreflectively), the existential impact of the look must be one of immediacy; i.e., it must be something we live or exist rather than something we infer through the mediation of the categories of reflective thought. Yet there is surely a problem in speaking of the experience of the body-for-others as involving both distance and immediacy. Once again, Sartre must have it both ways, and, once again, this equivocal stance creates difficulties.

Although Sartre's description of the other's body portrays it in a relatively straightforward way as an object consciousness posits as transcendent, what he says about the body-for-others is confusing. Insofar as it involves the immediate experience (of) being looked at, it seems to belong within the first ontological dimension, but, insofar as it involves the distance of reflective objectification, it seems to belong in the third dimension. These two dimensions, however, are defined as polar opposites in conscious modality: the first is nonthetic/prereflective, and the third is thetic/reflective. One is tempted to forestall such difficulties by ignoring the body-for-others and regarding the second ontological dimension of the body exclusively in terms of the other's body. This is not a viable alternative, attractive as it might seem, because it would undermine essential aspects of the third ontological dimension of the body.

Although Sartre's identification at the level of the second dimension of the other's body and the body-for-others has already been shown to be suspect in light of the differences between them just set forth, it should also be pointed out that this identification creates an internal inconsistency. It will be seen in the following discussion of the third ontological dimension of the body that the other's experience of my body must remain hidden from me; it is at best an empty and unfulfillable intention of mine. Although I may and, according to Sartre, do analogically identify the other's body (for me) with mine (for him), this inference by analogy can never be substantiated intuitively in direct experience. Hence, the *a priori* identification Sartre introduces at the level of the second dimension is necessarily groundless according to the claims he makes at the level of the third dimension. From whose standpoint could it be seen that "the way in which my body appears to the Other" amounts to the same thing as "the way in which the Other's body appears to me"?

C. The third ontological dimension of the body

The third ontological dimension of the body is that at which I reflectively apprehend my body as "my being-there-for-others." The reflection that takes place at this level enables me to effect "the analogical identification of the Other's body with mine"; i.e., I am now able "to think that 'my body is for the Other as the Other's body is for me' " (*BN,* 354). At the level of the third ontological dimension of the body, "I exist . . . for myself as known by the Other" (*BN,* 351). But I cannot know my-body-as-known-by-the-other: my body as object for the other is not an object for me. "The object-state of my body for the Other is not an object for me and cannot constitute my body as an object; it is experience as the flight of the body which I exist" (*BN,* 354). It is a consequence of "the look" that the other knows me in a way in which I can never know myself. "The Other *looks* at me and as such he holds the secret of my being, he knows what I *am.* Thus the profound meaning of my being is outside of me; imprisoned in an absence" (*BN,* 363). Furthermore, one gets the strong impression from Sartre's analysis of love and language that the other could not divulge this secret, were he to try. Hence, at this level, "my body is designated and alienated" (*BN,* 353). In other words, the third ontological dimension of the body involves the realization on the part of consciousness that it inhabits "two essentially different [and irreconcilable] orders of reality."

The structure of Sartre's explication of the body, when analyzed, reveals some interesting quirks. The body-for-itself is defined as the body apprehended from the perspective of the first person by consciousness in a nonthetic, prereflective mode. The body-for-other is arbitrarily equated with the other's body and the latter defined as the body apprehended from a third person standpoint by consciousness in a nonthetic, prereflective mode. The third ontological dimension of the body is the body apprehended by consciousness on the basis of the following series of reflections.

1. As sensing/knowing, the body is not the object of consciousness in a thetic mode.
2. As sensed/known, the body is the object of consciousness in a thetic mode.
3. In thetic modes, the object of consciousness is not the consciousness positing it (i.e., the body known as object is an other in relation to the knowing/positing consciousness).
4. Consciousness can know the body it inhabits only as the body of an other.
5. Consciousness coincides with the body-for-itself (but cannot know this body).
6. Consciousness is alienated from the body it knows.

It is clear that Sartre has defined the body-for-itself as sheer immanence and the body-for-others as sheer transcendence. Structurally, there is no significant difference between his account of the body-or-itself and that of the prereflective *cogito:* both are defined in terms of an immediate presence to itself that necessarily eludes thematic comprehension; both are experienced in a manner that is essentially solipsistic. Similarly, the body-for-others is described in such a way as to eliminate the possibility of its being known or experienced in a nonempty way. The body-for-itself and the body-for-others *must,* then, be different orders of reality for Sartre. Regardless of the evidence pointing toward their *de facto* unity, that unity is a *de jure* impossibility within the framework of Sartre's account.

Sartre's account of the body bifurcates it into two perfectly irreconcilable poles: the body as knower-which-cannot-be-known and the body as known-from-an-alien-standpoint. Although reflection may lead me to posit a unitary ground for both, it can never explain how such a unity is possible. Nor is it possible, within Sartre's account, to know the body I experience or to experience the body I know. What I can know and experience is the absolute alienation of the two poles. In brief, Sartre has described in his three ontological dimensions of the body (1) the body as pure immanence (which is devoid of corporeality), (2) the body as utter transcendence (which precludes bodily self-consciousness),[12] and (3) the body thematically experienced as the impossibility of any rapprochement between (1) and (2).

It would be difficult to find a better example (outside of Descartes, himself) of the paradox generated when immanence and transcendence are reified and defined as ontological spheres which are ultimate and mutually exclusive. The phenomenal theme I experience as my body (the third dimension) thus becomes explicated as the absolute incompatibility or alienation of the dual poles underlying it (i e., the first and second dimensions, the body as immanent or for-itself and the body as transcendent or the body as the other's body).

III. Merleau-Ponty's Critique

The problem before us is that of reconciling the immanent with the transcendent aspects of the lived body. The claim has been entered that there is a difference in formal structure between (what we have termed) the Cartesian and the phenomenological attempts at reconciliation. We have tried to show that, although he is known as a phenomenologist, Sartre's attempt to find separate grounds for the immanent and transcendent aspects of embodiment is essentially Cartesian and leads to failure, insofar as it results in an ontological dualism which fails to explain how a reconciliation is possible: Sartre leaves us with two mutually exclusive realms of being.

The formal structure of the phenomenological understanding of embodiment differs from the Cartesian in that it grounds the immanent and the transcendent components of incarnate experience in the same lived body. Insofar as the lived body can be identified with the phenomenal body, the thesis of the ontological primacy of phenomenon accords with the claim that the lived (or phenomenal) body is primordial and the ground of both immanent and transcendent aspects of embodiment. The major difficulty here lies in showing immanence and transcendence to be compatible without violating their diversity or the tension between them. In his treatment of this issue, Merleau-Ponty addresses himself to the same phenomenon, "double sensations," that Sartre focused upon.

The term "double sensation" was used by classical psychology to refer to one of the facets of the body that makes it unique among (or different from) other objects, viz., when I touch one hand with another I have the "double sensation" of touching and being touched. Merleau-Ponty and Sartre concur in rejecting both the term and the description offered by classical psychology of what happens when the body experiences itself; however, their reasons for rejecting the classical standpoint are significantly different, as are the explanations they propose in its stead.

We have seen Sartre's position on this issue. "To touch and be touched . . . these are two species of phenomena which it is useless to try to reunite by the term 'double sensation.' In fact, they are radically distinct, and they exist on two incommunicable levels" (*BN,* 304). The body is either subject (being-for-itself) who is touching or object (being-for-others) that is touched; to be both at once is impossible: there can be no such thing as a double sensation.

Merleau-Ponty objects to the term because it reduces experience to the entertaining of sensuous contents or the having of sensations. In its analysis of "double sensations," classical psychology adopts the position of impersonal or objective thought: it regards the body as an object with several unusual features, one of which is the capacity of entertaining "double sensations." From the standpoint of the lived body, however, Merleau-Ponty describes the phenomenon at hand as one in which "I apprehend my body as a subject-object, as capable of 'seeing' and 'suffering' " (*PP,* 94–95). His point is that the body's experience of itself cannot adequately be described in terms of the model "sensor receiving diverse sensa" because such models systematically ignore what it is to be a lived body. He goes on to argue that the body's "equivocal status as touching and touched" is one of the "*structural* characteristics of the body itself" (*PP,* 95).

The crucial difference between Sartre and Merleau-Ponty that comes to light here is this: whereas Sartre relegates the body as subject and the body as object to two distinct and incommunicable levels, Merleau-Ponty claims that it is an essential structure of embodiment to exist on both levels simultaneously, but ambiguously. This claim needs (and will receive) further explication, but for the moment it should be noted that Merleau-Ponty's statement that "I apprehend my body as a subject-object" instantiates the formal structure to which allusion was made earlier: immanence (body as subject) and transcendence (body as object) are grounded in the same (admittedly ambiguous) reality, that is, the lived body.

Which of the two accounts in contention here is the more adequate? Both purport to be phenomenological descriptions, yet they offer conflicting explications of the same phenomenon: Might the issue be settled by returning to the things themselves?

First-hand experimentation is once again indecisive: what I seem to experience tends to merge with my expectations, with what I think I ought to experience. This is an instance of what Merleau-Ponty calls the "experience error"; I project into my perceptions themselves my theoretical persuasions about the nature of perception. Hence, in this case, experimentation would serve mostly to corroborate standing prejudice. Appeals to first-hand experience typically have little persuasive value in philosophical debate.

Let us grant to Sartre that thematic reflective determinations about the nature of the body as sensing tend to miss or distort the experience of sensing. Still, can it be that the body as subject (as nonthetic sensing) is, as Sartre claims, distinct from and incommunicable with the body as object (i.e., as sensed thematically)? Were this the case then, for example, when I bring my index fingers together, no question could arise as to which is sensing and which is sensed: in reflective and thematic modes, I can know only objects; the finger I attend to must, by virtue of the thematization involved in attending to it, manifest itself as an object. If, however, there is some question or doubt or ambiguity in the experience, if the finger I attend to is objectlike, but not manifestly and univocally *only* an object (i.e., if it is an object which manifests itself in a peculiar way unlike other objects), if I am unsure as to whether it is now sensed or sensing, then Sartre has overstated his case. The point here is that, for such questions as these to arise, the body as sensed and the body as sensing cannot be as distinct and incommunicable as Sartre portrays them.

We noted in passing that Sartre's description of the body-for-itself is structurally akin to his account of nonthetic self-consciousness, (i.e., the prereflective *cogito*). Attendant upon every thematic intention or positing of an object, there is a prethematic, nonpositional or nonthetic consciousness (of) the conscious act itself. In sense perception, then, every positing of an object as sensed would involve a nonpositional awareness (of) sensing the object. A subsequent explicit act of rejection might thematize the earlier nonthetic awareness (of) sensing, but such reflective thematization would necessarily objectify (i.e., posit as its object or theme) that awareness and transform it into that experience of an other. This accords with Sartre's thesis that the prereflective *cogito* is the nonthetic awareness that consciousness always has (of) not being the object of which it is positional conscious. In the phenomenon (misleadingly) called "double sensation," the body-for-itself (the body-as-sensing) would be nonthetically aware (of) itself as not being its theme (the body posited as a sensed object); the theme would be the body of an other (i.e., the body of a consciousness which is not—or is *other* than—that of the body-for-itself). By subsuming bodily experience under the model he has generated for consciousness in general, Sartre renders the body's nonpositional self-consciousness (the body-for-itself) discontinuous from positional consciousness of the body as an object of sensation (the body as sensed). The *ontological* consequences of this standpoint follow from the negation inherent in his conception of the prereflective *cogito:* the body-for-itself is aware (of) itself as not *being* (as *being* other than) what is sensed positionally. The body as sensed, therefore, must be the body of an other or, given the identification Sartre makes, the body-for-others. The fundamental ontological distinction between the body as sensing and the body as sensed—he has said that they are "two essentially different orders of reality" (*BN,* 304)—corresponds to (more accurately, is an instance of) the ontological distinction he draws between consciousness as such and its objects. In both cases, the ontological distinction sets the realm of immanence absolutely apart from the realm of transcendence.

Nonetheless, the nonpositional awareness (of) the body as sensing and the body's positional awareness of the objects (including itself) which it senses are portrayed as (1) coincident in time and (2) experiences of a unitary consciousness. Granting the first point does not, however, substantiate the second. As stressed above, Sartre's distinction is ontological—the body-for-itself *is* not the body-for-others—it cannot be construed as merely an epistemological distinction between differing cognitive modes of apprehending one reality. There is, indeed, an epistemological distinction involved, (i.e., that between thetic and nonthetic modes of consciousness), but, for Sartre, the epistemological distinction both entails and is grounded upon the ontological distinction. This being the case, one wants to know how the body as sensing and the body as sensed are related.

The relation Sartre ascribes to the first and second ontological dimensions of the body is the negative relation of alienation constituting the third ontological dimension. The crucial point here—and the one that bears on the issue of double sensations presently at hand—is that there is a qualitative difference between (1) the alienation attributable to the body as subject over against the body as object and (2) the alienation of the body as subject (or consciousness as such) and objects at large (objects other than the body as object). If one allows that there is a qualitative difference between my positional awareness of my body and my positional awareness of other objects in the world, then Sartre encounters a serious difficulty. Because he has explicated the alienation inherent in my positional awareness of my body in terms of the objectification characteristic in *all* positional or thematic acts, Sartre cannot allow for any essential differences between such diverse but thematic acts as the experience of my body as object, that of another's body as object, or that of any inanimate thing as object: lacking any nonaccidental means of differentiating them, the experience of my body as object stands in danger of being assimilated to the experience of any object whatsoever. That Sartre is, in fact, led to accept such an assimilation is borne out by the identification of the body-for-others and the other's body upon which his treatment of the second ontological dimension of the body depends.

It may be granted to Sartre that there are cases in which the experience of my body does not differ in any essential way from the experience of objects at large, including the bodies of other people. Accordingly, we find Merleau-Ponty speaking of apprehending my body, not as mine but "in some general aspect" as "an impersonal being" (*PP,* 82). Again, in the same context, he makes reference to "the anonymity of our body" (*PP,* 85).[13] However, in focusing upon this aspect of experiencing one's body, Sartre leaves no theoretical room to allow for the possibility of experiencing—in thematic modes—one's own body as one's own. He equates thematization with objectification and interprets the latter as precluding any authentic or fulfilled (as opposed to empty) sense of selfhood.

Sartre does allow for positing the body as mine by grouping a set of objective determinations ("states" and "qualities") into a synthetic totality denoted as "me," but this "me" is synthetic in the other sense as well: it is not experienced, but is created by fiat (*ex nihilo*) in the self-deceptive attempt to endow an originally and intrinsically anonymous experience with the semblance of a personal grounds.[14] In other words, reflection attributes to the body a personality or identity which is spurious (inasmuch as that selfhood or identity is not genuinely present in one's experience of the body) by imposing upon it an "I-concept" ("the objective and empty support" of specific actions).[15] Thus, Sartre denies the possibility of *experiencing* my body thematically as my own (i.e., in a manner qualitatively different from the way in which I experience other bodies, animate and inanimate), and relegates any experience masquerading as such to the domain of illusion and self-deception.

Apart from the fact that Sartre's account is violently counterintuitive (this alone, of course, does not suffice as grounds for rejecting his claims), it tends to be at odds with itself. That is, given the radical ontological distinction between the body-for-itself and the body-for-others, it is difficult to make sense of the notion of alienation, which plays a relatively important role in the third ontological dimension of the body. "Alienation" connotes more than mere difference, mere otherness. It conveys the idea of estrangement and exclusion, and has overtones of disappointed expectations. To be different is not necessarily to be alien. Alienation arises when hopes and anticipations of inclusion and familiarity are thwarted and frustrated by exclusion and estrangement. Physical objects are not alien (although they are different and other) unless, of course, they are culturally symbolic: one does not typically expect to find communal solidarity in their midst. People, classes of people, and cultural *milieux* appear alien when a fundamental ground of communality which was tacitly presupposed is withdrawn or found wanting. In the present context, then to find a difference between the body one lives (and experiences nonthetically) and the body one knows (by thematic reflection) is to experience alienation only if that otherness appears where one had anticipated solidarity.

Sartre is certainly correct in describing as alienation the otherness, the feeling of being cut off, we experience in our attempts to know and understand our own and other incarnate selves. But he cannot account for the disappointment by virtue of which the otherness we encounter is experienced as alienation. The disappointment is unintelligible apart from anticipations; and these, in turn, must be grounded in experience. In brief the anticipations of communality which, when disappointed, produce alienation presuppose a realm of experience in which my body is intimately mine (and the body of the other appears in the context of a fundamental solidarity).

Although Merleau-Ponty does not mention Sartre's name in the following passage, it is clear (from the terminology, if nothing else) that the attack is aimed in that direction:

> we must ask why there are two views of me and my body: my body for me and my body for others, and how these two systems can exist together. It is indeed not enough to say that the objective body belongs to the realm of "for other" and my phenomenal body to that of "for me," and we cannot refuse to pose the problem of their relations, since the "for me" and the "for others" coexist in one and the same world, as is proved by my perception of an other who immediately brings me back to the condition of an object for him. (*PP,* 106 n.)

The problem of the relations between the body-for-itself (i.e., my body for me) and the body-for-others is the problem that has created the difficulties for Sartre we have just enumerated: as Merleau-Ponty points out, they must "coexist in one and the same world," yet Sartre has relegated them to different and incompatible spheres being (i.e., the immanent and the transcendent). The experience of alienation which is central to Sartre's description of the third ontological dimension of the body is an instance of just this kind of relation between the body-for-itself and the body-for-others which Sartre has rendered impossible by his initial polarization of the *relata.* As we have just tried to show, if any sense is to be made of the notion of alienation, it must be done within a context which can accommodate both immanent and transcendent aspects of embodiment (i.e., a context such as the realm of communality mentioned above, in which alienation occurs as the transcendently grounded disappointment of immanent anticipations of solidarity).

Merleau-Ponty describes such a realm of communality[16] and argues that it is primordial. The context in which the argument appears is a discussion of the problem of intersubjectivity—an issue only tangential to the present topic. Here, the point at stake is this: the alienation that Sartre depicts as an outgrowth of the ontological distinction and incommunicability between the body-for-itself and the body-for-others would, in reality, be impossible, were that distinction as radical as he claims.

IV. Conclusion

Returning to the central issue—the relative merits of the formal structures of the Cartesian as opposed to the phenomenological understanding of embodiment—we may draw the following conclusions. The bifurcation of being into the mutually exclusive realms of immanence and transcendence implicit in the Cartesian explication of the lived body engenders a parallel bifurcation of the body into irreconcilable poles (the body as subject, the body as object). This results in an anthropology that portrays man as ontologically schizophrenic. The thrust of the critique of the Cartesian standpoint lends weight to its alternative. In this, the phenomenological approach, immanence and transcendence are treated as aspects of embodiment which are grounded in the same reality, the lived or phenomenal body. This characterization construes the real as the phenomenal and as intrinsically ambiguous.

As noted in the first section of this essay, however, Sartre also defends the thesis of the ontological primacy of phenomena. Yet we have seen that, intent notwithstanding, his actual account of embodiment is clearly dualistic; instead of describing a unitary phenomenal reality, Sartre comes up with three ontologically discontinuous levels: the body portrayed as indistinguishable from the sheer immanence of consciousness or being-for-itself, the body as a transcendent thing which is effectively in-itself, and the body reflectively experienced as the impossibility of reconciling the first two polarized dimensions.

Our first conclusion, then, is that to define immanence and transcendence as mutually exclusive and consequently as requiring grounds in discontinuous orders of reality is to perpetuate some form of dualism in which the union of mind (or consciousness) and body will inevitably remain as unintelligible in principle as it is manifest in fact.

More specifically, the attempt to ground incarnate consciousness in a sphere of pure immanence defined without reference to embodiment (or, as is the case with Sartre, defined negatively with regard to the body) necessarily renders the incarnation of consciousness a mystery. As shown above, Sartre's description of the first ontological dimension of the body, the immanent aspect, is structurally equivalent to his description of the prereflective *cogito:* the sheer presence to itself of the knowing/sensing function which is absolutely autonomous, conscious (of) itself as not being whatever phenomenal theme it is conscious of, hence, absolutely discontinuous from the lived body as phenomenal theme. The attempt to ground the body's consciousness in a necessarily disembodied *cogito* (or a *cogito* which is not necessarily embodied) is to make the question of how the body is conscious impossible to answer. Indeed Sartre's understanding of the being of consciousness creates an ontological disjunction between consciousness and any object posited as a theme of consciousness. It follows *a fortiori* that consciousness and body as phenomenal theme are ontologically disjunct.

Merleau-Ponty's account of the tacit or prereflective *cogito* has much in common with Sartre's, but they differ on two crucial points. The first is that, for Merleau-Ponty, the tacit (i.e., prereflective) *cogito* is defined in terms of bodily self-consciousness at the prereflective level. In his view, the original *cogito* is the lived body's unreflective awareness (of) itself (sometimes called the "body image"). Here, there is no question of bringing discontinuous entities together; it is rather a matter of understanding consciousness and body as primordially inseparable.

The second point of difference centers around Sartre's claim that consciousness is always prereflectively aware (of) itself as *not* being the object it posits as its theme. Hence, as we have seen, for Sartre, to be consciousness is to be ontologically disjunct from the world of objects. For Merleau-Ponty, however, there is an ontological continuity between consciousness, body, and world. "Inside and outside are inseparable. The world is wholly inside and I am wholly outside myself" (*PP,* 407).[17]

These are crucial differences because upon them rests the *de jure* possibility of conscious incarnation. The ontological implications of the "not" in terms of which Sartre defines the prereflective *cogito* leave him but two mutually exclusive alternatives in treating the mind-body issue: either the body is identical to consciousness (his first ontological dimension) or it is a "different order of reality" (the second dimension). Sartre opts for both, then creates a third dimension defined as awareness of the incompossibility of the first two. The primordial continuity of consciousness, body, and world which is written into Merleau-Ponty's definition of the tacit *cogito* replaces the radical dualism consequent upon

Sartre's "not" with an ambiguous coincidence in which to be conscious is essentially to be embodied.

Only with the emergence of the explicit (Cartesian) *cogito,* which is a relatively late and sophisticated development, does consciousness become thematically aware of itself. The point here—and our second conclusion—is that the autonomy of thought which is presupposed by Cartesian dualism (and which makes the task of explaining its incarnation impossible) is neither primordial nor absolute: what degree of independence thought acquires it must work to gain, and it remains always to some extent circumscribed by its original incarnation.

Finally, the problematic areas which came in the course of discussion—"double sensations," alienation, communality—all remain inexplicable unless the lived body is acknowledged to be consciousness incarnate, primordially both immanent and transcendent, ambiguously subject and object of its own experience. Hence, our third conclusion: although recognition is given on both sides to the *de facto* union of the body as subject (its immanent aspect) and the body as object (its transcendent aspect), if this union is to be understood (i.e., if we are to comprehend its *de jure* possibility), then the formal structures of the requisite explication must be that which we have called "phenomenological" where the two conflicting poles are regarded as emanating from both unitary and ambiguous reality, the phenomenal body which we live.

The question of the merit of Merleau-Ponty's own positive account remains open. Whether immanence and transcendence can be reconciled within a unitary phenomenal order, whether the notion of ambiguity serves to resolve the problem or merely to skirt the issue, whether the category of bodily self-consciousness, bodily intentionality, and so forth provide the elements of a credible description and viable theory of incarnate consciousness: these considerations are taken up in another essay currently in preparation and cannot be handled here.

Nonetheless, we do claim to have demonstrated the inevitability of failure in one kind of approach to the mind-body problem and thereby to have shown at least the promise of greater success within a standpoint deliberately constructed in such a way as to correct the essentially neo-Cartesian mistakes just enumerated.

Notes

1. The thesis of the ontological primacy of phenomena is discussed in my essay, "Gestalt Theory and Merleau-Ponty's Concept of Intentionality," *Man*

and World 4, no. 4 (1971), and will be treated in depth in forthcoming manuscripts.

2. Albert Camus, *The Myth of Sisyphus,* trans. Justin O'Brien (New York, 1955), 6.

3. Maurice Merleau-Ponty, *Phenomenology of Perception,* trans. Colin Smith (London: Routledge and Kegan Paul, 1962), 95. Hereafter *PP.* References to the French edition (Paris, 1945) will be abbreviated as *Pp.*

4. Although some of his critics are disposed to deny that Merleau-Ponty concerns himself with critical inquiry into "possibility conditions" and interpret him as confining himself exclusively to the business of "pure description," in fact, much of Merleau-Ponty's discourse is devoted to the task of showing how it is possible (among other things) for consciousness to be incarnate. The standpoint being developed here is that embodiment, or union of soul and body in one reality, is *de jure* impossible and inconceivable outside of such a framework as Merleau-Ponty's ontology. Although one typically finds a *de facto* union of the psychical and the physical asserted or presupposed within philosophical contexts whose theoretical structure, if adhered to with rigorous consistency, should rule out such a union in principle. As we intend to show, Sartre provides an instance of this kind of mistake. Merleau-Ponty's ontology, in contrast to Sartre's, will here be regarded as setting forth the conditions under which the incarnation of consciousness is possible. However, it must be borne in mind that these possibility conditions are not to be understood merely as transcendental presuppositions; they are also descriptions of that reality in which embodiment is a fact.

5. "It seems to me that Sartre's analysis of the body, while it is undoubtedly a subtle and penetrating study, is infected with a bias deriving from his implicit acceptance of the Cartesian dualism, an acceptance moreover which does not seem to be noticed by him." Richard M. Zaner, *The Problem of Embodiment* (Netherlands, 1964), 111.

6. Jean-Paul Sartre, *Being and Nothingness,* trans. Hazel Barnes (New York, 1956). Hereafter *BN.*

7. Couched in Heideggerian terms, Sartre's claim is that the first ontological dimension of the body does not fall within Heidegger's ontological dimension of "*readiness-to-hand*" (*Zuhandenheit*). Merleau-Ponty, by contrast, maintains, not so much that sense organs have the same ontological status as instruments, but that instruments can acquire the same status as sense organs: e.g., the blind man's stick becomes an extension of his arm:

> The blind man's stick has ceased to be an object for him, and is no longer perceived for itself [*pour lui-même*]; its point has become an area of sensitivity, extending the scope and active radius of touch, and providing a parallel to sight. In the exploration of things, the length of the stick does not enter expressly as a middle term: the blind man is rather aware of it through the position of objects than of the position of objects through it. . . . To get used to a hat, a car or a stick is to be transplanted into them, or conversely, to incorporate them into the bulk of our body. (*PP,* 143)

8. The parentheses are used in accordance with Sartre's convention to distinguish nonthetic consciousness (of) something which is not thematized or posited as an object from the thetic or positional consciousness of a thematic object.

9. "The body-for-itself-for-others" is my phrase and not Sartre's. (His title for this section is simply "The Third Ontological Dimension of the Body.") The rationale for this characterization should become evident in the ensuing discussion.

10. Zaner, *The Problem of Embodiment,* 119. Also, see 74–83.

11. More than mere convenience is at stake here, as will become apparent in the sequel.

12. The phrase "bodily self-consciousness" is here meant to refer to the possibility (discussed below) of the body sensing itself as both subject and object of sensation when, for instance, one rubs one's hands together.

13. The phrase is awkward in both French and English. In the original text, it appears as "*l'anonymat de notre corps*" (*Pp,* 101).

14. Jean-Paul Sartre, *The Transcendence of the Ego,* trans. Forest Williams and Robert Kirkpatrick (New York, 1957), 71ff., "The Constitution of the Ego as the Pole of Actions, States and Qualities."

15. Ibid., 90. "The body and bodily images . . . consummate the total degradation of the concrete I of reflection to the 'I-concept' by functioning for the 'I-concept' as its illusory fulfillment. . . . The body . . . serves as a visible and tangible symbol for the I." It is noteworthy that in this essay Sartre argues that the I (or ego) is transcendent and has no place in the immanent sphere of consciousness.

16. See *PP,* part 2, chap. 4, "Other Selves and the Human World." Further discussion of problems relating to intersubjectivity may be found in Merleau-Ponty's essay "The Child's Relations with Others," in *The Primacy of Perception,* ed. James Edie (Evanston: Northwestern University Press, 1964), 96–155.

17. "When I reflect on the essence of subjectivity, I find it bound up with that of the body and that of the world, this is because my existence as subjectivity is merely one with my existence as a body and with the existence of the world, and because the subject that I am, when taken concretely, is inseparable from this body and this world" (*PP,* 408). See also *PP,* 377.

10

Touch and Vision: Rethinking with Merleau-Ponty Sartre on the Caress

Glen A. Mazis

Despite the proliferation of inquiries into the myriad facets of sexuality, and more specifically into those of sexual intercourse or intimacy, there remains little questioning of what are the basic structures of meaning of this phenomenon. This is the case despite the widespread recognition since Freud that sexuality is a pervasive current of existence vital to one's identity and relationship to others and the world at large. In this paper, sexual intimacy will be questioned in its constitution of distinctive possibilities of perception, interpersonal perception, embodiment, affirmation of finitude, and a realization of community. Given the confines of this paper, these meanings can only begin to be delineated, and can be best approached through a specific focus, chosen here as the caress. By focusing on the meaning of the caress, it will be shown that one comes immediately to the most distinctive possibilities of meaning of sexuality. Also, by focusing on the caress, the perspective to be presented here can be seen in its disagreement with that of Sartre's in *Being and Nothingness*—one of the few thoroughgoing and probably the most famous or infamous treatments of the pervasive significance of sexual intimacy. It is my contention that Sartre's descriptions of sexual intimacy are misguided. They are misguided by a set of assumptions that underlie Sartre's philosophy as a whole and which he imposes on the phenomenon of sexual intimacy, rather than allowing what is distinctive about this phenomenon to reveal itself.

It must be noted that it is my intention to investigate the structure of sexual intimacy in its fullest possibilities to be an expressive and revealing dimension of existence, as distinct from studying either the deviations from its distinctive significance or the diminutions of its power to reveal and express. Like language, which for the most part is not used in its power to reveal or arouse wonder or create authentic community, but rather is inexpressive and tranquilizing, as Heidegger puts it,[1] so too sexuality often appears having lost its distinctive expressiveness. Most avenues of expression and discovery are gained only with an awareness, effort, commitment, and loosening up of one's taken for granted world. This does not usually occur. However, this does not alter the unique possibilities that comprise its structure and can be recovered. This is what is sought here of sexual intimacy. Accordingly, deviations from these primary possibilities are of interest only in considering what they lack that might shed light by contrast on the primary possibilities we seek.

Retouching Sartre's Description of the Caress

Sartre views the caress as ultimately aiming at a possession of the other by passing through a "double reciprocal incarnation"[2] in which I reduce myself to "a *touched* passivity in such a way that my body is made flesh in order to touch the Other's body with its own passivity, that is, by caressing itself with the Other's body rather than by caressing her" (*BN*, 507). By caressing the other, according to Sartre, I begin a cycle where each consciousness is swallowed up by the heavy passivity of the body as enchanting object. This cycle continues as we each further sink down into this heavy passivity by becoming touched through the other. The ultimate aim of this process, Sartre states, is "that of being 'absorbed by my body as ink is by a blotter,' that of being reduced to my pure being-there" (*BN*, 513). Through this transformation I become like the rest of the "world of desire" which is "a destructured world which has lost its meaning, a world in which things jut out like fragments of pure matter, like brute qualities" (*BN*, 513). For Sartre, this means that the caress is a "shaping" in which I make the other be flesh in this sense: "the caress reveals the flesh by stripping the body of its action, by cutting it off from the possibilities which surround it; the caress is designed to uncover the web of inertia beneath the action—i.e. the pure 'being-there'—which sustains it" (*BN*, 507).

What is distinctive then about the caress is the utilization of the power of one's touch in revealing a certain dimension of existence called here by Sartre the "world of desire." However, what is striking in Sartre's initial conceptions of the power of touch is that his descriptions of its structure are informed by his previous analyses of the power of vision and, more specifically, that of the look.

The power to strip the person of surrounding possibilities, to cut through the web of action to a pure "being-there," and to drain the world of meanings in becoming reduced to brute qualities, is the power that Sartre has previously attributed to the look: "But in order for me to be what I am, it suffices merely that the Other look at me. . . . Thus for the Other I have stripped myself of transcendence. . . . I grasp the Other's look at the very center of my act as the solidification and alienation of my own possibilities. . . . But suddenly the alienation of myself, which is the act of being-looked-at, involves the alienation of the world I organize" (*BN,* 351–353).

This power of the look to strip away and appropriate which, as we shall uncover, stems from vision's characteristics becomes for Sartre the basis of his description of the caress. As a matter of fact, Sartre explains the significance of the act of caressing by making an analogy to the look: "similarly my look caresses when it discovers underneath this leaping which is at first the dancer's legs, the curved extension of the thighs" (*BN,* 507) which reveals the dancer's nakedness for the first time. Sartre also states that the caress has succeeded when not only is the other "flesh *to my eyes,*" but is also "flesh *in his own eyes*"—both expressions emphasizing the visual. In considering the caress, Sartre seems to have overlooked the most striking characteristics of touch, and instead continues to describe this phenomenon using not only the phrases of vision, but also according to sight's characteristics. At this point, it would be helpful to delineate and contrast the differing significance of touch and vision.

Touch and Vision

Merleau-Ponty in his *Phenomenology of Perception* points to an understanding of the senses as distinct contributors of differing strands of meaning which nevertheless form a whole. He recognizes the importance of distinguishing "that touching is not seeing,"[3] and that "the sense of touch is not spatial as is sight" (*PP,* 222). To admit that "the senses are distinct from each other," and also to admit at the same time that the distinct elements only appear within a whole, makes this distinction such that "we can recognize it without any threat to the unity of the senses" (*PP*, 225). What is distinctive about touch became increasingly important to Merleau-Ponty: "There is a circle of the touched and the touching, the touch takes hold of the touching."[4] In other words, the experience of touching is not unidirectional: one cannot neatly bisect the experience of touch into the act of touching and the passively touched object. In the very act of touching, one is touched in turn. Rather than the traditional dichotomy of activity versus passivity, one finds a reciprocity in touch.

To Merleau-Ponty, this was significant insofar as the reciprocity of tactile apprehension was a reservoir of significance that washes through the other senses in their unity of style. Although the senses are a whole in our perceptual grounding in the world, each sense has a founding role of depositing certain significances to which all the others will resonate and elaborate. As the previous quotation indicated, Merleau-Ponty believed that touch opened up a distinctive spatiality that uniquely leads to this reciprocity of the touched-touching, of the perceived-perceiving.

To touch or to be touched entails to be close to something or someone. This can be understood in purely physicalistic terms of being "up against." However, the phrase itself, "to be close to something or someone," has an interesting ambiguity that stems from its other usage which indicates a communing, an experienced loss of intervening boundaries, a sharing of worlds. It is interesting to note that the emotions are said to *touch* one, or that one feels this or that emotion. The language of emotions is a tactile one. The language of rational reflection or a distanced reflection is a visual one in which one *sees* things, something *dawns* on one as new *insight* is achieved. The world of vision, besides being a world most distinguished by distance and boundedness, is essential to the world of taking. Sartre states, "What is seen is possessed" (*BN*, 738). In other words, the experience of sight is marked by an agent acting to make something differentiated from himself his own. Insofar as our ways of knowing have followed this paradigm of vision, they have been an act of aggression or confrontation,[5] for as Sartre states in full: "What is seen is possessed, to see is to *deflower*. If we examine the comparisons ordinarily used to express the relation between the knower and the known, we see that many of them are represented as being a kind of *violation by sight*" (*BN*, 738).

For Sartre, these characteristics of sight and of knowing as an appropriating of something in a confrontation to make it one's own, suggests to him "the idea of sexual intercourse," of a "carnal possession," a "violation," a "penetration" and "caress" (*BN*, 738–740). Sartre, in investigating the aggressive, appropriative aspect of sight, is led to sexuality, and in exploring sexuality, he is led to the confrontation of sight, of the look. There is admittedly an opening up and penetrating into space given to one by vision that can lead it to have the characteristic that Sartre has pinpointed in his descriptions. However, it is touch which is essential to the caress, and it would seem to be more revealing of its significance to explore what is distinctive of touch and not of sight.

The distinct shared quality of spatiality involved in touching and being touched grounds a meaning which is inseparable from this dimension of experience:

> my hand, which is felt from within, is also accessible from without, itself tangible, for my other hand, for example, if it takes its place among the things that it touches, and is in a sense one of them, opens up finally a tangible being of which it is also a part. Through this crisscrossing within it of the touching and the tangible, its own movements incorporate themselves into the universe they interrogate . . . and finally a veritable touching of the touch, when my right hand touches my left while it is palpating the things, where the "touching subject" passes over to the rank of the touched, descends into things, such that touch is formed in the midst of the world.[6]

In touch, the distinction between touching subject and touched object blurs: in other words, the distinction between activity and passivity dissolves. Rather than a confrontation and appropriation, there is a permeability of boundaries and an opening up of interpenetration, of communion.

This is the distinguishing possibility of touch, and like all possibilities can be achieved to a greater or lesser extent, and is never realized in an absolute sense—which would be a permanent, perfect reciprocity. Rather, the experience of touch hovers along a continuum that can approach the pole of activity and passivity, given the context of the experience. However, there is always this undercurrent of reciprocity with the world that is present in every experience of touch, no matter where it is along this continuum. Up to this point, we have spoken of touch in general, and not what is unique about the caress that is shaped by touch, and what in turn infuses this sense as a result of this founding phenomenon of the caress.

The Caress and Its Significance

The possibilities of touch we have pointed to fully emerge in interpersonal perception, and are uniquely realized in the caress, an experience in which one's openness to the other becomes the theme. Each way the world can be revealed to us is altered and expanded when one begins to explore how I and the other are revealed to one another, and this interpersonal significance is an abiding possession of each mode of apprehension and structures them—often overlooked by philosophers. This is true of touch.

It was briefly mentioned that, although the tactile experience tends toward a reciprocity of touching and touched, often this circle is broken and leans to one side or the other:

> To begin with, we spoke summarily of a reversability . . . of the touching and the touched. It is time to emphasize that it is a reversability always imminent and never realized in fact. My left hand is always on the verge of touching my right hand touching the things, but it never reaches coincidence: the coincidence eclipses at the moment of realization, and one of two things always occurs: either my right hand really passes over to the rank of the touched, but then its hold on the world is interrupted; or it retains its hold on the world, but then I do not really touch it.[7]

What Merleau-Ponty seems to be bringing to our attention is that at least insofar as the tactile experience comes to my attention as a focus of awareness, the reciprocity of the experience tends to be unstable and vacillate between becoming more passive or active. However, Merleau-Ponty's descriptions center on my apprehension of the inanimate world or of myself.

In the interpersonal tactile experience, it is the reciprocity of touching that is more stable, and any experiences of passivity or activity that are fleeting and unstable.[8] One can through a deliberate act of consciousness or by attempting to adopt a certain impenetrable attitude toward the other approach not being touched by the other while touching the other, such as a doctor must assume in his examinations, or also approach not touching the other while one is being touched, the correlative stance of the patient while being examined by the doctor. However, outside of highly structured situations designed to forestall this, these are ephemeral attitudes that are washed away by the tide of reciprocity in the interpersonal tactile experienced.[9] Although this is the case in all interpersonal tactile experience, this is even more cogently the case in the situation that builds upon this characteristic of touch, affirms it, and brings it to one's existence as a foundational experience: the caress.

In sexual intimacy, the situation of desire gives the caress the opportunity to maximize and heighten the reciprocity of touch. It is the surpassing of the distinction of activity and passivity in the caress and in the sexual act that can take place at the height of its expressiveness and lead to an overcoming of the confrontation between lovers, giving them the distinctive respite of community. Through the surpassing of the distinction of activity versus passivity in the touch of the caress, there is opened up within sexual intimacy a copresence with the other in which neither is subject or object. Rather, both are interlocking existences who can affirm their embodiment as medium of reciprocal contact through the shared project of desire, rather than sentenced to being isolated, alienated, and acted upon or retaliating.

It must be emphasized that this is not a coincidence, for there is an acute sense of self-awareness; but, if sexual intimacy is successful, it is not the distressing self-consciousness that scalds one in alienated rejection of being embodied, but rather the joyful affirmation of being delimited, and not limited, by this unique body. There is a self-aware acceptance or even celebration of being consciousness-inseparable-from-body that allows one to take up one's embodiment, as distinguished from a distancing self-consciousness of reflection that fights embodiment. In the caress, one is separated from the other, but only insofar as it is in the act in which my body assumes its most sweeping possibility of dissolving barriers of confrontation through reciprocity and being radically *with* the other. This is the magic of the world of desire, where self-identity and coexistence both reach their most feverish pitch, and yet contralogically permeate each other.

In returning to Sartre's characterization of the caress, there are several revisions to make. Rather than being reduced to a "*touched passivity*," as Sartre states, one becomes a touched-touching through the reciprocity of the loving caress of sexual intimacy. Rather than having one's consciousness absorbed like ink into a blotter by the body in order to "sink down" into "heavy passivity," one's consciousness shines within and through the flesh as an acceptance of one's possibilities as an embodied consciousness; for it is not the case that through the caress one is reduced to a fascinating object for the other as subject, but rather one is affirmed and affirming through this reciprocity as a separate coexistence. Rather than the caress being a reduction of the living possibilities from the flesh—a "stripping away" to make it "pure being-there," as Sartre said—it is an attempt to touch in both an emotional and literal way these possibilities as affirmed through the body.

This means that we are to take Sartre's use of the loving glance or visual caress in the opposite manner to the way he presented it. Insofar as Sartre turned to the power of vision to deflower, to strip away, to violate, and to possess, in order to describe the caress, he chose those characteristics of sight that were most opposed to the particular power of touch that permeates the caress. Rather than a manipulative "shaping" of the body into mere flesh or a dominating "stripping away," the touch of the caress is a respectful opening up of the flow of possibilities through the flesh. In a visual sense, the touch of the caress sparks a translucency of the flesh that allows the lived body to reveal within itself the glow of the attributes and possibilities of the consciousness of the other that one is affirming. Insofar as vision shares in the possibilities of touch within the unity of the senses, one can bestow upon the other a caressing glance that affirms this aura of the other's attributes and possibilities as permeating the flesh in sexual intimacy.

This is the opposite of Sartre's claim that a caress would be like the look that suddenly divests a dancer of the aura of the grace and beauty of her body as an expressive acting out of possibilities in order to reveal her stark nakedness. Rather, the visual equivalent of the caress is precisely the way of regarding the dancer before she was reduced to stark nakedness: when her body appeared only within the web of significant action, glowing with possibilities that were born in her graceful movements. As Sartre did say of this type of regard, although he did not consider it a caress: "Nothing is less 'in the flesh' than a dancer even though she is in the nude" (*BN*, 506). It is the contention here that this is exactly how one is copresent with the other through the caress and in desire: one is nude with the other but is not seen as naked in the sense of merely being an inert body.

In the loving regard, one is seen within the web of one's actions and possibilities. Therefore, one can be comfortable or even pleased by this nudity, because it does not strip away one's identity and reduce one to a pure object. Sight borrows a lesson from tactile experience as here one uses vision not to register the other at a distance or deflower or violate or even unmask the other, but rather one *touches* the other with the regard of one's glance, and allows the other's visual appearance to *touch* one with the atmosphere of their entire being. Here, vision too approaches the surpassing of the distinction of activity and passivity in which, within one's loving regard, one is able to let the other be, to use Heidegger's phrase. As Sartre has rightly characterized, however, for vision this is a difficult balance to maintain without the particular spatiality of vision eventually making one aware of the possibilities of confrontation and alienation; indeed, one discovers in the visual caress of desire a pressing need to transform this visual exchange into a tactile one as the sustaining communication of a coexisting reciprocity.

We must note then that this description of the visual caress is in direct contradiction to Sartre's notion: "But the caress reveals the flesh by stripping the body of its action, by cutting it off from the possibilities which surround it: the caress is designed to uncover the web of inertia beneath the action, i.e. the pure being-there—which sustains it . . . to caress with the eyes and to desire are one and the same" (*BN,* 507). It is my contention that insofar as one looks at the other in this way, reducing the other's body to mere flesh in the sense of a pure, passive being-there, one is not caressing, and is using sight's characteristics in a way antithetical to loving sexual intimacy. This is part of why Sartre's descriptions of loving sexual intimacy are doomed to contradiction and breakdown. Sartre's misunderstandings of this phenomenon, which extends to his assessment of one's relationship to embodiment, to the alterations in perceptions that creates a "world of desire," and to the place of rhythm, interpenetrating space, and play within sexual intimacy are all part of his basic assumptions that man stands first in confrontation with others and the world, in a flight from anxiety in the face of freedom. However, the delineation of these other phenomena within sexual intimacy are topics for further discussion.

Notes

1. Martin Heidegger, *Being and Time,* trans. John MacQuarrie and Edward Robinson (New York: Harper and Row, 1962), 165, 214, 222–24.

2. Jean-Paul Sartre, *Being and Nothingness,* trans. Hazel Barnes (New York: Washington Square Press, 1966), 506. Hereafter *BN.*

3. Maurice Merleau-Ponty, *Phenomenology of Perception,* trans. Colin Smith (New York: The Humanities Press, 1962), 224. Hereafter *PP.*

4. Maurice Merleau-Ponty, *The Visible and the Invisible,* trans. Alphonso Lingis (Evanston: Northwestern University Press, 1968), 143.

5. Indeed, this is how Sartre depicts the essence of one's relations with others. One can predict this view once vision is given primacy in interpersonal perception.

6. Merleau-Ponty, *The Visible and the Invisible,* 133–34.

7. Ibid., 147–48.

8. Note how this parallels Sartre's observations about the world of emotion. Sartre points out how one can describe the emotions as an activity or passivity in some cases, but when one considers the interpersonal realms these rational superstructures used to categorize situations "cave in when the magical aspect of faces, of gestures, and of human situations is too strong." Jean-Paul Sartre, *The Emotions: Outline of a Theory,* trans. Bernard Frechtman (New York: Wisdom Library, 1948), 85. Sartre recognized that there was another level of experience that came to the forefront in the interpersonal situation that could not be described by our traditional distinctions and that in regard to the emotions he called "the world of magic."

9. It is significant in this regard to note that psychiatric patients may reach the extreme of a dissociation of the structures of their world that they may become alienated from feeling any reciprocity in the touch with the loss of what is normally constitutive of one's existence—showing both that one can turn away from this reciprocity, but also that it is an alienation: that the diminution of this reciprocity is part of the breakdown of the structure of existence.

11

The Body and the Book: Reading *Being and Nothingness*

Joseph S. Catalano

In *Phenomenology of Perception,* Merleau-Ponty reminds us of the words of Edmund Husserl's assistant, Eugen Fink, that phenomenology is wonder in the face of the world and a corresponding return to things.[1] Still, Husserl, Sartre, and Merleau-Ponty wrote about phenomenology, and certainly we come across their thoughts only in books. On one level I do not want to make very much of this; that is, I do not claim that the philosophical enterprise can be reduced to the act of writing. There is no need for me to take such a heavy burden upon myself since my point is a simple hermeneutical one, namely, that certain books have a unity that is more than the sum of their chapters.

If this observation is not obvious, it is because the purpose of writing philosophy, like the purpose of writing history, is usually to impart information that leads to a certain insight about reality, and, in this respect, the goal of the writing is clarity of expression. Writing with verve and color may increase our enjoyment, but the written word suited to philosophy seems to be the simple expository one of the type that we find exemplified in good encyclopedia articles.

Nevertheless, as Merleau-Ponty would say, neither reality nor history fall into neat divisions. There is more than one *corpus* of philosophical writings that fit into neither a literary nor a usual expository genre. The Platonic dialogues, the majority of the works of Nietzsche and of Kierkegaard, as well as the dialectic in all its forms, each have a non-expository aspect to their written forms. To be more precise, as I am using the term "expository," its main characteristic is that the author writes not only as an expert in a field but from the perspective of an expert. He or she informs us rather than leads us to see the matter for ourselves. This is not quite right either because in good expository writing arguments and examples are given, and, from that perspective, the writer does help us to grasp the point being discussed. Perhaps, it is best to formulate the difference between the usual philosophical expository writing as initiated by Aristotle and the kind that we get in the Platonic dialogues negatively. There is a sense in which Plato keeps us in the dark about his own conclusions in a way that Aristotle does not. Further, this difference is not merely one of a writing technique; it is an aspect of the philosophies themselves.

Still, one might object that a phenomenological procedure attempts to describe phenomena without the constraints of *a priori* criteria, and to this extent, it would seem appropriate that the act of writing not be itself burdened with a particular methodology. On the other hand, one can legitimately question whether this is possible; even the attitude that phenomenology should be written in a series of loosely connected descriptive tracts is itself a constraint on the act of writing, a constraint that, if followed through, would lead to the analytical requirement that philosophical reflection never be on the whole of reality. Indeed, this restraint would rule out Merleau-Ponty's *Phenomenology of Perception,* which has its own distinctive unity.

Whether these introductory remarks are helpful or not, my point is that Merleau-Ponty presents his thought in *Phenomenology of Perception* much differently than does Sartre in *Being and Nothingness.* Compared to Merleau-Ponty's phenomenological study, Sartre's work keeps us in the dark about what is happening in the book until we reach the pivotal chapter on the body. More, importantly, in both cases the writing techniques are related to the philosophies being expounded. This difference in the ways the writing is wedded to the philosophy explains to some extent why Merleau-Ponty's work is generally not misread in the way that is true of Sartre's book. Indeed, any comparison between Sartre and Merleau-Ponty encounters the embarrassment of the dual Sartrean canons, a fact that does not exist with Merleau-Ponty's work. The situation is further confusing because some Sartreans tend to concede *Being and Nothingness* to Merleau-Ponty's criticisms of it. I will attempt to show that this is a mistake, that it misses the crucial role of the body in Sartre's philosophy, and, consequently, the dialogue between the two thinkers is never placed on the proper level.

Specifically, there are two fundamentally diverse readings of Sartre's major text on ontology, one that reads it as espousing a quasi-Cartesianism that is precariously close to what Merleau-Ponty in *Phenomenology of Perception* identifies as the intellectualist view of the self and the world, and the other which views *Being and Nothingness* basically as a dialogue with Heidegger's *Being and Time,* a dialogue in which Sartre accepts the fundamental Heideggerian critique of panoramic consciousness and all traditional dualisms. I accept this second reading. It was my first reading of the text, and, as Merleau-Ponty says, we perhaps never get beyond our first reading. More importantly, even after twenty-five years of reflection, I think that it is the right reading. Also, it gives us a richer Sartre and makes the subsequent works themselves more interesting.[2]

In this expository essay, I want to first compare the way the writing in both books reflects the philosophies expressed in them. Secondly, I will then proceed to a fuller discussion of the unique way the body functions both as a chapter in Sartre's *Being and Nothingness* and in the philosophy expressed in this book.

Reading *Phenomenology of Perception*

Phenomenology of Perception is reader-friendly. It is almost impossible to misread the work. This does not mean that the work is easy or that it cannot be interpreted differently. Rather, the discourse is direct in the sense that, as a good teacher, Merleau-Ponty lets us know immediately where he stands, and he continues to inform us about the overall perspective on his philosophy. True, one must become acquainted with the way Merleau-Ponty continually frames his own thoughts between positions that he considers extremes, without explicitly warning us in advance that the early views merely introduce his own thought. But one soon becomes accustomed to this casual dialectic, and, regardless of questions we might have about Merleau-Ponty's thought, the work as a whole is so well written that it is almost impossible to misread.

What prevents a major misunderstanding is the way each chapter is the whole of the book, from one particular perspective. The book is fairly large, and if you do not finish the work, you will, of course, have an incomplete understanding of the book and of Merleau-Ponty's thought, but not a gross misinterpretation. This written methodology fits Merleau-Ponty's philosophy, a philosophy which invites us to witness our connections within the world and among other people, not as disinterested observers, but as coming from a network of interrelations and reciprocities. In one sense it does not matter where you begin the book, you will be brought back to the whole.

Of course, this is an oversimplification. The chapters of Merleau-Ponty's phenomenology do unfold with an inner logic. For example, like Sartre, Merleau-Ponty explains why he introduces the formal discussion of the body with "psychological considerations" (*PP,* 63). Then, too, it seems to me, that there is a gradual building to the last two chapters of part 2, "The Thing and the Natural World" and "Other People and the Human World." Also, by saving the discussions of the *cogito,* temporality, and freedom for the last section, Merleau-Ponty is not only reversing what he sees to be the Heideggerian and Sartrean orders of being and discussion, but he is indirectly telling us what he thinks of the *cogito,* temporality, and freedom, namely, that they have already been considered as aspects of the web of relations that is our involvement in the world and among others.

Phenomenology of Perception is partly an attempt to answer *Being and Nothingness,* just as Sartre's own work seems to be a reply to Heidegger's *Being and Time.* That is, the encounter is not merely of a philosophy with a philosophy but with a book to a book. My reservation about the success of Merleau-Ponty's work has nothing to do with my opinion about his philosophy. I will come to that. Rather, I am concerned with the inner dialogue with Sartre. Whether Merleau-Ponty has misread Sartre is, on one level, irrelevant for his own project. There is a sense in which every philosopher since Aristotle simplifies his or her predecessors in order to make a point. To the degree that the simplification gets to the heart of the earlier thought, we can have no quarrel with the thinker. But Merleau-Ponty's reading of Sartre is of a different order.

One of the problems is that, except for the last chapter on freedom, Merleau-Ponty seldom mentions *Being and Nothingness.* His objections against the intellectualist position in which the perceptions of the world become states of consciousness, as well as those against the scientific conception of the body as an object among other objects, and his arguments opposed to an absolute consciousness that constitutes the world, do not explicitly mention Sartre until we get to the last chapter, "Freedom." Still, the earlier discussions must, indirectly at least, be against Sartre, or the last chapter would have no roots. But this is the problem. Merleau-Ponty has made his case against Sartre before he formally discusses him, and by the time we get to the last chapter on freedom "the chips are down."

The relation between the two books is complex, and I am not prepared to deal with all the aspects. Nevertheless, it is clear that there is a fundamental disagreement between the two thinkers, and, at times Merleau-Ponty touches on this difference. The main difference between their philosophies does indeed concern our constituting of the world, and, in a more general way, it concerns the prime phenomenological issue of the advent of the human reality within being. But, since Merleau-Ponty insists on viewing the constituting consciousness as some intellectual force, he misses Sartre's basic point about the body's constituting of the world. For example, to anticipate my discussion, it is clear that Sartre holds to neither an intellectualist nor an empiricist view of sensation. Sensation is, for Sartre, primarily a mode of the body's being-in-the world, a mode that opens these doors into reality rather than others, for example, the door into color. By reducing this selectivity to an intellectualist position, Merleau-Ponty is able to dismiss it with the neat objection that all constituting makes the object constituted lucid, and thus all depth, surdness, and mystery of the world is removed. But if the relation of consciousness to the world is that of matter to matter, that is, the matter of an active and organic consciousness delineating its world, then Merleau-Ponty's objections are not to the point, or, at least, they are not to the point in the way he is making them.

Reading *Being and Nothingness*

Being and Nothingness is not reader-friendly. Sartre does not wish to mislead us, but he does require that we read the book as a whole, and that we follow his attempt to disclose how we pass through our body in our engaged activities. In this sense, the chapters cannot be separated from the whole. What distracts from the book's overall rigorous unity is the mixture of stylistically striking language and abundant use of commonplace examples that are relatively easy to read with a rigorous phenomenological procedure. For example, one could fill a dozen anthologies with articles dealing with the examples of the waiter and flirt in the chapter on bad faith and on the notion of bad faith itself, and I suspect that the majority would have little to do with the main thrust of Sartre's argument, which is to show that the negation which distinguishes one thing from another arises from the lack of identity of the self with its selfhood as this is evident in our bad-faith attitudes toward ourselves. That is, the chapter, "Bad Faith," is not a tract on bad faith as such, but a progression in a reflection that is, for the most part, of one piece.

The distinctive unity of *Being and Nothingness,* a unity that reveals the unique role of the body in Sartre's book and in his thought, comes about both through his use of language and the organization of his chapters. I will first briefly consider his use of language and then proceed to the organization of the chapters. To repeat, in both instances, I am concerned not merely with the structure of Sartre's book but with the philosophy expressed in the sentences and chapters.

Unlike his monographs, his essays, and his interviews, Sartre's major philosophical writings, *Being and Nothingness, Critique of Dialectical Reason,* and *The Family Idiot,* each distinctly unite writing with the philosophy expressed. Sartre's language begins as a contextualism in *Being and Nothingness,* and it emerges as an explicit but very distinct nominalism in *Critique of Dialectical Reason* that is more fully developed in *The Family Idiot.* I have discussed aspects of Sartre's unique nominalism elsewhere, and here I will limit myself to the contextualism of *Being and Nothingness.*[3]

Sartre's contextualism arises from two methodological procedures. First, Sartre's arguments and examples are directed only to the issue at hand. An author will frequently adopt this procedure *ad hoc.* For example, a writer may say that a stronger proposition might be true, but, for the present purposes, the weaker one will make the point. Sartre's argumentation, however, consistently and ruthlessly aims at establishing only the minimum that is needed to make the particular point at hand. This method is in direct opposition to Merleau-Ponty's own writing, and it amounts to more than the claim that one cannot write about everything at once.

Sartre's writing in *Being and Nothingness* implies the gamble that the reader will be extremely attentive to the issue being discussed and "bracket" any other issues until the proper place for its discussion. The result is that the chapters of *Being and Nothingness* do not function as the chapters of *Phenomenology of Perception.* For example, the description of questioning the world, as given in the first chapter of the book, "On the Origin of Negation," seems *not* to arise from a body. If you do not finish the book, if you do not get to the chapter on the body, you can be misled, although, if you read carefully, Sartre's numerous examples would remind you that he is implicitly discussing the body.

Part of the result of using words in such a way that the main discussion is limited only to the issue at hand is that terms, such as "for-itself," "in-itself," "consciousness," "objectivity," and "alienation," become completely contextual. None of these terms have a univocal meaning, although they do have contextual similarity. For example, there is no in-itself in the sense that we ever come across a pure in-itself that is not already modified by the for-itself. The in-itself is neither the Parmenidian One nor the Kantian thing-in-itself. Rather, in each instance, the in-itself points to the contribution of being to thinghood and the for-itself to the contribution of the conscious organic body. But this formulation, as Sartre himself warns us, can be misleading. The for-itself does not contribute any*thing* to thinghood; it merely delineates and highlights *this* rather than *that.*

> The world is human. We can see the very particular position of consciousness: being is everywhere, opposite me, around me; it weighs down on me, it besieges me, and I am perpetually referred from being to being; that table which is there is being and *nothing* more; that rock, that tree, that landscape—being and *nothing* else. I want to grasp this being and I no longer find anything but *myself*.[4]

Thus, on the primary ontological level, the in-itself is the fact that the being of phenomena is not reducible to the whatness of phenomena; for example, the being of yellow is not the whatness of yellow. Because of this, yellow will always have a depth and a mystery that is not reducible to our perception of it. Still, the world would not be differentiated into colored things without sight. When Merleau-Ponty claims that he has escaped the dilemma of the for-itself and in-itself, the dilemma is largely invented, although in the concluding remarks, I will consider their divergent views on passivity.[5]

I interpret the anthropocentrism of *Being and Nothingness* to be the claim that we have the world that we have because we have the body that we have. A star is a very human thing and consciousness is a very material thing. In *Being and Nothingness,* however, Sartre does not aim at preaching these anthropocentric conclusions to us; rather his purpose is to lead us to recognize the interdependence between consciousness and the world. This interdependence reveals that the world exists independently of our concepts about it, but not independently of the advent of human consciousness within matter. This interdependence between bodily consciousness and the world is real, although it is not a reciprocal relation. Here we touch upon a real difference between the thought of Sartre and Merleau-Ponty, but I want to temporarily postpone this discussion until the conclusion.

The organization of the chapters also reflects the way Sartre's book unites writing with phenomenological reflection. As a book, *Being and Nothingness* moves from the abstract to the concrete whole in such a way that the whole is always present, even if it is not being examined. This methodology and use of written language keeps the background as it were bracketed until the general nature of the question and the questioner have been examined in the introductory chapters. Thus in chapter 1 of part 1, "The Problem of Nothingness," Sartre's major point is to begin the destruction of a philosophy of presence by showing that the possibility of questioning things can arise only by an entity that is itself not a thing. To the extent that I ask, "Is it raining?" I pass through the very body that makes this question possible, and I am conscious only of the question and the possibility of its answer. The world and the background of interpersonal relations exist, but the immediacy of the experience is just that of the concrete question and the possibility of an answer.

Being and Nothingness is an attempt to rework the phenomenological method so that the act of writing becomes formally identified with the kind of reflection that reveals what is most basic to being and also what is first known. Sartre reverses the usual Aristotelian expository mode that leads us to understand the most basic issues from what is more easily understood. Sartre thus weds the philosophical method to the act of writing in such a way that the reader is led to make the philosophical "reduction" and "destruction" in a personal way. In order not to interfere with the reflection itself, the reader is not informed about what is happening until that place where methodology and content naturally meet, that is, two-thirds into *Being and Nothingness,* where Sartre finally moves the human body out of the background and into thetic awareness, and we are asked to become explicitly conscious of the bodily nature of all knowledge and all consciousness. Sartre writes: "But what is important above all else, in ontology as elsewhere, is to observe strict order in discussion" (*BN,* 218). And "it is most important to choose the *order* of our bits of knowledge" (*BN,* 303). Finally, "If we wish to reflect on the nature of the body, it is necessary to establish an order of reflection which conforms to the order of being" (*BN,* 305).

This ordering of bits of knowledge is the written attempt to establish an order of reflection that corresponds to the order of being; that is, it is a new use of the phenomenological method that attempts to reveal the human body not as an object among other objects, but as the condition for knowing natural kinds. The condition itself remains in the background; that is, although a question and stance about the world arise from our body, they do not arise from our body as known. In our engaged activities, we pass through our bodies, and thus neither the body nor sensation appears until the world itself is shown to be human and until we realize that all our questions about being are human ones.

The Body and the Book

The general task of the language of *Being and Nothingness* is to gradually reintroduce the lived horizon into thetic consciousness in such a way that natural kinds and interpersonal relations emerge not as fixed by some panoramic consciousness, but as related to the fact that reality is impregnated by organic consciousness. Since my purpose is both to examine the way the chapter on the body fits within *Being and Nothingness* as a whole and to show how the arrangement of chapters reflects Sartre's philosophy, it will be useful to have the book's general outline before us:

Introduction: The Pursuit of Being
Part One: The Problem of Nothingness
  Chapter One: The Origin of Negation
  Chapter Two: Bad Faith
Part Two: Being-for-Itself
  Chapter One: Immediate Structures of the For-Itself
  Chapter Two: Temporality
  Chapter Three: Transcendence
Part Three: Being-for-Others
  Chapter One: The Existence of Others
  Chapter Two: The Body
  Chapter Three: Concrete Relations with Others
Part Four: Having, Doing, Being
  Chapter One: Being and Doing: Freedom
  Chapter Two: Doing and Having
Conclusion

If we look at this outline as giving a list of parts and chapters that could be read more or less independently and that are united by the loose structure that is found in the expository writing which is evident in Merleau-Ponty's own works, then it does seem that Sartre has little regard for the human body. But if we keep in mind Sartre's overall methodology, which is to reveal the degree to which the world is human because of the advent of bodily consciousness within matter, it becomes clear why and how the book pivots about the chapter on the body in part 3. In Sartre's methodology, a direct, expository approach to the body would effectively mean that we examine our body as an object. It would not help to claim, "Look, I want to consider the *lived* body." If these are the first words that the phenomenologist utters about the human body, then, for Sartre, he or she unknowingly enters within the conceptual and linguistic framework that already accepts the body as an object.

Our body is first out in the world; it is in things having color, sound, textures, and as being here rather than there. Because of the depth of the body, things have depth. It is the body that establishes the condition for the possibility of perception, and it is the body that gives depth to the horizon of perception. Phenomenologically, we move from the body as it differentiates matter into a world to other people as bodies that in turn reveal our body to us as the lived center of relations. No doubt this is more anthropocentrism than Merleau-Ponty would allow; for he would immediately remind us that the other is already in the world, and thus the center of relations is never an individual. But the level of discussion is not the same. Merleau-Ponty's basic concerns are not those of Sartre, or, at least, the primacy of the concerns are not the same.

Sartre's ontology is primarily concerned with the way a world comes to be through the human body, and the way each body is in its own way a solution to the problem of being. One human body, or as Sartre claims in *The Family Idiot,* one organism, is enough to give us a world. True, a lone human organism would not give us the world as we know it conceptually. On this conceptual level we are indebted to others; for we know the world and ourselves only by first interiorizing the way others see the world and us. Sartre does not deny this; nevertheless, in the early chapters he is concerned with the basic differentiation of matter into things, and, on this level, even one organic existence would organize a world about it, and it would do so without being aware of itself as a body, even though that is exactly what it is. That this is Sartre's view is evident if we return to two of the previous quotations and fill in some of the earlier sentences:

> Perhaps some may be surprised that we have treated the problem of knowing without raising the question of the body and the senses or even once referring to it. It is not my purpose to misunderstand or to ignore the role of the body. But what is important above all else, in ontology as elsewhere, is to observe strict order in discussion. Now the body, whatever may be its function, appears first as the *known.* (*BN,* 218; my italics)

And again:

> The problem of the body and its relations with consciousness is often obscured by the fact that while the body is from the start posited as a certain *thing* having its own laws and capable of being defined from outside, consciousness is then reached by the type of inner intuition which is peculiar to it. . . . But these difficulties all stem from the fact that I try to unite my *consciousness* not with *my* body but with the body *of others.* . . . it is most important to choose the *order* of our bits of knowledge. (*BN,* 303)

From a phenomenological perspective, the human body as such is a late appearance, and this claim is true even of the lived body. To repeat again, in our engaged activities we pass through our bodies. By using what he calls "pure reflection," the phenomenological task is to move the lived body out of the background into our philosophic awareness.[6] Thus, once the body has been separated from the world, the phenomenological task is to describe how we proceed from a lived awareness of the body to a conceptual understanding of it.

We are thus led to see that the notion of body is not univocal; that is to say, there is no general notion of body that includes rocks and human bodies. Nevertheless, only matter exists, for nothingness is not a being, but the distinctive matter of the human body. The nothingness of the first part of *Being and Nothingness* is, in the second part, shown to be the self's lack of identity with its selfhood. In the third and fourth parts, this lack of identity of the self with its selfhood is shown to fracture matter into a world, not by making the world out of some primordial goo, but by showing how the qualities of the world are just the ones they are because of matter's relation to the body. Again, Sartre writes:

> Far from the relation of the body to objects being a problem, we never apprehend the body outside this relation. . . . A body is a body as this mass of flesh which it *is* is defined by the table which the body looks at, the chair in which it sits, the pavement on which it walks, etc. . . . The body is the totality of meaningful relations to the world. (*BN,* 344)

Merleau-Ponty would want these remarks to have been made earlier, and he would no doubt wish to qualify them in two ways. First, he would insist that the relation between the body and the world is more or less reciprocal, or, at least, more ambiguous, and he would also note that we cannot limit ourselves to one body.[7] "Thus, to sum up, the ambiguity of being in the world is translated by that of the body, and this is understood through time." For me the notion of ambiguity is empty unless it signifies that being somehow reaches to us without our first questioning it. Unfortunately, Merleau-Ponty does not press the issue of ambiguity and that of our bond with being. "Thus we refute both intellectualism and empiricism by simply saying that *the world has meaning*" (*PP,* 177).[8] The Sartrean question is: Does it have this meaning of itself, and if so how did it acquire it? Can we have Aristotle's nature without the separated substances? Or are we to hold to a quasi-Hegelian union of mind and matter?

Fundamentally, I think that Merleau-Ponty and Sartre are concerned in their two early works with different problems, although at times their concerns do indeed meet.[9] On his own level, Merleau-Ponty is almost without peer. "The gesture does not *make me think* of anger, it is anger itself" (*PP,* 184). In general, however, unlike Merleau-Ponty and more like Heidegger, Sartre is primarily concerned with the ontological bond of the human conscious body with the world. I understand Sartre to be holding to a kind of "world-making," in which each existence is an existential "solution" to the problem of being; for example, the choice of an active or passive response to the world. "My ultimate and initial project—for these are but one—is, as we shall see, always the outline of a solution of the problem of being" (*BN,* 463). From the perspective of world-making, Sartre can be understood to be ontologizing Nelson Goodman's and Hilary Putnam's later claims about how our language makes our world.

World-making does put Sartre in opposition to Merleau-Ponty, but not in the way Merleau-Ponty conceives it. Both the world-making and the difference in Merleau-Ponty's conception of it emerge if we turn to Sartre's view of sensation and to what he terms the various levels on which the body can exist.

Sartre claims that the usual approach to sensation and perception reverses the proper ontological order. Sensation and perception are not first ways of getting to know about the world or the existence of others; rather, they are that through which we are a being-in-the-world. The realization that our consciousness is in the form of a body with senses is simultaneously the awareness that our world and our presence in it are situational. For, while it is contingent that we be here rather than there, it is not contingent that we must be either here or there. Reciprocally, while there is no necessity that this tree be approached from here rather than from there, it is necessary that it be visible or touchable only from here or there.

On the other hand, the remarkable thing about our awareness of things is that we are not explicitly aware of our perception as arising from a perspective. We are aware of the sunset, of looking out a window, of reading or running, and only upon reflection are we aware that we do all of these things from this angle or perspective rather than some other.

> Therefore *my* body is a conscious structure of my consciousness. But precisely because the body is the point of view on which there cannot be a point of view, there is on the level of the unreflective consciousness no consciousness *of* the body. . . . In short, consciousness (of) the body is lateral and retrospective; the body is the *neglected,* the "*passed by in silence.*" And yet the body is what this consciousness *is;* it is not even anything except body. The rest is nothingness and silence. (*BN,* 330)

This is the crucial point. For Sartre, we cannot phenomenologically start with sensation, for the senses are not merely a knowing of things but a revealing and discriminating of matter into things. In this primary bond of the body to the world, we pass through the body and discover it in the world. Initially, this phenomenological process gives the impression that the world is constituted by some mind. But, consciousness is the body, and nothingness is, in the concrete the flesh of the body. At least I recommend this reading of Sartre's "nothingness," and it initiates, I think, an interesting dialogue between the two thinkers.[10]

Sartre's phenomenological reflection, a reflection that is also a "destruction," is revealed in the way *Being and Nothingness* pivots about the chapter on the body. The book and the reflection are of one piece. When we have retraced the body in the world to the body as the source of the continuity of things over time, we then become aware of what Sartre calls the three dimensions of the body. Once properly placed, these are fairly readable, with one caveat. Whereas Merleau-Ponty situates his own view amidst relatively brief descriptions of positions that he regards as errors, Sartre's minor dialectic is more extensive. First, Sartre continues at great length in these alternate views, and second, he does not, for the most part, consider them so much as errors as misconceived stages in the understanding of the body. Thus, the body and the senses are indeed objects, but their objectivity follows from their primary lived condition. This gives Sartre the so-called "dimensions" of the body.

I do not think that this is the place to repeat a commentary on the dimensions of the body. It may be useful to once again repeat that on the first ontological level we have no notion of sensation, nor does sensation make any sense on this level. True, we are intentionally thrown out toward the world by our senses; but this primary intentional awareness is not sensation. We touch, we read, we write, we hear, and we taste; but in all these instances we are first and foremost aware of the melon we are touching, the text we are reading, the letter we are writing, the person we are listening to, and the wine we are tasting. We *are* our hands, eyes, ears, or mouth. This does not mean that the rest of our body disappears or that the world or others are not important. Rather, when I am prereflectively engrossed in an activity, my consciousness is one with that activity; the totality of my body, the world, and others are the ground on which and from which I act. Of course, it is true that I am reading using my eyes, sitting in this chair, from which the light comes from this direction, and that the entire ensemble including the book have been made by others. But when I am engrossed in a perception or an activity, I pass through all of this, and I have no point of view on my own bodily perceptions or actions.

When, however, I see someone reading a book or looking at a friend, I then become aware that these activities are done through the eyes, and I attribute to the other an activity that philosophers call "sensation." I now return and interpret the use of my senses as "sensations." I begin to have a conceptual awareness of my body precisely as it is a knowing organism within the world in the midst of others. On this conceptual level, it is indeed proper to speak of sensations.

This approach, when and if it is understood, which is seldom, may still leave a Heideggerian unhappy. What about the *Mitsein?* Should not our relation to the other be on the first ontological level? I have already mentioned that the primary issue for Sartre is one of world-making. Apart from this, however, the issue of our union with others also concerns the degree to which we give full weight to the contingency of human existence, not attempting to hide the ontic beneath the ontological. We cannot avoid the partly confusing and embarrassing aspects of conflict described in chapter 3 of part 3, "Concrete Relations with Others." I think that it is best to accept these as quasi-historical *a priori,* even though it took Sartre some time to realize this. In either case, conflict can be overcome, and it emphasizes the fact that reciprocity is constituted. My friend Peter confronts me as an irreducible contingent fact; he is this corporeal, fleshy consciousness. "What for the Other is his *taste of himself* becomes for me the Other's *flesh.* The flesh is the pure contingency of presence" (*BN,* 343). Further, every individual is like Peter: each person is a unique and contingent happening, and the bond between people is positive only to the degree that we have made it to be so.

We thus constitute ourselves and our natures, and the growth in Sartre's thought consists in a greater understanding of the social dimensions of this constitution. The movement from *Being and Nothingness* to *Saint Genet,* and then to *Critique of Dialectical Reason,* and finally to *The Family Idiot* is a progression in awareness of the social and historical realms of this constituting. For example, it is Flaubert's mother who is responsible for molding his body so that he could not get beyond passive activity, although what Flaubert did with that limitation is another question.

Conclusion

Being and Nothingness unfolds a phenomenological reflection that reveals the degree to which the world is human. Sartre is not involved in the type of constitution that Husserl refers to in *Cartesian Meditations.* It is not the mind but the fact that consciousness appears through organs that differentiates the world into things. This revealing that is a distinguishing of things does not imply, as Merleau-Ponty would have us believe, that being must thereby be lucidly known with no depth. The fact that we make a hat does not mean that we know all about the materials used. Of course, Sartre is not referring to a neo-Aristotelian matter-form relation. The senses are more like doors that we open on reality, revealing it to have color, sound, textures, etc. What we find when the door is open, is another matter.

True, Sartre frequently refers to lucidity, but again the term is contextual. Primarily, terms such as lucidity and translucency imply that we are immediately bonded to being and not merely to its "whatness." These terms do not at all imply conceptual clarity either about reality, ourselves, or others. Indeed, this is explicitly denied by Sartre both in the way the entire book unfolds, placing misunderstandings, for example, about sensation, in their proper phenomenological place, and showing, particularly in the chapter "Existential Psychoanalysis," how we misconceive our ego.

I understand the key difference between Sartre's philosophy, on the one hand, and Heidegger and Merleau-Ponty's thought, on the other hand, to consist in Sartre's anthropocentric stance, and this stance is again evident in Sartre's use of language. If human consciousness, human freedom, and human understanding is all that there is, then these qualities can justifiably be described as absolute. Limitations in consciousness, freedom, or understanding are simply more accurate ways of describing these qualities, and they remain absolute. The only way we could refer to the qualities of freedom, consciousness, and understanding as not absolute is if we secretly believed that there might be another source limiting them. And, I think that, unlike Sartre, Merleau-Ponty (and Heidegger) desires such a source, even if he does not explicitly mention it in *Phenomenology of Perception.*

That Sartre's anthropocentric stance is what separates the two thinkers is again evident in Merleau-Ponty's objection to Sartre's notion of freedom in the last chapter. Merleau-Ponty attempts to show that a rock is difficult to climb not merely because of a human project, but because of the relation of the mountain to what human legs can ordinarily perform: "Whether or not I have decided to climb them, these mountains appear high to me, because they exceed the body's power to take them in stride" (*PP,* 440). One does not have to imaginatively place the body on Sirius to realize that the real issue is why anyone should be concerned with climbing mountains at all. I am perfectly happy taking all mountains in stride with my eyes.

Merleau-Ponty's objection is more focused when he considers why the climber yields to his fatigue: "But here once more we must recognize a sort of sedimentation of our life: an attitude towards the world, when it has received frequent confirmation, acquires a favored status for us"

(*PP,* 441). Granting that Sartre minimized the degree to which others, particularly our parents, can constitute our passivity, we are still left with an important question about the climber who gives into his fatigue (see *BN,* 453–56). The point is that he could have gone on until he collapsed.

On the other hand, we see here the difference in perspectives. For Sartre, ontology does not examine the genesis of a project. Sartre becomes concerned with these questions in his philosophical biographies, such as on Genet and particularly Flaubert. But always the point will be that passivity is constituted, if not by our project, then by others. And, more importantly, we never know that predispositions are primary, and, in the final analysis, our freedom is what we do with what has been given to us.

Still, there is an important point here, and it concerns the status of passivity and receptivity. Let us assume that one person has a predisposition, arising from whatever causes, to be passive. The Sartrean point is that passivity can never be neutral; it always encounters us as meaningful, for example, as something to fight against or as something to yield to. The general anthropocentric issue is whether Being, precisely as it is receptive, reaches out to us. For Sartre, this reaching out could only come from a specific direction, and, as such, the invitation could only come from another mind, transcendent to the world.

I think that Merleau-Ponty wants more than his objections to Sartre indicate. The so-called turn from *Being and Time* to *Time and Being,* and the movement from the *Phenomenology of Perception* to *The Visible and the Invisible* go in opposite directions to Sartre's growth from *Being and Nothingness* to *The Family Idiot.* For Sartre, the doors to reality open only from our end. Our bonds to nature and to others are not reciprocal in the sense that reciprocity is taken to be an *a priori* positive, nurturing bond. Precisely as they are meaningful structures, passivity and reciprocity are always constituted, if not by the individual, then by the family and the social structure. Heidegger, Marcel, Jaspers, Buber, and, I think, also Merleau-Ponty desire to justify a poetic, passive openness to reality. Some slight breeze blows open a door within being, and some spirit beckons. For Sartre, our bodies open all the doors within being, and, in the social order, we create the doors to be opened. Hope for a better humanity indeed exists, but only insofar as we create the conditions for the possibility of this hope.

Notes

1. Maurice Merleau-Ponty, *Phenomenology of Perception,* trans. Colin Smith (London: Routledge and Kegan Paul, 1962), xiii. Referred to in quotations as *PP.*

2. I am not alone in reading *Being and Nothingness* in relation to Heidegger's *Being and Time.* See, e.g., Joseph P. Fell, *Heidegger and Sartre: An Essay on Being and Place* (New York: Columbia University Press, 1979). I do not agree with a good deal of what Fell has to say, but, for the most part, he places the discussion on the proper level, and he does not have most of the problems with *Being and Nothingness* that many Sartreans have. Also, I have discussed the Sartrean canon in my *Good Faith and Other Essays* (Lanham: Rowman and Littlefield, 1996), 6–9.

3. See Joseph S. Catalano, *Commentary on Jean-Paul Sartre's "Critique of Dialectical Reason, Vol. 1: Theory of Practical Ensembles"* (Chicago: University of Chicago Press, 1986), 14–17; 90–91; 136–37, and passim.

4. Jean-Paul Sartre, *Being and Nothingness,* trans. Hazel E. Barnes (New York: Philosophical Library, 1956), 218. All quotations are from this translation and cited as *BN.*

5. *PP,* 215. Actually, there is little of consequence in this entire chapter that is in opposition to Sartre.

6. I have discussed pure reflection elsewhere, although not in comparison with Merleau-Ponty's objections. See Joseph S. Catalano, *Commentary on Jean-Paul Sartre's "Being and Nothingness"* (New York: Harper and Row, 1974; with new preface, Chicago: University of Chicago Press, 1980), 126–31; also see my commentary on Sartre's *Critique,* 42–45; 194–95.

7. Long before Donald Davidson proposed anomalous monism as a solution to the apparent dualism of mind and matter, Sartre had given us a nonreductive materialism, that is, a monism of matter in which the human organism is not reduced to the thinghood of other material kinds. Indeed, human organic unity is the source of the unity of all other natural kinds, and, from this perspective, Sartre indeed gives a unique role to the human body.

8. I think that this expression does reflect Merleau-Ponty's thought, and yet I am aware that to some extent I have taken it out of context. The discussion has to do with communication and the nature of the sign, and not with what I call world-making. On the level that Merleau-Ponty is considering signs, the world is indeed meaningful; the point is this level assumes the initial advent of human existence within matter. In general, this is another aspect of the divergent emphasis of the two philosophies.

9. For example, "To be a body, is to be tied to a certain world, as we have seen; our body is not primarily *in* space; it is of it" (*PP,* 148). But this is not true world-making, and further the entire progression of the chapters on the body shows that Merleau-Ponty is not really interested in the question of the body's constitution of the world.

10. See Maurice Merleau-Ponty, *The Visible and the Invisible,* trans. Alphonso Lingis (Evanston: Northwestern University Press, 1968). In his introductory remarks (liv), Lingis notes the importance of flesh in *Phenomenology of Perception* and, as he says, "The Flesh . . . is not just a new term for what the *Phenomenology of Perception* (but already Sartre's *Being and Nothingness*) brought to light." He then continues to note the development of the notion. In my view of *Being and Nothingness,* flesh is the invisible through which the world is made visible. I do

not think this is Merleau-Ponty's view, although, at present, I am not clear about this aspect of his thought. Also, in pushing Merleau-Ponty even slightly in the direction of the later Heidegger, I may be doing him an injustice. I am simply trying to make sense of his general view of interconnections that seem to arise from the body and yet are not to be limited to it.

PART 4

FREEDOM

12

Sartre, Merleau-Ponty, and Human Freedom

John J. Compton

Jean-Paul Sartre and Maurice Merleau-Ponty are commonly recognized to have shared in defining the project of an "existential phenomenology" which would seek to evoke and interpret primordial structures of human "being-in-the-world," of the way we "live" our relationship to the natural world, to other persons, to history and culture "prior," in some sense, to the overlay of reflective thought and prior in particular to the explanatory accounts of the special sciences. Inevitably, such a project requires a delicate balance between a recovery of hidden and unknowing experiences, on the one hand, and some guiding, interpretive framework, which directs attention to and provides the most general concepts for understanding those experiences on the other: the experiences should validate the broad conceptual framework, and the conceptual framework should disclose, and thus afford more comprehensive insight into, the fundamental experiences. Just as inevitably, therefore, differences in the conceptual framework, as between different investigators, should be expected to yield corresponding, pervasive differences in the phenomenologies in question. And differing, perhaps only subtly differing, emphases in the characterization of certain primary experiences should tend to reinforce broadly different framework concepts.

So it is with Sartre and Merleau-Ponty. And yet it is difficult to know how to put their relationship. On the one hand, it is arguable that the conceptual framework—the ontology—of Merleau-Ponty differs so fundamentally from that of Sartre that, at virtually every point, the nuance given to common phenomenological themes is distinctive to him. For

Merleau-Ponty, being-*with* is the way we are "in" the world. His most formative insight was that human being-in-the-world forms a *unifying* structure *within* which individual self-consciousness arises and *within* which the perceptive and active encounter with others, with natural things, and with historical-cultural practice, must be seen to take place. Dialectical reciprocity among the elements of a "synergic system," self-others-world, is the fundamental reality to be evoked.[1] For Sartre, by contrast, being-in-the-world is marked by the sharpest *distinctions* among these elements. Self-consciousness is to be found in a consciousness *without* a self (if always at or out alongside one) and *without* things and others and history (if always at or out alongside them). Negativity, distancing, conflict, and above all the nondialectical opposition between human consciousness as *for-itself*, as a nothingness of being, and everything else, or being, *in-itself*, is the fundamental reality to be evoked.[2] Sartre's and Merleau-Ponty's interpretive frameworks may thus be taken to be strictly incompatible.[3]

On the other hand, it is also arguable that virtually everything in Merleau-Ponty is, or could be, in Sartre, that these two friends from school days, notwithstanding political differences, are at bottom philosophical allies, and that the differences between their phenomenologies, such as they are, are of shading or emphasis only, rooted in the differences between two strong personalities and "fundamental choices" of values.[4] If one reads Sartre carefully, if one thinks about what he seems to want to say and in places does say, one can find Merleau-Pontyian texts, one can discover the immense debt that Merleau-Ponty owes him, and one can be led to read him in a fresh, more sympathetic way. On balance, as well as for the present purpose, however, I find it crucial to underscore the respects in which Merleau-Ponty "responds to" Sartre by reappropriating his thought within an original vision of his own, but not, I hope, at the expense of responsiveness to the sense in which Merleau-Ponty also offers us "Sartre saved from himself."

I want to explore Merleau-Ponty's critique of Sartre in the period of their "classical" works, *Being and Nothingness* (1943) and *Phenomenology of Perception* (1945), by focusing upon their interpretations of human freedom.[5]

Interpreting Freedom

The issue is whether freedom is best understood as categorical, as what human existence simply is, such that at every moment the entire meaning of our lives is at stake, or whether it is better understood as contingent, as a power, characteristic of our actions only in some measure, through which conditions having at least a general and fragmentary meaning independent of us are brought to some successful resolution. It is appropriate that Sartre should begin his book by invoking freedom, for, in his usage, freedom is experienced in the anxiety that accompanies the spontaneity of consciousness anterior to, and the same in, all actions. Equally appropriately, Merleau-Ponty offers his own analysis of freedom only in the final chapter of *Phenomenology of Perception,* and in explicit response to Sartre, since it is Merleau-Ponty's counterthesis that "if indeed it is the case that our freedom is the same in all our actions, then it cannot be held that there is such a thing as *free action* . . . [and] the idea of action, therefore, disappears" (*PP,* 436–37). This for the reason that free action is experienced and can be understood only as it arises "against a background of life from which it is entirely, or almost entirely absent," or in which it is genuinely imperiled (*PP,* 437). Merleau-Ponty believes that the attempt to counter a reductive causal determinism by means of a freedom outside all effective constraints is bound to be inadequate: instead of a view that takes us to be things, it is of no help to propose one that risks supposing us to be pure spirits. Merleau-Ponty links Sartre, despite the latter's protestations, with Kantian and other rationalistic tendencies of thought which fail to offer a faithful phenomenology of concrete, as distinct from abstract freedom, and argues that only within a significantly different ontological framework from Sartre's—specifically one that places *reciprocity with the environment* at the center of human reality—can an experientially adequate account of free action be rendered. Let us see how he proceeds.

Situation and Motivation

For both Merleau-Ponty and Sartre, the fundamental phenomenon to be elucidated is that of a "situated" freedom. "We shall use the term *situation,*" says Sartre, "for the contingency of freedom"—i.e., for the given, limiting conditions under which freedom appears, for the state of affairs in reference to which one must act (*BN,* 487). The distinctive Sartrean interpretation, however, is that this given, "which is there only *in order not to constrain* freedom, is revealed to this freedom only as *already illuminated* by the end which freedom chooses" (*BN,* 487). It is only by reference to the freely projected end that the situation is found to be lacking, troubling, threatening, or favorable, and thus motivating, for an agent. Necessarily, every action is motivated; but motives are not psychic things, nor are they causes; they are features of the situation defined and felt, as motivating, through an agent's free intentions in action. So Sartre continues, "there is freedom only in a *situation,* and there is a situation only through freedom. Human-reality everywhere encounters resistance and obstacles which it has not created, but these resistances and obstacles have meaning only in and through the free choice which human-reality is" (*BN,* 489).

Not so, thinks Merleau-Ponty. Our chosen ends do not simply constitute those meanings. Rather, to be situated is to find, precisely *prior* to any explicit choice of ends, that one is already engaged with a meaning-*ful* world which both solicits and resists. "Our freedom does not destroy our situation," Merleau-Ponty writes, "but gears itself to it: as long as we are alive, our situation is open, which implies both that it calls up specially favored modes of resolution, and also that it is powerless to bring one into being by itself" (*PP,* 442). The term "situation" stands not only for the contingency of freedom, then, but for its available possibilities of expression. Motives are *not* causes in any straightforward sense, right enough. But "one phenomenon may release another, not by means of some efficient cause . . . but by the meaning it holds out . . . [by] a sort of operative reason" (*PP,* 50). Motivating features of situations carry anonymous disposing power which makes free action necessary precisely by making it possible.[6]

Sartre does not dispute this. He acknowledges the efficacy of motives and asks us to recognize that this does not absolve us from choice. The issue, however, is whether he can account for this efficacy. Consider, for example, the parable of the climber and the crag, in which Sartre treats the motivating role of circumstances from the natural environment: "Here I am at the foot of this crag which appears to me as 'not scalable.' This means that the rock appears to me in the light of a projected scaling. . . . Thus the rock is carved out on the ground of the world by the effect of the initial choice of my freedom" (*BN,* 488). So far, the meaning-giving power of the for-itself. But, he adds, "what my freedom cannot determine is whether the rock 'to be scaled' will or will not lend itself to scaling. This is part of the brute being of the rock" (*BN,* 488). Sartre intends to be a radical realist, after all: there *is* the brute in-itself confronting us. Still, this rocky in-itself can have no determinate character *as motive* for me; that is, its specific resisting or cooperating power cannot be explained by reference to it as in itself. So Sartre says, "The given in itself as *resisting* or as *aid* is revealed only in the light of the projecting freedom. . . . The rock will not be an obstacle if I wish at any cost to arrive at the top of the mountain. On the other hand, it will discourage me if I have freely fixed limits to my desire of making the projected climb" (*BN,* 488). The "coefficient of adversity of the given," as

Sartre puts it, is a relation between the cliff and my freedom. But such a relation has no ontological status, no weight, and no efficacy. On Sartre's ontological framework, it can only be assimilated to freedom, and there is no limitation to my freedom outside myself.

Now hear Merleau-Ponty's response:

> When I say that this rock is unclimbable, it is certain that this attribute, like that of being big or little, straight or oblique, and indeed like all attributes in general, can be conferred upon it only by the project of climbing it, and by a human presence. . . . [But w]hether or not I have decided to climb them, these mountains appear high to me, because they exceed my body's power to take them in its stride. . . . Underlying myself as a thinking subject there is, therefore, as it were, a natural self which does not budge from its terrestrial situation and which constantly adumbrates absolute valuations. . . . Insofar as I have hands, feet, a body, I sustain around me intentions which are not dependent upon my decisions and which affect my surroundings in a way which I do not choose. . . . they are not of my own making, they originate from outside me, and I am not surprised to find them in all psychophysical subjects organized as I am. (*PP,* 439–40)

In short, you are quite right, friend Sartre, that a human presence confers meaning upon objects in the world, but quite wrong to understand this presence in terms that make it a matter of personal choice. We are systems of body intentions before we are persons. Vital interests and skills prestructure our interactions with the environment: they allow us to discover, as perceptually given, the initial resistances and cooperations of things; they dispose us to shared patterns of generally adaptive behavior; and they constitute the background against which deliberate choices are made and personal histories develop. This is what it means for us to be "embodied" subjects: we are entangled in *real* relations, i.e., relations of *reciprocal determination of meaning,* with the order of nature, with other persons, and with institutions, through our bodies. This is why we cannot be spectators and why it is necessary for us to adjust ourselves to things. On Merleau-Ponty's terms, this is what Sartre needed to have said in order adequately to interpret the very human engagement with the world he was most anxious to proclaim.

Embodiment

Of course, Merleau-Ponty's complaint is paradoxical, since Sartre himself views human being as an embodied subject and embodiment as a contingent way of "existing" or "living" the world. But Merleau-Ponty follows Marcel's original notion of embodiment more closely than does Sartre. For Sartre, to be embodied is simply *to exist as situated,* to occupy a place and time, to be in certain circumstances and conditions, and thus to be "the necessity of existing as an engaged, contingent being among other contingent beings" (*BN,* 309). We have to choose the meaning of these situating conditions. For Merleau-Ponty, on the other hand, to be embodied is *to find the meanings of situations and our responses to them already generally shaped* as well. "Although our body does not impose definite instincts upon us from birth, as it does upon animals, it does at least give to our life the form of generality. . . . The body is our general medium for having a world" (*PP,* 146). It is the necessity we live of "endowing the instantaneous expressions of spontaneity with 'a little renewable action and independent existence,' " of which habit is a form (*PP,* 146). It seems to Merleau-Ponty that Sartre can have no room for the phenomenon of habituation or for the weight of habit upon our freedom and the openings habit provides for it.

He recalls Sartre's fable of the friendly hike. After hours of walking in the hot sun, I finally give up, throw down my knapsack, and fall beside it. Why? Was it the pain and fatigue? No, precisely not, at least not as causes acting externally upon me. My friend shares these feelings, but is ready to go on. The truth is that I have *decided* to quit, while he has not. And the reason is that my companion and I *live* our feelings of pain and fatigue differently—he flexibly and with a kind of relish, according to his fundamental choice of values, and I, inflexibly, mistrustfully, and finally as useless, according to mine.

Now our two philosophers are fully agreed on the chief import of this story for the meaning of freedom: it is that while I might indeed have done otherwise than I did do, it would have been at the cost of modifying my entire way of being in the world. Both agree that there would be this "cost." The difference lies in how each understands it. "This modification is always possible," says Sartre (*BN,* 464). "But here once more we must recognize a sort of sedimentation of our life," says Merleau-Ponty, "an attitude towards the world, when it has received frequent confirmation, acquires a favored status for us . . . having built our life upon an inferiority complex [for example] which has been operative for twenty years, it is not *probable* that we shall change" (*PP,* 441–42).

Since, for Sartre, nothing outside of freedom can restrict our freedom, there can be no probabilities or generalities of behavior, only *de facto* projects, in actions expressing our fundamental choice of values against an indefinite realm of pure, anxiety-producing possibility. But, says Merleau-Ponty, "Generality and probability are not fictions, but phenomena; we must therefore find a phenomenological basis for statistical thought" (*PP,* 442). And the basis is the way in which I necessarily "make my abode in" certain attitudes and patterns of action which genuinely incline although they do not compel. This taking up an abode in inherited evaluations, thus requiring that I live *out of* them as within me, not against them *as outside* me, is precisely what a Sartrean for-itself cannot do. For this would be to be "between the psychic and the physiological, between the for-itself and the in-itself," which is categorically impossible on Sartre's ontology (*PP,* 122). And yet, human embodiment just *is* this "being between."

Had Merleau-Ponty pursued the fable further, he could have gone more deeply; Sartre cannot, in the first instance, allow for the special insistence of the fatigue and pain *as such,* which makes them *mine* and requires that I learn to "live" them in some way whatever else I may do.[7] All situating conditions, as in themselves, have to be on a par. Through his radical experiment of reading all "objects" out of consciousness, Sartre makes it impossible to be conceptually open to—although he describes—the intimacy and passivity and opacity of bodily conditions, not only of fatigue and pain, but of hunger, desire, and perception, which mediate the world to us. On Merleau-Ponty's view, these bodily experiences are not to be grouped with some total in-itself which is alien to us but which we "have to be"; they are intentional, already meaning-laden, already expressive *of* us in our relatedness to the environment. The reason we must take account of fatigue and pain is that they are our own incipient behavioral tendencies; they are biologically-functionally "fitted" to slowing down, stopping, or redirecting our activity. For me to yield to them or to resist them is not to be acted upon by an external cause, true enough, but neither is it simply to express some chosen attitude in face of them. It is rather *to identify myself in them.* It is to take them as body intentions which form part of the motivating basis for my habitual attitude and which I affirm or modify as I choose.

For Merleau-Ponty, then, concrete freedom rests upon our voluntarily mobilizing *in*voluntary, body intentions into generalized attitudes toward the world which themselves function involuntarily as background for, while being modified by, specific choices.[8] To speak of body intentions, or even of these general attitudes, as "choices," as Sartre does, is, from this perspective, at best a reminder that we are in part responsible for them, since they are ours and are modifiable. Not only is the concept of a "fundamental choice" of values self-contradictory, since choice requires a field of already value-laden possibilities from which to choose, but this way of speaking obscures the very prereflective and involuntary character of the way in which we live our fundamental values upon which Sartre rightly insists. And it distorts the gradual social-historical process by which generalized attitudes, and thus our choices, are formed, as well.

Sociality and History

For both Sartre and Merleau-Ponty, our being with others in various institutions such as a language, family, race, class, or nation, each with its own history, is essential to our situation. To be so situated is to tend, prior to any particular choice, to perceive the world and to act in it in certain predelineated ways, in customary settings, and according to established roles. I am a father, worker, black, voter, and so on. The issue for freedom is how to understand such institutional realities and our relationship, as individuals, to them.

For Sartre, they mark out alienation from others, the fact that "each man finds himself in the presence of meanings which do not come into the work through him" (*BN*, 520). Instituted social relations have their status as "outside" me unavoidably, as what I have to be, but yet, as with every other aspect of the situation, not as a constraint. For they are sustained in existence only through the free choice of their meaning as I "surpass" them in my projects. Sartre reflects upon a worker in 1830 who simply suffers his poverty as natural and does not act against it. How does being "oppressed" or "working class" become effective in his life? It does not become a motive for action until he projects a different condition, and he will not take his situation as unbearable until he becomes able "to conceive of a social state in which these sufferings would not exist" and for the sake of which a resolution is possible (*BN*, 435). The thesis, once more, is that motivating conditions are defined as parts of actions, not as antecedent causes of them. A worker does not become "working class" because of economic conditions or economic forces; he is in such a condition or subject to such forces only insofar as he has already determined to revolt.

Not so, responds Merleau-Ponty. This leaves the *coming to be* of his class consciousness wholly unaccounted for; it fails to capture the fact that social coexistence is a process within which we are incorporated without being made into things. In history, there are fragmentary meanings which "court" our freedom, and "there is an exchange between generalized and individual existence, each receiving and giving something" (*PP*, 449–50). Our worker will have noted that other workers in a different trade have, after striking, received wage increases. A severe economic decline may have destroyed his and others' savings. In various ways, he finds himself in a life synchronized with the lives of others. Class consciousness is in the making! So Merleau-Ponty concludes,

> It is, therefore, true that I recognize myself as a worker or a bourgeois on the day I take my stand in relation to a possible revolution . . . but [it is not] an unwarranted evaluation, instantaneous and unmotivated; it is prepared by some molecular process. . . . the intellectual project and the positing of ends are merely the bringing to completion of an existential project. . . . they spring from my present and past and in particular from my mode of present and past coexistence. (*PP*, 446–47)

We are here in the presence of a very different understanding of social relations from that of Sartre, one which affirms the primacy of being-*with* others, indeed of being "between" self and others, rooted at a basic level in involuntary intentions joining us through our bodies, and, only within this reality, allowing the possibility of alienation and conflict.

And we have a very different understanding of temporality. Sartre is sometimes said to have treated consciousness as instantaneous and to have made each moment of our lives one which we create, like God, *ex nihilo*. Yes and no. Yes, in that, notoriously, Sartre treats the past as in itself a mere contingency, the meaning of which I determine in my present choice. No, in that, with Merleau-Ponty, he recognizes that our "temporalization" contains no absolute moments. There is a structure of becoming in which the present fuses a projected future with a retained past (*BN*, 465–66). The flaw, however, from Merleau-Ponty's perspective, is that there is no *passivity* in this becoming, no sense in which it is *received and undergone* by us as part of a wider field of temporal being. It is the temporality of a pure, individualized consciousness, a disembodied consciousness with no depth in a generalized, natural, and historical process with its own meaning-structure independent of our choice (*PP*, 453). The structure of temporality has been conflated with that of choice, and choice with that of an absolute choice: each moment *is* a creation for Sartre, not in the sense of being cut off from prior moments, but in the sense of being a choice with no ground outside of itself.[9] Our freedom is not that of a God who creates moments one by one, but of a God who creates the meaning of time itself from above time and may, at any moment, recreate it entirely afresh. This is what Merleau-Ponty rejects. His, interestingly enough, is the more pagan vision of the freedom of an earth-bound deity who creates not from above but from within, not by fiat but by growth, not out of absolute power but out of hope for what might come to be through what is beyond him. In the last analysis, in Sartre's apotheosis of unconditioned choice, we do not choose: "Past motives, past reasons, present motives and reasons, future ends, all are organized in an indissoluble unity by the very upsurge of a freedom which is beyond reasons, motives, and ends" (*BN*, 450). Thus, "The result is that a voluntary deliberation is always a deception" (*BN*, 450). And nothing is ever done, for it must be chosen again. For Merleau-Ponty, on the contrary, it is precisely conditioned choice that is effective choice: "The fact remains that I am free, not in spite of, or on the hither side of, those motivations, but by means of them. For this significant life, this certain significance of nature and history which I am, does not limit my access to the world, but on the contrary is my means of entering into communication with it" (*PP*, 455).

Concluding Reflection

What, finally, does this difference come to? As I have said, it seems to me to reflect differences in understanding human situatedness, motivation, embodiment, social relations, and temporality. But behind these lies a cosmological difference as well. Sartre's most formative experience is that humans are outsiders in the world, whereas for Merleau-Ponty it is that we are in communication with it. For Sartre, everything natural is suspect; for Merleau-Ponty it is full of significant power. Sartre can see nothing between the undifferentiated and meaningless mass of physical existence, as in *Nausea,* on the one hand, and the spontaneous upsurge of human consciousness, on the other. Consciousness occasions in being the only meaning it can have. And anything in us, among things, or from others, that seems to have stable significance and power must be viewed as the threat of being in itself. Merleau-Ponty, however, sees nature primarily in biological terms, as an environment for life: he is able to envision a hierarchical nature with levels of significant order ranging from the physical through the vital to the human.[10] Human being, for him, is lodged, if always ambiguously lodged, within such a nature and is able to bring certain of its potentialities to cultural and historical expression. This is why "actual freedom is not on the hither side of my being, but before me, in things" (*PP*, 452).

Notes

Presented in an APA Symposium on French Responses to Sartre: Merleau-Ponty and Levinas, 30 December 1982. Alphonso Lingis was a cosymposiast and Peter Caws commented. See *Journal of Philosophy* 79 (1982); 588–96 and 596–97, respectively, for their contributions.

1. Two recent, albeit very different, studies underline this theme in Merleau-Ponty's ontology: Samuel Mallin, *Merleau-Ponty's Philosophy* (New Haven: Yale, 1979); and Gary Madison, *The Phenomenology of Merleau-Ponty* (Athens: Ohio University Press, 1981).

2. See Klaus Hartmann, *Sartre's Ontology* (Evanston: Northwestern University Press, 1966).

3. This is Merleau-Ponty's own sense, as he reflects on the matter in 1960: "I take my starting point where Sartre ends, in the Being taken up by the for-itself—It is for him the finishing point because he starts with being and negentity and *constructs* their union. For me it is structure or transcendence that explains, and being and nothingness (in Sartre's sense) are its two abstract properties." This is from the working notes at the end of *The Visible and the Invisible,* trans. Alphonso Lingis (Evanston: Northwestern University Press, 1968), 237. Sartre too believes, on reflection, that his and Merleau-Ponty's ontologies are incompatible, as he tells us in the "Interview with Jean Paul Sartre" of 1975 to be found in *The Philosophy of Jean-Paul Sartre,* ed. P. A. Schilpp (LaSalle: Open Court, 1981), 43.

4. This perception is nicely expressed by Mikel Dufrenne, "Sartre and Merleau-Ponty," in *Jean-Paul Sartre,* ed. Hugh J. Silverman and Frederick Elliston (Pittsburgh: Duquesne University Press, 1980) (printed below 279–89). A more radical view to the effect that Merleau-Ponty consistently misread Sartre and that the distinctive ontological emphasis in Merleau-Ponty's thought is itself already in Sartre, is forcefully developed by Monika Langer, "Sartre and Merleau-Ponty: A Reappraisal," in Schilpp, *The Philosophy of Jean-Paul Sartre,* 300–325 (printed above 93–117).

5. Page reference in parentheses are to these texts—*BN* for Hazel Barnes's translation of *Being and Nothingness* (New York: Philosophical Library, 1956); and *PP* for Colin Smith's translation of *Phenomenology of Perception* (New York: Humanities Press, 1962). Plainly, by restricting myself to these works I "freeze" the evolution of their thought, but I believe that what is revealed of their differences at this stage continues to be determinative for understanding their relationship. The most significant shift, in the matter of freedom, occurs in the *Critique of Dialectical Reason* as Sartre modifies his early heroic view of the complete isolation and openness of choice. In no small measure, this shift, at the level of political and historical understanding, came about through the influence of Merleau-Ponty. See Sartre's reminiscence, "Merleau-Ponty," originally printed in *Les Temps modernes* (October 1961), but translated by Benita Eisler in *Situations* (New York: Braziller, 1965) (printed below 565–625). Also see Sartre's interview, "The Itinerary of a Thought," in Sartre, *Between Existentialism and Marxism* (New York: Morrow Quill Paperbacks, 1979).

6. Merleau-Ponty's response here resembles that of causal theorists of action when confronted with the conceptual analyst's point, strongly resembling that of Sartre, to the effect that one's motives cannot be said to be causes of one's action since they are not specifiable independently of the meaning of the action

itself. Merleau-Ponty's response is that the conceptual connectedness of motives to action does not preclude, but may rather be seen to require, acknowledgment of their efficacy in bringing about the action. This is because their efficacy lies precisely *in* their meaning, in their way of disposing us to the appropriate action. Merleau-Ponty has available to him a more flexible view of causation than the Humean one, with the result that he can join Sartre in rejecting causation in the external or efficient sense while using it in the form of intentional or motivational causation. It is for lack of this latter concept that Sartre, and some other conceptual analysts of action, seem forced into their impossibly abstract doctrine.

7. Alphonse de Waelhens put this point incisively in his study of Merleau-Ponty's philosophy, *Une philosophie de l'ambiguité* (Louvain: Publications Universitaires de Louvain, 1951).

8. It was Paul Ricoeur who developed this thesis into a complete phenomenological exploration of the reciprocity between voluntary and involuntary elements in forming choices, carrying out actions and coming to terms with the ultimate limits of our embodiment: *Freedom and Nature,* trans. Erazim Kohak (Evanston: Northwestern University Press, 1966).

9. It is in this sense that he himself characterizes his view as one in which the awful freedom of the God of Descartes, for whom freedom and creation are one and the same, is returned to human beings: "La Liberté cartésienne," reprinted in Sartre, *Situations,* I (Paris: Gallimard, 1947). Sartre's conflation of phenomenological constitution with creation is the theme of Dagfinn Føllesdal's "Sartre on Freedom," in Schilpp, *The Philosophy of Jean-Paul Sartre,* 392–407.

10. The contrast between Sartre's and Merleau-Ponty's responsiveness to biological thought—even as late as Sartre's *Critique,* in which organic categories become newly important for him—is explored by Marjorie Grene in *Sartre* (New York: New Viewpoints Press, 1973), chap. 7. The limits of Sartre's philosophy of nature and science are thoughtfully put by Peter Caws in his *Sartre* (Boston: Routledge and Kegan Paul, 1979), esp. 90–93.

13

Freedom: Merleau-Ponty's Critique of Sartre

Ronald L. Hall

In this essay, I want to examine Merleau-Ponty's understanding of freedom as it is discussed in the last chapter of *Phenomenology of Perception*[1] with the aim of specifying the points at which it is an explicit critique of Sartre's view of freedom. To set the stage for this, I will give a brief exposition of Sartre's view derived from *Being and Nothingness*.[2] Providing this background will allow us to present Merleau-Ponty's view of freedom as a polemical response to Sartre's and hence facilitate our task of critically comparing the two views.[3]

Sartre is very intent upon dissociating himself from traditional (Cartesian) discussions of freedom, which tend to focus on *the will* and the mind-body problem of how the will can move the physical body. Sartre wants to refocus the discussion on the phenomenon of *action*, which by its very nature presupposes the integration of mind and body. To those who have been swinging on the Cartesian pendulum for too long, this suggestion to dismount and start over sounds attractive and promising.

Though Sartre does refocus the discussion on the phenomenon of action, it is not so clear as to whether he has really gotten away from the Cartesian framework. Action, he says, is on principle *intentional*. As he begins to elaborate on this definition of action, however, the slip back into Cartesianism becomes increasingly evident. If one can be truly said to have acted, then, in Sartre's words, "he knew what he was doing, or if you prefer, he intentionally realized a *conscious project*" (*BN*, 559). Indeed, the argument seems to culminate in the claim that action is based on the actor's unencumbered, lucid choice of himself as his own conscious project. This freedom of the *pour-soi* is absolute. There seems, in fact, to be no positive basis for relating the freedom of the *pour-soi* to the utterly passive, determined *en-soi*. The only relation between the two seems to be negative, i.e., the *pour-soi* is not the *en-soi*, just as the *res cogitans* in the Cartesian system is defined as *not* being extended (*res extensa*).

Negation is the very essence of the human reality for Sartre, and this power of negation is the very heart of freedom. He says, "if negation comes into the world through human-reality, the latter must be a being who can realize a nihilating rupture with the world and with himself; and we established that the permanent possibility of this rupture is the same as freedom" (*BN*, 567). Along the same line, Sartre comments, "freedom in its foundations coincides with the nothingness which is at the heart of man. Human reality is free because it *is not enough*. It is free because it is perpetually wrenched away from itself and because it has been separated by a nothingness from what it is and from what it will be" (*BN*, 568). And again, he writes,

> Freedom is precisely the nothingness which is *made-to-be* at the heart of man and which forces human reality to *make itself* instead of *to be*. As we have seen, for human-reality, to be is to *choose* oneself; nothing comes to it either from the outside or from within which it can *receive or accept*. . . . Thus freedom is not a being; it is *the being* of man—i.e., his nothingness of being. (*BN*, 568)

Actions, being intentional, always aim at what is *not*, and attempt to bring what is not into being what is. Take as an example a very simple intentional action: I am sitting at my desk, and I begin to sense a lack—I am thirsty. My conscious project then is literally a projecting toward what is not, the acquiring of that which will satisfy my thirst. My action of getting a drink of water was thus not motivated by an actual state of affairs in the past or present, rather it was motivated by a future possibility which my action tries to bring into actuality. As Sartre puts it, "No factual state whatever it may be is capable by itself of motivating any act whatsoever. For an act is a projection of the for-itself toward what is not, and what is can in no way determine by itself what is not" (*BN*, 562).

This conception of freedom, Sartre thinks, moves us considerably beyond the Cartesian view of freedom. The Cartesian view is basically that the will is perfectly free, while the "passions of the soul" are determined mechanically. Thus we have the basic duality of a free power, in conflict with, and always trying to master, a whole nexus of determined processes.

Sartre finds the Cartesian view of freedom unacceptable on the grounds that it is unintelligible that a free spontaneity could *act*. He asks,

"On what would it act? On the object itself (the present psychic fact)? But how could it modify an in-itself which by definition is and can only be what it is?" (*BN*, 570). But the situation is also the same the other way around. Spontaneity cannot act on a determined in-itself and the determined in-itself cannot act on spontaneity. "Thus any synthesis of the two types of existents is impossible; they are not homogeneous; they will remain each one in its own incommunicable solitude" (*BN*, 570).

Not only is it true that it is impossible to make intelligible a relation between a free will and a set of determined passions in the Cartesian system, it is also true, Sartre claims, that Descartes misconceived the very nature of the passions themselves. Sartre argues, against Descartes, that the passions of the soul are not determined processes of a mechanical body but, like the free will, are autonomous nihilations. Passions, for Sartre, are like free actions in being intentional. To have a desire, for example, is to sense a lack and to posit an end; a passion is a project and an enterprise; a passion is a nihilation. "And if nihilation is precisely the being of freedom, how can we refuse autonomy to the passions in order to grant it to the will?" (*BN*, 571).

We have not yet come to the point at which Sartre thinks his own view of freedom radically diverges from the Cartesian system. This radical divergence, he argues, will allow us to short-circuit the dilemma of free will and determinism. What then is this radically new "post-Cartesian" starting point?

The will itself, Sartre says, presupposes a more fundamental freedom, what he calls *original freedom*. The passions, which the will is supposed, on the Cartesian system, to be opposed to, also presuppose original freedom. The example Sartre cites here is helpful. If I am threatened, I can run away, or stand firm. To run away is an act of passion and to stand firm an act of rational will. Both presuppose, however, the same end, though neither posited this end, viz., the end of life as a supreme value. This end, Sartre argues, is posited by original freedom, and the will or the passion is but a mode of relation to that end. Original freedom posits my ends and the relation I choose to have toward those ends. Original freedom decides whether I shall act passionately or voluntarily, irrationally or rationally. No longer is will opposed to passion; both are grounded in a more radical, more fundamental choice.

Sartre's own language may be helpful in summarizing this point. He says that volitions, like the passions, "are certain subjective attitudes by which we attempt to attain the ends posited by original freedom. By original freedom, of course, we should not understand a freedom which would be *prior* to the voluntary or passionate act but rather a foundation, which is strictly contemporary with the will or the passion and which these manifest, each in its own way" (*BN,* 572–73).

According to Sartre, I am constantly choosing myself in original freedom, and this determines my attitudes toward the ends which I posit. As he puts it, "Actually it is not enough to will, it is necessary to will to will" (*BN,* 573). In the face of danger, when I act from will that means I have chosen myself as a rational, courageous, willful creature: I have willed to will. But if I react emotionally, by fleeing or fainting, I act out of passion, I choose myself as fearful, or as fainting: I will to not be willful. The for-itself is thus "the free foundation of its emotions as of its volitions" (*BN,* 574).

This, then, is a brief outline of Sartre's very familiar theory of human freedom. It is clear that in it he thinks he has overcome the dilemmas of the Cartesian system by founding both the will and the passions in a deep, inarticulate, but absolute and unfettered original freedom. We have yet to settle, however, the question as to whether or not Sartre has really moved significantly beyond the Cartesian dilemma. It is this question that we must keep in mind as we now move on to consider Merleau-Ponty's own view of freedom and its comparison to that of Sartre.

Setting Sartre's view alongside that of Merleau-Ponty, we are immediately struck by the similarities. There is ample evidence of their friendly dialogue on the subject of freedom. Yet there is an undercurrent of criticism that turns out to be a very radical disagreement between the two. My hunch is that the difference between the two will be crucial in the question as to which of the two has moved more radically toward a truly post-Cartesian definition of freedom.

In the last chapter of *Phenomenology of Perception,* Merleau-Ponty recapitulates his basic argument for the primacy of perception, though within the specific context of a discussion of freedom. The argument for the primacy of perception is an argument directed against the lingering ethos of Cartesianism in empiricism and intellectualism, especially as it manifests itself in the many forms of the mind-body problem. In the context of the discussion of freedom, that dichotomy presents itself as a choice between scientism's causal determinism and absolute freedom divorced from the outside.

It is interesting to note the similarities of the two sides of the controversy that Merleau-Ponty is trying to circumvent. Both the determinists and the proponents of absolute freedom agree that if the self is involved in the world of nature, culture, body, etc., freedom is eclipsed. But both conceive of the world in an objectified sense. Because the scientistic interpretation reduces man to a thing within the world, understood as the totality of things, there can be no freedom at all. In order to save freedom, the absolutist doesn't challenge this view of the world, but accepts it, which is shown by his lifting of the self out of that situation that burdens its freedom, i.e., the objectified world. Because both conceive of the world in an objectified way, both end up objectifying the self, one in the direction of thinghood and the other in the direction of a discarnate intellect.

Merleau-Ponty, like Sartre, will have nothing to do with any compromise here. He will not allow us to be free in some actions, or free to some extent and determined in others. The reason for this is that once I am free in one action, then I can no longer be counted as a thing in the world, and hence the very presupposition of the scientistic challenge to freedom collapses. Hence no compromise will do. We need a more radical approach.

In Merleau-Ponty's critique of the proponents of choice as an unencumbered act of a pure, lucid consciousness, this more radical approach begins to be disclosed. The problem with the absolutist is that he confuses freedom with deliberate conscious, intentional action and explicit choice. On this point, both Merleau-Ponty and Sartre seem to agree—we need to ground consciousness in a more fundamental prereflective relationality to the world. Merleau-Ponty says, "There is free choice only if freedom comes into play in its decision, and posits the situation chosen as a situation of freedom" (*PP,* 437). But what is the nature of this prethematic relationality to the world? This is perhaps where the real divergence can be seen. For Sartre the original relationality to the world seems to be an original *freedom,* but for Merleau-Ponty it seems to be something different. Free choice, for Merleau-Ponty, is grounded not in a more fundamental, original free choice, as in Sartre, but in a more fundamental, original horizon of *meaning* which makes free choice possible. Free choice presupposes a field of meaning, not a more fundamental free choice.

What is this primordial field of meaning? In Merleau-Ponty's view, it is a prereflective field of meaningful possibilities that I find myself in, which I do not freely posit. This field of meaning is my givenness, so to speak. It is the horizon that I dwell within prior to the objectification of the world and myself. This field of meaningful possibilities is my situation and forms the very means of my freedom. Without such a field there would be nothing to do, no way to exercise freedom. "There is not freedom without a field" (*PP,* 439).

This field of meaningful possibilities which freedom presupposes and which is constituted dialectically in my prereflective perceptual rapport with the world has at least three fundamental characteristics: spatiality, temporality, and intersubjectivity.

Consider first the spatiality of my body in relation to my ambience as an aspect of my prereflective field of meaning. Being a body is not here an obstacle to freedom but its very *conditio sine qua non,* and the same is true of the world. The world that I am prereflectively oriented within presents itself as a field of possible projects, and as such does not hinder freedom but brings it into being. The very idea of an obstacle to freedom already presupposes meaning. Merleau-Ponty says,

> Even what are called obstacles to freedom are in reality deployed by it. An unclimbable rock face, a large or small, vertical or slanting rock, are things which have no meaning for anyone who is not intending to surmount them, for a subject whose projects do not carve out such determinate forms from the uniform mass of the in-itself and cause an oriented world to arise—a significance in things. (*PP,* 436)[4]

And further he writes, "It is, therefore, freedom which brings into being the obstacles to freedom, so that the latter can be set over against it as its bounds" (*PP,* 439). And again he says, "The mountain is great or small to the extent that, as a perceived thing, it is to be found in the field of my possible actions" (*PP,* 442). The natural, spatial horizon is the place of my freedom, the means of its actualization, and I am certainly not free in spite of my situation but by means of it.

The prereflective field of possibilities which provides room for freedom is also temporal. The very notion of possibility implies the not-yet, i.e., the future. Freedom emerges only within historical continuity which connects this future with both the present and the past. Merleau-Ponty argues against the intellectualistic idea of time as a series of discrete instants. The idea of an initial, instantaneous, reflective choice of a self-constituting consciousness is a confusion, since choice presupposes a prior commitment and future consequences, i.e., continuity. As Merleau-Ponty says,

> If freedom is doing, it is necessary that what it does should not be immediately undone by a new freedom. Each instant, therefore, must not be a closed world; one instant must be able to commit its successors and, a decision once taken and action begun, I must have something acquired at my disposal, I must benefit from my impetus, I must be inclined to carry on, and there must be a bent or propensity of the mind. (*PP,* 437)

A basic element of historical continuity, of course, is the past—our historical, cultural situation into which we are thrown. Merleau-Ponty does not look at this past as that from which we must disentangle ourselves, *à la* Sartre, but rather it is seen as the means of our freedom: "Our freedom does not destroy our situation, but gears itself to it: as long as we are alive our situation is open, which implies both that it calls up specially favored modes of resolution and also that it is powerless to bring one into being by itself" (*PP*, 442).

The third aspect of the prereflective field of possibility in which personal freedom originates is intersubjectivity. Reacting again to Sartre's conception of the other, Merleau-Ponty says:

> Another person is not necessarily, is not even ever quite an object for me. And in sympathy, for example, I can perceive another person as bare existence and freedom as much or as little as myself. The-other-person-as-object is nothing but an insincere modality of others, just as absolute subjectivity is nothing but an abstract notion of myself. I must, therefore, in the most radical reflection, apprehend around my absolute individuality a kind of halo of generality or a kind of atmosphere of sociality. (*PP*, 448)

And in an even more direct attack on Sartre, Merleau-Ponty writes:

> My life must have a significance which I do not constitute; there must strictly speaking be an intersubjectivity. . . . I am an intersubjective field, not despite my body and historical situation, but on the contrary, by being this body and this historical situation and through them all the rest. . . . I can no longer pretend to be a cipher, and choose myself continually from the starting point of nothing at all. (*PP*, 448, 452)

This intersubjective matrix again does not limit my freedom but on the contrary is the means of my becoming a person capable of free and responsible acts.

The concept of a field of meaning is clearly primary for Merleau-Ponty. That is, freedom would not be possible without such a field. Freedom emerges from within the world and presupposes an integral prereflective relationality of self and world that Cartesianism tries in vain to establish on a purely reflective level. For Merleau-Ponty a person must already be intertwined in a world of meaning before a personal act of freedom can exist.

Now here is the fundamental difference between Sartre and Merleau-Ponty: for Sartre freedom creates meaning and hence is more fundamental, while for Merleau-Ponty meaning is more fundamental and is presupposed by freedom. For Sartre, we are condemned to be free; for Merleau-Ponty we are condemned to meaning.[5]

This major, radical difference allows us to see to what extent Sartre is still bound in the Cartesian framework and to what extent Merleau-Ponty has given us a radical alternative. Sartre's own criticism of Descartes comes back to haunt his own view: How can we render intelligible the claim that the free self *creates* meaning in an utter vacuum of meaning? The Cartesian ego, like Sartre's free self in its original choice of itself, lacks a place to stand to launch its decision, or better it lacks a body related to the world as the context of free choice. Sartre simply pushes the old Cartesian problem of how a spontaneity can act on an object back to the level of prereflective original freedom, without solving it. On the level of original freedom the problem still persists: How can I choose myself and posit ends if I do not presuppose a field of possible projects? Prior to the unfettered act of original freedom such a field of possible projects does not exist. Indeed original freedom, for Sartre, constitutes *ex nihilo* this field. But how was it a choice *of* anything, a choice between possible projects?

For Merleau-Ponty, the matter is different. Freedom is a phenomenon situated in a field of meaning. Freedom is the task of deciding upon the many possible meaningful projects that loom before me in the world. Freedom is not so much a power of nihilation as it is a power of appropriation. By situating the self bodily in a meaningful relation to the world prior to reflection, Merleau-Ponty has refused to objectify either the world or the self. For such an incarnate self, the Cartesian problem, Sartre's problem, has been dismantled literally before it can "get off the ground."

What Sartre does not adequately see, I think Merleau-Ponty would say, is that the historical given of a particular place and time is not presented, at least at the immediate prereflective level of experience as a *task only,* something to be overcome, but it also presents itself as a gift. As Kierkegaard has so eloquently put it: "actuality (the historical actuality) relates in a two-fold way to the subject: partly as a gift that will not admit of being rejected, and partly as a task to be realized."[6] By concentrating only on the task of being a person, Sartre misses the point that when I come to choose, to take up my task, I do so in a setting which is, in the most literal sense, *given* to be *received.* Prior to the level in which my presence in the world as a gift to be received is taken up by me as the field of my projects, i.e., prior to my body's coming to relate itself to itself, I cannot be said to have emerged in the fullest sense as a free and responsible person. And yet, every free action, every task taken up, has its origin in and retains its relation to my prereflective presence in the world which is my body in its relationality to its environment. Sartre's program seems to stall in the dimension where freedom is viewed under the categories of obstacle/task; Merleau-Ponty, on the other hand, breaks through to see the richer dialectic of freedom as being that of giving/receiving *and* obstacle/task. Merleau-Ponty does not deny the tasks of personal existence but grounds those projects in a deeper sense of the world's presence to me as a gift to be received.

Notes

1. Maurice Merleau-Ponty, *Phenomenology of Perception,* trans. Colin Smith (New York: Routledge and Kegan Paul), 1962, 434–56. Hereafter *PP.*

2. Jean-Paul Sartre, *Being and Nothingness,* trans. Hazel E. Barnes (New York: Washington Square Press, 1956), 559–711. Hereafter *BN.*

3. Of course I realize that using these chapters as representative of the views of Merleau-Ponty and Sartre tends to freeze the two protagonists in positions taken in the 40s. I also realize that they continued, until Merleau-Ponty's untimely death (1961), that friendly dialogue on freedom. For example, in Sartre's *Search for a Method* (1960), he says, "Man is for himself and others, a signifying being" (152). This may sound like Sartre has come closer to Merleau-Ponty's position. However, I think this is a superficial similarity hiding a deep disagreement: as we will see, for Sartre, man, "the signifying being," creates meaning in an original act of freedom, whereas for Merleau-Ponty, man becomes free in a received context of meaning. Their original disagreement persists.

4. The example of an unclimbable rockface as an obstacle to freedom is Sartre's own example, and of course Merleau-Ponty is aware of this (See *BN,* 627). Other "surface" similarities also are clearly discernible, e.g., Merleau-Ponty's field characteristics of spatiality, temporality, and intersubjectivity are strikingly close, and purposefully so, to Sartre's "My Place, My Past, My Fellowman" (*BN,* 629ff.). But again these are only surface similarities. When Merleau-Ponty says, "There is no freedom without a field" (*PP,* 439), we may wonder how far this is from Sartre's "Man encounters an obstacle only within the field of his freedom" (*BN,* 628). Yet the difference is crucial. It is the difference between a field constituted in an act of original freedom (Sartre) and a field of meaning already given in perception within which freedom becomes actual (Merleau-Ponty). One other example of the surface similarity and the deep difference: Sartre says, "there is freedom only in a *situation,* and there is a situation only through freedom" (*BN,* 629). Merleau-Ponty would agree there is freedom only in a situation; he would disagree that the self in an absolute original freedom constitutes that situation.

5. Merleau-Ponty's stress on meaning is already apparent in the preface of *Phenomenology of Perception.* For example, he says, "In the silence of primary consciousness can be seen appearing not only what words mean, but also what things mean: the core of primary meaning round which the acts of naming and expression take shape" (*PP,* xv). It is important to note here also that "meaning" is only one of the possible translations of the French *sens.* It can also be translated as "directions," "sense," "tenor," etc. Yet there is a common strand, as Merleau-Ponty

says, “In all the uses of the word *sens,* we find the same fundamental notion of a being orientated or polarized in the direction of what he is not, and thus we are always brought back to a conception of the subject as *ek-stase,* and to a relationship of active transcendence between the subject and the world” (*PP,* 430).

6. Søren Kierkegaard, *The Concept of Irony,* trans. Lee M. Capel (Bloomington: Indiana University Press, 1971), 293.

14

Merleau-Ponty's Criticisms of Sartre's Theory of Freedom

Jon Stewart

The history of the development of the personal and professional relationship between Jean-Paul Sartre and Maurice Merleau-Ponty is a long and complicated one. They knew each other over a period of many years and in a number of different roles and contexts. They were acquaintances as school comrades from a very early age and later became colleagues in the Resistance and on the editorial board of *Les Temps modernes*. Their thought, despite their many differences, was bound together as tightly as their lives, and their collective intellectual output can be seen as a sort of dialogue. Jean Hyppolite, the Hegel scholar who was the lifelong friend of both men, describes their relationship in his eulogistic essay on Merleau-Ponty in the following terms: "We must insist on the living and never interrupted dialogue with Jean-Paul Sartre. They were both counted as existentialists, whether to criticize them together or to oppose the one to the other. Between them it is a matter of a dialogue where at the same time they opposed and complemented one another."[1] Taking up this insight that Sartre is Merleau-Ponty's chief interlocutor and that their philosophical works constitute a sort of dialogue, I would like to explore one of the most important points of contact in their intellectual debate, namely the issue of human freedom which played such an important role in virtually all of French existentialist philosophy.

In Sartre's celebrated play, *The Flies*, it is Jupiter who proclaims, "The painful secret of gods and kings is that men are free."[2] This proclamation can be seen in many respects as the starting point of Sartre's thought. Most commentators would agree that the central thesis of *Being and Nothingness,* if not of the entirety of Sartre's philosophy, is that of human freedom.[3] This theme runs throughout his essays, novels, theater pieces, political works, book reviews, and sundry introductions and prefaces, and can be found in every period of his intellectual development.[4] Thus, to dub Sartre's thought a "philosophy of freedom" or to attach to his person the epithet "philosopher of freedom," as some scholars have done, is by no means inappropriate.[5] The theory of freedom constitutes in many ways the centerpiece of *Being and Nothingness* from which many of the work's other theses are derived. Any attempt to provide here a general overview of Sartre's lifelong struggle with the concept of freedom would necessarily fall short, since such an overview has been made the subject of book-length studies.[6] Given that the theory finds without a doubt its most detailed and systematic exposition in that work, for the purposes of this essay I wish by and large to confine myself to Sartre's account of freedom in *Being and Nothingness,* alluding to other texts only in order to illustrate the aspects of his theory which are expounded there.

Although Sartre in his own lifetime never published the ethical theory that he had promised in the final pages of *Being and Nothingness,*[7] nevertheless, as the recently published *opus posthumous* shows,[8] he was genuinely concerned to develop such a theory as a second part of the ontological system begun in *Being and Nothingness.*[9] Therefore, it is clear that in *Being and Nothingness* Sartre sets as his end the establishment of the ontological basis for human freedom, since he intends later to derive ethical consequences from it. Sartre confirms this later when he says that the theory of freedom presented in *Being and Nothingness* was not exactly what he originally meant to say: "What I wanted to say is that one is responsible for oneself even if the acts are provoked by something outside the self."[10] Thus, the emphasis is on the moral aspects of the theory which are only briefly touched on in *Being and Nothingness* itself in the short section "Freedom and Responsibility," where Sartre tries to draw conclusions about the nature of responsibility on the basis of his ontological account of freedom. The moralizing tone of this section is unmistakable: "The essential consequence of our earlier remarks is that man being condemned to be free carries the weight of the whole world on his shoulders."[11] In order to derive this extreme and severe concept of responsibility, Sartre's first task is to establish a wide-ranging notion of human freedom. He tries to do just this in the first two sections of the chapter "Being and Doing: Freedom" in *Being and Nothingness,* which constitutes the first half of part 4 of the work. This chapter is divided into three rambling sections, each devoted to different aspects of his theory of freedom and action.

We should note here that Sartre modified some of his more radical views on this subject in the course of his intellectual development, and these modifications themselves have in turn been the source of much discussion. The theory of freedom eighteen years later in *Critique of Dialectical Reason* is not the same as that in *Being and Nothingness,* and his account of the powers of socialization only eight years later in *Saint Genet: Actor and Martyr* seems to contradict some of the basic tenets of his early work. As one can readily observe from his comments in a number of interviews,[12] Sartre tempers considerably his claims about the absolute scope of freedom. However, aside from this amendment, the precise nature of the modifications is far from clear, and there is a great deal of work to be done in the literature before anything resembling a consensus is reached. Nevertheless, some have argued that there is more continuity on this issue between the early and the late Sartre than is generally acknowledged.[13] For our purposes here, I wish to leave to the side the issue of the continuity of the early and late thought and to limit my account primarily to Sartre's early philosophy and above all to *Being and Nothingness.*

Although freedom cannot be regarded as the central thesis of *Phenomenology of Perception,* the final chapter of that work is dedicated solely to this problem and tries to draw conclusions about this issue based on the account of experience and perception that Merleau-Ponty elaborates in the rest of the book. Equally important for our purposes is the fact that this short chapter represents one of the most serious challenges to Sartre's theory ever issued. Nowhere else in the entire *Phenomenology of Perception* does Merleau-Ponty discuss Sartre's philosophy more directly, and in many ways he seems to take the theory of freedom as paradigmatic for Sartre's thinking as a whole. This criticism of Sartre is in many ways revelatory for understanding much of the basic orientation of Merleau-Ponty's philosophy in its own right.

In the present essay, I wish to take up an analysis of this final section of *Phenomenology of Perception,* where Merleau-Ponty issues his famous criticism of Sartre's view. I will isolate and systematically analyze his counterarguments to Sartre's position as discrete units, evaluating their merits in terms of Sartre's theory. Thus, I have organized my discussion according to the individual objections that he raises. Instead of trying to recount exhaustively Merleau-Ponty's criticisms, I have attempted to isolate the principal ones in order to treat them in some detail. I will ultimately argue that Sartre has the theoretical equipment to deal with Merleau-Ponty's charges and that his theory is not as naive as it is often portrayed as being. Moreover, I will claim that, in the final analysis, Merleau-Ponty's criticisms are not necessarily inconsistent with Sartre's view.[14] This thesis runs contrary to most of the accounts in the secondary literature which are more sympathetic to Merleau-Ponty's critique.

The Conceptual Problem of Freedom

According to Merleau-Ponty's first counterargument, there is something fundamentally incoherent about the very idea of radical freedom. Instead of criticizing Sartre's theory from without, Merleau-Ponty tries to demonstrate how Sartre's theory renders the very notion of freedom unintelligible. His criticism can thus be seen as an immanent critique. Merleau-Ponty argues that if, as Sartre says, every action is free and we are at absolutely every moment free in a uniform fashion, then the very concept of freedom would be destroyed, since a free *act* would not be possible:[15]

> The result, however, of this first reflection on freedom would appear to be to rule it out altogether. If indeed it is the case that our freedom is the same in all our actions, and even in our passions, if it is not to be measured in terms of our conduct, and if the slave displays freedom as much by living in fear as by breaking his chains, then it cannot be held that there is such a thing as *free action,* freedom being anterior to all actions.[16]

This way of conceiving the issue makes freedom a sort of background for all of human existence, which proves to be self-contradictory upon closer examination. Sartre's view makes freedom independent of any particular action and by so doing destroys the very concept of action. In order to establish freedom, we must attempt to determine certain characteristics of action as criteria by which we can distinguish a free act from one that is not free. But when any action at all counts for free by virtue of the fact that freedom is synonymous with consciousness or existence in general, then the idea of freedom is rendered meaningless. Freedom would simply be a fundamental way of being in the world or as Merleau-Ponty puts it, our "primordial acquisition" or "the nature of consciousness" (*Pp,* 499; *PP,* 437). Freedom conceived in this way rules out the possibility of isolated acts that we can readily identify as free since, indeed, every act is free: "It will not be possible to declare: 'Here freedom makes its appearance,' since free action, in order to be discernible, has to stand out against a background of life from which it is entirely, or almost entirely, absent. We may say in this case that it is everywhere, but equally nowhere" (*Pp,* 499; *PP,* 437). In order for the very concept of freedom to make sense, there must simultaneously exist its opposite, i.e., nonfreedom or limitation. These two concepts mutually determine one another and make each other conceptually intelligible. Sartre's theory, however, wishes to insist on the one and entirely do away with the other. This is, as Merleau-Ponty points out, quite problematic since the two concepts are clearly complementary. In order to be able to talk about free actions at all, we must know what counts for a nonfree action. There must be a sphere of nonfree actions against which the free ones can stand out and be recognized as free in the first place.

If freedom is the fundamental way of being in the world that always characterizes human beings and every act is *ipso facto* a free one, then the concept of freedom becomes meaningless, since there is nothing which could constitute a genuine obstacle to it. Whatever I do, I do freely, and there is nothing that stands in the way: "There are merely intentions immediately followed by their effects" (*Pp*, 499; *PP*, 437). This destroys our notion of freedom by removing all intermediary elements between intentions and actions which we usually consider to hinder or limit our freedom in some way. If freedom "is to be describable as freedom, there must be something to hold it away from its objectives" (*Pp*, 500; *PP*, 438). If all potency is immediately actuality and every intention in itself an action, then we can no longer talk of freedom at all. From this initial counterargument, Merleau-Ponty concludes that there must be certain fixed aspects of the world which could conceivably serve as obstacles to our freedom and against which genuinely free acts stand out as free. He calls this a "field," and in the next argument he tries to distinguish different elements which might be thought to characterize it.

Sartre's theory lends itself to this criticism in many ways, since it seems as if it has confined freedom to mere freedom of thought and by so doing has made it such that we are always free. Whatever happens, it seems we are always ultimately free to think what we will. This comes out well in *The Flies* when Jupiter says to the insolent Orestes, "If you dare to claim that you are free, then it would be necessary to boast the freedom of the prisoner bound in chains at the bottom of a dungeon, or of a crucified slave." We can probably assume that Orestes' response is Sartre's as well: "Why not?"[17] Elsewhere Sartre revels in similar paradoxical formulations. He begins an essay from the period shortly after the Liberation by saying, "We were never more free than under the German Occupation."[18] If we are free according to this view even under such circumstances as the Occupation, then when are we ever not free? It is precisely in this context that Merleau-Ponty takes up a discussion of freedom in his essay "The War Has Taken Place," which was published in the same year as *Phenomenology of Perception*. There Merleau-Ponty claims that the kind of absolute or existential freedom which Sartre outlines is in fact empty or meaningless. Sartre argues that even in the most dire of existential situations man is free. During the Occupation, one nevertheless always had the freedom of thought—to approve, to disapprove, etc. But precisely this kind of freedom is limited to a sphere where it can only be thought and never realized. Merleau-Ponty writes, "This is no reason to surrender all that is exterior and to confine ourselves to our thoughts, which are always free, even in the mind of a slave. This division of interior and exterior is abstract."[19] Merleau-Ponty, roughly following Hegel's criticism of stoicism in *Phenomenology of Spirit,* reproaches Sartre for holding an empty stoic view of freedom.[20] An abstract freedom is always a limited freedom, i.e., limited to thought, and thus this freedom is in the final analysis no freedom at all. Stoicism historically appears at periods of helplessness and oppression; the Roman Empire presented such a time as did the Occupation of France. During the Occupation, one was free to withdraw from the world and dwell in the realm of thought: "we were not denied Plato or Descartes or rehearsals at the Conservatory on Saturday mornings. We could begin our adolescence all over again, return to our gods and great writers as if they were vices."[21] But this kind of stoic escapism cannot count for real freedom, and it appears instead merely as "the reveries of captives" (*Sens,* 260; *SNS,* 147). Freedom, according to Merleau-Ponty, only makes sense if it is accompanied and empowered by real possibility: "no effective freedom exists without some power" (*Sens,* 261; *SNS,* 148). He writes, "A judgment without words is incomplete; a word to which there can be no reply is nonsense; my freedom is interwoven with that of others by way of the world" (*Sens,* 260; *SNS,* 147).

It is important to note that Sartre operates with two different notions of freedom, only one of which is addressed here by Merleau-Ponty. There is first the fundamental sense in which we are always free to choose our project. Here freedom characterizes what we are as human beings and distinguishes us from objects. This notion has been referred to as "ontological freedom"[22] or "categorial freedom."[23] In other words, for Sartre it is the very ontological nature of consciousness to be free. Freedom is our way of being-in-the-world. In this sense, it is the same as consciousness. It is this conception of freedom that Merleau-Ponty's first argument rightly takes issue with. Clearly, on this ontological account, the very notion of freedom is in jeopardy; however, there is another more measured notion of freedom in Sartre, which can be called "freedom in situation"[24] or "contingent freedom."[25] This is the kind of freedom we have when we choose the means for a given end; thus, it is "contingent" with respect to the posited end and takes place only in a "situation" determined and created by that end. It is clear that Merleau-Ponty recognizes both of these notions of freedom,[26] but he seems to address only one of them with this criticism.

In many ways Sartre seems to be his own worst enemy by presenting his theory with so many paradoxical formulas which so readily lend themselves to misinterpretation. It is clear that with all the slogans aside, Sartre never denies that there are obstacles to our freedom. In fact, in his account of the situation and specifically of the environment, he says explicitly that the existence of obstacles is necessary for the very concept of freedom (*EN,* 563ff.; *BN,* 506ff.). He agrees with Merleau-Ponty that there must be a separation between intentions and action for freedom to make sense. On this point it seems that there is ultimately no conflict between the two.

Freedom, the Field, and Sedimentation

Our intuitive notion of freedom as autonomy is one that involves commitment and responsibility. In the philosophical tradition, theories of freedom are often accompanied by theories of morality, and, as we have noted, it is clear that Sartre as well wants to derive moral conclusions from his theory of freedom. Above all, he wants to be able to derive a strong notion of human responsibility. But according to Merleau-Ponty's second counterargument, the theory of radical freedom rules out the very possibility of a meaningful conception of responsibility, since it conceives of action simply as an isolated monadic instant entirely separated from the past and the future:

> The very notion of freedom demands that our decision should plunge into the future, that something should have been done by it, that the subsequent instant should benefit from its predecessor and, though not necessitated, should be at least required by it. If freedom is doing, it is necessary that what it does should not be immediately undone by a new freedom. Each instant, therefore, must not be a closed world. (*Pp,* 499; *PP,* 437)

Free acts must be acts that have meaningful results and which imply commitments. If each act can immediately be erased by the next without there being any meaningful pattern of logic behind them, and no continuity of character in the individual can be discerned in this chaos of freedom, then we cannot talk about genuine autonomy or ethical responsibility which rests on some conception of concern or commitment to a general conception of moral obligation to other human beings. Freedom cannot be seen as isolated instances.[27] A free act must be one that is performed in the context of a freely chosen project, one that is done in accordance with the project. If, however, there is not a project that fixes the background or horizon of action, and one merely acts arbitrarily, as if by whim, then we cannot talk about moral responsibility or rationality.

Merleau-Ponty indicates that there must be stable factors or intelligible structures in our behavior by which our actions can be perceived as free in the first place. Such structures constitute our rootedness or, as Merleau-Ponty says, our "sedimentation" in the world:

> Unless there are cycles of behavior, open situations requiring a certain completion and capable of constituting a background to either a confirmatory or transitory decision, we never experience freedom. The choice of an intelligible character is excluded, not only because there is no time anterior to time, but because choice presupposes a prior commitment and because the idea of an initial choice involves a contradiction . . . freedom . . . must have a *field,* which means that there must be for it special possibilities, or realities which tend to cling to being. (*Pp,* 500; *PP,* 438)

The fact that humans tend to act in ways that display certain regularities does not contradict freedom but on the contrary is the very condition for it. Merleau-Ponty states his thesis here succinctly: "there is no freedom without a field" (*Pp,* 501; *PP,* 439).

Merleau-Ponty goes on to outline different aspects of the factical field which Sartre's theory seems to smooth over. He begins by granting Sartre's claim that any number of characteristics and qualities of objects do not inhere in things themselves but rather only come to light in terms of our freely chosen project. Thus, the rock is for one person scalable, for another beautiful, and for another something more or less indifferent. But Merleau-Ponty undermines the complete relativity that Sartre seems to ascribe to such judgments by indicating the fixed nature of certain facts ordered inside of a particular judgment or project. Granted that my project to climb the rock makes it appear against the categories of scalable or not scalable, this does not contradict the fact that certain rocks are more scalable in themselves than others and that my project has not determined this relation. By virtue of our body, we are rooted in a determinate manner that we have not chosen and cannot change. We have, as it were, a natural self from which we cannot budge. We are embodied, and this constitutes our natural limit. This is a fact about the world and about the nature of the rocks relative to one another and judged against the common criterion of my project. Such facts constitute the field against which freedom acts.

By way of further elaborating the notion of a field or our sedimentation in the world, Merleau-Ponty talks about "a natural self" (*Pp*, 502; *PP*, 440) in a way that sometimes seems to imply that there is some predetermined, fixed ontological entity called the human subject. However, his claim need not be construed as being so strong. In his analyses he points out certain universal ways of human perception that point to a kind of natural subject which need not imply any ontological commitment about the nature of man. He refers to his earlier account of perception (*Pp*, 304; *PP*, 263) where he pointed out that certain figures are universally conceived and organized by the human mind in the same way. His example in this chapter is a series of dots which the human mind spontaneously orders and seizes as six pairs of dots:

> It is as if, on the hither side of our judgment and our freedom, someone were assigning such and such a significance to such and such a given grouping. It is indeed true that perceptual structures do not always force themselves upon the observer; there are some which are ambiguous. But these reveal even more effectively the presence within us of spontaneous evaluation: for they are elusive shapes which suggest constantly changing meanings to us. (*Pp*, 503; *PP*, 440)

This universality of experience implies certain fixed structures in human thought which are not determined as a result of a cognitive act of the will. These cognitive or perceptual structures make experience possible in the first place since without them, "we would not have a world" (*Pp*, 503; *PP*, 441). They are also necessary for human communication and intersubjectivity which would seem to be problematic given Sartre's account.[28] The structures of perception, although themselves not something that we can freely choose, thus constitute one such given field which makes freedom possible in the first place. Merleau-Ponty adds that perception is not the only sphere where a field is given or fixed: "This is true not only of an impersonal and, generally speaking, abstract function such as 'external perception.' There is something comparable present in all evaluations" (*Pp*, 503–4; *PP*, 441).

Merleau-Ponty's counterargument here does not seem to compel agreement, since Sartre responds by way of anticipation to this issue in the section, "My Fellowman," where he outlines a number of universal linguistic, social, and psychological structures which seem to be imposed on the individual without his assent. Sartre says that we are thrown into a world in which techniques have a meaning which we have not given them. In other words, we come into a world where other people have already created certain meanings for things: "One may recall, for example, the innumerable host of meanings which are independent of *my choice* and which I discover if I live in a city: streets, houses, shops, streetcars and buses, directing signs, warning sounds, music on the radio, etc."[29] The objection to the theory of freedom issued by this section is that such adventitious universal structures, meanings, and techniques seem to constitute a limit to human freedom since after all, we do not personally create them. The meanings of, for example, a train schedule or a traffic sign cannot be altered by an act of my free will. Not only are the meanings of objects determined adventitiously and without my help, but also the meaning of my very being is also determined in a thousand different ways by the language I speak, the social skills and competences I have acquired, and so forth. These things distinguish me from people from other countries and other social classes, yet these meanings have not been consciously chosen by me in the exercise of my freedom. Predictably enough, Sartre argues that we are free only in the context of such universal structures and techniques. In this section, Sartre discusses at some length the nature of language as an example for all such preestablished universal structures which come from without and whose meaning is not determined by the individual or his project. We do not need to examine his account of language here in great detail, and I will only touch on it here to the extent necessary for illuminating his account of freedom and facticity.

We seem to be limited by our fixed historical situation and the level of technological, social, and linguistic development of our culture. As Sartre notes, the subject is thrown into a world in which he apprehends various techniques of the instrumental complexes of others as objects or patterns of conduct. The individual freely historicizes those techniques and accepts them as part of his world. By doing so, one is responsible for the world one has so constituted. Sartre says, "By arising in a world in which Pierre and Paul speak in a certain way, stick to the right when driving a bicycle or a car, etc., and by constituting these free patterns of conduct into meaningful objects, the for-itself is responsible for the fact that *there is* a world in which *they* stick to the right, in which *they* speak French, etc." (*EN,* 579; *BN,* 521). The act of the collective other thus becomes constituted as an object by the for-itself. Sartre argues, "This historization, which is the effect of the for-itself's free choice, in no way restricts its freedom; quite the contrary, it is *in this world* and no other that its freedom comes into play" (*EN,* 579; *BN,* 521). In other words, by historicizing the world, the for-itself gives itself a context within which its freedom can operate. This does not mean that we are free to choose the society or culture that we live in or the language we speak, but rather we choose ourselves as existing in a particular society or culture: "For to be free is not to choose the historic world in which one arises—which would have no meaning—but to choose oneself in the world whatever this may be" (*EN*, 579; *BN*, 521).

Sartre continues by arguing that it is absurd to think that the techniques of one's time restrict human possibilities. It is perfectly obvious that different ages at different stages of development have developed differing techniques. The question is now whether we can say that a certain past age, for example, was somehow less free since it did not know modern technology. Is someone living in the Middle Ages not free since he does not have at his disposal the use of the automobile or the airplane? This absurdity seems to be what the objection raised here is implicitly committed to. Clearly, these possibilities only appear to us since we are wont to see them as representative of our own techniques. Someone living in the Middle Ages has clearly accepted and historicized a world with very different techniques which would preclude his perception of the possible use of the automobile or the airplane on his horizon of experience. Although people in the Middle Ages could not possibly have imagined our current level of technology, this cannot be seen as a limit to their freedom.[30] Their freedom existed in the sphere of their own level of technological development. It would be a perverse and philosophically uninteresting notion of freedom which required as its condition that one have at one's disposal every single possible technique from every conceivable age. On such a view, one would not be free unless one could freely choose to speak a language not yet invented or employ a technology not yet developed. Thus, this objection is implicitly committed to a wholly implausible conception of freedom which we need not entertain further. For Sartre, the sphere of freedom that we are concerned with is that localized inside of a given network of meanings and techniques.

The upshot of Sartre's discussion here about universally predetermined meanings amounts to seeing such meanings merely as so many aspects of the facticity of the human condition. As Sartre says, the universally defined meaning of a thing "is not distinguished from the quality of the in-itself" (*EN*, 568; *BN*, 511). Thus, although we do not create these significations or techniques any more than the climber creates the crag, nevertheless it is through our projects that these things take on the meaning and value that they do for us in the context of our own lives. The existence of such universal structures cannot therefore be seen as limiting one's freedom any more than any other aspect of one's facticity limits it.

Generally speaking, it is by no means clear how Merleau-Ponty's conception of a "field" differs from Sartre's conception of facticity or the situation. It is clear that Merleau-Ponty recognizes Sartre's account of freedom in situation, since years later he says explicitly, "human beings, as Sartre presents them in *Being and Nothingness,* are situated beings."[31] Sartre would clearly grant that there are universal structures of perception which are a part of what makes us human, just like walking upright or the use of language. He even grants that we do not choose these: "each man finds himself in the presence of *meanings* which do not come into the world through him" (*EN,* 577; *BN,* 520). The question is whether or not such structures represent a threat to Sartre's theory or can be conceived of as truly limiting our freedom. Clearly, according to Sartre's discussion in the aforementioned section, they do not. Thus, we need some demonstration that these universal structures actually limit freedom in a way that Sartre's theory does not allow. Lacking this, it appears that Sartre and Merleau-Ponty are also ultimately in agreement on this issue.

The Social Order and History

Merleau-Ponty's last major counterargument involves demonstrating the phenomenological rootedness of human beings in social and historical conditions. He gives an extended and provocative analysis of social class that is intended as a criticism of Sartre's apparent claim that one is always spontaneously free to choose oneself and thus one's identification with a particular social class.[32] What Merleau-Ponty points out is that social class is not merely a question of free decision but rather is a way of being-in-the-world.[33] He gives examples of a factory worker and a day laborer and describes their unhappy social experience. He writes, in such cases "one cannot in any case talk about a choice . . . it is enough that I should be born into the world and that I exist in order to experience my life as full of difficulties and constraints—I do not choose so to experience it" (*Pp,* 507; *PP,* 444). My experience in a social class is not something which I have determined through the exercise of my freedom. It belongs rather to the facticity of the situation. But this situation does not determine me absolutely either. One's perception of oneself in a certain class is based upon a perception of a common experience that one shares with others, "in a certain basis of co-existence."[34] As Merleau-Ponty says, "Thus to be a bourgeois or a worker is not only to be aware of being one or the other, it is to identify oneself as worker or bourgeois through an implicit or existential project which merges into our way of patterning the world and co-existing with other people" (*Pp*, 510–11; *PP*, 447). What assigns us to a particular social class is not an arbitrary act of the will but rather our common experience with others who share our lot and with whom we identify. These common experiences, which last a lifetime, shape who we are and cannot be seen as the object of free choice. Merleau-Ponty concludes,

> For class is a matter neither for observation nor decree; like the appointed order of the capitalistic system, like revolution, before being thought it is lived through as an obsessive presence, as possibility, enigma and myth. To make class-consciousness the outcome of a decision and a choice is to say that problems are solved on the day they are posed, that every question already contains the reply that it awaits; it is, in short, to revert to immanence and abandon the attempt to understand history. (*Pp*, 509–10; *PP*, 446–47)

The attempt to see class affiliation as merely a matter of personal choice is deeply misguided since it badly underestimates the way of being in the world common to members of various classes and to those with common experiences.

This counterargument is, however, something of a strawman, since Sartre's theory does not commit him to claiming that one freely or arbitrarily chooses one's social class. In fact, he discusses at some length how common language and techniques in some sense make us what we are in terms of class affiliation. He agrees that these various techniques shape one's way of perceiving and of being-in-the-world: "to be a Savoyard is not simply to inhabit the high valleys of Savoy; it is, among a thousand other things, to ski in the winters, to use the ski as a mode of transportation" (*EN*, 570; *BN*, 513). These techniques and habits are what makes one person French and another German, one person bourgeois, another proletariat. The essential question is whether or not these things represent a threat or limit to freedom. Once again it is clear from Sartre's analysis of freedom in situation that they do not. These techniques provide us with a certain modality of being-in-the-world, and the exercise of freedom takes place within this sphere.

Merleau-Ponty then turns to the issue of history and offers a *reductio ad absurdum* in refutation of what he perceives as Sartre's view that every individual act of history is one that issues from an absolute freedom that is not grounded in any past or tradition. The result would be, he claims, that there would be no identifiable meaning or trends in history which obviously do exist and can be discerned by any astute observer.[35] He writes,

> If indeed I made myself into a worker or a bourgeois by an absolute initiative, and if in general terms nothing ever courted our freedom, history would display no structure, no event would be seen to take shape in it, and anything might emerge from anything else. . . . History would never move in any direction, nor would it be possible to say that even over a short period of time events were conspiring to produce any definite outcome. (*Pp*, 512; *PP*, 449)

This would rule out any talk of historical movements,[36] as Merleau-Ponty illustrates with the persuasive example of the Napoleonic dictatorship in 1799. According to Sartre's purported view, Napoleon's rise to power would be simply a question of the free choice of one man. For Merleau-Ponty, on the other hand, although Napoleon's will and ambition doubtless played a role, there was also a much larger historical context which made these events possible. Instead of it being purely a question of individual personalities, it was the general historical moment which in a sense presented itself: "What is known as the significance of events is not an idea which produces them, or the fortuitous result of their occurring together. It is the concrete project of a future which is elaborated within social co-existence and in the One before any personal decision is made" (*Pp*, 513; *PP*, 449). For Merleau-Ponty, there is a social-historical context of a universal "one" or anonymous collectivity which is prior to any cognitive volition or desire. There are thus two factors involved: individual free will and a fixed historical context. These two stand in a constant dialectical interaction: "There is an exchange between generalized and individual existence, each receiving and giving something" (*Pp*, 513; *PP*, 450). There is thus a reciprocal movement between the faceless forces of history and the will and ambition of individuals.

Sartre is not blind to this kind of argument, and in his account of freedom, he himself uses a great number of historical examples. Although it is true that he ascribes an important role to individual initiative in history, as his example of the conversion of Clovis illustrates (*EN*, 501; *BN*, 446), nevertheless it does not follow that for him history is chaotic or unintelligible. On the contrary, he claims that history is coherent first in terms of the present historical configuration and second precisely in terms of the goals of the individual figures involved. The events of the Napoleonic dictatorship are important for us given the course of history since then and given our own present political agenda. There is a meaning and λογος in history, but it is one that we seek out. Secondly, it is precisely the goals and ambitions of the individual historical actors which gave history its meaning. This is the point of Sartre's example of Clovis. One cannot distinguish between his ambition, his action and the historical meaning of his work. His ambition is his action, and its meaning or structure is simply an interpretation of this ambition, i.e., Clovis wanted to expand Roman influence in Gaul. Thus, Sartre's view neither reduces history to random actions or particular individuals nor does it render it impossible to distinguish meaning and structure in history. Finally, Sartre is also aware of the weight of the historical context as is evinced by the section, "My Past." He grants that such factical elements exist, but the key point is his denial that they in any way threaten our freedom. Merleau-Ponty's account of the reciprocal relation between the historical context and the individual in no way contradicts Sartre's fundamental intuition, since even in this reciprocal relation the individual remains free.

Freedom as Reciprocity

At the end of his criticism of Sartre, Merleau-Ponty, after having rejected Sartre's view, presents his own theory of freedom. The central thesis of Merleau-Ponty's theory of freedom is that the individual is a preset structure of cognition, history, intersubjectivity, etc. and that these structures, far from causing one to be determined or taking away from one's freedom, in fact make freedom possible in the first place. In a fashion parallel to his account of history, he argues that there is a reciprocal movement between the individual and the world: "The world is already constituted, but also never completely; in the first case we are acted upon, in the second we are open to an infinite number of possibilities. . . . we exist in both ways *at once*. There is, therefore, never determinism and never absolute choice, I am never a thing and never bare consciousness" (*Pp*, 517; *PP*, 453). The world and the individuals who inhabit it mutually condition each other. The world shapes the individual by its preformed meanings and structures. The individual is thrown into a world and is obliged to adapt himself to these structures and techniques. He learns a language and specific forms of social competence, etc. Although he seems to be determined in this sense, he is nevertheless free in his turn to shape the world. Language and social techniques are after all human inventions which change with time. Humans are free to modify and improve the institutions and techniques which have been handed down to them. In this sense they shape the world by an exercise of their autonomy. There is thus a reciprocity between the individual and the world, and it is only in this domain that we can speak of freedom.

Although Sartre couches the matter rhetorically in a much different way, it seems that his theory, in fact, is not so distant from Merleau-Ponty's account of reciprocity. Although he denies straightforwardly that the world or the in-itself can ever serve as a motive for action, nevertheless Sartre does admit the existence of universal structures and techniques as a fundamental fact of human existence. Nothing stands in the way of his admitting that these clearly do determine and shape us as individual agents. However, Sartre refuses to grant that this fact limits our freedom in any way. Thus, he can perfectly well grant Merleau-Ponty's account of reciprocity, merely by indicating that the sphere of freedom which he has outlined as freedom in situation exhibits both sides of the reciprocal movement. I am always in a concrete situation which is determined in many different ways apart from myself and my project, but yet I am always free to determine other aspects of it by my free choice of particular ends.

Not surprisingly the two different conceptions of freedom that we are presented with here issue from two radically different conceptions of the individual human subject. According to Sartre's dualistic view, the for-itself is fundamentally distinct and separate from the world. Thus, it is the subject or the for-itself alone which is entirely responsible for the creation of meaning and for the positing of particular projects. For Sartre the individual is and must be free, since there is no genuine interaction with the world that might hinder freedom. Thus, the individual can never be hindered in his projects by the world but rather only by limitations which he himself posits and recognizes. The fundamental ontological concept for Merleau-Ponty is not the dualistic split of for-itself and in-itself but rather the more Heideggerian sounding notion of being-with. For Merleau-Ponty we are always already situated in the world. The question of interaction is thus unproblematic, since we are constantly in reciprocal and dialectical interaction with the world. Thus, freedom for Merleau-Ponty is conceived of as reciprocity. Although the world can influence and shape our actions, it does not follow that we are not free. At bottom there are two different ontologies at work from which spring two competing views of freedom. The differences in these views for the issue of freedom are, however, not as radical as is often thought.

Notes

1. Jean Hyppolite, "Existence et dialectique dans la philosophie de Merleau-Ponty," *Les Temps modernes* 17, nos. 184–85 (1961), 230.

2. Jean-Paul Sartre, *Huis clos suivi de Les mouches* (Paris: Gallimard, 1947), 200.

3. See Simone de Beauvoir, *La Cérémonie des adieux* (Paris: Gallimard, 1981), 505. Hereafter *CA*. Here Sartre says explicitly, "*Being and Nothingness* is a work about freedom."

4. For a very useful general overview of the development of this concept in Sartre's philosophy, see de Beauvoir, *CA*, 492–527.

5. Cf. Maurice Natanson, "Jean-Paul Sartre's Philosophy of Freedom," *Social Research* 19 (1952), 364–80. R. Guerra Tejada, "Jean-Paul Sartre, filósofo de la libertad," *Filosofía y Letras* 15 (1948), 295–312.

6. Cf. Jürgen Hengelbrock, *Jean-Paul Sartre: Freiheit als Notwendigkeit—Einführung in das philosophische Werk* (Freiburg: Alber, 1989); Christina Howells, *The Necessity of Freedom* (Cambridge: Cambridge University Press, 1988); István Mészáros, *The Work of Sartre,* vol. 1: *Search for Freedom* (Hassocks: The Harvester Press, 1979).

7. *EN,* 692; *BN,* 628. *EN=L'Être et le néant: Essai d'ontologie phénoménologique* (Paris: Gallimard, 1943); *BN=Being and Nothingness,* trans. Hazel E. Barnes (New York: Philosophical Library, 1956).

8. Jean-Paul Sartre, *Cahiers pour une morale* (Paris: Gallimard, 1983). In English as *Notebook for an Ethics,* trans. David Pellauer (Chicago: University of Chicago Press, 1992).

9. Cf. Jeanson's work, which emphasizes the ethical aspects of *Being and Nothingness.* Francis Jeanson, *Le Problème moral et la pensée de Sartre* (Paris: Seuil, 1947). In English as *Sartre and the Problem of Morality,* trans. Robert V. Stone (Bloomington: Indiana University Press, 1980).

10. De Beauvoir, *CA,* 498.

11. *EN,* 612; *BN,* 553. Cf. Orestes' statement in *The Flies:* "I have done my act, Electra, and it was good. I will carry it on my shoulders like a ferryboat will carry its travelers" (Sartre, *Huis clos suivi de Les mouches,* 210).

12. De Beauvoir, *CA,* 497ff. Cf. also Sartre. "Sartre par Sartre," *Situations,* IX (Paris: Gallimard, 1972), 99–134.

13. For example, Margaret Whitford, *Merleau-Ponty's Critique of Sartre's Philosophy* (Lexington: French Forum Publishers, 1982), 58–59. George J. Stack, "Jean-Paul Sartre: Consciousness and Concrete Freedom," *Philosophy Today* 19 (1975), 305–25; Norman McLeod, "Existential Freedom in the Marxism of Jean-Paul Sartre," *Dialogue* 7 (1968–1969), 26–44.

14. This is basically in agreement with John O'Neill's thesis in his "Situation and Temporality," *Philosophy and Phenomenological Research* 28 (1968), 413–22.

15. Cf. Whitford, *Merleau-Ponty's Critique,* 63.

16. *Pp,* 499; *PP,* 436–37. (*Pp=Phénoménologie de la perception* (Paris: Gallimard, 1945); *PP=Phenomenology of Perception,* trans. Colin Smith (London: Routledge and Kegan Paul, 1962).

17. Sartre, *Huis clos suivi de Les mouches,* 227.

18. Jean-Paul Sartre, *Situations,* III: *Lendemains de guerre* (Paris: Gallimard, 1949), 11. Cf. Simone de Beauvoir, *La Force des choses,* vol. 1 (Paris: Gallimard, 1963), 332.

19. *Sens,* 259–60; *SNS,* 147. *Sens=Sens et non-sens* (Paris: Nagel, 1948); *SNS=*

Sense and Non-Sense, trans. Hubert L. Dreyfus and Patricia Allen Dreyfus (Evanston: Northwestern University Press, 1964).

20. Cf. de Beauvoir, *CA,* 497, 505. Cf. Hazel E. Barnes, "The Discovery of Freedom," in her *Sartre* (Philadelphia: J. B. Lippincott Co., 1971), 35.

21. *Sens,* 260; *SNS,* 147. Cf. *Situations,* III, 23–24.

22. Whitford, *Merleau-Ponty's Critique,* 56.

23. John J. Compton, "Sartre, Merleau-Ponty, and Human Freedom," *Journal of Philosophy* 79 (1982), 579; reprinted above 176.

24. Whitford, *Merleau-Ponty's Critique,* 57.

25. Compton, "Sartre, Merleau-Ponty, and Human Freedom," 579ff.

26. Cf. *Signes,* 196; *Signs,* 155. *Signes=Signes* (Paris: Gallimard, 1960); *Signs=Signs,* trans. Richard C. McCleary (Evanston: Northwestern University Press, 1964).

27. Whitford, *Merleau-Ponty's Critique,* 75.

28. Cf. ibid. 71.

29. *EN,* 568; *BN,* 510. Cf. *Pp,* 399; *PP,* 347. Cf. Jean-Paul Sartre, *Les Carnets de la drôle de guerre* (Paris: Gallimard, 1983): "One seizes the world only through a technique, a culture, a condition; and in turn the world so apprehended presents itself as human and returns to human nature" (137).

30. *EN,* 579; *BN,* 522: "For him, who has no relation of any kind with these objects and the techniques which refer to them, there exists a kind of absolute, unthinkable, and undecipherable nothingness. Such a nothingness *can in no way* limit the for-itself which is choosing itself."

31. Maurice Merleau-Ponty, "La Philosophie de l'existence," *Dialogue* 5 (1966–67), 316. In English as "The Philosophy of Existence," trans. Allen S. Weiss, in *Texts and Dialogues: Merleau-Ponty,* ed. Hugh J. Silverman and James Barry, Jr. (New York: Humanities Press, 1992), 135; reprinted below 498.

32. Cf. Whitford, *Merleau-Ponty's Critique,* 74. This is the view of some critics but not of Sartre. Lessing for instance writes, for Sartre, "I am free to construct my own social and political world." Arthur Lessing, "Walking in the World: Sartre and Merleau-Ponty," *Human Inquiries* 11 (1971), 44.

33. Cf. C. M. T. Hanly, "Phenomenology, Consciousness and Freedom," *Dialogue* 5 (1966), 337; reprinted above 78.

34. *Pp,* 509; *PP,* 446. Cf. *Pp,* 416; *PP,* 362: "Despite cultural, moral, occupational and ideological differences, the Russian peasants of 1917 joined the workers of Petrograd and Moscow in the struggle, because they felt that they shared the same fate; class was experienced in concrete terms before becoming the object of a determinate volition."

35. Whitford, *Merleau-Ponty's Critique,* 76; Compton, "Sartre, Merleau-Ponty, and Human Freedom," 585ff; above 182ff.

36. That there is a structure in history does not imply any ontological claim: "We are not asserting that history from end to end has only one meaning, any more than has an individual life. We mean simply that in any case freedom modifies it only by taking up the meaning which history *was offering* at the moment in question, and by a kind of unobtrusive assimilation" (*Pp,* 513; *PP,* 450).

PART 5

POLITICS

15

Sartre and Merleau-Ponty: An Existentialist Quarrel

Graham Daniels

The ideological dispute that occurred between Camus and Sartre in 1952 is familiar enough to the general reader; so much so, that it perhaps overshadows a similar quarrel, of considerable importance in the history of modern French thought, which took place three years later—this time, between Sartre and Merleau-Ponty. While various accounts of this particular episode have appeared in the context of some more broadly based studies,[1] a separate presentation of the main issues it involved will be, it is hoped, of interest to the less specialized reader.

The relationship between Merleau-Ponty and Sartre is well described in the long article which Sartre devoted to his friend after his death in 1961, and published in a special number of *Les Temps modernes.*[2] They had known each other as students in the twenties, but it was the Second World War which really brought the two men together and led them to explore their common interest in philosophies of existence and phenomenology. In 1943, they decided they would one day found a review. When *Les Temps modernes* appeared in 1945, Merleau-Ponty's role and authority were equal to Sartre's, but he would not allow more than mention of his name on the editorial board. He was, Sartre asserts, their political guide, more left-wing than himself, and on occasions testily so. Compared with his younger colleague, Sartre suffered in the eyes of Marxists and communists from the strongly subjective trend in his thinking and also from the notoriety that existentialism enjoyed in the early postwar years. Yet both philosophers shared many common assumptions, repudiating the ideas of historical necessity and materialism in their cruder forms, seeking to enlarge the implications of Marxism, and, in the class struggle, coming down heavily in favor of the proletariat. Within the limits of a watchful skepticism, the policy of *Les Temps modernes* was then, as it has remained, anticapitalist, and prorevolutionary; its general aim, Sartre says, was to bring about a better understanding between communist intellectuals and middle-class left-wing intellectuals. This task was soon to become a more urgent one. In 1947, highly suspect to the left, the R.P.F. was formed and achieved sweeping victories in the municipal elections; Ramadier eliminated the communists from his ministry, and the Marshall Plan was proposed. In 1949, Sartre and others attempted to form a mediatory left-wing party, the R.D.R.[3] This venture soon failed. It had received only lukewarm support from Merleau-Ponty; perhaps, Sartre suggests, he felt they would have more influence with the communists by belonging to no party at all, than one which, rightly or wrongly, might be seen as a political rival. Soon, communist sympathizers were to be faced with more serious problems. In 1949 came the revelation that concentration camps existed on a large scale in the U.S.S.R. David Rousset, one of the cofounders with Sartre of the R.D.R., wrote attacking them in *Le Figaro littéraire,* and, in January 1950, Merleau-Ponty replied in *Les Temps modernes.*[4] He took up an uneasy midway position between partial blame of the Soviet Union and a persistent belief in the historical mission of the proletariat, and, as he had done when seeking to justify the Moscow trials in *Humanism and Terror* (1947),[5] pointed out once again that so-called liberal values were often a verbal alibi for the numerous acts of oppression practiced by the Western powers in the name of democracy. In this way, he continued to give communism the benefit of the doubt, and his article had the wholehearted support of Sartre—appearing, in fact, with both their names appended to it. Yet both were experiencing deep anxieties that would lead in the one case to disillusionment, in the other to a more radical political alignment. It was the outbreak of the Korean War which crystallized this process. Merleau-Ponty, having tried to present the Moscow trials and the Russian concentration camps in a relatively favorable light, appears now to have lapsed into skepticism. He suggested to Sartre that political commentary be dropped altogether from their review, and there followed in the history of *Les Temps modernes* a period when it depended heavily upon its regular contributors: "*pendant l'interrègne, entre 1950 et 1952, un navire sans capitaine recruta lui-même des officiers qui en évitèrent la perdition*" ("In short, during the interregnum, between 1950 and 1952, a vessel without a captain recruited, by itself, the officers who saved it from perdition" [reprinted below p. 600]), as Sartre puts it.[6] His own silence was broken by what he calls his "conversion," which followed upon the Henri Martin affair and the arrest of Jacques

Duclos in 1952. Merleau-Ponty's skepticism was now to be countered by a fulgurating revelation on Sartre's part: "*Les derniers liens furent brisés, ma vision fut transformée: un anti-communiste est un chien, je ne sors pas de là, je n'en sortirai plus jamais*" ("An anticommunist is a rat. I couldn't see any way out of that one, and I never will" [reprinted below p. 601]), writes paradoxically the former advocate of indefinitely renewed choice.[7] The first act of his conversion was to begin the series of articles entitled *The Communists and Peace*[8] in which he was more vehement and less critical of the Soviet Union than Merleau-Ponty had ever been. Their relationship now developed into one of mutual exasperation, and it needed only an example of editorial high-handedness from Sartre, in 1953, to bring about Merleau-Ponty's resignation from *Les Temps modernes*.[9]

But theirs was not yet an open disagreement. This was not to come until nearly two years later, when Merleau-Ponty attacked Sartre's interpretation of Marxism in *Adventures of the Dialectic* (1955).[10] Sartre himself did not reply to this, but Simone de Beauvoir did, with his approval, and there appeared in *Les Temps modernes,* under her name, a vitriolic, if partly justified article, castigating the former political director of that review.[11] She could not help defending a philosophy she had made her own against Merleau-Ponty's distortions of it, she would later write, adding: "*quant à lui, il ne m'en voulut pas, ou du moins pas très longtemps; il pouvait comprendre les colères intellectuelles*" ("There were no hard feelings on his side, at least not for very long. He could understand intellectual anger").[12]

These are the bare outlines of a dispute which virtually brought to an end a personal and professional relationship between two of France's leading philosophers. As we have so far presented it, it appears to be largely the outcome of historical events. There were, of course, other causes, some of which Sartre, often with a note of puzzlement, seeks to explore. But Professor Kwant rightly insists that the origins of their disagreement are to be sought also in contrasting philosophical assumptions. Beneath the political aspirations that united the philosophers for a decade there had always subsisted elements of potential conflict. The point may most usefully be made by a brief comparison between some of the ideas expressed in *Being and Nothingness* (1943)[13] with their counterparts in Merleau-Ponty's *Phenomenology of Perception* (1945).[14] These works firmly established the philosophical reputation of their respective authors. Both were conceived within the phenomenological tradition, and both had been written when the joint venture of *Les Temps modernes* was embarked upon, and yet they clearly contain the seeds of future dissent.

In *Being and Nothingness,* the fundamental distinction which Sartre makes between the *en-soi* and the *pour-soi* before raising in any detail the problem of the body's involvement in the world, or the subject's relationship with other subjects, readily conveys the impression that the world of objects is quite distinct from the human consciousness that reflects them, and gives consciousness, in its turn, an excessively subjective bias. Moreover, the thinking subject himself, for Sartre, seems to be isolated within each moment of time; while it is consciousness, or *liberté,* that permits man to select fields of interest, and impose meaning on the world by the process of exclusion, or negation, this same operation involves him in a continual temporal *ex-stasis:* "*La liberté, c'est l'être humain mettant son passé hors de jeu en sécrétant son propre néant*" (*EN,* 65). ("Freedom is the human being putting his past out of play by secreting his own nothingness" [*BN,* 28].) Hence, we experience our lives as a constant process of rupture, reassessment, and renewal, and the tension which results from this is frequently emphasized: it is the experience of anguish (*EN,* 72). Unlike Merleau-Ponty, Sartre does not yet adopt the term "existential" or any of its derivatives to characterize his *own* philosophy, but the importance he accords to choice and anguish already constitutes a significant difference between the two works under consideration.[15] In his world, anguish and conflict are recurrent and inevitable factors: "*J'émerge seul et dans l'angoisse en face du projet unique et premier qui constitue mon être, toutes les barrières, tous les garde-fous s'écroulent, néantisés par la conscience de ma liberté,*" he writes (*EN,* 77). ("I emerge alone and in anguish confronting the unique and original project which constitutes my being; all the barriers, all the guard rails collapse, nihilated by the consciousness of my freedom" [*BN,* 39].) To be sure, he presents this experience as a reflective act, a pause, so to speak, in situational activities and relationships that make up our nonreflective contact with the world and men (*EN,* 73–77). It is true, also, that Sartre had begun the first part of his study by insisting briefly on "[*une*] *totalité qu'est l'homme dans le monde*" (*EN,* 38) ("[a] totality which is man-in-the-world" [*BN,* 4]) and by situating the act of interrogation "*sur le fond d'une familiarité préinterrogative avec l'être*" (*EN,* 39) ("on the basis of a pre-interrogative familiarity with being" [*BN,* 4–5]); furthermore, he later seeks to resolve what could appear as an "insurmountable dualism" by again insisting that consciousness is synthetically linked with, and dependent upon, being, by virtue of its intentionality (*EN,* 711, 712). The fact remains that, in contradistinction to Merleau-Ponty, it is not so much this "naive" contact with the world that he concentrates upon, as the consequences of his initial distinction between consciousness and undifferentiated being. Hence the impression, already commented upon, of what one recent critic has said "might prove to be subjectivism and dualism in a new guise,"[16] and of a dichotomy whose result, writes Thévenaz, is to give

"Sartre's ontology a dogmatic, not to say a scholastic, look from the beginning."[17]

Merleau-Ponty, on the contrary, emphasizes in the *Phenomenology* the essential incompletion of the phenomenological method; philosophy is, in his view, an infinite meditation (*Pp,* xvi). Reflection is undertaken against an unreflected background of experience; there is no inner man, it is in and through the world that man knows himself (*Pp,* iv, v), and this he does neither as a passive recipient nor as constitutive consciousness (*Pp,* chap. 4). As Jean Hyppolite has pointed out,[18] it is clear from the outset that, in contrast to Sartre, there is a strongly antidualistic tendency in Merleau-Ponty's thinking. The latter frequently emphasizes, for instance, the role played by perceptual judgment, in which subject and object merge: "*la perception est justement cet acte qui crée d'un seul coup, avec la constellation des données, le sens qui les relie—qui non seulement découvre le sens qu'elles ont mais encore fait qu' elles aient un sens*" (*Pp,* 46) ("perception is just that act which creates at a stroke, along with a cluster of data, the meaning which unites them—indeed which not only discovers the meaning *which they have,* but moreover *causes them to have a meaning*" [*PP,* 36]). The latter part of this quotation implies that as perception becomes an attentive act, it creates new syntheses from sensations already given; but it always operates against an indeterminate background of experience that is our inherence in the world, what he calls on one occasion "*le langage muet que nous parle la perception*" (*Pp,* 60) ("This is the silent language whereby perception communicates with us" [*PP,* 48]). We are far removed from the sense of separation from the world, and the resultant tension between fascination and dread, to which Sartre's thought constantly inclines. For here, subject and object are involved in a process of endless interaction.[19] Similarly, in the social sphere, contact between individuals occurs naturally, at a prepersonal level, our perceptions overlapping as those of "anonymous" perceiving subjects (*Pp,* 405). An important consequence of this is that Merleau-Ponty is led far from the solipsism that never seems far below the surface in Sartre's philosophy. For instance, on one occasion he discusses the notion of the gaze which, it will be recalled, is an essential factor in Sartre's description of alienation; he implicitly contradicts his colleague by saying that we may experience the gaze of others as painful not because we are fundamentally separated from them, but because in some situations observing or being observed can take the place of a more positive relationship: "*l'objectivation de chacun par le regard de l'autre n'est ressentie comme pénible que parce qu'elle prend la place d'une communication possible*" (*Pp,* 414) ("the objectification of each by the other's gaze is felt as unbearable only because it takes the place of possible communication" [*PP,* 361]). The social sphere, for Merleau-

Ponty, far from being one in which strife is inevitable, constitutes, like the natural world, a *Lebenswelt: "Notre rapport au social est, comme notre rapport au monde, plus profond que toute perception expresse ou que tout jugement"* (*PP,* 415) ("Our relationship to the social is, like our relationship to the world, deeper than any express perception or any judgment" [*PP,* 362]). Sartre's emphasis on the negating role of consciousness is, similarly, absent from the *Phenomenology,* as Professor Alexander pertinently reminds us,[20] and likewise, it is the organic and continuous nature of our experience rather than its constant disruption that Merleau-Ponty draws attention to: "*Ce que nous avons vécu est et demeure perpétuellement pour nous, le vieillard touche à son enfance*" (*Pp,* 450) ("What we have experienced is, and remains, permanently ours; and in old age a man is still in contact with his youth" [*PP,* 393]). Sartre is brought more openly into the debate in the last chapter of the *Phenomenology,* though even here reference to his thought is still largely implicit, and an open confrontation is avoided. Professor Kwant examines these points of divergence in some detail; for our present purposes, it will be necessary to mention one or two instances only. Like Sartre, Merleau-Ponty accepts volition as an organic act, involving the whole personality, but integrates it into a more open approach to the notion of freedom itself. He cannot agree, with Sartre, that we are either totally free (hence totally responsible), or not free at all. The past, and our situation in the world, necessarily impose a pattern and limitations on us (*Pp,* 505). To Sartre's belief that obstacles exist only because we have freely chosen to consider them as such (*EN,* 569) he replies, without specifying whose viewpoint he is contesting, that there are bodily intentions which we do not really choose, and spontaneous evaluations which we share with our fellow men (*Pp,* 503). Sartre is more often refuted by implication than actually named, but Merleau-Ponty's irritation with certain trends of his thought is, nonetheless, quite apparent. Indeed, in an otherwise sympathetic essay published in the same year as the *Phenomenology,* Merleau-Ponty wrote of *Being and Nothingness:*

> *À notre sens, le livre reste trop exclusivement antithétique: l'antithese de ma vue sur moi-même et de la vue d'autrui sur moi l'antithèse du pour-soi et de l'en-soi font souvent figure d'alternatives au lieu d'être décrites comme le lien vivant de l'un des termes à l'autre et comme leur communication.*"[21]

> In our opinion the book remains too exclusively antithetic: the antithesis of my view of myself and another's view of me and the antithesis of the *for itself* and the *in itself* often seem to be alternatives instead of being described as the living bond and communication between one term and another.

Simone de Beauvoir's reply to Merleau-Ponty would later provide a counterbalance to his neglect of the more situational aspects of Sartre's thinking. Our own concern is not to seek to rectify this neglect, but to indicate important differences in emphasis that the pressure of events was subsequently to amplify. A further contrast should be mentioned before this brief comparison is concluded. It is significant that Sartre, who had become acquainted with the work of Marx eight years or so before that of the phenomenologists,[22] should nevertheless, in *Being and Nothingness,* formulate his ideas on class relationships without direct reference to Marx. Despite the fact that the work was published in 1943, one senses the rigor of its author's "Cartesianism" rather than the shadow of possible censorship. For Sartre's views on class conflict are derived from his own theories of alienation and reification and are argued as a logical consequence of his initial premises. In the process, theory predominates over factual illustration; while he draws on the idea of capitalist oppression, historical and economic considerations are otherwise absent from his argument. Class consciousness arises for Sartre not so much through the experience of shared hardship, or community of effort, as through the gaze of an alienating third person (*EN,* 491–93). Class unity cannot be experienced from within, but occurs as the result of some menace outside the class; it is an extension of the conflict that all human relationships represent for this philosopher, and which he constantly emphasizes (*EN,* 502). Merleau-Ponty's approach to Marxism was to be more empirical, and less assertive in its implications. A lengthy footnote in his *Phenomenology* proposes an "ambiguous" interpretation of historical materialism, neither denying the influence of economic pressures on society, nor on the other hand making these the pale reflection of some more general existential drama (*Pp,* 199). When, in his final chapter, he returns to the theme of class relationships, it is again to steer a middle course between excessively objective and subjective interpretations, to avoid the alternatives of the *pour-soi* and the *en-soi,* as he puts it, discreetly suggesting the identity of at least one dualistic culprit (*Pp,* 506). He emphasizes class awareness as an ambiguous experience, once again, and sees it as imperceptibly rather than consciously evolving toward crises such as revolutions; the party-class relationship, which will later prove such a bone of contention between him and Sartre, represents a similarly organic process (*Pp,* 508). This idea of a reciprocal relationship between action and formulated intention, he no doubt largely derived from Marx; at all events, it is in a Marxist context that it will continue to preoccupy him for a decade. As in the present instance, he will also continue to emphasize the cumulative pressure of events rather than any factor of individual choice they may exemplify. In this chapter of the

Phenomenology, we find him stating that while we give history its meaning, it is a meaning that history itself has already proposed to us, or as he again puts it: "*le sens des événements . . . s'élabore dans la coexistence sociale et dans l'On, avant toute décision personnelle*" (*Pp,* 513) ("the significance of events . . . is elaborated within social co-existence and in the One before any personal decision is made" [*PP,* 449]). So that for him, choice tends to consist in the lucid appraisal and assumption of a given situation rather than in the ability to effect radical change: "*Je ne peux manquer ma liberté que si je cherche à dépasser ma situation naturelle et sociale*" (*Pp,* 520) ("I can pass freedom by, only if I try to get over my natural and social situation" [*PP,* 456]), as he says on the concluding page of his thesis, significantly adding, a few lines later, that the role of the philosopher is to teach us to see both things and historical situations clearly. Militancy, for Merleau-Ponty, would always be tempered by the need to understand and explain. Even his most radically inclined political writings, the articles reprinted in *Humanism and Terror,* were to combine a belief in the historical mission of the proletariat, a justification, or at least sympathetic understanding, of Stalinist political violence, and a considerable degree of political hesitation. We even find there, on one occasion, the philosopher who made such widespread use of the concept of ambiguity, and saw it as an integral part of all human experience, unexpectedly hoping for guidance from "*une nouvelle pulsation de l'histoire . . . un mouvement populaire sans ambiguïté*" (*Ht,* xix) ("a fresh historical impulse . . . a popular movement without ambiguity").[23] There always was, of course, much more to his social and political thinking than the "*nostalgie d'un âge d'or de la révolution*" that Simone de Beauvoir saw there;[24] yet, already in 1945, the emphasis he places on the preconceptual and the intersubjective nature of human experience appears, despite a more overt appeal to Marxism, to suggest an underlying attitude that could come to differ radically from Sartre's and lead him, politically speaking, to a far less radical position.

The focal point of their subsequent quarrel was the articles which Sartre would subsequently describe as the first act of his "conversion": *The Communists and Peace,* begun in 1952 and concluded in 1954.[25] In these, Sartre set out to account for the failure of the communist-organized demonstration and strikes of 28 May and 4 June 1952. Underlying his lengthy and detailed argument are certain theoretical assumptions, the main ones being the familiar Marxist belief that truly human values are the prerogative of the working class,[26] that the Communist Party is the only proper representative of the French proletariat,[27] and the frequently developed corollary that, without the party, the working class will lose its identity and lapse into passivity. He has not overlooked his original view that class awareness is the product of a baleful gaze, directed at the class from without, but the circumstantial nature of these writings and his own intellectualist development lead Sartre to a much more overtly Marxist and historical analysis of the situation. Already in 1946, he had somewhat played down the notion of the gaze, if not of reification itself, in his "Materialism and Revolution." In this challenge to modern Marxists, his own concepts had often had a familiar Marxist ring about them; work, for instance, he saw as a transformation of the material world which gave man a concrete sense of meaning of freedom,[28] or afforded an example of "*un type primordial de rapport entre les hommes*" ("a primordial form of human interrelationship").[29] But on the subject of actual class cohesion, Sartre had had little to say; the reader was left to assume that it followed automatically from the shared experience of oppression, or from each worker's desire to extend his discovery of freedom to all men. With *The Communists and Peace,* however, the trend away from ontology toward practical politics is taken a stage further, as the problem of class identity now comes to the forefront as a major issue. Even here, let us note, this is not so much a new development as an old idea refurbished, and reemphasized in the light of changing political circumstances; Sartre had already expressed strong reservations over the viability of any collective identity generated from within the group, what he had there called the *nous-sujet,* in *Being and Nothingness* (*EN,* 496–98). He now takes the same attitude toward a specific class, the proletariat, sees it as an amorphous mass requiring direction from above,[30] and frequently attacks those who believe a class capable of survival without political direction; this view, he rejects as an *illusion spontanéiste,* and opts instead for an authoritarian organization of the masses, and claims that only within the disciplinary framework of the communist party can freedom have any meaning for the worker.[31]

To a Marxist of Merleau-Ponty's stamp, as to Claude Lefort, who had already quarreled with Sartre over them,[32] these articles seemed to have a dangerously totalitarian trend. They became, in 1954, the main target for his attack on communism in *Adventures of the Dialectic.* Almost half of the work, in which he examines the possibilities and abuses of Marxist dialectics, is devoted to a sustained onslaught on his ex-colleague's political thought. The title of this section, "Sartre and Ultrabolshevism" (parodied by Simone de Beauvoir's reply: "Merleau-Ponty and Pseudo-Sartreanism"), reflects his belief that Sartre and present-day communism have in common their terrorist tendencies and an absolutely gratuitous authoritarianism. In Sartre's case, he is intent on tracing these characteristics back to their origins in what we have already seen him consider to be an excessively subjective philosophy. Sartre had played this down in his new-found adhesion to communist policies; Merleau-

Ponty is determined to bring it back into the foreground. So to the texts specifically under consideration, he more or less tacitly appends *Being and Nothingness*: "*Toute la théorie du Parti et de la classe chez Sartre dérive de sa philosophie du fait, de la conscience, et par-delà le fait et la conscience, de sa philosophie du temps,*" he declares (*Ad,* 144). ("Sartre's entire theory of the party and of class is derived from his philosophy of fact, of consciousness, and beyond fact and consciousness, from his philosophy of time.")[33]

Sartre's "ultrabolshevism" is seen, initially, in the sense of urgency he attributes to the situation he describes—a Manichean attempt to bypass middle-of-the-road criticism, argues Merleau-Ponty, who believes politics to be too subtle a business for this kind of absolute attitude (*Ad,* 140, 141). This is a viewpoint we might have expected of him, as is also his emphasis on the quasi-organic evolution of doctrines and organizations. For he goes on to say that, when Sartre allows himself to be carried away by the urgency of the present situation, he is being more theoretical than practical: "*Ne pas parler du prolétaire, de la classe en soi, et du Parti éternel, c'est ici faire une théorie du prolétariat et du Parti comme créations continuées, c'est-à-dire comme morts en sursis*" (*Ad,* 144). ("Not to speak of the proletarian, of the class in itself, or of the eternal Party is here to make a theory of the proletariat and of the Party as continued creations, that is to say, as the dead reprieved from death" [*AD,* 105; reprinted below p. 363].) Sartre had, in fact, given considerable attention to the historical struggles of the French working class, but this is an aspect of his argument that Merleau-Ponty chooses largely to ignore, preferring to undermine the ontological basis of Sartre's Marxism. For Sartre's militancy, he claims, originates in his conception of freedom; its origins are, then, voluntaristic, for in the last analysis, it represents Sartre's vision of man as being constantly projected toward change and action (*Ad,* 144, 146). The party, likewise, emerges not as an organization with an historical past, but as a further aspect of the militant's pure will to action (*Ad,* 147). In short, Merleau-Ponty argues that Sartre's support for communism is based on his personal theories rather than on a proper understanding of the movement; his concept of the party merely represents the projection of his subjectivism into the realm of collective action. In the process, the party assumes the burden of desperate choice which Sartre originally placed on each individual, loses its inner cohesion, and becomes authoritative and omnipotent.

He then contrasts Sartre's approach with that of Marx, who had seen the party-class relationship as one existing between two inseparable factors that shape history through a process of mutual enlightenment (*Ad,* 159). If the party is able to define historical truth, it is only because it is in immediate contact with the everyday life and realities of the class it represents; this perpetual interchange between reality and theory is what

Marx's idea of the *praxis* refers to (*Ad,* 157). Sartre argues as if the party cannot be judged to be wrong unless the working class openly declares it to be so, and explains the failure of the strike of June 2 by saying that the workers abstained for personal reasons. Precisely, agrees his critic, but personal reasons of the kind which Sartre instances form the very basis of political judgment (*Ad,* 164). He is, in fact, confronting Sartre with those same notions of tacit evaluation and preconceptual choice which he had emphasized in the *Phenomenology,* but placing them more openly in a Marxist context. He then goes on to repudiate any narrow causal explanation of the respective roles of party and proletariat (*Ad,* 167), and to dismiss, with a rather more liberal view of Lenin than in *Humanism and Terror,* Sartre's attacks on the *spontanéistes* (*Ad,* 169–74). Yet as he proceeds he is obliged to recognize that inherent in the class struggle is a paradox that runs counter to the intentions of Lenin, and more so to those of Marx; circumstances may oblige the party to assume a dictatorial role which it is afterwards loath to relinquish. This occurred with Stalinism, when an authoritarian regime replaced one based on a reciprocal relationship, and the notion of the praxis became distorted into a cult of action directed by the few. Sartre's misinterpretations of Marx lead in this selfsame direction (*Ad,* 174–85).

So Merleau-Ponty begins to take a more positive stand than he had done in *Humanism and Terror,* and several of the comments he now makes echo Camus's distinction between revolt and revolution in *The Rebel* (*Ad,* 278, 281); for he proceeds to describe a situation in which, in his view, the idea of the ultimate revolution has degenerated into a cynically utilized myth, justifying apparently endless terrorism and aggression. What he must now ask Sartre, and ultimately himself, is how long one can continue to give Marxism the benefit of the doubt when its practice is at such variance with its premises. One waits, and not in vain, for the word "liberalism" to appear in a far more favorable sense than hitherto in his writings. This it does as he outlines his hope for the emergence of a new, noncommunist left. But his political program remains somewhat vague, and is not connected, in these pages at least, to the idea of a new left which was widespread at this time (1954–55) or to the nature of Mendès-France. What is most noticeable here is the basically interrogative nature of Merleau-Ponty's approach to politics. The meaning he would himself give to involvement, in contrast to Sartre's implied leap in the dark, comes much nearer to reflection than to action. Should it not, he suggests, really mean self-interrogation and criticism as one comes into contact with history? (*Ad,* 262). Sartre's view, he continues, is based on a mistaken understanding of the nature of freedom; but as he seeks to correct this, he merely repeats that experience precedes and founds conceptualization, that choice is not a sudden but a cumulative process, rooted in our past experience. We transcend the infrastructure which shapes our lives, and rise above determinism, when we consent to "*Vivre naïvement ce qui s'offre à* [*nous*] *sans ruser avec la logique de l'enterprise, sans l'enfermer par avance dans les limites d'une signification préméditée*" (*Ad,* 265) ("it is by attempting simply to live what is offered me, without playing tricks with the logic of the enterprise, without enclosing it beforehand inside the limits of a premeditated meaning" [*AD,* 197; reprinted below p. 434]). It was, no doubt, remarks of this kind that gave rise to Simone de Beauvoir's acid comment that for the author of *Adventures of the Dialectic,* "*il suffit de rêver pour être un homme d'action*" ("It will suffice to only dream to be a man of action").[34] For Merleau-Ponty was clearly abandoning what had been reasonably cohesive political sympathies without defining in any detail what was to take their place. In fact, such a definition, except in terms of a kind of liberalism based on a minimum of *a priori* assumptions, was no longer possible. For he concludes this work by divorcing ideology from politics, and repudiating the doctrine which might, for him, have brought the two together. After attacking Sartre's brand of Marxism, he now dismisses his own as "*un marxisme de vie intérieure,*" a kind of categorical imperative in favor of the proletariat (*Ad,* 312).

It had, of course, been much more than this. Marxism had been a philosophical as well as a moral temptation for him. In an essay dating from 1945, he suggested various ways in which phenomenology was indebted to Marx,[35] and there are many parallels that could be made, on the basis of this essay, between Merleau-Ponty's own ideas and his view of Marxism as a nonscientific, nondeterministic philosophy. Here and elsewhere, Marx offers him a contextual and historical view of man in which everything, from physical objects to ideologies, is interrelated. It is the writings of the early Marx that he most readily refers to, seeing there the outline of an "ambiguous" philosophy that at once takes account of historical and economic pressures and avoids simple causal explanations. In this way, he deprives Marxism of much of its militancy and dogmatism, and makes it complementary to his own thinking. What had particularly appealed to him was Marx's idea of elucidation through action: the *praxis.* Implicit in the *Phenomenology* and some of the early essays printed in *Sense and Non-Sense,* the basis of the party-class relationship in *Humanism and Terror,* it becomes a concept of central importance in *Adventures of the Dialectic:* "*Le sens profond, philosophique, de la notion de praxis est de nous installer dans un ordre qui n'est pas celui de la connaissance, mais celui de la communication, de l'échange, de la fréquentation*" (*Ad,* 70) ("The profound philosophical meaning of the notion of praxis is to place us in an order which is not that of knowledge but rather that of communication, exchange and association" [*Ad,* 50]), he writes there on one occasion. There is no need to emphasize the link between such a concept and the general trend of the *Phenomenology of Perception.* When he discusses the *praxis,* we feel that his own investigations as a phenomenologist are seeking their most natural outlet in the realm of political philosophy.

Yet when he turned away from Marxism, this was no sudden awakening: its attraction for him had all along been accompanied by some degree of skepticism. In the immediate postwar years, he had on occasions confronted it, as an interpretative philosophy, with a contemporary situation which it seemed incapable of elucidating (*Sens,* 217, 302). His political attitude had been constantly one of nonalignment; it was his emphasis, not his general direction, which changed. The political program he outlined in 1945 (*Sens,* 302) was similar, in his desire for a lucid appraisal of the situation and his wish to steer a middle course between East and West, to that advocated at the end of *Adventures of the Dialectic,* ten years later. The important difference was that his cautious support for communism and his belief in the proletariat had now been dropped, and the fascination of Marxism, broken.

The quarrel with Sartre must therefore be seen as a conflict of basic viewpoints, exacerbated by events, and centering around a social and political philosophy toward which their respective attitudes became increasingly divergent. Their dispute is largely the result of their individual adventures with dialectical materialism; and for this reason, one of the weaknesses of Merleau-Ponty's attack on Sartre is its impersonality; he isolates the latter's Marxism from its process of development, and its origins in a commonly shared enterprise. Despite his scathing comment on it (*Ad,* 169), Sartre's "Materialism and Revolution" (1946) had been written in the same spirit as many of the early comments on Marxism of Merleau-Ponty himself; it was an attempt to correlate the aims of existentialism and Marxism, insofar, at least, as Sartre seeks to repudiate the dogmatic accretions of Marxism.[36] Indeed, in his tribute to Merleau-Ponty, Sartre goes so far as to give the younger philosopher the credit for his own political education, saying that he had guided him away from near anarchy toward involvement, and that *Humanism and Terror* had provided him with both a method and an objective.[37] This may be an overstatement, but it points to the irony of a situation in which something approaching a reversal of positions has occurred. The breach between them was never entirely healed; but whereas, in the preface to *Signs* (1960) Merleau-Ponty's irritation with Sartre the thinker yields before a warm appraisal of Sartre the man, the divorce between Marxism and philosophy is now made absolute. Marxism, in contrast to Sartre's treatment of it in "Marxism and Existentialism,"[38] is relegated to the status of a secondary truth—"*une vue de l'histoire et non pas le mouvement en acte de l'histoire*" ("a view of history and not the movement of history")—and Marx has become a "classic."[39] Phenomenology regains its autonomy as Merleau-Ponty comments: "*La politique des philosophes, c'est celle que personne ne fait*" ("the politics of philosophers is what no one *practices*"),[40] and advocates a return to "*une philosophie d'autant moins liée par les responsabilités politiques qu'elle a les siennes . . . qu'elle ne joue pas aux passions, à la politique, à la vie, qu'elle ne les refait pas dans l'imaginaire, mais dévoile précisément l'Être que nous habitons*" ("a philosophy which is all the less tied down by political responsibilities to the extent that it has its own, and . . . [does not *play* at passions, politics, and life, or reconstruct them in imagination] but discloses exactly the Being we inhabit").[41] Remarks of this kind separate Merleau-Ponty more radically than ever from the viewpoint of the *Les Temps modernes* group. But he had not withdrawn into an ivory tower after writing *Adventures of the Dialectic;* the generalized program of its conclusion found concrete expression in his support for Mendès-France, and the political articles he wrote for *L'Express,* some of which were reprinted in *Signs.* The presence of these acts as a corrective to any excessively one-sided view of their author's development; and, illustrating the comments he had made on communism and parliamentarianism in the abstract framework of *Adventures of the Dialectic,* they constitute an indispensable appendix to an overtheoretical work.

It was political crises of first magnitude which drew Merleau-Ponty out in this way, and, not surprisingly, the same crises brought his position and Sartre's closer together, at least for a time. The Hungarian Revolt, the Algerian War, the return to power of de Gaulle, all led them both in the same general direction—though, as M. Burnier comments, Sartre remained in character by taking the more radical course. But this time, there was no unifying factor, such as their joint editorship of *Les Temps modernes,* to emphasize what they had in common and cement over their basic philosophical differences. At the time of his death, Merleau-Ponty was once more working on a refutation of Sartre's method;[42] and Sartre was left to pursue alone that quest for a synthesis of Marxist and existentialist philosophy which had once represented the most positive aspect of their relationship.

Notes

1. See Rémy C. Kwant, *The Phenomenological Philosophy of Merleau-Ponty* (Pittsburg: Duquesne University Press, 1963); and M.-A. Burnier, *Les Existentialistes et*

la politique (Paris: N.R.F., 1966). The most sustained attempt at a synthesis of the philosophical and political approaches to date is by A. Rabil, *Merleau-Ponty: Existentialist of the Social World* (New York: Columbia University Press, 1967).

2. *Les Temps modernes,* no. 184 (1961). Reprinted in *Situations,* IV, 189–287.

3. A succinct account of this is given by P. Thody, in *Jean-Paul Sartre* (Hamish Hamilton, 1964 edition), 202ff.

4. Reprinted in *Signes* (Paris: N.R.F., 1960), 330–43.

5. Maurice Merleau-Ponty, *Humanisme et terreur* (Paris: Gallimard, 1947). Hereafter *Ht.*

6. Jean-Paul Sartre, *Situations,* IV (246).

7. Ibid., 248.

8. *Les Temps modernes,* nos. 81, 84–85 (1952), no. 101 (1954). Reprinted in *Situations,* VI, 80–384.

9. Sartre, *Situations,* IV, 259. The unnamed author of the articles which provoked the dispute was apparently P. Naville (see *Les Temps modernes,* nos. 86, 90, 1953). Rabil misreads Sartre's account in this instance in *Merleau-Ponty,* 121 and n.

10. Maurice Merleau-Ponty, *Aventures de la dialectique* (Paris: Gallimard, 1955). Hereafter *Ad.*

11. Simone de Beauvoir, "Merleau-Ponty et le pseudo-Sartrisme," *Les Temps modernes,* nos. 114–15 (1955), 2072–2122.

12. Simone de Beauvoir, *La Force des choses* (Paris: N.R.F., 1963), 342.

13. Jean-Paul Sartre, *L'Être et le néant* (Paris: Gallimard, 1943). Hereafter *EN.*

14. Maurice Merleau-Ponty, *Phénoménologie de la perception* (Paris: Gallimard, 1945). Hereafter *Pp.*

15. Cf. Rabil, *Merleau-Ponty,* 30, 31.

16. Ian W. Alexander, "The Phenomenological Philosophy in France: An Analysis of Its Themes, Significance and Implications," in *Currents of Thought in French Literature* (Oxford: Blackwell, 1965), 348.

17. Pierre Thévenaz, *What Is Phenomenology?* (Chicago: Quadrangle Books, 1962), 71. It will be recalled that Thévenaz is generally far more appreciative of Sartre's achievement than this isolated comment might suggest. He, too, brings out, with considerable insight, differences between Sartre and Merleau-Ponty.

18. Jean Hyppolite, "Existence et dialectique dans la philosophie de Merleau-Ponty," *Les Temps modernes,* no. 184 (1961), 230.

19. Cf. Colin Smith, *Contemporary French Philosophy* (London, 1964): "Where Merleau-Ponty differs from Sartre is in recognizing that we do achieve significant contact, that is, meaning-giving contact, with our world, etc." (132).

20. Alexander, *The Phenomenological Philosophy in France,* 346.

21. Maurice Merleau-Ponty, *Sens et non-sens* (Paris: Nagel, 1948), 125, hereafter *Sens; Sense and Non-Sense,* trans. Huber L. Dreyfus and Patricia Allen Dreyfus (Evanston: Northwestern University Press, 1964), 72.

22. Jean-Paul Sartre, *Questions de méthode* (Paris: N.R.F., 1967 reprint), 26, 55.

23. Maurice Merleau-Ponty, *Humanism and Terror,* trans. John O'Neill (Boston: Beacon Press, 1969), xxiii.

24. De Beauvoir, "Merleau-Ponty et le pseudo-Sartrisme," 2121; below 488.

25. For a good general summary of this, see Thody, *Jean-Paul Sartre,* 204–14. Present page references are taken from *Situations,* VI.

26. Sartre, *Situations,* IV, 87.

27. Ibid., 85, 86.

28. Jean-Paul Sartre, *Matérialisme et révolution,* as reprinted in *Situations,* III, 197, 199, 203–6.

29. Ibid., 180.

30. Sartre, *Situations,* VI, 377. Cf. also 195, 197, 207.

31. Ibid., 250, 251.

32. Claude Lefort, "Le Marxisme de Sartre," *Les Temps modernes,* no. 89 (1953). Lefort sees Sartre's concept of freedom as having undergone a radical change. Sartre's "Réponse à Claude Lefort," to which Merleau-Ponty refers, appears in the same number of *Les Temps modernes,* and is reprinted in *Situations,* VII.

33. Maurice Merleau-Ponty, *Adventures of the Dialectic,* trans. Joseph Bien (Evanston: Northwestern University Press, 1973), 105, hereafter abbreviated *AD;* reprinted below p. 363.

34. De Beauvoir, "Merleau-Ponty et le pseudo-Sartrisme," 2122; translated by Veronique Zaytzeff below, p. 489.

35. Maurice Merleau-Ponty, "Marxisme et philosophie," in *Sens et non-sens,* 221–41.

36. Marx is admittedly only a background figure in this essay, Sartre's avowed concern being to refute the uncritical materialism of contemporary French Marxists. Nevertheless, in three footnotes he specifically identifies his own views with those of the early Marx (*Situations,* III, 184, 210, 213).

37. Sartre, *Situations,* IV, 215.

38. In "Questions de méthode," *Les Temps modernes,* nos. 139, 140 (1957). Reprinted as the first part of *Critique de la raison dialectique* (1960), and as a separate volume in 1967. Sartre here echoes Merleau-Ponty's criticism when he acknowledges the disparity between Marxist theory and practice, and criticizes voluntaristic Marxism. But as opposed to Merleau-Ponty, he still considers that Marxism offers the only valid overall view of modern man, one which existentialism is called upon to complement.

39. Merleau-Ponty, *Signes,* 16, 17; *Signs,* trans. Richard C. McCleary (Evanston: Northwestern University Press, 1964), 11.

40. Merleau-Ponty, *Signes,* 10; *Signs,* 5.

41. Merleau-Ponty, *Signes,* 20; *Signs,* 13.

42. Maurice Merleau-Ponty, *Le Visible et l'invisible,* ed. Claude Lefort (Paris: N.R.F., 1964), section headed "Interrogation et dialectique," 75–141. What appears to begin as a favorable reevaluation of *L'Être et le néant* (cf. 80, 90) turns out to be a further repudiation of a method in which the dialectical process is not taken far enough.

16

Vicissitudes of the Dialectic: From Merleau-Ponty's *Adventures of the Dialectic* to Sartre's Second *Critique*

Ronald Aronson

Volume 2 of Sartre's *Critique of Dialectical Reason,* published posthumously in 1985, takes up where volume 1, published in 1960, left off. Beginning from the Marxian premise that class struggle is the motor of history, how, Sartre asks, can we "conceive of a struggle between individuals or between groups being dialectically intelligible?" In other words, in studying a conflict, can we see each side's action as participating in the creation of a larger history, as leading beyond itself to progress and development, as proceeding by contradiction and transcendence? Can a meaningful historical or social whole emerge "when we are confronted by two actions: in other words, by two autonomous and contradictory totalizations?"[1]

These questions merely continue, after Sartre's pause to conclude volume 1 and prepare it for publication, the train of thought whose basic direction and concepts have already been carefully established. To be sure, Sartre spent the opening pages of volume 2 specifying, focusing, and circumscribing this train of thought, but he also clearly indicated that it is no more than the continuation and completion of volume 1.

In fact, for much of the way a single, coherent, and well-developed manuscript, volume 2 allows us our first full understanding of the *Cri-*

tique's goals. Most studies of the first volume have presented a self-sufficiency and completeness not inherent in the book's achievement, but imposed by Sartre's subsequent decision to abandon the project without finishing it. As a result, "the *Critique*" has usually meant the specific structures of volume 1 rather than the larger historical process into which they are to be inserted in volume 2;[2] or indeed, scholars have usually taken the (reversible) passage from one structure to another as the totalizing study of history of volume 2 rather than a highly abstract preliminary sketch of its elements and their modes of combination and transformation.[3] Since the publication of the second volume, however, we have been permitted new ways of viewing the purposes and analyses of the first, as well as Sartre's entire career.[4]

A Glimpse of Volume 2

In taking up "the same structures as those brought to light by [the first volume's] regressive investigations," volume 2 seeks "to rediscover the moments of their inter-relations, the ever vaster and more complete movement which totalizes them and, finally, the very direction of the totalization, that is to say, the 'meaning of history' and its truth."[5] The structures laid out in the first volume—individual praxis, the practico-inert, the series, the fused group, the sworn group, the institution, social classes—are intended in the second as "the condition of a directed, developing totalization."[6]

Sartre will pursue this in the first quarter of volume 2 by exploring how separate and contending actions conspire to create totalizations. To totalize, we know from volume 1, is to draw together into "the developmental unity of a single process" what appear to be separate actions and entities—"the re-interiorization of the different moments in a synthetic progression."[7] In volume 1 we have repeatedly seen individual or group praxis totalize, but volume 2 turns to the real historical world of fragmented, contending, and convicting praxis. Can there be a "totalization without a totalizer"—one not produced by a single individual or group praxis, but which emerges against or in spite of anyone's intentionality yet advances some process of historical development? Hegel had spoken of the "cunning of reason" when lodging the dialectic in a progress operating behind the back of individuals. For Sartre any such totalization can only occur through the praxis of individuals.

Thus he will study two boxers each trying to defeat the other and explore the larger totalities they create and which create them. He will then explore the dialectical theme of contradiction, asking how two subgroups in conflict can be said to further the larger group's purposes in their struggle. And then he will describe, in close detail, the deformed yet still significant product of individuals, subgroups, groups, or classes in conflict. Under the concept of antilabor, he will examine entities produced in and by the conflict yet intended by neither.

Sartre's specific example of antilabor, the slogan "socialism in a single country," will be explained as resulting from the conflict between Stalin and Trotsky for Soviet leadership in the 1920s. With this example Sartre will initiate a new direction of volume 2, a major interpretation of Stalinism occupying nearly half of its pages. Framed by a variety of formal goals which diverge from Sartre's search for the totalization without a totalizer—to study the action of groups on series, to observe the "totalization of envelopment" under the conditions of individual sovereignty, and to trace the sovereign individual enveloped by his own praxis—these interconnected analyses will show the Revolution deviating far from its original goals *in order to survive.*

The final quarter of volume 2 will then wander strikingly from this line of thought. It will shift rather abruptly to explore the ontological status of the particular totalization Sartre has been describing—the totalization of envelopment dominated by Stalin. In a change from dialectical reason to ontology Sartre will ask about its "real-being." He will justify this as avoiding the idealism implied by saying that everything takes place within the praxis-process of history. This discussion will return to the root terms of *Being and Nothingness,* being-in-itself and being-for-itself, but will struggle to connect them with *need* and *praxis,* root terms of the *Critique.* In its last pages, volume 2 will stress the difference between analytical and dialectical reason. Then, before the manuscript breaks off, its original goals unmet, Sartre will conclude by reaffirming dialectical reason as the master logic of the human world.

Why the Dialectic?

A detailed explication of these themes is, of course, the province of a book-length study.[8] In this essay I want to focus on the general direction of the first three quarters of volume 2, and ask what it tells us about Sartre's purpose in writing the *Critique.* Its publication allows us to return to, and fully understand, his *starting point:* What brings Sartre to the dialectic in the first place? Why is it that, aligning himself with Marxism, he both asks about the meaning and direction of history *and* seeks to root his exploration in the activities of individuals? Why his concern that we create *and* are controlled by the dialectic? More basically, why did Sartre undertake this *a priori* study of the nature and meaning of dialectical reason?

The answers evolve slowly, internally, in the body of volumes 1 and 2. But at the outset we can glimpse two features of volume 2 having important bearing on the question. First is Sartre's concern, throughout the first quarter of the manuscript, to prepare the ground for understanding history as a "totalization without a totalizer." This, after all, was the explicit if unachieved goal of volume 2. Second, Sartre devoted nearly half of volume 2 to understanding why the Bolshevik Revolution turned out as it did. For Sartre, then, dialectical reason leads to history, and even more, to the specific history of the first society to be organized by those committed to dialectical reason. But why study a totalization without a totalizer in the first place, and why the Bolshevik Revolution?

To answer these questions I will, for the bulk of this essay, situate the *Critique* beyond itself, in the intellectual and political history of which it is such an important moment. Volume 2 makes clear the extent to which the *Critique*'s directions were set by the larger debates over Marxism. We can understand what provoked Sartre to undertake this particular project by looking beyond its texts themselves.

Moving Toward Marxism

As the culmination of Sartre's complex movement toward Marxism, the *Critique* crowns a period that began twenty years earlier in a prisoner-of-war camp after the fall of France. In slow, definite stages between 1940 and 1957[9] Sartre first became committed to political activism,[10] to socialism,[11] to developing an integration of thought, writing, and political activity,[12] to building a noncommunist democratic socialist movement,[13] to close relations with the Communist Party and the Soviet Union, to using Marxism as a tool of analysis, and then, in *Search for a Method* and the *Critique,* to Marxism as a philosophy.

Although (as we know from *Nausea*) Sartre was thoroughly alienated from bourgeois France in the 1930s, he enthusiastically embraced phenomenology but remained largely indifferent to Marxism as providing an alternative orientation. Still, something about Marxism drew and fascinated him, as he later noted in *Search for a Method:* "it was not the idea which unsettled us; nor was it the condition of the worker, which we knew abstractly but which we had not experienced. No, it was the two joined together. It was—as we would have said then in our idealist jargon even as we were breaking with idealism—the proletariat as the incarnation and vehicle of an idea."[14]

In his apolitical days, the appeal of Marxism was neither the philosophy nor the movement, but the *connection* between the two. In this way, historical materialism, criticized by Sartre in his very first published essay, offered something no other philosophy could aspire to and challenged this philosopher to his roots.[15] At the same time it repelled him by its emphasis on dominant structures and forces which are not immediately accessible to translucent and spontaneous consciousness. Man is not free, Marxism was saying to the Sartre bent on demonstrating freedom.

Before the war, Sartre had been yearning to encounter the real world. During the Occupation and after the war the sheer organized power of the Marxist movement of the working class—the French Communist Party (P.C.F.)—continued to draw him toward it and define his capacity to act. In 1945 Sartre, along with Simone de Beauvoir, Maurice Merleau-Ponty, Raymond Aron, and others, launched *Les Temps modernes,* which soon became a major force as a political and cultural journal of the non-P.C.F. left.[16] Functionally, Sartre and Merleau-Ponty were its coeditors, although the latter, whom Sartre regarded as his political mentor, was the journal's political editor.

By the postwar period Sartre had accepted certain Marxist themes: the class struggle, the goal of a classless society, the leading role of the proletariat in attaining it, and the emphasis on action as central. But his own action, the engagement of a writer, still put little weight on the social and economic forces emphasized by Marxism. Again and again, he found himself appealing to the spontaneity of consciousness and the power of words to influence it, as in *What Is Literature?* first published in *Les Temps modernes* in 1947. And so this socialist activist still kept his distance from Marxism. During this period Sartre saw himself as being to the right of Merleau-Ponty, whose "hard hitting, severe and disillusioned Marxism"[17] wanted a greater recognition of historical contingency than Marxism had allowed, but who still called for close adherence to "the effective policy of the Communist Party."[18]

With characteristic self-confidence, in 1946 Sartre wrote "Materialism and Revolution" as an alternative to Marxism: it offered existentialism to the left, including the communists, as a philosophy of freedom befitting a movement of liberation. Sartre attempted to show how human freedom became alienated under capitalism, and could be fully realized under socialism. The original version of this abstract philosophical essay quarrels with Stalin's *Dialectical and Historical Materialism,* but shows neither a direct reading of Marx nor an appreciation of history, economy, and society as central themes underlying political analysis.

It is interesting to note that Merleau-Ponty was presenting his own sophisticated reflections on communism and history in the journal during this very period. Merleau-Ponty brilliantly laid out the dilemma of the noncommunist sympathetic to proletarian revolution but troubled by its bloody and dictatorial outcome in the Soviet Union as well as by the passivity of the French working class: "It is impossible to be an anti-Communist, and it is not possible to be a Communist."[19] Through essays on the writings of Arthur Koestler, the trial of Bukharin and Trotsky's mode of thought, Merleau-Ponty considered the decisive issues of revolutionary violence and the deviation of the Soviet Union from original Bolshevik goals. Because history is human contingency and not an inevitable process working itself out, he argued that we must still wait on events before deciding how communism has turned out. In the meantime, whatever its imperfections in the world before us, Marxism is the only humanistic philosophy committed to realizing itself in the world. Its agent, the proletariat, "has not achieved power anywhere in the world,"[20] but still "threatens to make its voice heard again. This is enough for us to regard the Marxist attitude as still attractive, not only as moral criticism but also as an historical hypothesis."[21] Merleau-Ponty thus proclaimed a widely influential "Marxist wait-and-see attitude."[22]

Sartre claimed that these essays, published in book form in 1947 as *Humanism and Terror,* caused him to be "converted" from his old individualism to politics. "This small dense book revealed to me the method and object. It gave me the push I had needed to release me from my immobility."[23] Method and object: Merleau-Ponty takes Marxism in its *historical* reality, seeking to deny none of the negative features of Soviet history or daily life, but refusing to divorce Marxism from its embodiment in that society. His realism insists that even if proletarian rule has not yet been realized by Soviet socialism, that society and the communist movement still deserve sympathy and patient waiting.

Three years later, in notes added for the republication of "Materialism and Revolution," Sartre foreshadows what will later develop into a rather different direction. He distinguishes "the Marxist scholasticism of 1949," which he still criticizes, from Marx's "much deeper and richer conception"[24] and indicates his intention to explore this later. Sartre, unlike Merleau-Ponty, was in the process of discovering a politically relevant *noncommunist* Marxism, one which was in closer sympathy to his own existentialism than communist orthodoxy had been.

This was to be followed by other decisive steps in Sartre's development which were, at the same time, steps away from Merleau-Ponty. In the intensifying Cold War, Sartre chose sides with the P.C.F. and the

Soviet Union against the West, citing the government's apparent attempt to suppress the communist party in the wake of the anti-N.A.T.O. riots against American General Matthew Ridgway in May, 1952. "In the name of those principles which it had inculcated into me, in the name of its humanism and of its 'humanities,' in the name of liberty, equality, fraternity, I swore to the bourgeoisie a hatred which would only die with me. When I returned precipitately to Paris [from Rome, where he heard about the events], I had to write or suffocate. Day and night, I wrote the first part of *The Communists and Peace.*"[25]

This essay set a new procommunist direction for *Les Temps modernes,* which had been drifting since the beginning of the Korean War due to Merleau-Ponty's self-imposed silence. We shall see that Merleau-Ponty in turn attacked this essay for its lack of historical or social grounding: influenced by the Cold War and discouraged about the Soviet Union, he was then moving in the opposite political direction, away from Marxism. Sartre, however, was simultaneously pursuing this grounding by self-consciously absorbing his own version of realism into his thought and action. Obviously influenced by Marxism and by his own failure to create a noncommunist left, as well as by Merleau-Ponty's original analyses, Sartre ruminated on what he increasingly came to call his "idealism." He first sought a way of making his ideas effective in the real world, and then sought a basis for action which was committed to liberation and grounded in reality. He had already pondered the problem in 1948 in *Dirty Hands,* producing the impressive character of Hoederer but killing him off and generating no resolution. The most successful intellectual and creative fruit of this process, appearing in 1951, was the brilliant dramatic search for a principle of realistic yet humane action, *The Devil and the Good Lord.*

Politically this began the period of Sartre's fellow-traveling. However he might disagree with the P.C.F. and the Soviet Union, he now appropriated Merleau-Ponty's earlier argument, in the process of being renounced by its author, that communism represented the only positive future of the great mass of humankind.[26] Accepting this thesis did not stifle his sharp intellect: these half-dozen years of his closest ties with the Soviet Union and P.C.F. were characterized by Sartre's critical-minded and original absorption of Marxism. By early 1956 he called it "the truth in motion and the royal road of knowledge." He cited Marxism against party versions of it, agreeing that the P.C.F.'s positions were usually correct, but declaring that intellectually, "Marxism in France has come to a halt."[27] Sartre had begun to see himself as one of the thinkers who would get it moving again. By the Hungarian invasion this independent Marxist was ready to break with the Soviet Union (and the P.C.F. for not condemning it) precisely *in the name of socialism and Marxism.*

The Specific Circumstance

Obviously Sartre would sooner or later need to reflect on the relationship of his original philosophical terms—most notably his Cartesian starting point in *Being and Nothingness* and his famous emphasis on individual freedom—to his growing Marxist intellectual and political orientation. Indeed, his abortive first ethics, *Notebooks for an Ethics,* began this task in the late 1940s, but at that time he talked of the class struggle "on the level of a concept; so long as it was not felt as a concrete reality, there could be no morality in it."[28] This leads us to one way of framing the *Critique:* Sartre's slow appropriation of Marxism in experience as well as theory, to the point of seeking to examine—and establish—it philosophically. The general lines of Sartre's itinerary led quite naturally to a full-scale theoretical encounter with the basic principles of historical materialism.

But what provoked Sartre to write the *Critique?* To answer this we must continue looking beyond its texts themselves—even if only to set them alongside another text, by Merleau-Ponty—close friend and collaborator become critic of Marxism and Sartre by 1955. The *Critique* project was developed in the context of a specific circumstance: the ending of the personal, intellectual, and political relationship between Sartre and Maurice Merleau-Ponty. Its ninety-thousand-word epitaph, *Adventures of the Dialectic,* asserted the obsolescence of communism and Marxism as well as the philosophical inadequacy of Sartre's alignment with them.

As we shall see, this quarrel focused the political and intellectual tensions of an entire generation. But to inquire about it is to encounter immediately a major problem: the intellectual histories of the postwar noncommunist French left ignore its decisive links.[29] Indeed, there has been virtual silence by commentators on the remarkable juxtaposition between two facts—Sartre's political mentor proclaimed his abandonment of the Marxist dialectic in 1955, and his former junior collaborator began a major project of affirming it a few months later.[30] Or yet more remarkably, as we shall see, that the one abandons the Marxian dialectic for the same reason that the other attempts to ground it: "it is precisely when the machine seems jammed [*semble coincée*] that it is appropriate to unravel the formal difficulties hitherto neglected until now."[31]

Does the incomprehension stem from the inherent difficulty of the two texts? As Raymond Aron wrote of *Adventures of the Dialectic,* "Out of 330 pages I do not think that there are more than half a dozen that would allow a reader who was not a professional philosopher to clearly grasp the point of these subtle analyses or the purpose of this long discussion."[32] Yet Aron, having seemingly grasped their point, made no reference to it when commenting at even greater length on Sartre's *Critique.* I would suggest, rather, that the two texts have simply not been studied side by side. When they are, it becomes evident, as Perry Anderson notes, that the *Critique* "was initially conceived as a direct response to the criticisms and objections put to [Sartre] by Merleau-Ponty"[33] in *Adventures of the Dialectic.*

Merleau-Ponty's Break with Marxism

Indeed, having moved into Sartre's and Merleau-Ponty's intellectual-political universe of the 1950s, it is impossible not to read the *Critique* as a reply to the challenge of Merleau-Ponty. The publication of Merleau-Ponty's self-consciously "post-Marxist" attack on Marxism, communism, and Sartre immediately caused a major stir. In a decisive moment in postwar intellectual history, it presented the rationale for Merleau-Ponty's departure from his common project with Sartre. *Adventures of the Dialectic* not only rejected Marxism as having been wrong all along, and thoroughly excoriated Sartre for his growing sympathy to communism, but proposed a "new liberalism" in its place.

In spite of its obtuseness, *Adventures* was sufficiently important to draw a response from Aron[34] as well as Roger Garaudy and other communist intellectuals.[35] And it provoked Simone de Beauvoir herself to write a reply attacking Merleau-Ponty's distortion of Sartre's thought into a "pseudo-Sartreanism" which ignored key conceptions of his ontology as well as his political and philosophical evolution.[36] In his eulogy of Merleau-Ponty, written in 1961, Sartre tersely suggests that he himself identified with her reply. "He wrote a book on dialectic, where he strongly took me to task. Simone de Beauvoir replied to him in *Les Temps modernes* in terms no less strong. This was the first and last time that we fought in writing. By publishing our dissensions, we almost made them irremediable."[37]

"We fought," but why did he not reply directly? The question is a personal and not a philosophical or political one, and its answer is to be found in Sartre's moving account of a broken comradeship. In his eulogy we can see Sartre treating Merleau-Ponty as an intellectual giant, the "throwback to anarchy" still learning from the man who "converted" him to a genuinely historical and social perspective.[38] And we see him still disagreeing, over the nature of the dialectic. Yet moving as it may be, the personal tone of "Merleau-Ponty *vivant*" tends to diminish the political charge of this historic split.

Sartre first describes the growing closeness of this deep personal-intellectual relationship and indicates his own profound debt to Merleau-Ponty as his political mentor. The two had shared many of the same tasks, the same attitudes, the same lines of analyses, a common language. By aligning himself with communist politics and Marxist realism while Sartre was still seeking a "third way," Merleau-Ponty in fact drew Sartre along with him.[39] After 1949 Merleau-Ponty slowly inched away from communism and then departed as the Cold War intensified. The Korean War, at first widely perceived in France as the beginning of World War III,[40] was his personal turning point. It told Merleau-Ponty that the Soviet Union was morally and politically no better than the great powers of the capitalist West. At *Les Temps modernes* he counseled silence—"Because brute force will decide the outcome. Why speak to what has no ears?"[41]—and had less and less to do with politics.[42]

Painfully, in great detail, Sartre describes their mounting political-personal estrangement. During this period of his own rapprochement with communism and Marxism Sartre behaved intemperately toward his collaborators on *Les Temps modernes,* especially toward Merleau-Ponty.[43] The storm began with *The Communists and Peace.* With its first part, published in July 1952, it "seemed as though I had planned a systematic refutation of our political editor, opposing, point by point, my views to his."[44] This was followed by Sartre's nasty reply to *Les Temps modernes* associate Claude Lefort's[45] harsh criticism, and by his high-handed excising of Merleau-Ponty's disavowing editor's preface from the proof of a Marxist essay on "the contradictions of capitalism." Merleau-Ponty resigned. Then, when *Adventures of the Dialectic* appeared in early 1955, Sartre demurred. Obviously shaken by the irreversible rupture with Merleau-Ponty, Sartre would soon make restraint in the face of attack his customary response.

Western Marxism

Adventures has puzzled analysts in part because of its apparent contradictoriness. After an introduction in which he announces his goal, the "liquidation of the revolutionary dialectic" (*AD,* 7), Merleau-Ponty briefly seems to champion the critical, nondogmatic "Western Marxism" developed by Georg Lukács. Lukács's *History and Class Consciousness* had emphasized the subjective revolutionary capacity of the proletariat as Marxism's theoretical and political core.[46] Yet Merleau-Ponty rejects this open-ended Marxism as incapable of capturing the dense social and economic structures that eventually came to dominate Bolshevik action. On the other hand, the variants of Marxism that paid heed to this plane of reality led to theoretical dogmatism and, ultimately but inevitably, political oppression. The problem, he argues, lies with the very notion of a revolutionary dialectic: after devoting nearly one-third of the book to criticizing Sartre's independent effort to justify communism, Merleau-Ponty renounces both Marxist philosophy and politics.

Merleau-Ponty is first attracted to Lukács because his kind of rigorous Marxism does not study events in order to "justify a pre-established schema. Rather it questions events, truly deciphers them, and gives them only as much meaning as they demand" (*AD,* 44). And yet it remains Marxism, pointing to the proletariat, and its consciousness, as the truth of history.

Merleau-Ponty praises Lukács for being committed to the proletariat as a force for "universal criticism" rather than as a "carrier of myths." Marxism is thus not a positivism which would present the answer to human history. "This 'philosophy of history' does not so much give us the keys of history as it restores history to us as permanent interrogation" (*AD,* 57). Merleau-Ponty values Marxism, then, as a critical coming-to-consciousness. When it "focuses everything through the perspective of the proletariat, it focuses on a principle of universal strife and intensifies human questioning instead of ending it" (*AD,* 57).[47]

Orthodox Marxism versus Western Marxism

If this dialectical Marxism seems to meet Merleau-Ponty's demands, it was suppressed by Leninist orthodoxy, with all its crude naturalism—its emphasis on the weight of the real world, moving on its own, at the expense of the subjectivity so central to Lukács. Both poles are present in Marx himself, but, Merleau-Ponty argues, Marx rejects the first as "pre-Marxist." What is the reason, within Marxism itself, why the dialectic reverts to naturalism?

Dialectical Marxism fits revolutionary moments—"soaring periods," according to the Marxist philosopher and proponent of Western Marxism Karl Korsch[48]—when the world seems capable of radical change, when human relationships appear transparently in social reality, when theory and practice are united. In other words, it expresses those malleable historical periods when the human subject seems fully able to shape human history. Yet although it achieved power, Marxism "could not maintain itself at that *sublime point*" (*AD,* 73) as the weight of economic reality imposed itself. The sense of human possibility began to recede before the urgency of material conditions. "The Marxism of the young Marx as well as the 'Western' Marxism of 1923 lacked a means of expressing the inertia of the infrastructures, the resistance of economic and even natural conditions, and the swallowing-up of 'personal relationships' in 'things' " (*AD,* 64). Lukács accepted the criticism of his book by the Comintern—"because his too supple and too notional dialectic did not translate the opacity, or at least the density, of real history" (*AD,* 66).[49]

Having seemed to approve Western Marxism, then, Merleau-Ponty quickly concedes its limits. Yet Leninist naturalism restored the weight of the objective world to Marxism by rooting the dialectic in *being* rather than in human subjectivity. Thus the dialectic is also placed beyond practice. Merleau-Ponty refuses to blame Leninism specifically for the breakdown of the various unifications envisioned by Lukács: it may well be that no revolution remains critical of itself, but this suggests that the Lukácsian vision is inherently unstable. Illusions aside of "a historical time which would be constantly agitated by this critical ferment" (*AD,* 90), at its conceptual core Marxism "bases the Party's interventions on forces which are already there and bases praxis on a historical truth" (*AD,* 85).

A single fatal action of Trotsky offers practical confirmation of this inherent theoretical weakness—Trotsky's remarkable passivity in the face of the party's degeneration and Stalin's rise to power. He seemed unaccountably blind to the fact that the party of the mid-1920s had ceased being revolutionary and democratic. "The dialectic was put to the test"—and failed—when Trotsky was unwilling and unable to split the party in order to save it.

He could not conceive of the party betraying the Revolution, and this faith paralyzed him, making impossible the call to arms which alone might have saved the Revolution. Merleau-Ponty blames the materialist dialectic—because it "postulates that if truth is anywhere, it resides in the inner life of the Party, which the proletariat has created" (*AD,* 82). The ascription of truth to the party is based on the belief in an objective historical process operating through, but independently of, human beings. Trotsky's inability to act reveals a "contradiction and ambiguity" in Bolshevism.

Trotsky's genuflection before the party[50] was preceded by Marx's own movement towards scientific socialism and "the idea of a socialism inscribed in facts" (*AD,* 85). In other words, if revolution is "engraved in the infrastructures of capital," a voluntaristic leadership is needed to decipher them and is entitled "to brush aside, by any means, oppositions which are only apparent" (*AD,* 85). Merleau-Ponty once again emphasizes the theoretical point over the political one, namely that in addition to the themes that we might find in Lukács of "the objective conditions of history and the will of men, there is a third order, that of the internal mechanism of revolutionary action, and that, within this order, from the beginning to the end of space and time, the proletarian revolution is never completely absent" (*AD*, 86–87). History contains, and praxis must realize, an immanent logic—meaning that Marxism grounds value in being rather than in human action. This implies that if the classless society is somehow "inscribed in the structure of capitalist production," the weight and laws of its being must sooner or later prevail. Trotsky's Marxist faith was sophisticated enough to allow for defeats and delays, and was made more supple by the development of ideas such as "permanent revolution" and "uneven and combined development." But he refused to consider one decisive hypothesis: "that a Party born of the proletarian movement and brought to power by it might not only degenerate but might actually turn against the Revolution" (*AD*, 87–88).

The failure is not only a political one, but is more basically the failure of a philosophy. Facing this, Trotsky would have had to have abandoned his illusions and acknowledged the prospect of a *permanent* and *essential* delay in history "fulfilling itself," instead of straining to make his philosophy emerge intact. But Trotsky was a Marxist.

> The dialectical schema must be retained: things must be realized and things must be destroyed, revolution saves everything and changes everything. In practice, depending on the moment, one or the other predominates; a zigzag movement replaces dialectical development. Purgings and the easing of tensions are made to alternate. The result is that each of these attitudes becomes the simple mask of the other. One creates from nothing in the name of truth, one uses violence with little scruple, since it is said to be inscribed in things. This is the Bolshevik mind, the thought of Trotsky; it is the crisis of Marx's thought and its continuation. Trotsky's fate is outlined in this philosophy which was to unite truth and action, but where one is simply an alibi for the other. (*AD*, 93)

This last point leads us to the philosophical heart of the book. In *Humanism and Terror* Merleau-Ponty had warned that "there comes a time when a detour ceases to be a detour, when the dialectic is no longer a dialectic and we enter a new order of history which has nothing in common with Marx's philosophy of the proletariat."[51] In 1946 he was not yet ready to say that this time had come, perhaps because he still retained residual hope that the philosophy might be fulfilled. By 1955 he conceded that a new order had been reached. He concluded that this was due to a philosophy which itself had been faulty from the outset. In volume 2 Sartre responds by taking up this challenge directly, using the Marxian dialectic itself to explain the deviation of the Marxian dialectic. Indeed, Sartre will develop Merleau-Ponty's very theme of deviation into one of the *Critique*'s most powerful tools, everywhere insisting on laying bare its underlying dialectical logic.

From Philosophy to History: The Obsolescence of Marxism

So far Merleau-Ponty's discussion may seem a bit puzzling. Any confusion thus far stems from the fact that his argument moves along two intersecting axes *and* shifts as it develops. Along one axis he shifts from seeking an authentic Marxism and appearing to find it, to discovering that Western Marxism is unable to express history's density, to concluding that Marxism's natural terminus lies rather in an objectivist dialectic which exalts the party as its keeper.[52] After locating what seems to be a philosophically adequate Marxism, he turns away from it insisting that history itself reduces *all* varieties of Marxism to a single effective one.

But is there no middle ground which stresses subject and structure, activity and history, chance *and* objective tendency?[53] Merleau-Ponty's "post-Marxism" seems to be crying out for precisely the great creative reconsideration carried out in an Italian prison by Antonio Gramsci, or in American exile by the members of the Frankfurt School.[54] Indeed, such a "living Marxism" is precisely the Sartrean hope, to be voiced immediately after *Adventures* appeared, in essays in *Les Temps modernes* (one of which mentions Merleau-Ponty's criticism of Sartre).[55] Sartre then began to fulfill the hope in *Search for a Method* and the *Critique.*

Merleau-Ponty's critique foredooms *all* such efforts to separate a more authentic Marxism from the official Marxisms, and to find there the possibility of a new political reorientation. His renunciation barred him from joining with that Marxism which, incubated in defeat, prison, and exile, as well as in response to his own challenge, would itself become a political force—in the Italian Communist Party, in the student movements of the 1960s, and in the explosion of the French left in 1968. Why didn't his formidable intellect seek to *develop* this Marxism? Unlike Sartre, he takes Marxism *as it is,* rather than seeking to fashion a more adequate one. Philosophically he argues that the entire enterprise is obsolete because it is wrong in the first place:

> there is not much sense in trying Bolshevism all over again at the moment when its revolutionary failure becomes apparent. But neither is there much sense in trying Marx all over again if his philosophy is involved in this failure, or in acting as if this philosophy came out of this affair intact and rightfully ended humanity's questioning and self-criticism. (*AD,* 91)

A second answer, a historical one, lies along the other axis of Merleau-Ponty's argument. Having learned his Marxist realism well,[56] Merleau-Ponty rejects defeated versions of Marxism precisely because history has made them into "ideas without historical equivalents" (*AD,* 204). For him, the only historically substantive Marxist dialectic is the victorious one, embodied in Stalinism.[57] Western Marxism's distance from power is the very token of its political irrelevance.

Thus the changing locus of Merleau-Ponty's argument: whatever may be its philosophical insufficiencies, Marxism has been invalidated by *history* itself. As a result "there is no longer much more reason to preserve these perspectives and to force the facts into them than there is to place the facts into the context of Plato's *Republic*" (*AD,* 93). Merleau-Ponty decisively ends the "wait-and-see Marxism" he announced a decade earlier. Because of the way events have evolved, there is no longer any reason to wait.[58]

Critique of Sartre

Atop this already complex argument Merleau-Ponty now seeks to build another of equal complexity, namely that Sartre's efforts to replace this obsolete philosophy with his own reveal both the inadequacy of communist politics and of Sartrean thought. Merleau-Ponty is writing this, of course, in 1953 and 1954, after Sartre has declared his alignment with the P.C.F. in *The Communists and Peace.* There Sartre tries "to declare my agreement with the Communists on certain precise and limited subjects, reasoning from my principles and not from *theirs.*"[59] He has performed only a single study that might be called Marxist, an analysis (in the third of these essays) of the bitter relations between the French bourgeoisie and proletariat since 1871. At the moment of Merleau-Ponty's critique, then, Sartre has politically identified himself with the P.C.F. and has tried his hand at historical-materialist analysis, but he has not yet begun the philosophical rethinking that will result in the *Critique.* In fact, Merleau-Ponty's attack will provide a powerful basis for this reflection.

Merleau-Ponty alternately attacks Marxism and compares Sartre unfavorably with it in an argument that shifts rapidly between several frames of reference: Marxism and Merleau-Ponty's "post-Marxist" rendition/critique of it, Sartre's embracing of the French Communist Party and Merleau-Ponty's critical account of it, Sartre's ontology and Merleau-Ponty's critical rendering both of it and its relation to Sartre's politics. Merleau-Ponty attacks not only *The Communists and Peace* but *The Psychology of the Imagination, Being and Nothingness,* and *What Is Literature?* arguing that Sartrean dualism has not changed over the twenty years spanning these works.[60] Sartre, his argument goes, lacks the subtle and sophisticated, if flawed, historical and social tools provided by Marxism and so has no way to ground his philosophy in the real world of proletariat and party; as a result, he uses absurd conceptions to justify a politics which in any case can no longer be justified by its original starting points.

The first section makes a relatively simple point: for Sartre political action is not rooted in social conditions, economic structures, or history, but is a creation *ex nihilo,* a "conversion," an "invention." If Merleau-Ponty had criticized Sartre's "philosophy of the subject" ten years earlier, in *Phenomenology of Perception,*[61] he now insists that Sartre, the "ultra-Bolshevik," remains stuck there. "Sartre's entire theory of the Party and of class is derived from his philosophy of fact, of consciousness, and, beyond fact and consciousness, from his philosophy of time" (*AD,* 105; below 363). Through its lenses majority rule, minority rights, democracy, control by the rank and file over the leaders—all dissolve before the fact that the party is, by definition, the power of the powerless.

Merleau-Ponty then compares what he regards as Marxism's overly objectivist conception of truth with Sartre's overly subjective one in which all "facts" must await the interpretation that gives them meaning. And yet, paradoxically, if Marxism's dogmatic sense of truth-in-being entails an exalted sense of the party, so does Sartre's subjective basing of all truth on consciousness. It is "the answer of consciousness, all the more peremptory because the course of things is so indecisive" (*AD,* 117; below 372).

In addition to the Party, Sartre transmutes each of the other key Marxist themes into his own: praxis, revolution, history, the proletariat. And in doing so he reveals his totally subjective, individualistic, and ahistorical perspective based on being-for-itself and "its inevitable correlate: pure being-in-itself" (*AD,* 142; below 388). Sartre melodramatically reduces history to the personal choices and actions of specific individuals, such as Stalin. Thus he rejects as absurd the idea that there can be a historical and social current such as Stalinism without the specific man, Stalin.

Merleau-Ponty now probes more deeply into Sartre's ontology, arguing that it fundamentally lacks the dimension of sociality. Inasmuch as the dialectic appears "only in that type of being in which a junction of subjects occurs" (*AD,* 204), Sartre's individualism must reject it. For him, on the contrary, being is not a common residence, but "a spectacle that each subject presents to itself for its own benefit" (*AD,* 204). His argument for the writer's commitment is based on the same philosophy of permanent revolution, a philosophy lacking mediations, lacking sociality, where consciousness encounters consciousness and everything must always be recreated from scratch. "Yesterday literature was the consciousness of the revolutionary society; today it is the Party which plays this role" (*AD,* 158; below 402). And the root of these common themes? "What continues to distinguish Sartre from Marxism, even in recent times, is . . . his philosophy of the *cogito*" (*AD,* 158; below 402).

Merleau-Ponty acknowledges that Sartre's historical study of French capitalism and the French working class has a tone which "in some passages is fairly new. It is no longer a tone of urgency or ultimatum but rather one of history" (*AD,* 172; below 413). But even a Sartre who has authentically moved onto the terrain of history and politics faces shipwreck due to the contortions the party demands of a fellow traveler who happens to be a writer. Merleau-Ponty mocks Sartre's commitment-from-a-distance which refuses to criticize the party. Sartre's "commitment is action at a distance, politics by proxy, a way of putting ourselves right with the world rather than entering it" (*AD,* 193; below 431)—all the natural product of a philosophy incapable of entering the world.

More genuine forms of commitment would begin with an *evaluation* both of the Soviet Union and the P.C.F., including asking whether revolution is "still the order of the day." Once we see communism detached from the dialectic which proclaimed it as bringing an end to history, it becomes secularized, deprived of its privileged position in our thought, one system among others. "If there is no logic of history" (*AD,* 183; below 422), communism must be judged by its actual results: and they are "not sufficient to prove that the proletarians' interests lie in this system" (*AD,* 182; below 422). It is impossible to prefer a system revealing "only the leaders' authority, manipulation of the masses, the rigging of congresses, the liquidation of minorities, the masquerading of majorities as unanimity" (*AD,* 183; below 422).

Keeping his freedom to himself, Sartre does not undertake such a critical analysis, but rather transmutes communism into Sartre. Instead of developing new categories and habits of thought upon encountering history and politics, Sartre's notion of commitment stems from "a conception of freedom that allows only for sudden interventions into the world, for camera shots and flash bulbs" (*AD,* 193; below 430–31). The root problem, once again, is Sartre's conception of consciousness: "a pure power of signifying, as a centrifugal movement without opacity or inertia, which casts history and the social outside, into the signified, reducing them to a series of instantaneous views, subordinating doing to seeing, and finally reducing action to 'demonstration' or 'sympathy' " (*AD,* 198; below 435). Missing in Sartre's thought is the entire "interworld which we call history, symbolism, truth-to-be-made" (*AD,* 200; below 437)—the world of mediations between men and men, men and things.

In the *Critique* Sartre will attempt to discover these mediations and, indeed, will attempt to ground social theory on praxis rather than consciousness. Even before the *Critique,* during 1956 and 1957, we shall see Sartre display a political independence and critical evaluation of the Soviet Union that Merleau-Ponty thought impossible. Then, most remarkably, in volume 2 he will deal with virtually each and every one of these specific criticisms, showing Stalinism as a social current inseparable from the specific individuality of Joseph Stalin, tracing the evolution of Soviet socialism and speculating on its possibilities for democratic revitalization.

What Remains of the Dialectic?

"But," Merleau-Ponty asks in moving toward a conclusion, "what remains of the dialectic if one must give up reading history and deciphering in it the becoming-true of society?" (*AD,* 205). Was it only a myth? Not at all. In the final pages Merleau-Ponty tries to rescue the dialectic for his project of liberal reform, by developing the thesis that there is indeed a dialectic of history and society, a movement of progress through the free play of oppositions. But the dialectic is not a revolutionary one pointing to an "end of history" and embodied in a specific class, such as the proletariat.

Revolutionary thought, in fact, is *not* truly dialectical, but utopian and dogmatic. After all, it projects a class that "will not be a new positive power which, after dispossessing the fallen classes, would in turn assert its own particularity; rather, it will be the last of all classes, the suppression of all classes and of itself as a class" (*AD,* 210). The problem is that "there is no dialectic without opposition or freedom, and in a revolution opposition and freedom do not last long" (*AD,* 207). Revolutionary power destroys the dialectic: "Precisely because it rules, the new ruling class tends to make itself autonomous" (*AD,* 209). To hope that the proletariat will be the last ruling class, and will suppress all classes *including itself,* is to project hopes and wishes that are not dialectical because they have no basis in fact.

In writing about the French Revolution, historian Daniel Guérin dreams of "an 'end of politics' out of which one is to make a politics.

Like 'proletarian power,' it is a problem that presents itself as a solution, a question which is given as an answer, the transcendence of history in ideas" (*AD,* 218).[62] After all, revolutions must defend themselves, and in so doing create weapons against their enemies and their adherents. This means that "revolution and its failure are one and the same thing" (*AD,* 219). All revolutionary advances yield new ruling classes, and therefore a "permanent decadence." Because ruling classes resemble each other *insofar as they rule,* even the dictatorship of the proletariat will become "something like a bourgeoisie" (*AD,* 220). Proletarian revolution is thus not only a dream, but a dangerous one: the more that we dogmatically assume that this class will cure history's basic problems, the more likely we are to erect a power beyond control.

As a result, Merleau-Ponty calls for a "new left"—a genuinely independent noncommunist left freed from "the pretension of terminating [the dialectic] in an end of history" (*AD,* 206) and capable of seeing the full complexity of society, social change, and the contest between the United States and the Soviet Union. This left will make the dialectic its living principle only by *accepting parliamentary democracy,* "the only known institution that guarantees a minimum of opposition and truth" (*AD,* 226). The complex "effort of enlightenment" Merleau-Ponty calls for is *not* possible under communism, but is possible in the West. And so he seeks an open-ended "new liberalism" which aligns itself with the proletariat but not the party, does not necessarily accept capitalism but certainly rejects the idea that social problems admit of "a solution the way a crossword puzzle does or an elementary problem of arithmetic" (*AD,* 227).

In 1946 he had described Marxism as follows: "Even if the Marxist dialectic did not take possession of our history, even if we have nowhere seen the advent of the proletariat as ruling class, the dialectic continues to gnaw at capitalist society, it retains its full value as negation: it remains true, it will always remain true, that a history in which the proletariat is nothing is not a human history" (*AD,* 228). Ten years later he renounces his earlier effort to separate Marxism as negation from the Marxist revolution that came to a halt in the Soviet Union. The disappearance of a neutral zone such as Czechoslovakia and the participation of the Soviet Union in the Korean War led Merleau-Ponty to conclude that, finally, the Marxist critique he had accepted yielded the communist actions he had rejected. And so he began the exploration leading to renunciation: "There must be something in the critique itself that germinates the defects in the action" (*AD,* 231). That something was the Marxist dialectic itself, with its sweeping vision of a future classless society.

It is because they are heirs of Marx that communists fail to see history as ambiguity and will, chance and choice, but rather pretend that truth is lodged in the historical unfolding of being. The root problem is already present in the *Communist Manifesto* when it proclaims that Marx's theoretical conclusions "merely express . . . actual relations springing from an existing class struggle, from a historical movement going on under our very eyes" (*AD,* 130; below 382). In fact the Marxist dialectic is a grand projection beyond the boundaries of human knowledge, while the dialectic itself, chastened by such adventures, would still describe conflict and transcendence, but without any hope that grand solutions are at hand. And so Merleau-Ponty renounces being a revolutionary, without renouncing the right to struggle against injustice—in the name, we may say, of the dialectic.[63]

Merleau-Ponty's Challenge

Could this total critique demand any less than a total reply? Merleau-Ponty fundamentally challenged his former close colleague *at the very moment* Sartre was moving toward theoretical Marxism. This is not to say that Sartre's political-theoretical energy over the next few years would be explicitly dominated by the task of satisfying Merleau-Ponty's criticisms. But in being occupied with intervening politically and carrying out a revitalization of Marxism, Sartre's work can be described *vis-à-vis* his former colleague as we have seen him characterize the unconscious meaning of *The Communists and Peace:* "a systematic refutation . . . opposing point by point, my views to his." In fact he would address virtually every significant issue Merleau-Ponty had posed, incorporating this powerful critique in seeking to go beyond it.[64] The result is a major effort at refashioning his own thought and Marxism as he assimilates the one to the other. Thus *Adventures of the Dialectic* forms an inevitable set of reference points in what will become Sartre's unique appropriation of Marxism.

"The Spectre of Stalin"

Sartre's first major response came in late 1956 and early 1957 in his famous articles in *Les Temps modernes* denouncing the Soviet invasion of Hungary and the P.C.F.'s knee jerk support for it, giving evidence of being the "completely new type of sympathizer"—independent, critical, able to say why he is not a communist—Merleau-Ponty hoped but doubted he could become.[65] He analyzed the "neo-Stalinist" intervention from a nonparty Marxist point of view, one which rooted it in a detailed account of Soviet history. Yet in words owing a great deal to Merleau-Ponty's earlier formulations, Sartre also forcefully affirmed his commitment to the communist project as the universal human project, in spite of its contradictions:

> For more than a century, under forms which change in the course of history, one movement alone has drawn the exploited on to lay claim, for themselves and for everybody, to the possibility of full and complete manhood; one movement alone has exposed in all its reality and defined the bourgeoisie as the exploiting class when all the rest treat it as the universal class; one alone produces through and by action an ideology which gives it understanding of itself as well as of others; that movement is the socialist movement taken in its entirety. This movement is the absolute judge of all the rest because, to the exploited, exploitation and the class struggle are their reality and the truth of bourgeois societies; it sees the deep meaning of working men and of operative processes because it cannot but tie them to the fundamental structure of history, because it is the movement of man in the process of developing himself.[66]

Above all, Sartre's premise explicitly rejected Merleau-Ponty's new position, in *L'Express* (drawn from the analyses we have just examined), that communism must be seen relatively as one fact among others, "without privilege." "Its aim," Sartre says, "is to give justice and freedom to all men; this basic intention cannot snatch it from history since, on the contrary, it is in and through history that it will come true" (*SS,* 89). Sartre rejects Merleau-Ponty's newfound "eagle's eyrie from which the evolution of people's regimes and of capitalist democracies could be jointly appraised" (*SS,* 90).[67] On the contrary, this state, this movement, "in spite of everything that has happened . . . still carries within it the likelihood that it may lead to socialism" (*SS,* 6).

Likelihood? In a telling reference to Plato, which ironically builds on Merleau-Ponty's original realism while explicitly refuting his equation of Marxism and the *Republic,* Sartre emphasizes that this "bloody monster which itself tears itself to pieces" (*SS,* 61) was indeed socialism. "That was socialism even in its primitive phase; there has been no other, except in Plato's heaven, and it must be desired as it is or not at all" (*SS,* 61). *This reality,* with its weaknesses, remains an authentic path to the future free society—the *only* path we can see today.

> And I quite see, in fact, that Merleau-Ponty is not very indignant about the Soviet intervention: if the U.S.S.R. is worth no more and no less than capitalist Britain, then, in fact, there is hardly anything else left for us to do except cultivate our gardens. To preserve hope, it is necessary to do the exact opposite: to recognize, in spite of the mistakes, the abominations, the crimes, the obvious privileges of the socialist camp, and to condemn with so much the more strength the policy which puts these privileges in danger. (*SS*, 91)

Thus does Sartre show signs of absorbing his mentor's lessons while trying to go beyond Merleau-Ponty's critique: he recognizes all the evils of communism in 1956, but as one who still embraces its project and, indeed, who seeks to use Marxist tools to explain these evils.

Search for a Method

Sartre's next response, equally forceful and equally famous, appropriately follows Merleau-Ponty's own trajectory and moves onto the theoretical plane. Published in September and October of 1957, *Search for a Method* explains, as Merleau-Ponty had demanded Sartre do,[68] why he is not wholly a Marxist (and by implication why he is not a communist). But it does so in asserting that Marxism is the "only valid interpretation of history."[69] Marxism is, indeed, "the philosophy of our time."[70] Because it is "simultaneously a totalization of knowledge, a method, a regulative idea, an offensive weapon, and a community of language," it forms "the humus of every particular thought and the horizon of all culture."[71] Merleau-Ponty's "post-Marxism" would thus have to be an illusion—either a veiled return to pre-Marxism or the rediscovery of ideas *already* contained in Marxism. One cannot go beyond living philosophies such as Marxism "so long as man has not gone beyond the historical moment which they express."[72]

Then why does Sartre not simply convert to Marxism? Why keep existentialism alive, as a parasitic ideology on its margin? First, because "Marxism stopped."[73] It was destined to be the unity of theory and practice, a guide to reshaping society. But when it became dominant—in the Bolshevik Revolution—its normal course of development was frozen. In the besieged Soviet Union "the free process of truth, with all the discussions and all the conflicts which it involves"[74] had to be curtailed. As a result, theory became separated from practice, "transforming the latter into an empiricism without principles; the former into a pure, fixed knowledge."[75] Where Merleau-Ponty had spoken of Marxism eventuating in opportunism or terror because of its ontological starting point, Sartre argues, on the contrary, that the historical situation itself generated such alternatives. Under urgent conditions, reality was violently assaulted, and theory became an absolute idealism.

Reality came to be understood through a network of *a priori* categories, as Marxism stopped paying attention to the specificity of individuals and events. "Men and things had to yield to ideas—*a priori;* experience, when it did not verify the predictions, could only be wrong."[76] As a result, today's "lazy Marxists" render all events—the Hungarian Revolution, Valéry's poetry—through abstract ideas which pretend to explain but give us no knowledge at all. To correct this we need, within and alongside Marxism, an approach which can return us to Marx by respecting and studying individuals and events in all their specificity. Again and again Sartre insists: "What is necessary is simply to reject *a priorism.*"[77]

The second, and related, reason for Sartre's refusal to embrace contemporary Marxism is that he takes its ideas not as knowledge but "as guiding principles, as indications of jobs to be done, as problems—not as concrete truth."[78] Even after accepting Marxism, "everything remains to be done; we must find the method and constitute the science."[79] While providing us with general keys, Marxism by itself does not allow us to understand, for example, how a specific individual of a specific class—such as Valéry the petty-bourgeois—chooses his specific individual path. Sartre uses precisely the theme—mediations—Merleau-Ponty had used in criticizing him. "Marxism lacks any hierarchy of mediations which would permit it to grasp the process which produces the person and his product inside a class and within a given society at a given historical moment."[80] For example, Marxism avoids seeing the way in which the family operates as the key mediation between the individual and "the general movement of history," yet is lived by the child "as an absolute in the depth and opaqueness of childhood."[81]

Next Sartre explores the ways in which mediations operate, especially through the family. Then, in the remainder of *Search for a Method,* he indicates his project of developing these mediations. He sketches the progressive-regressive method as the path to understanding how an individual internalizes the elements of his situation and then reexteriorizes them as his project. The specifics of these discussions need not occupy us here, but Sartre's general intent is decisive for appreciating the alternative he develops to Merleau-Ponty's abandonment of Marxism. We have seen Merleau-Ponty flatly oppose "Western Marxism" to "naturalistic Marxism," the subjective dialectic to the objective dialectic. He found the first to be a historical irrelevancy outside of great revolutionary moments, the other as accounting for history's weight and the urgency of social pressures, but by lodging the dialectic in the facts themselves. When he concluded that the subjective dialectic led to an unrealizable fantasy and the objective dialectic to the oppressive reality of Soviet communism, Merleau-Ponty left himself no choice but to abandon both.

Sartre, on the other hand, looked for the links between the two, the process whereby *each* created the other—as did Gramsci and the Frankfurt School. He rejected Merleau-Ponty's either/or, searching instead for the subjective roots of the objective alienations and the objective root of the subjective possibility—at one and the same time. There is no question, he insisted, of *adding* a method to Marxism. The dialectic itself must—and can—be developed to be adequate to the human beings who are its objects. In doing so, we will avoid opposing individuality to generality, chance to necessity. Sartre, for example—in opposition to Merleau-Ponty's claim that Stalinism is a general phenomenon separable from the personality of the individual[82]—wants to show that a historical situation does not demand general traits which can be met by a number of individuals, but rather *creates* and *asks for* the very individual who pushes it forward.[83] In seeking to create a Marxism which takes full account of the individual, Sartre seeks "not to reject Marxism in the name of a third path or of an idealist humanism, but to reconquer man within Marxism."[84]

Merleau-Ponty had attacked Marxism, above all, for lifting the moving force of history out of human hands and lodging it in an apparently autonomous sociohistorical process—this is what he meant by his remarks that the truth and direction of history were inscribed in being. If the subjective dialectic was impotent, this objective dialectic had resulted in terror and the cult of the party. In contrast Sartre understands that an adequate Marxism—or social philosophy of any stamp—has to explain *both* the density and weight of history *and* the transforming activity of human subjects. Merleau-Ponty had seen both statically, as opposing camps, and so had not thought beyond them. As a result, he could not fail to regard each as equally incorrect. Sartre, on the contrary, now shows his full distance from Merleau-Ponty by looking forward to developing an analysis which takes account of each side in terms of the other:

> If one wants to grant to Marxist thought its full complexity, one would have to say that man in a period of exploitation is *at once both* the product of his own product and a historical agent who can under no circumstances be taken as a product. . . . [As Engels said,] men make their history on the basis of real, prior conditions . . . but it is *the men* who make it and not the prior conditions. Otherwise men would be merely the vehicles of inhuman forces which through them would govern the social world. To be sure, these conditions exist, and it is they, they alone, which can furnish a

> direction and a material reality to the changes which are in preparation; but the movement of human praxis goes beyond them while conserving them.[85]

Until Marxism learns this lesson, existentialism will continue to exist as a philosophy demanding that it "reintegrate man into itself as its foundation."[86] How will this reintegration be accomplished? First, in a *critique of dialectical reason* which performs its basic theoretical steps, and secondly by encouraging other work which, collectively, completes this task. "From the day that Marxist thought will have taken on the human dimension (that is, the existential project) as the foundation of an anthropological knowledge, existentialism will no longer have any reason for being."[87]

The Daunting Task

And so Sartre turns to create the *Critique.* If these two brief prefaces have already turned out to equal the entire length of Merleau-Ponty's *Adventures,* Sartre's effort has only begun. He will try to show that another Marxian dialectic exists than the one Merleau-Ponty has prematurely rejected, and that this dialectic *both* bears the weight of the world *and* is wholly produced by human beings. But to see the light of day this dialectic must be liberated from the "organicism" which sees society and history as moving on their own.

To set the dialectic straight and account for its deviation, especially in isolation from others who had been attempting the same task, was to be a daunting project of world-historical import. No wonder, then, Sartre worked as if a man possessed. De Beauvoir describes the fury with which he wrote: "for hours at a stretch he raced across sheet after sheet without rereading them, as though absorbed by ideas that his pen, even at that speed, couldn't keep up with; to maintain this pace I could hear him crunching corydrame capsules, of which he managed to get through a tube a day."[88] And in the evenings, exhaustion, alcohol, more alcohol.

The result, even unfinished, was a manuscript separated into two volumes, *five times* the length of Merleau-Ponty's farewell to Marxism. Sartre's hello to Marxism is an entirely new and original work, one which scarcely mentions Merleau-Ponty, but bears the mark of his critique on every page. Let us now return to our opening questions and see how its most general purposes absorb and frame the issues we have been exploring.

The Critique as Theoretical Praxis

Let us be clear upon returning: volume 1 develops the abstract elements for an understanding of history; volume 2 seeks to develop that understanding. It is the progressive study which recombines the themes of the regressive half, volume 1, into a whole whose meaning it interrogates. We have seen Merleau-Ponty argue that Soviet communism's weaknesses and brutality are rooted in historical materialism's philosophical weakness—to inscribe the dialectic as rooted in being itself, as if *events themselves* unfolded toward communism. The *Critique*'s very first section will respond by distinguishing "critical dialectic"—which self-consciously traces the subjective-objective movement of history—from "dogmatic dialectic"—which lifts history beyond the human beings who are its source. Thus the dialectic, which is "both a method *and* a movement in the object,"[89] *went astray* historically, in praxis itself, and at this moment calls for a critique to set it back on track. As "the living logic of action,"[90] it can only appear in its true light, as "the rationality of praxis"[91] to one who performs the *Critique* "in the course of praxis as a necessary moment of it."[92] Sartre's praxis, more specifically, is to ascertain the limits of the dialectic after Stalinism: "the *abuses* which have obscured the very notion of dialectical rationality and produced a new divorce between praxis and the knowledge which elucidates it."[93]

Such a critique makes sense only *after* the dialectic "was posited for itself in the philosophies of Hegel and Marx," then had become the algebra of twentieth-century socialist revolution, and then "Stalinist idealism had sclerosed both epistemological methods and practices. It could take place only as the intellectual expression of that re-ordering which characterizes, in this 'one world' of ours, the post-Stalinist period."[94] If the "totalizing activity of the world" had led to a "divorce of blind unprincipled praxis and sclerosed thought, or in other words the obscuring of the dialectic," the movement of de-Stalinization now makes a critique of dialectical reason both possible and necessary, indeed urgent. Merleau-Ponty, then, had contemplated, but not seen beyond, this frozen "naturalism" that developed under the conditions faced by the Soviet Union after 1917: Sartre's project is not to reject the dialectic or claim to go beyond it in a "post-Marxist" way, but to *perform the intellectual labor necessary to free it from rigidification.*

This, then, is Sartre's most general goal: to revitalize the dialectic by determining its "validity and limits." He seeks to free it from the Stalinist sclerosis under which Merleau-Ponty had encountered it and which he had mistaken as the only possible Marxist dialectic. The decisive question of Sartre's theoretical praxis, after laying out the abstract elements of dialectical comprehension in volume 1, occupies the first quarter of volume 2: Can there be a totalization without a totalizer? In other words, once we abandon Stalinist dogmatism (with its Marxist warrant reaching back to Engels and even to some texts of Marx himself), do struggles themselves produce a larger history? Like Merleau-Ponty, Sartre would reject seeing history as a hyperorganic process unfolding through individuals—this is one of the second volume's recurrent themes. But if so, how do individual human beings and social classes, in their separate and contending praxes, produce something larger that Marxists have mistaken for *laws* of history and society and have inscribed in being?

This, the second volume's first question, is precisely the one Sartre must answer if he is to validate Marxism in the face of Merleau-Ponty's withering attack. Sartre himself is keenly aware of the stakes:

> Marxism is rigorously true if history is totalization; it is no longer so if human history is decomposed into a plurality of particular histories or if any case within the relationship of immanence which characterizes struggle, the negation of each adversary by the other is on principle *detotalizing.* Certainly, we have neither the project nor the possibility of showing here the full truth of dialectical materialism—which we will without doubt attempt elsewhere, in a book devoted to anthropology, which is to say to struggle as such. Our single goal is to establish whether in a practical ensemble torn by antagonism (whether there are multiple conflicts or they are reduced to a single one) the breaks themselves are totalizing and entailed by the totalizing movement of the ensemble. But if in fact we establish this abstract principle, the materialist dialectic, as a movement of history and of historical understanding, need only be proven by the facts it illuminates, or if one prefers, need only be itself discovered as a fact and through other facts.[95]

And so the entire *Critique,* indeed the fate of Marxism itself, hangs on the theoretical praxis of volume 2. Strikingly, just before posing this, Sartre echoes the very same thought expressed a dozen years earlier, then renounced in 1955, by Merleau-Ponty: it is today when "the machine seems to jam" that we should solve these long-neglected problems. In 1946 Merleau-Ponty had already indicated the path for explaining why: "It is jammed [*c'est enrayée*] when the revolution was limited to an undeveloped country" (*AD,* 228). The remarkable parallel emphasizes the remarkable fact: Merleau-Ponty's rejection of Marxism becomes Sartre's challenge and opportunity.

The Critique as Political Praxis

Yet this is only part of the story. In the idea that he abandoned to Sartre, Merleau-Ponty raised a second fundamental issue, which Sartre is not yet ready to approach in volume 1. As we have seen, it is historical and political, as well as philosophical: Why the deterioration of Bolshevism into the phenomenon known as Stalinism? Was it inherent in the Bolshevik Revolution itself, or indeed in *any* revolution, as Merleau-Ponty increasingly came to believe? Is it a *result* of the revolutionary dialectic, as Merleau-Ponty suggests? Or may it rather be explained as Merleau-Ponty earlier suggested, by *using* the dialectic to analyze a specific historical outcome of a praxis undertaken under certain conditions? In following the latter thought Sartre will ask: What is the historical *logic* of the blockage of the dialectic known as Stalinism?

As I indicated earlier, however, Sartre will study Stalinism by posing a variety of other, formal questions which, taken together, move volume 2 away from its original goal. While only an extended study can make clear the relationship between Sartre's formal goals and substantive analysis in this part of volume 2, we may at least note that Sartre's formal goals may be taken for themselves. Indeed, editor Arlette Elkaïm-Sartre has managed to develop titles and a table of contents for publication with only two parenthetical references to the Soviet Union. Yet the formal goals serve to frame a remarkable chronological study of the praxis-process of Bolshevism-Stalinism occupying half of volume 2. It is a major interpretation of the phenomenon of Stalinism.

Although most readings of volume 1 have lacked the framework to see this, volume 2 and a comparison with Merleau-Ponty's critique allow us to discern the concrete political purpose at the heart of Sartre's project:[96] in the act of thawing the dialectic, to trace the praxis-process of its freezing. Sartre set out in volume 2 to sketch why the Bolshevik Revolution followed the course it did, and to explore the prospects of its evolving into a different socialism. The fate of the Revolution had been one of Sartre's major concerns even before his adherence to Marxism, explored in the ten years before beginning the *Critique,* not only in *The Communists and Peace, The Spectre of Stalin,* and *Search for a Method,* but in the plays *Dirty Hands* (1948), and *The Devil and the Good Lord* (1951) and the screenplay, *In the Mesh* (1946). Spurred on by Merleau-Ponty as well as by his own interests, in the *Critique* Sartre now poses the question of revolutionary success-cum-deterioriation as, remarkably, the central historical experience within and around which his social theory develops.

The specific studies of volume 1 begin with the storming of the Bastille and seem to point to the French Revolution. The study of the passage from the group-in-fusion to the Terror to the institutionalization of the revolution, to bureaucracy and the cult of personality, becomes increasingly suggestive of Stalin rather than Napoleon, at the end referring to him by name.[97] Considered by itself, volume 1 may not allow us to say confidently that in its central sections Sartre meant to understand the Russian Revolution through the French. But this impression is strengthened not only retrospectively, by the clearly anticipatory analyses in *The Communists and Peace* and *The Spectre of Stalin,* but above all by the central pages of volume 2.

There, Sartre explores under the rubric of "contradiction" the general problem of oppositions developing within a revolutionary group. Then, under the rubric of "antilabor" he studies the Trotsky-Stalin conflict and its unintended product, "socialism in a single country." He explores, under the formal concern for examining the interaction of groups and series, Bolshevik political practice in the early 1930s (including collectivization and industrialization). He shows how the Revolution deviated itself in order to save itself. And then he studies the singularization of sovereignty, specifically under the "cult of personality." This leads him to inquire about the totalization of envelopment under Stalin which organized every aspect of Soviet life, from the workers' sexuality to the writers' literary praxis. Finally, as an example of the individual sovereign himself being enveloped by the totalization he has created and presided over, he takes up the question of Stalin's anti-Semitism during his final years. In sum, this sustained work on the Soviet Union, equal in size to Merleau-Ponty's entire *Adventures,* poses and answers the question of questions: Why Stalin?

Conclusion: Separation of Theory and Practice

I have situated the *Critique* project, and especially the two questions that together take up the bulk of its second volume, within Merleau-Ponty's challenge to Marxism and Sartre. Sartre's project forms one of the great undertakings of twentieth-century thought. Yet as the "*inachevé*" placed on its title page attests, Sartre abandoned volume 2 without having answered its main question. Although he leaves us tools and suggestions for further study, Sartre himself was not fated to complete the *Critique.*

One reason is certainly its remoteness from any meaningful social forces or movements. In his very formulations, Sartre tends to separate the dialectic as method from the dialectic as content—the tools of dialectical reason are developed in volume 1 *in order to then* be deployed in volume 2 for determining whether history is dialectical. Sartre seeks to construct a universal and *a priori* understanding of the formal conditions of history, one which places praxis in the abstract, but not yet anyone's specific praxis, such as the proletariat or that of the class struggle, at its center.

On the one hand, this weakness is rooted, as I have argued in *Jean-Paul Sartre—Philosophy in the World,* in the very structure of Sartre's thought. His Cartesianism ultimately separates him from social and historical reality, in spite of his Herculean efforts to overcome that separation. Yet, as any critique must acknowledge, living history does not provide Sartre with the basis for thinking his way beyond the dualism at the heart of his thought. It is quite appropriate, after all, that he *asks* about a totalization without a totalizer: living history itself has not made the answer self-evident. In other words, I am suggesting, the problem is not only a *theoretical* problem, and it is certainly not Sartre's alone. *In fact,* and not just in theory, theory became separated from practice. We have already seen Sartre explain this in *Search for a Method:* real history forced the break. It is precisely the history Sartre traces in volume 2 that separates the work tracing it from the social forces which alone can revitalize the dialectic in reality.

And yet as I have indicated above, neither Sartre nor Merleau-Ponty were quite as isolated as they seemed. Neither realized that dialectical Marxism kept developing, even in defeat. As Perry Anderson succinctly captures both the development and the defeat:

> from 1924 to 1968, Marxism did not "stop," as Sartre was later to claim; but it advanced via an unending detour from any revolutionary political practice. The divorce between the two was determined by the whole historical epoch. At its deepest level, the fate of Marxism in Europe was rooted in the absence of any big revolutionary upsurge after 1920, except in the cultural periphery of Spain, Yugoslavia and Greece. It was also, and inseparably, a result of the Stalinization of the Communist Parties, the formal heirs of the October Revolution, which rendered impossible genuine theoretical work within politics even in the absence of any revolutionary upheavals—which it in turn contributed to prevent. The hidden hallmark of Western Marxism as a whole is thus that it is a product of *defeat.* The failure of the socialist revolution to spread outside Russia,

> cause and consequence of its corruption inside Russia, is the common background to the entire theoretical tradition of this period.[98]

The richest of several currents of Marxian thought to develop in these years between Lukács and Sartre, that originating in the Institute for Social Research, bore the stamp of defeat. More academic than political from its founding in 1923, it reflected the enormous psychological distance from active politics of all those who, in Anderson's words, "were statutorily debarred from the revolutionary unity of theory and practice demanded by the eleventh thesis on Feuerbach."[99]

The *Critique* is fated to follow along this path of separation, sometimes unconsciously, in fundamental ways a work of theory apart from praxis. But for a Sartre barred by its bureaucratized and Stalinized character from genuine interaction with a communist party or a workers' movement, there were simply no alternative paths open. His thought was not, could not be, tied to a political force. His own political trajectory shows this definitively. In writing, as founder/editor of *Les Temps modernes,* and as activist, Sartre himself tried again and again, without finally feeling successful, to connect thought and action.[100] No doubt, Sartre was not as aware as were the members of the Institute for Social Research of the ways in which this alienation entered into his concepts themselves.[101] But aware or not, the pressures and absences keeping the *Critique* from real struggles were defined by history itself. Yet, as in the case of the Frankfurt School, this situation limited, but did not doom, its intellectual products. Along with the work of the more self-conscious Herbert Marcuse,[102] Sartre's unfinished analyses would become taken up and used as tools in the struggles of the next generation.[103] And they remain before us today, containing keys and guides as we continue to pose their unanswered questions.

Notes

1. Jean-Paul Sartre, *Critique de la raison dialectique,* vol. 2: *L'intelligibilité de l'histoire* (Paris: Gallimard, 1985); Quintin Hoare, trans., *Critique of Dialectical Reason,* vol. 2: *The Intelligibility of History* (London: Verso, 1991), 4–5.

2. See, e.g., Pietro Chiodi, *Sartre and Marxism* (London: Harvester, 1976).

3. See, e.g., Mark Poster, *Sartre's Marxism* (London: Pluto, 1980).

4. My own study of Sartre's career benefited from access to volume 2. See *Jean-Paul Sartre: Philosophy in the World* (London: Verso, 1981). See also "Sartre's Turning Point: *Critique de la raison dialectique,* II," in *The Philosophy of Jean-Paul Sartre,* ed. P. A. Schilpp (La Salle: Open Court, 1981).

5. Jean-Paul Sartre, *Critique de la raison dialectique,* vol. 1: *Théorie des emsembles pratiques* (Paris: Gallimard, 1985); this is a newly established and annotated text edited by Arlette Elkaïm-Sartre with an annotated table of contents by Juliette Simont and Pierre Verstraeten. The original edition, still widely used, was published in 1960. The English translation, made from the original edition, is by Alan Sheridan-Smith, *Critique of Dialectical Reason,* vol. 1 (London: Verso, 1976). This statement is found in the current edition on 183; in the 1960 edition on 156; in the English version on 69.

6. Vol. 1, 184 (1960, 156); trans., 69.

7. Vol. 1, 135 (1960, 115); trans., 15.

8. This essay is drawn from the first chapter of my *Sartre's Second Critique* (Chicago: University of Chicago Press, 1987).

9. The following story is presented in detail in my *Jean-Paul Sartre,* esp. 107–242.

10. "But it was above all a moral position, and my ideas were naive in the extreme." *Sartre by Himself,* a film directed by Alexandre Astruc and Michel Contat,1977; screenplay translated by Richard Seaver (New York: Urizen, 1979), 50.

11. The first political group he formed included Simone de Beauvoir and Maurice Merleau-Ponty. It was a short-lived Resistance organization called Socialism and Liberty.

12. In *Les Temps modernes,* which first appeared in October 1945. See Sartre's editor's introduction to the first issue, *Situations,* II (Paris: Gallimard, 1948), 9–30.

13. The short-lived organization was named the Rassemblement Démocratique et Révolutionaire. See Jean-Paul Sartre, David Rousset, Gerard Rosenthal, *Entretiens sur la Politique* (Paris: Gallimard, 1949).

14. Jean-Paul Sartre, *Questions de méthode, Critique,* vol. 1, 29 (1960, 23); *Search for a Method,* trans. Hazel Barnes (New York: Vintage, 1963), 20.

15. Jean-Paul Sartre, *La Transcendence de l'ego* (Paris, 1965); *The Transcendence of the Ego,* trans. Forrest Williams and Robert Kirkpatrick (New York: Noonday, 1957), 105.

16. The story of *TM* is best told by Michel-Antoine Burnier's excellent *Choice of Action* (New York: Vintage, 1969). Sartre describes his relationship with Merleau-Ponty on the journal in his eulogy, "Merleau-Ponty *vivant,*" in *Situations,* IV (Paris: Gallimard, 1964); "Merleau-Ponty," in *Situations,* trans. Benita Eisler (Greenwich: Fawcett, 1966). For this and other biographical information see Annie Cohen-Solal, *Sartre: A Life* (New York: Pantheon, 1987).

17. Sartre, "Merleau-Ponty," 168.

18. Quoted in Burnier, *Choice of Action,* 36.

19. Maurice Merleau-Ponty, *Humanism and Terror,* trans. John O'Neill (Boston: Beacon Press, 1969), xxi.

20. Ibid., 156.

21. Ibid., 156–57.

22. This is Merleau-Ponty's description from *Adventures of the Dialectic* (Evanston: Northwestern University Press, 1973), 228. Hereafter *AD.* In *Humanism*

and Terror he speaks of a "comprehension without adherence" which acknowledges both the negative features of communism and that Marxism offers the only adequate moral critique of capitalism and the only meaningful philosophy of history (148–57).

23. Sartre, "Merleau-Ponty," 174; above 580.

24. Jean-Paul Sartre, "Matérialisme et révolution," in *Situations,* III (Paris: Gallimard, 1949); "Materialism and Revolution," trans. Annette Michelson, in *Literary and Philosophical Essays* (New York: Collier, 1955), 198.

25. Sartre, "Merleau-Ponty," 198; above 601.

26. It is especially striking to see Sartre citing Merleau-Ponty's original words in his 1961 eulogy. See ibid., 183–84.

27. Jean-Paul Sartre, "Le Reformisme et les fétiches," in *Situations,* VII (Paris: Gallimard, 1965), 117–18. For Sartre's fascinating rejoinder to a P.C.F. intellectual's reply (in which he emphasizes that the halt is temporary), see "Réponse à Pierre Naville," ibid., 119–43.

28. *Sartre by Himself,* 78.

29. George Lichtheim (*Marxism in Modern France* [New York: Columbia, 1966], 89–102) develops Merleau-Ponty's argument and then notes Sartre's attitude toward Marxism without showing either Sartre's own development or the relationship between the two. Arthur Hirsch (*The French New Left: An Intellectual History from Sartre to Gorz* [Boston: South End, 1981]) indicates the relationship between Merleau-Ponty's *Adventures of the Dialectic* and Sartre's *Critique* in which "Sartre took the criticism seriously and incorporated much of it into his later *Critique*" (49). But after this promising beginning, Hirsch adds not a word to show how Sartre did so. In *Existential Marxism in Postwar France* (Princeton: Princeton University Press, 1975) Mark Poster seems totally unaware of any connection between the two works, or that their personal-political collaboration *should* lead Sartre to take the criticism seriously. In *Choice of Action* Burnier mentions each work but without suggesting any connection between them. Pursuing the development of dialectical Marxism, Scott Warren (*The Emergence of Dialectical Theory* [Chicago: University of Chicago Press, 1984]) explores Merleau-Ponty's attack but unaccountably ignores Sartre's *Critique* altogether.

30. Thomas R. Flynn, almost alone among students of Sartre, notes that Merleau-Ponty virtually "invite[s]" the writing of the *Critique* [by arguing] that Sartre lacks a social philosophy of mediations" (*Sartre and Marxist Existentialism* [Chicago: University of Chicago Press, 1984]). Pietro Chiodi (*Sartre and Marxism*) spends a good deal of time discussing *Adventures of the Dialectic,* but none showing its internal role in the *Critique.* It is surprising that Monika Langer's study of the relationship between *The Communists and Peace* and *Adventures* does not look beyond 1955 to explore Sartre's reflection on the issues raised by his former friend and colleague. Langer rather unhistorically chooses to assert the correctness of the Sartre of 1952–54 against the Merleau-Ponty of *Adventures* instead of following Sartre's own response ("Sartre and Merleau-Ponty: A Reappraisal," in Schilpp, *The Philosophy of Jean-Paul Sartre*). And most surprisingly, in two separate books Raymond Aron ignores Merleau-Ponty's role in provoking the *Critique,* even after

contributing a trenchant analysis of *Adventures,* which includes reference to de Beauvoir's reply (see below n. 32 and *History and the Dialectic of Violence* [New York: Harper and Row, 1975]).

31. Sartre, *Critique,* vol. 2, 16. Merleau-Ponty, summarizing his 1946 position before renouncing it in 1955: "But the Marxist dialectic continues to play across the world. It jammed [*s'est enrayée*] when the revolution was limited to an undeveloped country, but one feels its presence in the French and Italian labor movements," (*AD,* 228).

32. Raymond Aron, *Marxism and the Existentialists* (New York: Simon and Schuster, 1969), 46.

33. Perry Anderson, *In the Tracks of Historical Materialism* (London: Verso, 1984), 36.

34. Aron contributed two articles, published in the review *Preuves* in 1956, and translated and republished in *Marxism and the Existentialists.*

35. Roger Garaudy, et al., *Mésaventures de l'anti-marxisme* (Paris, 1956).

36. Simone de Beauvoir, "Merleau-Ponty et le pseudo-Sartrisme," *Les Temps modernes,* nos. 114–15 (June–July 1955); her reaction is described in *The Force of Circumstances,* trans. Richard Howard (Harmondsworth: Penguin, 1968), 331–32.

37. Sartre, "Merleau-Ponty," 220; below 619.

38. Ibid., 176; below 582.

39. Sartre suggests that Merleau-Ponty, much closer to the P.C.F. during this period, accompanied him in his involvement with the R.D.R. only "in order not to disavow me" (ibid., 180; below 585).

40. Ibid., 189–92, 197; below 593–96, 600.

41. Ibid., 189; below 594.

42. Ibid., 188–97; below 593–600.

43. See ibid., 198–206; below 601–8.

44. Ibid., 199; below 601–2.

45. Lefort had been close to Merleau-Ponty.

46. Georg Lukács, *History and Class Consciousness,* trans. Rodney Livingstone (Cambridge, Mass.: MIT Press, 1971).

47. Merleau-Ponty is already being more stringent here than in *Humanism and Terror,* where he argued that "Marxism is not a philosophy of history; it is the philosophy of history and to renounce it is to dig the grave of reason in history. After that there can be no more dreams or adventures" (153). By 1955 he had clearly renounced the possibility of "dreams or adventures."

48. For a discussion of and selection from Korsch, see Douglas Kellner, *Karl Korsch: Revolutionary Theory* (Austin: University of Texas Press, 1977).

49. For a discussion of the orthodox criticism of Lukács, see Russell Jacoby, *Dialectic of Defeat* (Cambridge: Cambridge University Press, 1981), 83–103.

50. Even as he was falling from power and under attack, Trotsky insisted that "none of us wishes to be or can be right against the party. In the last instant the party is always right, because it is the only historic instrument which the working class possesses for the solution of its fundamental tasks . . . I know that one ought not to be right against the party. One can be right only with the party and through

the party because history has not created any other way for the realization of one's rightness." Isaac Deutscher, *The Prophet Unarmed* (New York: Oxford University Press, 1958), 139.

51. Merleau-Ponty, *Humanism and Terror,* 150.

52. Commentators have remarked on the political ambivalence of *Adventures.* According to Aron, for example, "Merleau-Ponty writes half of his book as if he were still a Marxist, the other half as if he no longer were" (*Marxism and the Existentialists,* 78). Merleau-Ponty succinctly presents this same deep understanding and apparent sympathy for Marxism alongside a fundamental critique of it in "The Yalta Papers," in *Signs,* trans. Richard McCleary (Evanston: Northwestern University Press, 1964), 274–77.

53. For a discussion of the evolution of Merleau-Ponty's politics and an excellent critique of *Adventures,* see Sonia Kruks, *The Political Philosophy of Merleau-Ponty* (Brighton: Harvester, 1981).

54. For a discussion of the vitality and revolutionary character of Western Marxism, see Jacoby, *Dialectic of Defeat.*

55. See n. 27 above.

51. For example, from the second thesis on Feuerbach, which ordains that practice is the criterion of truth.

57. See Jacoby, *Dialectic of Defeat,* 11–36, for a provocative discussion of "conformist Marxism" and the cult of success.

58. As I mentioned, he saw its sponsorship of the Korean War as a decisive indication that the Soviet Union was just another great power. He discusses this in *Adventures,* 228–30.

59. "Les Communistes et la paix," in *Situations,* VI (Paris: Gallimard, 1964); *The Communists and Peace,* trans. Irene Clephane (London: Hamish Hamilton, 1969), 62.

60. This charge was the one that most angered de Beauvoir. See "Merleau-Ponty et le pseudo-Sartrisme."

61. Maurice Merleau-Ponty, *Phenomenology of Perception,* trans. Colin Smith (London: Routledge and Kegan Paul, 1962), 434ff.

62. Translation changed.

63. That his commitment stayed alive, as well as his deep interest in Marxism and communism, is amply evidenced in the second half of *Signs.*

64. Merleau-Ponty did not choose to reply to Sartre, even as Sartre reaffirmed his commitment to the C.P.F. in the face of Merleau-Ponty's critique (in his "Réponse à Pierre Naville") and used Merleau-Ponty's original ideas against his newer ones (see below). Nor did Merleau-Ponty choose to publicly discuss the *Critique,* published in early 1960. Instead, he chose, in the introduction to *Signs,* completed in September 1960, to comment at length on why Sartre drew near to communism when he did, referring to Sartre's essay on Paul Nizan in *Situations,* IV.

65. See *AD,* 187; below 426.

66. "Le Fantôme de Staline," in *Situations,* VII. *The Spectre of Stalin,* trans. Irene Clephane (London: Hamish Hamilton, 1969), 4. Hereafter *SS.* Translation

changed. Compare with *Humanism and Terror,* 149–60, and "The U.S.S.R. and the Camps," in *Signs,* 263–73.

67. This is succinctly formulated in a post-Hungary essay collected in *Signs,* "On De-Stalinization" (303). Merleau-Ponty himself had criticized this stance ten years earlier, in *Humanism and Terror,* 185–86.

68. See *AD,* 165–170; below 407–13.

69. *Questions de méthode* (hereafter *QM*), 30 (1960, 24); trans., 21.

70. *QM,* 36 (1960, 29); trans., 30.

71. *QM,* 21 (1960, 17); trans., 6–7.

72. Ibid.

73. *QM,* 31 (1960, 25); trans., 21.

74. *QM,* 31 (1960, 25); trans., 22.

75. Ibid.

76. *QM,* 31 (1960, 25); trans., 23.

77. *QM,* 44 (1960, 36); trans., 42.

78. *QM,* 40 (1960, 33); trans., 35.

79. Ibid.

80. *QM,* 57 (1960, 47); trans., 56.

81. *QM,* 57 (1960, 47); trans., 62.

82. See *AD,* 144–45; below 390–91.

83. *QM,* 70–71 (1960, 58–59); trans., 83. This prefigures Sartre's major discussion of Stalin, explored in Sartre's Second *Critique,* chap. 6.

84. *QM,* 71 (1960, 59); trans., 83.

85. *QM,* 73–74 (1960, 61); trans., 87.

86. *QM,* 131 (1960, 109); trans., 179.

87. *QM,* 132 (1960, 111), trans., 181.

88. De Beauvoir, *Force of Circumstances,* 385.

89. *QM,* 140 (1960, 120); trans., 20.

90. *QM,* 156 (1960, 133); trans., 38.

91. *QM,* 157 (1960, 134); trans., 39.

92. *QM,* 156 (1960, 133); trans., 38.

93. *QM,* 166 (1960, 141); trans., 50.

94. *QM,* 166 (1960, 141); trans., 50.

95. Sartre, *Critique,* vol. 2, 25.

96. The exceptional reading of the *Critique* confirms the rule; it is based on a study of volume 2. See Perry Anderson, *In Tracks of Historical Materialism,* 70–72.

97. See *QM,* 743–46 (1960, 628–31); trans., 660–63.

98. Perry Anderson, *Considerations on Western Marxism* (London: Verso, 1976), 42.

99. Ibid., 60.

100. See my *Jean-Paul Sartre,* 157–79.

101. Marcuse's *One-Dimensional Man* (Boston: Beacon, 1964) is probably the best example of a social critique painfully aware of itself as lacking the agency which could make it historically true. Interestingly enough, it was published at almost the same time as the *Critique.*

102. For an excellent discussion of Marcuse's lifelong project of rethinking Marxism—and its political effect—see Douglas Kellner, *Herbert Marcuse and the Crisis of Marxism* (Berkeley: University of California Press, 1984).

103. This point is developed by Mark Poster, *Sartre's Marxism,* as well as by André Gorz, "Sartre and Marx," in *Western Marxism* (London: Verso, 1977).

17

Merleau-Ponty and the *Critique of Dialectical Reason*

Thomas R. Flynn

In an inflammatory chapter of his *Adventures of the Dialectic*[1] entitled "Sartre and Ultrabolshevism," Merleau-Ponty savaged the political theory of his erstwhile friend and colleague Sartre with the usual incisiveness, if not with accustomed moderation. The scandal caused by this essay and by Simone de Beauvoir's intemperate reply is a matter of history.[2] What I should like to assess is the difference Merleau-Ponty's criticism may have made in Sartre's major study of social theory, the *Critique of Dialectical Reason*,[3] then in the process of being written. I say "may" because claims of philosophical influence are difficult to warrant, especially in the absence of explicit avowals. Still, it is worthwhile reading the *Critique* in light of Merleau-Ponty's challenge for the focus this lends to Sartre's argument in that somewhat repetitious and prolix text. So I shall first summarize Merleau-Ponty's criticism of Sartre's political and social theory prior to the *Critique* (sec. I), assess the accuracy of his claims regarding Sartre's early work (sec. II), and consider relevant passages from the *Critique* as responses to Merleau-Ponty's remarks (sec. III).

I

Although Merleau-Ponty commented on Sartre's philosophy on different occasions throughout his career, his major remarks on the social theory for our purposes occur in *Adventures*.[4] The context is a broad attack on the Marxist use of dialectic as the instrument of the "universal class" that finds its *Aufhebung* in the proletarian revolution.

What interests Merleau-Ponty about Sartre's defense of the communists is that it is based on principles patently opposed to theirs, ones which by their very nature entail the failure of the dialectic as they understand it. The conflict lies between the "subjectivism" of Sartrean existentialism and the extreme "objectivism" of the Marxist dialectic, sometimes tempered by revisionists like Lukács by being restricted to the level of society as "second nature." The Marxist view, whether diluted or full strength, ascribes objective "truth" and necessity to historical events and relations, which surpass the intentions and responsibilities of individuals. The meaning and historical efficacy of individuals' actions are mediated by their socioeconomic class at a particular point in its historical relations with other classes. Thus the Marxist dialectic "quantifies over" classes as collective subjects and objects of history.

Sartre's existential social theory, as Merleau-Ponty sees it, "founds communist action precisely by refusing any productivity to history and by making history, insofar as it is intelligible, the *immediate* result of our volitions. As for the rest, it is an impenetrable opacity" (*AD,* 97–98; below 357; emphasis mine). It is for lack of mediation that he sees the death of dialectic in Sartre's philosophy. Instead, Sartre offers us a voluntarism, a "pure creation," an individualist philosophy of pure act. Unlike Husserl, whose "teleology" of consciousness led him "to the threshold of dialectical philosophy" in his later work, Sartre holds "there are men and things, and there is nothing between them except cinders of consciousness. There is no other truth than the truth of consciousness, and doing is absolute rootless initiative" (*AD,* 138 n.; below 444–45, note 37). Given this disregard for mediations, "one feels," Merleau-Ponty concludes, "that for Sartre the dialectic has always been an illusion" (*AD,* 98; below 357).

Why this rage for the immediate? Merleau-Ponty locates the root of Sartre's difficulties with dialectic in his philosophy of consciousness, the ontology of *Being and Nothingness* which bifurcates reality without recognizing that interrelation which allows efficacity to the nonconscious and a certain passivity to consciousness itself. In Sartre's ontology, Merleau-Ponty insists, "there is no mediation between 'pure fact' which has whatever meaning one wants to give it, and decision, which gives the fact only one meaning." "The mediation," he argues, "would be the probable, the meaning that the facts *seem* to recommend" (*AD,* 114; below 370). The realm of the probable and the ambiguous, the locus of politics and history for Merleau-Ponty, eludes Sartre.

The immediacy of this philosophy of consciousness is mirrored in Sartre's understanding of temporality, which values the atemporal instant as the cutting edge of choice, freedom, and responsibility. This too relieves Sartre of the weight of the past and the lure of the future—the stuff of politics—and enables him to combine a rationalistic disdain for the probable with a commitment to pure, self-sustaining action that at its limit "becomes . . . theater" (*AD,* 118; below 373). "Sartre's entire theory of the Party and of class," Merleau-Ponty concludes, "is derived from his philosophy of fact, of consciousness, and . . . of time" (*AD,* 105; below 363).

If the failure to mediate historical action is the first weakness in a political theory generated from Sartre's existentialist ontology, Merleau-Ponty discovers two others, equally debilitating to the dialectic, namely, the absence of a concept of objective possibility and an inability to accommodate specifically social predicates.

The absence of mediating factors that keeps Sartre's social philosophy necessarily abstract and inapplicable is particularly marked in the matter of what Weber and Lukács call "objective possibility" (see *AD,* 128; below 379). Marxist dialecticians employ the metaphors of "ripeness" and "boiling point" to denote that objective stage when otherwise indifferent actions and events become historically decisive. If the socioeconomic relations are not appropriate, all the genius or enthusiasm in the world will not effect significant historical change. But for Sartre, as Merleau-Ponty interprets him, "the possibilities are all equally distant—in a sense at zero distance, since all there is to do is to will, in another sense infinitely distant, since we will never be *them,* and *they* will never be what we have to be" (*AD,* 132; below 383). Freed from anchorage in the world of concrete possibilities, Sartrean consciousness floats above the give-and-take of ambiguous reality, a kind of spectator awareness (*conscience de survol*).[5]

Perhaps his *coup de grâce* is Merleau-Ponty's claim that Sartre cannot build a social theory, dialectical or not, on the looking/looked-at ontology that grounds interpersonal relations in *Being and Nothingness:* "For Sartre, the social remains the relationship of 'two individual consciousnesses' which look at each other" (*AD,* 152; below 396). In contrast, Merleau-Ponty offers his own positive alternative: "[Social] relationships are no longer the encounter of two for-itselfs but are the meshing of two experiences which without ever coinciding, belong to a single world." And he recalls the inadequacies of pure consciousness and immediacy by asking "whether," as Sartre says, "there are only *men* and *things* or whether there is also the interworld [*l'intermonde*], which we call history, symbolism, truth-to-be-made" (*AD,* 200; below 437). In effect, what Sartre promises us is a morally motivated theory of history; what he delivers, Merleau-

Ponty implies, is the juxtaposition of existential for-itselfs in mutual opposition—i.e., no social theory at all.

II

What is the accuracy of these charges? Although delivered against the essays subsequently issued as *The Communists and Peace* with "A Reply to Claude Lefort,"[6] the basis of Merleau-Ponty's criticism is Sartre's ontology of *Being and Nothingness,* published nine years earlier. The substance of de Beauvoir's defense is that Merleau-Ponty acted in bad faith by leveling such charges, since he knew full well Sartre was reassessing his social theory.[7] Is *The Communists and Peace* a faithful application of Sartre's existentialist social ontology? Or does de Beauvoir's defense hold, at least that Merleau-Ponty could have known better, for the evidence was present even in *The Communists and Peace?*

Let me acknowledge at the outset that each protagonist is partially correct. Merleau-Ponty has accurately diagnosed the major inadequacies in Sartre's existentialist ontology for grounding any viable social philosophy. But de Beauvoir has correctly sensed that, in his political fervor, Merleau-Ponty overlooked the significance of those shifts and adjustments which, with the wisdom of hindsight, we can now perceive even in *The Communists and Peace.*

Of the many such changes in that later work, three specifically come to mind. The first is Sartre's replacing the discourse of consciousness with that of praxis, which will figure so centrally in the *Critique.* Merleau-Ponty dismisses what we now recognize as a significant change as merely another name for "pure action" (see *AD,* 132; below 383). Though Sartre at this point has yet to draw the implications of this move for a dialectical understanding of human history, Merleau-Ponty seems unwilling *a priori* to allow him such a shift.

Second, Sartre's lengthy discussion of the economic Malthusianism of nineteenth-century industrial capitalists—repeated in the *Critique* and in his Flaubert study—evinces a growing awareness of objective possibility and structural injustice: "The meanness is in the system" (*CP,* 183). He likewise recognizes the weight of objective possibility when noting that "it is history which shows some the exits and makes others cool their heels before closed doors." As he explains: "The historical whole determines our powers at any given moment, it prescribes their limits in our field of action and our real future; it conditions our attitude toward the possible and the impossible" (*CP,* 80). No doubt Merleau-Ponty is justified in pointing out that Sartre joins the anarchists in emphasizing oppressive praxis over impersonal exploitation—such will be the fulcrum of his humanism to the very end—but this scarcely precludes respect for the influence of the latter, a sense of its sociohistorical pressure. The *ad hoc* character of *The Communists and Peace* counsels us to regard it as merely symptomatic of the evolution Sartre's thought is undergoing rather than as providing the terminus of that development itself.

Finally, there is ample evidence in this work that Sartre has come to acknowledge the specificity of the social. One instance is his discussion of the proletariat moving from mass to class, from object to subject of history, a discussion that clearly anticipates his famous analysis of the series and the group in the *Critique* (see *CP,* 81, 207 ff.). Although he has not yet formulated the ontology to systematize these insights, he has already set the limits of the discussion; he is aware that social wholes are neither organic entities nor atomistic chains: "No one believes any longer in the proletariat fetish, a metaphysical entity from which the workers might alienate themselves. There are men, animals, and objects. And men are real and individual beings who are part of historical wholes and are comparable neither to atoms nor to the cells of an organism" (*CP,* 89).

Here, too, Merleau-Ponty seems insensitive to the change he is witnessing. He insists that the "social world" Sartre describes in *The Communists and Peace* is one against which Sartre's own thinking is in revolt, that Sartre merely finds there "an incentive to transcend it [the social world] and to begin again *ex nihilo* this entire disgusting world" (*AD,* 137–38; below 385). That would seem to be the case only if one is convinced that the ontology of *Being and Nothingness* is the norm, that it is incapable of significant change, and that any counterevidence must be read as either an apparent exception to an inviolable rule or an inconsistency.

Yet Merleau-Ponty's remarks are most telling, even prescient, when he links Sartrean subjectivism and voluntarism with the *violence* that necessarily attends any fusion of social wholes out of pure consciousnesses. As he observes, "it is the *cogito* which gives to violence its Sartrean nuance" (*AD,* 159; below 402); and again, "choice, freedom, and effort become conquest and violence in order to become everyone's affair" (*AD,* 163; below 406). Indeed, violence continues to flavor Sartre's social theory not only in his preface to Frantz Fanon's *The Wretched of the Earth,*[8] where it reaches its climax, but in the concept of "fraternity-terror" that covers the pledged group in the *Critique.* Sartre never solved the problem of social violence to his satisfaction. In one of the last public statements given before his death he avowed: "To tell the truth, I do not yet see clearly the true relationship between violence and fraternity."[9] If Merleau-Ponty is correct, this is because Sartre never fully rejected his philosophy of the *cogito* and the rationalism it presumed.

III

Sartre admitted Merleau-Ponty's basic objection when, in an interview published a decade after the *Critique,* he allowed *a propos* of *Being and Nothingness:* "My early work was a rationalist philosophy of consciousness."[10] But by subsuming this into a philosophy of praxis, I am arguing, Sartre short-circuited the cluster of difficulties marshalled against him in *Adventures.* As was so often the case, he anticipated in his popular writings philosophical concepts and distinctions subsequently elaborated in more specialized works. This is the relation between *The Communists and Peace* and the *Critique.* If the former gives evidence Sartre is changing his social philosophy, certain passages in the latter sound as if they were written with Merleau-Ponty's criticism ringing in Sartre's ears. They counter each of the charges we have discussed.

The philosophy of praxis, for example, enables Sartre to achieve a real dialectic that overcomes, or at least basically tempers, the dichotomies of *Being and Nothingness.* Sartre is particularly intent on accounting for the materiality of praxis and thus for the reality of the dialectic that it grounds. So he turns from the mutual gaze of consciousnesses (the source of interpersonal relations in *Being and Nothingness*) to generate his dialectic out of "the initial contradiction between the organic and the inorganic," that is, between lack and need as negation and double negation respectively (*CDR,* 80). "In so far as body is function, function need, and need praxis," he argues, "one can say that *human labor,* the original praxis by which man produces and reproduces his life, is *entirely* dialectical" (*CDR,* 90). By understanding the basic human project as a doing, not a looking, Sartre evades the accusation of spectator consciousness and makes possible a *common* praxis (where a common gaze had been out of the question).

This materiality of praxis affects temporality as well. In Sartre's view, the potentially cyclical synthesis of change and identity that marks primitive societies is disrupted by "the contingent and inescapable fact of scarcity" (*CDR,* 82). In the time of elementary praxis, need "transforms the totality as future reality into possibility" (*CDR,* 83). Material scarcity qualifies human history as a tale of competition and conflict. He never addresses the implication that time would become cyclical in a nonprimitive society of material abundance.

As if to counter directly the charge of excessive immediacy, Sartre proclaims: "The crucial discovery of dialectical investigation is that man is 'mediated' by things to the same extent as things are 'mediated' by man" (*CDR,* 79). The quality of this mediation, whether positive or negative, cooperation or struggle, depends on the fact of scarcity. And the lack of material goods merely underscores the dimensions of passivity and activity that characterize praxis and the "inert" material environment respectively. Sartre now speaks of a "dialectic of passivity," namely, "the way inertia itself becomes dialectical through having the seal [of praxis] placed on it" (*CDR,* 67n.). He cites the paradoxical counterfinality that by hoarding gold, for example, a state may in fact impoverish itself through inflation. Examples of such dialectical intelligibility abound in the *Critique,* giving full measure to the passive element in human affairs without admitting some *initial* efficacy to impersonal forces in history—a stand incompatible with Sartrean humanism. Indeed, the entire *Critique* is a skein of mediations and mediations of mediations, leading Althusser to proclaim Sartre "the philosopher of mediation *par excellence.*"[11]

Again, the matter of objective possibility figures so centrally in the *Critique,* the upshot of which is that in a world of material scarcity the only real, albeit fleeting, freedom occurs in the group, that we need not comment further on this aspect of Sartre's "answer" to Merleau-Ponty. Besides, we have already seen that the concept is fully operative in *The Communists and Peace.* Suffice it to say that objective possibility functions in the later work particularly as "exigency" which "imposes a certain content on the future towards which it is transcended" (*CDR,* 235). This contributes to Sartre's *via media* between economic "determinism" and the kind of "pure creation" Merleau-Ponty criticized so severely.

As if to correct the impression given Merleau-Ponty by *The Communists and Peace,* Sartre now urges: "There are only men and real relations between men."[12] And he later explains: "'Human relations' are in fact inter-individual structures whose common bond is language and which actually exist at every moment of history" (*CDR,* 99). He even adopts Merleau-Ponty's term "interworld" (*l'intermonde*) as he urges sociologists to determine "the type of reality and efficacy appropriate to the collective objects which people our social field and which may be conveniently called the intermundane" (*SM,* 76).[13] Indeed, Sartre's whole project of constructing "a structural, historical anthropology" (*SM,* xxxiv) in the *Critique* occurs in the very realm of the interworld that Merleau-Ponty called for.

Are we to conclude that the *Critique* is at least in part a response to Merleau-Ponty's criticism of Sartre's early social philosophy? As I noted at the outset, we can scarcely expect a strict demonstration of that claim. But I hope to have made clear that many of the basic flaws which Merleau-Ponty noted in Sartre's existentialism are remedied by his taking a dialectical turn in the *Critique,* even to the point of adopting Merleau-Ponty's use of the "interworld" as the proper locus for social phenomena. Given the immense respect Sartre continued to maintain for Merleau-Ponty, even after *Adventures,*[14] it is reasonable to suppose that the latter's strictures were in Sartre's mind as he explicitly addressed the very issues for which he had been taken to task in that work.

But the subjectivist thrust of Sartre's thought and hence his "existentialism," though chastened, survived these shifts. Insofar as Merleau-Ponty's criticism constitutes the challenge that a Sartrean existentialist social philosophy is impossible, the *Critique* is a counterdemonstration *ambulando.* The social ontology of that work defends the "existentialist" values of individual freedom and responsibility in the midst of properly social identities and predicates. Thus Sartre remains true to his abiding conviction that "a man can always make something out of what is made of him."[15] Whereas roughly the first half of his career was bent on showing that "a man can always make something," the second increasingly respected and analyzed the "what has been made of him."

Notes

1. Maurice Merleau-Ponty, *Adventures of the Dialectic,* trans. Joseph Bien (Evanston: Northwestern University Press, 1973). Hereafter cited as *AD.*

2. See her "Merleau-Ponty et le pseudo-sartrisme," *Les Temps modernes* 10 (June–July 1955), 2072–2122. The controversy is recorded by Michel-Antoine Burnier in *Les Existentialistes et la politique* (Paris, 1966), 101–3.

3. Jean-Paul Sartre, *Critique of Dialectical Reason,* trans. Alan Sheridan-Smith (London, 1976). Hereafter cited as *CDR.*

4. For a list of the principal texts where Merleau-Ponty assesses Sartre's philosophy, see Margaret Whitford, *Merleau-Ponty's Critique of Sartre's Philosophy* (Lexington, 1982), 149 n. 6. I have not discussed the long and important chapter of *Le Visible et l'invisible,* "Interrogation et dialectique," because it appeared after the *Critique* and it is unlikely that Sartre was familiar with the notes on which it was based.

5. Actually, the expression "*conscience de survol*" is Sartre's and is used to criticize the young Flaubert's incapacity for genuine praxis (see *L'Idiot de la famille,* 3 vols. [Paris, 1971–72], vol. 2, 1558). Sartre had already introduced the phrase "*projet de survol*" in *Being and Nothingness,* trans. Hazel E. Barnes (New York, 1956), 486 (hereafter cited *BN*); French edition (Paris, 1943), 566. Merleau-Ponty turns the expression against Sartre in *Le Visible et l'invisible* (Paris, 1964), when he accuses him of employing "*une pensée en survol*" (99).

6. Jean-Paul Sartre, *The Communists and Peace,* with "A Reply to Claude Lefort," trans. Martha H. Fletcher and Philip R. Berk, respectively (New York, 1968). Hereafter *CP.*

7. See "Merleau-Ponty et le pseudo-sartrisme," esp. 2122 n.; below 491, note 7.

8. Frantz Fanon, *The Wretched of the Earth,* trans. Constance Farrington (New York, 1968).

9. Jean-Paul Sartre, "L'Espoir, maintenant . . . ," *La Nouvel Observateur,* no. 801 (17 March 1980), 58.

10. Jean-Paul Sartre, "The Itinerary of a Thought," in *Between Existentialism and Marxism* (New York, 1974), 41.

11. Louis Althusser, et al., *Lire le Capital,* 2 vols. (Paris, 1965), vol. 2, 98.

12. Jean-Paul Sartre, *Search for a Method,* trans. Hazel E. Barnes (New York, 1968), 76; see also 162. Hereafter cited as *SM.*

13. Professor Barnes, in a note to her translation, rightly points out the common source of this term for both Merleau-Ponty and Sartre in the Epicurean concept of space between the worlds (see *SM,* 76 n.).

14. See Jean-Paul Sartre, "Merleau-Ponty," in *Situations,* IV (Paris, 1964), 189–287.

15. Sartre, "Itinerary of a Thought," 35.

18

Sartre and Merleau-Ponty

Mikel Dufrenne

Translated by Hugh J. Silverman and Frederick A. Elliston

Within Parisian intellectual circles, Sartre is no longer fashionable. Our present situation does not yet provide the distance needed to measure his work and to assign him a place in the history of ideas. On the other hand, posthumous judgments and laurels of a meager immortality make little difference, particularly to Sartre. But let us make no mistake: whatever the ebbs and flows of fashion may be, Sartre is profoundly present for our present age. We are all Sartreans—perhaps because, on the whole, Sartre is not Sartre. But he would certainly like to be the elusive power of reflection that is faithful only to a thoroughly generous inspiration. For this reason, outside academia and professional circles Sartre is *the* philosopher, the incarnation of militant philosophy—just as Picasso embodies painting.

Apparently, however, opposition to Sartre thrives among specialists. What is the counterposition? On the one hand, it is the philosophy of the concept, authorized by scientific, semiological, and structuralist knowledge. On the other hand, it is the philosophy of nonphilosophy—sometimes in terms of traces, sometimes in terms of flux. Nevertheless, has not Sartre contributed to knowledge and to analytic reason just as much as he has contributed to dialectical reason? And if we hold that knowledge is the ally of power, that science becomes ideology and that philosophy must have at least some force, must we not still look for the first manifestation of this force in Sartre? For him, philosophy ceases to be the authoritarian and totalitarian discourse of the master. It exists only by way of a subjectivity that "bursts forth towards the world" (following Sartre's interpretation of Husserlian intentionality).[1] Philosophy is carried out by the practice of a philosopher who writes plays, attempts a political reassessment, supports the Russell tribunal, creates a journal and acts with militancy on many terrains.

Despite this philosophical burgeoning, Sartre cannot claim a monopoly on philosophy. As for his contemporaries within the French context, another philosopher—Maurice Merleau-Ponty—can be set off against Sartre. They were once very close: classmates at the École Normale, comrades in battle at *Les Temps modernes,* a solid friendship that later dissolved between them. We know of the emotion with which Sartre recalled their friendship on the occasion of Merleau-Ponty's premature death. And yet they diverged. Without crossing swords overtly they unequivocally maintained their dignity. Must we therefore, in turn, put one in opposition to the other—perhaps even to the extent of taking sides?

We cannot ignore the reasons that separated them. Their reasons were serious, yet they acted without excessive seriousness. Both were profoundly ethical—that is, political. What caused the break was Merleau-Ponty's attitude toward the communist party in *Adventures of the Dialectic* (1955). This position was no longer the reticence of *Humanism and Terror* but an outright refusal. This is very significant. For French intellectuals, the communist party did not cease to be a problem, and did not cease to create problems. Witness the sometimes theatrical movement of adherence and resignation and even, most recently, the turns that *Tel Quel* has taken. The problem is above all that of allegiance to the party in Moscow. Today this subordination is undoubtedly less strong. It is even more intolerable now that the Soviet state has betrayed the Revolution and its only ambition is to be a partner—the equal—of the United States. Yet in France, the communist party continues to be the party of the proletariat. For a long time it was impossible—at least until 1968—to undertake any action in the streets, to work in spite of, or even outside the party. Can we disengage ourselves from all the workers whom the party unites and who are the living force of the proletariat? Can we be content to say that these workers are mystified and neutralized? Thus, we adopt a good conscience—at little cost to ourselves. Must we sacrifice the solidarity and efficacy that is too easy for the privileged to reject in favor of purity? It makes little difference today whether purity flies the colors of the impure, the perverse, and the schizoid. Purity always runs the risk of being a pretext for someone's resignation. Sartre never resigned from his position as a beautiful revolutionary soul, and as one who passively awaits a miracle.

Neither Sartre nor Merleau-Ponty ever believed that they could situate themselves outside history and become disinterested toward the present. They were both committed initially side by side at *Les Temps modernes.* Yet even then they were committed in terms of their different styles. When Merleau-Ponty in *Adventures of the Dialectic* distanced himself from his friend, he left Sartre with a moral project of the Kantian sort. Simone de Beauvoir became indignant, as if it were shameful to be a Kantian. And yet Merleau-Ponty was not wrong. Even if Sartre's commitment does not have the rationality of a formal imperative (which, for Kant, is supposed to be forged into empirical choices), it acquired the character of an absolute decision. Nourished within bourgeois culture, Sartre chose to put himself unreservedly at the service of the oppressed. His was an original and, we might add, unreflective or nontheoretical choice, because it remained prior to all deliberative reflection on history. The *Critique of Dialectical Reason* was not published, and not even written, until 1960—whereas the break with Merleau-Ponty occurred in 1955. This choice induced Sartre to join in common cause with the communist party, at least on precise and limited subjects. Whatever the case, he certainly knew that the party is the instrument of Russian imperialism, that the Revolution in the Soviet Union had been stifled by the bureaucracy and the police, and that the proletariat was in no way a dictatorship that could prepare for the abolition of the state. But he also knew that the party in France is, objectively speaking, the sole force capable of rallying the proletariat, because the proletariat recognizes itself in the party. Sartre refused, therefore, radically to cut himself off from the party. Merleau-Ponty made a different choice. Indeed, he chose not to choose. He did not offend history by throwing himself into it. Rather, he maintained his distance, just because he considered himself already thrown. This passive commitment within history preserved him from an active commitment. The unreflectedness that surrounded him—the complexity and opacity of historical situations—brought him to a reflection that compelled him to "decipher the probable" without compromising itself with radical options. Their situation parallels the relationship between Hume and Kant.

Thus, what separates Sartre from Merleau-Ponty is a tactical problem. But their divergence expresses the difference between two beings-in-the-world, one who is more abrupt, more willful, more concerned with disengaging himself from his context; the other who is more reserved, more subtle, more prudent. This inevitable difference reverberates in their philosophies. But does it extend to the point of placing them in opposition? I would like to show that little by little Sartre's thought, especially when he wrote the *Critique,* cautions above all that his philosophy does not conflict with that of Merleau-Ponty.

In 1955 Merleau-Ponty became hardened to what he could not accept in Sartre, even to the point of caricature: the passion for freedom, the idea of a radical upheaval of the for-itself outside the shadows of the in-itself, and what he calls "the folly of the *cogito*." And certainly Sartre forcefully affirms the irreducibility of the subject. Yet consciousness is not always purely personal. Since it is self-consciousness, nothing issues forth from it. But the dualism to which this initial affirmation seems to lead is not the last word. Acts of consciousness are not pure acts; choices are not sovereign decisions. And indeed, as Francis Jeanson has indicated, Sartre describes images of the bastard in his novels and plays: "Roquentin, Orestes, Mathieu . . . three failures in freedom." Freedom fails to interrogate itself, to take itself as an end. It is found only when it is engaged in an action in which it forgets itself. In effect, the for-itself always has an obligatory relation to the in-itself. At the end of *Being and Nothingness,* beyond the dualism that a "phenomenological ontology" suggests, Sartre asks a "metaphysical" question in order to determine whether this relation can be articulated within a totality. It is perhaps true that this totality must always remain "both indicated and impossible," that we can no longer be Spinozists. To think this totality would be to think God, and furthermore to think myself as God. For in me the for-itself is first advanced to the in-itself without alienating itself. And I am a bastard more easily than God is.

This totality is no less lived because it is unthinkable. It is not mastered within a dialectic but lived in ambiguity. The philosophy of *Being and Nothingness* could also have been called a philosophy of ambiguity, as de Waelhens and others have described Merleau-Ponty's work.

First there is the fact—the metaphysical fact, if you like—of birth. The for-itself bursts forth abruptly. It acts in accordance with a celebrated formula: "carried by the in-itself, the for-itself is born." Yet the umbilical cord will never be cut. Consciousness will not cease to live this relation to the object that defines its intentionality. It is a power of "bursting forth toward the world," and it is only that. The relation of the self to the self that accompanies this burst does not constitute the subject as an object. Let us stress the "burgeoning" rather than the aim (*visée*). This substitution of terms is the measure of the distance between Sartre and Husserl. Sartre would not be tempted by the idealism whereby the aims (*visées*) of consciousness are constitutive acts and in which consciousness is accorded a properly transcendental status. Quite the contrary, there is the charter of a fundamental realism that would hear all of its fruit within the confrontation with Marxism: "Existentialism and Marxism aim at the same object; but Marxism has reabsorbed man into the idea, and existentialism seeks him everywhere *where he is*—at his work, at his home and in the streets."[2] Being-in-the-world is presence to the world. The critique of representation that is intoxicated by contemporary thought finds its source here: the world is not my representation; it is what I am present to and there is no "I" except at the heart of this presence. Merleau-Ponty had already described the dissolution of the pact that perception effects between man and the world. He had taught us that there is no more an interior man than an external world. In doing so, was he not following Sartre's teachings? We must admit that presence to the world is not neutral. Being-in-the-world is not only openness onto the world, it is also compromised by it to the extent that its presence is mediated by the body. The relation of the for-itself to the in-itself, in that it is obligatory and unthinkable, is therefore the relation of freedom to facticity. Sartre has not forgotten this, for it is through the body as body that I am in the world. It is possible that certain formulas from *Being and Nothingness* appear to refine the body, making it into a sign rather than a reality; for example, Sartre describes the body as "the necessity of my contingency."[3] But Sartre also knows that this contingent form is man's destiny. It is not only the matter in him that gives him balast but also the form that informs him and thereby determines and limits him. That I am my body signifies that I am not what I want; and life that animates me preserves in me without me. No matter what the impact of the psychic on the somatic, I cannot measure its effects nor measure its effects of the inverse relation. For me to be living signifies that the relation of the for-itself to the in-itself cannot be categorized. But there is still more: being-in-the-world is not just compromise: it is also betrayed. And here Sartre's thought ultimately goes in the same direction as that of Merleau-Ponty.

After being-alive, another dimension of being-in-the-world must be considered: being-in-society. If Merleau-Ponty in *The Structure of Behavior* was more explicit than Sartre on the theme of life, Sartre in the *Critique of Dialectical Reason* is more explicit than Merleau-Ponty on the theme of society, for the *Critique*, published in 1960, is a response to objections that Merleau-Ponty had raised in 1955. Merleau-Ponty contested Sartre's earlier account of the primary opacity of social life, within which consciousness is incarnate. Sartre held that history has a meaning, but it is neither clear nor distinct, and no dialectic can master it. However, such a dogmatic philosophy of history is a trap. From this, Merleau-Ponty took up the challenge, but his was no less categorical than Sartre's. Moreover, we might even ask whether his conclusion was justified. If history carries us and moves us like life, can we disengage ourselves from it in order to interrogate it from without? To be within the world or to be within history is always at the same time to be both inside and outside. But then the philosopher, sanctioned by history, appeals to its wisdom and recommends a reformist attitude. This is still a choice, as with Sartre, of a revolutionary attitude, neither more nor less justifiable by a philosophy of history. What distances Merleau-Ponty from Sartre is precisely this existential choice, more so than any doctrinal partisanship.

But in fact, Sartre has attempted to justify his choice or in any case to clarify it. He has striven to think history or at least to "establish the basis for a prolegomenon to any future anthropology."[4] In other words, to do what Merleau-Ponty should have done would be to do for social life what he had done with natural life. Merleau-Ponty showed that the natural world, which is our own environment and which he calls the transcendental field, is entirely opaque to us. Perception is the emergence of a lived meaning for the body in its presence; a world is expressed across appearances; and the arts bear witness to this world by taking up a movement of blossoming. Now why does the social dimension of the work not reveal itself in perception, too? To inhabit the world (to repeat Hölderlin's expression) is always to co-inhabit, to grasp the already articulated presence of others at least as a watermark on the things themselves. The social is abandoned to feeling, and extends to aesthetic experience. Meanwhile, Sartre does not explore the meaning of history according to a "phenomenology of perception" and thus he does not explore it as an extension of Merleau-Ponty.

Sartre speaks of intelligibility more than sense. The *Critique* is, in a Kantian way, the search for the conditions of intelligibility within the social. Sartre understands this intelligibility as comprehension,[5] following the traditional opposition between comprehension and explanation. This allows him to refuse the intelligibility of the natural sciences as elaborated by analytic reason. In *Being and Nothingness* the principle of intelligibility always resides in the immediate transparency within the relation of the self to itself, which defines the for-itself as consciousness (of) self and whereby understanding is primarily self-understanding—i.e., consciousness of the self. But the great novelty of the *Critique* consists in substituting praxis for consciousness. Because the relation of the for-itself to the for-itself—if not of self to self—is necessarily mediated by matter, Sartre appeals at the same time to dialectic: "The *praxis* of men is the sole intelligible reality" (*CRD,* 674; *CDR,* 717). Why? Because praxis is still consciousness. And could we not also say that all consciousness is praxis, that every relation to the world—even passive relations such as emotion—is still in some respect active? Sartre does not develop this point. What he underlines in praxis is rather his relation to matter as "worked matter." And what interests him is that it can communicate its intelligibility to the whole sociohistorical field. How can it do that? By totalizing.

"Totalization" is the key word here. At the end of *Being and Nothingness* totality already appeared as a metaphysical problem, but in that case it made no difference whether it was confronted or neglected. Its meaning, however, has changed: as far as the for-itself is concerned, emphasis has shifted from consciousness to praxis, and the in-itself is henceforth the matter on which praxis affixes its seal; "matter as a passive totality is revealed by an organic being seeking its being" (*CRD*, 167; *CDR*, 81). First, the totality does not exist by itself. We do not encounter it, we do not undergo it except as a provisional product of a totalizing act. In nature there is no totality. Outside of the act that brings the object together (outside of perception, we might say) or outside of the act that unifies a practical field (in other words, outside of work), there is only multiplicity and exteriority. All meaning and everything social, to the extent to which the totality makes sense, remain suspended in a subjectivity but hereafter of a practical sort. Furthermore, intersubjectivity, the confrontation of consciousnesses, and the look of the third party are no longer thematizations of the social: "The relation of reciprocity and the relation to the third party are not in themselves social" (*CRD*, 308; *CDR*, 255). This relation of the practical organism acting on the environment occurs in a context that is affirmed by materialism. In this respect, a whole theory of individual totalizing praxis serves as a prelude to a theory of the social. To totalize is to confer unity on the practical field by a project. From this it follows that totalization implies matter. And here already the dialectic that inaugurates history—and which in truth is antidialectical, as Sartre would say—will play a role such that we can call it, with Adorno, a negative dialectic: not a surpassing but a return. This misfortune of praxis is indicated in several ways. First, man makes himself inert in order to act. This, we dare to say, is not very convincing, for one can choose to make oneself inert without alienating the individual. We could even extend the analysis to show how means too often pervert the ends or become themselves the ends such that man sees himself as stealing meaning from his own enterprise. The history of the Russian Revolution provides a rather probing example of this shift. Here we have rejoined the Sartrean theory: the totality turns itself back against the totalization while totalizing man finds himself totalized by the matter he has totalized. He submits to the history he has made. But this submission demands that we also take the other into consideration. And indeed the other is always already there: individual praxis is never solitary. The individual's unhappiness arises because the first relation between men is always one of opposition. No longer is it owing as in *Being and Nothingness* to the look of the other objectifying me and stealing my world from me, in other words, to each consciousness pursuing the other's death. Rather, it is owing to each praxis entering into competition with the other—because "the practical field is originally conditioned by scarcity" (*CRD*, 269; *CDR*, 331). Matter is always at the heart of human relations, and in this case each person is excessive in relation to the other. Scarcity is the fundamental fact—the necessity of our contingency, just as the body in *Being and Nothingness* was that which orients all history.

Scarcity is assuredly an evil. But all evil cannot be attributed to scarcity. Evil comes from the success of totalization in the totality. For what becomes individual praxis also becomes common practice instituted in the group: "the unity of exteriority" is opposed and often substituted for "the unity of interiority." "Any social field is constituted to a large extent by structured ensembles of groupings that are always both praxis and practico-inert, even though either one of these characteristics may constantly tend to cancel itself out" (*CRD*, 307; *CDR*, 254). Passing through a series of admirable analyses, Sartre describes two phases of the social. The first is the place of a possible liberation when the group is truly totalizing. It is linked by a common enterprise and does not bind itself as does the heated group of rioters at the moment of a revolutionary action. The second is the place of alienation when the group cools down, institutionalizes, and hardens itself, when objectivity becomes inertia—the fall into materiality.

Is all this so far from Merleau-Ponty? By moving in a direction counter to that of Merleau-Ponty, does Sartre open up the possibility of a science or philosophy of history? No, but he does indicate the possibility of an experience rather than a concept. The intelligibility that he first proposes is not what is demanded by knowledge. To understand is not to explain. To understand is to resume, to reincorporate, to participate. On the other hand, should history be studied theoretically? In the *Critique* presented as only the first volume of a larger projected study, Sartre says nothing about history as a totalizing act of becoming. In the process of formalization, he notes only the abstract elements of social reality. He joins them according to a logical genesis that remains explicitly indifferent to chronology. This formalization is at the heart of the real whose intelligibility he guarantees but does not situate historically. Certainly, totalization can have some relationship to time. It is also the unity lived by the subject of temporal *ekstases.*

But what is the relation between this unity and the flow of a transindividual act of becoming? What sort of grounding is available to a becoming whose subjectivity is intelligible? But must we trap Sartre in his own questions? Whether he holds to his promises or not, we must not expect that he will provide a theory of history similar, for example, to Althusser's—namely, a structuralist theory that explains instead of understands and which relegates the subject to an all-encompassing ideology, which renounces its right to think how the structure is operated or lived. Sartre can be only partially structuralist. The structure must be thought, but we cannot think it like a thing—simply in terms of exteriority. The structure is the object of a negative dialectic that is at the same time "the inert object of calculation when seen as an ossification without taking account of totalization or an effective power activated by the praxis of each and every person" (*CRD,* 503; *CDR,* 500). Anthropology cannot place the human in parentheses. He who is attached to the lived must take into account what Van Gogh called the terrible human passions. We no longer write treatises on the passions; rather, we make a strong case for desire. By mystifying it with elements of *eros* and *thanatos,* or at least by depersonalizing it, one might still write a libidinal history devoid of a subject. But such a study is nevertheless about historical subjects, which in the last analysis are individuals—not necessarily the great men or names inhabited by a will to power, but anonymous people lost in the masses. In them, we show the relationship between the libido and their work.

Sartre, in his own way, does refer to the passions. Instead of desire, he speaks of violence. When in conflict, he says, men continually try to remove themselves from it. However, violence does not derive its full meaning from its use in a historical totalization. How can we understand torture without also appealing to sadism? Must we suppress "the incredible ferocity of the English proprietors in the nineteenth century," even though it is "quite deliberate"? (*CRD,* 694; *CDR,* 742–43). If the theory does not account for that aspect of violence, it will construct only abstract models and in turn will undergo the same failures as bureaucracies. On the practical plane, bureaucracies juggle statistics or strategies without considering the incredible courage of the Vietnamese. By accounting for the human, the theory also encounters the inhuman. What was nonhuman in inert matter becomes antihuman through the mediation of historical agents. A theoretician—when his name is Sartre—cannot remain indifferent to this presence of evil. His theory finds a more stringent link with its practice than epistemologists derive from Marxism, which is animated by indignation and anger—the avatars of generosity. Lucidity loses nothing there. Something from history is revealed in sentiments that actively engage man in history, and his historical moment, just as something from the world is revealed to perception where a body proves itself in the flesh of the sensory.

Sartre and Merleau-Ponty are not so different in their opening up of the transcendental field. However, we would say that Sartre indicates a greater debt to dialectic as the spring of history and the instruments of its intelligibility. Yet what is primarily intelligible is the praxis that, like consciousness, is a relation of the self to itself. If we say that the totalization that it accomplishes is dialectical, it is on the basis of a rather uncertain meaning of dialectic. What is properly dialectical is a return or circularity: man is mediated by things to the same extent that things are mediated by men. True dialectic is this antidialectic that steals from man the meaning and fruit of his enterprises. Antidialectic is this fall of totalization into the totality that confers on the group the objectivity of inertness. For

> the group in fact does not exist anywhere except *everywhere,* that is to say, it belongs to each individual *praxis* as an interiorized unity of multiplicity. . . . If we abandon every mystical or magical interpretation, then it is clear that this ubiquity not only signifies that no new reality has been incarnated in each individual, but on the contrary that it is a question of a practical determination of everyone by everyone, by all and by oneself within the perspective of a common praxis. (*CRD,* 506; *CDR,* 507)

When the group cools down, becomes fixed, and is immobilized in a structure—in short, when it becomes institutionalized—it escapes praxis to some extent and takes on the consistency of the inert. Sartre effectively illuminates this status of the practico-inert or the subjective-objective as the bastard reality of society, and, why not say, of ambiguity? It is precisely ambiguity that Sartre is describing, and dialectic helps him to systematize it. But he does so without producing a complete system, that is, without proclaiming a path that is simultaneously chronological in dealing with the experiences of consciousness and logical in dealing with the becoming of the concept—in other words, the truth of consciousness. In short, Sartre succeeds without opposing a dogmatic epistemology to Merleau-Ponty's phenomenology.

While Merleau-Ponty wrote—and rewrote—a *Phenomenology of Perception,* Sartre wrote a *Critique of Dialectical Reason.* In the end, the problems they confront are not the same: Merleau-Ponty's world is above all the natural world; Sartre's world is the social world. Even if their approaches, despite all appearances, do not diverge radically, their emphases are different. Must we say that this difference is insignificant? No, philosophy is not a competitive game between doctrines, a trial case upon which fashion provisionally passes its verdict. It is not a question of determining who is right and who is wrong, as if some sovereign court could decide—God's judgment or that of history. Yet this difference can govern choices. We must not choose as if we were choosing between two consumer goods. Rather, this difference is at the very least a matter of orienting our sympathies.

Notes

1. See Jean-Paul Sartre, "Intentionality: A Fundamental Idea of Husserl's Phenomenology," trans. Joseph P. Fell, *Journal of the British Society for Phenomenology* 1, no. 2 (1970), 4–5.

2. Jean-Paul Sartre, *Critique de la raison dialectique* (Paris: Gallimard, 1960), 28. Henceforth cited in text as *CRD*. English translation of this introductory essay is entitled *Search for a Method,* trans. Hazel E. Barnes (New York: Knopf, 1963), 28. Henceforth cited in the text as *SM.*

3. Jean-Paul Sartre, *L'Être et le néant* (Paris: Gallimard, 1943), 371; *Being and Nothingness,* trans. Hazel E. Barnes (New York: Philosophical Library, 1956), 309.

4. Sartre, *Critique de la raison dialectique,* 153; *Critique of Dialectical Reason,* trans. Alan Sheridan-Smith, ed. Jonathan Rée (London: New Left Books, 1976), 66. Henceforth cited in the text as *CDR.*

5. "*Compréhension*" can also be translated as "understanding" or "*Verstehen.*"

PART 6

AESTHETICS

19

The Aesthetic Dialogue of Sartre and Merleau-Ponty

Marjorie Grene

Merleau-Ponty's discussions of painting, together with his criticisms of Sartre, show up strikingly the contrast of their philosophies. I shall use the comparison of the two philosophers' views on art to illuminate their treatment of four basic existential concepts. These are: first, being-in-a-world; second, the concept of the lived body; third, communication; and fourth, freedom.

Let me first recall the biographical background of the aesthetic dialogue I propose to examine. Sartre and Merleau-Ponty belonged to the same generation of students at the Sorbonne and the same circle of friends; Merleau-Ponty is mentioned occasionally in Simone de Beauvoir's autobiography. He is the only one of this circle (unless Raymond Aron is included) who became an academic: he was professor at the Sorbonne from 1949 and held the Chair of Philosophy at the Collège de France from 1951 until his death in 1961. In 1945 he had joined with Sartre in founding the literary and philosophical review, *Les Temps modernes,* but resigned a few years later over the issue of Sartre's relation to the Communist Party. His attack on Sartre was formulated in a chapter of his *Adventures of the Dialectic,* "Sartre and Ultrabolshevism,"[1] to which Simone de Beauvoir replied in a counterattack: "Merleau-Ponty and Pseudo-Sartreanism." The breach seemed to be complete; but the former friends were in fact reconciled: Sartre recounts their meeting in this connection, in the issue of *Les Temps modernes* published in memory of Merleau-Ponty after his death. Indeed, the first essay in Merleau-Ponty's book, *Signs,* published in 1960, is dedicated to Sartre, and the preface to that collection suggests that the renewal of their friendship was at least in part occasioned by Sartre's moving introduction to the posthumous work of a mutual friend, Nizan. In fact, the bitterness of Merleau-Ponty's attack on Sartre was the measure, in my view, of the depth of his admiration for him and for de Beauvoir. Merleau-Ponty was a philosopher for whom artistic creation was a central theme, the paradigm, as we shall see, of the human condition, and they were *his* artists: it was they who, in their novels and plays, exhibited concretely the common philosophical concern of all of them. He had said as much publicly and eloquently on a number of occasions. And then they let him down.

The quarrel, on the surface, was political, but, as Merleau-Ponty himself said in the ultrabolshevism essay, their difference went much deeper: it was, he said, both as personal as possible and as general as possible: it was philosophical.[2] Their quarrel brought to the surface, in other words, a very deep-seated difference in their ways of looking at the world. One can put it briefly by saying that while Sartre is *a man of words,* Merleau-Ponty is *a man of vision.* It is this contrast that I want to elaborate, starting from the problem presented by Sartre's literary criticism and working back to the foundation of the problem in the premises of his philosophy.

The existential approach to literature involves trying to see a writer's work as expressive of his "project," his fundamental way of being human. Every one of us, in his life, is engaged in making of his given situation a composition, an organic whole, that is uniquely his; an artist does this in and through his work, which therefore speaks to us of his particular style of being-in-the-world. Now this approach in criticism can be very illuminating indeed, trying, as it does, to achieve, and to speak from, an understanding of the artist as a whole man, deeply engaged in a human task. An example of successful existentialist criticism, for instance, is Sartre's account of Flaubert in his *Search for a Method.*[3] Flaubert's origin in the middle class does not *make* Mme. Bovary, neither do his particular circumstances, his domineering father, his brilliant elder brother, his own effeminacy: but all these circumstances, both general and particular, are the conditions upon which, the limits without which, he, freely and uniquely, created his own being in his work. They are, to put it in very un-Sartrean terms, the matter to which he, by his own act, gave unique and significant form. In highlighting this relation between life and work, the remarks on Flaubert scattered through *Search for a Method* add a new dimension to one's understanding of *Bovary,* and that is the final test of significant criticism.

Yet if one looks over the pages upon pages of Sartrean critical writing, which proliferate as only a review editor's publications can, such passages as the Flaubert ones seem to represent an unstable equilibrium between two apparently incongruent extremes. On the one hand, Sartre often falls back, in his evaluation of literatures into a perverse *inwardness,* an extreme subjectivism where all relation to the world is vehemently renounced: and on the other hand, in his lengthy and equally vehement pronouncements on committed literature, he evaluates other writers exclusively for their *external* significance, for their "social message." In the former mood he elevates Genet, thief, homosexual, and narcissist, to sainthood; in the latter, Marxist or quasi-Marxist frame of mind, he finds in Richard Wright's *Black Boy* the greatest American literary work, simply, one must suppose, because of the social wrongs with which it is preoccupied. Now of course one might say that these two opposite tendencies, one wholly subjective, the other wholly objective in its critical standards, are at one in their Marxist affiliation: that is, they both express admiration for a literature of rebellion against the emptiness and stupidity of bourgeois society. But this is an indirect and superficial unity. It is not only the fact that Genet is a reject of his society, a prisoner and a pervert that attracts Sartre to him—though that helps: he really wallows in Genet's total isolation, as such. For him, Genet represents a last, inverted transformation of the medieval ordered universe. Chesterton said, he reminds us, "that the modern world is full of Christian ideas run wild." And *Our Lady of the Flowers,* he is confident, would have confirmed him in his view: "It is an 'itinerary of the Soul toward God,' the author of which, run wild, takes himself for the creator of the universe. Every object in it speaks to us of Genet as every being in the cosmos of St. Bonaventura speaks to us of God."[4]

When Sartre wrote in *Being and Nothingness* that man is a useless passion who tries to become God and fails, he had not yet met Genet. For Genet has succeeded in precisely this Sartrean task, the task of Sartrean man: and it is the total rejection of the world that enables him to succeed: "This absence of connection with external reality," Sartre says, "is transfigured and becomes the sign of the demiurge's independence of his creation. . . . In the realm of the imaginary, absolute impotence changes sign and becomes omnipotence. Genet plays at inventing the world in order to stand before it in a state of supreme indifference."[5]

And what is this self-created world in which Genet is God? It is the last phase of what Plato in the *Gorgias* calls a plover's life, savoring endlessly the only material left to a human being who has cut off the whole external, human world from any relation to himself: i.e., those physical pleasures devised by the most ingenious devotion to the stimulation of his own body by itself. Such a life has little to do with the concern for social justice that is supposed to characterize "committed literature": indeed, it is its very contrary.

Why this strange see-saw in Sartre's critical writing? The first step on our way to an answer to this question we may find in his theory of the imagination.[6] The imaginary, for Sartre, is pure negation. I stand as a consciousness, over against the world; to *imagine* is to cut myself off from the objects that confront me, to deny them. Imagination therefore is simply denial, an emptiness. That is why Genet, outcast, imprisoned, and denied all instruments but his own ingenuity, so dramatically embodies Sartre's ideal of the imaginative life. But if, out of such an empty inwardness, I project the world again, envisage action in the world, a relation to others, this projection is itself deformed and distorted by the emptiness of its source. The denial of a denial does indeed produce assertion of a sort, but a mechanized, abstract assertion, not an insight into concrete situations. It is literature committed on principle, not immersed in history. What Sartre looks for in committed literature is "totalization," the full swing round from the void of imagination as he sees it. But history is *never* total, and his theory of committed literature remains as unreal, as remote from the feel of concrete action, as the void of imagination itself. So Sartre swings, in his literary theory, as in his ontology, between the two abstractions nothingness and being, being and nothingness. If he does occasionally, as in the passages on Flaubert, halt at a midpoint between the two extremes, it is *despite* his philosophical method, not because of it, that he manages to do so.

But Sartre himself is a novelist and playwright. Why should he hold so strangely abstract a theory of literature? To take the next step in our answer, we must look back briefly at the course of his year in the early thirties at the French House in Berlin, studying the phenomenology of Husserl. One of Husserl's central concepts, which especially impressed him, is the concept of *intentionality*. Every thought, Husserl had insisted, is by its very nature directed toward an object—not necessarily an external, physically existent object; indeed for the phenomenological study of thought it is irrelevant whether the object in fact exists or not. But what is essential is the *directedness* of thought. The pure "I think" of Descartes is not, as he had thought it, self-contained, but turned outward beyond itself to that of which it is a thought. But the conscious mind, the ego, is therefore, Sartre argued, *nothing but* this relation to its object. In itself, it is empty. If A consists in a relation to B, and B is subtracted, what is left is *nothing*. And that is just what happens when I subtract the outward direction of my thought. If I turn inward to myself, if I look for the content of my own subjectivity as such, what I find is just exactly *nothing*.[7] The same message, applied this time explicitly to the visual arts, is conceived by

Sartre's essay on Giacometti, the artist who was obsessed by vacuum—the very contrary, as we shall see, of Merleau-Ponty's Cézanne. Thus Sartre writes:

> Ironic, defiant, ceremonious and tender, Giacometti sees empty space everywhere. Surely not everywhere, you will say, for some objects touch others. But this is exactly the point. Giacometti is certain of nothing, not even that. For weeks on end, he has been fascinated by the legs of a chair that did not *touch* the floor. Between things as between men, the bridges are broken, and emptiness seeps in everywhere, every creature concealing his own.[8]

It is this fascination with emptiness, with nothing, that, for Sartre, marks the imagination and all its world in the visual arts as well as in the literary. Imagination is the denial of the full, the out-there; what it makes, in here, is—nothing.

Why this all or none attitude? The answer lies yet another step back in Sartre's philosophical history. De Beauvoir, in her memoirs, remarks of herself and Sartre in their early days together, "We were Cartesians; we thought we were nothing but pure reason and pure will." This is quite literally true of Sartre's thinking: his Cartesian premises fix irrevocably the limit of his thought.[9]

For Descartes, the mind was wholly self-explicit, luminously aware of each clear and distinct idea in turn, the sum of which taken together composed the totality of knowledge. And over against this area of pure intellectual transparency, the material world was equally explicitly there to be known. Both these, mind and matter, Descartes believed to be substances, independently existent, though dependent at every moment on God to recreate them. Now Sartre has certainly abandoned the seventeenth-century conception of substance, of independent self-existent entities, as well as the conception of an all-powerful, nondeceiving God to support our knowledge of them. All that is left him, then, of the Cartesian heritage, is the demand of total explicitness, the refusal to see any lurking opacity behind what can be clearly formulated, thoroughly apprehended, arbitrarily chosen. Add to this shrunken remnant of Cartesian reason the vector of intentionality, the tie of thought to its object, and you have the truncated dialectic that is Sartre's philosophy, the unending oscillation between a meaningless other out-there and an empty center in-here.

However Sartre has elaborated the relation of the self, and, in particular, of the writer, to society, he has never abandoned or broadened the limits of his philosophy. Take the relation of my consciousness to my body. My body, says Sartre, is the necessity of my contingency, the stubborn flaunting by myself to myself of the limits of my project, of my fancy. We have here subjectivism versus its denial, sheer being versus the subjectivity that is *its* denial. This is but the first stage of the irresolvable conflict that is to follow. Beyond this most intimate otherness, all contact with external things or agencies equally represents their threat to myself. For if my self-consciousness is but the denial of them, they are the denial, the annihilation of my self-consciousness. Thus the chestnut root nauseates Rocquentin. Thus, *a fortiori,* every other person, himself a denier of the world of which he makes me part, threatens me with extinction. And Sartre's social perspective, finally, the perspective of committed literature, looks out, not on any concrete I-thou relationship, any communion in submission to a common cause: that would be the self-deception of bad faith. On the contrary, his social perspective looks out upon a great web of such I-other conflicts, where each is entangled by the threat of all the others and so, despite themselves, they weave themselves into a society. Union here can be only indirect, through common hatred: "Hell is the others."

All this follows closely and clearly from Sartre's philosophical starting point. In arguing that this is so I have, as I mentioned earlier, been restating in large part Merleau-Ponty's criticism of Sartre. But Merleau-Ponty also reproaches him in another way. He is, he says, too much of a writer.[10] This is at first sight a puzzling statement. What seems to be wrong with Sartre is that he lacks the breadth of starting point needed to allow communication with his fellow men; but surely writers do want to communicate. How is it then *as a writer* that Sartre conceives the self as so isolated, the world of imagination as a dimensionless void? Ironically, Sartre himself, in the first volume of his autobiography, published since Merleau-Ponty's death, has both illuminated and amply justified his friend's reproach. The book, of course, is called *Words,* and the title is brilliantly chosen, for he shows us there how from early childhood he lived in a fictional world, a world made by himself in and through romancing, in and through words, taken not as a means of reaching out to others, but as a means of hiding himself from them and building inwardly an imagined kingdom all his own. It was a kingdom where, as Merleau-Ponty said, "all is significance";[11] but luminously, unequivocally significance, where the ambiguities, the silences, the unsayable realities that underlie all living speech could be forgotten or denied. This strange unchildlike childhood already expresses the quality of existence Merleau-Ponty was describing by the phrase "too much a writer" or that I was trying to convey in calling Sartre "a man of words."

It is this quality too, that strains and stultifies Sartre's use of existential concepts in philosophy. Consider briefly the four concepts listed above. First, Heidegger's *being-in-a-world* becomes for Sartre not so much being-in as being-over-against; it is confrontation, not indwelling, I *against* the other. The *person* as mind and body, secondly, is, as we have seen, but the narrowest arena of this opposition. Third, *communication,* the relation to other persons, remains forever the expression of contradiction and antagonism. Strictly speaking, there are only my words; but no hearer to address them to. And finally, what of Sartrean freedom? Plainly, on Sartre's premises, in terms of the dialectic of being and nothingness, we are *indeed* condemned to be free. Freedom is unqualified and absolute but impotent. The Sartrean hero seeks his own act but, unless in the perverse inversions of a Genet, he can never find it. For like Sartrean imagination, and indeed as the very being of the imaginer, it is essentially denial over against, never within, the world, that world which alone could give it concrete embodiment.

Merleau-Ponty begins, according to his own statement, where Sartre leaves off, not with the imaginary, sundered from the real, but with the union of real and unreal, of affirmation and denial, that marks our living experience.[12] This statement, however, is not quite accurate, since Sartre, starting from the two bare abstracts, being and nothingness, is unable to achieve a viable synthesis between these contraries. What Merleau-Ponty's statement does truthfully convey, however, is, for one thing, the kinship of his thought with Sartre. They both move intellectually within the sphere of influence of the phenomenology of Heidegger and Husserl, and, as I have already suggested, Merleau-Ponty's thought often resonated closely to Sartre's own literary work. But Merleau-Ponty's statement also puts, if not precisely, the very sharp opposition that does in fact separate the two. Merleau-Ponty begins, not where Sartre *does* leave off, but where he ought to arrive and cannot, i.e., with the concrete situation of the individual person, projecting, not an abstraction, but himself. For the phenomenon Merleau-Ponty starts from and remained with as this problem is not the emptiness of Sartrean imagination, but the fullness of real, embodied, ongoing perception, perception not over against the world, but in it.

It was visual perception, in particular, that especially concerned him (hence my slogan "man of vision") and for him the paradigm case, the activity that uniquely shows us what perception is, was the activity of the painter. Not the writer making fables for himself, but the artist making a world—*our* world—through eye and hand and canvas: that is the person we should look to to learn both what the world is and what we are. In his earliest book, *The Structure of Behavior,* he had already suggested that it is through art that human transcendence, our way of being-in-the-world, can best be understood.[13] And in an essay, "Eye and Mind," written the year before he died, he was still haunted by this theme. For the painter, he believed, withdraws behind the world to make the world afresh. It is not, Cézanne said, a picture the painter is trying to create but a piece of nature itself. And of Cézanne, who is for him the painter *par excellence,* Merleau-Ponty says: "His work seems to us inhuman because it is making humanity, going behind the every-day human world, creating the hidden handling of experience through which we make our world the world it is, through which we people it with objects." He does this, Merleau-Ponty says, by using the impressionists' discoveries, and then transcending them to restore the object. Impressionism, he says "was attempting to reproduce in painting the effect objects have as they strike the eye or attack the senses. It represents them in the atmosphere where we perceive them instantaneously with absolute shape bound to each other by light and air." Now to get this effect, it was necessary to use only the seven colors of the prism, eliminating ochre and the earth colors, and also to take into account the reverberation of complementary colors. Thus if it was a question of grass, not only green but its complement red must be hinted at as well. And further, of course, the impressionists conveyed the airiness they wanted by breaking up the local hue itself. So, Merleau-Ponty says, "a canvas which no longer corresponds to nature, point by fine point, restores by the interaction of its parts the general truth of the impression." But Cézanne went further than this. He used not only the seven colors of the prism, but eighteen colors: six reds, five yellows, three blues, three greens, one black. "And this use of warm colors and of black, show," Merleau-Ponty argues, "that Cézanne wishes to represent the *object,* to rediscover it behind the atmosphere." "At the same time," Merleau-Ponty continues, "he renounces the division of hue and replaces it by graduated mixtures, by an unfolding of chromatic shadows on the object, by a color modulation which follows the form and the light received by the object." But the fact that color dominates the pattern, does not, he says, have the same meaning in Cézanne as in Impressionism: "The object is no longer obscured by reflections, lost in its relations with the air and with other objects; *it is us though a secret light glowed within it, light emanates from it, and there results an impression of solidity and matter.*"[14]

Yet if modern painting has wrestled with such problems with new theories and new techniques, the task of the painter through the ages has been a constant one: to reveal and remake the achievement of visual perception which in our routine lives we perform without focal awareness or reflection. "The visible in the layman's sense forgets its premises," he remarks in "Eye and Mind."[15] The painter recalls these premises, and so exhibits them to us explicitly, at a reflective level, as it were, yet immediately, in our perception of the painting, so that we see, not simply the object, but the object *as* we see it: we reenact our seeing. In *Night Watch* the hand pointing at us in the center of the painting is caught again in profile as shadowed on the captain's body. It is this kind of fusion of nonfusible aspects, Merleau-Ponty argues, which makes us "see things and a space." But in perception *of* things and space, we see *through* such play of contrary aspects: it points *to* the thing, and does so by its own self-concealment. To see the thing, says Merleau-Ponty, it was necessary not to see the very premises on which in fact our vision rests. It is this act of seeing *from* the play of aspects *to* the thing in space that the painter reveals to us.

But in the act of vision so revealed we have found the world not so much over against us as around us. Seeing is not only a confrontation, but an indwelling. It is "having at a distance," and this "bizarre possession" too the painter reveals to us. Merleau-Ponty rebukes Berenson for praising Giotto's "evocation of tactile values"; painting "evokes" nothing, he insists, "least of all the tactile." On the contrary, "it gives visible existence to what lay-vision believes invisible, it brings it about that we have no need of a 'muscular sense' to possess the voluminousness of the world." The vision of the painter, doubly mediated—indeed, triply, though our seeing, of it—this "devouring vision," as he calls it, "beyond the 'visual data', opens upon a texture of being whose separate sensory messages are but the punctuation or the cesuras, and which the eye inhabits, as a man inhabits his home."[16]

"The eye inhabits being, as a man inhabits his home": a very tissue of "category-mistakes," yet a true, and, for the philosophy of perception, a revolutionary statement. However complex an achievement vision may be—and if we think of its neurological foundation it is immensely complex—in its phenomenological being, in its "what," it is immersion in the world: a distanceless distance, a living *in* that extends the existence of the seer to the outer limits of his seeing, and concentrates the seen in him as its center. Our visual perception is the most striking example of what Plessner calls "mediated immediacy." And this immediacy of the mediated, necessarily forgotten in the pragmatic use of sensory input, is, again, just what the painter is striving to demonstrate. He reverses the ordinary direction of outgoing, practical vision: the world fascinates him, draws him to it. Thus a painter confesses: "In a forest I have sometimes felt that it was not I who was looking at the forest, I have felt on certain days that the trees were looking at me. I was there, listening."[17] Merleau-Ponty inserted in the original edition of "Eye and Mind" a print of Klee's *Park bei Luzern* which vividly exemplifies this mood. Yet at the same time, *through* this receptivity, the painter creates the visible world, and himself, its viewer and inhabitant: "I expect to be inwardly submerged, buried. Perhaps I paint in order to rise up."[18]

Out of this immersion in the world, then, the painter makes the world, and shows us how, through "making" it, we have immersed ourselves in it. This interpretation of the painter's task is illustrated, for example, in Merleau-Ponty's discussion of Cézanne's "return to color" in his later work. Cézanne himself said of color: "it is the place where our brain and the universe meet." What did he mean by this? It was not, Merleau-Ponty assures us, a question of finding colors "like the colors of nature"; it was a question of seeing, and working, in "the *dimension* of color, which creates, of itself for itself, identities, differences, a materiality, a something." Not that this gives us a "recipe for the visible": there is no such recipe, not in color any more than in space. But "the return to color has the merit of leading a little closer to the 'heart of things' "—though it is "beyond the color envelope as it is beyond the space envelope."[19] The color technique of *Portrait of Vallier* illustrates Merleau-Ponty's point here: the whites used among the colors, he says, "have . . . the function of shaping, or cutting out a being more general than being-yellow or being-green or being-blue." But the most striking example is that of the late watercolors. Whatever the merits or demerits of Merleau-Ponty's interpretation of Cézanne in general, his description here is perspicuous: "in the water-colors of the last years," he writes, "space, of which one would suppose that it is self-evidence itself and that for it at least the question *where* does not arise, space itself radiates about planes which we cannot assign to any place." We have rather "the superposition of transparent surfaces," the "floating movement of planes of color which cover each other, advance and retreat."[20] Nor is it a question here, he insists, of adding "another dimension to the two dimensions of the canvas, of organizing an illusion or a perception without an object, the perfection of which would be to resemble as much as possible our empirical vision." "For the depth of a picture (and likewise its height and breadth) comes from we know not where, to present itself, to grow out of the frame. The painter's vision is no longer a looking at an *out-there,* a 'physical-optical' relation, solely with the world. The world is no longer before him through representation: it is rather the painter *who is born in things* as if by concentration and as the coming to itself of the visible."[21] Thus the painter bodies forth the emergence of the visible as the birth of our being, the emergence of ourselves as seeing beings, and of the world as the colored, spatial sphere in which we are.

We must beware, therefore, of the sort of talk that puts qualities, feelings on the canvas. The painting, once achieved, haunts us as the world does when we have shaped it into a world. The painting is not on the canvas, nor at the place, if there is one, represented by it. It is ambiguously and embracingly here, nowhere, and everywhere. Cézanne's *Mont Sainte Victoire,* transcending the "moment of the world" when he painted it, will be always wherever people have eyes to see. "It is made and remade from one of the world to the other, differently, but no less actually than the hard rock above Aix."[22] To deny this is to misread radically the painter's gift. In this connection Merleau-Ponty made explicit his opposition to Sartre on the theory of visual art. Sartre had written of Tintoretto's *Road to Golgotha:*

> That yellow rending of the sky above Golgotha is an agony made into a thing, an agony that has turned into a yellow rending of the sky, and is suddenly submerged by . . . the qualities of things, their impermeability, their extension, their blind permanence. . . . That is to say, it is no longer legible, it is like an immense vain effort, forever stopped halfway between heaven and earth, meant to express what the very nature of things prevents them from expressing.[23]

Thus the painting is, for Sartre, in the last analysis, a thing, over against me, threatening me, like every other thing. What "feeling" it does convey is, he says, a little "haze of heat" hovering about the canvas. To this Merleau-Ponty replied: "This impression is perhaps inevitable among professionals of language, the same thing happens to them that happens to all of us when we hear a foreign language which we speak badly: we find it monotonous, marked by too strong an accent and flavor, just because it is not ours and we have not made of it the principal instrument of our relation with the world."[24] But for the painter, he continues, and for us too if we devote ourselves to living in painting,

> the sense of the painting is much more than a little haze on the surface of the canvas, since it was capable of demanding this color and this object in preference to any other and since it commands the arrangement of the picture as imperiously as a syntax or a logic. For the whole picture is not in these little local agonies or joys with which it is besprinkled; they are only components in a total sense less pathetic, more *legible* and more enduring.[25]

Merleau-Ponty illustrates his point by retelling the anecdote of the innkeeper of Cassis who was watching Renoir at work. Renoir, intently watching the sea, was painting washerwomen at a stream. "He kept gazing," the puzzled onlooker said, "at I know not what and then changed one little corner." How can one look at the sea in order to paint a freshwater stream? How could the sea tell Renoir about the washerwomen's brook? "The fact is," says Merleau-Ponty, "that every fragment of the world—and in particular the sea, so riddled with eddies and waves, so plumed with spray, so massive and immobile in itself, contains all sorts of shapes of being, and by its manner of reply to the onlooker's attack, evokes a series of possible variants, and teaches beyond itself, a general manner of saying what is."[26] Painting, in short, embodies our openness to being. Even in speech, and more strikingly in the arts that speak through silence, it is the ineffable ground of being itself that the artist seeks to encounter and that addresses us through his work. All meaning means what cannot be said; even the most formal signs carry their significance not in themselves but in what they signify, in what we understand *through* them. And in painting we have, visible and incarnate, the concrete expression of this tension, this reverberation between sign and signified, meaning and what is meant. This is intentionality, not caught between two unattainable abstractions, but at home. The painter shows us our being-in-the-world in its original quality, drawn to being and within it, yet, within it, absent from it in our withdrawal, in our gaze. For this tension of being and distance-from-being, again, is not a see-saw like that of Sartre's being and nothingness, but a living unity-in-separation: ineradicably equivocal, bright and shadowy at once, with the opacity and the luminousness of being itself: "In this circuit," says Merleau-Ponty, "there is no rupture, it is impossible to say where nature ends and man or expression begins. For it is voiceless Being itself which comes to us here, in vision, to show forth its proper meaning."[27] That is why, Merleau-Ponty argues, the dilemma of representative versus abstract art is badly stated: No object is ever *wholly* like its "representation," and at the same time even the most abstract painting "represents" reality: it is in this sense that "the grapes of Caravaggio are the grapes themselves."[28]

Painting, then, shows us paradigmatically the character of our being-in-a-world. It does so, secondly, because, as the art of and through vision, it displays as no other activity can the single equivocal unity of the person, a unity which Merleau-Ponty expresses in the phrase *le corps vécu, the lived body,* and which can perhaps be better expressed in English by speaking of embodiment of the person as *embodied.*

The painter, Valéry said, brings his body with him; and indeed, Merleau-Ponty comments, we could not imagine a disembodied spirit *painting.* Nor, for that matter, would speech be possible for a pure mind, detached from tongue or pen. Speech is significance in sound or ink or chalk; it is mental and physical at once. Even so, a Sartrean life of words, of a pure verbalizing consciousness, is at least a possible illusion. If thought is, as Plato said, the dialogue of the soul with itself, we can at least imagine it running on, cut off from reality, in a kind of ghost world. But every painter, however "abstract" his style, is working, with arm and hand, to shape physical material, colors and lines. The painter at work stands, for Merleau-Ponty, for the bodily rootedness of all creative activity.

But, you may well ask, why only painting? Why not sculpture? Why not music? The sculptor shapes material with his hands, much as we try, in our projection of ourselves into the future, to shape the contingent material of our lives. And even better, perhaps, the composer working with sounds shapes a temporal material, he gives significant form to successive as well as simultaneous events. The shape of a human life, surely, is much more closely mirrored here than in the quiescent two-dimensional surface of a picture. If life itself may be described as *configured time,*[29] then it is music that we should take as the art that can best teach us what we are. The ear is as truly embodied spirit as the eye. And admittedly, Merleau-Ponty did say, in *The Structure of Behavior,* that it is art in general that best reveals the way in which we fashion our biological environment into a human world. But it is certainly the case of painting in particular that haunted him to the end of his life.

For it is painting that is most plainly and purely the art of vision, and for Merleau-Ponty it is visual perception that most clearly expresses the way we live our bodily lives. For one thing, vision is presence in absence: in it our very being is fused with distant objects, we become part of them and they of us. Moreover, the awareness of what is visible embraces at the same time an invisible: when I look at an orange, I see the whole round object even though only one aspect of it is strictly present to my eyes. True, when I hear a passing car, I hear a car, not just a noise of which I then proceed to judge: that is a car. My perceptive grasp of things is always already interpretative. That fact remains, whatever sense I use as my example. Indeed, Merleau-Ponty himself insists that perception in its living existence is kinaesthetic: we grasp, through our senses and more than our senses, through the whole complex series of transactions with the world that constitutes experience, the presence about us of other things and other lives. It is only in analysis and reflection that we separate the five senses and learn to understand their distinctive achievements. Despite this common basis of cooperation among the separate or separable channels of sense, however, there is a special way in which visual perception illustrates the character of the lived body. Vision exemplifies as no other sense does what we may call the mutuality of subject and object. I not only see, I am in part visible to myself, and I am wholly visible to all others. I can look at other people, and they can look at me. This seems so obvious as to need no statement, let alone the tortuous paragraphs and pages that Merleau-Ponty devotes to his theme.

But it is, all the same, the kind of obvious truth which has far-reaching philosophical consequences when you look at it more closely. A Sartrean consciousness gazing at another person must either make him an object or succumb to becoming one himself: there is no mutuality of gaze. Even a dumb object, Rocquentin's chestnut root, by its very existence makes my consciousness absurd. But, Merleau-Ponty insists, vision is already *as such* vision *by* a visible body: it is not subject fighting to the death with object, consciousness against body, but always and in its very essence the two in one. So he says, in one of the most pregnant statements of his favorite—indeed, almost his obsessive—theme:

> Visible and mobile, my body is numbered among things, it is one of them, it is caught in the tissue of the world, and its cohesion is that of a thing. But because it sees and moves itself, it holds things in a circle around itself, they are an annex and a prolongation of itself, they are encrusted in its flesh, they form part of its full definition and the world is made of the very stuff of the body. These reversals, these antinomies are different ways of saying that vision takes place or develops out of the medium of things, there where a visible being sets about seeing, becomes visible for itself and for the vision of all things.[30]

Again, this paradoxical direct-indirectness, this active passivity of vision, Merleau-Ponty believes, is quintessentially expressed in painting. This system of exchanges once given, he says, "all the problems of painting are there. They illustrate the enigma of the body and it justifies them." Cézanne had said: "Nature is within." Merleau-Ponty comments: "Quality, light, color, depth, which are out there before us, are so only because they awaken an echo in our body, because it makes them welcome." And from this inner echo, "this fleshy formula of their presence that things evoke in me," springs the painter's creation: the seen at one remove, yet immediate, even more immediate, in its reflective reality: "a trace, visible in its turn, where every other eye will rediscover the motives which support its inspection of the world." The painting, in short, is "a visible to the second power, fleshy essence or icon of the first."[31]

Thus painting is far from being an "image" in the sense of an unreal copy of some prosaic reality: it has its nature in the very "duplicity," as Merleau-Ponty calls it, of perception itself. Now in fact this thesis of the ambiguity of perception and especially of the interplay of perceiver and perceived, is a favorite motif of painters. They like to present, for example, that most striking and uniquely human phenomenon: the mirrored image of ourselves, which shows us ourselves in a kind of half reality as others see us. A mirrored life is a uniquely human life: no other animal can live in this strange, ambiguous relation to its own body; consider, for example, the complex mirrorings of Velasquez's famous court scene, *Las Meninas*. Matisse's fascination with painting himself painting expresses a kindred theme. The painter is immersed in the visible world, struggling to express its visibility, yet he himself, doing this, is visible to himself doing this. Both cases—the mirror, and the painter painting his own activity of painting—generate an infinite regress which expresses the very heart of human reflectiveness. Not a still bright center of consciousness, but an inexhaustible proliferation of level upon level of significance constitutes human thought.

But every level, every shade of meaning, however it transcend the here and now, is, again, rooted in bodily presence. Modern philosophy, under the spell of the scientific intellect, has forgotten this truth, Merleau-Ponty argues, and the insights of modern painting can show us where philosophy has failed. Modern thought, he says in "Eye and Mind," is dominated by operationalism: that is, by the belief that all problems can be solved by the experimental manipulation of precisely specified variables. But significance never floats freely on the surface of things, as a scientistic philosophy would seem to suppose it does. It is always grounded in the being of the living, embodied individual; but individual life can only be *lived,* not said; in its opacity it eludes the formalisms of science, however powerful. The archetype of an operationalist theory of vision, for Merleau-Ponty, is Descartes's *Dioptrics,* where, as one might expect, vision is a matter of pure geometry, wholly transparent to the clear intellect. Descartes, Merleau-Ponty points out, shows little interest in painting: had he done so, he would have needed a different ontology. But when he does talk about it, what interests him exclusively is line and form. He might work out a theory of engraving, though even this would be, on his view, as it is not in fact, a mere copying of the geometry of the real extended world. But color in its living nature, color as it captures us, as we dwell in it, is wholly alien to a Cartesian mentality. Consider again the play of color which the impressionists have taught us to see. This is a reality of which the Cartesian theory of perception can give no account.

Perspective, too, in its bodily reality, is something different from the pure geometrical perspective of the intellect which interested Descartes. Merleau-Ponty points out, for example, how Cézanne uses the actual distortion of a line as seen. There is a portrait of Mme. Cézanne in which the border on both sides of the body fails to make a straight line; "but we know," he writes, "if a line passes under a large band of paper, the two visible segments appear dislocated." Similarly, in the portrait of Gustave Geffroy the table at the front spreads out before us—for when the eye traverses a broad surface, its images are taken from different points of view, and so the total surface is warped. "Cézanne's genius," he says, "is through the total arrangement of the picture to make the deformations in perspective cease to be visible in themselves when we look at them in the lump; and they only contribute, as they do in natural vision, to give the impression of an order in process of birth, an object in process of appearing, of collecting itself under our eyes. There is nothing less arbitrary than these celebrated deformations."[32] Indeed they are only in theory deformations; for in fact they restore the living reality which the intellect in its arbitration distorts.

Merleau-Ponty's account of what I have called the mutuality of vision, moreover, exemplifies also my third point of comparison with Sartre. Our being-in-the-world is indwelling as well as confrontation; and the world we dwell in is necessarily inhabited not only by things but by other persons too, by all those who see me, just as I see them. Communication is not an insoluble problem for Merleau-Ponty as it is for Sartre, but the given from which we start: the very emergence of myself as a center of experience reveals me as one among others. However isolated the painter in his struggle with the visible, therefore, he is struggling with, he is bringing into being, a common human world. The innkeeper did not understand what Renoir was doing at the seashore, but still the work Renoir created was there to speak to him and to all of us of the human condition, of the being in which together we are all immersed. So it is, again, that Cézanne's *Mont Sainte Victoire* can speak to all men always, everywhere.

The painter's place in the history of his art, moreover, Merleau-Ponty believes, shows us, more immediately than the history of literature can do, the nature of tradition. Each generation of painters has to deny the style of its predecessors and at the same time profits by their example; yet for all the painter's efforts to renew his art, the paintings of the past are there, present to us still. The writer, on the other hand, in writing, remakes language, and the literature of the past becomes at least partly obsolete, accessible to us only by an intellectual effort. It needs a verbal as well as imaginative exertion to read Chaucer; Giotto is there still, as near at least as Padua or Florence. Literature is more contemporary but also more temporary. The problem of painting, in contrast, is a quasi-eternal one, embodying, therefore, a single unbroken tradition. It remains, Merleau-Ponty says, "an abortive attempt to do what is always still to be done,"[33] yet an attempt which, in this forever uncompleted endeavor, unites men of each generation mutely but profoundly with the whole human past. "The field of pictorial meanings has been open," he writes, "ever since a man appeared in the world." This is so just because painting so truly mirrors the embodied situation:

> The first drawing on the walls of caves founded a tradition only because it inherited another: that of perception. The quasi-eternity of art merges with the quasi-eternity of incarnate existence, and we have in the exercise of our body and of our senses, insofar as they insert us in a world, the means of understanding our cultural gesticulation insofar as it inserts us in history. . . . The continuous attempt at expression establishes a single history—as the hold of our body on every possible object establishes a single space.[34]

Here again communication with the past, as with the present, is the very ground out of which human existence springs. Temporally as well as spatially we dwell in and come to individual awareness out of our communal being.

History is a favorite theme of existential philosophers, yet Merleau-Ponty is the first writer in this tradition to found the historical being of man in communal existence. Existentialism is known with some justice as a philosophy of the lonely, alienated individual; but for Merleau-Ponty the dimension of human togetherness, both the communication of man with man and the immersion of the individual in a communal heritage, is a presupposition of human life. The painter speaks to his contemporaries of the world they see and of the way they see it; and he echoes a voice as old as man himself. It would be irrelevant here to compare Merleau-Ponty's conception of history or communication in general with that of other philosophers like Jaspers or Heidegger. But let me just look back briefly to compare the lesson Merleau-Ponty draws from painting with Sartre's theory of committed literature. For Sartre, the ego is not only isolated from others, but is itself simply a negation of the objects to which it is, in essence, a relation: it is the amputation by itself of itself from being. In committed literature this nonexistent existent, this empty ego, projects itself outward again to form a program of social action. This produces, however, as Merleau-Ponty rightly insists, not a literature of concrete activity, a reflection of history as lived, but an abstract, and false, equation of art with politics. It produces propaganda.

Here again, Sartre's premises allow him no other issue; and once more, we can express this limitation of his thought by pointing to his fascination with words, words for their own sake, not for their meaning, i.e., for what they point to, but cannot articulate. Speech itself, Merleau-Ponty reminds us, is grounded in silence. Even a novel has to speak, not in words, but through them; it has to signify through speech an unspoken reality, a style of life, that transcends words: "it expresses tacitly, like a painting."[35] But it is this *tacit* ground of speech which makes communication possible. There is no good in speaking if my hearer has ears but hears not and his hearing is silent. That is why painting so usefully exhibits the nature even of speech in its primordial functioning of what Merleau-Ponty calls "speaking speech" rather than mere language. Painting is the struggle for expression through silence, its voice is the voice of silence; and this paradigm, cut off from the abstract explicitness of language, can effectively exhibit, therefore, both the tacit ground of each act of communication, and the communion, through the "voices of silence," of each with all. It breaks the circle of verbalization and brings us face to face with one another in the world. It points toward the resonance of those occasions when we encounter one another, and toward the shared encounter with being, potentially reflective but never wholly reflected, which constitutes our common human destiny.

I listed at the beginning four concepts I wanted to mention in connection with Merleau-Ponty's view of art. So far I have referred to three of these: being-in-the-world, embodiment, and communication. Where for Sartre we have consciousness against the world, we have, for Merleau-Ponty, indwelling as the ground of confrontation. Where for Sartre we have the conflict of mind with body, and the internecine war of self against self, we have, with Merleau-Ponty, on the one hand, the integrity of the lived body, and on the other, the organic participation of the individual in a common cultural world. Finally, there remains the contrast in their conceptions of freedom. It is here that Merleau-Ponty's discussions of paintings and painters come closest to the practice of Sartre in his best literary criticism, yet we can see plainly in this case also how far he stands from Sartre in his basic philosophical beliefs.

In his reflections on painters and their lives, Merleau-Ponty practices what Sartre had christened "existential psychoanalysis," i.e., he examines the artist's life as bearing on his work, and expressing it insofar as an artist's life *is* a life becoming expression. But that does not mean that the life, even in its hidden origins, determines the work. It is the man as artist in his whole projection of himself into the world that the existential critic seeks to understand; and that means to understand the work in its intrinsic significance, for the work is the artist's project, his freedom realized. When Van Gogh, Merleau-Ponty says, in painting *Crows over a Wheatfield,* sought to "go further," this was not a question of going one step further in a beaded causal sequence; the "further" expresses the tension that always subsists between the man who is not yet and the one who is already.[36] This is the pull of the future, full of significance not yet realized, upon a past waiting to be made significant. It is not a question here either of a one-level series of causal determinants and their effects, nor of a pure "spiritual" meaning, subsisting in a cloud-cuckoo land all on its own. Rather there is an essential polarity between the painter's life as ground and material of his work and the work as significant expression of and through the life. Thus Cézanne, Merleau-Ponty argues, would appear to an outside observer a schizoid type; even his good friend and biographer Bernard could fail to see the relevance of his sufferings to his task as a painter, could see them as mere weaknesses or eccentricities. And yet Cézanne's life has a bearing on the work, and expresses it, since in the last analysis Cézanne's life is the life "which this work demands."[37] In his practical criticism, in other words, Merleau-Ponty shows us the same equilibrium between the artist's work and his world which Sartre also exhibits in his accounts of Flaubert or Baudelaire. For Sartre, however, as I have tried to argue, this delicate balance of work and life, of significance and sheer happening, is always endangered by the Sartrean demand of *total freedom*. In a Sartrean free act I must make not only my decision and my act, but the very standards by which I must decide. I make the world; singly and suddenly, I become God. But in fact I do no such thing—and so I become a useless passion, fallen back from the hopelessness of my infinite demands upon absurdity and despair. The ontology of being and nothingness, in other words, cannot in fact provide an adequate theory for the practice of existential criticism; Sartre's philosophy belies his best critical insights. In contrast, Merleau-Ponty's theory of freedom is adapted to the needs of his practical criticism, which in turn confirms his theory. First, freedom for him is not literal and final, as for Sartre, but, like the lived body whose freedom it is, ambiguous. Cézanne is both schizoid sufferer *and* reshaper of the visibility of things. These are not two legs of a see-saw, but two aspects of the inescapable ambivalence, the iridescence of the very texture of our lives.

Secondly, freedom for Merleau-Ponty is indirect. The painter wrestling with a problem that grips him, struggling for expression with the material of line and color, the material of his experience, is displaying human freedom *through* the demands of his determinate situation, not somewhere else, over against them. Cézanne, says Merleau-Ponty, struggled and suffered and doubted to the end his power to do what in fact he was magnificently engaged in doing. "We never see our freedom face to face,"[38] not because, like Sartrean freedom, it is an impossible ideal, but because it is so real, woven into the intricate stuff of life itself.

And finally, freedom is never finished. Indeed, it *is* that openness to the future which most deeply marks our being-in-the-world. Painting, we have seen, is always, in Merleau-Ponty's view, an abortive attempt to say what still remains to be said. It is a continuous grappling with a problem which remains always still to be solved. The intellect, he writes in the closing, paragraphs of "Eye and Mind," is disappointed by this conclusion: Are we to go on always asking the same question, moving in a circle, in a state of continuous stupor? "But this disappointment," he writes, "is that of the imaginary in a mistaken sense, which demands a positivity that exactly fills its void. This is the regret at not being everything."[39] This seems to be his final comment on the imaginary of Sartre. But the frustration we face here in our intellectual being is compensated by a broader view: "if we can establish neither in painting nor indeed elsewhere, a hierarchy of civilizations nor speak of progress, this is not because some destiny holds us back; it is rather because in a sense the first painting of all already reached into the depths of the future." Its task was not complete, but open: resonant of the future: "if no painting absolutely achieves the aim of painting, if indeed no work absolutely achieves itself, every creation changes, alters, illuminates, deepens, confirms, exalts, recreates or creates in advance all the others."[40]

In conclusion, I should like to think of the next and final sentence—the last of Merleau-Ponty's last complete work—as a hope also for his own uncompleted task, which may well reverberate in the future in ways unsuspected by himself. "If," he says in conclusion, "creations are not an acquisition, it is not only because, like all things they pass away, it is also because they have almost all their lives before them."[41] This is, as against Sartre, Merleau-Ponty's principal merit. His arguments lack the dialectical rigor of Sartre's, they "circle round and round the same landscape." But it is a landscape, not a bundle of abstractions; we can live in it, philosophically, and even build in it, with help from a few like-minded thinkers, a conceptual home.[42]

Sartre is the last of the Cartesians. He shows us, brilliantly and maddeningly, the impasse to which in our time the modern mind has come. Merleau-Ponty, groping, obsessed with one paradox—the paradox of visual perception—over-rhetorical, yet speaks to us as one of the first truly post-Cartesians. He gives us, if not a philosophy—perhaps not even a philosophy of visual art—a foundation on which we can build, and equally, to echo his own paradox, a view of the horizon toward which we can hope to move. The man of words alone is by profession the man of alienation; his philosophy is uncurably a philosophy of alienation. The man of vision may teach us, in contrast, how to begin to build a philosophy of indwelling. He shows how in our very distance from things we are near them, he recreates conceptually, as, for him, the painter does iconically, our mediated immediacy, our attachment through detachment, the very core of our way of being-in-a-world, the puzzle of our freedom.

Notes

This essay was originally written for the Fine Arts Festival of the University of Wisconsin, Milwaukee.

1. Maurice Merleau-Ponty, *Aventures de la dialectique* (Paris: Gallimard, 1955), 131ff.

2. Ibid., 253. In what follows I have relied heavily on a number of Merleau-Ponty's discussions of Sartre, including some of the working notes in his posthumous and incompleted work *Le Visible et l'invisible,* but in order not to pepper my argument with references, I have not stopped to mention at each stage the Merleau-Pontyian text which supports my own reasoning. This work, like most of those referred to, is now available in translation in the phenomenological series of Northwestern University Press.

3. Published in *Critique de la raison dialectique,* vol. 1 (Paris: Gallimard, 1960), and translated by Hazel Barnes as *Search for a Method* (New York: Knopf, 1963).

4. Introduction to Jean Genet, *Our Lady of the Flowers* (London: Blond, 1964), 47.

5. Ibid., 53.

6. See Jean-Paul Sartre, *L'Imaginaire* (Paris: Alcan, 1940). Translated as *The Psychology of the Imagination* (New York: Rider, 1950).

7. See Jean-Paul Sartre, *The Transcendence of the Ego* (New York: Noonday Press, 1957). First published in *Recherches Philosophiques* (1936).

8. Jean-Paul Sartre, *Situations* (New York: Fawcett World Library, 1966), 126. Cf. on the same page: "Giacometti is a sculptor because he carries his vacuum along with him, as a snail its shell." But compare also the treatment of Giacometti as graphic artist in a contrary sense in Merleau-Ponty's *L'Oeil et l'esprit* (Paris: Gallimard, 1964), 24.

9. I have argued this in detail elsewhere: cf. my "Tacit Knowing and the Pre-Reflexive Cogito," in *Intellect and Hope* (Durham: Duke University Press, 1968), or my review of Manser's *Sartre,* in *Mind* 78 (1969), 141–52.

10. Cf. Maurice Merleau-Ponty, *Aventures de la dialectique,* 271.

11. Ibid.

12. Jean-Paul Sartre, *Le Visible et l'invisible* (Paris: Gallimard, 1964), 290.

13. Maurice Merleau-Ponty, *La Structure du comportement,* 5th ed. (Paris: Presses Universitaires de France, 1963).

14. Maurice Merleau-Ponty, "Le doubt de Cézanne," in *Sens et non-sens* (Paris: Nagel, 1948), 15–44, 19–21.

15. Merleau-Ponty, *Le Oeil et l'esprit,* 29–30. Merleau-Ponty's account here comes close to Polanyi's theory of tacit knowing; my use of "from-to" in particular is borrowed from him. See, e.g., *The Tacit Dimension* (New York: Doubleday, 1966), or *Knowing and Being* (New York: Routledge, 1969), and my introduction to the latter.

16. Ibid., 26–27.

17. Ibid., 31.

18. Ibid.

19. Ibid., 67–68.
20. Ibid.
21. Ibid., 68–69.
22. Ibid., 35.
23. Jean-Paul Sartre, *Situations,* II, 61. Quoted in "Le Language indirect et les voix du silence," in *Signes* (Paris: Gallimard, 1960), 49ff., 69.
24. Ibid.
25. Ibid.
26. Ibid., 70.
27. Sartre, *L'Oeil et l'esprit,* 86–87.
28. Ibid., 87.
29. See A. Portmann, "Die Zeit im Leben des Organismus," reprinted from *Eranos Jahrbuch in Biologie und Geist* (Freiburg: Herder, 1963), 123ff.
30. Merleau-Ponty, *L'Oeil et l'esprit,* 19.
31. Ibid., 21–22.
32. Merleau-Ponty, *Sens et non-sens,* 34–35.
33. Merleau-Ponty, *Signes,* 99.
34. Ibid., 87.
35. Ibid., 95.
36. Ibid., 71.
37. Merleau-Ponty, *Sens et non-sens,* 35.
38. Ibid., 44.
39. Merleau-Ponty, *L'Oeil et l'espirit,* 92–93.
40. Ibid.
41. Ibid.
42. In particular, e.g., Polanyi, Portmann, Plessner, perhaps also David Bohm. See my *Knower and the Known* (Faber and Basic Books, 1966), and *Approaches to a Philosophical Biology* (Basic Books, 1969). On the side of experimental psychology, J. J. Gibson's *The Senses Considered as Perceptual Systems* (Ithaca: Cornell, 1966), seems to me also to show a striking convergence with this philosophical tendency.

20

Situation and Temporality

John O'Neill

In the following discussion I shall restrict myself for the most part to Sartre's essays collected in the volumes, *Situations,*[1] since what follows is intended largely as an introduction to *Situations,* IV,[2] and in particular to the long essay therein on Sartre's relation to Merleau-Ponty. The ultimate purpose of the discussion is to suggest that there is perhaps a greater similarity in the views of Sartre and Merleau-Ponty on the phenomenology of perception, expression, and history than is likely to appear if one relies upon a number of conventional interpretations of Sartre and then turns away in order to study Merleau-Ponty. I am aware, of course, that the two friends became enemies over their differences. But I am suggesting that Sartre's tribute to Merleau-Ponty and his later work in the *Critique of Dialectical Reason* represent an ultimate comprehension which was always present. It has been argued that Sartre's identification of consciousness and imagination condemns individual consciousness to a comedy of errors, degeneration, and self-enchantment. Similarly, Sartre's conception of individual freedom as any awareness of the conflict between *l'être-en-soi-pour-soi* and the being that lacks being opens up an abyss which individual freedom can never overleap.[3] Together these views involve the difficulty that the flux of individual consciousness and the futility of its passions resist identification with any historical process which aims at the realization of political values willed as such for all men. The Sartrean individual is crippled by the burden of a radical freedom which is essentially indifferent to the structures of language, history, economy, and society.

In my own view, much of the critical literature has concentrated upon the antithetical nature of Sartre's philosophy because it has dealt only with the epistemological and/or ontological *ekstasis,* but has not attempted to understand the latter as secondary structures within the temporal *ekstasis* which is the diasporatic unity of all the intramundane multiplicities of being. Time is the opening in being through which there can be meaning (*sens*) which is neither transcendental nor opaque but rather a schema of the practical truth or physiognomy of things. Thus time is the hollow in being in which is conceived the value of being-in-itself for the being who lacks being or self-coincidence. Time is the arrow of being, the dialectical surge which continuously sweeps up its starting points into fresh, but equally distant totalizations of the human project:

> Thus Temporality is not a universal time containing all beings and in particular human realities. Neither is it a law of development which is imposed on being from without. Nor is it being. But it is the intra-structure of the being which is its own nihilation—that is, the *mode of being* peculiar to being for itself. The For-itself is the being which has to be its being in the form of Temporality.[4]

We shall not properly understand Sartre's concept of situation as a matrix in which the act is born in a revelation and recovery of being unless we preserve its temporal *ekstasis.* Situation is a secondary structure which can be made and unmade in the temporalization of an original project which is never present in a global view, but reveals being at the place where being opens to gesture, expression, and conduct. It is thus the appropriation of a world that is present to a being which undertakes to make itself through acts which polarize the world as value and instrument—i.e., the human world.

The structure of the human world is essentially linguistic. It is through language that we assume responsibility for events either in the past or future which are the necessary but otherwise insufficient conditions of the act; hence the unities of time, place, and actions.[5] It is the task of the play and the novel as employed by Sartre to recuperate the mysterious depth which the decision to act opens up in the commonplace world, which otherwise bears us away from our acts and covers them over as soon as they are done. Literature is action because of the intentional structure of the word, and its situations are correlative with the historical structure of the world. There are, however, at the extreme limits two literary techniques which are alien to the intention of the authentic novel. Though they seem to be opposites, naturalism and *l'art pour l'art* are in practice two species of objectivism, i.e., an unsituated perspectivism which produces a decomposition of time and duration. Writers who employ either technique construct novels according to what Sartre calls the eidetic imagery of bad faith—handing over the freedom of their characters to the past, or moving them like creatures who have pawned their future in order to maintain their author's omniscience. The true novelist draws the reader into the situation of his characters as an accomplice to actions which unfold with the characters and polarize the flow of events as acts polarize the scenes in a play.

The technique of the naturalist or near-realist does not, according to Sartre, produce genuine novels. The naturalist fails because he attempts to construct the novel out of events which have only a Humean history and never any intrinsic meaning. But then it might be argued that Hume is the first philosopher of the absurd, as Camus, Hemingway, and Dos Passos are the great novelists of the absurd. What each reveals to us is that man's customs are merely veils which hide the abyss between man and nature. None of our routines ever succeeds in establishing a "qualitative ethic." Outside of the idea, we experience only a sequence of radically contingent events which turn up without qualitative adhesions, yet with a density of their own in the feelings. Although the philosophy of the absurd scrupulously avoids the orientations of bad faith, Sartre nevertheless denies the status of the novel to Camus's *The Stranger*, as he does for similar reasons to Hemingway's *Death in the Afternoon*. In each case, Sartre's objection is that the technique of these writers is not to use words to integrate the absurd into a human order, but to juxtapose a transparent sequence of events and an order of meaning correspondingly opaque. Similarly, in Dos Passos the technique of accumulation by conjunction is employed to represent events which borrow prefabricated meanings through the public declarations of the characters. But in Dos Passos ("the greatest writer of our time") the characters maintain a hybrid existence between their own lived time and the collapsed time of reported events into which they are driven in the conflict between character and the destiny which is their lot in capitalist society.

The lack of transcendence in the writings of the naturalists, which has its source in their metaphysical decomposition of time, is likewise the defect of an author such as Mauriac, who views his characters *sub specie aeternitatis*, a technique which also fails to grasp the nature of lived time essential to the novel.

> A novel is a series of readings, of little parasitic lives, none of them longer than a dance. It swells and feeds upon the reader's time. But in order for the duration of my impatience and ignorance to be caught and then moulded and finally presented to me as the flesh of these creatures of invention, the novelist must know how to draw it into the trap, how to hollow out in his book, by means of the signs at his disposal a time

> resembling my own, one in which the future does not exist. If I suggest that the hero's future actions are determined in advance by heredity, social influence or some other mechanism, my own time ebbs back into me; there remains only myself, reading and persisting, confronted by a static book. Do you want your characters to live? See to it that they are free.[6]

Characters whose future is congealed in the gaze of the author are reduced to *things* which have a *destiny* but no life that the reader can share from the inside.

The fate of Mauriac's characters is revealed in his use of third-person statements. The latter function ambiguously to designate the other, viewed solely from the outside, and simultaneously, while preserving a certain *aesthetic distance,* to draw us into the intimacy of the subject on the basis of shared experience. But in Mauriac's use the ambiguity of the third person loses the dimension of aesthetic distance and is employed to set us up in judgment over the characters. Suddenly, out of his own omniscience, Mauriac gives us the key to his character. Thereafter, "Thérèse's 'pattern of destiny,' the graph of her ups and downs, resembles a fever curve; it is dead time, since the future is spread out like the past and simply repeats it."[7] In Mauriac there are no time-traps, objects have no resistance or impenetrability, and conversations never stumble, meander or grope toward meaning—everything is lucid. But lucidity is the novelist's sin of pride. It is the denial of the principle of relativity which applies both to physical and to fictional systems (the novel as a whole, as well as the partial systems of which it is composed, the minds of the characters, their psychological and moral judgments). In short, "novels are written *by* men and *for* men. In the eyes of God, Who cuts through appearances and goes beyond them, there is no novel, no art, for art thrives on appearances. God is not an artist."[8]

Sartre's conception of the novel may be further illustrated by turning to his recent comments on the novels of Nathalie Sarraute and André Gorz which, like those of Nabakov, Waugh, and Gide, represent an attempt to use the novel against itself in order to reflect upon the genuine nature of the novel. The result is what Sartre calls the *antinovel,*[9] understood as a creative experiment which explores the novel as a metaphysical trap for the storyteller and the reader. Sarraute takes as her theme the realm of the *commonplace,* much like Dos Passos. The trick of the novelist is to shuffle off the problem of the relation of the individual to the universal by resorting to the commonplaces of character, moral opinion, and of art, especially the novel itself. Through such devices the threat of subjectivity is contained within the realm of the objective. Feeling is centrifugal and consensual, feeding upon the exchange of generalities, in flight from itself.

Sarraute subjects the novel to a confrontation with its possibility of inauthenticity. Gorz, however, pushes the novel into an extreme situation in which the words have yet to inhabit its principal character. We witness the birth of an order in which every moment involves the risk of a regression. The pages of the book murmur to us, but they do not speak in the first person for the very reason that they are in search of a self:

> What reassures us, however, is that we perceive, behind the hesitations of life and language, an arid, trenchant and frozen passion, a steel wire, stretched between the lacerations of the past and the uncertainty of the future. An inhuman passion ignorant of itself, an uneasy seeker, a lunatic silence within the heart of language. It bores a hole through the reader's time, dragging this stream of words behind. We shall have faith in it.[10]

The experiment undertaken in Gorz's novel is the search for the *act* which justifies the shift from the third person to the first person. Otherwise we all remain kidnapped by the other. "They spoke of us as 'He' years before we were able to say 'I.' We had our first existence as absolute objects."[11] It is this circumstance which causes us to be careless of our human nature, whereas Gorz's traitor, by the effort he has to appropriate every human emotion, reminds us that the human species does not exist.

The error common to those writers whom Sartre refuses to recognize as novelists is that they adopt a position external to their characters. This in effect involves a double error, namely, that the writer fails to understand his own immersion in time as well as that of his characters. These writers treat time as a datum, either as a sociological or a theological assumption. The result is that their art is reduced to the revelation of the spectacle of being and falls into the category of consumption rather than production, or *praxis*. The genuine novelist is obliged to analyze his own historical situation and its effects upon his metaphysical assumptions and literary techniques. This is the task which Sartre undertook in a lengthy essay *What Is Literature?,* where he makes it clear that the novelist's creation of character is an integral factor in the historical process in which man makes himself at the risk of losing himself.

The intention of Sartre's survey of the history of literature is not to separate its future from its past or near-present. Indeed, Sartre is not *surveying* the history of literature in any ordinary sense at all. It is only in the light of a literature which is for-itself that its separation from its modality as action identifies it as *having been* a literature of *hexis* and consummatory destruction. The task of literature is to reveal the human situation in order to surpass it toward a community of freedoms. Its own history is internal to the ideal relationship of generosity and freedom which it forges between the writer and the public. In the past, literature fell into the category of consumption because it had adopted a metaphysics in which being and having were identical. Thus literature professed to offer through indulgence the fulfillment of being, the appropriation of being through the spectacle of being. By contrast, the literature of *praxis* starts from the metaphysical assumption that being is appropriated only through the act of making itself. The literature of *praxis* is always a literature *en situation.* It inserts itself into the world of gestures and instruments which reveal the world in the act of transforming it.

The late nineteenth-century bourgeoisie had employed artists and writers to convince itself that it was capable of useless, gratuitous passions, such as adultery and stamp-collecting. For a class which practiced honesty out of interest, virtue through unimaginativeness, and fidelity from habit, it was satisfying to be told that its daring exceeded that of the seducer or highwayman. Under these conditions, the writer, himself formerly a useless passion, became a functionary in producing a *literature of alibis,* titillating the bourgeoisie with a fictional identity of the categories of production and consumption.

Surrealist literature which followed attempted to recreate the identification of literature with consumption radicalized as the pure act of destruction. It embarked upon the destruction of bourgeois subjectivity by pushing its rationality to the limit, in all automated irrationalism which consumes the contours of every object in a radical self-contradiction. In reality, the surrealists merely bracketed the world in order to celebrate its symbolic destruction. Their conception of violence was instantaneous, gratuitous, and scandalous, but not such as could undertake a protracted struggle in which the categories of means and ends are essential to the definition of the political situation.

It was the forties which altered the pace of history and the ratios of good and evil so as to confront every individual with a situation in which to act was to play one's hand irredeemably in the certainty that destruction and evil were absolute realities. For previous generations evil had been only an appearance, a detour for freedom. Henceforth good and evil were equally absolute because their consequences for collective destruction could no longer be foreseen contemplatively, but required deliberation through action or resistance. Under these conditions the individual lived on the frontier between his own humanity and man's inhumanity to man. In these circumstances, the relativity of things could only be conveyed through a *literature of extreme situations* which involved the reader in the predicament of characters without guarantees. It was no longer possible to create a literature of ordinary situations when each day a man somewhere chose between humiliation and heroism, between the polarities of the human condition.

Finally, in the period of postwar capitalist reconstruction, literature had once again to situate itself relative to the processes of production and consumption. In a context characterized equally by the highest levels of production in history and the most profound sense of alienation, it becomes the task of literature to reveal the power of the productive process over the producer, as did Hesiod in an earlier day, but to relate this alienation within the total project whereby man makes history his own history. The writer engaged in such a task must create what Sartre calls a *total literature,* which is simultaneously a literary and political activity in which the writer and the reading public communicate man to man, on the model of a socialist society.

The power of nihilation or freedom whereby consciousness becomes aware of what is lacking in its condition is not an act of pure reflection or simple withdrawal. The fundamental project which I am is progressively revealed through an ensemble of real existents which simultaneously separate me from my ends and are structured secondarily as means or obstacles to my purposes. Values come into the world only through the being which carves into the plenitude of being its own lack of being:

> We shall use the term *situation* for the contingency of freedom in the plenum of being of the world inasmuch as this *datum,* which is there only in order not to constrain freedom, is revealed to this freedom only as already *illuminated* by the end which freedom chooses. Thus the *datum* never appears to the for-itself as a brute existent in-itself; it is discovered always *as a cause* since it is revealed only in the light of an end which illuminates it. Situation and motivation are really one. The for-itself discovers itself as engaged in being, hemmed in by being, threatened by being; it discovers the state of things which surrounds it as the cause for a reaction of defense or attack. But it can make this discovery only because it freely posits the end in relation to which the state of things is threatening or favorable. (*BN,* 487–88)

My situation is never reducible to the dead-weight upon me of my body, my place, my past, my environment, my death, my relation to the other. The significance of each of these structures unfolds only within my situation as a practical field in which my decision to act qualifies the facticities of place or environment. It is only in the light of my undertaking that things acquire a coefficient of adversity, that is to say, are designated simultaneously as *data* which have to be assumed by my action and as *possibilities* illuminated by my needs. It is through the exigency which I exist in order to become what I am that nothingness is added to the plenitude of being:

> It is because freedom is condemned to be free—i.e. cannot choose itself as freedom—that there are things; that is, a plenitude of contingency at the heart of which it is itself contingency. It is by the assumption of this contingency and by its surpassing that there can be at once a *choice* and an organization of things in *situation;* and it is the contingency of freedom and the contingency of the in-itself which are expressed *in situation* by the unpredictability and the adversity of the environment. Thus I am absolutely free and absolutely responsible for my situation. But I can never be free except *in situation.* (*BN,* 509)

Thus we are in language as we are in the body; that is, as a vehicle of expression, an excarnation of particular purposes or detotalizations of the total human project. In speech we unveil the world, name its objects, and describe situations in order to transcend them. It is the poet who does not pass beyond words to the practical utilities which they furnish. To the poet these connections are purely magical. He uses words to produce word-objects or images of the world, but not to *express* a certain situation like the writer of a political pamphlet who intends to transform the situation in the light of his description. Every creation of the genuine artist, far from being a finished object opens on to the entire world, calling forth the freedom of his public:

> Each painting, each book, is a recovery of the totality of being. Each of them presents this totality to the freedom of the spectator. For this is quite the final goal of art: to recover this world by giving it to be seen as it is, but as if it had its source in human freedom. But since what the author creates takes on objective reality only in the eyes of the spectator, this recovery is consecrated by the ceremony of the spectacle—and particularly of reading. We are already in a better position to answer the question we raised a while ago: the writer chooses to appeal to the freedom of other men so that, by the reciprocal implications of their demands, they may readapt the totality of being to man and may again enclose the universe within man.[12]

The artist's creation, therefore, appeals to a kingdom of ends for which terror and beauty are never simply natural events but simultaneously an *exigency* and a *gift* to be integrated into the human condition.

Whenever the artist is separated from his public, his work loses its quality as an imperative and is reduced to a purely aesthetic object. In turn the artist is forced to substitute the formal relationship between himself and his art for the relationship of commitment and transcendence between the artist and the public. Under these conditions, works of art function not as outlines of the total man, but as treasures whose scarcity is the measure of the absolute poverty of man, whose eternity is the denial of human history.[13]

Together Sartre and Merleau-Ponty were the enemies of "high-altitude thinking." But, as Sartre tells the story, the two became estranged by everything they had in common. The thought of Merleau-Ponty was labyrinthine; its anchorage in the body, its passion unity. By contrast, Sartre allows his own thought to appear overlucid, dialectical and, even worse, optimistic in the face of Merleau-Ponty's brooding silence. The events of history forced the two to quarrel over the spontaneity of the proletarian revolution and its organization, the nature of individual and group life, in the course of which they embroiled everything each had ever stood for:

> Beneath our intellectual divergences of 1941, so calmly accepted when Husserl alone was the cause, we discovered, astounded, that our conflicts had, at times, stemmed from our childhood, or went back to the elementary differences of our two organisms; and that at other times, they were between the flesh and the skin; in one of us hypocrisies, complicities, a passion for activism hiding his defeats, and, in the other, retractile emotions and a desperate quietism.[14]

Sartre generously conceded that it was from Merleau-Ponty that he "learned history" and the testimony to this is his *Critique of Dialectical Reason.* To some this may suggest the relative inferiority of *Being and Nothingness* to *Phenomenology of Perception* and the consequent failure of Sartre's identification of the categories of literature and politics. This is the old criticism of Sartrean lucidity that I have suggested is unjust to Sartre's phenomenology of temporality and situation which is the foundation of his novels and plays and his most recent studies of history and social structure.

Notes

1. Jean-Paul Sartre, *Situations,* I–III (Paris: Gallimard, 1947–49). Essays from *Situations,* I and III, have been published as *Literary Essays,* trans. Annette

Michelson (New York: Philosophical Library, 1957), and most of *Situations,* II, has been published as *What Is Literature?* trans. Bernard Frechtman (New York: Philosophical Library, 1949). Quotations are from the English translations.

2. Jean-Paul Sartre, *Situations,* IV (Paris: Gallimard, 1964); *Situations,* trans. Benita Eisler (New York: George Braziller, 1965). There is a fascinating history of an alternating conception of environment as a deterministic force (*milieu*) and as a beneficent shell or field (*ambiance*), a point where the thought of Heidegger, Sartre, Marcel, and Jaspers might be related. I refer to the essays of Leo Spitzer, "*Milieu* and *Ambiance:* An Essay in Historical Semantics," *Philosophy and Phenomenological Research* 3 (1942–43), 1–42 and 169–218.

3. Iris Murdoch, *Sartre: Romantic Rationalist* (New Haven: Yale University Press, 1959).

4. Jean-Paul Sartre, *Being and Nothingness,* trans. Hazel E. Barnes (New York: Philosophical Library, 1956), 142. Hereafter *BN.*

5. F. Jameson, *Sartre: The Origins of a Style* (New Haven: Yale University Press, 1961).

6. Sartre, *Literary Essays,* 7.

7. Ibid., 19.

8. Ibid., 23.

9. Sartre, *Situations,* 195.

10. Ibid., 336.

11. Ibid., 345.

12. *Literature and Existentialism,* trans. Bernard Frechtman (New York: Citadel Press, 1962), 57–58; in the original *Situations,* II, 106–7.

13. Sartre, "The Artist and his Conscience," in *Situations,* 205–24.

14. Ibid., 296.

PART 7

PRIMARY TEXTS AND DOCUMENTS

21

Philosophy and Political Engagement: Letters from the Quarrel between Sartre and Merleau-Ponty

Translated and Presented by Jon Stewart

Translator's Introduction

The three letters presented here come from the crucial period of the quarrel between Sartre and Merleau-Ponty in July 1953 that ultimately resulted in the latter's retiring from *Les Temps modernes,* the journal that the two men had jointly edited since the war. These letters were only recently released for publication by the families of Sartre and Merleau-Ponty and first appeared in *Magazine littéraire* in 1994,[1] with a brief introduction by the journal's editor, François Ewald, who has generously allowed them to be translated and published in this collection.

In order to appreciate the importance of these letters, it is necessary to know something about the context in which they were written and the background of the conflict between Sartre and Merleau-Ponty. The dispute that reached its head in these letters had been brewing for at least three years. Merleau-Ponty, though not a member of the Communist Party, had for some time been an advocate of communism as works such as *Humanism and Terror* attest, and this affiliation was naturally reflected in *Les Temps modernes.* In 1950 at the outbreak of the Korean War, however, Merleau-Ponty began to distance himself from Soviet communism after judging that the Soviet Union was the initiator of the conflict. In "Merleau-Ponty *vivant*," Sartre recalls how Merleau-Ponty considered it inappropriate for *Les Temps modernes* to comment on the war and in effect muzzled the journal with respect to political issues.[2] At that time Merleau-Ponty resigned from his post as political editor of the journal while continuing in his capacity as editor-in-chief. This silence on politics lasted for two years during which it continued to rankle Sartre, who began to have more and more sympathies for communism. This must certainly be seen as the first precipitating factor in the eventual conflict.

The second came in 1952 when Sartre declared his wholehearted affiliation with communism. As he tells the story,[3] it was the French government's arrests of the communists and of their leader Jacques Duclos in the wake of anti-American demonstrations which caused his conversion. The manifesto which announced his new political views was a series of articles entitled *The Communists and Peace,* the first of which appeared in *Les Temps modernes* in the same year.[4] Merleau-Ponty was not always informed or consulted about the content of these articles ahead of time. Sartre's radical new political stance alienated a number of the colleagues at *Les Temps modernes;* some, like Merleau-Ponty, tolerated it quietly, while for others it became the source of an open conflict.

The third factor was just such an open conflict between Sartre and Claude Lefort, one of Merleau-Ponty's former students and a colleague at *Les Temps modernes.* Lefort was critical of Sartre's new political orientation, and the two agreed to write articles criticizing each other's position in the journal itself.[5] These articles[6] were lively and did not shrink from *ad hominem* abuse. Merleau-Ponty played the role of mediator, and in his capacity as coeditor had, for the sake of the journal, to persuade both parties to omit from their texts the most venomous rhetoric. The result of the exchange was ill-feeling among all three men.

The final cause and, according to Sartre, the immediate factor precipitating the conflict came in 1953 and concerned an article for the review that was proposed by a Marxist acquaintance of Sartre. The article was submitted to the journal at a time when Sartre happened to be out of town, and for this reason it fell into Merleau-Ponty's hands. Merleau-Ponty, as editor, found the article to be one-sided and affixed to it a somewhat apologetic and even critical note to the readers. When Sartre returned, he was infuriated by the note that Merleau-Ponty had added without consulting him.[7] He in turn removed it without discussing the matter with Merleau-Ponty, who in turn was infuriated when he noticed the note's omission in reading the galley proofs for the number. At this time Sartre had left for Rome where he was wont to take his vacations. As Sartre portrays the events,[8] Merleau-Ponty called him immediately once he saw that his prefatory note had been omitted without his consent and threatened to resign from the journal. The two were on the telephone for two hours and the conversation doubtless provided much of the basis for the material in the ensuing letters presented here.

This is the moment that the letters featured here begin. Sartre, still in Rome, having considered the matter for a time and discussed it with Simone de Beauvoir, writes a letter to Merleau-Ponty in order above all to reproach him for his lack of political engagement. He criticizes Merleau-Ponty for assuming an apolitical position, which lacks social awareness and concern. On a more personal level, Sartre is especially annoyed by a lecture that Merleau-Ponty gave at the Collège de France, the subject of which was precisely the relationship of philosophy to politics. In this lecture, Merleau-Ponty discussed, among other things, Sartre's political views in a way which Sartre took amiss. In his letter, Sartre then criticizes Merleau-Ponty for the inconsistency of, on the one hand, having no political standpoint himself while, on the other hand, criticizing others who are politically engaged. It seems that in their telephone conversation Merleau-Ponty proposed as a solution to write a text for *Les Temps modernes* stating his own political views. In this way he could make his own views clear independently of the controversial article on capitalism. In his letter Sartre, however, says that he cannot accept this solution and vows that he will refuse to print any such text on the grounds that Merleau-Ponty, by not being politically engaged in recent events, has forfeited his right to enter into a political discussion in the forum of *Les Temps modernes*. In short, Sartre vows to stifle Merleau-Ponty's article in the journal which they both founded and of which they were both editors.

The second letter featured here is Merleau-Ponty's response. He outlines at length his own position, arguing, first, that there never was a time when he was not politically engaged and, second, that although he discussed Sartre's political views in his lecture, he never criticized them in any way that would be cause for offense. As evidence of the latter, he encloses with the letter his lecture notes. These are somewhat schematic but begin to read more like a finished text when Merleau-Ponty takes up his discussion of Sartre. (He had perhaps rewritten this part more clearly just for Sartre's sake on the occasion of this letter.) In his response to Sartre, Merleau-Ponty outlines what he understands political engagement to amount to. He argues that the need to give a running commentary in the public eye on political events as Sartre does leads one to distort and misunderstand the individual events by taking them out of their larger social and historical context. A more accurate and insightful political analysis, one more in keeping with the tools and education of a philosopher, can only be given when it is based on a more thorough study of the entire context in which the individual events take place. Merleau-Ponty argues that he is not obliged to choose between one of the two power blocks of the Cold War, and, by not choosing, he is in no way adopting a naive or apolitical stance. The realm of philosophy is simply different from that of party politics. He ultimately underlines his inability to accept Sartre's censorship of his work and vows to send him his article on politics in the coming few months.

In the third and final letter, Sartre, still in Rome, writes to Merleau-Ponty and proposes a meeting upon his return to Paris at which they might have the opportunity to resolve their differences face to face. He avoids entering into polemics anew and merely cautions his friend to avoid reading too much into his actions and words. Finally, he relates how the rumors surrounding their quarrel have important and, for him, negative political results. Specifically, he is particularly worried about the fact that the political right is able to make use of Merleau-Ponty's criticisms for their own cause. This then works against the political agenda that Sartre proposes.

It is not clear whether a meeting of reconciliation ever took place between the two men once Sartre returned to Paris. If it did, then Sartre does not mention it in his account of the dispute. With what concerns the article on politics that Merleau-Ponty proposes, it is likely, as Ewald suggests,[9] that it ultimately became the basis for the book *Adventures of the Dialectic* or specifically for the long chapter therein entitled "Sartre and Ultrabolshevism." In any case, this conflict did end the cooperative work of the two men and caused Merleau-Ponty to resign from the journal that he helped to found. He would never write in the journal again. The dispute between the two men remained open until they met at a conference in Venice in 1956 where they effected a partial reconciliation. In the years that followed, the two men saw each other only fleetingly.

These letters are useful for a number of reasons. They provide a great deal of information about the nature of the dispute, much of which is omitted for whatever reason from Sartre's extended account in "Merleau-Ponty *vivant*." They therefore give a somewhat different view of the dispute than Sartre presents and thus serve as an invaluable source of historical and biographical information. For example, while Sartre cites the episode of the prefatory note to the article on capitalism as divisive in the conflict, this issue is never mentioned once in the letters. Moreover, Sartre never mentions threatening to stifle Merleau-Ponty's article, and he, likewise, never mentions the fact that he was rankled by Merleau-Ponty's lecture. In the letter we have here, it is clearly the issue of the censorship of his work that annoys Merleau-Ponty the most. There is also no mention of Merleau-Ponty's retiring from the journal.

Although the dispute here is certainly to a fair degree personal in nature, these letters are also of philosophical value and are not merely a reflection of the petty bickerings of two self-indulgent French intellectuals. Here what is at issue is the office of philosophy itself and its responsibilities and obligations with respect to political engagement. Both men are clearly vexed by the demands that the Cold War seems to make on intellectuals and are at pains to know exactly how to react and what their responsibilities are both to themselves and to their reading public. These letters also give an important picture of the political and intellectual climate of the times.

With respect to the translation of these letters, my primary goal has been to present a readable English text. In order to do so, I have had to make numerous changes in punctuation and have in a few places inserted paragraph breaks. The result is that something of the informality and spontaneity of the letters has been lost, while, I hope, a degree of clarity and readability has been gained. I have added a handful of explanatory notes above all in order to aid the reader unfamiliar either with the political context in France at the time or with specific philosophical terms.[10]

1. Sartre to Merleau-Ponty

exact date uncertain

at Albergo Nazionale,
Piazza Monecitorio
Rome
until July 18 [1953]

My Dear Merleau,

I've waited a long time to respond to you because I've hesitated a long time. I also wanted to discuss the matter with Beaver[11] who had left before me. At present I am certain of my response: I cannot accept your solution. I am going to try to tell you why in all friendship. Don't get angry and just listen to me.

You criticized my position directly and indirectly, in conversation with me and publicly. I just defended myself. As if your position were correct and as if I had to justify myself for not accepting it. Why did I do that? Because that is the way I am. I'm terrified of making an accusation, be it to defend myself or those people whom I love. But ultimately we must do so. But the true response to make to you is this one: I do not approve of your position, and *I blame you.* Fine, you know what I'm talking about. That you withdraw from politics (that is, what we intellectuals call politics), that you prefer to dedicate yourself to your philosophical research, is an act that is at once legitimate and unjustifiable. I mean, it is legitimate *if* you are not trying to justify it. It is legitimate if it remains a subjective decision which concerns you alone, and no one has the right to reproach you for it. And you prove, in fact, that you are right with what concerns you if the result of this retreat is—as I hope, believe me, with all my heart it will be—a book, *The Prose of the World,* which will be as new and as rich as *Phenomenology of Perception* or *Humanism and Terror.* At bottom it goes back to the question of *vocation.* You are conscious of the fact that that is your vocation, and you prove it through your books, and *you are right.* Fine. But if, in the name of this individual gesture, you discuss the attitude of those who remain in the *objective* domain of politics and who try somehow or another to make decisions based on motivations that are objectively valid, then you in turn deserve to be criticized by an objective judgment. You are no longer someone who says, "I would do better to abstain," but you are rather someone who says to others, "*it is necessary* to abstain."

I avow that I was pained to read in *L'Express* a review of a lecture that you gave to some students and where you said publicly that I was wrong. Yes, I made allowances for the journalistic language, and I'm certain you spoke of me politely and in a friendly manner. Believe me that my sensitivity is not the problem here. I just say that the statements that you made, if not against me, then at least against my present position, have their immediate resonance *on the right* and take on an objective meaning, which there can be no mistaking. You will say that you can't do anything about that: regardless of what you say, be it finely or delicately put, people will still always come to this conclusion: a philosopher is wrong today to speak out on the North Atlantic Treaty, the policy of the French government, etc., etc. Or rather one can speak out if one refuses both the blocks or the parties which oppose each other but not if one judges *a* policy to be more dangerous than another. In a word, the philosopher of *today* cannot take a political position. This doesn't correspond to a criticism of my position in the name of another position but to an attempt to neutralize it, to put it into parentheses in the name of a nonposition. You pretend that it is necessary to know what the Soviet regime is in order to choose. But since one always chooses in ignorance and since it is not reserved *for us* to know, it would be in bad faith to see this problem *of principle* as an empirical one. And then, above all, it is not a question of us entering the communist party but of reacting as we think in conscience we ought to in urgent cases such as, for example, the

European army, the war in Indochina, etc., etc. You reproach me for going too far, for getting too close to the communist party. It is not impossible that you are right on this point and I am wrong. But I reproach you and even more severely for abdicating under these circumstances when it is necessary to make a decision as a human being, a Frenchman, a citizen, and an intellectual, and for using your "philosophy" as an alibi. You are not philosophy, Merleau, no more than I am or Jaspers (or anyone else). One is "philosophy" when one is dead and when posterity reduces you to a few books. In our lifetime, we are people who, among other things, write books on philosophy. Your lecture at the Collège de France was not at all convincing if you hoped by it to become philosophy. In that sense, it was wholly lacking. Let's take this first problem, this prefatory question: Is something like philosophy possible? It would be admirable if it were only a matter of a self-portrait of a painter, and even of a self-justification. But ultimately, with it being taken as such, it forbids you to judge the nonphilosophers. It could only be a matter of zoology: the species "philosopher" would be described and fixed (supposing that one accepts your premises) and would not be related to any of the other species. Among them communication seems difficult: you arrive at the problem at the end of the analysis, but in my view you do not treat it. And after all not a word of your lecture allows one to know if the "dreamy presence" [*présence songeuse*] of which you speak was a characteristic which was accidental, historical, pathological, or on the contrary a fundamental choice. This *dreamy presence* I do not recognize as like mine; my *being-there*[12] . . . as we say, is not of this kind. It can mean that I am not a philosopher (that's what I believe), or that there are other ways of being a philosopher. It is therefore absolutely impossible to criticize my position as you have done in the lecture reviewed by *L'Express* in the name of this pseudo-essence of philosophy, which is in my opinion only an extrapolation from your own psychology and its projection into the domain of values and principles.

My conclusion: your position can be neither admirable nor defensible. It is the result of the pure exercise of your right to choose for yourself what suits you best. If you try to criticize anything at all in the name of this position, you play the game of the reactionaries and of anticommunism; everything hangs on this point.

Don't conclude from this that I don't think my position is criticizable. It surely is and indeed from all points of view, on the condition that the points of view are already political, that is, that they translate an objective stance founded on objective motives. Someone from the M.R.P.[13] can criticize my assessment of the war in Indochina, a socialist can criticize my conception of the communist party, but no one has the right to do it in the name of the phenomenological εποχη.[14]

What bothers me about you is that I have not seen you intervene either for the Rosenbergs or for Henri Martin or in principle against the arrests of the communists (your presence at the Committee for the Defense of Freedoms is truly too dreamy for anyone to think it efficacious) or against those who want the international expansion of the war in Indochina. (I speak of your present position because before your sudden change in 1950 you had already passionately condemned this war.) Here it's a matter of human reactions to immediate demands. Only someone who has satisfied these demands can, in my opinion, criticize me in *Les Temps modernes,* that is, can engage in a political dialogue. In a word, I pose to my critic a prefatory question: What about you, what are you doing today? If you are not doing anything, then you don't have the right to make political criticisms; you have the right to write your book, but that's all. Believe me that I say it without irony: I think your choice to be rigorous ought to be restricted to the pure reflection about history and society. But you don't have the right to play both games. And if you want my whole opinion, it is only a subjective passion which makes you take this contradictory position (contradictory since you want to destroy a certain politics—that of people who think like me—by refusing to have one yourself). You want to condemn as fast as possible those who might condemn you.

I don't have the stomach or the right to condemn your present position. I am ready to recognize that your position and mine are perfectly compatible and can exist even today. But for precisely this reason I condemn vigorously and without hesitation your attempts to condemn me. I will certainly not give them any hospitality in *Les Temps modernes* because then I would risk annoying my readers. All attempts from the left are permissible: I mean all those which allow (1) that political problems are posed to all people and that it is not permissible to elude them even under the pretext that they cannot be solved, and (2) that those who—whatever might be their severity toward the communist party—consider that it is not permissible to ignore a party which receives between five and six million votes. These two conditions seem to me to rigorously rule out your present position. Moreover, I tell you what's more that my "change" in position has not brought with it any change in the clientele of *Les Temps modernes.* There are some new subscriptions, no cancellations of the old ones, and the renewals are normal. This signifies, I think, that I have changed at the same time as our public. You recall, on the contrary, the growing irritation of the readers when you refused to take a position on the war in Korea? This point of view is also important: your position for the readers of the journal seemed a step backwards, a way of protecting oneself. I conclude that *you* wanted to justify yourself; but it seems to me (and, moreover, not because I have *personal* motivations) that *they* paid no heed to it. They want you to explain the situation in accordance with objective principles which they think they have in common with the journal.

This is what I wanted to say. I would want that you not regard it as an unfriendly gesture. (To be perfectly candid, the unfriendly gesture is rather the one that you made in giving that lecture against me and without warning me except for by a word thrown incautiously into our conversation at the Café Procope. This is what Beaver calls "an indiscreet point of abuse." But I would not dream of reproaching you for it.) Just weigh everything well. It seems to me that your position is not such that it could today be expressed in *Les Temps modernes.* You have not accompanied us in our efforts (the Rosenbergs, Henri Martin, Indochina, the Committee for the Defense of Freedoms, etc.), and so I, therefore, do not see in the name of what you, *as a part of the team,* would criticize us. I would like, dear Merleau, that everything here remain on the ambiguous terrain of politics and that you not forget even for a moment our long friendship.

Amicably, J. P. Sartre

P.S. My response obviously concerns the *article on politics.* Concerning the notes, of course, I'm not going to respond since you do not say whether you intend to make these notes apolitical or to make use of them as an indirect way of introducing an opposition into *Les Temps modernes.*

2. Merleau-Ponty to Sartre

8 July [1953]
Paris

Dear Sartre,

The subject of the lecture which your letter mentions three times ("Philosophy and Politics Today") was determined months ahead of time, as the printed programs of the Philosophical Faculty at the Collège show. Having given it on the 29th of May, I saw you again two days later at the meeting of *Les Temps modernes,* and you could have spoken about it more at that time if you had wanted to. Before having held the lecture and when

I announced it to you at the Café Procope, I did not think of explaining to you point by point what I would say there, but these things came into our conversation. Moreover, it was at this moment which was agreed on between you and me that I was preparing an article on politics for the journal, and you did not find anything wrong in the fact that I would say in the lecture some odds and ends that would then appear later in *Les Temps modernes* since it was after all only a matter of odds and ends. Lecturing a bit longer than an hour altogether, I spoke of your political position for no longer than the last fifteen minutes. And in the fourteen pages of notes that I had prepared and that I have before me, there are *two* of them which are about you and two concluding pages giving my views on political engagement. You will find enclosed an outline of the lecture (where I give the last two paragraphs more relative space than they actually had). I defy you to find there anything shocking. At Lyon, at the Sorbonne, at the Philosophical Faculty at the Collège and abroad, I have *always* discussed publicly your theses (and at the Philosophical Faculty at the Collège, three years ago, I discussed those of *The Second Sex*). . . . Certainly this time, the difference between you and me was much more obvious, but the tone was no different. I was not only courteous, that goes without saying, but also the listeners were sensitive to the sympathy for your thought which appeared, they told me, in my manner of discussing it. Finally, I was very careful to say nothing which was inspired by our private conversations and which was not able to be explained by your published texts. To give a lecture *about you,* there was no lack of material. I did not say one tenth of what I could have said regarding your recent political works, and, for example, nowhere did I enter into a discussion of the notions of class, party, etc. I confined myself to putting up a signpost. If the reactionaries rejoice at a divergence of this kind, there are two positions one can take: the one is to direct the argument in order to transform the divergence into hostility. That is what you do, and this makes them the judges of our debates. The other would be to show them that what separates me from you does not put us in two opposing camps. This is what I propose and you refuse.

Not being in agreement with you, what could I do? If we together had stopped a political position of the journal, it would have been unfriendly—or rather, it would have been a treason—to discuss it publicly. But you never deliberated with me the least of your political decisions. You first presented to me, as something already decided, the project of leaving France in the case of an occupation. (I do not forget that you offered to help me, but you were not disposed to raise any questions about the matter itself.) Some time later later, I learned incidentally in the course of a conversation that you had finally decided to remain, come what may. It's true that these decisions had a quite personal side, but the matter was not any different with respect to the orientation of *Les Temps modernes*. I learned from the press of the creation of the R.D.R.,[15] and I learned by reading the journal of your present position with respect to the communist party. (The price of all this for me was that I appeared ridiculous when I said and wrote that you thought only of a joint action for limited objectives with the communist party, and when I vigorously defended you on this basis, only having found out too late about your position in the course of a conversation that we would not have had if I had not insisted on it, that the work in common with the communists had led you beyond the point of departure and that, for example, you would no longer consider as valid your published works.) How could I have been held responsible for positions that you wanted to guard so jealously as *your own*? If you found it unfriendly of me that I discussed your positions, I myself find hardly friendly the silence with which you have taken them up. Talent and literary importance aside, which are not at issue here, we owe to each other the same consideration because I was stimulated by what you published concerning politics pretty much in the same way you were stimulated by me. (No one outside the journal ever imagined that I was so little informed about your change.) The day when it was necessary to speak of the well-known affair of the camps, I brought you a text and asked you to sign it with me. You never did anything like that for me. But ultimately this way of acting was practicable. At least it implied that you gave me full right to discuss your views publicly. Even though orally and in writing you cite *Humanism and Terror* in accordance with your views, you name me, not without malice, for bringing up the case of Lefort in connection with my own, and in passing you mention, not without sarcasm ("one knows the song," you say), the bad readers who see the social between the in-itself and the for-itself, and the better readers have recognized me in these lines. To renounce speaking of your theses, I would have to renounce having an opinion.

Precisely, you say, I ought not have an opinion. By a "sudden change" that you date at 1950, I allegedly withdrew from politics in order to do philosophy, a decision which can be contested as little as that of being a mountain climber but which can have no more political meaning than that and which cannot pretend to be admirable. There would be a contradiction in discussing a political position in the name of a "nonposition" and in "playing both games." I could write an article on politics only in order "to condemn as fast as possible those who might condemn me" because I am not comfortable with myself—personal affairs to which the readers pay no heed. . . .

What you call my "sudden change" is above all a sudden awakening of your attention, and my "subjective" decision, a small crack in the "objective" world which you have construed for yourself for some time now. I have never changed in the will to do philosophy, and I told you this one day around 1948, when you asked me why I didn't stop teaching. My action in *Les Temps modernes* for several years, as much as Sartre's action for some months during the war in the bulletin of the movement, always tended to bring the facts toward their theory. . . . When I wrote the editorials on Indochina or on the general strike, it was never without malaise, it was more or less inevitable on these subjects. They were usually quite short, and I did them because they fit with the rest. And I did not put my name on *Les Temps modernes* because I did not want to be acknowledged as a contemporary writer, even at the end of the war. I did not follow your advice to enter the C.N.E.[16] and to write for *Les Lettres françaises* because I did not want to officially become a writer of the resistance.

In no way did I renounce writing on politics in 1950; on the contrary, I always thought that *The Prose of the World* would have a second part on Catholicism and a third part on the revolution. In September 1951, I gave a lecture in Geneva of which a good part was on politics, and it was a virtue in the atmosphere of the place.

I decided after the Korean war, and this is an entirely different matter, no longer to write on events as they presented themselves. I did this for reasons which belong to the nature of that period and for other reasons which are permanent. Let us omit the latter since they are not decisive.* Engagement on *every* event taken on its own becomes, in a period of tension, a system of "bad faith." . . . There are events which permit or rather demand that one judge them immediately and even in themselves, for example, the condemnation and the execution of the Rosenbergs. . . . But most of the time, the event cannot be appreciated in the entirety of a politics which changes the meaning of it, and it would be an artifice and a ruse to provoke the judgment on each point of a policy instead of considering it in its consequence and in its relation to that of its adversary. This would permit one to swallow in its detail that which would not be accepted in the big picture, or, on the contrary, to make odious at one blow the little truths which, when seen together, are in the logic of the struggle. You and I have admitted that it was in this that the

*To write about the event of the day when one does not belong to a party (and even if one, as a member of a party, is brought to philosophy) demands and simultaneously hinders one from elaborating the principles. Your commentary from May 28 made you hope to write your book on history and yet hindered you from beginning.

inadmissible ruse of anticommunism and also the ruse of the communist policy could be found. If we did not sign the Stockholm Appeal, it is because it tried to bring in, with a condemnation of the atomic bomb, which to be sure no decent human being can fail to support, a solution favorable to the U.S.S.R. in all situations of force. And this is still what hinders me from taking a position on the war in Korea or on the invasion of Laos. To consider the situation of South Korea, one easily justifies the *political* intervention of North Korea. To consider the invasion of Laos in itself, one has for those who do it as much sympathy as antipathy for those who oppose it. But this is not the entire question. In a globally strained situation, and even without imagining in the least that the U.S.S.R. pulls all the strings, it is artificial—and deceptive—to act as if the problems were posed one by one and to break up into a series of local questions what is historically a unity. *If one wants coexistence,* one cannot demand that the capitalist world attribute to the "social movements" what, in this case, is also military occupation, and if one does, it's because one does not want coexistence but the victory of the U.S.S.R. If, because the invasion of South Korea and of Laos are *also* social movements, you say that they are *only* that, that the ruse is in the matter and not in the communist party, then it is no longer peace that you are for but rather the global victory of communism, preferably without war, and you no longer count on maintaining the peace except on the indecision of the capitalist world. . . . This is why, while being wholly against the international expansion of the war in Indochina, I did not want to write *at the moment of the invasion of Laos.* I was not angry that this threat weighed on the communist politics. Coexistence and peace have these demands. One must believe that I was not so wrong since by not signing the Stockholm Appeal, we did not pass into the camp of the partisans of the atomic bomb since the communists consequently proposed for our signature texts much less full of ruses, the Vietminh renounced its offensive, the North Koreans accepted the armistice, and one saw finally the outline of a true policy of *détente.*

To become engaged on every event, as if it were a test of morality, to make a politics into your own cause without realizing or without saying it to your readers, you refuse without reflection a *right of correction* which no serious action renounces. And since above all the communist governments, which are even more capable than the others of going back on their decisions, would do so, you finally find yourself alone on the positions that the communists have abandoned—which just proves that they were not the only tenable ones for them, and by refusing to stand security for the military action of the communists, the noncommunist left played its role, which is to favor a policy of *détente.*

One more thing, if you say that we have not occupied ourselves with the aspect which takes the events in the eyes of the anticommunist and that is to *play the game of the reactionaries,* then you suppress in thought the capitalist world and you do not act for coexistence. This is why I suggested several times that we put into the journal whole studies rather than premature positions, in short to aim at the head of the reader and not at the heart, which is, moreover, in keeping with our manner and that of the journal. There I found the action of a writer, which consists in the comings and goings between the event and the general opinion, and not attacking (in the imagination) every event as if it were decisive, unique, and irrecoverable.

This method is closer to politics than your method of *constant engagement* (in the Cartesian sense). For, at the same time, it is more philosophic because the distance that it contrives between the event and the judgment which one makes of it disarms the trap of the event and allows one to see its meaning clearly. I therefore have no need to separate philosophy from the world in order to remain a philosopher—and I have never done that. You must have listened to the opening lecture of which you spoke with a lot of suspicion in order to have understood it as you did. I took care to speak of Socrates in order to show that the philosopher is not someone who simply produces books but who is in the world. I attacked those who place philosophy outside of time, and I have in no way made an *alibi* of it as you can read, among other things, in the text which I send you: "the philosophic absolute is nowhere, it doesn't ever take place anywhere, it is therefore never elsewhere, it must be defended in each particular event . . . ."** Since I spoke of philosophy at the beginning of a course on philosophy, it was legitimate, I think, to consult inductively some empirical cases of "philosophers." I found their common trait to be in equivocation, and I do not know how you could disagree on this point when considering the history of philosophers and their buffooneries. But I tried to say that equivocation is bad philosophy and that good philosophy is a healthy ambiguity because it affirms the basic agreement and disagreement *de facto* between the individual, others and the truth and since it is patience which makes them all work together in some way or another. I said that, understood in this way, philosophy was perhaps a stranger to professional politics,*** but not to people. (What

**You see that the final words exaggerate in your sense.

***At least officially. In speaking to the students, I quoted Lenin's words as reported by Gorki concerning musicians, words which one can apply to literature and philosophy: " . . . often I cannot listen to music. It gets on my nerves. One wants to say sweet nothings and caress the head of people who, living in a hell, can an irony: I thought, in writing these words, of your talk at Vel d'Hiv that Suzo[17] heard while I was with my mother at Menton, and which, she had told me, touched the public in such a way that the people there felt a dangerous freedom that was unusual in politics.) One has not shown that this philosophy is possible since it is the person himself who is paradoxical, incarnate, and social. If philosophy were not these things, there would be nothing to say or to do; there would be nothing valuable and everything would be meaningless. You ask me if it is a fundamental choice. It is better than a choice, it is that which makes everything possible; it is the fact itself of *human living* to which we are, as you say, "condemned." There is neither an essence of philosophy nor myth nor justifying phantasm. I don't believe that these ideas are my own or that they are so foreign to you. That which, for me, is turned into a *dreamy presence* is the consequence among certain people who, when faced with the difficulty of making everything work together, tend to crawl back up into to their shells. For others, like you, the difficulty rather provokes a leap of affirmation, and they throw themselves ahead breaking everything. But I don't doubt that the same thorn pesters them both, and, in order to doubt this, one would have to forget everything you wrote, that is, everything that you are up until the new order, in any case, everything that makes people listen to you.

I don't accept the benefit of that pure kindness that one reserves for ordinary animals and the sick and which inspires you to let me do philosophy on the condition that it be only a pastime. Even if philosophy does not choose between communism and anticommunism, it is a position in the world, not an abstention; it is by no means reserved for the philosopher by profession, and it manifests itself outside of his books. I spent an afternoon writing a manifesto for Auriol regarding the arrest of Duclos and the prosecutions of the communists. They asked to me to sign one that was naive and full of ruses, which was pure form. I preferred to write one which showed in the anticommunist campaign of the government an expedient for conjuring away the discussions about the European army, the policy of N.A.T.O., etc. I always said that the Committee for the Defense of Freedoms ought to be open at every level to communists. I also said that the Committee did not have to negotiate with any organization regarding the sending of official representatives.

---

create such beauty. Now today, it is impossible to caress the head of anyone. They'll tear off your hand with a bite. One must hit them over the head, hit without pity, even though from a theoretical point of view we are against all violence." Hm! Hm! What a devilishly difficult duty. I love the frank admission of this divergence which is not hostility.

If the communists think that this again would forbid them access to the Committee, it's because they are trying to compromise it rather than to work together with it; it's because they continue the policy of a unity, which is a trap.

Contrary to what you say, I signed for the petition for the Rosenbergs drawn up by a lawyer of the Conseil d'Etat, the memorandum of which was excellent, and I wholly refused to speak at the meeting at Vel d'Hiv, which was organized by the communists for the same night that the execution took place, and which was by nature designed to make Eisenhower decide against a pardon, as if his own cruelty were not enough. I signed one, a little while ago for the Turkish intellectuals, whom the Turkish government keeps in prison and wants to judge summarily, also for a Frenchman from Morocco, whom the government dismissed because he had been expelled by General Gillaume. In a lecture given to students for the Committee for the Defense of Freedoms, I said in substance to the students, who thanked me with an statement signed by their representatives, "defend the communists, don't be communists." A big step would be made the day when in the governments, in the businesses, one would see that there is a core of people, who though themselves not communists, are absolutely resolved to defend freedoms, even to the benefit of the communists. This line is not easy to take, but at least it is a line. It does not give you the right to say that I "ignore" the communist party or that I "elude political problems under the pretext that they cannot be solved." I take them at a level where there is not any necessity to be a communist or an anticommunist in the hope that these two positions will be surpassed by the evolution of the international political order. The expression the *noncommunist left,* which you like to make use of, cannot have any other meaning. For your part, you make it shrink every time that you use it, like the skin of the ass.[18] If, in order to deserve the label and to have the right to discuss with you, one must have intervened not only for the Rosenbergs and also against the arrests of last year but also, and namely, for Henri Martin and at the moment of the invasion of Laos, I hardly see anyone at *Les Temps modernes* except you yourself, who can discuss with you.

Such are the thoughts which I nurtured and by which I wanted here not, please note, to *justify* but to *explain* my behavior. I do not flatter myself for being without *psyche* (neither without cares nor without emotions; in friendship you will have been able to think of what concerns this winter). But, as you somberly say, this doesn't interest others. What's important is that one can find what is true, firm, and valuable for everyone in examining rigorously a total "state of the soul." Now I say that everything that I just wrote is consistent and that in order to see there only morose dreams and subterfuge, you yourself must be sunken down in yourself. Your procedure, which in the final analysis is to interpret others psychologically, supposes that you mistake the train of your thoughts for the trains of events. Do you believe therefore that you are wholly in the world, do you think that you alone can escape to existential psychoanalysis and that the anger which I saw in you was *perfectly saintly?* You make a merit out of your silence toward me. I do not share your opinion. Since it was shot through anyway with some words which showed above all cynical humor: like the day when you told me in a glacially cold tone that my opening lecture was "amusing," and in an irritated tone regarding the Collège, "I hope that you are going [to] subvert all this a little," and in a tone shaking with violence that research between the in-itself and the for-itself was "vague thoughts" and that if you were a professor today and were to teach *Being and Nothingness* or the *Phenomenology of Perception,* you would have the impression of treason. That was enough to make one tremble, but not enough to shed light on the matter. You don't discuss things with me, you simply *blame* me. This is just the opposite of the way I have always acted toward you. I'm not going to change, as you say, "even a little." But it is nevertheless necessary that you know that your behavior, seen from the outside, is highly "psychological," that precisely the presumption of acting in accordance with objective principles is the most arrogant form of "the law of the heart"[19] and that finally many people know that your subjective opinion is the ground for the lamentable picture that you have had of me since 1950.

Since the Korean War the cause of the left has been more and more lumped together in communism, the cause of noncommunism tended to be confounded with the reaction since the "hard-line" policy of Stalin and the bellicose policy of America drew everything to themselves. We two from the beginning responded to this situation in different ways. You thought that it was between these that it was necessary to decide and that one ought to choose one of the parties or at least prefer one of the policies as the "least dangerous." For me, on the military field, they became soldiers, and I thought that it was necessary to refuse to opt in this case and to struggle against all military exploitation of the situation (I was enchanted by the first articles from Dzélépy which I received myself), and, on the contrary, to exploit every chance of *détente.* This position flattered my penchant for theory? Let's suppose it's true. I am not an angel. But your position was no less personal, no more admirable. Since it was not objective relations in the universe of politics which made you decide, it was your being-there—you wanted to be present day for day *at the events,* opposed to and against everything since "everyone is responsible for everything before us"; this does not mean that you were present at the *total event* of the last years (indeed, it's even clear for me that you were passed by)—and instead it was your heart, your most personal manner of feeling your relations to the world and to the times which intervened to make you decide here. My silence was ambiguous? Having numbered the public enemies, you, accepting to become engaged on each episode, appeared franker than me. You were no less ambiguous in the final account since there was (as I just said) something fallacious in your engagement in every episode, something confused in the mixture of an unconditional pacifism (which you held at the beginning) and a conditional pacifism (that of the communists) and in your gradual change in position from the unity of action based on objective limits to global sympathy. I didn't want the event to force my hand, and you didn't want to make a retreat. I don't see where you got the right to blame me: to blame me is not to blame yourself. And since you have so little respect, you must know that one can also be *annoyed* by your position; indeed, I was the day when I saw that you had decided to emigrate in case of an invasion: if we had decided to emigrate, we might have done more justice to communism in our articles and exhorted the public to see its value, rather than to have been assuring ourselves of avoiding its inconveniences. Our disagreement today is no different: to continue to define oneself as a noncommunist with the conviction that if the war doesn't take place, popular democracy would inevitably come, and it would be necessary to work within that framework—to recommend—Marxism, as you told me some time around April—this is already to live in spirit and to write in the popular democracy. In both cases, a fixed future, and since one keeps it secret, one maintains the present position and gives to it something clandestine. When one is too frank about the future, one is precisely not frank about the present. Here I don't blame you, but responding to your blaming me, I have the right to say that there is a position that is passive in tone just like mine. It is an easy task for you to construct and live in a future which is entirely personal. I look rather into the present and leave it undecided and open as it is. It is not that I construct another future (one could do it and the greater the rupture between Europe and America and the greater the change in the communist policy in Russia, the more these things are probable). It's not that I am a "rebel" and still less a hero. My relation to the times is constituted above all by the present, that's all. I don't dream of imposing it on you. I say merely that it has its value, and I won't allow that one make it out to be an error.

With respect to the relation to the "objective" world and to history, which you make the sole criterion, it has not served me so badly. I do not boast of it too much: I could predict neither Stalin's death nor its consequences, and it's somewhat by chance that my *being-there* has come down correctly. At least you ought to admit that it was not so faulty to place in brackets the period which began with the Korean War and which was finished at present and that, on the contrary, your own being-there played some real dirty tricks on you. It made you inattentive to an entire side of the issue. *Les Temps modernes* had still not, since March, said a word about the new policy of the U.S.S.R.—"The Communists and Peace"[20] treated the communist problem in a limit-situation, thus under the form of an alternative (either the party such as it is or the atomization of the proletariat), and as happened in emergencies, you took a position without worrying too much about the content, without examining the life of the party in the last forty years, its ideology, its history. During this time, the situation became less strained, the life and the history of the party continued. Perhaps you would have been closer to the facts by performing the true political function of a writer, which consists in showing oneself to be in a struggle with one's difficulties of objectifying oneself before others: by writing the "Memoirs of a slimy rat."

You see now what I think of the conclusion of your letter. To be sure, I have never demanded that you accept ahead of time the article which I prepared. But to refuse it ahead of time, to make someone keep quiet who has also had his readers and who has thus contributed to making the journal what it is, to withhold from him the ability to speak out at the moment when opinions are changing just because there is no agreement, and in order not to have to say it, to hinder him from stating his true position on the same questions which were treated earlier, that is what I call an "imperceptible point of abuse." I never thought myself to be on the editorial board of the journal due to the "moral rights" which you speak of often and indeed once again a month ago on the telephone. On the contrary, I only want to reclaim my due when I want to write there one more time. It would only be in order that the readers could appreciate in the articles and beyond all them, as one says, our real differences. You would not have to write a response since the article would essentially treat Marxism, communism, and your analyses only to the degree demanded by the study of the latest phase. It would be easy for you to underscore the official line of the journal in a prefatory note—and even why not, to say that you threw me out. These are the responsibilities which one cannot elude. Whether you want it or not, in a few months you will have this article in your hands, and one will see—knowing as you do that I will give it to no other journal—if you are a man to stifle it. You said at the beginning of winter that nothing has changed at the journal. At least one thing has: until now, we have imposed silence only on collaborators and unworthy nationals.

Concerning the chronicle which I told you about and which, according to my plan, will be on very diverse subjects, for its sake I intend to remain present at *Les Temps modernes*—and also in order to make money. Your letter indicates to me that the first motivation is without value for you. You don't suppose, I imagine, that the second suffices for me to accept a censor?

You speak to me of your friendship. Alas! I heard you say (perhaps to Beaver) that you no longer believed in personal relations, that there were only common work relations. How can you, other than with condescension, speak of friendship at the moment when you make an end of this work? When I think of all these years, I see a lot of benefits coming from your side—and believe me, I do not forget any of them. But regarding friendship, I'm not certain. For my part, on the contrary, I do not reduce you to the behavior that I saw you perform, and you have no reason to constantly do things in order to be assured of my friendship.

M. Merleau-Ponty

P.S. A. Before leaving, Lefort showed me the second text that he had written. At the moment when your letter arrived, I was going to write you regarding this matter. This response is such that, not being able to ask Lefort for corrections since he feels hurt, justly in my view, I don't want to come to plead for its insertion as I did at the Café Procope. I made him aware of this, and I inform you of it now so that everything will be clear. But certainly, the incident is over.

It has played, I think, an important role in our disagreement. You didn't understand what freedom I allowed a former student, even toward me—nor that by making him retract five pages and by letting him send you the rest, I had tried with this freedom to effect a reconciliation, which I owed you. I fear that you made an allusion to Lefort when you write that I criticized you "indirectly." But no. It was neither a maneuver, nor a direct attack.

B. I saw Germaine at the journal before receiving your letter, and she asked me questions about the coming numbers. I should tell you that by mutual agreement we judged it preferable given the political differences that the coming numbers be written entirely by you. I added (without responding to you since I believed the matter understood) that it would change nothing in my relations with the journal and that I was preparing an article and that I would be without a doubt writing a chronicle next winter. I leave the matter there. It is not my job to inform Germaine (or Julliard, whom I have stopped visiting for around a month now).

C. The gossips are starting. Anne-Marie Cazalis is going around saying that a letter from you dated from Venice has informed her of our "quarrel." (She is asking people "which side" they are on and declares that everyone is wrong who is not on your side.) To be sure, I don't believe a word of it. But you sometimes put in the dossier of the others information which is more or less on a par with that.

Summary of the Lecture

1. Classic concept of the relations between philosophy and politics. Philosophy as possession of the universal includes politics.
2. Hegel. Philosophy in principle only totalizes the movement of the world and its self-understanding. In reality, it's philosophy which decides which state of the world is "the maturity of reality" and that everything which comes afterwards is only a "stationary history."

In fact, history here is a disguise for philosophy; Hegel remains surreptitiously classic and does not question the philosophical power of totalizing. Engels in *Feuerbach* shows that the idea of the state perfectly annuls the revolutionary movement of the dialectic. Except for this, philosophy after Hegel becomes an elucidated experience: philosophy is "the head of the proletariat" for Marx, the philosopher is "the guinea pig of existence" (Kierkegaard).
3. Marx. In order to make philosophy young again, Hegel saw the world as completed and decadent. Marx takes the world as beginning and removes philosophy from its role as the final instance. But philosophy is subordinated to history only in that it wants to separate itself from it. As a practical-critical activity, coming and going between the fact and meaning, it lives and even "realizes itself" in history. The expectation of a new goddess in the *Dissertation on Epicurus and Democritus*. It's a matter of giving to "truths" their "passions" and to "passions" their "truth" (*XVIII Brumaire*). When one has left a time which is defined by its "lack of decision," rationality will be reborn or rather it will simply be born.

The intersection of the real and the rational is made by the very existence of the proletariat, which is an effect of capitalism, but also the attraction of a reversal of the relations between nature and human beings, the problem and the solution are given together, the revolution is already there, the future is in the present, the decision has already been made, the "specter of communism" (*Manifesto*) which haunts Europe. The existence of the proletariat, the conquest of power by it and, in perspective, the end of classes constitute a sole event-norm, which is the realization of

philosophy and the regulator of politics. In this sense there is a Marxist classicism: "to destroy" precisely in order "to actualize" (philosophy).
4. Today. Characterized by (A) the crisis in the idea of revolution and (B) the accelerated decadence of liberalism.

A. The crisis in the idea of revolution. The criterion of a valid compromise is no longer (Lenin) the growth of the "consciousness" of the proletariat but the safeguarding of its "interests" (Hervé)—interests about which it can be mistaken. In fact, in Europe (not in Asia) since 1945 the revolutions have been made "from above." Revolutionary violence presents itself as a defense of the established order (and the opponents are condemned as criminals according to common law). In these conditions, can there be consciousness of emancipation, and is the power objectively taken over by the proletariat? Is the regime of the proletariat or for the proletariat? And in the second case, isn't the distance between the power and the proletariat always the object of history? There is no longer any surplus value, but is one moving toward a homogeneous society? Does the regulator of politics function? Is it in order to actualize it that one destroys the universal philosophy? Is it toward a higher truth that consciousness is surpassed?

Symptoms: the generalization of the secret, passage of the clandestine to criticism, from revolutionary action to terrorist action, from professional revolutionary to adventurer, at least in judging from the people who have sympathy for a communist sympathizer like Malraux (Borodine). Politics of culture: comparison of the "classic" texts of Engels, Lenin himself, Lukács on art and literature, which recognize in art and literature the force of distinct expression of their value of employment in the immediate struggle and of the conceptions such as those of Jdanov.

This makes one doubt that these new societies can reclaim the "historical mission" of "actualizing" philosophy.

B. The accelerated decadence of liberalism. It is more and more certain that a politics of consciousness is deception: criticism of the idol of freedom, the point of honor of the "free world," which one ultimately reserves for the friends of freedom and which thus becomes an emblem of war.

There is always solidarity of philosophy and politics, but in the bad not in the good: they do not succeed in living together, they suffer together. Consciousness can be experience, but the facts do not respond to this demand.
5. Sartre's position. The notion of engagement expresses philosophically this situation: it identifies freedom and makes it, posits the circularity of an absence which is presence (one is free to become engaged) and of a presence which is absence (one engages oneself in order to be free).

The lack of mediation sought in Marx is the immediacy of the inward and the outward. If it decidedly does not succeed in making the one pass into the other, it can end by being either a subjectivism or an extreme objectivism.

At the beginning, the relatively optimistic conception of engagement: it's not a matter of choosing between the existing politics, but of elaborating the one "total" conception. (The creation of *Les Temps modernes* and later of the R.D.R.) Insofar as the situation becomes strained and the political reality avoids the effort that one makes in order to reorganize it and to change its meaning, it becomes evident that engagement amounts to, if not accepting as definitive the formulation by antithesis (communism/anticommunism), at least indicating a preference. That is to give a partial response, by withholding the motivations of this response ("for reasons which are mine and not theirs").

The difficulty with this position: if the reasons are different, so also is what one chooses. Sartre's motivations: peace and the lot of the proletariat. Motivations of communists: peace under certain conditions and power of the proletariat understood as a dictatorship of the party. Thus, either the agreement is a misunderstanding or communism today is closer to a philosophy of engagement than the Marxist philosophy of history. (It is a remarkable fact that Sartre, a non-Marxist, would be closer to the communists than many self-proclaimed Marxists.) Sartre says perhaps what the communists would say if they thought their action through to the end. But then why don't they say it and still make use of the proletarian philosophy of history? Perhaps this ideology is necessary for them in order that the present hierarchy might appear as a premise of the classless society. Sartre sees communism above all as an opposition to bourgeois society and shows that without this opposition, the proletariat would no longer have its defenders. The communism in power is something else and poses other questions. As much as the situation is not thought out and returns to a philosophy which expresses it badly, it remains confused.

Even the paradox in the politics of culture: the conception of engaged literature is tied to the literature of action more tightly than in Engels and Lukács, who are considered as representatives of classical Marxism. They have for the writer of the class-based society a respect which is also a disdain: Balzac is reactionary but precisely his reactionary passions make him see and paint coarsely the new people of the nineteenth century. Sartre wants neither this respect nor this disdain: he does not want the writer, if he thinks of himself as a human being, to save himself as writer. He puts literature and political action together on a unique plane of the event, because they belong to a sole enterprise, to a sole time. In fact, the communist politics of culture is more "existentialist" than the theoretical writings of Lukács. Is there truly an agreement between his "existentialism" either voluntary or unconscious and the conscious existentialism of Sartre?

Conclusion. In my view engagement cannot go so far as to accept even provisionally the dilemmas given in politics of today. This would mean not that there is no engagement but that it cannot go to the heart of the events when the two blocks are a reality. This would be a failure of engagement only if there were, on the one hand, human subjects and, on the other hand, the field of diplomatic and/or military events and if as a result of the refusal to say yes or no to events one by one leaves room only for subjectivity or a separated philosophy. But in reality we don't live in two orders, that of consciousness and that of the event-object. There's not a separated philosophy, and the plan of events is a limit which is attained only by the head of state or the party in certain decisive moments. The greatest part of action takes place in the intermediate space between the events and the pure thoughts, neither in things nor in spirits, but in the thick stratum of symbolic actions which operate less by their efficacy than by their meaning. To this zone belong books, lectures, but also meetings. And likewise one can say the same when one puts into circulation critical weapons, instruments of political consciousness, even if they cannot serve the moment and cannot adjudicate the issue among the adversaries. Even Sartre's political action remains an "action of disclosure." It is valuable and it serves like his books, like the very good books, in that it makes one think. It puts in an unequal light the crisis of relations between philosophy and politics which is also a crisis in philosophy and a crisis in politics. (The final lines are more or less word for word.)

3. Sartre to Merleau-Ponty

29 July 1953
[postmarked]

My Dear Merleau,

Your letter certainly calls for a response point by point. But it would be better in my view to do it *vive vox.* For me this exchange of written criticisms has had the beneficial effect of "purging the abscess," as one says, or of starting to purge it. It would be necessary that certain things be written in part and that in part that they also have a more meditated form. But at length the benefit would be changed into an inconvenience because one always makes rougher what one thinks by writing it down. It was certainly not my intention to make a list of charges, and I'm sure it wasn't yours either. If we see each other, the fact alone of getting together and of listening to each other would serve to smooth out the angles and to remove the hardness of the reciprocal "accusations." Therefore, I return the 18th in the morning, and if you can give me word or call me the same day, I am at your disposition any afternoon.

There is only one thing that I want to say to you since it would prepare our meeting again: for God's sake, don't interpret my intonations or my physiognomies as you do, that is, wholly askew and emotionally. I don't know if my tone was "glacially cold" when I spoke of your course at the Collège de France, but what I do know is that I very much appreciated your lecture and was completely sympathetic to it. (Michelle will tell you so.) If there were reservations, it was after the reading of the little work (you sent to me) and *in light of* our discussion. Moreover, my reservations did not touch on the lecture as such, but what came across in it of your present position. If I appeared glacially cold, it's because I always have a kind of timidity about congratulating people. I don't know how to do it, and I'm aware of this. It's certainly a character trait, and I admit it to you, but it has no relation to what you infer from your observation. When I said that I would have the impression of treason by teaching *Being and Nothingness,* I meant that a simple account *today,* that is ten years later—in an evolving situation and which we all have lived and rethought day by day—of a thought, which at the time was born of pure reflections of classical and non-Marxist philosophy, would seem to me by nature to make the students who want to follow me go backwards, to send them back again to an epoch when one could think without reference to Marxism (or at least when one thought one could do so), whereas the duty of philosophy *today* is to confront Marx (exactly as his duty in the middle of the last century was to confront Hegel).

Fine, but does this mean that I renounce *Being and Nothingness?* Not for a moment. That I consider it a product of my youth? Not at all. All the theses of *Being and Nothingness* seem to me just as true as in 1943. It's just that I say that those theses had in '43 an open future before them. To repeat them today without giving them the future that they imply is at once to betray my thought *today* and to betray *them.* Put differently, I need to write a book *today* on history and morality (and politics) such that one can, according to it, reaffirm *Being and Nothingness* without betraying it in its details. You see that it is far from an emotional outburst. At present what does my physiognomy express when I speak? I don't know, but someone who knows me better than you must have without doubt found me "convinced" but certainly not emotional (in the sense in which you take it). It happened that Michelle was there when I said to you about the Collège de France that "you are going to subvert all this, etc." I asked her if I gave the impression of being irritated, and she was dumbfounded by the question. She knew full well that it was a statement of *no importance.* I hate scandals and bold little initiatives of professors to make something modern, and I would certainly not want to change the Collège de France if I were there. These are things one says with a laugh but which are not worth worrying about for five minutes. And I think, likewise, that you were entirely correct for going there, and I would have done the same thing in your place. So why would I have been irritated? ("I would have done it in your place" doesn't mean "if I had been you," but, for example, "if I hadn't written any plays and earned so much with theater to stop teaching." Indeed, if it had been possible for me.) It is wholly false that I would blame you. Look, on the contrary, at the development of our "quarrel." Who was annoyed first? Who discussed the matter first? Who made the criticism? You. For my part, I defended myself, and it's as a result of your lecture that I, in my turn, made some remarks about your position. Moreover, you reproached me the other day for gratuitously and in principle supposing that you were always and in every point in agreement with me. Today you reproach me for spending my time blaming you. I know that these two judgments are not at all incompatible, but it would nevertheless be necessary to make them a bit more nuanced in order to make them go together.

All this in order to say not that you shouldn't interpret me, but just be prudent and don't do it based on *a priori* principles. I give you a hint for our discussion next time: it's that I regret our disagreement, and I will be in a more reconciliatory mood. Therefore, please, don't read into this any anger or any vindictiveness. If I spoke "three times," as you say, of the lecture you gave, believe me it was not because I felt hurt by it. I am convinced that you spoke of me in a friendly manner. It's for the following reason: *objectively* people are saying: "Merleau-Ponty must find Sartre's position very dangerous if he can come to disavow his colleague and friend publicly." Who says this? You say, "the reactionaries." Not at all, and I don't make them in any way judges between us. But I have rushed into an enterprise: for right or wrong I want to try, in accordance with my means as an intellectual, to form a left allied with communism. Your position exploited by the right necessarily influences those intellectuals who see you as a brake. It goes without saying that it matters little that one has written this or that in the *L'Express,* what counts is that you *act against me.* The friendship of your tone has nothing to do with that. Or even, that's what's so aggravating: "He must find it dangerous. You see the precautions that he is taking and his friendship with Sartre. But he has judged that it *was necessary* to say this, etc., etc., etc. . . ." Concerning the rumors which are circulating about our quarrel, I ask you very seriously to believe that I am *for absolutely none* of this. I have neither spoken nor written about it to anyone aside from three or four people who are as I say "in my family" (Bost, Beaver, Michelle).

All this does not reach the heart of the question but only my feelings. I would like to see you to save our friendship and not so that I can lose it. That's what I want you to know. Look: one more interpretation. I did not say to Beaver that I didn't believe in personal relationships. I said that personal relationships have a concrete meaning only if they are based on common undertakings. I wanted to condemn by this certain relationships (just the contrary of the kind I have with you) which I have with certain people. People ask me to dine together with them and at the table we speak without any kind of link except that of being one of the "*intelligentzia de gauche.*" But this never meant that the only relation between people is that of work. *In the course of* the undertaking relations are born (trust, fondness, intimacy, relations of characters, and also conversations on all kinds of subjects, dinners, trips, etc., etc.). Doesn't this reduce to a truism? Does this makes me an imperialist, a feudal lord, who has a heart so hard that he cannot be concerned with people who have their utility for him in the capacity of the work they do? Let's drop this. In any case, I am your friend and want to remain so. I think that you would recognize that you yourself are "emotional" when you write that I threw you out of the journal while you quit from the editorial board *in spite of me* when I returned from Saint-Tropez.

Therefore, until soon I hope (with the Italian mail, you might receive this letter after my return) and farewell.

J. P. Sartre

Concerning the twenty-five thousand francs, I don't understand why you don't take them other than a whim. You made a proposition to me: this is the means I propose of earning and keeping them at the journal. I responded to you, "no, in my view it's not a good way." That meant, let's find another way, that's all.

Notes

1. "Sartre, Merleau-Ponty: les lettres d'une rupture," *Magazine littéraire,* no. 320 (April 1994), 67–85.

2. Jean-Paul Sartre, "Merleau-Ponty *vivant*," *Les Temps modernes* 17, nos. 184–85 (1961), 304–76, (hereafter *TM*); in English as "Merleau-Ponty," trans. Benita Eisler, in *Situations* (New York: Braziller, 1965), 188–92; below 593–96 (hereafter *Sits.*).

3. Sartre, *TM*, 347; *Sits.*, 198; below 601.

4. Jean-Paul Sartre, "Les Communistes et la paix, 1," *Les Temps modernes*, no. 81 (July 1952), 1–50. Part 2, nos. 84–85 (October–November, 1952), 695–763. Part 3, no. 101 (April 1954), 1731–1819.

5. Sartre, *TM*, 353–54; *Sits.*, 204; below 606.

6. Claude Lefort, "Le Marxisme et Sartre," *Les Temps modernes*, no. 89 (April 1953), 1541–70; Sartre, "Réponse à Claude Lefort," ibid., 1571–1629.

7. Sartre, *TM*, 355; *Sits.*, 205–6.

8. Sartre, *TM*, 355; *Sits.*, 206; below 606–7.

9. "Sartre, Merleau-Ponty: les lettres d'une rupture," 69.

10. I would like to thank Darío González for his invaluable assistance with the translation of these letters.

11. Beaver: Sartre's nickname for Simone de Beauvoir.

12. Being-there: *être-là*, French for the German *Dasein*, central term from Heidegger's philosophy intended to capture the lived experience of human beings in their concrete situations.

13. M.R.P.: Mouvement Républicain Populaire.

14. εποχη: the act of withholding judgment or putting in brackets what is epistemologically unknowable. A central concept in Husserl's phenomenology that Sartre takes up in *Being and Nothingness*.

15. R.D.R.: Rassemblement Démocratique Révolutionnaire, political party founded in 1948 by George Altman, David Rousset, and Jean-Paul Sartre. The party attempted to form a political left independent of the communist party. Sartre left the party in 1949 after David Rousset was obliged to turn to American unions for financial reasons.

16. C.N.E.: Comité national des écrivans, i.e., National Committee of Writers, founded secretly in 1943.

17. Suzo: sc. Suzanne Merleau-Ponty.

18. The skin of the ass: an allusion to Balzac's novel of the same name.

19. The law of the heart: a well-known form of consciousness in the "Reason" chapter of Hegel's *Phenomenology of Spirit* intended to capture various forms of self-willed individualism of German Romanticism.

20. See n.4 above.

22

Sartre and Ultrabolshevism (from *Adventures of the Dialectic*)

Maurice Merleau-Ponty

Translated by Joseph Bien

Thus, since Marxist philosophy believes it possible to express the weight of social reality only by situating the dialectic wholly in the object, the dialectic in action responds to adversity either by means of terror exercised in the name of a hidden truth or by opportunism; in either case, the dialectic wanders from its own line. But it is one thing to experience this and yet another to recognize and formulate it. It was only implicitly that Trotsky resigned himself to this when, in his last years, he said that the course of things would perhaps call into question the Marxist thesis of the proletariat as ruling class and of socialism as heir to capitalism. The communists are very far from this admission. For them, to the very degree that the dialectic is a failure, it must remain in force: it is the "point of honor," the "justification" of an immense technical labor in which it never appears in person. In both meanings of the word, one does not "touch" the dialectic, because one does not change anything and because one does not use it. If, as Lukács says, the social is a "second nature," the only thing to do is to govern it as one governs nature: through a technique which allows discussion only among engineers, that is to say, according to criteria of efficiency, not according to criteria of meaning. The meaning will come later, only God knows how. This will be the business of the future communist society. For the moment it is only a question of "laying the foundations," using means which no more resemble their ends than the trowel does the masonry which it serves to construct. Once the machinery of production, which Marx took for granted—and which was indeed not present in Russia and is even less evident in China—has been built, state production will of itself put forth its socialist and communist consequences, and one will see humanism and the dialectic bloom and flower, while the state fades away.[1] This would be fine if Soviet society, in order to create the machinery of production, did not establish machinery of constraint and did not organize privileges which, little by little, make up the true shape of its history. But this the communists do not see, because their eyes are fixed on the dialectic. They take its failure into consideration (and in this sense they know it is a failure), since at every opportunity they avoid the dialectic with great care. But *with the same movement* they place it in the future. It is the same thing to no longer believe in the dialectic and to put it in the future; but it is seen to be the same thing by an external witness, who contents himself with the present, not by someone who commits the fraud and who lives already in his intended ends. The dialectic thus plays precisely the role of an ideology, helping communism to be something other than what it thinks it is.

Given this state of affairs, it was good that an independent philosopher attempted to analyze communist practice directly, without the mediation of ideology. The language of the dialectic and of the philosophy of history has been so fully incorporated into communism that it is a completely new undertaking to describe communism without using it. Such is the extreme interest of the essays recently published by Sartre.[2] Here the dialectical cover is drawn back, communist action is considered as it is at present, as it would be by someone who had forgotten its history; in short, it is "understood" in itself. Here, for the first time, we are told what a communist should say to defend communism clearly and without recourse to the presuppositions of tradition.[3]

Sartre "understands" communist politics, justifies it from the proletarian point of view, and thus (to a degree to be specified) makes it his own for reasons quite different from those of the communists and, as he says, "by reasoning from *my* principles and not from *theirs*" (*Cp,* 706; *CP,* 68). His principles are, in truth, not only different from those of the communists, they are practically opposed to them; and what Sartre contributes is a brief on the failure of the dialectic. While the communist philosophers, Lukács among them, formally preserve the principle of a historical dialectic and simply drive it back into the in-itself of the "second nature"—which, it is true, infinitely extends the field of mediations, separates the communist enterprise from its final meaning, and defers their confrontation indefinitely—Sartre founds communist action precisely by refusing any productivity to history and by making history, insofar as it is intelligible, the immediate result of our volitions. As for the rest, it is an impenetrable opacity. To be sure, this extreme subjectivism and this extreme objectivism have something in common: if the social is a second nature, it can be modified, like the other, only by a technician, in this case a sort of political engineer. And if the social is only the inert and confused residue of past actions, one can intervene and put it in order only by pure creation. Whether it be in the name of a theoretical knowledge which the party alone possesses or in the name of an absolute nonknowledge (since, if history is chaos, then anything is better than what exists at present), the party's action is not subject to the criteria of meaning. The philosophy of pure object and the philosophy of pure subject are equally terroristic, but they agree only about consequences. As for their motives, these remain in a position of rivalry. The ruin of the dialectic is accomplished openly with Sartre and clandestinely with the communists, and the same decisions that the communists base on the historical process and on the historical mission of the proletariat Sartre bases on the nonbeing of the proletariat and on the decision which, out of nothing, creates the proletariat as the subject of history.

Sartre then relatively justifies the communists, in their action rather than in what they think and in the philosophy they teach; moreover, if this philosophy is itself "understood" as an auxiliary myth, the kind of truth that one attributes to it is symbolic and not the kind that it lays claim to. One feels that for Sartre the dialectic has always been an illusion, whether it was in the hands of Marx, of Trotsky, or of others; differences arise only in the manner of speaking, of justifying action, of staging the illusion; in its essential features, Marxist action has always been pure creation. The "truth" of history has always been fraudulent and the discussion of the party always a ceremony or an exercise. Marxism has always been the choice of the proletariat, which, historically, does not exist, in opposition to the other, which does; and the pretense of transcending internal oppositions has always been Platonic: one can only leap over them. Sartre, then, does not see any reason to distinguish in the history of Marxism between important and decadent periods, between founders and epigones. He never confronts communism with the dialectic which it claims. Better equipped than anyone to understand and explain communism as it is, in relation to the traditional ideologies with which it covers itself, Sartre does not do this, precisely because, for him, the profound meaning of communism lies—well beyond dialectical illusions—in the categorical will to bring into being that which never was. He never asks himself why no communist would dream of writing what he is writing, even though communists do it every day, or why no communist would base his action on repudiation of the dialectic, even though this is the only thing to do if those who are nothing historically are to become men. It is enough for him that communism should finally be like this within the context of his thought. That communists conceive and justify it otherwise, this, he is sure, changes nothing in the meaning of communism. Communism is here "understood" and relatively justified to a second degree, not as it sees itself, but as it is—in other words, as Hegel teaches it, as the philosopher sees it. If Sartre would openly give his reasons, if he would say that communism is a more profound pragmatism, he would expose to broad daylight the divergence between theory and practice, the crisis of communist philosophy, and, beyond philosophy, the change in meaning of the whole system. If he "understands" communism correctly, then communist ideology is deceitful, and we can ask the nature of the regime which hides itself in the philosophy it teaches instead of expressing itself there. If Sartre is right in grounding communism as he does, communism is wrong in thinking of itself as it does; it is not, then, entirely what Sartre says it is. Ultimately, if Sartre is right, Sartre is wrong. Such is the situation of the loner who incorporates communism into his universe and thinks of it with no regard for what it thinks of itself. In reading *The Communists and Peace,* one often wonders—without finding an answer, since the quotations from Marx are so equitably distributed—what distinction Sartre makes between Marx, the ideologies of Soviet communism, and his own thought. As a good philosopher, Sartre packs this whole company into his thought. In it and in it alone—once his negation of history and historical truth and his philosophy of the subject and of the other as intrusion are supposed—Marx, Lenin, Stalin, and Duclos are, in the main, indistinguishable from one another and indistinguishable from Sartre. But even that is left unsaid: in saying it he would emphasize the change in communism from Marx to the present day, and this change is for him only apparent. His interpretation remains implicit. From this there results a certain reticence in him, and, in us who read him, a certain uneasiness. We would very much like it to be said that if Duclos and Trotsky are equally legitimate heirs of Marxism and if non-Stalinist Marxists are traitors, it is only so for someone who does not believe in the dialectic. Because of a lack of precision on this point, Sartre's analysis, which was to enlighten the reader, simply adds to the confusion.

In the above, we were anticipating, and indeed we had to in order to place Sartre's theses within our own study. In *The Communists and Peace,* then, we will look for the indication of this new phase, which we will call ultrabolshevism, in which communism no longer justifies itself by truth, the philosophy of history, and the dialectic but by their negation. Next we shall have to ask ourselves whether one must draw from Sartre's premises the conclusions he does, whether they can ground any form of communism, whether this completely voluntary communism is tenable, and whether it is not based on an idea of revolution which such a form of communism in itself renders impossible.

Someone may object that it is premature to appraise Sartre's first analyses; we cannot know precisely what implications he himself attributes to them, since they are to be completed later. He has stated that, after he has shown how the communist party expresses the proletariat, he will show in what way it does not, and it is only then that one will be able to see how communism and noncommunism are reconciled in his mind and in his action. The problem is comparable to Christian philosophies confronted with historical Christianity. One always wonders whether for them religion is the true philosophy or whether, on the contrary, philosophy is the truth of religion, which includes the former; or rather one wonders how a peaceful coexistence is established between them, for if truth is on only one side, the Cold War continues. Sartre will thus leave behind the terrain of historical terror. He will say why he does not become a communist, in what way his "understanding" is different from adherence, in what way his reasons for approving the communists remain distinct from their own, and finally he will construct a mixed universe where the action of communists and that of a noncommunist left can unite.

But still, the published analyses must leave room for these developments, and this is the point toward which our study is directed. It seems to us that if we accept Sartre's analyses, the debate is closed by a desperate justification of communism which does not admit of restriction, nuance, or motive, properly speaking, because it belongs to the sphere of morality: communism is not to be judged, to be put in place, or to be reconciled with anything other than itself. Its action is not to be measured by any criterion other than itself because it is the only consequential attempt to create, out of nothing, a society where those who are nothing become men and because this "antiphysis," as Sartre readily says, this heroic enterprise, tolerates no sort of condition or restriction. If indeed for him these views represent only the thoughts of a communist sympathizer, and if they must be joined to others to arrive at his true conclusion, our discussion will do no more than anticipate his own. If, on the contrary, he accepts them as they are, we are justified in saying even now why they do not convince us. Briefly, this is so because (1) the conception of communism that Sartre proposes is a denunciation of the dialectic and the philosophy of history and substitutes for them a philosophy of absolute creation amidst the unknown; (2) if this philosophy is accepted, communism is an undetermined enterprise of which one knows only that it is absolutely other, that, like duty, it is not subject to discussion, nor is it subject to rational proof or rational control; (3) finally, this action without criteria, precisely because it is without criteria, can obtain from those who are undecided only a reserved sympathy, an absent presence. This action will scarcely be strengthened by them and still less will it be changed. Finally, the noncommunist left will be "noncommunist" in its reasons, not in its actions. This is exactly why, instead of serving it, it can be harmful to the coexistence of communism and noncommunism.

I

Sartre's study is first of all an appeal to the facts. It is true that today the most active part of the working class adheres to the C.P. and C.G.T.[4] It is thus true that any failure of the C.P. lessens the weight of the working class in the political struggle and that those who celebrate as a victory of the working class the failure of a strike called by the C.P. are abandoning the existing working class, which is in the majority communist. The anticommunist leftist extricates himself by calling the working class's weariness "lucidity" and by calling its disgust "revolutionary spirit." He advances with an imaginary proletariat toward a revolution finally freed from communist tutelage, and he dignifies with the name "proletarian politics" a politics which triumphs or suffers at the same time as the government of Mr. Pinay.[5] Sartre asks him: *What are you doing?* If the world were to stop at this instant and you were judged by your perverse glee, you would be one who applauded the collapse of the working class. You say that a distinction must be made, that you celebrate the event as a defeat of the C.P. and as the awakening of a liberated working class, but you know very well that most of the time politics is the art of organizing equivocations and attacking the adversary's flank. When the government arrests J. Duclos and organizes a test of strength, it is not openly after unionism or the working class: it is only a question of a party leader. But when the strike called to defend him fails, general strikes are thereby assailed in advance, apathy is established in the working class, and it is the working class which is weakened. In the moment, and facing the event, this failure of the C.P. is a failure of the working class. If you treat the communist party as enemy number one and conceive your politics accordingly, your enemy number two, capitalism, is relatively your ally; for if you are *first of all* concerned with weakening the communist party, you will have neither the time nor the taste to weaken its adversaries. If today the communist party is against you, the existing proletariat is against you, and you speak only in the name of an ideal proletariat; at this minute you express only thoughts—not, as your Marxism would demand, the worker's movement itself.

All of this is true and had to be said. Sartre poses the question in urgent terms and in the present moment: he who is not with the C.P. is against it and against the proletariat which surrounds it. One can reply, however, that any opposition accepts the risk of destroying the movement that it wants to reform and that, if it did not accept this, no organization would ever reform its politics. If one did not at times compare today's proletariat to that of tomorrow's, if one did not thus dare to prefer the ideal proletariat to the existing one, there would be no proletarian politics. There would then be in each case only a blind fidelity to what the proletariat's party does, and one would not even know if the party still merited its name. No politician, and, indeed, especially not those of the communist party, will accept being judged on an isolated moment of his action. No politics responds to an event simply by "yes" or "no," none renounces the right of posing the problem in a different way than it is posed in the moment; for there is the past, where this trap has been prepared, and there is the future, where one can work to remove its bait and render it harmless. A politics which should lack any recourse against the factual situation and its dilemmas would not be a living politics; it would be that of a dying man reprieved, yet threatened at each moment with appearing before his judge. "I was abroad, my relations with the communists were good but certainly not excellent . . . all the more reason to hear of the failure of the strikes with indifference . . . yet the news produced just the contrary effect on me" (*Cp,* 705; *CP,* 67). All right. Everyone thinks in terms of the event, but it is from afar, while traveling, that the crisis is a clap of thunder in the midst of silence. The politician saw it coming, and when it bursts he is already thinking of tomorrow. In short, he thinks it and he lives it, he is not in the position of saying "yes" or "no."

Sartre reserves in principle the right to refuse the ultimatum of facts: "To be a traitor, you don't have to be accused of treason by the Communists" (*Cp,* 5; *CP,* 8). The communist party can cause the working class to be against us, but not us to be against it. The entreaty of consciousness remains and, with it, the right for us to step back, consider the event, and ourselves give a meaning to what we are doing. But the situation, the "smiles from the Right," put us in imminent peril of treason, for—and this is the decisive point—the consciousness which withdraws from the dilemma and wishes to confront the C.P.'s politics with a certain idea of revolution *will find nothing in the facts which permits it to decide whether or not the C.P.'s politics is revolutionary* or to sketch another revolutionary line. The solidarity between the working class and the C.P. is not an accident, a jumble supported by the C.P. and exploited by the government. It is legitimate and will never cease, for there is no way to distinguish communist politics from the proletarian movement. They say that the strike of June 2 bears the mark of the C.P.: the preference given to illegal means, the confusion of the political and the economic, the devotion to Soviet diplomacy—this is communist, not proletarian. For Sartre there is no assignable difference between the C.P.'s politics and proletarian violence. It is not only mentally and through a regrettable error that the workers' movement forms a coalition with the C.P. and the U.S.S.R., it is in reality. And it is not only by a correctable oversight that the anticommunist of the left allows his hatred of communism to overflow to include proletarian violence; it is because, even though he is a "Marxist," he has, as a result of being outside the working class, such as it is, stopped thinking as it does, and, through communism, it is the working class that he is rejecting. Certainly one cannot demonstrate that the revolutionary end requires a June 2, *this* illegality, *this* mixture of the economic and the political, *this* support of the security of the U.S.S.R.; but neither can one demonstrate the contrary. Equivocalness is in things. It is history that is equivocal. "As always, the facts say neither 'yes' nor 'no' " (*Cp*, 8; *CP*, 11). The use of illegal means? But they are the proletariat's means, since bourgeois law is made against the proletariat. The jumble of the economic and the political? But it is the very law of the proletarian, because he never has access to pure political life (particularly when an electoral law annuls a good part of the communist suffrage), because political action is simply that which aims at the whole of the social apparatus, and because, in abstaining in this domain, the proletariat would be like a body without consciousness. The devotion to the U.S.S.R.? But the U.S.S.R. is the country of the revolution; and even if the revolution is everywhere, and everywhere inescapable, how can it measure the support it owes to its first bastion? If communist politics can always by some expedient attach itself to revolutionary violence, though it cannot be derived from it, a consciousness which attempts to evaluate it freely cannot make any effective use of its freedom. It is "yes" or it is "no," and that is all. The "yes," just like the "no," is willful and is uttered equivocally. The C.P. is always justifiable by the permanent reason that its violence is *perhaps* nothing other than proletarian violence. The "yes" is barely distinguishable from the "no," just as, with Kierkegaard, faith was barely distinguishable from incredulity. The C.P. has, in any case, a negative mission: it is perhaps not the revolution, but surely it is not capitalism. It is perhaps not pure proletarian violence, but that certainly is not absent from what it does. Consciousness as pure negation, when confronted with facts which on the contrary, say "neither 'yes' nor 'no,' " can engage itself outside only if it finds a negation there which resembles it and in which it recognizes itself: as negation of bourgeois society and emblem of proletarian violence, the party is a double of consciousness. Consciousness can discuss what the party does; it will, in fact, never finish discussing it. It remains free. But it will employ this right of scrutiny only with respect, for such a right must never compromise the essential esteem that consciousness holds for the party as the vehicle of its negations. This decision is *a priori* and of another order.

Thus from an observation, the solidarity of the working class and the C.P., one has passed to a principle, because the facts have, as one might say, several meanings or none at all, and they receive a single meaning only through freedom. Sartre's entire theory of the party and of class is derived from his philosophy of fact, of consciousness, and, beyond fact and consciousness, from his philosophy of time. He often says that he is not making a theory or speaking of either the ideal proletariat or the party in general; rather, he looks at what is taking place in France today. But it is this reference to the present as such which is theory. There is theory precisely in this manner of treating the event as ineffaceable, as a decisive test of our intentions and an instantaneous choice of the whole future and of all that we are. This is to imply that political questions can and should be posed and resolved in the moment, without looking back to the past or repeating it. It is to accept the confrontation with the singular. This twisting, which in the event forever unites what appeared separable, places in opposition what was only other. Not to speak of the proletarian, of the class in itself, or of the eternal party is here to make a theory of the proletariat and of the party as continued creations, that is to say, as the dead reprieved from death.

The militant, the party, and the class are going to be born out of similar urgencies. They will be the replies that a will which has no basis in things gives to the trap of events. Let us not even speak of birth, for they come from nowhere, they are only what they have to be, what they make themselves. The militant is not a worker who militates; he is not a certain past of suffering which makes itself political action. The sufferings belong to the producer, to "the concrete man" (*CP,* 731; *ET,* 96), and it is beyond the concrete man that the active proletarian appears. His sufferings would reduce him to yielding if a pure refusal did not make him a militant. Sartre has always thought that nothing could be the cause of an act of consciousness. In the past Sartre spoke at least of "mild forces" and "motives." Today he still speaks of "the reciprocal conditioning of both progressive impoverishment and permanent revolution" (*RL*, 1611; *CP*, 278), but for him this is statistical and secondary thought. In all strictness, the proletarian is not the condition of the militant, and the fact that the revolutionary will does not arise completely armed out of misery is enough for Sartre to act as if it did not arise from it at all, and to see it appear *ex nihilo* as an "invention," a refusal of the worker's condition,[6] a "conversion" by which the worker "dies and is reborn." Lagneau said that to live will always be to take the trouble to live.[7] He who takes this trouble is not the worker overwhelmed with misery and fatigue. It is that in him, beyond despair and also beyond hope, that says "no" to this life and transforms it into another. One must not even speak of decision here, that is to say, of the deliberation between possibilities and of the motives which prefigure it. "Freedom has descended on me like an eagle" is more or less what Orestes said in *The Flies*. In the same way, the revolutionary will of the militant is more himself than his life. It does not come out of what he was but out of the future, out of nonbeing, where from now on he places himself. ". . . if action takes hold of him, he will believe: action is in and of itself a kind of confidence. And why does it take hold of him? Because it is possible: he *does not decide* to act, he acts, he *is* action, subject of history" (*Cp*, 717; *CP*, 80–81; modified). The militant believes in the revolution and the party as Kant's moral subject believes in God and immortality: not that the will attaches itself to an external being, but, on the contrary, because it is gratuitous, prior to any motive, and pure affirmation of value, the will additionally postulates in being what is necessary for its fulfillment. The will believes only in itself, it is its own source. The revolution cannot come from the worker, and especially not from the skilled worker. He has a recognized value, he is encumbered with his talent, he is not ready for the rape of freedom. He supposes that man exists and that all that is necessary is to arrange society. Liquidate merit, says Sartre. The only valid humanism is that of absolute destitution, just as Lagneau's God was the more acceptable since he had no basis in being. "Man is yet to be made: he is *what man lacks,* what is *in question* for each one of us, at every instant, what, without ever having been, continually risks being lost" (*Cp*, 1792; *CP*, 200). In other words, man is a duty-to-be [*devoir-être*] and even a pure duty, since it is difficult to see how man could be man without losing his value. It is the bite of duty or of nothingness into being, into freedom—the bite that Sartre once called "mortal," "deadly"—which constitutes the militant.

It will be asked why the militant is active in the communist party and not, like Lagneau, in the Union pour l'Action morale.[8] It is because, for Sartre, the will as absolute is only the interior truth and because there is a different view of the subject (different and the same, since it is his own freedom which is affected and compromised by the gaze of one in misery): the view the other has of him and, in particular, the most miserable of the others. Freedom recognizes itself in this misery, which is, as it were, its derision or caricature, a destitution which is not its own but which, on the contrary, invites it to capitulate. Because for Sartre the other is not a vague double of myself, because, born in the field of my life, the other overturns it, decenters my freedom, and destroys me in order to make me reappear over there, in a gaze which is fastened on me, it is not, as with Kant, beyond this life, or even, as with Lagneau, prior to life, within oneself, on the level of the pure relations of friendship and the society of minds, that *making* imposes its postulates; it is in this life, in the space that separates me from and links me to the other, and which gradually envelops the whole world.

Yet, at this very moment and in this passing to the outside, something attests to the fact that we remain within the philosophy of the subject. It is precisely that the party, like the militant, is pure action. If everything comes from freedom, if the workers are nothing, not even proletarians, before they create the party, the party rests on nothing that has been established, not even on their common history. Either the party of the proletarians never will exist or, if it exists, it will be their continued creation and the emblem of their nonbeing, itself a pure act or relationship, like the categorical imperative from which it was born. There will thus be a single party (*Cp*, 760; *CP*, 128–29), and no factions within it. "The linking organism must be pure action; if it carries with it the least seed of division, if it still conserves in it any passivity—sluggishness, self-interest, divergent opinions—who then will unify the unifying apparatus?" (*Cp*, 760; *CP*, 128–29). If there is only one organization, its decisions being "the only possible ones" (*Cp*, 766; *CP*, 129), then that organization is the proletariat itself, and in it the proletariat is all that it can and should be (ibid.). If there are several organizations, their decisions, even majority decisions, are no more than accidents. Since other decisions are possible, the leaders are no longer the proletariat itself; and to say that the leaders are good is already to say that they could be bad (*Cp*, 716; *CP*, 79). The masses, "instead of asserting themselves in a unanimous reaction, are made to choose one of several likely politics" (ibid.). Since it destroys the proletariat, pluralism is not even to be discussed. One must therefore say that the party is by definition the bearer of the proletarian spirit. It is an order in the sense of monastic and professional orders. It has received the sacred trust of a certain inspiration or of a certain honor and administers it with full powers. In it the three meanings of the word "order" are united. "[It is] an Order which makes order reign and which gives orders" (*Cp*, 759; *CP*, 128). It should not be said that it expresses the proletariat *because* the militants elect the leadership or even *because* they tacitly approve it. It has an eternal and total mandate from the single fact that without it there would be no proletariat. The Hegelian state is society in substance because it is the emergence of an idea preexisting in society. The party, on the contrary, is the proletariat in substance because before it there was no proletariat. What one calls the confidence of the proletarians is thus not a state of mind or a feeling which could decrease or increase; it is like a condition of being [*un sentiment d'état*]: if there is a proletarian, he has confidence in the party. It is a feeling which does not need to be felt. It is inscribed or implicated in the necessity for the proletariat, which is nothing, to have a party if it is to exist historically; and finally it is inscribed in the thought of Sartre, who conceives these possibilities and their relationships. Proletarian history is thus or it is nothing: it is made not of opinions which are expressed and communicated but of missions entrusted as a bottle is thrown into the sea, of investitures received as a consecration, formed in the absolute by a will without means and without condition, because the creation of a proletariat and of a proletarian society is itself an unprecedented enterprise, contrary to everything that until now has been called nature and history. Any idea of controlling the leaders is therefore out of the question. What does the opinion of a majority, and, even less, that of a minority, mean with regard to the party's infinite task, which is to make something out of nothing? They are only opinions, while the party has at each instant no other choice than to be or not to be. They are thus "almost nothing: soreheads, outsiders: the majority disregards them and declares unanimity" (*Cp*, 715; *CP*, 78). The liquidation of minorities[9] is already germinating at the birth of the proletarian party. Because the unanimity of decisions in the party is only a way of saying that the decisions were taken at the risk of the death of the party, that they carry all the chances of the proletariat's survival, and because this condition of risk is permanent, any decision is, by nominal definition, "unanimous." This regime without secret ballot, without a minority, without an opposition, calls itself "real" democracy—not because it extends the formal guarantees of a bourgeois regime to the realities of government and production, but because it creates out of nothing the power of the powerless, an enormous undertaking which cannot afford contestation. The militant's function is, therefore, to "obey orders."[10] It is true that Sartre does not identify the proletariat with the party apparatus.[11] With good reason he protests that the apparatus would be nothing if it were not supported by the proletarians, but they in turn would be nothing if they did not support it. They do not obey it as an external urgency: it is rather that the militant is, in the philosophical sense, in ecstasy in the party and is completely transformed in it, so that obedience to orders is his highest activity, making him in turn pure action: "the Party is his freedom." One may ask whether to obey without criticizing, without examining, without taking a certain distance, is still to be active. But in the urgent situation—which is always the case for the proletariat—to act is not to choose or to decide: "To criticize is to stand back, to put oneself outside the group or the system, to consider them as objects" (*Cp*, 755; *CP*, 123). "Doubt and uncertainty: these seem to be intellectual virtues. But [the worker] must struggle to change his condition, and these virtues of the mind can only paralyze action . . . and he, precisely, needs to believe that there is a truth. Since he cannot work it out alone, he must be able to trust his class leaders profoundly enough to believe he is getting the truth from them" (*Cp*, 758; *CP*, 127). Action does not come from the worker, who existed before the party; it is localized in the life of the party. Only starting with his initial conversion will he discuss, within the framework of the party, "the problems which the Party submits to him and . . . within the context of the principles which the Party gives to him" (*Cp*, 761; *CP*, 130). In other words, the question can only be one of "enriching," of "going beyond" party politics in its own direction, of accelerating this politics and preceding it toward its goal. Resistance to party action never comes from a proletarian, for the worker disqualifies himself as a proletarian as soon as he resists. Resistance, therefore, never has the value of a judgment but exists in the party only as the remains of inertia, as a relic of its prehistory. The militants and even the masses are justified in respect to the party if they go further in their attack than it does.[12] For once, they have felt more clearly than the party the alternative between action or death which is the perpetual law of the party and have felt the original *delay* (*RL*, 1606; *CP*, 272; modified) of all proletarian action, which occurs because its action is not founded in an existing class and because it is the invention of a future. But the outdistancing of the party by the masses presupposes them already formed and organized by it; the current which overflows the party comes from the party. Even then it is not subject to proceedings other than its own or judged according to other criteria than its own: it is their haste and feverishness, which are justified in respect to it, it is the state of urgency, of which, nine times out of ten, it is the most sensitive detector, it is the law of all or nothing, its fundamental law, which brings it back to itself. This exception cannot by definition be extended to the case where the masses leave the party, nor can it found a control of the party by the masses.[13]

A fabric of imperious wills which do not allow gradations, itself pure action or nothing, the party does not leave much of anything to the class. There is a way of living, of dressing, of eating, of envisaging life and death, love and work, finally a way of thinking which comes from the worker's condition as producer. These are the traits that one can describe like the habits of a species; they are the wrinkles of the proletariat, the marks of its enslavement. It is the class as discouraged, inactive, and historically dispersed. It is the class which "objective" sociology willingly describes in order to keep the proletariat inactive. For indeed, Sartre says, when sociology returns to primitive societies, it willingly takes the class as a living and significant whole. One could reply that the class in primitive societies is in fact largely constituted by participation in mythical relationships and that, on the contrary, in advanced capitalism the relationships of production predominate, and that in the former case one might "understand" and in the latter case describe objectively. It is labor lost. One is suspect for being too interested in what the proletarians eat and think. This is to push them down into what they are, to distract them from what they have to be and from the party. And the only way to escape the reproach completely would be to renounce, as communism does, saying anything about the proletarians. Let us rather speak of the party, where they die and are reborn. But what will there be even to say about the party? Thus duty closes the mouth of knowledge. Let us not even say that the class shows or hides itself, that it strengthens or weakens itself. Let us say that it "makes, unmakes and remakes itself endlessly" (*RL*, 1573; *CP*, 237; modified). History is voluntary or nothing. "Classes don't just happen to exist, they are made" (*Cp*, 732; *CP*, 96). The proletariat "exists only by acting. It is action. If it ceases to act, it decomposes" (*Cp*, 732; *CP*, 97). "The class is a system in motion: if it stopped, the individuals would revert to their inertia and to their isolation" (*Cp*, 733; *CP*, 98). "A class *organizes itself*" (ibid.), says Sartre, probably meaning to say, not that it organizes itself, not that others organize it, but that in a single movement which is without subject, being the exchange of the workers and the party, the workers invent themselves as militants and pure action comes into being. Between the worker and the militant, the unbeliever and the converted, the militants and the party which "tolerates" their discussion, the relationships are inflexible because they are inflexible to the highest degree between the proletariat and the bourgeoisie. It is the entire social fabric which becomes as fragile as glass. It is all history which becomes a duel without intermission, without oversights, without chance, under the accusing gaze of the moral imperative. The passivity of the workers is the activity of the bourgeoisie working on the worker's world and setting out there, like so many traps, near occasions of treason. To invoke the class against the party, to judge the party by the measure of the class, is the bourgeoisie's cleverest victory, since it scatters the proletariat from behind and spares the bourgeoisie a frontal attack. In order to reply to this bourgeois aggression which comes from everywhere, Sartre does not seem to count very much on a counteroffensive: but the bourgeoisie also has its "slippery customers," and a conquering politics would sweep them along and rebuild the unity of the party in action. Perhaps he will speak of it later on. But this dialectic dissolves the contours; one no longer knows where the enemy is, where the ally is. For the moment, Sartre stresses them; to pass a judgment on the C.P. that was a political act would require nothing less than the C.P. Thus, by virtue of the principle of identity there is no judgment of the C.P., especially not in the name of the class. At the very moment when the proletariat evades a party-directed strike, Sartre solemnly writes that it "*recognizes itself* in the test of strength which the C.P. institutes in its name" (*Cp*, 49; *CP*, 55). This is because "recognition," like "unanimity," no longer designates verifiable relationships. These words are no more than a manner of expressing a solidarity which *would* be realized in death, or an oath exchanged outside of life. Those that did not strike put the proletariat in danger, since the party went the distance for the proletariat; and as the party can always completely commit itself and play double or nothing, it is threatened with death and infallible any time it wishes to be. But as this common peril of party and class unites them, not in what they are and do but only in defeat, the general and formal approbation that Sartre gives to the party does not tie him to a particular policy that the party may decide to follow at a particular moment. If, instead of the lighting of death, in which the shadows of the proletariat and the party merge, the sun of discussion were to reappear in broad daylight, as it does in Sartre's third article, the reader would perhaps find Sartre preparing a wise politics of a united left against economic Malthusianism.

II

He clearly differs from Marx by his conception of the equivocalness of facts. We have seen that in the area of facts Sartre dismisses both sides, communism and anticommunism, that for him there is no rigorous confrontation of idea and fact and no means of establishing whether or not the idea is realized in fact. With a few dialectical modifications, the idea covers any fact; and indeed it must, for it is the expression of the existing proletariat, and, in a given moment, the party action is the entire existence of the proletariat. "Facts" are always circumvented by decisions. They give us no means of appeal against decisions which, in any case, do not *result* from discussion and which, regardless of what they may be, continually engage the fate of the proletariat and are thus its decisions.

From time to time there is, of course, an external verdict—the party fails, the masses ebb, pure action stops and reconsiders itself. But even then one never knows exactly to what the facts said "no." The failure allows of opposing interpretations, and it is still in obscurity that one makes one's choice. The fact, insofar as it exists, does not carry its meaning, which is of another order: meaning is dependent on consciousness and, just for this reason, can in all strictness be neither justified nor excluded by the facts. We encounter, therefore, only facts invaded by consciousness. Nothing can enlighten the party or its militants. They never have to deal with truth but with views which already are biases. There is no mediation between "pure fact," which has whatever meaning one wants to give it, and decision, which gives the fact only one meaning. The mediation would be the probable, the meaning that the facts *seem* to recommend. But this shaky meaning cannot ground the politics of the proletariat, which itself is improbable and which begins to exist only by lightning-quick decisions against all facts. One does not even see here on what basis a discussion could be carried on, for discussions suppose a situation to which one attempts to fit a meaning. One applies a meaning and then another and takes whichever works the best, but it is not a question of doing it for the best. Under pain of leaving the universe to the bourgeoisie, it is a question of doing what will work, and why would this be what is most probable? Sartre does not even think that the party unravels the situation; it gropingly tries its keys (*RL*, 1587; *CP*, 253). What would one discuss, since it is not a question of interpreting the world but of changing it, since pure data (if there were any) and a decision are without common measure, and since, finally, the data themselves are not pure and give us only the reflection of other decisions?

Marxism well knows that any situation is ambiguous. How could it be otherwise, since the consciousness that one has of a situation is still a factor of that situation, since there is here no separation of the observer and the observed or any objective criterion for knowing whether one should wait or forge ahead toward the future? Nothing is more Marxist than the mixing of fact and meaning, with the exception that Marxism does not mix them in an equivocation but in a genesis of truth, does not crush two adversaries into each other, but makes of them two stakes along the same road. For Sartre conscious awareness is an absolute. It gives meaning; and in the case of an event, the meaning it gives is irrevocable. For Marx, conscious awareness, that of the leader like that of the militants, is itself a fact. It has its place in history, it either answers to what the period expects or it does not, it is complete or partial. At its birth it is already *in* a truth which judges it. And if, at the moment, we do not indeed have any external model with which we can compare it, the trial that it undergoes in party discussion, the reception it receives there, the power that it either does or does not have to carry the proletariat along, to increase consciousness and power in it—these are the criteria of truth. Not in the sense of conformity of theses to a ready-made reality—that, indeed, would not be Marxist. Truth is to be made, but to be made according to what the proletariat and its adversaries are and do in the same moment. What is this dubious relationship, Sartre would say? Is or is not the meaning of the present given in it? It is neither given in it nor created out of nothing. It is elicited from the present, and such is the function of a congress. Here it is a matter of confronting theses and an existing proletariat, not as one compares two things, but by explaining the theses, by speaking to the proletariat, by giving it an understanding of itself and of its worldly situation that it does not have. If in the end it recognizes itself in these views, they become true, not by nominal definition and because the proletariat stakes its life on them, but because in a philosophy of praxis, where the world does not exist completely without man, this view that the proletariat has of itself—once it has taken stock of its strengths and everything has been accounted for—is the present form of the truth. Ideas are neither received from the proletariat by the party nor given by the party to the proletariat; they are *elaborated* in the party, and it is on this condition that they represent the maximum clarity that the proletarian present has of itself. Sartre does not envisage this adjustment of action to the situation because he always considers only decisions that are already made. Considered at its birth, however, action is first of all a *view;* it proposes immediate and distant objectives, it follows a line, it has a content, it supposes an examination, it is not "pure action." Reading Sartre, one would believe that the party's action is a series of *coups de force* by which it defends itself against death. But such *action* would be mere convulsions. If there is action, it is necessary to elicit information, facts, a discussion (even when it would be only the discussion of the leader with himself), arguments, a preference given to this rather than that—in short, the probable, which Sartre does not want because he looks at it as a pure rationalist and sees it as a lesser certitude. And yet he has elsewhere said, profoundly, that the whole of the perceived world is probable. Let us add that that is its way of existing: the probable is another name for the real, it is the modality of what exists. In this sense the party's line is probable: not as an uncertain opinion, but as the position which has been disengaged through the confrontation of the proletariat and its "consciousness" and to which this confrontation gives an absolute authority, since, right or wrong as regards the future, the "line" is at the moment the maximum of truth that history can claim. This is all very fine, Sartre would say, but where, then, are these criteria, where is this truth to which one subordinates the party? Where is this revolutionary line when, without the party, there would be only fluctuating masses? Where is this proletarian history on which the party is dependent when, without it, there would be no proletariat at all? A truth always means that someone is judging. It must be either the militants or the leaders—and if one leaves it to the militants, the proletariat is lost. Who will judge the *true* line, the *true* situation, the *true* history? The Marxist reply is: no one, *which is to say,* the party as laboratory of history, as contact with the proletariat and its consciousness, as elucidation of the present, of itself the becoming of truth. There is no external criterion by which one can measure the party's action, but there is an internal logic by which one recognizes it. Sartre is at the highest point of realism, since he reasons under the category of pure fact and since political time is atomized for him into a series of decisions taken in the presence of death; he is also at the highest point of formalism, since what is put indiscriminately into question each time is the unqualified and naked existence of the party and the proletariat. Marxism wanted to be a philosophy of contents. If Sartre is right, history has separated what Marxism had united: that is to say, the proletariat or the party and a certain sense of their becoming, the existing proletariat and the leaders' idea of it. The party's Marxist fidelity is not a fidelity to a wager but to general outlooks which the majority and the opposition have in common and which are not *continually* questioned. For a Marxist the meaning of events is to be found only in the party, not by virtue of a permanent equivocalness—because the party manufactures meaning and the proletariat is always compromised by what is done in its name but rather by virtue of an immanent truth which magnetizes the party's decisions.

All of Sartre's divergences with regard to Marx are given in this one, for his rigid conception of the party is only the counterpart of the equivocalness of facts: it is the answer of consciousness, all the more peremptory[14] because the course of things is so indecisive. The party as pure action is nothing but an ideal, says Sartre. But it is difficult to see how pure action could have gradations in reality: it is either completely pure or it is nothing. On these grounds, it is aggression and tends toward physical struggle. In fact, it will have to transform itself into a "line," situate itself according to a certain perspective, and direct this perspective. On the day after the June 2 strike, Sartre said buoyantly that the Central Committee had already solved its family quarrel with the working class. Subsequent events have shown that things are not so simple. Whether it is in the Central Committee or in the party—and it is ordinarily in the Central Committee at the same time as in the party—a perspective must be developed. In order to struggle, it is not enough to know that capitalism is the enemy. This enemy must be found here and now; one must know under what disguise it hides itself, whether a given strike is a provocation or whether, on the contrary, it foretells a movement of the masses. This examination knocks the wind out of pure action, because several estimations are possible and because the best one is subject to discussion. Besides, if the proletariat, which is nothing, can count only on itself, it is defeated in advance. It must assail the adversary, not in a frontal attack, but on its flanks or its rear; it must understand the bourgeoisie's internal functioning. Here again there are many probabilities to be evaluated. There is no action worthy of the name which is "pure action." Pure action, the "unanimous" party, are the action and the party seen from outside; and if Sartre entered within, he, like everyone else, could no more abstain from discussing than from breathing. Ultimately, pure action is either suicide or murder. Generally, it is an imaginary (and not, as Sartre believes, an ideal) action. When it tries to impose itself on things, it suddenly returns to the unreal from which it was born. It becomes . . . theater. From this come both the extraordinary description of the May 28 demonstration as "street theater," in which the Parisian population plays the part "Parisian population" (*Cp*, 696; *CP*, 57) and Sartre's sympathy for the demonstrations in which the proletariat "shows itself."[15] The ardent negation which was to inspire a pure action becomes an exhibition, the duel becomes a show or an exchange of gazes. And Sartre says correctly that this is only a last resource, to which one resigns oneself when there is nothing else to be done. But starting from his principles, any action tends to end in such a way. It remains to be seen whether the working-class leaders can in any case give the excuse that there was "nothing else to be done," if they are ever allowed to organize shows, since the police weapons are not made of pasteboard. The May 28 demonstration was indeed something of that sort. The analysis of the neoproletariat and of mass syndicalism given by Sartre in his third article makes it clear that we have come to this point. Unskilled workers, who very often are not militant and do not elect or control their leaders, do not have any political action. They do not know, says Sartre, how to maneuver in the face of capitalism, how to exercise pressure on it, how to use tactics, much less strategy. Suddenly they move to explosive strikes from which it is extremely difficult to predict whether or not a mass movement is heralded, strikes which the apparatus therefore hardly controls and with regard to which it is always either ahead or behind. All this is somewhat likely and reflects fairly well the ways of the working movement and of today's communist action. It remains to be seen whether this indeed is action as Marxism has conceived and practiced it. Sartre writes (*Cp*, 722–23; *CP*, 83) that the neoproletariat has lost its grip on history, that the distance between everyday problems and the revolution has increased tremendously. During the great periods of the working-class movement, the demands and problems of the working class formed a whole, they were leading to an overthrow of capitalism which was to resolve them and, with them, the problem of modern society. It was not then a question of pure action. For the party, the question was to organize the proletariat's hold on the social whole and to transform this into victory, to extend, concentrate, and push to its maximum effectiveness a struggle already inscribed in the relationships of production and in their partial demands. "Already inscribed?" Sartre will say. "But this is the retrospective illusion. You are projecting into a former reality what has been accomplished by the Party's action." Not at all. We are saying that the working class, guided by the party, endowed by it with differentiated means of perception and action, was nonetheless functioning in the party in a completely different way than as a driving force for which the party invented the means of operation and determined the use. In an organism there is no action without a nervous system, but the nervous system endows an organism with a life which it is not adequate to explain. There is also the part played by humoral regulation, by experience, and most of all by a mobilization of all these resources in the face of a perceived situation to which one must respond. In the party, without which, indeed, it would be inert and virtually like a body without brains, the working class accomplishes real work. Its choice is not only between a conversion that would identify it with the apparatus and a discouragement that would reduce it to a state of mass; it more or less takes part in the action, and the party takes account of this action and considers it not mere caprice, but like the indications of a thermometer. Sartre writes that the party gives "orders" to the workers. The Marxists used to say "watchwords," and the whole difference is there. The party gives the militant something to will beyond himself: a line, a perspective of action, both established after an examination, not only of the relations of force, but also of the way the proletariat lives and interprets the situation. There is an ebb and flow of the proletariat living politically in the party. Sartre once said that the party itself has a history. Yes, and to speak like Max Weber, it is made up not only of its *zweckrational* actions, of their consequences, and of the new decisions taken by the party in their presence. It is the history of the party's efforts to utilize the ebb and flow that are the respiration of the class and of the entire society. The class's history does not explain the party's, nor does the party's history explain the class's. They are coupled to each other; together they are only one history, but one in which class reactions count as much as party actions. It is therefore essential for the party to include this plurality or this inertia which Sartre refuses it and which is its flesh, *the principle of its strength and, in other moments, of its weakness,* and the control wheel which for the moment holds it back but which tomorrow may take it beyond the ends which it proposed. For the historical ebb and flow, of which the party is the interpreter and consequently a very special component but never the cause, Sartre substitutes the conversion of the masses to the party and their atomization when they withdraw. It is thus natural for him to conceive the party's action[16] as a "technique for the masses," which "churns" them like an emulsion, makes them "curdle" like butter, or maintains them in a state of "affective erethism" (*CP,* Part 3). It is just the opposite of an action in which the party and the working class jointly live the same situation and thus make the same history—not because all the proletarians see their action as clearly as the leaders, not because the party alone conceives it, but because the action works on them and disposes them to understand the party's watchwords and carries the apparatus itself to its highest degree of tension. Sartre intends to prove that the workers' abstention during the June 2 strike does not amount to a judgment of the C.P.'s politics by showing that they all had personal motives: one says that he was tired of politics, another that the Workers' Federation [*Force Ouvrière*] did not budge, a third that one does not strike during a month of paid holidays, and finally another that he has three children and his wife was recently ill. But it is precisely this recourse to personal motives which is a political judgment. If the party had a hold on the masses (and the masses a hold on history), personal motives would be outflanked. Sartre reasons as if the political life of the masses were on the level of judgment; and before admitting that they disapprove of the party, he waits until they say that the party is wrong. But neither adherence nor divergence, neither working-class history nor revolutionary history are of this order: the party's watchwords do or do not count, do or do not exist for the worker, depending on their relation to the situation that he is living and on this situation itself. The judgments he makes of the party and the importance he gives to his private life convey this tacit engagement, which is the essential factor. Marxism believes that in ordinary moments history is an accumulation of symbols that day by day inscribe themselves more or less clearly on the record of the past, fade or intensify, leaving a practically unreadable residue; but at other moments history is caught in a movement which attracts and submits to its rhythm an increasing number of facts. Political decisions prepare these moments and respond to them, but they do not create them. In the so-called revolutionary situations, everything works as a system, the problems appear to be linked, and all the solutions seem included in the proletariat's power. In the chaos of history these moments of truth furnish Marxist action its landmarks, and it guides itself by them. Marxist action never sets up the revolution as a goal that one can imagine but rather makes it spring out of the concatenation of the demands, of their convergence, of their collaboration, a process which calls the entire state apparatus into question and finally makes a new power emerge in opposition to the old. Not that the party does away with politics by means of a fortuitous confluence of favorable circumstances, but because at these privileged moments all its initiatives succeed, the social whole responds marvelously, and the logic of the struggle makes the proletariat emerge into a revolution that they would have perhaps not dared make if it had been proposed to them as an end. It is this life of the party and of the proletariat in the historical situation, this event which confirms itself as it goes along, like a fire or a snowball, that one cannot express by the idea of pure action. Sartre sometimes admits of degrees of historical equivocalness,[17] as he sometimes speaks of proletarian currents that the party decodes (*RL*, 1607; *CP*, 273) and even of a dialectic between the party and the masses (*Cp*, 1572; *CP*, 236). This is odd if the masses are nothing politically and if the party is their political existence. One asks what is left of the dilemma: stick to the party or disappear, and of the formal condemnation: whoever distinguishes the proletariat from the party betrays the proletariat. But never does he consider, in order to reduce these tensions, anything but "concessions, accommodations, compromises,"[18] or perhaps, when they are not possible, pure action, which is to say, force. Yet he never evokes the basic Marxist hope of resolution in *true* action, that is to say, action fitted to internal relations of the historical situation, which await nothing but action to "take," to constitute a form in movement. In other words, Sartre never speaks of revolution, for the truth to be made is in Marxist language precisely the revolution. He undoubtedly feels that such is not the order of the day, and this appears unquestionable to us. But what is the C.P.'s action without the revolution? What is left of the immanent guarantee that the revolution brought to the party? The stratagem of men substituted for that of things, pure action substituted for the conflagration of a society, this is perhaps the expedient of communism confronting a history in crisis. But the expedient, produced by the crisis it attempts to hide, will not bring history back to a Marxist course; it prepares something else, and what it is remains to be seen.

What opposes Sartre's theses on class are not only "optimistic nonsense," the monadic class, spontaneity which "needs only to be directed,"[19] the "proletariat which grows all alone like a very gifted student," the "fruit-proletariat," the "flower-proletariat," which "has to do only with itself, with its own activity";[20] rather it is the Marxist conviction that the class is not placed before the militant like an object that his will molds or manipulates but that it is also behind him, ready to understand his politics, if this politics is explained to it. The question is not to know who, from the class or the party, makes the proletariat's political history. These problems of causality, which have very little meaning in nature, have even less when dealing with society. No one holds that in advance of the party the class contains a complete proletarian politics folded up inside it and that all that is necessary is to unfold it. But neither does the party's general staff have such a plan; it invents proletarian politics in contact with the masses and as their expression. "This is quibbling," says Sartre, "for if expression could determine this immense tidal wave, then expression is also action" (*RL*, 1609; *CP*, 275). Who says the contrary? But it is an action of the proletariat, not by nominal definition and because it is the party's action, not by the inspiration of the "revolutionary instinct," but because the proletariat adopts it, finds itself in it, and makes it its own. Sartre writes that even in 1936 the movement expanded only when *L'Humanité* (May 20 and 24) had analyzed the first three strikes and underlined "the novelty and the similarity of the methods of combat." Thus the party's press plays an essential role in "a supposedly spontaneous movement" (*Cp*, 1807 n.; *CP*, 218 n.). But who said that the proletariat cannot see without eyes or that political facts do not count in the movement of the masses? It has been said, and it is quite another thing, that through the party's apparatus, using its means of information and communication, the proletariat is born to a political life which is not to be confused with the general staff's orders. What stops Sartre from admitting this substantial action—in which there is neither pure authority nor pure obedience and which, in its culmination, is called revolution—is a philosophy in which meaning, seen as wholly spiritual, as impalpable as lightning, is absolutely opposed to being, which is absolute weight and blindness; and certainly this philosophy is the opposite of Marx's. "No one believes any longer in the proletariat fetish, a metaphysical entity from which the workers might alienate themselves. There are men, animals, and objects" (*Cp*, 725; *CP*, 89). Marx, on the other hand, thought there were relationships between persons "mediated by things," and for him revolution, like capitalism, like all the realities of history, belonged to this mixed order. For Marx there was, and for Sartre there is not, a coming-to-be of meaning in institutions. History is no longer for Sartre, as it was for Marx, a mixed milieu, neither things nor persons, where intentions are absorbed and transformed and where they decay but are sometimes also reborn and exacerbated, tied to one another and multiplied through one another; history is made of criminal intentions or virtuous intentions and, for the rest, of acceptances which have the value of acts. Sartre today is as far away from Marx as when he wrote "Materialism and Revolution," and there is nothing inconsistent in his work. What he disapproved of in the communists was materialism, the idea, well or poorly formulated, of a dialectic which is material. What he today appreciates in them is the disavowal of historical "matter," of class as the measure of action, and of revolution as truth.[21]

Truth, revolution, and history, then, are the things at stake in the confused, or too clear, discussion that Sartre bases upon the notion of *spontaneity*. There is indeed one meaning of this word that Marxism does not have to consider. This involves what Lenin called "primitivism," the myth of a revolution based completely on economic premises and of workers' action limited exclusively to this domain. But there is another sense of the word which is essential, not only for Marxism but even for Bolshevism, since it merges with the sense of proletarian revolution: the masses' entry into politics, the common life of the masses and the party. If Lenin never renounced the word or the thing called "spontaneity,"[22] it was for a reason which he makes implicit in a far-sighted passage: all things considered, "spontaneity" and "consciousness" are not alternatives, and if one eliminated spontaneity from the party's theory, one would deprive it of any means of being the proletariat's consciousness. Lenin wrote that

> the very talk of "estimating the *relative* significance" . . . of spontaneity and consciousness itself reveals a complete lack of "consciousness." If certain "spontaneous elements of development" can be grasped at all by human understanding, then an incorrect estimation of them will be tantamount to "belittling the conscious element." But if they cannot be grasped, then we do not know them, and therefore cannot speak of them.[23]

These lines, directed against those who advocated spontaneity [*les spontanéistes*], also work against the worshipers of consciousness, since they show that, in spite of some momentary lags, spontaneity and consciousness vary in the same sense. The general staff does not have supersensible faculties, and it is difficult to see on what the party itself could be based in order to decide upon a politics if not on the proletariat's situation in different countries and on their "spontaneous" reactions. And even if it is necessary to coordinate and rectify them, it is still to the proletariat that one must speak, it is to the proletariat that the party line must be explained and made familiar and natural. Lenin never imagined the relationship of party to proletariat as that of a general staff to its troops.[24] The class has an apprenticeship in political life which enables it to understand what the party does and to express itself in the party, as we express ourselves in what we say, not without work and effort but not without profit to ourselves as well. It is not enough for the proletariat to follow; the party must direct it, to quote a well-known text, "in a way so as to elevate and not to lower the general level of consciousness, of revolutionary spirit, of the capacity to struggle and of proletarian victory."[25] The party is not the Calvinist Church: means which are too human precisely because they are in the service of a being beyond being. It is the initiation of the proletariat into political life, and in this regard it is neither end nor means for the proletariat. It is not an end, as Sartre implies when he writes that the party gives orders, nor is it "means," as he ends up writing in completing his first analysis (*RL*, 1572; *CP*, 236). Are my profession and my children ends or means, or both? They are nothing of the sort, certainly not means for my life, which loses itself in them instead of using them; and they are much more than ends, since an end is *what* one wants, and since I want my profession and my children without measuring in advance where this will lead me, which will be far beyond what I can know of them. Not that I dedicate myself to something I do not know—I see them with the kind of precision that belongs to existing things, I recognize them among all others without completely knowing of what they are made. Our concrete decisions do not aim at closed meanings. The party has value for the militant only through the action to which it calls him, and this action is not completely definable in advance. It is, like everything which exists, like everything we live, something in the process of becoming an expression, a movement which calls for a continuation, a past in the process of giving itself a future—in short, a being we can know in a certain *way*. We have said elsewhere that a proletarian power leads toward internationalism, to appropriation by the workers of production and the state, and to modern production, even though the necessary detours are to be explained to the workers. Anti-Semitism or police masquerades are excluded because either one of them clouds proletarian consciousness. Sartre somewhere makes fun of those purists who still speak of the day when Stalin proclaimed socialism in one country. He says that on that day the angels cried. It is, however, true that Marxism is touchy about certain points because it believes that history is a whole, that each detail counts, and that together they make a healthy or unhealthy historical landscape. For a Marxist, to speak on behalf of the proletariat does not mean one has unlimited powers; and precisely because a democratic consultation in the bourgeois manner is impossible, it is even more necessary to ballast the party's action with the counterweight which guarantees against historical delirium: the proletariat's agreement. The workers are not gods, but neither are the leaders. The joining of the proletariat and the leaders is the only certain sign in a history full of irony; as Lukács said—using Weber's expression—it is here that the proletariat's *objective possibility* appears, not the proletarians' thought, not the thought the general staff believes they have or attributes to them, but what is left, completely hammered down, after the confrontation between the party and the proletariat. Lenin never sacrificed spontaneity to consciousness; he postulated their agreement in the common work of the party because he was a Marxist, that is to say, because he believed in a politics that attests to its truth by becoming the truth of the proletarians. He went very far in the art of compromise, maneuver, and trickery. He was not one of those supercilious ideologues who endlessly confront the party's line with a concept of revolution, that is to say, with a revolution in ideas. But precisely because he was not an ideologue, he did not put consciousness or conception on one side and obedience or execution on the other. Contrary to Sartre, he did not give a free hand to the leaders "at their own risk." For him the leaders were ahead of the working class, but "only a step ahead." There was no criterion or geometrical definition which, in the abstract and outside a given situation, permitted one to say what is or is not proletarian. But there was a practical criterion: whatever can be explained to and be accepted by the proletariat, not through pure obedience but in conscience, is proletarian. The Party's action is not to be judged on a detail any more than a man is to be judged on a tic or a mole; rather it is judged on a direction taken, on a way of doing things, and, in the last analysis, on the militants' relationships with it.

One might answer that the Bolshevist pretension of making a *true* politics was never more than an illusion, that it served only to ground the authority of power more solidly. For if it is true that the classless society is already present in the infrastructures of capitalism, if the internal mechanism of capitalist production is like a particular and aberrant case of socialist production, in terms of which it must be understood and which is in some sense already there, then the initiatives of proletarian power find their guarantee once and for all in things and are justified in advance. How could one limit them? They are only there to liberate a revolution toward which the productive forces are moving. The "delivery" can be difficult. There is a logic in things which tends to make the remnants of capitalism regenerate themselves, even if only in people's minds. Revolution, then, is not made all at once; it comes at the end of an endless purification, it demands a party of iron. But the underground reality of socialism guarantees these violences and grounds them in truth. Since socialism is true, endowed with a truth which is accessible only to the readers of *Capital,* the party of the proletariat, and more exactly its leaders (who have read *Capital*), see better than anyone else the true path toward socialism; the orientation they give to the party also *must* be true, the consciousness they have of the proletarian situation *must* coincide with the spontaneous reactions of the properly enlightened proletariat. Ultimately, how could they want something which was not true? The assurance of being the carrier of truth is vertiginous. It is in itself violence. How can I know what God wants unless I try it out, asked Coûfontaine?[26] If I succeed, it is because God was with me. In the same way, the Bolshevik in power, assailed as he is by contingencies, is even more tempted to dare because, being in the darkness of everyday politics and incapable of getting from universal history a solution for today's problems, he is assured of acting according to truth only if he succeeds: it was then permitted by things and by the ineluctable truth of socialism. Here the relationship is reversed: at the start, the action of the party and its leaders succeeded because it was true, but the truth of the moment is accessible only through action; one must try things out, and what will succeed was true. When one identifies spontaneity and consciousness, Bolshevist vertigo is not far away; and this is what Sartre pushes to its limit. One is not far from thinking that the party's decisions are *eminently* "spontaneous" and that, *by definition,* they translate the movement of history. This is what Sartre says, but this is not what Lenin intended. Lenin gave consciousness the obligation of informing itself about everything the proletariat spontaneously does or says and of explaining to the proletariat its own direction. But in the end his formula, which we recalled earlier—consciousness *cannot* be unaware of spontaneity, the leaders *cannot* lose sight of the proletariat's spontaneous reactions—suddenly authorizes a state of frenzy belonging to the leader alone, if indeed he is the one who estimates the importance and the meaning of these spontaneous reactions. And how could it not be he, since he has the best knowledge of long-run and short-run perspectives? The workers do not understand? They will understand tomorrow, and they will be grateful to the leader for having preceded them toward truth. It is not only truth in the sense of "scientific socialism" which grounds violence. Even when the truth is dialectical, it is dogmatic. It is understood that revolutionary action conserves in sublating, destroys only for the sake of realizing, that it saves everything, that it reconciles the individual and the party, the past and the future, value and reality. But this return to the positive takes place only after negation: first of all, it is necessary to destroy, to sublate; and in order to put into motion the dialectical functioning that so delights classical minds, the revolutionary power must be solidly established. The classless society reconciles everyone, but to get there it is first of all necessary that the proletariat affirm itself as a class and make its own the state apparatus which served to oppress it. Those who will be shot *would understand* tomorrow that they did not die in vain; the only problem is that they will no longer be there to understand it. Revolutionary violence insults them most grievously by not taking their revolt seriously: they do not know what they are doing. Such are the poisoned fruits of *willed truth:* it authorizes one to go ahead against all appearances; in itself it is madness. "A specter is haunting Europe—the specter of communism."[27] Communism is not only in things; it is even in the thoughts of the adversary. There is a historical imagination which forces communism into his dreams. And the proletarian power would hesitate? "The theoretical conclusions of the Communists are in no way based on ideas or principles that have been invented, or discovered, by this or that would-be universal reformer. They merely express, in general terms, actual relations springing from an existing class struggle, from a historical movement going on under our very eyes."[28] Knowing this, how could one hesitate to step over an obstacle?

This is indeed how the Bolshevik in power reasons, this is why he has to collide with Stalin someday, and this development, as we have already said, was prepared by the idea of a materialistic dialectic. But between Stalinist communism and Lenin, and even more so between Stalin and Marx, there remains the difference that Lenin, who was not a philosopher but who understood the party's life in the most precise Marxist sense, broke up the *tête-à-tête* between truth and the theoretician and slipped a third party in between the dialectic of things and its reflection in the leader's mind. This third party was the proletariat, and the golden rule was to do nothing which could diminish its consciousness or its power. This was not a rigorous conceptual criterion, and one could ask for yet another criterion to guide its application; but the rule was very clear when applied to a long enough development, and it was explicit, at least as far as the party's style was concerned, that is to say, pedagogic, not military. The *Theses on Feuerbach* philosophically defined Marxist action as "objective activity." The materialism of former times had understood matter only as inertia and left the monopoly of activity to idealism. It was necessary to arrive at the idea of activity on the part of the object, and particularly on the part of the historical object. This heavy activity was the counterweight to the dialectical exploits of the theoretician confronting truth alone. These fragile barriers defended the essence of Marxism, the idea of a truth that, in order to be completely true, must be *evolved,* not only in the solitary thoughts of the philosopher who ripened it and who has understood everything, but also in the relationship between the leader who thinks and explains it and the proletariat which lives and adopts it.[29] The barriers have been swept away, but one cannot speak of communism without mentioning the incident. Sartre describes a communism of pure action which no longer believes in truth, revolution, or history. The October generation, like the young Marx, believed in an action which *verifies itself,* in a truth which comes to be in the life of the party and the proletariat. It was, perhaps, a chimera. At least it was—to speak as Sartre does, but without smiling—the Marxist "something or other."

III

One could show that Sartre strips this halo from each of the Marxist notions that he uses by placing each in the light of his philosophy and, moreover, that he accounts in this way for today's communism point by point. The same term "praxis" that the *Theses on Feuerbach* used for designating an activity immanent in the object of history Sartre uses for designating the "pure" activity which makes the proletariat exist in history. The Sartrean "something or other"—radical freedom—takes possession of praxis. Sartre used to say that there is no difference between imaginary love and true love because the subject, being a thinking subject, is by definition what he thinks he is. He could say that a historically "true" politics is always an invented one, that only by a retrospective illusion is this politics seen to be prepared within the history where it intervenes, and that, in a society, revolution is self-imagination. According to Sartre, praxis is thus the vertiginous freedom, the magic power that is ours to act and to make ourselves whatever we want, so that the formula "everything which is real is praxis, everything which is praxis is real" (*Cp*, 741; *CP*, 107)—in itself an excellent way of specifying the relations between Marx and Hegel—ends up meaning that we are what we contrive to be and, as for everything else, we are as responsible for it as if we had done it. The possibilities are all equally distant—in a sense at zero distance, since all there is to do is to will, in another sense infinitely distant, since we will never be *them,* and *they* will never be what we have to be. Transferred to history, this means that the worker who adheres to the party at the same time rejoins a possibility which is nothing other than himself, the external reflection of his freedom, and that yet he will never be this militant that he swore to be because he is the one who swears. In both cases—because the party and the revolution are both very close and infinitely far apart—there is no path which leads from that which was to that which will be, and this is why party politics cannot be, properly speaking, "just" or "false." There are, of course, foolish decisions and wise decisions, the party either is or is not informed; but the question is never, as it is in battles, one of knowing the adversary's strength and weakness; there are no internal collusions to break it up, just as there is no internal norm of action in the proletariat. Action is *the only possibility,* not because it rigorously translates the themes of proletarian politics into today's terms, but because no one else is proposing another possibility. If, in an opaque history, rationality is created by party action and you are in conflict with the party—the only historical agent (all the more so if it eliminates you)—you are historically wrong. If it gets the better of you, it knows better than you do.[30]

When he is not giving an absolutely new and Sartrean meaning to Marxist notions, Sartre takes them as they present themselves in today's communism (and the two operations are not by any means mutually exclusive). So is it with the idea of revolution. He observes, as we have said, that in the great periods of working-class history revolution was the culminating point or the horizon of everyday demands. The everyday struggle opened onto the social totality, and there was a dialectic of demands and of revolution. Today, he adds, revolution has withdrawn; it is out of sight. Nowhere does he ask if, when revolution withdraws to infinity, it truly remains the same.[31] Like the communists, he continues to speak of "reformists" and of "revolutionaries."[32] He retains the language of 1917 and thus keeps the moral benefit of the proletarian revolution for the communists. Now, if the revolution is the horizon of labor struggles, it is already present when the proletariat emerges, and the movement toward emancipation does not stop with it; revolution is a process, a growth. If, on the contrary, everyday action does not have a hold on history, revolution is a convulsion, it is at once explosive and without a future, and the revolution of which one still speaks becomes a future *state,* of which one knows only that it will reverse the present relationships. It is no longer the truth of the existing society and of every society; it is a dream which passes itself off as truth but which, as far as everyday life is concerned, is only a comforting beyond. In a word, it is a myth. Sartre does not say so, but this is where his thought leads.[33] Skilled workers, the neoproletariat, who do not know how to struggle,[34] are, he says, still revolutionaries. What could they expect from the existing order? But the question is precisely to know whether revolutionaries and a revolution still exist in the Marxist sense when there is no longer a class which, because of its situation, possesses, in addition to the will to change the world, the means of doing it and of giving life to a new society. When one bases a politics on the neoproletariat's historical nonexistence, it cannot be the same politics as one which was based on the proletariat's political existence. What one will have is not the already present and never completed revolution, the permanent revolution, but rather continuous acts of rupture in the name of a utopia. "The revolutionary *élan* . . . postulates the ends all at once in order to call for their immediate realization" (*Cp,* 1815; *CP,* 226). Of course, this radicalism is an illusion, and the explosion of revolt has a future only if it puts itself in the party's service. The power which is lacking in the proletariat must pass to the party which fights in its name. Then serious action begins, and Sartre lets it be understood that the proletariat is not to control it;[35] and just as the party, in organizing strikes with dual objectives, artificially connects the daily struggle to the revolutionary ends, so, too, will the revolution itself be the party's concern. It is for the same reasons that the masses want everything right away and that they will have to wait indefinitely on the party's wisdom for that which their madness demands immediately. The revolution is in an incalculable future precisely because it is wanted immediately and unconditionally. It is thus really utopia, with the single exception that a party of iron receives the mission of realizing it. The revolution of which Sartre speaks is absent in the sense in which Marxism said it was present, that is to say, as the "internal mechanism" of the class struggle; and it is present in the sense in which Marxism believed it distant, that is to say, as the "positing of ends." The notion of permanent revolution, which Sartre gladly takes up, changes meaning in his hands. It was the sometimes premature action of the revolutionary class against the power of the possessing class, an action prolonged beyond the insurrection and directed against the inertia of its own apparatus; for Sartre it becomes the permanent anxiety of a party which torments and tears itself apart, because, being the proletariat's party, it rests on nothing and because it itself lives in terror. Self-criticism, which was the definition of the proletariat as *Selbstaufhebung* and which was to confront the apparatus with its sustaining historical forces, with the revolution already present, is falsified when one leaves to the apparatus the task of organizing it.[36] Revolution, not as truth and as history's horizon, but as the Party's staging of a future without antecedents, is not *the same revolution* carried to another moment in time; it is another enterprise, which has in common with the first only the negation of bourgeois society. In the only passage in which he defines it, Sartre calls revolution "outstripping the Other toward the unlimited task." Marx thought: outstripping the other *and itself*. Without these two words, revolution is defined only by its antagonism toward the class that it eliminates. This is no longer the Revolution, the founding anew of all things under the aegis of the last class, a creative imbalance which, once in motion, will not stop—history supporting itself on itself to rise above itself.

Sartre, however, is not unaware of the historical field in which the revolution, and consequently all Marxist politics, is established. The apparent paradox of his work is that he became famous by describing a middle ground, as heavy as things and fascinating for consciousness, between consciousness and things—the root in *Nausea*, viscosity or situation in *Being and Nothingness*, here the social world—and that nonetheless is in revolt against this middle ground and finds there only an incentive to transcend it and to begin again *ex nihilo* this entire disgusting world.[37] Once again in the present work he sketches one of the horrified descriptions which make him an incomparable showman of enigmas, even if one does not agree with his way of going beyond them in a *coup de force* of action. There is, then, a social field onto which all consciousnesses open; but it is in front of them, not prior to them, that its unity is made. My own field of thought and action is made up of "imperfect meanings, badly defined and interrupted" (*RL*, 1581; *CP*, 245). They are completed over there, in the others who hold the key to them because they see sides of things that I do not see, as well as, one might say, my social back, my social body. Likewise, I am the only one capable of tallying the balance sheet of their lives, for their meanings are also incomplete and are opening onto something that I alone am able to see. I do not have to search very far for others: I find them in my experience, lodged in the hollows that show what they see and what I fail to see. Our experiences thus have lateral relationships of truth: all together, each possessing clearly what is secret in the others, in our combined functioning we form a totality which moves toward enlightenment and completion. We are sufficiently open to others to be able to place ourselves mentally in their perspective, to imagine ourselves in them. We are in no way locked inside ourselves. However, the totality toward which we are going together, while it is being completed on one side, is being destroyed on the other. Despite the fact that we accept others as witnesses, that we make our views accord with theirs, we are still the ones who set the terms of the agreement: the transpersonal field remains dependent on our own. The open, incompleted meanings that we see in the social world and that, in acting, we allow to be seen are nearly empty diagrams, far in any case from equaling the fullness of what others and ourselves are living. These meanings lead an anonymous life among things, they are indecisive actions which run off the track along the way or even change into their opposites as soon as they are put into circulation. There is practically nothing left in them of our precise aims, which go directly to their meaning and of which they are the external mark. "Intentions without consciousness, actions without subjects, human relationships without men, participating at once in material necessity and finality: such are generally our undertakings when they develop freely in the dimension of objectivity" (*RL*, 1624; *CP*, 292). This is what Marx had in mind when he spoke of relations among persons mediated by things.

> Marx sees . . . that the very work of man, becoming a thing manifests in turn the inertia of a thing, its coefficient of adversity; he sees that the human relationships which man creates fall back again into inertia, introducing the inhuman as a destructive force among men. We dominate the environment by work, but the environment dominates us in turn by the rigidified swarm of thoughts we have inscribed there. (*RL*, 1605; *CP*, 271)

Yet, far though Sartre appears to be from his dichotomy between things and men, he has not gotten any closer to Marx, because for Marx this suspect environment can ignite. Just as it vegetates and proliferates in false thoughts and pseudo-things, it can also escape from equivocalness when what happens here answers to what happens over there, when each event projects the process further in the very direction it was already moving, when an "internal mechanism" leads the system beyond any immobile balance; this is what one calls revolution. For Marx, good and evil come from the same source, which is history. For Sartre, the social whole never starts moving by itself, never yields more movement than it has received from "inassimilable" and "irreducible" consciousnesses; and if it escapes from equivocalness, it can only be through an absolute initiative on the part of subjects who go beyond its weight and who decree, without any previous motive and against all reason, that precisely what was not and did not seem possible to be, be done. This is why Sartre, who so well described "intentions without consciousness, actions without subjects, human relationships without men, participating at once in material necessity and finality"—but as residual phenomena, as furrows or traces of consciousness in what is constituted—uses all his severity to call to order those who look for something between being and doing, object and subject, body and consciousness.[38] It is because in reality, for him, as soon as one reflects, there is nothing there. Intentions without consciousness are phantasms. Intention without consciousness: this monster, this myth, is a way of expressing that, reflecting on events, I find a meaning which could have been put there either by myself or by another subject, or again, considering a complex of signs, I find myself obliged to give to each one a meaning which depends on the meaning of all the others, which itself is not yet fixed, and thus that the totality of meaning precedes itself in its parts. But of course it is I who make my passivity out of nothing. There is no real intention in the social whole, no meaning immanent in signs. Sartre has not changed since *The Psychology of the Imagination*,[39] where he rigidly distinguished between the "certain," the meanings of pure consciousness, and the "probable," that which emerges from the phenomenological experience; or, if he has changed, it is in the sense that he expects even less of the probable. He is the same philosopher who, analyzing the act of reading, saw nothing between scribbling, a book in its physical existence, and the meaning attributed to it by the reader's consciousness. The in-between, that is to say, the book taken according to the meaning ordinarily given to it, the changes of this reading which take place with time, and the way in which these layers of meaning accumulate, displace each other, or even complete each other—in short, the "metamorphosis" of the book and the history of its meaning, and my reading placed within this history, understood by it, included by it as a provisional truth of this book—none of this, for Sartre, prevents the canonical form of meaning from being the one I personally bring into existence by reading or prevents my reading, expressly considered, from being the measure of any other. We cannot avoid putting the thoughts we have formed in reading it into the pages of the book resting on the table, and this is what one calls a cultural object. At a higher level we imagine Julien Sorel as a wandering ghost haunting generations, always different in each one, and we write a literary history which attempts to link these apparitions and form a truth of Julien Sorel, a genesis of his total meaning. But, for Sartre, this universe of literature or of culture is an illusion: there is only the Julien Sorel of Stendhal, *and* that of Taine, *and* that of Leon Blum, *and* that of Paul Bourget; and they are so many incompossible absolutes. The idea of a truth of the whole is vague. It is an idealization of *our* view, which indeed takes in all things but only from one point of view. The total Julien Sorel has no more reality than the haze of consciousness we see appearing beneath the steel forehead of the electronic automaton when he responds too well to what *we* see as promises or threats around him. At most one can accept a sort of consolidation by which the intentions without consciousness (that is to say, the thoughts that *I* would formulate if I let myself be guided by a certain common meaning of the signs) manage to compose themselves or, rather, mass together and weigh on our perception of the social world and on our action. A residue of residues, a distant effect of drowsy thoughts, this mechanism of significations could not in any case create a new meaning or bring history toward its true meaning. If there is truth—one should rather say that, for Sartre, *there will be truth*[40] when praxis has completely destroyed and rebuilt this jumbled world—it will come with the spark of consciousness which will bring us into being, myself and the others, in the only comprehensible way, that of being-for-itself. Contrary to appearances, being-for-itself is all Sartre has ever accepted, with its inevitable correlate: pure being-in-itself. The mixed forms of the For Others [*du Pour Autrui*] urge us at every moment to think about "how nothingness comes into the world." But the truth is that it does not come into the world or that it remains there only for a moment. Ultimately there is pure being, natural and immobile in itself, a limpid mystery which limits and adds an outside to the transparency of the subject or suddenly congeals and destroys this transparency when I am looked at from outside. But even then there is no hinge, no joint or mediation, between myself and the other; I feel myself to be looked at immediately, I take this passivity as my own but at the same time reintegrate it into my universe. All the so-called beings which flutter in the in-between—intentions without subjects, open and dulled meanings—are only statistical entities, "permanent possibilities" of present thought; they do not have their own energy, they are only something constituted. If one wants to engender revolutionary politics dialectically from the proletarian condition, the revolution from the rigidified swarm of thoughts without subject, Sartre answers with a dilemma: either the conscious renewal alone gives its meaning to the process, or one returns to organicism.[41] What he rejects under the name of organicism at the level of history is in reality much more than the notion of life: it is symbolism understood as a functioning of signs having its own efficacy beyond the meanings that analysis can assign to these signs. It is, more generally, expression. For him expression either goes beyond what is expressed and is then a pure creation, or it copies it and is then a simple unveiling. But an action which is an unveiling, an unveiling which is an action—in short, a dialectic—this Sartre does not want to consider.[42] The relationship between persons can indeed become caught in social "things," can be degraded in them, and can extend its bleak consequences endlessly; this relationship is not visible in things, it is *made* and not observed. In Sartre's thought, as in the *Critique of Pure Reason*, the consciousness of a connection comes from the consciousness of a pure connecting principle. From there comes the Kantian question which he always asks: Who will decide? Who will judge? From where does the synthesis come? And if one wants to measure the party against a historical norm: "Who will unify the unifying principle?" The absolute authority of the party is the purity of the transcendental subject forcefully incorporated into the world. This Kantian or Cartesian thought sees only organicism in the idea of an unconstructed unity. Yet Marx was not an organicist. For him it is indeed man who makes the unity of the world, but man is everywhere, inscribed on all the walls and in all the social apparatuses made by him. Men can see nothing about them that is not in their image. They therefore do not at every moment have to reassemble and recreate themselves out of an absurd multiplicity; everything speaks to them of themselves, and this is why there is no sense in asking whether the movement comes from them or from things, whether it is the militant who makes the class or the class which makes the militant. Their very landscape is animated; it is there, as well as in them, that tensions accumulate. That is also why the lightning flash which will give its decisive meaning to all this is not for Marx a private happening in each consciousness. It goes from one to the other, the current passes, and what is called becoming conscious [*prise de conscience*] or revolution is this advent of an interworld. If, on the contrary, one thinks that the social world is "obscure and all too full of meaning" (*RL*, 1588; *CP*, 253)—obscure because it does not of itself indicate its meaning; too meaningful because it indicates several of them, none of which is truer than the other (which amounts to the same thing), and the truest, if such exists, is not the revolutionary meaning—that would tend to justify a liberal rather than a revolutionary politics, for one cannot sanely attempt to recreate history by pure action alone, with no external complicity. Pure action, if it wants to remain pure, can only arrange the world and obliquely intervene by opposing, not force to force, but the trickery of freedom to the force of being. To want to change the world, we need a truth which gives us a hold on adversity; we need, not a world that is, as Sartre says, opaque and rigidified, but rather a world which is dense and which moves.

Because he always moves from open and uncompleted meanings to the pure model of a closed meaning, such as it offers itself to lucid consciousness, Sartre is obliged to ascribe all historical facts to actions dated and signed by persons, and he is led to a sort of *systematic mythology*. For example, he says that, in order to show that the politics of the U.S.S.R. and that of the C.P. are not revolutionary, it would be necessary to "show that the Soviet leaders no longer believe in the Russian revolution or that they think the experiment has failed" (*Cp*, 10; *CP*, 13). The reader asks himself how, even if confided to us, disillusioned confessions could ever settle the question. Could one not take exception to them by showing that, whatever the leaders' beliefs, they have inherited a system which is neither that of the Russian nation nor within reach of a universal solution? And if, on the contrary, their intentions are still revolutionary, how could this knowledge allow one to judge the system, which either does or does not exploit the workers, which either does or does not express the historical mission of the proletariat? But the fact is that for Sartre there is no deciphering of truth of a society, because no deciphering ever expresses anything but a personal, more or less ample, *perspective* and because degrees of truth are worth nothing when it comes to deciding, that is to say, to presuming everything. The idea of a party being revolutionary in spite of itself seems to him the height of absurdity (*Cp*, 742; *CP*, 108), like the idea of Stalinism without Stalin (*RL*, 1614; *CP*, 281). The reader says to himself that, nevertheless, in the countries it occupied at the end of the war, the U.S.S.R. was by its position in conflict with the interests of the bourgeoisie without, for that reason, calling upon the proletariat to manage the economy; or that the same revolutionary ebb which made Stalin possible prepared in all countries the mold for the same type of politics, the alternation of opportunism and terror. But this kind of analysis looks for the content of the historical fact: revolution is the negation of the bourgeoisie and the power of the proletariat, Stalinism is the alternation of rotten compromise and pure violence. Yet as soon as one examines the content, the historical reality unfolds: each fact is this, but also that; one can decide only through balanced considerations, according to the *dominant* characteristic; in short, one penetrates, according to Sartre, into the order of the probable and the equivocal, one no longer measures revolution by its own standard. If one wants to understand it, one must not begin the infinite analysis of a society, one must not ask oneself what communism *is,* for that is questionable and thus immaterial. One must return to its sources in the will of one or several men and thereby restore a pure negation, because freedom is only secondarily will of this or of that: these are its momentary aspects, and revolution distinguishes itself from power only as a power of not doing. Thus historical judgment returns from revolution to the negation which is its principle, from Stalinism to Stalin, and here hesitation is not in order: one will readily agree that the power of the U.S.S.R. is not that of the bourgeoisie, that Stalin's fundamental choice was not the return to capitalism. The revolutionary ebb, the equivocal character of a regime which is new but which is not the revolution, these flowing notions have no place in a negative analysis or in an analysis of *pure intentions.* They would have a place only in analyses of dulled actions, of "intentions without subject." Revolutionary ebb and flow—bastard notions in which actual conditions, negligences, abstentions, and decisions are mixed—have no place in a universe where there are only men, animals, and things. Either *things*—"*historical* circumstances," the "*vital* necessity to intensify production" (*RL,* 1618; *CP,* 284–85)—explain the decisions of the man Stalin, and then one is not "allowed" (*RL,* 1621; *CP,* 288) to speak of exploitation and one must continue to speak of revolution, since the choice was between Stalinism and nothing; or else Stalin could have done something different, he chose badly, he is guilty, but then one must not try to "understand" him. In any case, there is no Stalinism without Stalin, nor any revolutionary in spite of himself. That Stalin's action was a reply to certain external "quasi-necessities," but a reply which exacerbated them and prepared for tomorrow new dilemmas in which, little by little, the revolution's meaning was changed and, with it, that of all the Marxist institutions and notions; that this very dialectic of wills and fortune is to be found throughout the world, because everywhere the signs of things have changed and, besides, what is done here serves as a model over there—Sartre does not have to consider these hypotheses because they are placed at the juncture of men and things, where, according to him, there is nothing to know, indeed nothing at all but a vague adversity which one must face up to in every possible way.

Now his reduction of history to personal actions authorizes unlimited generalizations, since Stalin or Malenkov, brought back to their fundamental choices are probably[43] the Revolution itself in new circumstances, and since Stalin the individual and Malenkov the individual thus with a single stroke rejoin Lenin and Marx beyond all the verifiable differences in their politics.[44] For Sartre it is illusory to attempt to judge history according to its "objective meaning": in the last analysis there is no objective meaning; all meanings are subjective or, as one might also say, they are all objective. What one calls "objective meaning" is the aspect taken by one of these fundamental choices in the light of another, when the latter succeeds in imposing itself. For example, for the proletariat, the bourgeoisie consists of those signed and dated acts which instituted exploitation, and all those who do not call these acts into question are considered as accomplices and coresponsible, because objectively—that is to say, in the eyes of the exploited—they assume these acts as their own. For the bourgeoisie, the proletariat is the worker who wants the impossible, who acts against the inevitable conditions of the social world. Between these two fundamental choices, no reading of history can arbitrate, no truth can decide. Very simply, one of them is the demand of life for all, the other for a few. The bourgeois choice is ultimately murder or, worse still, degradation of other freedoms. The revolutionary choice is ultimately freedom for all. The decisive reading of history depends, then, on a moral option: one wants to exist against others, or one wishes to exist with everyone; and the true perspective in history is not the one that accounts for all the facts, because they are equivocal, but that which takes into account all lives. "To look at man and society *in their truth,* that is to say," Sartre writes, "with the eyes of the least-favored" (*CP,* 1793; *ET,* 201). Thence comes the necessity of a mythological reading of history which reassembles into a single bundle wills scattered throughout the world; some are courageous and cynical, others are insipid and timid, but little matter: this is the share of things, of circumstances; the intention does not vary, it is virtue or crime, emancipation or exploitation. Since men and things are face to face (let us forget animals, for which Sartre, as a good Cartesian, should not care very much), wills do not continue living a decadent or fertile life in the things they mark. They are the brief signals a consciousness makes to another consciousness, separated from it by the wall of being. If those who receive them are thereby inspired, they have the entire merit or blame of what they are doing; they are not continuing anything, they are beginning anew. The 1954 Malthusian bourgeois really committed the Versailles 1871 crime. On 28 May 1952, the communist party was really the same people who acted in 1848 and who formed the Commune. Neither the politics of the bourgeoisie nor that of the C.P. is to be examined historically as the exact or inexact renewal of a tradition, the meaning of which perhaps changes, like a near-sighted action, starting from a well or badly understood present which would have to be confronted with its truth. In replacing men in a historical scenario, one could find them less noble or less base. For Sartre, on the contrary, Duclos[45] is Marxism, and Mr. Pinay is Mr. Thiers, since Pinay and Duclos live off what Thiers and Marx did, take it upon themselves, and are responsible for it, and since infinitely distant men pierce the wall of things and live in the same world, suddenly reappearing very close, identified, lost, and saved together. By this inevitable reversal, extreme personalism makes history into a melodrama, smeared with crude colors, where the individuals are types. There is only a single monotonous fight, ended and begun at each moment, with no acquisition, no truces, no areas of abatement. Those periods of apparent relaxation in which the historian deludes himself into making up perspectives, into distributing both merit and blame, into passing from the bourgeois to the proletarian point of view and afterwards reconciling them in a larger view, are unreal for those who have seen the drama. If the proletariat does not advance, it retreats; if it is passive, it is because the bourgeoisie is active or rather because the bourgeoisie is the only class in the world and the proletariat has been fragmented, it is because the universe is bourgeois. Even then, in truth, there is only the *tête-à-tête* of contradictory positions, of the class which is and of the class which is not.

And even the struggle of the proletariat and its party is nothing outside the signed and dated acts which stake it out; from bourgeois to bourgeois there is a solidarity of interests, but not from worker to worker. Their only common interest would be to not be workers. "I encounter in myself, in all men, in all groups and even in all classes, the presence of the Other, not only as a stranger to whom one is opposed in complicity, but as the objectifying power which penetrates us, divides us, and makes us possible traitors in the eyes of the other members of the group" (*RL*, 1615; *CP*, 282). The workers' unity is always to be remade; they are no less tempted by their adversaries than by their fellows, they have not many more ties among themselves than with the bourgeoisie, and the problem is to erase by means of the class other and through struggle the ineffaceable otherness of the individual other. The bourgeoisie and the proletariat are struggling only because the bourgeoisie is compact, while the proletariat is opposed to itself; and this is to say that for the proletariat the struggle begins under almost desperate conditions. There can be a truth, a rationality of the bourgeoisie as a servicing of certain interests; there is in it a given sociality. The values of truth and reason are in complicity with it because it is in its interest to make people believe that man and the world are thinkable and therefore already made. The proletariat will be true if it itself acts; but for the moment it rises up in history only under the form of magical connections, and history shows in it its mystical essence. For it is not difficult, but also not convincing, to link consciousnesses through interests, that is to say, through things, through calculations and estimations of probable results, or through customs, which are only the reflection of this quiet possession, the point of honor of interests. History—or metahistory—truly begins when men are linked through what they are not—through what they do; and that is communism.

Here all is to be constructed, and the oppositions are not arbitrated by things to be defended: the party is at the heart of the proletariat as an other, and within communism each party is an other for its fraternal party. Precisely because it links each one to the others from the inside, because the stake for everyone is life itself, the relationship is one of rivalry, with that background of love that goes with rivalries, but also with their false relaxations, their false fraternity. It is a mixture of independence and submission, a "no" which ends up being "yes" and which waits only for a little violence to change into "yes"; it is always a provisional "yes," always to be reexamined after the surrender. Thus we find in Sartre terms which are not very Marxist: the class "surrenders itself" to an authority which, following Lefort, he is not afraid to call "military" (*RL*, 1621; *ET*, 288). He says that the masses of 1919, which disavowed the old unionism and even their own representatives, "*would have condescended to submit themselves* only to an iron hand implacably fighting the constant unbalance of mass formations" (*Cp*, 1788; *CP*, 197; my emphasis). Like a woman they condescend, they condescend to surrender themselves, they wait to be forced, to be taken. Strange confidence. Confidence is distinct from vertigo and social eroticism only when it is confidence in an action, in a politics: but this sober confidence is impossible if the proletarian politics is without precise criteria, if the facts "say neither 'yes' nor 'no.' " This confidence will therefore be hollow and infinite: "the working class has coherence and power only in so far as it has confidence in the leaders: . . . the leader interprets the situation, illuminates it by his plans, at his own risk, and the working class, by observing the directives, *legitimizes* the authority of the leader" (*RL*, 1606–7; *CP*, 272). "[L]acking a minutely detailed knowledge of all events—possible only for the historian and in retrospect—it is confidence alone which will persuade a worker that he has not been fooled and that the sacrifices accepted were legitimate" (*Cp*, 8; *CP*, 10). The proletariat thus really gives itself without condition or limit, and the leaders exercise a priesthood: no matter what they do, they are consecrated. "When a Communist makes known the interests or the feelings of the proletariat, rightly or wrongly, it is *in the name* of the proletariat that he speaks. But I am very much afraid that you, Lefort, speak only *about* the class" (*Cp*, 1582; *CP*, 246). "Rightly or wrongly" makes one reflect: for if it is wrongly, the damage is serious. Lefort makes inoffensive remarks about the class. The communist makes the class itself speak incorrectly. At least, Sartre will answer, he makes it speak. And if one starts debating whether or not he makes it speak correctly, who will judge? The proletarians? They do not always take a correct view of things, and Marx and Lenin were the first to say so. However, no one knows better than the proletarians whether or not they should stick to the party's politics, and the party is judged according to whether or not it succeeds in carrying this weight along behind it. There is nothing like this in Sartre, there is no exchange between those who conceive the politics and those who execute it: the leader gives a meaning to the situation, the class carries out the orders. And what if the leader is wrong? "How can he be wrong?" replies Sartre. One can be wrong about the path to take when the path exists; but when it is entirely to be made, and when the proletarian condition does not define a strategy or a tactics, even the choice of a difficult line is not an error, since there is no true path and since what is essential is, not that the proletariat's existence be exactly translated by its politics, but rather that the proletariat exist and give life to the party. The path chosen is the only one possible and is *a fortiori* the best. There is no conceivable adjustment between the principle of communist politics and its line, the principle being of the order of duty, the line of the order of fact. One can therefore prove *a priori* that the party's politics is, in general, the only one and the best one; this is not a question of experience.

> Even if he were more concerned with the apparatus than with his comrades, [the militant's] particular interest is the general interest; his personal ambitions, if he has any, can be achieved only by inspiring in the masses a confidence that is renewed daily; and he will inspire confidence in them only if he agrees to lead them where they are going. In a word, he must be *all of them* in order to be himself. (*Cp*, 1805; *CP*, 216–17)

Let us make no mistake: *this daily renewed* confidence is not a judgment made on documents, which would demand deliberation and a probabilistic assent: we know that the masses never judge the party when they say "no." Let us not believe either that Sartre is satisfied with the Maurassian reasoning which proved the king's utility by showing that his interest was the same as the nation's. Sartre knows very well that when it is a question of interests one can always discuss the best way to serve them. But here discussion is meaningless, and the leader *is* the proletariat *a priori* or by definition, because the proletariat is nothing at all and can be nothing except in its leaders and because the link between them is timeless and eternal. It can either hold or break, not slacken or tighten. Thus, when

Sartre speaks of a daily renewal, it is a way of expressing that each day it could suddenly break, but it is not a question of control. Between the proletarian and the militants, between the militant and his leaders, then, there is literally an identification: they live in him and he lives in them. If there are only men and things, if each consciousness wishes the death of the other, how does one jump over the abyss to the other? This is accomplished before our eyes. It is the party. The worker gives himself to his leader so that "in his person" the group exists; the leader thus has "charismatic power"; he lives in the group, as consciousness lives in the body, as an immediate presence which does not need to command to be obeyed. Who commands, since the leader is leader only through the militants' devotion? Who obeys, since the militant himself has made the leader's power? "If there is a leader, everyone is leader in the name of the leader," not only because he makes others obey him, but especially because, in obeying the leader, it is one's own better self that one obeys. Undoubtedly this principle brings back painful memories. But what is to be done? If the militant and the leaders are not linked by an action, by a political content, nothing remains except the encounter of absolute existences, sadomasochism, or, if one prefers, what Sartre once called magic or emotional action, that which throws itself directly toward its end or which awaits everything from the sorcerer. How can it be otherwise if there is neither degree nor path between the actual society and the revolutionary society? A *coup de force,* a methodical fetishism, are necessary. These analyses have the benefit of helping one understand how backward forms of sociability and the cult of the leader have reemerged even in communism. When men wish to create things *ex nihilo,* then the supernatural reappears. Thus arise Sartre's religious formulas: the party and the class are ideally "pure linking, the relation which surges up wherever two workers are together" (*Cp,* 761; *CP,* 129–30). But as a result, communism crosses over into the realm of the imaginary, it is the outer limit of the vertiginous encounter of persons, it is the imaginary become institution or myth. There is an encounter rather than a common action because, for Sartre, the social remains the relationship of "two individual consciousnesses" which look at each other.[46]

We are far from Marxism. The Bolsheviks knew that it is not easy to reconcile truth with struggle, that the party's truth in battle is not absolute truth, and that in battle it yet has absolute value. "Our 'truth,' of course," wrote Trotsky,

> is not absolute. But *as in its name we are, at the present moment, shedding our blood,* we have neither cause nor possibility to carry on a literary discussion as to the relativity of truth with those who "criticize" us with the help of all forms of arms. Similarly, our problem is not to punish liars and to

> encourage just men amongst journalists of all shades of opinion, but to throttle the class lie of the bourgeoisie and to achieve the class truth of the proletariat, irrespective of the fact that in both camps there are fanatics and liars.[47]

History is action. The acts and the words of a party and a government cannot be judged according to the single criterion of what is true; rather one must consider the whole, form "truth" with force, impose a truth which, for the moment, is class truth and only later will be everyone's truth. *But it is already a class truth.* One cannot prove it by principles or by facts, by deduction or by induction; one can legitimize it by dialectic, that is to say, by having this truth recognized by the proletarians—by the "workers' democracy," Trotsky said; against the bureaucracy, Lenin said, at the end of his life. This guarantee is theoretically imprecise. Even the October 1917 revolution and the proletarian uprising are proof only when seen through the lenses of Marxist thought, by the quality of the facts rather than by their number, provided one uses an appropriate reading, which does not impose itself as a statistic or as a crucial experiment. But if there is neither an objective proof of the revolution nor a sufficient speculative criterion, there is a test of the revolution and a very clear practical criterion: the proletariat must have access to political life and to management. At least in this, class truth certifies itself as truth, if not in the eyes of the others, at least in the eyes of the proletarians. History is not the unfolding of a ready-made truth; but from time to time it has a rendezvous with a truth which is made and is recognized in the fact that the revolutionary class, at least, functions as a whole and that in it social relationships are not opaque, as they are in a class society. The watchwords of the "democracy of the masses" or of "constant struggle against bureaucracy" have no precise meaning in Sartre's perspective. Party democracy is always "mass democracy," without a minority, without deliberation. In comparison to the menace which constantly threatens the proletariat, the revolution's manner of being—democratic or bureaucratic—is practically insignificant. But at the same time, the entire history of Bolshevism and of the revolution also becomes insignificant, and this is why Sartre speaks so little of it. The revolutionary choice is really a choice of "something or other."

IV

We have perhaps dwelt a little too long on the metamorphoses through which praxis, revolution, history, the proletariat, and the party, taken in the sense Marx conceived them, are transformed into their Sartrean homonyms. If it were necessary to approach the philosophical and fundamental difference, one would say that, for Sartre, the relationships between classes, the relationships within the proletariat, and finally those of the whole of history are not articulated relationships, including tension and the easing of tension, but are the immediate or magical relationships of our gazes. The truth of a society is seen through the eyes of its least-favored member, not in his fate or in his role in production, and even less in his action; rather, it is seen in his gaze, the sole expression of a pure need, without means and without power. Relationships between persons stop being mediated by things; they are immediately readable in the accusation of a gaze. "Pure action" is Sartre's response to this gaze, which, like it, reaches its aim from a distance. We are in the magical or moral universe. The misery and exploitation of the least-favored are final arguments; and, as Péguy said, the city wherein a single man suffers injustice is an unjust city. But when revolution thus motivated ceases being a thought in order to become a deed, we will have to apply the same criterion to it, since there is no other, unless we wish to give up all points of reference and sink into the revolution as into a delirium. And if we look for the truth of the U.S.S.R. in the gaze of the least-favored—a political prisoner or simply the lowest-level unskilled worker—it is doubtful whether this gaze would be one of benediction. We will rightly refuse to judge on this basis, saying that it is necessary to situate the facts in their context, the present in the future which it prepares, the episode in the total action. And this is to speak politically. But it is also to consider suffering, misery, and death as elements of the whole, to make them the touchstones and revealers of the truth of that whole; it is to situate this truth elsewhere. And, since it would be a bit too much to look for the truth of the whole in the spirit of the leaders when one refuses to read it in that of the led, it is to grant an "objective" meaning to the enterprise and to come back to the problem of Marxist action as action in the realm of the probable—something that had been put aside a bit too quickly. The gaze of the least-favored thus has to be taken into account, but along with the geographical, historical, and political circumstances. This is an immoral attitude, but that is the way it is. The political man is someone who speaks about other people's deaths as statistical items. It is perhaps even still more immoral to ground a political revolution on morality. There is not in the present stage of our knowledge, and there may never be, a theoretical analysis that would give the absolute truth of a society, which would sort out societies as a teacher sorts the bluebooks written on the same subject, by students of the same age, in the same amount of time, and with the help of the same dictionaries and grammars. Since the original situations are not the same, since the "objective" possibilities are not computable, since one never exactly knows, for example, what Russia would have become without the revolution, political and historical judgment will perhaps never be objective; it will always be a bastard judgment. But precisely for this reason it escapes morality as well as pure science. It is of the category of action, which makes for continual oscillation between morality and science.

If this category does not appear in Sartre's analyses, it is because the social can enter his philosophy of the *cogito* only by way of the *alter ego:* if I am a thinking being, only another "I" can contest the thought that I have of myself. Inversely, the other can have the status of a self only by taking it away from me, and I can recover it only by reacting to the magic of the gaze with the countermagic of pure action. "Sociality" as a given fact is a scandal for the "I think." How could the "I think" take within itself the qualifications, opaque as things, which belong to it because of its insertion into a history? The scandal does not disappear but is at least stifled if one remakes history and the world, and such is the party's function. Although the enlarged *cogito,* the philosophy of For-Others, does not confine itself to the perspective of self on self, it is inside this perspective that it must introduce what puts this position into question. The social never appears openly; it is sometimes a trap, sometimes a task, sometimes a menace, sometimes a promise, sometimes behind us as a self-reproach, sometimes in front of us as a project. In any case, it is never perceived or lived by man except as incompleteness [*décomplétude*] and oppression, or in the obscurity of action. It is the absolute of the subject who remakes himself when he incorporates the point of view of others, which he was dragging along behind him like a hardship, and he reappears after he has digested it, confirmed in himself, strengthened by the trial. With Sartre, as with the anarchists, the idea of oppression always dominates that of exploitation. If he is not an anarchist, it is because he suddenly passes from the poetry of the subject to the prose of the world at the same time as he passes from the for-self to the for-others. But the other is still a subject, and, to establish his rights, magical means are necessary. Behind the prose and discipline of the party we have seen sorcery abound. One should not exactly say that the determinations attributed to me by the other's gaze are true; rather one should say that I am responsible for them, that I must, and that I can, modify them by acting in such a way as to put them in agreement with what I am in my own eyes.

It has not been sufficiently noted that at the very moment when he appeared to take up the Marxist idea of a social criterion of literature, Sartre did it in terms which are his alone and which give to his notion of historicity an absolutely new meaning. In *What Is Literature?*[48] the social is never cause or even motive, it is never behind the work, it does not weigh on it, it gives neither an explanation nor an excuse for it. Social reality is in front of the writer like the milieu or like a dimension of his line of sight. In choosing to write on this subject and in this form, he chooses to be the buffoon of the bourgeoisie or the writer of a potential and unlimited public. He therefore takes a position with respect to history; and since in any case he speaks of it, he will not know what he says, he will not be a writer, unless he speaks unmistakably about history. If not, he cheats, for he contributes to a drama which he agrees to see only in the dark mirror of literary anxieties. The task, in short, was to transform into meanings formed by myself what formerly passed for my historical determinants, to return to the *cogito* its truth by thinking my historical situation and making it one of my thoughts—and Sartre believed then that literature is capable of this conversion. If the *action* which he proposed was only one of *unveiling*, it was nonetheless irreplaceable. Literature seen as consciousness brought a revolutionary ferment, it changed the world in showing it, it had only to show the world to change it. Literature was, he said, the consciousness of a society in permanent revolution. This is why he approached the communist question only as a writer, to know whether it was possible for one to be a communist and remain a writer. Literature, if it was not revolution itself, was eminently revolution because it introduced into history a permanent element of imbalance and contestation by showing what can endure in obscurity but cannot support scrutiny. Today in Sartre's conception of the social the action of unveiling gives way to pure action. The writer in search of a potential public or of the universal is no longer the motor of the revolution. To be squared away with the social, it is no longer sufficient to unveil it and to make it an object of consciousness. One thought that in *What Is Literature?* Sartre was attempting to engage literature. He was attempting, at least as much, to disengage politics from the dilemmas of the times. Today, on the contrary, it appears that he holds these dilemmas to be insurmountable. The writer no longer surpasses man. The writer wants to be "a man who writes." Sartre no longer believes the demands of the action of unveiling to be *a priori* the same as those of a valid or revolutionary society—which was still a way of believing in salvation through literature. The truth of a society or of a history is no longer dependent on a specialist of truth, the writer; it is in the gaze of the least favored, who is never the writer. Now it is no longer the writer who appeals to the reader's freedom; it is the gaze of the oppressed which appeals to man's action. It is no longer literature which animates a society in permanent revolution; it is the party which makes this society. But there is a constant in this development: whether it is the appeal of the writer to the potential public and the response of the benevolent reader in the transparent universe of literature, or the call of the proletarian to the writer, who, as a man, recognizes in return pure action in the opaque universe of history—whether white magic or black—the social link remains immediate. Sartre's permanent revolution, whether effected by the party or by literature, is always a relationship of consciousness to consciousness, and it always excludes that minimum of relaxation that guarantees the Marxist claim to truth and to historical politics. A Marxist does not expect literature to be the consciousness of the revolution, and this is exactly why he will not admit in principle that it be made a means of action. He respects the writer as the "specialist" which Sartre despises, and he despises the writer where Sartre respects him: when the writer thinks himself capable of thinking the present. Writers are writers: they are men of speech and of experience; one should not ask of them to think "objectively" the historical totality. Trotsky said, and Lukács more or less agrees, that it is enough for them to have their honor as writers, and whatever they say, even what is tendentious, is recoverable for the revolution. Ultimately the writer's ideas are of little importance. Balzac's reactionary ideas make him feel and picture the world of money, and Stendhal's progressist ideas do not give him any advantage as far as this is concerned. There is a center of history, which is political action, and a periphery, which is culture. There are infrastructures and superstructures. Things do not go along everywhere at the same pace. A writer fulfills his role when he presents typical situations and behavior, even if the political commentary remains to be done, even if the work, as Engels said, is without a thesis. For Sartre, on the contrary, since there is not a single history behind us to which both our literature and our politics belong, since their unity is to be made by us, since he takes them at their common source, consciousness, then, if they are to touch things, literature must deal with politics, and action must stick to the event as in a novel, taking no distance. Marxist action was a world; it went on at all levels, near and far from everyday life, at both long and short terms. The vagueness that reigned in the theory of superstructures allotted culture a certain margin: sometimes culture was extended in the direction of political orders, and sometimes the many imperishable texts condemning sectarianism were recalled. Marx and Lenin said that in communist society there would no longer be painters or writers but rather men who painted or who wrote. But this would be in the communist society, after an immense historical work on man, and not in the immediate future. For Sartre, it is now that literature and politics are the same struggle on the single plane of events. In a word, for the Marxists consciousness can be mystified; for Sartre consciousness is in bad faith. For the Marxists there are fools; for Sartre there are only scoundrels.

Thus he exhibits a generalized suspicion in which one again finds the tone of the communist rather than Marx. How could it be otherwise? History is waste, except for the history that is created by the "potential public," now by "the gaze of the least-favored." In both cases, how is it possible to wait without betrayal? How are we to allow for these partitionings—politics, culture—between the subject and his world, partitionings which deaden the virulence of the subject? Whether as a permanent spectacle or as a continued creation, the social is in any case before consciousnesses and is constituted by them. Yesterday literature was the consciousness of the revolutionary society; today it is the party which plays this role. In both cases history, in regard to everything in it that is living, is a history of projects. History is understood by that sighting of the future which belongs only to consciousnesses and not, as with Marx, by the point called revolution, where the past grows hollow, is raised above itself, and is seized by the future.

What continues to distinguish Sartre from Marxism, even in recent times, is therefore his philosophy of the *cogito*. Men are mentally attached to history. The *cogito* perseveres in its claim to be everything that we are, taking as its own even our situation before others. This carries it far, as far as the obscurity of "pure action." There is a madness of the *cogito* which has sworn to recapture its image in others. But in the end it is the *cogito* itself which demands its own disavowal and puts itself in question, first by the clarity of thought and then by the obscurity of devotion. One finds several times in these articles of Sartre's a movement of thought which is the Cartesian movement. Show us, says Sartre to Lefort, this class or this history which you say are not made by the party. Separate them from it so that we can touch them with our fingers. Produce the acts which would not have taken place without them. This challenge is not as conclusive as it seems to be. Sartre is too much of a philosopher to cherish illusions on the "method of differences." He well knows that no one can isolate the efficacy of a single element in a whole, separate what belongs to the class from what belongs to the party, or, finally, examine history as a thing. He well knows that this causal or empiricist process is impossible. But from the fact that the social is a totality, it does not follow that it is a pure relationship of consciousnesses; and yet that is the very thing which, for Sartre, goes without saying. Since no historical reality is without contact with consciousnesses, history and revolution are nothing but a pact of thoughts or of wills. When consciousness intervenes, it does so as a sovereign legislator, because it is consciousness which gives meaning, because meaning is not more or less, because it is not divisible, because it is all or nothing. One recognizes the *cogito*. It is the *cogito* which gives to violence its Sartrean nuance.

There is indeed a Sartrean violence, and it is more highly strung and less durable than Marx's violence. The personal tone of the polemic with Lefort was surprising. Lefort, writes Sartre, "wants to anchor himself in the intellectual bourgeoisie." That kind of talk, if it is not a personal imputation, an allusion to the adversary's personal history, and, in short, aggression—but this cannot be the case, for clearly Sartre has no information about the man—then it is simply a manner of speaking. It is an allegorical way of saying that *if* Lefort had the same ideas as Sartre about the proletariat, the C.P., Marxism, history, subject and object, and freedom, and yet could decide against the C.P., this could only be for base reasons. One will easily agree to this. But is Lefort Sartre? Here is the question that Sartre forgets. Is what he thinks so true that any resistance would be impure? But he will say that Lefort is a Marxist and consequently a realist. Thus, if Lefort does not join the C.P., he renounces in practice working with and for the proletariat, and, using his language, I have the right to say that he prefers the other side. I neither attribute nor oppose my views to him, I place him in contradiction with himself. With himself? The whole question is there. It is certainly true if we are dealing with a pragmatic Marxism, realistic in the "bourgeois" sense, or with Marxism as seen by Sartre; but is this Lefort's Marxism, and, in the face of the immense Marxist literature, can Sartre presume that his own interpretation imposes itself on every man of good faith? We also believe and have said in an earlier chapter [of *Adventures of the Dialectic*] that the notion of a Marxist without a party is an untenable position in the long run and that it refutes the Marxist conception of history and even of philosophy. But one does not have to see this immediately. In the meantime, to rally to the party in the dark is a pragmatic solution, but not a more Marxist one. For a reader of Marx who is not used to these *coups de force* it is natural to hold both ends of the chain and try to reweld them. To put him in contradiction with himself is then to smother a problem or to insinuate that there is none. The type of discussion which opposes, in Marx, the necessity of the whole to the contingency of historical details, which opposes in the spontaneists, the passivity to the activity of the class, and which opposes, in Lefort, Marxism to the critique of communism contributes and proves nothing when one is dealing with an author of any merit. Contradictions are the sign of a search, and it is this search that counts. To pin down the "contradictions" is to treat the adversary as an object; he is a Marxist, therefore he should think this or that. And what if he understands Marxism in another way? And what if his "contradiction" was already in Marx? And what if Lefort and Marx, like Sartre himself, are people who try to understand, who are Marxists when they can be and something else when there is no other way? And what if Lefort, instead of trying to anchor himself in the intellectual bourgeoisie (there are certainly less indirect means of doing it), was trying to understand the nature of revolution or truth in history? And what if one were to lend him a little of that freedom to be himself that Sartre does not begrudge himself? To place an adversary in contradiction *with himself* is fundamentally an arbitrary decision to express oneself only tacitly, by means of a Marxism that one rethinks but that one presents as Marxism itself; it is to claim for oneself the right to be undecided or vague while refusing it to the adversary. You who are Marxist, says Sartre, you should join the C.P. But I, who teach you so well your Marxist duty without, fortunately, being a Marxist, I keep my freedom intact. The very difficulties that are called maneuvers in others are in Sartre only the proof of a free spirit. If Lefort asks himself questions about revolution and about truth, it is *so that he will not have to join the C.P.* If Sartre does not join the C.P., it is *because he is asking himself these questions or others.* This is unequal treatment; Sartre is plainly more conciliatory toward Sartre than toward Lefort.

Why all that, and is it not merely a question of temper? It is much more serious than that. What gives this strident tone to the discussion is Sartre's effort to annex history to his philosophy of freedom and of the other. Freedom as he conceives it is unstable and tends toward violence. Freedom is not at first an infinite power that we would notice in ourselves; it presents itself trapped and powerless: it is a quality which marks our entire life and which makes this life our charge. It is as if at each moment everything that has made us, everything from which we benefit, and everything which will result from our life were entered in our account. Sartre has even evoked the Kantian myth of choice and its intelligible nature in order to show that freedom first appears in the past as freedom to be found again, freedom lost. This is what he has so well expressed in saying that we are condemned to freedom. To say that we are free is a way of saying that we are not innocent, that we are responsible for everything before everyone as if we had done it with our own hands. Freedom, which Sartre, like Descartes, distinguishes absolutely from power, is almost identified with the simple existence around us of a charged field in which all our acts immediately take the aspect of merits and demerits. To live is to wake up bound like Gulliver at Lilliput, as if in a former life one had already disposed of oneself. It is to attempt to make up this perpetual delay, to transform into actual freedom the prenatal freedom which is there only to condemn us. Freedom is behind us, or perhaps in front of us; never are we able to coincide with it. Perhaps we can reverse the order of things: by living the future we put ourselves ahead of ourselves. We will never be on time. And this movement toward the future will be violence, as is our relationship to a world already there, and concerning which we have not been consulted. The other's gaze is nothing but another mark of this original delay, which comes from the fact that we are *born*. The image of me that the other evokes is once again an elsewhere that I will never be able to overtake and yet that I must overtake, since, as I acknowledge in shame, I am also over there in this gaze which I do not challenge. This accusation from outside takes up anew my grievance against myself. In private life and in literature there is some relaxation: I speak to others, I act with them, with them I move beyond my condition at birth and they, theirs, toward a common future or toward the world taken as spectacle. In action, or in the action of unveiling which is literature, there is a relationship of calling and response. This solution is more apparent than real, for the relationship with the other is never symmetrical; rather, it is always one of the two who proposes, the "common" life is his project, and even the effort he makes to associate the other to it is the product of his good will. The mutual project remains an individual one for the fundamental reason that the future lives only in consciousness, it never truly descends *between* us. The calling of one freedom to another through literature is even more illusory, since the call is always from the writer to the reader. What happens when one comes to the social bond, when it is a question of uniting the near and the far in a common enterprise in that social space in which everything becomes deadened and dissipated? Then the apparent liberalism which exists in common life and in literature is denounced. There is a liberalism for the internal use of the bourgeoisie because it manages its society like a private enterprise and forms its unity, as a couple does, through common "interests." But this community excludes others. And the others are not even united by the common exile: they suffer the same things at the same time, that is all. In the proletariat, insofar as it calls for a society which would be total or true, each life is condemned to the solitude and the surrender which defined consciousness in its first meeting with the other. So that, here too, a common future, a history, may efface the initial situation, it is necessary to make them out of nothing, it is necessary to set up pure wills—absolute commands, absolute obedience, indistinguishable because they are absolute—which will create history, since it was not given to us even in a relative sense, as was friendship or love. Everyone found himself by means of a common life, at least through things done together: he who loves, that is to say, who wants to be loved, found himself completed by these things (with the condition that he forget that the other's love is also nothing but the will to be loved and that the other also lives the enterprise as his alone; but in action this turning back upon oneself is suspended, and the two mirages confirm each other). In social life there are no things done together. They must be invented. One must here create from nothing the milieu of a common enterprise or history, and one must even create the subjects of this enterprise: the party. There is no point in demanding here that each consciousness find itself through common action: it must transform itself and be converted into action. The "I think" was able to recover itself through the common life with the other; but where this common life does not exist, the "I think" must explode, it must first create the common life. Thus in Sartre what gives to the gaze of the least-favored its absolute authority and to the party its historical monopoly, and consequently the duty of absolutely respecting communism, is the fact that the initial discord of the other with me and of me with myself lives again undisguisedly and imperiously in the discord between the bourgeoisie and the proletarians and that it demands a solution for which the elements this time are not given. It is Sartre's ontology that determines that history as a common future be sustained by the pure action of a few, which is identical to the obedience of the others. Choice, freedom, and effort become conquest and violence in order to become everyone's affair.

This violence thus does not come from temper; or rather temper, like all things, is, in a philosopher, philosophy. It is already there when freedom and impotence, the past and the future, the present and the distant, the I and the other, the gaze of the least-favored and the party that claims it, are immediately united by the simple negation that separates them, are united one to another and all together in violence. When negativity descends into the world and takes possession of it by force, when it wants to become history immediately, everything that opposes it appears as negation and can be put pell-mell in the same bag. These mixtures, these short cuts, are the counterparts of the short circuit which goes directly from freedom to the party. This is why Lefort is the philosopher of the young executives.[49] It is not so much due, as one sees, to Lefort and the young executives as it is to Sartre.

Is violence Sartre's last word? Surely not, and for a fundamental reason, which is that pure violence does not exist. It is not pure in the case of the Bolsheviks; it hides behind truth, and, as we have seen, this is what makes it implacable. In reality ultrabolshevism throws off this cover: truth and reason are for tomorrow, and today's action must be pure. But this is also to say that ultrabolshevism is only adhering to the principles of communism, to its desire to change the world. Pure action is only the root of freedom; as soon as it is applied, it is in a world of "probable" relations in a situation where it must find its way and accept mediations. In truth, this is where politics begins. The approbation in principle of the party remains philosophical. It concerns communism only as the negation of the bourgeoisie, as thought or as conception, and not, except in certain of its "aspects," as that which bears the name of communism over there, in the sun or in the snow. It does not extend to the "probabilistic" consequences. The absolute choice, the choice of existence, beyond all the reasons, is violent only when it does not present itself as a choice but takes itself for the law of the world. It tacitly imposes its own categories on others under the pretext that no one is supposed to ignore the world—the world such as it has been chosen by the thinker. But as soon as the choice is justified and declared, the discussion starts all over again. The pure will to change the world is nothing but inner life so long as we are not told how to do it. As long as this is not done, as long as Sartre is not a communist, the judgment that "Lefort wants to anchor himself in the intellectual bourgeoisie" means only that Sartre wants to cut himself loose from his own anchorage [*se désancrer*] at any cost. Lefort's "bad faith" is a projection of Sartre's own good faith, which will be sorely tried when he has to move beyond principles. Sartre presents his polemic as a first phase, after which he will say how the C.P. also does not express the proletariat. But if he expresses it only *quatenus,* Sartre becomes a slippery customer once more. Sartre's ontology, which was moving toward a C.P. existing in ideas as its only possible issue, takes up a distinct existence and surveys the C.P. with a glance. Sartre's conclusion is no longer pure action; it is pure action contemplated from a distance—in other words, sympathy. On the concrete political terrain Sartre may tomorrow reappear pacified, conciliatory, and universalist, as he *also* is.

V

Sartre's "reasons" are at the other extreme from those of Marxism, and it is because the dialectic has broken down that he defends communist politics. What conclusions now have to be drawn? For in showing Sartrean and Marxian motives to be parallel, we have not implied that Marx, rather than Sartre, was right; we were trying to restore the Marxist spirit only in order to show what is new in Sartre's analysis. To read Sartre with Marx's eyeglasses would be deliberately to ignore the real question that his studies raise—although he does not raise it himself—which is whether revolution in the Marxist sense is still the order of the day. It would also be to add to the confusions he creates, to obscure the debate ourselves, to conceal under Marx's authority a post-Marxian evaluation of history, which, on the contrary, must be made explicit. We have stressed that the return of dogmatism in its scientistic form to an offensive role, the isolation of the dialectic in being, and the end of philosophical Marxism signaled disillusion and difficulties in Marxist theory and practice. This was not done in order to now confront Sartre with this same philosophy, with this same ideology whose crisis is perfectly attested by his own analyses. As a description of existing communism, Sartre's antidialectic appears to us to be hardly questionable. We are only saying that it raises the question of the nature of communism, and we reproach him only for not having raised this question himself. Our problem would be his if only he had formulated it as a problem instead of acting as if the whole thing were a matter of "common sense." If in fact, as we believe, communism is what Sartre says it is, what attitude can and should one have toward it, and how can one evaluate Sartre's attitude?

Must we say that of course we can no longer expect either the accession of the proletariat to management, to politics, and to history or the homogeneous society—in short, what the dialectic promised—but that, anyway, that was only the final "optimistic twaddle" which experience has eliminated and that communism remains *on the right road,* that it is the proletariat's *only chance,* offering in the present a *progressive* regime and, for the future, a *revolutionary* perspective? Must we say that, beyond an official philosophy which is a collection of curiosities, beyond uncivil behavior toward intellectuals, beyond its undoubtedly superfluous violence, communism is still preferable? "The Stalinist movement throughout the world," wrote F. Jeanson,[50]

> does not appear to us to be authentically revolutionary. Yet it is the only one which claims to be revolutionary, and, particularly in our country, it has organized the great majority of the proletariat. We are therefore at one and the same time against it, since we are critical of its methods, and for it, since we do not know whether the authentic revolution is not a chimera, whether the revolutionary enterprise does not first have to go along these paths before it is able to establish a more human social order, or whether the perversions of this enterprise are not, given the actual context, preferable, all in all, to its pure and simple annihilation.[51]

An odd way of thinking. One has a certain idea of "authentic" revolution; one verifies that the U.S.S.R. is not a revolution in this sense; one then wonders whether authentic revolution is not a dream; in the name of this doubt one keeps the label "revolutionary" for a regime which may perhaps mend its ways; but, as this future is vague, one says only that it will be "a more human social order." These lines give the entire essence of "progressism," its dreamy sweetness, its incurable bullheadedness, and its padded violence. At the very bottom, there is always "authentic" revolution. This is what is at the end of the journey and what justifies it. And, certainly, the paths are indirect, but they are the paths of revolution. Why not think rather about the goal and the "more human social order"? In all this, how very little is asked about what one *does* outside. How much one feels that it is only a question of the relations of the self to itself. There is something of this sort in certain of Sartre's lines, as, for example, when he writes: "[The] 'Stalinists' would agree without hesitation that neither the authoritarian Party nor the Soviet state can be envisaged as the definitive form of proletarian organization" (*RL*, 1616; *CP*, 283). The reference to the revolution or to "proletarian organization" at the moment when one observes that the regime is far from it, without any precision about the turning point which will bring it closer or about the forces which will impose this turning point, this oscillation from what one sees to what one dreams thus contaminating the real with the imaginary (without thereby achieving any true resemblance) and obscuring the harsh present under the haze of a fictitious future—these techniques recall the devices of physicists who encumber a theory with auxiliary hypotheses so as to avoid recognizing that it does not clarify what happens. If the Marxist revolution were a *general idea*, there would be nothing to say against this play of the imaginary and the real, of expediency and utopia. But the dialectical idea of revolution is no more an advance toward "some more human social order" than it is a "chimera" or a star in the farthest reaches of the future.[52] Revolution in its beginnings is rupture, because revolution is the seizure of power by the proletariat. The rupture is always to be renewed, for revolution is also self-suppression of the proletariat as a class. It is thus a process, but not an "advance" in the vague and "bourgeois" meaning of the word. It is an identifiable becoming because it always moves toward the development of the proletariat in consciousness and in power. Even in its beginnings, in its atypical forms, it is never a *perhaps*. When Lenin proposed the N.E.P., he was not content with vague allusions to the future; he explained and made the path accepted. Revolution as a "perhaps" is Marxist action disjointed between a utopia situated at infinity and a completely different present that it sanctifies. If one has to class the revolutionary dialectic as "optimistic twaddle," let us no longer speak of revolution.

The "perhaps," a formula of doubt as well as faith, aims at that which is absolutely beyond our grasp. How can the most categorical undertaking that exists be founded on a sigh? The communists are right to value the dialectic. Without it they are only progressists, and the progressist, left to himself, vegetates. In reading Sartre, one sometimes believes that he has set himself the task of proving that revolution is impossible. How could this proletariat which has lost its hold on history keep a historical mission? How could it propel an emancipated society if it is no longer skilled labor, know-how, and a capacity for management and for struggle but is only a "need" lacking political consciousness and power? Whatever the efforts of the C.P., how can one make a proletarian revolution with a neoproletariat? It will not be a proletarian revolution. But then what? Sartre's analysis presents communism as absolutely undetermined. He does not have in common with it a view of history, of its possibilities or its articulated causalities. He values communism because it has at its center the gaze of the least-favored. This is a great deal, because this argument can ground any kind of politics; and it is very little, because he defends it only in a formal manner and in terms of its internal principle. The reader gets the feeling that, for Sartre, communism is something holy but also something one talks about and looks at, something which remains remote and inaccessible. One has less respect and more passion for what one lives. For Sartre it is not a social fact that one examines as best one can, that one attempts to understand in its distinctive features, using the same criteria that are used for judging other societies. We lack information. I defy you, he says to Lefort, to prove according to the rules of historical criticism that the Russian working class disavows the regime (*RL*, 1619; *CP*, 286). A return to historical reality would be healthy if it were a question of refuting those who speak of opposition in Russia as a fact because it results from their principles. But it is not facts that Sartre reminds us of; it is our ignorance of facts. It would only be fair to observe that what is hidden is precisely that which renders the adversary's proof difficult. If Sartre readily resigns himself to this state of affairs, it is because he does not burden himself with the task of proving his position; for him it is enough that it cannot be disproved. And since it does not appear that we will be getting information for quite a while, communism becomes a negative being or even, like the moon and the sun, one of those "ultra-things" that are seen only from afar. Or finally, torn from the world, floating equidistant between things and Sartre's gaze, it is like those tenacious appearances which no judgment can situate. Just as these appearances reside this side of articulated space, so, too, communism lies this side of proof.

If one must really get rid of all the optimistic twaddle that lies between the subject and the object—spontaneity, initiative of the masses, meaning of history—and leave the brute will of the leaders face to face with the opaque necessity of things, such extreme realism cannot be distinguished from an extreme idealism. Men—proletarians and even leaders—are no more than beings of reason. What do you want the leader to do if not to lead the revolution, says Sartre. He is himself only in being everyone, he is nothing without the proletariat. This is to suppose that there are beings who are living definitions, whose existence is fully included in their essence. This is to forget that, from the day when the dialectic is only in the leaders' minds, from this very fact and without further inquiry it is no more than an accessory of power. The proletariat of which Sartre is speaking is not verifiable, debatable, or living. It is not a phenomenon but is rather a category delegated to represent humanity in Sartre's thought. Since the proletariat is nothing when it does not adhere to the party, it never is the party but is only a nameless mass which can be detached from it. It exists immediately through obedience, and it ceases to exist immediately through disobedience. It is not a historical reality with advances, peaks, declines, or variable historical weight. Like an idea, the proletariat exists in the instant; and if Sartre refuses it "spontaneity," this is only because the party and history must appear by *spontaneous generation*. Sartre reproaches the Trotskyites with fabricating beyond observable facts a "real" proletariat which does the opposite of what the existing proletarians do. But this is the way Sartre himself operates, with the exception that, not being a Marxist, he does not bother to garb his proletariat in historical reality. "Spontaneity" passes to the side of the leaders and the militants because here, at least, we know what we are talking about, we are among men or among consciousnesses. But that is to say that the proletariat is an idea of the leaders. The proletariat is suspended above history, it is not caught in the fabric, it cannot be explained, it is cause of itself, as are all ideas. No conceivable method can reveal its historical presence, absence, or variations. The proletariat subsists through any disobedience, since, as soon as it disobeys, it is no longer it that disobeys. Obedience does not make it grow, because obedience is included in its definition. If some fact or symptom emerges to testify to its presence and its force, this is accepted only condescendingly; for when, on the contrary, such facts are lacking, nothing is changed as regards the proletariat's essence, which is always to obey the party. The party continues to "represent" it historically. The proletariat is untouchable because it exists only in the pure action of the party, and this action exists only in Sartre's thought. All detectors and proofs are superfluous when it is a question of capturing an essence, and this is undoubtedly why Sartre airily takes them or leaves them. When the proletariat is not visible on the terrain of class struggle, he turns to legislative elections and has no problem in showing that the proletariat is still there, for it is electing communist deputies. But the same secret vote falsifies everything when the bourgeoisie imposes it on the trade unions. It breaks the workers' unity of action, destroys the proletariat as a class, and hides historical reality; we are therefore invited to look for the proletariat in the class struggle and in the democracy of the masses, a democracy which is not obliged to prove itself through a bourgeois-style vote. On 2 June 1952, the proletarians did not follow the party. In his articles Sartre comments that the proletariat was not involved. By definition it was not involved since it is obedience to the party. Let us translate: it is a definition and exists only in Sartre's mind. One might be tempted to see things differently. One could note that the C.P. is sanctioned as a parliamentary party, that it does not perform its functions on the street. One might remember, then, that it gained votes from outside the working class, that for a time it was part of the government, that perhaps its voters are themselves "progressists" rather than revolutionaries, that the essence of its action is no longer the strike, the insurrection, or the revolution, which for the party are now only means in the parliamentary and diplomatic struggle. But this would be to make the party enter history, when it is supposed to make it; it would be to subordinate the party's authority to "probabilistic" discussions. It is better, if one wants certainty, to remain on the terrain of pure action and of the proletariat as idea, which allows neither exaltation nor discouragement, which is always absent and always present, which is the party's thought—or rather Sartre's thought. For the party itself has the weakness (or the cleverness) of providing proofs of its spontaneity: it makes itself responsible for failures and exculpates the masses. This is a language for the initiated, Sartre says to the party, and I understand you at once—it is not your role to put the blame on the masses, but the masses do not judge the party when they do not follow it. Sartre is uncompromisingly rigid when the question concerns the duty of the masses or even of the party. Until now the only point on which he has reproved the party is the communiqué in which the party avowed its failure. Sartre, for his part, "note[s], like everybody else, the discouragement of the masses," but he "still do[es] not know whether the policy of the C.P. bears the responsibility for it" (*RL*, 762; *CP*, 131). How, indeed, could the party move away from the proletariat which it makes? Rather, it is the masses which renounce being the proletariat. Yet here one feels that Sartre would like to take a break. For if the C.P. is not wrong, if the masses as masses can only fall back into dispersion, one does not see too well to whom one should attribute the crisis. To the bourgeoisie, of course—but one cannot ask it to change. To the noncommunist Marxists, who encourage the masses in secession? Certainly. But they are outside history. One is at dead center, there is really nothing to do. Humanism based on need, which does not define a strategy, calls us to an abstract duty, to respect for the C.P. in its essence; but this sympathy, sometimes too demanding, since it does not even accept the C.P.'s retraction, sometimes too docile, since it always approves of the party when it charges forward, is not in any case a collaboration or an action. It is an operation in Sartre's mind that in no way establishes a relation between him and existing communism. Existing communism is in itself Sartrean since it exercises unjustifiable choice. It is Sartrean as a theme, as an object of analysis or of representation; but it can neither live nor acknowledge itself as an unjustifiable choice, and, in this sense, there is no Sartrean communism.

Sartre's attitude—assent in principle to pure action and agreement on particular points—leaves him free with regard to what is essential to communism, that is to say, communist action, the effort that translates pure action into applied action. And for this very reason his attitude permits him only to oscillate between rebellion and forbearance. The agreement on the principle of pure action is situated at the root of history, where the proletariat and the party are only names for the I, the other, and freedom. In short, it does not make the philosopher emerge from his own thought. In truth, politics begins only afterwards, when it is a question of knowing how pure action will be embodied. On this plane the agreement on particular points or even on numerous aspects of communism looks rather like reticence. For it means that pure action does not necessarily lead to all the consequences that communist politics derives from it and that when pure action defines itself as a politics the problem remains completely untouched. Sartre stresses that whatever he said to lay the foundation of communism in principle leaves him entirely free to evaluate the C.P. and communism in what they do. Lefort makes a value judgment on the C.P.; "I am not going to correct you," Sartre says (*RL*, 1622; *CP*, 289). To Lefort he opposes only the impossibility of making a judgment without endangering the existence of the party and the proletariat. In the end he appears to accept this risk, since he admits that "the discussion is open" on the question of exploitation in the Soviet Union (*RL*, 1619; *CP*, 286). His sympathy for numerous aspects of the communist enterprise is a question of common sense and does not carry with it an evaluation of the whole. This he expressly reserves (*RL*, 1615; *CP*, 282). He even has an opinion about some decisions of pure action that the C.P. attempts to impose; for example, he judged the demonstration against Ridgway "inopportune" (*Cp*, 705; *CP*, 67). We are not crushed between the party's authority and the masses' discouragement. Undoubtedly one must get beyond their quarrel, understand the reasons for it, compare the party's politics to the masses' attitude, and find in this analysis a way of joining them once more. This is what Sartre appears to be attempting in his third article, and its tone in some passages is fairly new. It is no longer a tone of urgency or ultimatum but rather one of history. We have seen that history is traversed by the mutually defiant gazes of the bourgeois and the proletarian; but the party's decisions, by the single fact that they are introduced into the life of the class, are relativized. Already in his "Reply to Claude Lefort" Sartre spoke of a dialectic between the masses and the party (*RL*, 1772; *CP*, 236), of a reaction of the masses organized around the apparatus (*RL*, 1600–1601; *CP*, 266), and this would seem to be incompatible with pure action.[53] If the masses do not suppress themselves as masses at the moment when they are organized into the party, if they continue to live in it, if there they are something other than a permanent possibility of annihilation, then their resistance to the apparatus can be something other than a betrayal. This is undoubtedly why the interpretation of the unsuccessful strike of June 4 as a disavowal of the party, at first categorically rejected, is in the end "not completely false" (*RL*, 1623; *CP*, 290). Seen from the angle of pure action, pluralistic unionism was the ruin of the labor movement (*Cp*, 716; *CP*, 79). Considered from a historical perspective, that is to say, as effect as much as cause, it is "in a sense . . . legitimate" (*Cp*, 1819; *CP*, 231). The distinction between politics and economics, first treated as a bourgeois maneuver, receives an acceptable meaning in the second article (*Cp*, 709; *CP*, 71–72); and, using the double-objective strikes, the third article analyzes the expedient that the party invented to reunite what history had thus separated. Like all alleged vices of the C.P., "bureaucracy" was taken in the first articles as one of those modalities of the proletarian movement which do not alter its essence and must be accepted in a realistic spirit. The Trotskyites' theses on bureaucratic society were not taken seriously. Indeed, a certain dosage of bureaucracy was necessary so that the proletariat, which is nothing, could be able to oppose *something* to the bourgeoisie's weighty apparatuses. In the third article, bureaucracy reappears as a trait common to all contemporary societies (*Cp*, 1803; *CP*, 213). Is there, then, a history which the bourgeoisie and the proletariat share and which leaves its mark on both of them? And is one not giving up the struggle when one takes a view that incorporates both oppressor and oppressed? Can one thus without betrayal take a certain distance in order to evaluate the present forms of communist organization? Sartre has given up the point of view of immediacy. The emotion of 1952 recedes. The C.P. continues to exist, and so does its uneasiness. The problems cannot be posed, nor will they be resolved, in haste. There is time. The precept of not being the enemy of the C.P. is not sufficient. There must be an analysis of the present which can go far back and an action that is not short-lived. It is not enough to know that without the C.P. the universe would be bourgeois. One cannot bring the masses back to obedience by this completely formal argument, reduce union pluralism to the bourgeois trick which it was in the immediate situation, conjure away "bureaucracy" and "spontaneity" as twin myths, or disregard the neoproletariat's impotence or compensate for it by an increase of authority. At last one speaks of politics, at last one has emerged from "certainty" and the inner life. But what remains of those massive certitudes with which we began, and how can they be reconciled with a positive politics? What is to be done if the C.P. refuses the concrete perspectives that we will propose to it? In his third article, Sartre insists on the fact of Malthusianism. It is a capitalistic fact, since the bourgeoisie manages our economy. Following the principle that holds a half-choice to be a choice of duplicity, the principle upon which his methodical mythology is based, Sartre presents even Malthusianism and the defense of small businessmen as a plot of the bourgeoisie. The remedy would thus be to destroy the bourgeoisie's power; but the world situation is such that, except in case of war, communism cannot soon take power in France. For the moment, the only efficacious struggle against Malthusianism is that of the neocapitalists. Should one therefore support them? But they may restore a semblance of health to dying capitalism. And, moreover, the defense of small business and trade is an article of communist action in parliament. The C.P. hesitates and the parliamentary group abstains when a government asks special powers to undertake this struggle. If pure action is paralyzed and deliberates, so much the more will this be the case for its sympathizer. In his third article, Sartre avoids the question by incorporating the analyses of Sauvy[54] and others in his indictment of the bourgeoisie. But the means compromise the end. For, in short, if the major crime of today's bourgeoisie is stagnation, and if only its most enlightened faction will, for the foreseeable future, be in a position to struggle against stagnation, is it not best to unite with it? What would the "least-favored" say if he had the right to gaze on these questions? And, since a gaze can grasp only the immediate present, where then is its immediate interest? When one leaves principles or intentions behind and attempts to understand what is happening in France today, one meets the C.P., not as pure action, but as applied action, as action which is also attempting to understand what is happening in France today and to reconcile these local necessities with all the other necessities of communist action. On both these grounds the C.P. can be considered by Sartre only as one political factor among others, and one not meriting particular attention. If, on the contrary, one holds to the party's prerogative in principle, it is useless and risky to enter into the discussion of concrete problems; the only thing to do is wait.

But just as it is distant, sympathy is so near that the sympathizer must be fooled when he is not fooling. He is not in the communist action and does not want communist power as such. He wants, one by one, the results which, for the communist, are stages of this action. He therefore accepts piecemeal what he refuses as a whole. It is sufficient to ask him the questions one at a time—and especially in a negative form: you are not in favor of atomic weapons? You are not, are you? Then you are going to sign this paper, which condemns them. You are not in favor of a few colonists' interests against those of colonial populations? You do not want the world to go up in flames because Laos is invaded? You will not, then, refuse to put your name on this petition against the internationalization of the war. The sympathizer realizes full well that elsewhere these protests have a positive aspect about which he is not consulted. But, as a sympathizer, he has agreed to decide what he does not want; he is only trying to achieve innocence. Questions are put to him the way he asks them himself, and he does have to agree with them. From time to time he find himself alone again: communism—which has a line of action, which does not proceed by single judgments, and which does not have to prove continuously that it is against capitalism—evacuates the positions that the sympathizer had sworn to uphold, leaving him there with his principles. The Vietminh's troops leave Laos; the C.P. proposes to the socialist party the very unity of action which Sartre said the communists should not be asked to initiate. The sympathizer then vaguely suspects that he and the communists are not altogether in the same world. But all the same, he is in order with himself, and, besides, some new protest will soon give him the occasion to link arms with men again. This is how serious politics forces the understanding into a corner. Or rather it is the understanding itself which sets the traps it will fall into, because it does not believe in the dialectic and reduces action to judgments the way Zeno reduced movement to positions, and because it has committed itself in advance to supply an action which is not its own with judgments which that action uses for other ends. Whether he judges for or against is of little importance; the sympathizer is outside action, if action is not a series of fulgurating judgments but the art of organizing the confluence of forces.

We do not mention these varying nuances and alternations of sympathy as signs of contradiction: speculatively speaking, it is not contradictory to respect the C.P. as the negation of bourgeois history and to judge it freely for what it is and for its daily action; the two things even complement each other very well, for they are not of the same order. One deals with a mental object, the C.P. insofar as it expresses the proletariat; the other deals with a historical being, the C.P. which perhaps does not express it. Without inconsistency the same man can maintain both representations, but he cannot follow their consequences in action, and his solution is to contemplate sympathetically. Sympathy is the action of those who are everywhere and nowhere: by their assent in principle they are morally in the party, but they remain outside because they discuss it piecemeal. This is an external opposition, an imaginary action. Criticizing in all solidarity is a formula of action only in the case of a true opposition working within the party and attempting to put its views forward. But the party does not want opposition, which is why the opposition remains outside; and Sartre has explained to us that the party is right. If he thus succeeds in respecting the party while judging it, such a delicate balance is maintained only on the strict condition that he not take part in either its or any other action and that he remain at a speculative distance. When one judges the party from outside and defers to it entirely, one dreams of a constructive opposition that in other respects one realizes is impossible. A dialectical Marxist communism has room for an opposition, but a Sartrean communism tolerates none, not even Sartre's, nor his own "reasons." The same reasons force him to respect the C.P. and force him not to join it.

There is thus no contradiction in Sartre's thought. Only it is a thought, not an action; and there is perhaps not much sense in dealing with communism, which is an action, by means of pure thought. Or, rather, let us say that there are two types of action: action of unveiling and action of governing. What is easy in one order is difficult in the other. The action of unveiling admits of reserves, nuances, omissions, and intermittencies, and it is incomparably easier to give a direction to a newspaper or a work of art than to a party or a government: the paper can endure anything, the readers fewer things, and the militants or the governed still fewer. The action of a party or a government cannot afford to lose contact even momentarily with the event: such action must remain the same and be immediately recognized throughout its different phases, it must comment practically on anything that happens, in each "yes" or "no" it must make the meaning of all the others appear (or, if it has variable principles, it must not change them too often). On the other hand, it is incomparably easier to navigate between communism and anticommunism (England and France did it at Geneva in 1954) than to reconcile in thought respect for and criticism of the party. Neither a government nor the C.P. itself is obligated to have an opinion on the Soviet camps or, if they have one, to state it. The writer and the journalist must declare their position, for they *unveil,* their universe is a canvas upon which nothing exists unless it is represented, analyzed, and judged. The newspaper is the truth of the world; it acts by showing. As a result of this, there arise insoluble problems or illegitimate solutions which are not those of political action. The action of unveiling has its easy times and its torments, which are those of contemplation. They are mandarin problems and solutions. The mandarin myth unites the phantasm of total knowledge with that of pure action. The mandarin is thought to be present by means of his knowledge wherever there is a problem, and capable of acting immediately from a distance, anywhere, as pure efficient cause, as if *what he did* occurred in an inert milieu and was not at the same time theater, a manifestation, an object of scandal or of enthusiasm. The spectator consciousness is too busy seeing to see itself as a "particular" consciousness, and it dreams of an action which also would be ubiquitous. Such is the naïveté and the hoax of narcissism. Knowing everything, the spectator consciousness also knows that certain people want to change the world. Consciousness makes room for them in its universe, comprehends them like everything else, and justifies them in terms of the very thing that challenges it. But it can follow them only in thought; it cannot be one of them and remain itself. And there is nothing surprising if in the end it does not know what to do. The drama is not only that of the writer; it involves every man: it is the drama of a being who *sees* and *does*. Insofar as he sees, he transforms whatever he sees into something seen; he is, one might say, a voyeur, he is everywhere present without distance; even among those who act, he insists on imposing his presence on them while knowing that they reject him. Yet, insofar as man acts, he cannot act without some perspective or refuse a minimum of explanation to those who follow the action. The worlds of vision and action are therefore different, and yet they act as cross-checks. This is why in the C.P., as in Sartre's work, the balance between the demands of seeing and those of doing is always difficult to obtain, and nothing *will remove* the difficulty. Marxism had conceived, not a solution, but a way of passing beyond the problem through the life of the party, which was supposed to take each person where he was situated and offer him a view of the whole, rectifying its perspectives by means of its action and its action by its perspectives. These illusions have been dispelled, and we still have two distinct ways of going to the universal: one, the more direct, consists in putting everything into words, the other consists in entering the game, with its obscurity, and creating there a little bit of truth by sheer audacity. One cannot therefore reproach the writer with a professional defect when he tries to see everything and restricts himself to imaginary action: by doing so he maintains one of the two components of man. But he would be quite mistaken if he thought he could thus glue together the two components and move to political action because he looks at it.

The compromise of being an external communist, of imposing on communism a gaze which comes from outside and which is not hostile, might be said to be the only possible attitude in a time when communism expels those who wish to see. While possible in the noncommunist world, it is not possible in the communist world. For here one must reason in the opposite sense: since communism has expelled its opposition, one therefore cannot be halfway into communism—one can only be in it completely or not at all. The weakness of Sartre's position is that it is a solution for someone who lives in the capitalist world, not for someone who lives in the communist world, although this is what is at issue here. He decrees coexistence between communism and the external opposition, but this has yet to be acknowledged by the C.P. At the very moment when Sartre attaches the greatest importance to the other, since he wants to see the noncommunist world through the eyes of the least-favored, it is still in terms of himself that things are ordered. At the very moment when he affirms only a sympathy of principle for communism, he places himself in the noncommunist world, and he is still not speaking of communism.

External opposition, all right; but he situates himself in such a way that one fears he may give up unveiling without being able to act. Internal opposition is impossible; therefore I carry it outside. But if it is not possible from the inside, it is even less possible from the outside. From the outside it is rivalry, threat. The oppositionist pays for his criticism, and this is why his criticism is an action. The external oppositionist never completely proves that he is faithful from a distance. He will not use the right of criticism that he reserves for himself for fear of abusing it. Because his relationships with the party are of a mental order only, they are broad and intermittent: regardless of what the party does, one can support it when one does not belong; and whatever one says in its favor is, like all things that have been said, to be said again tomorrow. True commitment would be practically the inverse: agreement not on principles but in an action that one is called upon to elaborate; agreement not on particular points but on a line which connects them; relationships, then, simultaneously differentiated and continual. Always present, always absent, the "slippery customer" is the spectator consciousness, and we have to ask ourselves whether commitment as understood by Sartre does not transform the relationships of action into relationships of contemplation: one dreams of touching the things themselves through action; to better get outside oneself, one agrees that it is only a question of preferring one or another of existing things or even that it is only a matter of *choosing* one without there being a preference of man as a whole. But this is actually how one proves that it is only a question of spectacle and of relationships of thought: since communism, for a communist, and in reality, is not just one of the existing things in the world, the U.S.S.R. over there, planning God knows what; and this masked giant is not something we can take or leave—we have to know and to say what we like and what we dislike and why, what we want and do not want from life. Direct contact with the thing itself is a dream. Except in certain instances, in the case of the executioner who chops off a head or the leader who decides on a war or an insurrection, all contacts with history are indirect, all actions are symbolic. The writer would act more surely by accepting this kind of action, which is eminently his, by reporting his preferences, his internal debates with communism, than by bringing to others the austere news of the choice he has made, out of duty, between existing things.

One will still say: all right, it is not a question of choosing the U.S.S.R. but rather of remaining faithful to what you think of capitalism and pursuing the consequences of this position. If capitalism overturns personal relationships by subjugating one class to another, if it even succeeds in depriving the oppressed class of any hold on history, dispersing it through the democratic game, which allows for all opinions but not for the enterprise of recreating humanity and beginning history anew, and if you do not want to become the enemy of the proletariat and of mankind by opposing this enterprise—if, additionally, you hold with Sartre that the dialectic, aside from a few privileged moments, never was anything but a cover for violent action, that the solutions for the communism of hope and for Western Marxism have remained on paper—then what is there to do except to open a credit account (which cannot be precisely measured in advance) to the only party that claims kinship with the proletariat, all the while reserving only your right to inspect the account? In a history which is without reason, in the name of what would you proclaim that the communist enterprise is impossible? This reasoning takes into account only intentions, not what one prefers or chooses; it tells us on what condition we will be irreproachable before the proletariat, at least in the short run, but it does not tell us how our action will liberate the proletariat. Yet it is the liberation of the worker that you are pretending to pursue. If the facts "say neither yes nor no," if the regime the proletariat desires is equivocal, and if, being aware of that and knowing the liabilities of the system, you help the proletariat establish such a regime, it is because you are thinking less of the proletariat than of yourself.

But whether there is a Marxist critique of capitalism which is still valid and which is not a moral judgment—this remains to be seen. The Marxist analysis of capital is indeed presented as "scientific," not as an always subjective perspective on history, and still less as a moral judgment. But because it *gives itself* the perspective of socialist production as the alternative to capitalism, there is thus scarcely any choice to be made, since the socialist future is hypothetically free of shackles, advance deductions, and the contradictions which make capitalism's existence a deferred bankruptcy. Yet now we know well, from the example of Soviet society, that other advance deductions, other shackles, and other contradictions may appear, once those of capitalism are suppressed; consequently, socialist production in Marx's sense once again becomes overtly what it always was: a *constructum* in the economist's mind. The choice is only among several types of social stratification, among several forms of the state. The disgraces of capitalism remain disgraces; they are certainly not erased by the eventual defects of the other system: but the disgraces of both systems are entered on a complex and "probabilistic" balance sheet, and a critique of one of the systems cannot by itself ground one's choice of the other. There is quite a difference between a critique of capitalism which believes it sees in it the last obstacle to the homogeneous society, the last bond before the liberation of true production, and a critique which perceives behind capitalism still other states, other armies, other elites, other police forces—all this constructed, as in capitalism itself, with institutions, myths, social symbols, human initiatives, and compensated errors, with no "natural" preordination. In the first case the critique is almost sufficient, because it is only the inverse of a positive truth. In the second case, it is conclusive only if one resolutely makes up one's mind on the basis of what one refuses and knows, without trying to know what one accepts in exchange. In other words, far from supplying a properly rational basis for the choice, this absolute critique is already the choice of noncapitalism, *whatever it may be.*

The fact is that the "objective" critique of capital hardly enters into Sartre's study. Inside an immediate or moral relationship of persons, he deliberately focuses on those that capitalism ruins, on those of whom we are starkly reminded by the gaze of the least favored. His idea therefore seems to be that, even undetermined and destined to unforeseeable results, the communist enterprise deserves a favorable prejudice because the least-favored demand it and because we are not to be the judges of their best interests. But can one say that they demand it? Sartre himself explains that the least-favored are hardly militant and do not support communist action or any other action. It is he who interprets the curse hurled by the proletariat at bourgeois power; it is he who decides that it is aimed only at bourgeois power and that the suppression of this power, even if it makes way for another oppression, is in any case preferable. To prefer anything to what exists now simply because the proletariat condemns it would be to give oneself a good conscience under the pretext of giving the proletariat its historical chance. This can be very costly to the proletariat and is, moreover, an illusion, for one yields less to the will of the proletariat than to the will one attributes to it. The same reasons which made the proletariat lose its hold on history also make us, for better or for worse, judges of its interests. As soon as we leave the domain of good intentions, we cannot do without an analysis of communism, we cannot rest with negations, we must become acquainted with what we prefer, or in any case choose, *for* the proletariat.

Now if one stops projecting on the U.S.S.R. the light of the classless society and of socialist production in Marx's sense, what one sees is not sufficient to prove that the proletarians' interests lie in this system. One sees industrialization and a higher standard of living, but one also sees the differences in salaries and positions, the personalities of people like Kravchenko,[55] the authoritarian party customs, the uniforms, the decorations, the self-accusation of the leaders, soon expressly contradicted by the power itself, the zigzags of power in the people's democracies, and the alternately opportunistic and suicidal politics of the fraternal parties in the noncommunist world. All of this, which is not open to debate, and which is public knowledge, says as clearly as possible that there is a state apparatus in the U.S.S.R., that it makes concessions on everything except state property and planning, which do not constitute socialism since they are made to support the cost of a managerial group and the lost opportunities caused by rigid leadership. All this does not make the U.S.S.R. an evil, or even an evil for Russia; but it does raise the question whether this is the concern of proletarians of all countries. Sartre says that one must "liquidate merit" and move toward a humanism based on need, the only one which is appropriate for the least-favored. As far as one can judge, it is rather the humanism of work which is the order of the day in the U.S.S.R., and the Soviet people seem to have set themselves the task of forming that working elite for which Sartre shows very little sympathy. Should one say that this is not definitive? But if there is change, it will be because the privileged of the regime will have judged it appropriate to share their privileges, which is good, but not very different from the concessions of a healthy capitalism. Sartre said that, since there is no dialectic, one can maintain the *aura* of revolution for communism such as it is. We would say that, if there is no dialectic, communism must be secularized. Capitalism may indeed be the exploitation of the working class. But if, despite what is professed by the communists, the social is inert in itself, an unpolarized chaos; if there is no historical moment, and even less a durable regime, in which all problems converge toward the power of a class which will suppress itself as a class; if there is only the leaders' authority, the manipulation of the masses, the rigging of congresses, the liquidation of minorities, the masquerading of majorities as unanimity: then how can we prefer this system, of which we know only one thing—that it is not what it pretends to be—and which probably does not know itself? If there is no logic of history, then communism is to be judged piecemeal; and favorable judgments, even on numerous "aspects" of the system, cannot give adherence to the whole as long as the whole is hidden. To secularize communism is to deprive it of the favorable prejudice to which it would be entitled if there were a philosophy of history and, moreover, to give it an even fairer examination, since one does not expect it to bring an end to history. There would undoubtedly be some features to touch up in the outline that we gave earlier, and they will be gladly rectified as the relevant information comes to our attention. It is essential for peace that communism stop being this ghost floating somewhere between transcendental freedom and everyday prose, which attracts both fervent sentiments and warlike dispositions.

If one decides to change the world and to overcome adversities, not together with the proletariat, but by giving it "orders," not by realizing a truth which comes to be in the course of things, but by manufacturing it out of nothing, in short, if one upsets the game in order to begin history again at zero, no one can say exactly what he is doing. The only thing which is sure is that the basis, the pure relationships of persons, will not be found again in things and that yet another state will be manufactured. It may be good, mediocre, or bad; that remains to be seen. But we will see only by placing the "revolutionary" country in common history; we will see nothing if we place ourselves in the perspective of the latest intentions of its leaders. For from then on there is nothing left to *learn*. Leaders change, Stalin's successors repudiate some of his acts. The sympathizer does not consider himself defeated. There was Stalin's action and perspective, there are Malenkov's and his colleagues'. The U.S.S.R., both obscure and too full of meaning, still says neither "yes" nor "no." On the other hand, the sympathizer always says "yes"—to Malenkov as before to Stalin. He is the friend of everyone because he does nothing. One must not tell him that under Stalin history was choked, that there were latent questions and a dynamic of the system which were not given expression. Those are beings of reason. There are men and things; things are mute, and meaning is only found in men. Thus history merges into official history. Those who have lived in the U.S.S.R. know that this is not the case and that Malenkov's or Stalin's action, and even planning itself, are episodes or aspects of an actual functioning of the U.S.S.R. which includes official decisions but also the unofficial cycles of production and of exchange, the makeshift measures of leaders behind schedule on the plan, the unwritten distribution of powers, the questions unformulated but present in opposition, "sabotage," and "espionage." Only God knows this true history, and one cannot judge the U.S.S.R. on the unknowable. But it would be a little bit less unknowable if the proletariat had a political life in the U.S.S.R. Then one could say that, whatever its defects for an absolute observer, the system is everything that a revolutionary dictatorship can humanly be. Without this guarantee, it cannot be judged. One cannot at the same time play both the game of truth and that of "pure" morality. If communism is true, it does not need so much respect; and if it is only respectable, this is because it is chiefly intention. To say, as Sartre does, that it *will* be true is to bet on our power of forgetfulness, on the dizziness of freedom and of the future, and, at the same time, to cover the bet with a veil of reason. But it was already objected to Pascal that an eternity of imaginary happiness could not possibly be the equivalent of a moment of life.

It seems to us, therefore, that one can draw only an agnostic conclusion from his analyses. To adhere in principle to a "pure action" which cannot be translated into facts without equivocation is to throw probabilities overboard in a domain where there is only the probable. Anyone who either closely or remotely associates himself with the communist enterprise for reasons like Sartre's thereby becomes impervious to experience. Agnosticism, on the contrary, is first of all the promise to examine, without fervor and without disparagement, all that one can know about the U.S.S.R. This is an easy promise if one does not keep communism within oneself as a remorse or resource, if one has exorcised the "optimistic twaddle" and can consider communism relatively. Agnosticism, despite the word, is here a positive behavior, a task—as, on the contrary, sympathy is here an abstention. It still remains to be clarified what politics can be deduced from this position. Let us say here only that acommunism (and it alone) obliges us to have a positive politics, to pose and resolve concrete problems instead of living with one eye fixed on the U.S.S.R. and the other on the United States. As to the benefits that communist action can reap from this frank politics, the rule is to face the stratagem of things and to thwart that of men. If the right to strike, political liberties, and the fulfillment of our promises to the colonies risks bringing communism, the risk should be run; for those who want to protect themselves from it have only to organize repression everywhere. On the contrary, men's stratagem—which presents as a politics of peace a politics which would give the U.S.S.R. victory without war, which breaks down the political problem into small problems of conscience and stakes out the path of communist actions with democratic protestations—this stratagem must be rejected, and all the more so if one is for a noncommunist left. The noncommunist left is not a left which fails to speak publicly about communism or one which, together with it, fights its enemies. To deserve its name, it must arrange a ground of coexistence between communism and the rest of the world. Now, this is in fact possible only if it does not adhere to the principle of communism: it is difficult to see why the communist world would grant the noncommunist one the concessions that are necessary from both sides to ground coexistence if those who negotiate with the U.S.S.R. declare in advance that it is in the right. One fears that a sympathetic attitude would prevent precisely those who want peace from working for it. When Sartre writes that "the U.S.S.R. wants peace," one feels uneasy in the same way as when someone gives his conclusions without giving his premises. Sartre surely knows that neither the U.S.S.R. nor the United States, nor any state with a long tradition, has ever chosen between peace and war. Only pacifist leagues and fascist states deal in these abstractions. The U.S.S.R. wants other things as well as peace, and for some time it has not appeared ready to sacrifice any of them for peace. It wanted peace but did not prevent North Korea from invading South Korea. Was this not an internal problem? Those who truly want peace and coexistence cannot dismiss as "internal problems" the communist movements that may go beyond the borders of the communist world. This does not mean that repression is called for. To hold or to surrender is a military alternative; the politics of coexistence is to act in such a way that this alternative does not arise. The noncommunist left is not practicing such a politics when it simply tells us that the U.S.S.R. wants peace. If it "understands" in communism, as the inevitable consequence of the proletarians' situation, what it cannot accept, when, then, can it say "no"? And if it says "no" only on details, by what right does it call itself noncommunist? Because it does not share the communist philosophy? But then the only freedom it retains for itself is the freedom to justify communism with different motives; it again becomes a pretext and a smoke screen. Shall one say that there are more things in communism than in all its philosophy, that there is a radical will to make be those who are nothing, a will which is not bound up with the letter of communism? This is quite certain. But for coexistence on this basis to be something other than a thought the noncommunist left has, it would at least be necessary that communism accept being right in terms of wider principles than its own, admit therefore that there are also reasons for not being communist—and this it has never done. If one wishes it to do so, one must not start by simply telling it that it is right. That is to tempt it on its weak point, which is to believe that it is alone in the world. One must, on the contrary, say that one is not a communist, and why. Coexistence is threatened when one of the partners understands the other without the other understanding him; and any agreement is illusory when one of the parties denies in thought the other's existence.

It happens that the U.S.S.R. seems to have understood all of this. It imposed an armistice in Korea, and it negotiated in Indochina when the Vietminh was near victory. It no longer seems to hold as impossible those buffer zones that Stalinism had suppressed. After all, it is a question of negotiating with America, not with sympathizers. The change probably goes further than one thinks. When Tito is rehabilitated and—who knows—tomorrow perhaps Slansky,[56] *objectively* one abandons the Stalinist principle according to which opposition is treason. Perhaps this is the end of ultrabolshevism.[57] In any case, to stay with the question of peace—and if really the problem is one of the relationship between the *communists and peace*—a noncommunist left should, in matters which depend on it, push communism in the direction indicated instead of proposing a spare-tire philosophy that justifies communism as it is and that, moreover, it cannot want.

Perhaps in the end this is what Sartre will do. This would be a completely new type of sympathizer, not one who acts out of the weakness of thought which prevents one from joining or breaking when one agrees or disagrees on what is essential and which prefers to refuse tacitly what in fact it accepts, or to accept tacitly what in truth it refuses. On the contrary, sympathizing boldly because he understands situations other than his own while remaining irreducibly himself, Sartre certainly does not stand before communism like an unhappy conscience before God; he visits but does not inhabit it, he remains in the universal, and it is rather communism that he transmutes into Sartre. Tomorrow he might invent a real ground of coexistence between noncommunism and communism. This will be true if he exposes himself more, and if he puts into a politics the freedom that he so jealously keeps for himself. A philosopher's temptation is to believe that he has really joined others and has attained the concrete universal when he has given them a meaning in his universe, because for him his universe is being itself. The true universal demands that the others understand the meaning that we give them, and until now the communists have never accepted as true the image that noncommunists have formed of them. But perhaps it is Sartre's idea that they are on the brink of doing it. He writes:

> It has happened over and over again, since the Congress of Tours, that "left-wing" men or groups proclaim their *de facto* agreement with the C.P. while at the same time stressing their differences of principle. And if their collaboration seems desirable to the Party, it accepted this alliance *in spite of* those differences. It seems to me today that the situation has changed, both for the Party and for us, in such a way that the Party must desire such alliances in part *because of* the differences. (*Cp*, 706; *CP*, 68)

Sartre does not mean, of course, that it is useful to the communists to rally noncommunists to serve as a smoke screen for them: this would not create the new situation of which he is speaking. No, this time the communists should seek an agreement with the noncommunists because there really is a politics common to them which not only tolerates differences of principle but demands them. This perhaps announces a reciprocal recognition between communists and noncommunists beyond the equivocations that we have emphasized—and which therefore needed to be emphasized.

One sees that what separates us from Sartre is not the description he gives of communism but rather the conclusions he draws from it. It is true that the divergence is all the more profound because it does not come from the facts but from the way they are taken, from the answer given to them, from the relationships that one establishes between the internal and the external. It is as personal and as general as possible; it is philosophical. When Sartre passed from a philosophy that ignored the problem of the other, because it freed consciousness from any individual inherence,[58] to a philosophy which, on the contrary, makes consciousnesses rivals, because each one is a world for itself and claims to be the only one—or when he passed from conflict between rival freedoms to a relationship of call and response between them—each time his previous views were at the same time preserved and destroyed by a new intuition that they put into contrast: the other was this impossibility that, nonetheless, the "I think" could not challenge; it was this enemy that, nonetheless, freedom fed with its own substance and from which it expected response and confirmation. In going from personal history or literature to history, Sartre does not for the time being believe that he is meeting a new phenomenon which demands new categories. Undoubtedly he thinks that history, like language in his view, does not pose metaphysical questions which are not already present in the problem of the other: it is only a particular case to be thought through by the same means that serve to treat the other. The class "other" is so established a phenomenon that the individual other is always in competition with it. The proletarian class exists only by the pure will of a few, as language exists only as carried by a consciousness which constitutes it. Consciousness manages to make prose a transparent glass, whereas it never reads unambiguously in historical action. What is certainly new in history is that the resolution to bring into being at any cost a society which excludes no one entails a whole mythology, whereas, in prose, consciousness immediately shows itself to be universal. But this particularity of history and politics does not make them another type of being: it is only men's freedom, this time grappling with *things* that thwart it and passing beyond them. Politics and action stand out over and against everything, like appendages or extensions of personal life, and this at the very moment when it is proved that they are something else. We wonder whether action does not have both servitudes and virtues that are of an entirely different order and whether philosophy should not explore them instead of substituting itself for them. We see proof of this in the fact that Sartre does not end up with a theory of action, that he is obliged to divide the roles between a sympathy limited to pure principles and to certain aspects of action, and an action which itself is completely in the in-between. Sympathy has meaning only if others move to action. Is it not their action which is an experiment of history—their action or another, if decidedly one cannot be communist—but assuredly not the relationship of sympathy, which is at times too close, at times too remote, to be political? Is not action made up of relations, supported by categories, and carried on through a relationship with the world that the philosophy of the I and the other does not express?

In truth, the question arose as soon as Sartre presented his conception of commitment, and it has accompanied his entire development of this idea. For, regardless of appearances, it is indeed a development at issue here, and Sartre in his present-day positions is not at all unfaithful to himself. Commitment was at first the determination to show oneself outside as one is inside, to confront behavior with its principle and each behavior with all the others, thus to say everything and to weigh everything anew, to invent a total behavior in response to the whole of the world. *Les Temps modernes* demanded of its founders that they belong to no party or church, because one cannot rethink the whole if one is already bound by a conception of the whole. Commitment was the promise to succeed where the parties had failed; it therefore placed itself outside parties, and a preference or choice in favor of one of them made no sense at a moment when it was a question of recreating principles in contact with facts. Yet something already rendered this program null and void and announced the avatars of commitment: it was the manner in which Sartre understood the relation between action and freedom. Already at that moment he was writing that one is free to commit oneself and that *one commits oneself in order to be free.* The power of acting or not acting must be exercised if it is to be more than just a word, but it remains, in the choice or after the choice, exactly what it was before; and indeed there was choice only in order to attest a power of choosing or not choosing, which, without it, would have remained potential. We never choose something for what it is, but simply to have done it, to construct for ourselves a definable past. We never choose to become or to be this or that, but to have been this or that. We are faced with a situation, we think we examine it and deliberate, but we have already taken a stand, we have acted, we suddenly find ourselves stewards of a certain past. How it becomes ours is what no one understands; it is the fact of freedom. Freedom is thus in every action and in none, never compromised, never lost, never saved, always similar. And certainly the presence of the other strongly obliges us to distinguish between behaviors which liberate others and those which enslave others, to reject the second, to prefer the first, to propagate freedom around us, to embody it. But this second freedom proceeds entirely from the first, the order is irreversible, and the preferences it leads to are always in the end pure choice. All that can be known about history and men, this encyclopedia of situations, this universal inventory that *Les Temps modernes* undertook, could not diminish by an inch the distance between radical and savage freedom and its embodiments in the world, could not establish any measure between it and a given civilization, a given action, or a given historical enterprise. For one commits oneself only to get rid of the world. Freedom is not at *work* there, it makes continual, but only momentary, appearances; and except in fascism, which fights it on all levels, it always recognizes itself in some aspect of a political system, be it on the level of intentions or on that of daily actions, and does not identify itself with any one system, for it has no means of summing up the total or the balance of an enterprise, a good not being able to redeem an evil or join with it in a comprehensive appraisal. One could thus denounce facts of oppression and speak of Blacks, Jews, Soviet camps, Moscow trials, women, and homosexuals; one could live all these situations in one's mind, make oneself personally responsible for them, and show how, in each one, freedom is flouted; but one would not find a political line for freedom, because it is embodied as much, or as little, in the diverse political actions which compete for the world, as much, or as little, in Soviet society as in American society. One can recognize in the principle of communism the most radical affirmation of freedom, for it is the decision to change the world; and one can also find unlimited good will in the heart of the American liberal, even though Puritan wickedness is never far away. This is why *Les Temps modernes* did not refuse the United States world leadership[59] at the very moment when it was attacking segregation and why, at the very moment when it was speaking of Soviet camps, it was preparing to make the U.S.S.R. the proletariat's only hope. One can confront freedom with individual acts or facts but not with regimes or large formations, for it always appears in them at some moments without ever being found in all of them. If "each person is responsible for everything before all others," that is to say, if one must take as one's own, in themselves and as if they were their own ends, each phase of an action, each detail of a regime, then actions and regimes are all alike and are worth nothing, for all of them have shameful secrets.

Commitment organizes for us a confrontation with situations the farthest removed from one another and from ourselves. This is exactly why it is so different from historical and political action, which does move within situations and facts, sacrifices this to obtain that, excuses the details in the name of the whole. As far as regimes and actions are concerned, commitment can only be indifference. If it attempts to become a politics, to invent its own solutions on the terrain of action, to impose its ubiquity, its immediate universal, on political life, it will only disguise as a double "yes" its double "no," proposing to correct democracy by revolution and revolution by democracy. It is then democracy and revolution which refuse to allow themselves to be united. What is to be done then? Should one continue the work of humanist criticism? It is good, indeed indispensable, that along with professional politicians there should be writers who, without mincing words, expose some of the scandals politics always hides, because it wraps them inside a whole. But as the situation becomes more tense and charged, commitment, even if it continues to be exercised according to its principles, becomes something else. Even though *Les Temps modernes* continued to distribute its criticism equitably, circumstances underlined some remarks, conjured away others, and gave the review an involuntary line. The study it published on the Prague trials was ignored, while what it said about the Indochinese war hit home every time. Sartre's essay on *The Communists and Peace* attests to this factual situation: since concrete freedom was not able to invent the solutions put forward there, or since these were not listened to, since circumstances have transformed his independent criticism into a political line and carried humanist commitment onto the terrain of action, Sartre accepts responsibility for a state of things which he neither wanted nor organized. When today he states a preference in principle for the U.S.S.R. and an agreement with the communists on particular points, he seems far from his initial conception of commitment; but it is not so much he that has changed as it is the world, and there is absolutely no inconsistency on his part. It remains true that freedom does not see its own image in any existing regime or political action. From communism it accepts only the internal principle of "changing the world," which is its own formula; and from communist action it accepts only some "aspects" or "particular points." No more today than yesterday is freedom made flesh, nor does it become historical action. Between freedom and what it does, the distance remains the same. Commitment is still the same brief contact with the world, it still does not take charge of it; it renders judgments only about very general principles or about facts and particular aspects of action. Quite simply, one today consents to make, if not a real balance sheet, at least an algebraic sum of these very general or very particular judgments, and one declares that it is more favorable to the U.S.S.R. Sympathy for communism and unity of action with it on certain particular points represent the maximum possible action in a conception of freedom that allows only for sudden interventions into the world for camera shots and flash bulbs. Today, as yesterday, commitment is action at a distance, politics by proxy, a way of putting ourselves right with the world rather than entering it; and, rather than an art of intervention, it is an art of circumscribing, of preventing, intervention. There is thus no change in Sartre in relation to himself, and today, in a different world, he draws new consequences from the same philosophical intuition. For Sartre, as for Descartes, the principle of changing oneself rather than the order of things is an intelligent way of remaining oneself over and against everything. The preference for communism without adherence to it, like yesterday's nonpartisan critique, is an attitude, not an action. Freedom projects its essential negation into communism and is linked to a few of its aspects; but it exempts from scrutiny, neither approving nor blaming communist action taken as a whole, the work which for thirty-five years has been eliciting concrete determinations from its principles. The paradox is only that he makes a contemplative attitude work for the benefit of communist action. We wonder whether, rather than ending up with this semblance of action in order to remain faithful to principles, this would not be, on the contrary, the time to reconsider them; whether, instead of reducing action to the proportions imposed by commitment, it would not be better to reexamine commitment as Sartre understands it; and whether, by so doing, we would not with a single stroke cure action of its paralysis and remove from philosophy its gag.

As first-rate philosophical experience, the development of Sartre's ideas, like any experience, needs to be interpreted. Sartre thinks that the difficulties of his position today come from the course that things have taken and leave his philosophical premises intact. We wonder whether these difficulties are not the uneasiness of a philosophy confronted with a type of relationship to the world—history, action—that it does not want to recognize. For commitment in Sartre's sense is the negation of the link between us and the world that it seems to assert; or rather Sartre tries to make a link out of a negation. When I awake to life, I find I am responsible for a variety of things I did not do but for which I take responsibility by living. In Sartre this *de facto* commitment is always for the worse; the existing world and history never call for anything but my indignation, and commitment in the active sense, which is my response to the original trap, consists then in building myself, in choosing myself, in erasing my congenital compromises, in redeeming them through what I devise as their issue, in beginning myself again, and in again beginning history as well. The very way in which Sartre boorishly approaches communism, not through the history of the undertaking, but by taking it in the present, in this instant, according to the promises or menaces it offers to a consciousness that wants to redeem itself through the future, shows clearly enough that it is not so much a question of knowing where communist action is going, so as either to associate oneself with it or not, as it is of finding a meaning for this action in the Sartrean project. Of course we know that no history contains its entire meaning in itself; it is obscure and too full of meaning as long as I have not put it in perspective. But there are perspectives which take into account all preceding perspectives (particularly those of the actors of the drama), which take them seriously, which attempt to understand them even if it means putting them in their proper place and establishing a hierarchy among them, which owe to this contact with the perspectives of others—with their divergences, with their struggle, and with the sanction that events have brought to these struggles—if not a demonstrative value, at least a certain weight of experience. History itself does not give its meaning to the historian, but it does exclude certain readings into which the reader has obviously put too much of himself and which do not stick closely enough to the text; and it accredits others as probable. For Sartre this probability is the same as nothing. But in rejecting the probable, it is theoretical and practical contact with history that he rejects; he decides to look to history only for the illumination of a drama whose characters—the I and the other—are defined *a priori* by means of reflection. By taking as his own the gaze that the least-favored casts on our society, by his willingness to see himself through these eyes, by extending an open credit of principle to the party and the regime that claim kinship with the least-favored, Sartre seems to have the greatest concern for the other. But Sartre hides his reasons from the other; it is not Sartre that is given to him, it is almost an official personage. The homage rendered to the principle of communism is not only accompanied by all sorts of reservations about the existing regime but is indeed itself a measure of opposition, since what Sartre honors in communism is "pure action," which it cannot be every day. Thus, despite appearances, the other is less accepted than neutralized by a general concession. The *cogito* empties like a container through the gap opened by the other's gaze; but since there is no meaning visible in history, Sartre finds himself caught in no perspective other than his own, a perspective in which he would have to confront himself. For him, to be committed is not to interpret and criticize oneself in contact with history; rather it is to recreate one's own relationship with history as if one were in a position to remake oneself from top to bottom, it is to decide to hold as absolute the meaning one invents for one's personal history and for public history, it is to place oneself deliberately in the imaginary. The operation has no other principle than my independence of consciousness, no other result than its confirmation: for others and for history it substitutes the role I decide to let them play; it justifies in principle, but it also limits and terminates, their intervention in my life. It limits impingements, circumscribes evil, transforms the ravenous outside demands into a pact, concludes with history an accord of unity of action which is actually an accord of nonintervention. From the single fact that it is a question of committing *oneself,* that the prisoner is also his own jailer, it is clear that one will never have other bonds than those one currently gives oneself and that one never *will* be committed. Descartes said that one could not at the same time do and not do something, and this is undoubtedly how Sartre understands commitment: as the minimum of coherence and of perseverance, without which one would have had only an intention, one would have tried nothing, one would have learned nothing about the direction to follow. But in reality Descartes's formula states an endless task: When one begins to act, when will one be able to say that one has finished the endeavor? If it fails, it immediately leads us to another action; and the major proof that Sartre's thesis is not a thesis of action is that it is not susceptible of flat contradiction: the esteem in principle for pure action remains intact no matter what existing communism is like. Commitment is so strictly measured out that one cannot conceive of any circumstance that could validly undo it: it can cease only through weariness. Action is another commitment, both more demanding and more fragile: it obliges one always to bear more than what is promised or owed, and at the same time it is susceptible to failure because it addresses itself to others as they are, to the history we are making and they are making, and because it does not relate to principles and particular points but to an enterprise which we put ourselves into entirely, refusing it nothing, not even our criticism, which is part of the action and which is the proof of our commitment. In order for that kind of commitment to be possible, I must not define my relationships with the outside by contract; I must stop considering my thoughts and the meaning I give to my life as the absolute authority, my criteria and my decisions must be relativized and committed to a trial which, as we have said, can never verify them in a crucial way but which can weaken them. This praxis is just the opposite of pragmatism, for it submits its principles to a continuous critique and tries, if not to be *true,* at least *not* to be *false.* Precisely because it agrees to commit itself to more than what it knows of a party and of history, it allows more to be learned, and its motto could be *Clarum per obscurius.* Choosing according to principles or incontestable details, but without ever seeing where his reticent action leads him, Sartre on the contrary practices *Obscurius per clarum.*

Behind these two commitments there are two meanings of freedom. One is the pure power of doing or not doing, of which Descartes speaks. Remaining the same over the entire course of an action, this power fragments freedom into so many instants, making it a continued creation and reducing it to an indefinite series of acts of positing which holds it at arm's length from annihilation. This type of freedom never becomes what it does. It is never a *doing*—one cannot even see what this word might mean for it. Its action is a magical fiat; and this fiat would not even know what it is applied to if what was to be done were not simultaneously represented as *end*. This freedom that never becomes flesh, never secures anything, and never compromises itself with power is in reality the freedom to judge, which even slaves in chains have. Its equally impalpable "yes" and "no" relate only to things seen. For the power of not doing the things that are done is null at the moment one is doing them, not only, as Descartes believed, because one thereby enters into the external domain where a gesture, a movement, or a word has to either be or not be, but also because this alternative is in force even in ourselves, because what we do occupies our field and renders us, perhaps not incapable of, but unconcerned with, the rest. The pure power of doing or not doing indeed exists, but it is the power of interrupting; and from the fact that defection is always possible, it does not follow that our life needs first to obliterate this "possible" or that it interposes between me who lives and what I live a distance that all actions would arbitrarily have to overcome. With this casing of nothingness, which is simultaneously the separation and the joining of freedom and its acts, both the fiat and the representation of an *end* disappear. Life and history are there for me, in their own mode, neither *ponens* nor *tollens:* they continue and are continued even when they are transformed. My thoughts and the sense I give to my life are always caught in a swarm of meanings which have already established me in a certain position with regard to others and to events at the moment when I attempt to see clearly. And, of course, these infrastructures are not destiny; my life will transform them. But if I have a chance to go beyond them and become something other than this bundle of accidents, it is not by deciding to give my life this or that meaning; rather, it is by attempting simply to live what is offered me, without playing tricks with the logic of the enterprise, without enclosing it beforehand inside the limits of a premeditated meaning. The word "choice" here barely has a meaning, not because our acts are written in our initial situation, but because freedom does not *descend* from a power of choice to specifications which would be only an exercise, because it is not a pure source of projects which open up time toward the future, and because throughout my present, deciphered and understood as well as it can be as it starts becoming what I will be, freedom is diffused. The meaning of my future does not arise by decree; it is the truth of my experience, and I cannot communicate it other than by recounting the history that made me become this truth. How then shall I date my choices? They have innumerable precedents in my life, unless they are hollow decisions; but in that case they are compensations, and therefore they still have roots. The *end* is the imaginary object that I choose. The end is the dialectical unity of the means, Sartre said somewhere; and this would have happily corrected his abuse elsewhere of this notion, if he had not deprived himself, by rejecting dialectical thought, of the right of recourse to an open consciousness.[60] When did a communist start being a communist, and when did a renegade stop being one? Choice, like judgment, is much less a principle than a consequence, a balance sheet, a formulation which intervenes at certain moments of the internal monologue and of action but whose meaning is formed day by day. Whether it is a question of action or even of thought, the fruitful modes of consciousness are those in which the object does not need to be posited, because consciousness inhabits it and is at work in it, because each response the outside gives to the initiatives of consciousness is immediately meaningful for it and gives rise to a new intervention on its part, and because it is in fact what it does, not only in the eyes of others but for itself. When Marx said, "I am not a Marxist," and Kierkegaard more or less said, "I am not a Christian," they meant that action is too present to the person acting to admit the ostentation of a declared choice. The declared choice is nearly the proof that there has been no choice. One certainly finds in Sartre something similar when he writes that freedom is not in the decision, that one's choices are dominated by a fundamental choice which is dateless and which is symbolized by the myth of the intelligible character. But everything takes place as if these thoughts do not intervene when it is a question for Sartre of taking a position in the present: then he returns to the ideology of choice and to "futurism."

Ultimately it is perhaps the notion of consciousness as a pure power of signifying, as a centrifugal movement without opacity or inertia, which casts history and the social outside, into the signified, reducing them to a series of instantaneous views, subordinating doing to seeing, and finally reducing action to "demonstration" or "sympathy"—reducing doing to showing or seeing done [*le faire au faire-voir ou au voir-faire*]. The surest way of finding action is to find it already present in seeing, which is very far from being the simple positing of something meant. A meaning, if it is posited by a consciousness whose whole essence is to know what it does, is necessarily closed. Consciousness leaves no corner of it unexplored. And if, on the contrary, one definitely admits of open, incomplete meanings, the subject must not be pure presence to itself and to the object. But neither at the level of the perceived, nor even at the level of the ideal, are we dealing with closed meanings. A perceived thing is rather a certain *variation* in relation to a norm or to a spatial, temporal, or colored level, it is a certain distortion, a certain "coherent deformation" of the permanent links which unite us to sensorial fields and to a world. And in the same way an idea is a certain excess in our view in regard to the available and closed meanings whose depository is language and their reordination around a virtual focus toward which they point but which they do not circumscribe. If this is so, the thought of thoughts, the *cogito,* the pure appearance of something to someone—and first of all of myself to myself—cannot be taken literally and as the testimony of a being whose whole essence is to know itself, that is to say, of a consciousness. It is always through the thickness of a field of existence that my presentation to myself takes place. The mind is always thinking, not because it is always in the process of constituting ideas but because it is always directly or indirectly tuned in on the world and in cycle with history. Like perceived things, my tasks are presented to me, not as objects or ends, but as reliefs and configurations, that is to say, in the landscape of praxis. And just as, when I bring an object closer or move it further away, when I turn it in my hands, I do not need to relate its appearances to a single scale to understand what I observe, in the same way action inhabits its field so fully that anything that appears there is immediately meaningful for it, without analysis or transposition, and calls for its response. If one takes into account a consciousness thus engaged, which is joined again with itself only across its historical and worldly field, which does not touch itself or coincide with itself but rather is divined and glimpsed in the present experience, of which it is the invisible steward, the relationships between consciousnesses take on a completely new aspect. For if the subject is not the sun from which the world radiates or the demiurge of my pure objects, if its signifying activity is rather the perception of a *difference* between two or several meanings—inconceivable, then, without the dimensions, levels, and perspectives which the world and history establish around me—then its action and all actions are possible only as they follow the course of the world, just as I can change the spectacle of the perceived world only by taking as my observation post one of the places revealed to me by perception. There is perception only because I am part of this world through my body, and I give a meaning to history only because I occupy a certain vantage point in it, because other possible vantage points have already been indicated to me by the historical landscape, and because all these perspectives already depend on a truth in which they would be integrated. At the very heart of my perspective, I realize that my private world is already being used, that there is "behavior" that concerns it, and that the other's place in it is already prepared, because I find other historical situations to be occupiable by me. A consciousness that is truly engaged in a world and a history on which it has a hold but which go beyond it is not insular. Already in the thickness of the sensible and historical fabric it feels other presences moving, just as the group of men who dig a tunnel hear the work of another group coming toward them. Unlike the Sartrean consciousness, it is not visible only for the other: consciousness can see him, at least out of the corner of its eye. Between its perspective and that of the other there is a link and an established way of crossing over, and this for the single reason that each perspective claims to envelop the others. Neither in private nor in public history is the formula of these relationships "either him or me," the alternative of solipsism or pure abnegation, because these relationships are no longer the encounter of two for-itselfs but are the meshing of two experiences which, without ever coinciding, belong to a single world.

The question is to know whether, as Sartre says, there are only *men* and *things* or whether there is also the interworld, which we call history, symbolism, truth-to-be-made. If one sticks to the dichotomy, men, as the place where all meaning arises, are condemned to an incredible tension. Each man, in literature as well as in politics, must assume all that happens instant by instant to all others; he must be immediately universal. If, on the contrary, one acknowledges a mediation of personal relationships through the world of human symbols, it is true that one renounces being instantly justified in the eyes of everyone and holding oneself responsible for all that is done at each moment. But since consciousness cannot in practice maintain its pretension of being God, since it is inevitably led to delegate responsibility—it is one abdication for another, and we prefer the one which leaves consciousness the means of knowing what it is doing. To feel responsible for everything in the eyes of everyone and present to all situations—if this leads to approving an action which, like any action, refuses to acknowledge these principles, then one must confess that one is imprisoned in words. If, on the contrary, one agrees that no action assumes as its own all that happens, that it does not reach the event itself, that all actions, even war, are always symbolic actions and count as much upon the effect they will have as a meaningful gesture and as the mark of an intention as upon the direct results of the event—if one thus renounces "pure action," which is a myth (and a myth of the spectator consciousness), perhaps it is then that one has the best chance of changing the world. We do not say that this margin we give ourselves serves only our personal comfort, by endowing knowledge and literature with a good conscience that pure action refuses them. If truly all action is symbolic, then books are in their fashion actions and deserve to be written in accordance with the standards of the craft, without neglecting in any way the duty of unveiling. If politics is not immediate and total responsibility, if it consists in tracing a line in the obscurity of historical symbolism, then it too is a craft and has its technique. Politics and culture are reunited, not because they are completely congruent or because they both adhere to the event, but because the symbols of each order have echoes, correspondences, and effects of induction in the other. To recognize literature and politics as distinct activities is perhaps finally the only way to be as faithful to action as to literature; and, on the contrary, to propose unity of action to a party when one is a writer is perhaps to testify that one remains in the writer's world: for unity of action has a meaning between parties, each one bringing its own weight and thus maintaining the balance of the common action. But between him who handles signs and him who handles the masses there is no contact that is a political act—there is only a delegation of power from the former to the latter. In order to think otherwise, one must live in a universe where all is meaning, politics as well as literature: one must be a writer. Literature and politics are linked with each other and with the event, but in a different way, like two layers of a single symbolic life or history. And if the conditions of the times are such that this symbolic life is torn apart and one cannot at the same time be both a free writer and a communist, or a communist and an oppositionist, the Marxist dialectic which united these opposites will not be replaced by an exhausting oscillation between them; they will not be reconciled by force. One must then go back, attack obliquely what could not be changed frontally, and look for an action other than communist action.

Notes

1. In his later years Stalin once again took up the thesis of the withering-away of the state.

2. "Les Communistes et la paix" (parts 1, 2, and 3), and "Réponse à Claude Lefort," which appeared as articles in *Les Temps modernes.* ["Les Communistes et la paix," part 1, appeared in vol. 8, no. 81 (July 1952), 150; part 2 appeared in 8, nos. 84–85 (October–November, 1952), 695–763; and part 3 appeared in vol. 9, no. 101 (April 1964), 1731–1819. "Réponse à Claude Lefort" appeared in vol. 8, no. 89 (April 1953), 1571–1629. They were later published in book form—"Les Communistes et la paix" in *Situations,* VI: *Problèmes du marxisme,* 1 (Paris: Gallimard, 1964), 80–384; and "Réponse à Claude Lefort," in *Situations,* VII: *Problèmes du marxisme,* 2 (Paris: Gallimard, 1965), 7–93.

Quotations from these essays in the present volume are taken from the English translation, *The Communists and Peace,* trans. Martha Fletcher, John Kleinschmidt, and Philip Berk (New York: Braziller, 1968). (The book includes both essays.) "Les Communistes et la paix" will be abbreviated as *Cp*; "Résponse à Claude Lefort" will be abbreviated as *RL*. The page numbers cited will refer first to *Les Temps modernes* (*Cp* or *RL*) and then to the English translation (*CP*)—TRANS.

3. In part 2 of *Cp,* Sartre writes, "the purpose of this article is to declare my agreement with the communists on precise and limited subjects" (*Cp,* 706; *CP,* 68). The title of the work indicates that in the beginning he was looking for agreement with them based on the single question of peace. Yet, in order to justify unity of action, Sartre attempts to say as much as one can say in favor of communist politics when one is on the left but is not a communist. This leads him to present it as the only politics possible for a communist party, to concentrate his criticism on the Marxist adversaries of the communist party, and finally to challenge their Marxism. On the terrain of Marxist discussion, this is to take a position. It is true that this is not Sartre's terrain and that he envelops Stalinists and Trotskyites in another philosophy—his own; but even when he stops arbitrating Marxist discussions to speak in his own name, the advantage given to the C.P. is not withdrawn. The C.P. remains grounded in Sartrean philosophy (although, as we will see, this is for reasons which are not its own). Sartre's accord with the party thus goes beyond the "precise and limited subjects" with which it started: " [I] do not hide my sympathies for many aspects of the Communist enterprise" (*RL,* 1615; *CP,* 282); and it is necessary to seek in *The Communists and Peace,* beyond the formulas of unity of action, for an attitude of sympathy.

4. C.G.T. is the abbreviation for the Confédération générale du Travail, which is the French communist trade union and one of France's largest unions.—TRANS.

5. Antoine Pinay was prime minister during the Fourth Republic.—TRANS.

6. In his "A Reply to Claude Lefort," Sartre explains that the worker refuses the wage system, not manual labor. Yet he had written in his first article: "Is there a worker's interest? It seems to me that the interest of the worker is to be no longer a worker" (*Cp,* 27; *CP,* 31). Sartre understands the revolution of existing conditions, of which Marx spoke, almost as a change in professions.

7. Jules Lagneau (1851–94) was a highly influential spiritualist and idealist philosopher known for his method of reflective analysis, which, starting with the "I," moved to universal spirit—TRANS.

8. Also see his posthumous works, *Fragments* and *L'Existence de Dieu.*—TRANS.

9. In part 3 of his study, Sartre describes this as a trait of mass trade unionism (*Cp,* 1812; *CP,* 223). But not a word indicates that no one knows where trade unionism is going on this path or that there is a problem that needs to be posed once again. On the contrary, sarcasm rains on the skilled workers. Does Sartre mean that we must just go along until chaos reigns and then begin everything anew with a system about which we know only that it will be something different? This is, perhaps, his perspective. Or does he mean, as one might believe from reading his third article [part 3], that a renovated capitalism would come out of the impasse, giving at least to the French proletarians the benefits of a type of

production of which until now they knew only the slavery? Sartre "understands" mass trade unionism so well that one does not see to what extent he is actually following it.

10. "They [the workers] give birth to the class when they all obey the orders of the leaders" (*Cp*, 760; *CP*, 128).

11. "Where have I written," he asks, "that the Party is identical to the working class?" (*RL*, 1572; *CP*, 236). When he writes, however, that the party is only the means by which the class is formed, or the string on the bunch of asparagus (RL, 1572; *CP*, 236), he is speaking of the apparatus. On the other hand, the entire party—the apparatus, the militants, and the sympathizers—is identical to the proletariat: "In a word, the Party is the very movement which unites the workers by carrying them along toward the taking of power. How then can you expect the working class to repudiate the C.P.? It is true that the C.P. is nothing outside of the class; but let it disappear, and the working class falls back into dust particles" (*Cp*, 761; *CP*, 130).

12. The masses "judge their leaders when their leaders follow them, but not when they don't follow their leaders" (*Cp*, 752; *CP*, 120).

13. In truth, this concession puts everything back in question because, if the masses are permitted to invoke the teaching of the party against its decisions, its essence against its existence as it is, one passes from the brute urgency which takes one by the throat to an appraisal of the urgency; and from then on, the discussion, previously limited to a contest of activism, will extend to everything. The apparatus will be able to maintain that the offensive is provocation and treason. The premium on activism is no longer in order as soon as one distinguishes strategy from tactics and as soon as the notion of offensive and defensive are relativized. The party, as Sartre conceives it, excludes even this rudiment of dialectic.

14. "Marx saw the necessity of a constant effort of emancipation *which needed to be all the more sustained as the working class saw its condition worsen further*" (*RL*, 1611 [our emphasis]; *CP*, 277).

15. *Cp*, 710; *CP*, 73. In Italy, after the assassination attempt against Togliatti [former Italian Communist Party leader], "the working class manifested its existence by an *act* before the nation, before Europe . . . the barriers explode and the proletariat *shows itself*" [modified].

16. In the neoproletariat phase. But not a word to say that this is a crisis of Marxist politics and a dead-end situation.

17. He who refused to distinguish between the U.S.S.R. and the revolution, the C.P.'s and the proletariat's violence, ends up speaking of a permanent tension between the U.S.S.R. and the fraternal parties, between the party and the proletariat (*RL*, 1616; *CP*, 282–83)—and a tension is not a mediation, but it does mark differences, and it poses a problem. He who refused as bourgeois the distinction between politics and economics now says that they are dissociated in contemporary history and that strikes with dual objectives are the artificial means invented to compensate for this quartering of history (*Cp*, 1778, 1815; *CP*, 189, 227). Thus, equivocalness in the strict sense—the indistinguishability

of contraries—appears as a limiting case, and the problem of dialectical unity is posed.

18. This is said with regard to the relations between the U.S.S.R. and the fraternal parties (*RL*, 1615; *CP*, 282).

19. It is true that Claude Lefort concluded in a previous article that revolutionary leadership poses a problem, and he indicated that a leadership was needed that would not isolate itself from the class, as the party does. But he never said that the class could act without organization or leadership.

20. Lefort wrote: "The proletariat has nothing to do with anything but itself, its own activity, *and the problems posed by its own situation in capitalistic society*" ("Le Marxisme et Sartre," *Les Temps modernes* 8, no. 89 [April 1953], 1555) [italics added]. He thus did not forget the struggle. He said that it begins at the level of production, that this struggle, which is the proletariat's condition, is the ground or ballast of its political action, and that therefore the other cannot, as Sartre says, "at any minute" pulverize the proletariat.

21. In a completely prospective philosophy such as Sartre's, the very formulas which rooted action in the class end up rooting the class in action. When Marx said to the proletariat that "its goal and its historical action are irrevocably and visibly traced out for it in the very circumstances of its life," one might have believed that the proletariat's historical role was already prepared in its existence. Sartre uses this text, but to describe the proletariat organized in a single labor union; the "circumstances of its life" which assign the proletariat a goal are thus those that it has first created in organizing itself (*Cp*, 715–16; *CP*, 78–79).

22. Precisely in *What Is to Be Done?* where he strongly criticized "primitivism," one can read: "Whoever doubts this lags in his consciousness behind the spontaneous awakening of the masses" (V. I. Lenin, *Collected Works*, vol. 5 [Moscow, 1961], 430); "the wave of spontaneous indignation, as it were, is sweeping over us, leaders and organizers of the movement" (441); "we were right in our opinion that the principal cause of the present crisis in the Russian Social Democracy is *the lag of the leaders* ('ideologists,' revolutionaries, Social Democrats) behind *the spontaneous upsurge of the masses*" (446); "the revolutionary movement is rapidly and spontaneously growing" (476); "[for] a circle of leaders . . . is capable of coping with political tasks in the genuine and most practical sense of the term, for the reason and to the extent that their impassioned propaganda meets with response among the spontaneously awakening masses, and their sparkling energy is answered and supported by the energy of the revolutionary class. Plekhanov was profoundly right, not only in pointing to this revolutionary class and proving that its spontaneous awakening was inevitable, but in setting even 'the workers' circles' a great and lofty political task" (447). The organization is thus at one and the same time made to amplify a spontaneity which is already political and to render political thought and action "natural" for the proletariat. Sartre, on the contrary, takes for granted that "the very essence of the masses forbids them from thinking and acting politically" (*Cp*, 1815; *CP*, 226).

23. Lenin, *Collected Works*, vol. 5, 394.

24. Sartre says that democratic centralism means permanent mobilization.

But one joins one's military unit under pain of death, and, at least in this regard, no mobilization is democratic. For Lenin "democritism" was impossible under an autocratic regime and in a clandestine party. But the elective principle "goes without saying in countries where there is political freedom." A completely straightfaced picture of the democratic control of the German Social Democratic Party follows. One will see that it is not a question of a formality: "Everyone knows that a certain political figure began in such and such a way, passed through such and such an evolution, behaved in a trying moment in such and such a manner, and possesses such and such qualities; consequently, *all* party members, knowing all the facts, can elect or refuse to elect this person to a particular party office. The general control (in the literal sense of the term) exercised over every act of a party man in the political field brings into existence an automatically operating mechanism which produces what in biology is called the 'survival of the fittest' " (Lenin, *Collected Works,* vol. 5, 478). Here is biology again, Sartre will say, and the fruit-proletariat. Not biology, but history, and the historical mission of the proletariat.

25. Lenin, *Collected Works* (1966), vol. 31, 74.

26. A character in Paul Claudel's play *L'Otage* (*The Hostage*).—TRANS.

27. *Manifesto of the Communist Party* (Moscow, 1952), 38.

28. Ibid., 61.

29. The Marxists had a word (which is no longer used except ritually) for designating the line which takes into account the objective situation as well as the spontaneous reactions. It was the accurate line, not the arbitrary one, not exactly *true,* as if the question were to copy an already-made history, but accurate—that is to say, at one and the same time efficacious and proletarian.

30. To this effect Sartre quotes a sentence of ours which places definitive judgment of each decision at the end of history. What appears to us to be outside the accurate line might, within the whole, appear indispensable. For our part, we immediately added: "But the resort to a judgment based on the future is indistinguishable from the theological appeal to the Last Judgment, unless it is simply a reversal of *pro* and *contra,* unless the future is in some sense outlined in the present, and unless hope is not simply faith and we know where we are going" (Merleau-Ponty, *Humanisme et Terreur* [Paris, 1948], 153–54; *Humanism and Terror,* trans. John O'Neill [Boston, 1969], 142–43), and this brought back the necessity of a comprehensible line. The recourse to a universal history that one imagines accomplished is pragmatism and nominalism in disguise. If we imagine ourselves to be spectators of a completed history, which, therefore, is the picture of all that humanity *will have been,* one can indeed say that we have before our eyes *all that was possible.* Hypothetically, the picture is complete; it is the picture of humanity; any other "possibility" we might like to imagine is out of the question, just as the particularities of a different species show nothing about those of a living species. But human possibility intermingles in this way with man's effective history only for a judge who, by hypothesis, is placed outside humanity and who is making its balance sheet—that is to say, for an absolute mind contemplating a dead humanity. No one who writes or makes history is in this position: they all

have a past and a future, that is to say, they *continue*. For them, therefore, nothing that has been is completely in the past; they relive as their own the history they recount or to which they give a sequel, and they evoke at decisive moments in the past other decisions which would have had a different sequel. There is history only for a historical subject. A universal, completed, and externally contemplated history makes no sense, nor does the reference to this definitive balance sheet or the hypothesis of a rigorous necessity in which, by hindsight, our decisions would solemnly be cloaked. "The only possible decision" means and will always mean only one thing: the decision that, in a field of action opening onto the future, and with the uncertainties which that implies, orients things within the realm of the probable in a direction desired by us and permitted by them. Universal history never is and never will be the total of what humanity has been. It will always be in process; it will be what humanity has been *plus* what it wanted and still wants through the one who speaks of it. There is, therefore, a play on words in saying that in universal history reality is all possibilities. It would be more precise to say that there is no universal history, if by that one means a completely real and accomplished history, because the historical reality of which we can speak has meaning only for a man who is situated in it and wants to go beyond it and therefore has meaning only within a framework of possibilities. We evoked the dream of an absolute justification of what is because it is, and the attitude "You are historically wrong since I liquidate you," only as traits of historical terror. We then showed that, precisely if the future is to be made, not to be contemplated, Marxism has no transcendent view at its disposal to justify its action and that, therefore, terror must open onto a "humanistic perspective" and revolutionary action must announce this future by certain unchallengeable signs in order that one may speak of a Marxist and revolutionary politics. It is just this confrontation of terror with a humanistic perspective that until now has been lacking in Sartre's studies. An immediate desire to change the world, resting on no historical buildup and including neither strategy nor tactics, is, in history, sentimentalism and vertigo of "doing" [*la loi du coeur et le vertige du "faire"*]. Sartre notes that Marxism has always admitted the dialectical necessity of the whole and the contingency of everyday history. From this he deduces that the militant, but not the theoretician, has the right to evoke diverse possibilities. "The theoretician can claim to provide us with an indubitable truth, on the condition that he confine himself to what is and does not concern himself with what *might have* been" (*Cp*, 741; *CP*, 107). Is it granting Marx too much to suppose that he never admitted this dualism of theory and practice, that he believed in a practical value of theory and a theoretical value of practice? And that, therefore, instead of opposing the dialectical necessity of the whole and the contingency of the details, it would be better to see whether there is truly a *necessity* in Marxism, whether the dialectic does not in its very definition include contingency? This is not the way Sartre reads Marx: he maintains the dichotomy of radical contingency and mythical rationality from which one easily arrives at Sartre's own conceptions. All that is necessary is to consciously recognize the myth as a myth.

31. Concerning the neoproletarian he writes: "True, he still believes in the

Revolution, but he only believes in it; it is no longer his daily task" (*Cp*, 1718; *CP*, 185).

32. *Cp*, 1819; *CP*, 231. He remarks, however, that certain professional workers revolt against "mass democracy" and yet agree with the C.G.T. on objectives and tactics. Must we say that they are "reformists" or "revolutionaries"? And is it not proof that these two common notions no longer enable us to understand today's history?

33. We have already quoted the text: "He, precisely, needs to believe that there is a truth. Since he cannot work it out alone, he must be able to trust his class leaders profoundly enough to believe he is getting the truth from them. In short, at the first opportunity, he will chuck these freedoms which strangle him" (*Cp*, 758; *CP*, 127).

34. "Need is only a lack: it can be the foundation of a humanism, but not of a strategy" (*Cp*, 1815; *CP*, 225).

35. The strike which includes occupying factories "in a socialist society no longer has a *raison d'être*" (*Cp*, 44; *CP*, 50).

36. We have attempted to indicate this decline of self-criticism (Merleau-Ponty, "Lukács et l'autocritique," *Les Temps modernes*, no. 50 [December 1949], 1119–21; [see also Merleau-Ponty, *Signes* (Paris, 1960), 328–30; *Signs*, trans. R. McCleary (Evanston, 1964), 261–64—TRANS.]) and to show how a dialectical process becomes its own opposite when a "pure" authority is put in charge of administering it. Lukács thought that the proletariat is self-critical because it is its own suppression as a class. The proletariat's power is, or will be, a power which is self-critical. He profoundly justifies self-criticism as the true faithfulness to self which is that of a life which makes attempts, corrects itself, and progresses as it goes. But what happens when, instead of wandering through the social body, negation and criticism are concentrated in power? When there are functionaries of negativity? What happens is that the criticism is only nominally self-criticism; the functionaries give to the person in question the task of pronouncing the very sentence which they were passing on him and, in the name of negation, organize for themselves the most positive power on earth. It cannot be stressed strongly enough that in Marxism's classical period the oppositionist was bound by the majority's decision but was justified in keeping his theses if he believed them to be right while waiting for the lesson of events to force their acceptance, with the single condition that he not use them as the emblem of a party within the party. It was a first sign of decadence to have erected it as a principle that the oppositionist should be broken, that is to say, forced to disavow his theses and charged with carrying out the decisions of which he disapproved. A second sign was the affirmation that true self-criticism is self-accusation and that the militant should dishonor the man he once was.

37. The paradox is only apparent, since it is necessary to have another background—the transparency of consciousness—in order to see the root, the viscous, or history in their obscene evidence. Husserl, who gave the first descriptions of embodiment and its paradoxes, offers another example of it, all the while continuing to place the philosophizing subject beyond their grasp as the one

who constitutes them or, at least, reconstitutes them. He acknowledged only that there was an enigma there: In what conceivable sense can one say, he wrote, that a philosopher's thoughts move with him when he travels? It was only at the end of his career that he propounded as primordial fact that the constituting subject is inserted within the temporal flow (what he called *sich einströmen*); that it is even his permanent condition; that consequently, when he withdraws from things in order to reconstitute them, he does not find a universe of ready-made meanings, rather he constructs; and that, finally, there is a *genesis of sense.* This time the paradox and the dualism of description and reflection were transcended. And it is toward the same result that Sartre turns. For him also, consciousness, which is constitution, does not find a system of already-present meanings in what it constitutes; it constructs or creates. The difference—and it is immense—is that Husserl sees even in this praxis an ultimate problem: even though consciousness constructs, it is conscious of making explicit something true anterior to itself, it continues a movement begun in experience, "It is voiceless experience, which must be brought to the pure expression of its own meaning." Thence the "teleology" (in quotation marks) of consciousness, which led Husserl to the threshold of dialectical philosophy, and of which Sartre does not want to hear: there are men and things, and there is nothing between them except cinders of consciousness. There is no other truth than the truth of consciousness, and *doing* is absolute rootless initiative.

38. *Cp,* 739; *CP,* 103. He has against them this argument, which is not absolutely decisive: "We know the stock answers" (*RL,* 1599; *CP,* 265).

39. Jean-Paul Sartre, *L'Imaginaire* (Paris, 1940); English translation by Bernard Frechtman (New York, 1948).

40. "Is it . . . irrationalism? Not at all. Everything *will be* clear, rational" (RL, 1588; *CP,* 253).

41. *RL,* 1608; *CP,* 272. And also: "If one wanted to expose the shameful finalism which is hidden under all dialectic" (*RL,* 1575; *CP,* 239). Sartre does not even seem to admit that at the level of the organism there is a problem of organicism or that, no matter how they may finally be grounded, meanings are operating before they are known. He speaks of Goldstein with an irritation which applies also to the *Critique of Judgment,* the idea of an agreement between understanding and its object, strangely prepared in the object itself.

42. Indeed, of literature he says spitefully that it is an "unveiling action, a strange action."

43. For once, Sartre here speaks in terms of the probable and the improbable. The Soviet leaders no longer believe in the Russian revolution? "It goes without saying that, even if this were true, which I strongly *doubt,* to prove it *would not be possible* today" (*Cp,* 10; *CP,* 13). But this is because here the probable is only a polite form of the *a priori,* an *a priori* which becomes shy around facts.

44. One will remark that Sartre says much about the working class, very little about communism or revolution, and nothing about Soviet society. He even gives as an argument in favor of communism our ignorance of the internal life of the U.S.S.R., whose side he readily takes. For him, the question does not lie there.

One can forever discuss the nature of Soviet society, the right and left opposition, Bolshevism and revolution as a social fact. None of this is decisive. What is decisive is the fundamental choice which lies behind these appearances. As for the rest, he says tranquilly, "the discussion is open." For him, communism is not something one makes or lives; rather, it is a human posture with which one "sympathizes."

45. Jacques Duclos: French politician born in 1896, communist party leader in the French National Assembly.—TRANS.

46. Here is the text:

> What has been called "charismatic power" proves well enough that the concrete unity of the group is *projective,* that is to say, that the unity is necessarily exterior to the group. The diffuse sovereignty assembles and is condensed in the person of the leader who subsequently reflects it to each one of the members; and each one, to the very extent that he obeys, finds himself, *vis-à-vis* others and outsiders, the repository of total sovereignty. If there is a leader, each one is leader in the name of the leader. Thus the "collective consciousness" is necessarily incarnated: it is for each one the collective dimension which he grasps in the individual consciousness of the other" (*Cp,* 1812 n.; *CP,* 223 n.).

47. *Terrorism and Communism: A Reply to Karl Kautsky* (Ann Arbor, 1961), 60. [Merleau-Ponty's italics.—TRANS.]

48. Jean-Paul Sartre, *Qu'est-ce que la littérature?* (Paris, 1948); English translation by Bernard Frechtman, *What Is Literature?* (New York, 1949).

49. The French is "*jeunes patrons,*" which might be more fully translated as "young owner-directors of medium- to small-sized businesses." In France there is a semipolitical liberal group that goes under the name Jeunes Patrons.—TRANS.

50. An important editor of *Les Temps modernes.*—TRANS.

51. *Les Temps modernes* (August 1952); 378. Despite the "we," I have never agreed with this text. [For years Merleau-Ponty wrote most of the political editorials for *Les Temps modernes,* was himself a cofounder and editor, and largely decided on the political writings of the review.—TRANS.]

52. The Marxist meaning of the word "progressism" or "progressist" is unequivocal: the progressist is he who in his field and without a full political consciousness thinks and acts in a way which helps the proletarian revolution. The idea of a "progressist party," that is to say, organized unconsciousness, is a humorous creation of the recent phase.

53. Sartre indeed said that pure action is an ideal and that the real party and the labor movement are a mixture of action and passion: "I do not think that one can interpret the present situation except as an inextricable mixture of action and passion in which passion temporarily dominates" (*RL,* 1623; *CP,* 290). But how is one to understand this mixture of fire and water? How is one to add up action and passion, when Sartre says that communist action is either pure or nothing? To speak of a mixture amounts to admitting that in periods of stagnation the political and social facts belong to neither the order of things nor the order of meanings. The reader suddenly wonders whether both "pure" action and pure passion might not be precisely ideologies or phantasms of historical stagnation

and whether, to get out of this, it is not necessary to return, moving beyond the crisis which has disassociated them, to the proletariat's hold on history.

54. The reference is to Alfred Sauvy, professor of social demography at the Collège de France. He wrote widely on population problems.—TRANS.

55. V. A. Kravchenko, author of the book *I Chose Freedom,* which revealed the existence of Soviet labor camps to the French left. The trial for defamation against the communist paper *Les Lettres françaises* was one of the more sensational issues in that period.—TRANS.

56. Rudolf Slansky, Czech politician, member of the communist guerilla resistance during World War II, later vice-premier of Czechoslovakia. Executed for treason in 1951 and "rehabilitated" in 1963.—TRANS.

57. The changes that have recently taken place in the Soviet government do not exclude this hypothesis. While they may put an end to the politics of *détente* which followed Stalin's death, they cannot restore the equivocal character of ultrabolshevism, of which Stalin was more than the emblem: he was its historical bearer. As we have said, ultrabolshevism exists only as dialectic in disguise. It could thus come apart either through the "liberalization" of the regime, which stressed pragmatism in the Stalinist period, or by evolving toward a "hard" regime without Marxist principles.

58. This philosophy was expressed in the article "La Transcendance de l'ego," *Recherches philosophiques* 6 (1936–37), 85–123.

59. Nos. 11–12, 244. [The word "leadership" is in English in the original text.—TRANS.]

60. It is a misunderstanding to believe that for Sartre transcendence opens up consciousness. One might say that, for him, consciousness is nothing but an opening, since there is no opacity in it to hold it at a distance from things and since it meets them perfectly where they are, outside. But this is exactly why it does not open *onto* the world, which goes beyond its capacity of meaning; it is exactly coextensive with the world.

23

Merleau-Ponty and Pseudo-Sartreanism

Simone de Beauvoir

Translated by Veronique Zaytzeff

When Merleau-Ponty discovered in the light of the Korean War that up until then he had confused Marx and Kant, he realized that he had to give up the Hegelian idea of the end of history and decided on the need to liquidate the Marxist dialectic. I do not intend to examine here the value of the logical process which slowly developed in conjunction with events, and led him to write *Adventures of the Dialectic.* But Merleau-Ponty involves Sartre in his own endeavor. He claims to find in *The Communists and Peace* an acknowledgment of the failure of dialectic; he criticizes Sartre for not having drawn the necessary conclusions and ascribes this failure to the "madness of the *cogito*" which allegedly defines Sartrean ontology. Sartre has so often been criticized without being read or at least, without being understood, that the very excess of errors committed in his regard usually deprives such errors of any importance. Merleau-Ponty, however, enjoys a certain philosophical prestige; he has known Sartre long enough that the public imagines that he knows his thought as well. Recently he has so forcefully exhorted his adversaries "to learn how to read" that one can presume that he knows how to interpret a text without prejudice and how to quote it without omission. Under these conditions, his travesty becomes a breach of confidence, and it must be denounced.

Sartre wrote *The Communists and Peace* in specific circumstances with a specific purpose;[1] Merleau-Ponty decides to look through it for a comprehensive and definite philosophy of history. He fails to find one there. Instead of admitting that Sartre did not include one, he calls Sartre's deliberate silences concealments, and in light of the Sartrean ontology proceeds to reconstruct what Sartre must think. He admits that when Sartre moved from one period in his philosophy to the next "each time his previous views were at the same time preserved and destroyed by a new intuition (*Ad,* 253; *AD,* 188; above 427). How do we *deduce* this *intuition* from Sartre's system? Merleau-Ponty's method, to say the least, is bold. But what is even more serious is that the philosophy to which our exegete refers contradicts on almost all points what Sartre has always professed. Since all Merleau-Ponty's interpretations presuppose the existence of this pseudo-Sartreanism—which he explicitly exposes only at the end of his study—I shall begin by showing the distance which separates his pseudo-Sartreanism from the authentic Sartrean ontology. Even a layperson will easily realize the enormity of the falsification.

I

Pseudo-Sartreanism is a philosophy of the subject; the subject merges with consciousness which is pure translucence and is coextensive with the world; its transparency is opposed to the opacity of the being-in-itself which possesses no signification [*signification*]; meaning [*sens*] is imposed on things by a decree of consciousness which is motivated *ex nihilo.* The existence of the other does not break this *tête-à-tête* since the other never appears except under the figure of another subject. The relationship between the I [*Je*] and the other is reduced to the look; each subject lives alone at the heart of that subject's own universe, a universe of which that subject is the sole sovereign: there is no interworld.

Sartre's philosophy has never been a philosophy of the subject, and he seldom uses this word by which Merleau-Ponty indiscriminately designates consciousness, the Ego [*Moi*], and humanity. For Sartre, consciousness's pure presence to self is not a subject: "It is as the Ego that we are subjects" (*EN,* 209; *BN,* 138); and "the Ego appears to consciousness as a transcendent in-itself" (*EN,* 147; *BN,* 79). On this basis Sartre has built his entire theory of the psychical field: "We, on the contrary, have shown that the self on principle cannot inhabit consciousness" (*EN,* 148; *BN,* 79). The psyche and the Ego which is its pole, are construed by consciousness as objects. Merleau-Ponty has so forgotten this fundamental thesis that he asserts Sartre used to say that there is no difference between imaginary love and true love because the subject is by definition what he thinks he is (*Ad,* 178; *AD,* 132; above 383).

His reconstructionist delirium leads him to contradict word for word the author he claims to interpret, for Sartre has developed at length in *The Psychology of Imagination* the concept that one must "distinguish between two irreducible classes of feelings: real feelings and imaginary feelings." "The real feelings and the imaginary cannot coexist by their very nature. It is a matter of two types of objects of feelings and of actions that are completely irreducible."[2]

By applying to love—the psychic object what Sartre used to say about pleasure—the immanent *Erlebnis*—Merleau-Ponty shows that he confuses consciousness, immediate presence to self, with the subject whose unveiling requires mediation. Thus, when he objects to the pseudo-Sartre: "It is always through the thickness of a field of existence that my presentation to myself takes place" (*Ad,* 268; *AD,* 199; above 436), he only repeats one of the leading ideas of *Being and Nothingness.* Faithful on this point to the Heideggerian thesis that human reality announces what it is based on the world, Sartre has always insisted on the reciprocal conditioning of the world and that of Ego [*Moi*]: "Without the world, there is no selfness, no person; without the person, there is no world" [*EN,* 149; *BN,* 80]. "The pure for-itself is itself down there, beyond its grasp, in the far reaches of its possibilities" (*EN,* 148; *BN,* 79–80). This is what Sartre calls the "circuit of selfness," and this idea is radically opposed to the one that Merleau-Ponty attributes to him when he remonstrates, with an uncalled for appeal to common sense: "The subject is not the sun from which the world radiates or, the demiurge of my pure objects" (*Ad,* 268; *AD,* 199; above 436).

If the subject creates the world by shedding light on it, the latter could not, of course, surpass the consciousness I have of it. "It is a misunderstanding," writes Merleau-Ponty, "to believe that for Sartre transcendence opens up consciousness. . . . It does not open *onto* a world, which goes beyond its capacity of meaning; it is exactly *coextensive with the world*" (*Ad,* 266 n.; *AD,* 197 n.; above 477, note 60).

What Merleau-Ponty simply fails to grasp here is the theory of *facticity,* one of the foundations of Sartrean ontology. My consciousness can only go beyond the world by engaging itself in it, that is by condemning itself to grasp the world in a univocal and finite perspective, and therefore to be perpetually overwhelmed by it: this is why there can be only an embodied consciousness. "We must be careful to remember that the world exists confronting consciousness as an indefinite multiplicity of reciprocal relations which consciousness surveys without perspective," writes Sartre [*EN,* 368; *BN,* 282]. "Thus by the mere fact that there is a world this world cannot exist without a univocal orientation in relation to me. I must *lose myself* in the world for the world to exist and for me to be able to transcend it. To surpass the world is precisely not to survey it but to be engaged in it in order to emerge from it; it is always necessary that a *particular* perspective of surpassing be effected. In this sense *finitude* is the necessary condition of the original project of the for-itself" (*EN,* 368ff.; *BN,* 283ff.). The body expresses "the necessity that there be a choice, that I do not exist all at once" [*EN,* 396; *BN,* 304]. Throughout his entire work, from *Nausea* to *Saint Genet,* Sartre devotes himself to describing the passion of the embodied consciousness; he has always portrayed man as overtaken by "the threatening and sumptuous opacity" (*Sits.* II, 254) of the world. How can one, then, without bad faith, define Sartrean consciousness as being *coextensive with the world,* when consciousness unveils the world through the unique condition of losing *itself* in the world?

This is not an inconsequential mistake. Merleau-Ponty's entire argument rests on the following thesis: for Sartre, signification is reduced to the consciousness that a subject has of it. But "for Sartre conscious awareness is an absolute. It *gives* meaning [*sens*]" (*Ad,* 168; *AD,* 115; above 370). Sartre's philosophy "is a philosophy in which meaning, seen as wholly *spiritual,* as impalpable as lightning, is absolutely opposed to being, which is absolute weight and absolute blindness" (*Ad,* 168; *AD,* 124; above 377).

It would suffice to skim through just one of Sartre's books to be dumb-struck with astonishment in the face of such assertions. Sartre never denied the principles which rule existential psychoanalysis. Quite the contrary, he deepened and developed them by applying them to various fields. For the task that Sartre assigns to existential psychoanalysis is "to explain the meaning which really belongs to things. The meaning of matter, the human sense, needles, snow, grained wood, of crowded, of greasy, etc. are as real as the world, neither more nor less, and to come into the world means to become familiar with these meanings [*significations*] (*EN,* 691; *EP,* 177). The secret meaning of snow is "an ontological meaning [*sens*]" and in order to decipher it one has "to compare strictly objective structures" (*EN,* 692; *EP,* 120).

Sartre, says Merleau-Ponty, "always moves from open and uncompleted meanings [*significations*] to the pure model of a *closed* meaning, such as it offers itself to lucid consciousness" (*Ad,* 193; *AD,* 144; above 390). But Sartre has written: "By meaning [*sens*] I denote the participation of the being of a present reality in the being of other realities, whether present or absent, visible or invisible, and eventually, in *the universe*" (*SG,* 283; *SGE,* 304). Therefore, far from being given by consciousness and closed, significations are real, objective, and opened *ad infinitum* into the universe.

The falsification here is so glaring that Merleau-Ponty himself takes note of it. He could not be unaware that Sartre's work presents a world in which every consciousness is engaged in things, a world in which all things bear a human meaning. Awakening for an instant from his delirium, the author recognizes that Sartre's work made him "famous by describing a middle ground as heavy as things and fascinating for consciousness, between consciousness and things—the root in *Nausea,* viscosity or situation in *Being and Nothingness,* here the social world" (*Ad,* 185; *AD,* 137; above 385). It would seem natural in explaining an author to take into account the author's work. Our exegete, however, disregards it due to a method which we see him use again and again and which I shall call "the ruse of paradox" [*le coup da paradoxe*]. Sartre's paradox is that he does not think what he thinks. Sartre's thought "is in revolt against this middle ground" (*Ad,* 185; *AD,* 137; above 385]. Merleau-Ponty equivocates with regard to the word "revolt," for he defines it as a will to transcend and implicitly makes it a radical negation. Against *Nausea, Being and Nothingness,* against everything Sartre has written, he maintains that Sartre's philosophy acknowledges nothing between the subject and being-in-itself.

To support this thesis, Merleau-Ponty makes use of another method, which is also typical of him, and which I shall call "the ruse of oversignification" [*le coup de la sursignification*]. He takes a sentence out of context, which by itself is nothing but a trite commonplace, assigns it a singular meaning and makes that a key to Sartre's thought. In a passage where Sartre challenges the myth of the fetish of the proletariat, of an entity, he writes "There are men, animals, and things" [*Cp,* 197; *CP,* 82]. This simply means that Sartre situated the debate on earth, in this world. Since he has explained himself frequently enough on the relationship of men and things, there is no need to treat that here. Merleau-Ponty chooses to understand: "Men and things are radically separated between the two of them there is nothing." Thanks to this short sentence, arbitrarily interpreted, Merleau-Ponty allows himself to throw overboard all Sartre's writings and to invent, as he pleases, "pseudo-Sartreanism."

The consequences of this travesty are of utmost importance; what will result is a philosophy of history with political conceptions radically opposed depending on whether the subject is enclosed in its subjectivity or deciphers in the world of objective meanings. Summarizing the debate he initiated, Merleau-Ponty writes: "The question is to know whether, *as Sartre says,* there are only men and things or whether there is also the interworld, which we call history, symbolism, truth-to-be-made" (*Ad,* 269; *AD,* 200; above 437). When he writes that in Sartre, "Consciousness which is constitution, does not find a system of already-present meanings in what it constitutes: it constructs or creates" (*Ad,* 186 n.; above 444–45; *AD,* 138 n. 37), he means to ban the idea of an interworld from Sartre's philosophy. Therefore, it must be emphasized that Sartre explicitly repudiates this theory of a creative consciousness: "In *my* world there exist objective meanings [*significations*] which are immediately given to me as *not having been brought to light by me.* I, by whom meanings come to things, I find myself engaged in an already meaningful world which reflects to me meanings which I have not put into it" (*EN,* 592; *BN,* 486).

To recall the existence of an objective meaning of things in Sartre is really belaboring the obvious; for example, one can reread *Saint Genet.* There one will see how Genet the child emerges in a world filled with meanings which impose themselves on him. Nevertheless, Merleau-Ponty unflaggingly repeats that for Sartre "things are mute and the meaning lies only within men" (*Ad,* 247; *AD,* 184; above 423). "*Wills* do not continue living a decadent or fertile life in the things they mark" [*Ad,* 198; *AD,* 147; above 392]. Now here are two texts of Sartre's among many others: "The industrial products that make up the urban landscape are the social will bottled and canned; they speak to us of our integration in society; men address us through the silence of these products, etc." (*SG,* 241; *SGE,* 257). "We rule the environment by work, but the environment dominates us in turn by the rigified swarm of thoughts we have inscribed there" (*RL,* 58; *CP,* 271).

We feel like smiling here when we see Merleau-Ponty oppose Marx and Sartre with the following: "It is man who makes the unity of the world, but man is everywhere. Men can see nothing about them that is not in their image; everything speaks to them of themselves. Their very landscape is animated" [*Ad,* 192; *AD,* 143; above 389 (a paraphrase)]. For Sartre had not waited for Merleau-Ponty's lessons to be able to think that: "The world is human," and to show us in urban or agricultural landscapes, in streets, in public gardens, in utensils, and natural elements the mirrors where at every step man rediscovers his own image; the voices which relentlessly speak to him of himself.

If Merleau-Ponty stubbornly maintains that Sartre ignores any interworld, it is due to the fact that in order to lead to the negation of history and dialectic, it is necessary to challenge at first all intersubjectivity, since an interworld would mean a mediation between subjects. Merleau-Ponty states: "In Sartre there is plurality of subjects but not intersubjectivity" (*Ad,* 275; *AD,* 205). "Contrary to appearances, being-for-itself is all Sartre has ever accepted, with its inevitable correlate pure being in-itself. . . . There is no hinge, no joint or mediation, between myself and the other; I feel myself to be looked at immediately, I take this passivity as my own but at the same time reintegrate it into my universe" (*Ad,* 275; *AD,* 205).

This text calls for several comments. First of all one finds in it a surprising confusion between the function of *assuming* and that of *integrating.* To assume my alienation is to take a moral stand that does not suppress the reality of alienation; the existence of the other means that I am thrown into a universe which, on principle, escapes me. "The fact of the Other is incontestable and touches me to the heart. I realize him through uneasiness; through him I am perpetually in danger in a world which is this world and which nevertheless I can only glimpse" (*EN,* 334; *BN,* 251). We ought to quote all the pages where Sartre describes this sort of "internal hemorrhage" through which my world flows toward the other. "*The flight is without limit;* it is lost externally; the world flows out of the world, and I flow outside myself. The Other's look makes me be beyond my being in this world and puts me in the midst of the world which is at once this world and beyond this world" (*EN,* 319; *BN,* 237). "The appearance of the Other causes the appearance in the situation of an aspect which I did not wish, of which I am not master, and which on principle escapes me since it is for the Other. That ignorance which, however, is lived as ignorance, that total opacity which can only be felt as a presentiment across a total translucency—this is nothing but the description of our being-in-the-midst-of-the-world" (*EN,* 324; *BN,* 241–42).

Here we are quite far from the idea of a consciousness coextensive with the world which reintegrates the other into its universe through an instantaneous decree. On the contrary, we see signs of the beginnings of a fluid relation between the I and the other, a relation which develops with time, which is never still, in short, the possibility of a dialectic. Sartre has given a precise example of this phenomenon in *Saint Genet:* when Genet assumes his being for the other, when he assumes the role of the burglar, he is far from finding himself as the "demiurge of his pure objects." The acts through which he attempts to recapture his being shape a new face for him that the other sees and which again escapes him. It is a process which does not result in any permanent synthesis: "A fathomless abyss separates the subjective certainty which we have of ourselves from the objective truth which we have for others" (*SG,* 548; *SGE,* 597).

The other mistake Merleau-Ponty makes is no less monumental: he imagines—and this is the central theme of his study—that in Sartre the I and the other have no other relation than the look which brings their pure subjectivity face to face. However, Sartre writes:

> Inasmuch as the Other is for him (the for-itself) the Other-as-a-look, there can be no question of techniques or of foreign meanings; the for-itself experiences itself as an object in the universe beneath the Other's look. But as soon as the for-itself by surpassing the Other toward its ends makes of him a transcendence-transcended . . . the Other as

> object becomes an *indicator of ends*. . . . Thus the Other's presence as transcendence transcended reveals given complexes of means to ends. (*EN,* 603; *BN,* 496).

Thus, the other is present to me in things under the guise of meanings and techniques: "The for-itself arises in a world which is a world for other it-selfs. Such is the *given.* And thereby, as we have seen, the meaning of the world is alien to the for-itself. This means simply that each man finds himself in the presence of meanings which do not come into the world through him" (*EN,* 603; *BN,* 496). Therefore, it is amusing to see Merleau-Ponty argue:

> A consciousness that is truly engaged in a world and a history . . . which go beyond it is not insular. . . . Unlike the Sartrean consciousness, it is not visible only for the other: consciousness can see him, at least out of the corner of its eye. Between its perspective and that of the other there is a link. . . . these relationships are no longer the encounter of two for-itselfs, but are the meshing of two experiences, which without ever coinciding, belong to a single world. (*Ad,* 269; *AD,* 200; above 436–37)

Throughout *Being and Nothingness* Sartre makes this point. And in answer to Lefort he writes "The other party is there, immediately accessible—if not decipherable—and his experience is there, *completing itself in my own or mine completing itself in his.* All these imperfect meanings, badly defined and interrupted, which constitute our real knowledge are taken into account there in the other who perhaps knows the answer" [*Cp,* 21–22; *CP,* 245]. And in a note Sartre adds: "But in any case while these values and these points of view which are not yours although combined with yours creep around everywhere to oppose you, and present themselves to you like systems of comprehensible relationships, they will always keep their irreducibility always different, always foreign; immediately present, yet inassimilable" (*RL,* 22; *CP,* 245). We can see that if Merleau-Ponty's thought is original in comparison with that of the pseudo-Sartre, it is less original when confronted with Sartre himself; this meshing without coincidence that he describes is exactly the mixture of the irreducible experiences so often evoked by Sartre.

Yet Merleau-Ponty is aware of the text I have just mentioned, and admits that for Sartre "there is, then, a social field" (*Ad,* 186; *AD,* 138; above 386). But he maintains that the social, according to Sartre, does not exist: " 'Sociality,' as a given fact is a scandal for the 'I think' " (*Ad,* 208; *AD,* 155). "From the fact that the social is a totality, it does not follow that it is a pure relationship of consciousnesses; and yet, that is the very thing which, for Sartre, goes without saying" (*Ad,* 214; *AD,* 159; above

402). Indeed, Merleau-Ponty says, Sartrean consciousnesses open onto a social field, but "it is in front of them, not prior to them, that its unity is made" [*Ad,* 186; *AD,* 138; above 386]. Intersubjective realities in Sartre "do not have their own energy, they are something constituted" (*Ad,* 191; *AD,* 142; above 389).

We have already said that the for-itself is necessary for a world to exist—Merleau-Ponty also accepts this idea—but the for-itself is far from *constituting* meanings, techniques, a reality that it would project out of itself in the manner of the Hegelian Spirit and where consciousness would find again exactly what it initially accepted. The unveiling of the world, performed in the dimension of intersubjectivity, reveals realities which resist consciousness and possess their own laws. It is difficult to know what Merleau-Ponty means by *own energy.* But what is certain is that he insinuates that in Sartre intersubjective realities exist and relate to one another only through a subjectivity which supports them; whereas Sartre, when he defined existential psychoanalysis, wrote: "The meaningful, because of the very structure of transcendence, is a reference to other transcendents which can be interpreted without recourse to the subjectivity which has established it" (*EN,* 692; *BN,* 121).

Merleau-Ponty is clearly in error when he writes that according to Sartre: "Language exists only as carried by a consciousness which constitutes it" (*Ad,* 254; *AD,* 189; above 427). For in *Saint Genet* Sartre sums up his conception of language as follows: "Language is *nature* when I discover it within myself and outside myself with its resistances and its laws which *escape me:* words have affinities and customs which I must observe, must learn: language is a *tool* as soon as I speak or listen to someone else; and words sometimes display surprising independence, marrying in defiance of all laws and thus producing puns and oracles with language; thus, the word is *miraculous*" (*SG,* 258; *SGE,* 276).

Merleau-Ponty must be victim of a strange delirium to think that Sartre denies the existence of mediating areas between the different topics called culture and literature. According to Sartre, the ideology of a class, for example, is an intersubjective reality, endowed with its *own energy* since it *produces* ideas. He writes in *Henri Martin:* "In other environments, children are immediately thrust into the ideology of their class, it enters them as the air they breathe; they read it on things; they learn it with the language; they never think about it, but always through it, since it is this ideology which produces and governs ideas" (*HM,* 24). He recognizes the same energy in literature whose periods are born without a recourse to subjectivity; one only needs to read *What Is Literature?* to be convinced. For example, one reads the following regarding surrealism: "It is the last phase of a lengthy dialectic process: in the eighteenth century literature was negativity; under the reign of the bourgeoisie, it went to the absolute and hypostasized state of negation, it became a many-colored process shimmering with annihilation etc., etc." The idea of the dialectic implies objective relations, and it also supposes that the unity of the social field is made both prior and subsequent to consciousnesses, for each stage is born of the preceding one. Merleau-Ponty claims that, according to Sartre, "the social is never cause or even motive, it is never behind the work," it is in front of the writer (*Ad,* 209; *AD,* 156; above 399–400). In fact, Sartre refuses the deterministic explanation of Taine, who saw a work as the product of its environment; however, he declares, he is far from "ruling out the explanation of the work by the *situation* of the man." The situation is based on what is given, which "is always discovered as a cause" (*EN,* 568; *BN,* 463); the situation includes a past which also always is given as a motive for our choices; the situation is defined through its relation to the society to which I belong. All the studies made by Sartre show us the literary work as one created from a society for a public which is itself defined by the historical moment; the social field appears both prior and subsequent to the society, and it cannot be otherwise since for Sartre, past and future are inextricably linked.

Merleau-Ponty is so convinced of the insularity of Sartrean consciousness that he has reduced reading, according to Sartre, to a mere subjective act. In a book, there would be: "Nothing between scribbling, a book in its physical existence, and the meaning attributed to it by the reader's consciousness" (*Ad,* 189; *AD,* 140–41; above 387). On the contrary, Sartre thinks that "all books contain in themselves the image of the reader for whom they are intended." The reader is engaged in history, so are the authors: "Between these men who are immersed in a same history and who equally contribute to it, a contact is established with the medium of the book" (*Sits.,* II, 177ff.). Besides, one knows just how many studies Sartre has devoted to "this concrete and imaginary object which is a literary work" (*Sits.,* II, 93). Not one of his critical essays would have been possible had he seen nothing in a book but scribbling and subjective meaning. He is so far from holding such an opinion that he used to reproach Mauriac for reducing the novel to a body of signs and intentions, when it should have the substantiality of a thing: "If it is true that a novel is a thing, as are a painting or a building, if it is true that one makes a novel with free consciousness and duration. . . . *End of the Night* (*Fin de la nuit*) is not a novel; at most it is a body of signs and intentions." Sartre had also written regarding *Sartoris:* "With the passing of time, novels become completely similar to natural phenomena: one forgets that they have an author, one accepts them as stones or trees" (*Sits.,* II, 7).

Nevertheless, Merleau-Ponty passes over all these texts which represent literature and reading as a form of intersubjectivity. And he maintains his thesis: "Whether as a permanent spectacle or as a continued creation, the social is in any case before consciousnesses and is constituted by them" (*Ad,* 213; *AD,* 158; above 402). This is blatantly untrue. Sartre opposed the spontaneity of the masses, as envisioned by the Trotskyites, with the idea of a passivity in which the weight of the social is *endured:* "Suppose the spontaneous action of the masses, instead of having the future in view, were reduced to being only a rebound of the past" [*Cp,* 229; *CP,* 114]. And throughout *The Communists and Peace* his analyses defined the worker's condition by a social field whose unity is behind them. To counter Merleau-Ponty's interpretation, I shall also quote the following passage—one of many possible texts—which is particularly conclusive:

> We cannot all be objects unless it be for a transcendent subject, *nor can we all be unless we first undertake the impossible liquidation of all objectivity;* as for absolute reciprocity, it is concealed by the historical conditions of race and class. . . . Thus, we usually live in a state of familiar and unthinking vagueness . . . we are not quite objects and are not quite subjects. The Other is that instrument which obeys the voice, which regulates, divides, distributes, and it is, at the same time, that warm, diffused atmosphere which envelops us. (*SG,* 542; *SGE,* 590–91)

We are a long way from the philosophy of the I and the other in which the only relationship between men is their immediate confrontation instigated by the look. The truth is that Sartre's entire ontology contradicts what Merleau-Ponty said it was. According to Merleau-Ponty one would find in Sartre "the demand of an *intuitive* philosophy which wants to see *all* meanings immediately and simultaneously"[*Ad,* 275; *AD,* 205]. Such a philosophy "poses everything in the instant" [ibid.]. Therefore "there is no longer any ordered passage from one perspective to another, no completion of others in me and of me in others, for this is possible only in time" (*Ad,* 275; *AD,* 205).

Nonetheless, one has seen that Sartre said of the experience of the other: "completing itself in my own or mine completing itself in his" [*RL,* 21; *CP,* 245]. But his philosophy is so far from being intuitive that he wrote in *Being and Nothingness:* "No consciousness, not even God's, can 'see the underside'—that is, apprehend the totality as such" [*EN,* 363; *BN,* 278].

Society is for Sartre a detotalized-totality which can never be reassembled for a subject; the relationships of individuals are not given to any of them in their immediacy, but imply the possibility of a dialectic and of a history unfolding in time. Merleau-Ponty's falsification tends to do nothing but deny this possibility. And now we will see how, from this rigged ontology, he interprets *The Communists and Peace* in such a way that he can find in it a negation of history, dialectic, and truth: the statement of a nothingness which would leave clear field to the pure dictate of the will.

II

In negating any interworld, any intersubjectivity, the pseudo-Sartre, obviously, negates history: "History is voluntary or nothing" (*Ad,* 153; *AD,* 112; above 368). It is made "of criminal intentions or virtuous intentions" (*Ad,* 168; *AD,* 124; above 377). History is "insofar as it is intelligible, the immediate result of our volitions. As for the rest, it is an impenetrable opacity" (*Ad,* 134; *AD,* 97–98; above 357). In fact, if "things are mute," the historical fact also must be mute. According to the pseudo-Sartre: "The fact, insofar as it exists, does not carry its meaning, which is of another order: meaning is dependent on consciousness" (*Ad,* 155; *AD,* 114; above 370). "There is no mediation between 'pure fact,' which has whatever meaning one wants to give it, and decision, which gives the fact only one meaning" (*Ad,* 155; *AD,* 114; above 370). This mediation must be the probable, which Sartre, according to Merleau-Ponty, "does not want." There is a new paradox here: "And yet he has elsewhere said, profoundly, that the whole of the perceived world is probable" (*Ad,* 158; *AD,* 116; above 371).

Sartre said it and never did refute it. In the second part of *The Communists and Peace,* he reproaches the Trotskyites for playing a double game: for reconstructing bourgeois history according to necessity and for reconstructing proletarian history according to the prospect of probability. He denies *them* the right to retrospectively invoke probability when they interpret history according to a dialectic fatality. Yet Sartre himself explicitly resorts to this concept; and the identity he established between reality and probability caused this implied concept to intervene in all his analyses. Yet, Merleau-Ponty states: "This probability for Sartre is like nothing." In order to substantiate this assertion, Merleau-Ponty resorts to a process which I have already mentioned: the ruse of oversignification, *le coup de la sursignification.* Sartre wrote that if one wants to judge the final objective of slogans proposed to the proletariat by the communist party, the bare facts do not explain anything: "As always, the facts say neither yes nor no. . . . One will come to a decision on the question only after taking a position on much vaster questions" (*Cp,* 90–91; *CP,* 11). The second part of this text clearly indicates that the first part is the simple reminder of a methodological postulate quite widely accepted: experimental sciences, social sciences, and history are in agreement when they recognize that facts speak only if they are studied and interpreted. Merleau-Ponty, by isolating the first sentence, turns this commonplace into a significant key of Sartrean thought. The fact, according to Sartre, would be definitely equivocal.

In the discussion in which he contrasts his own position with Lefort's, Sartre clearly says that he merely refuses "the experience-which-contains-its-own-interpretation" [*RL*, 33; *CP*, 253]. He underscores the ambiguity of the fact: "First of all, facts are not as neat as you say: they must be reconstructed, then *each of them* is at once obscure and all too full of meaning. . . . All objective structures of the social world present themselves as an initial confusion to the worker's subjectivity. Nothing is elucidated, nor are there absolute guarantees: resignation and revolution simultaneously illumine the situation, but their relationship is always in flux." But immediately he adds that one can resolve the ambiguity: "Everything *will* be clear, rational, everything *is* real, beginning with that resistance to deciphering; but it takes time" (*RL*, 33; *CP*, 253).

Merleau-Ponty acknowledges that for Marx, too, "any situation is ambiguous." And even, he says, "nothing is more Marxist than the mixing of act and meaning." Then why does he claim that Sartre is condemned to negate the historical reality which is recognized by Marx? It is because, he answers, "Marxism does not mix them in an equivocation but in a genesis of truth" [*Ad*, 156; *AD*, 114; above 370]. Interpreting with bad faith the lines of Sartre that I have just quoted, Merleau-Ponty retains "the facts are obscure and all too full of meaning" [*sursignification*]. But Sartre had said that each fact in itself is equivocal, not that it is impossible to explain it by means of other facts. One finds a specific example of this process of elucidation in the passage of *Henri Martin* in which Sartre questions the meaning of the tracts posted by Martin: "Considered in its objective reality, the act informs us *up to a certain point*. . . . Beyond that, there is total indetermination and one would not be able to judge it without relating it to the universe" (*HM*, 185).

Yet, we have seen that Sartre concluded: "Everything will be rational." The time needed for deciphering is not infinite, as Merleau-Ponty suggests; if it were, it would in practice suppress any criterion. This is the time needed to interpret the meaning of any experience. Elsewhere Sartre says: "The difficulties which we have already encountered bring us back to the usual idea of experience: an obscure mass of consequences without premises, which require a number of men to decipher" [*RL*, 33; *CP*, 254]. If we keep these lines in mind, we will find the dialogue Merleau-Ponty has with the pseudo-Sartre highly comical: "What is this dubious relationship," demands the pseudo-Sartre enamored with Cartesian clarity. "Is or is not the meaning of present given in it?" (*Ad,* 157; *AD,* 115; above 371). And Merleau-Ponty, who knows existential ambiguity, answers: "It is neither given in it nor created out of nothing. It is elicited from the present, and such is the function of a congress" (*Ad,* 157; *AD,* 115; above 371). The real Sartre had spoken clearly about a deciphering which requires time and several hands to decipher it. He adheres to the Marxist idea of a genesis of truth since he had written "everything *will be* clear." This having-become truth [*vérité devenue*] has nothing to do with pseudo-Sartre's willed truth [*vérité voulue*] of which Merleau-Ponty says "it authorizes one to go ahead against all appearances; in itself it is madness" [*Ad,* 176; *AD,* 130; above 381–82]. One has the right to ask whether Sartre's paradoxes and madness could be, in fact, explained by this commentator's lack of comprehension.

As a matter of fact, falsehoods keep cropping up. Having wrongly asserted that for Sartre "conscious awareness gives meaning" [*Ad,* 156; *AD,* 115; above 370, a paraphrase], Merleau-Ponty adds: "And in the case of an event, the meaning it gives is irrevocable" (*Ad,* 156; *AD,* 115; above 370). Relying on Marx, he reminds Sartre that: "Conscious awareness . . . is itself a fact, it has its place in history" (*Ad,* 157; *AD,* 115; above 370), and that "I give meaning to history only because I occupy a certain vantage point in it" (*Ad,* 269; *AD,* 199; above 436). Yet Sartre had written in *Being and Nothingness:* "There is only the point of view of *engaged* knowledge. This amounts to saying that knowledge and action are only two abstract aspects of an original, concrete relation" (*EN,* 370; *BN,* 284). Sartre applies this concept to history. The main theme of his "Reply to Albert Camus" is that under no circumstances can consciousness withdraw from history, since any awareness is a historical fact: "If I believed that history is a pool of filth and blood . . . I would look twice before diving in. But suppose that I am in it already, suppose that, from my point of view, even your sulking is the proof of your historicity" [*RC,* 123; *Sits.,* 102]. The meaning, reached by the historically situated consciousness, is so far from being *irrevocable* that Sartre wrote: "Thus, human history would have to be finished before a particular event, for example the taking of the Bastille, could receive a *definitive* meaning. . . . He who would like to decide the question today forgets that the historian is himself historical; that is that he historicizes himself by illuminating history in the lights of his projects and of those of his society. . . . Thus it is necessary to say that the meaning of the past is perpetually *in suspense*" (*EN,* 582; *BN,* 477).

The text just quoted utterly refutes Merleau-Ponty's assertion: "For Marx there was, and for Sartre there is not, a coming-to-be of meaning in institutions" (*Ad,* 168; *AD,* 124; above 377). For neither the meaning of institutions nor that of events is, according to Sartre, irrevocable; it historicizes itself in the context of the *praxis,* and this brings us back to our opposition to the madness of a willed truth, to the idea of a having become truth. The meaning is given neither *ex nihilo* nor inexorably: it emerges from the facts, and it is criticized in light of history.

However, this history according to the pseudo-Sartre is only a history of persons; since, according to him, there exist only men and things, he is forced to translate "the reduction of history to personal actions" (*Ad,* 196; *AD,* 146; above 391). Such an assertion is surprising, since for the real Sartre the person can truly be understood only through history: it is this view which emerges in *What Is Literature?* among other texts, and also in *Saint Genet,* where Sartre writes:

> In order for a man to have a history, he must evolve, the course of the world must change him in changing itself, and he must change in changing the world, his life must depend on everything and on himself alone, he must discover in it, at the moment of death, a vulgar product of the age and the singular achievement of his will. (*SG,* 288–89; *SGE,* 310)

In *The Communists and Peace* he is even more decisive. The complete text that Merleau-Ponty truncated is, as a matter of fact, as follows: "There are men, animals, and objects. And men are real and individual beings who are part of historical wholes" (*Cp,* 197; *CP,* 89). Elsewhere Sartre clarifies:

> The historical whole determines our powers at any given moment, it prescribes their limits in our field of action and our real future; it conditions our attitude toward the possible and the impossible, the real and the imaginary, what is and what should be, time and space. From there on, we in turn determine our relationship with others, that is to say, the meaning of our life and the value of our death: it is within this framework that our Self finally makes its appearance. . . . It is history which shows some the exits and makes others cool their heels before closed doors. (*Cp,* 184; *CP,* 80)

Thus, the person depends on its Ego and its acts upon historic conjunctures; one must not forget that for Sartre the act is something quite different from the intention which animates it: by falling into a world which is alienated from us our wills escape us: "The event transforms our best intentions into criminal desires not only in history but even in family life" (*SG,* 548; *SGE,* 597). Although the meaning of the event always reflects a conscious intention, it possesses an *objective* meaning. "It matters little then whether strikers or demonstrators *intend* to make revolution *objectively,* every mass demonstration is revolutionary," writes Sartre (*Cp,*

356; *CP,* 210). And he shows in *The Communists and Peace* how the action of skilled workers objectively takes a reformist meaning which no will has subjectively chosen to attribute to it.

Since history is a history of persons according to the pseudo-Sartre, history is nothing more than a "History of projects" (*Ad,* 213; *AD,* 158; above 402), where the past plays no role. One has already seen how false this thesis is with regard to the history of literature. In *The Communists and Peace,* Sartre continually reminds us to be alert to the Trotskyites and alert to Lefort: "This confused history, so full of delays and lost chances, in which the working class seems to exhaust itself in catching up an earlier delay, whose path is often disturbed by exterior violence, wars, etc." (*RL,* 59–60; *CP,* 272). He insists—we shall go back to it—on the singular characteristics the French proletariat owes to its singular history; to this confused past which is neither the immediate result of personal wills nor an impenetrable opacity. And he radically condemns sociological interpretations which snap their fingers at history. "For having begun by eliminating history, the anti-Communist is constrained to reintroduce it at the end in its most absurd form" (*Cp,* 256; *CP,* 134).

At any rate, Merleau-Ponty says, this history is discontinuous, it does not envelop the becoming of a truth, since: "An intuitive philosophy poses everything in the instant" [*Ad,* 275; *AD,* 205]. The result must be that Sartre envisions political action as a pure present, since "Political time is atomized for him into a series of decisions taken in the presence of death" (*Ad,* 159; *AD,* 117; above 372). "Political questions can and should be resolved in the moment, without looking back to the past or repeating it" (*Ad,* 144; *AD,* 105; above 363).

We could oppose to Merleau-Ponty the fact that in Sartre no reality is instantaneous, that the theory of temporality, elaborated at length in *Being and Nothingness,* inextricably solders different moments of time, that the present perpetually recaptures the past by fleeing toward the future and that it is nothing else but double *ek-stasis.* Merleau-Ponty would probably retort with the ruse of the paradox: in politics, Sartre disowns his previous work. We could then remind him that, in *The Communists and Peace,* Sartre speaks of a "true time of the dialectic," that he writes about the masses: "In point of fact, their most elementary desire is separated from its object by the universe, and can be satisfied only by long and exacting labor" [*Cp,* 376; *CP,* 225]. Merleau-Ponty will answer that, as a matter of fact, in the last part of *The Communists and Peace,* Sartre "has given up the point of view of immediacy" [*Ad,* 233; *AD,* 173; above 414]. Nevertheless, it is from this point of view that Merleau-Ponty will continue to interpret the whole of Sartre's essay. Then, we are justified in asking Merleau-Ponty whether the fears that the incoherence he notices in Sartre might indicate a defect in the method he uses. Sartre's last essay would contradict his entire work, and each part of this essay would contradict each one of the others. Would it not be the commentator's role to restore the unity of the work and situate elements in the whole instead of interpreting each one of them separately and opposing it to everything else? Perhaps then he would notice that Sartre did not have to give up the point of view of immediacy, but faithful to his earlier thought, he had never adopted it.

What are Merleau-Ponty's bases for claiming the contrary? Is it because Sartre in *The Communists and Peace* proposed to study a specific moment in history? Therefore, according to him, moments can be isolated! says the deeply shocked Merleau-Ponty. Let us look at his proof more closely. Sartre has written "Leaving eternal France at grips with the proletariat-in-itself, I am undertaking to explain events rigorously defined in time and space by the peculiar structure of our economy, and the latter in turn by certain events of our local history."[3] This attitude, which is the one adopted by historians in general, also the very one often adopted by Marx himself and Lenin, appears to Merleau-Ponty as being singularly Sartrean: "But it is this reference to the present as such which is theory. There is theory precisely in this manner of treating the events as ineffaceable [?], as a decisive test of our intentions [?] and an instantaneous choice of the whole future and of all that we are [?]" (*Ad,* 144; *AD,* 105; above 363). The method used here by Merleau-Ponty is what one can call "the ruse [*coup*] of gratuitous affirmations." I have emphasized each one with a question mark. The text is even more stupefying, since Sartre wrote *The Communists and Peace* against those anticommunists who sought to treat the events of May 28th and those of June 4th as ineffaceable, to judge them as the decisive test of the proletarians' intentions and the expression of an instantaneous choice. Sartre, on the contrary, maintains that they were only a "negative sign" and as such "decipherable with difficulty." It is impossible, says Sartre, if one limits oneself to the present, to know if masses have disavowed something, or what they have disavowed. "We are dealing with local and day-to-day history, opaque, in part contingent, and the connection between the terms is not so tight that we cannot vary some of them within certain limits without modifying all the others" (*Cp,* 234; *CP,* 118). Hence he considers that a reference to the pure present can never suffice to shed light on the event.

Merleau-Ponty pursues his indictment by using a new method, "the ruse [*coup*] of dichotomy." He traps his adversary in a false alternative: "Not to speak of the proletarian, of the class in itself, or of the eternal Party is here to make a theory of the proletariat and of the Party as continued creations, that is to say, as the dead reprieved from death" (*Ad,* 144; *AD,* 105; above 363). Merleau-Ponty is a professor of philosophy at the

Collège de France; how does he dare to propose the dilemma: the idea or the continued creation? Doesn't he know of systems—phenomenology, for example—which, going beyond Plato and Descartes, endow existents with a temporal dimension without immobilizing them in eternity? Does he really ignore the fact that one can negate *the-idea-in-itself* while believing at the same time in history, dialectic, and time? Nonetheless, Merleau-Ponty does not bring forth any additional weightier arguments to support his assertions regarding Sartre's treatment of the dialectic. In the name of the intuitive philosophy which he attributes to Sartre, Merleau-Ponty calmly writes: "Today Sartre says that the dialectic is twaddle" (*Ad,* 312; *AD,* 232). "It is a brief on the failure of the dialectic that he contributes" (*Ad,* 133; *AD,* 97; above 356). "One *feels* that for Sartre the dialectic has always been an illusion" (*Ad,* 135; *AD,* 98; above 357).

There is no text of Sartre's that authorizes these assertions. Sartre did call the finalist optimism which usually hides behind dialectics "twaddle," but not the dialectic itself. He does not believe that history can receive its information from some sort of idea-force, foreign to the men who make it, a force which would drive history with a sure fatality toward a happy ending. Nor did Marx accept this idea. He wrote: "History is only the activity of man pursuing his own ends." Sartre adopts these words as his own (*RC,* 123; *Sits.,* 102); according to him the dialectic is the product of our activities, which fall into a world where they *thingify* themselves and escape according to the dimension of the for-others, and immediately motivate new activities. It is precisely because historical dialectic is correlative to the dialectic originally implied in temporality and to the dialectic implied in the relationship of the for-itself with the for-others, that historical dialectic is so remote from being "twaddle" and Sartre is for far from negating it, that he describes—as we have seen—the history of literature in a dialectical form. And he writes: "The processes of capitalism are dialectical (*RL,* 44; *CP,* 261). "Hegelian universal idealism is intensified by an all embracing tragic sense, and in Marxism too, there is the process of capital and the drama of man; two inseparable aspects of the same dialectic."[4] "But how could you even conceive of what Trotsky called 'the dialectic of the heads of the party and the masses'?" (*RL,* 15; *CP,* 240). "Marxist dialectic is not the spontaneous movement of the Spirit, but the hard work of man to enter a world which rejects him" (*RL,* 58; *CP,* 271). "Marx has allowed us to recover true dialectical time" (*RL,* 59; *CP,* 272). How can Merleau-Ponty feel that Sartre negates the dialectic when Sartre writes down in black and white: "In truth, there are dialectics and they reside in facts; it is for us to discover them there, not put them there" (*RL,* 370; *CP,* 221).

Merleau-Ponty goes as far as to claim that: "An action which is an unveiling, an unveiling which is an action—in short, a dialectic—this

Sartre does not want to consider" (*Ad,* 192; *AD,* 142; above 389), while Sartre keeps on saying that any action is an unveiling, any unveiling is an action. I have already quoted the text where Sartre says: "Knowledge and action are nothing else but two abstract sides of an original and concrete relation." This is one of the theses developed in *Being and Nothingness* and found at the source of *What Is Literature?* "The engaged writer knows that the word is action: he knows that to unveil is to change and one cannot unveil unless one projects to change." If the *act* of unveiling is strange, it is because of the type of redoubling it implies: it poses as an *end* one of its immediate dimensions. But, in the relation of consciousness to act, as well as in the relationship of the Ego and the other, and of the past and the future, all the conditions for a dialectic are present, according to Sartre.

III

If there is no history, no truth, no temporality, no dialectic, then the meaning of events is imposed on them by decree, and the action is reduced to a discontinued series of arbitrary decisions. Such is the central theme on which Merleau-Ponty based his pseudo-Sartreanism. He announces in the introduction of his study on Sartre, that Sartre substitutes for a philosophy of history "a philosophy of absolute creation amidst the unknown" [*Ad,* 138; *AD,* 101; above 359–60]. Communism then becomes "an undetermined enterprise . . . that, like duty, is not subject to discussion nor is it subject to rational proof" (*Ad,* 138; *AD,* 101; above 360). According to this conception "the Party's action is not subject to the criteria of meaning" (*Ad,* 134; *AD,* 98; above 357). "Doing is absolute rootless initiative" (*Ad,* 186 n.; *AD,* 138 n.; above 445, note 37). The militant, the party, and the class are going to be born out of a "will which has no basis in things" [*Ad,* 144; *AD,* 105; above 363, a paraphrase].

We know well enough that Sartre has never admitted that an act could take place without cause nor that a creation could be brought about *ex nihilo.* "The freedom of the for-itself is always engaged; there is no question here of a freedom which could be undetermined and which could pre-exist its choice" (*EN,* 558; *BN,* 455). "The structure of the choice necessarily implies that it be a choice in the world. A choice which would be a choice in *terms of nothing,* a choice *against nothing,* would be a choice of nothing and would be annihilated as choice" (*EN,* 559; *BN,* 456). "Our decisions gather into new syntheses and on new occasions the *leitmotif* that governs our life" (*SG,* 397; *SGE,* 428). "The act transforms the possible into reality" (*SG,* 397; *SGE,* 428). "One does something with or to something" (*EN,* 566; *BN,* 461). There is no need to supply additional passages. Merleau-Ponty remembers quite well that for Sartre "freedom is not in the decision" (*Ad,* 266; *AD,* 198; above 435). Yet, once again he shakes off any scruples, thanks to the ruse of paradox [*coup du paradoxe*], and makes Sartre contradict his own work. "Everything takes place as if these thoughts do not intervene when it is a question for Sartre of taking a position in the present: then he returns [?][5] to the ideology of choice and to futurism."

We shall restrict our comments here to Sartre's political thought and ascertain if, according to him, the revolutionary will, the class, and the party are indeed born out of "no basis in things." Merleau-Ponty assures that: "In all strictness, the proletarian is not the condition of the militant, and the fact that the revolutionary will does not arise completely armed out of misery is enough for Sartre to act as if it did not arise from it at all, and to see it appear *ex nihilo*" (*Ad,* 145; *AD,* 106; above 364). As Orestes in *The Flies,* the militant sees that freedom has descended on him like an eagle, and he becomes revolutionary by decree. Such is the meaning that Merleau-Ponty attributes to Sartre's text: "Man is yet to be made: he is what man lacks" [*Cp,* 256; *CP,* 200]. Merleau-Ponty claims that these words mean that man is a "duty-to-be [*devoir-être*] and even a pure duty" [*Ad,* 146; *AD,* 107; above 364]. "It is the bite of duty or of nothingness into being, into freedom—the bite that Sartre once called 'mortal'—which constitutes the militant" (*Ad,* 146; *AD,* 107; above 364). And Merleau-Ponty amusingly asks: Why isn't Sartre militating instead for the *Union for Moral Action?*

I am afraid that Merleau-Ponty, who advises against reading Sartre with Marx's glasses, here, borrowed—God only knows for what reason—those of Lagneau. Had he not done so he would have understood this text he so arbitrarily truncated, quite differently. As a matter of fact, Sartre, has written: "The new proletarian cannot claim the least merit. . . . Yet, *fatigue* and *misery* overwhelm it: *it must die* or *obtain satisfaction.* On what, then, will it base its demands? Well, precisely on nothing.[6] Or, if you prefer, on the demands themselves. The need creates the right. . . . This new humanism is a need itself; it is lived hollowly like the very sense of an *inadmissible frustration* . . . for the unskilled worker, man is yet to be made, etc." (*Cp,* 343; *CP,* 200). Hence, the bite that nothingness inflicts on the being is called, here, not freedom, but need. Merleau-Ponty is the only one to claim that in Sartre the revolutionary will, in order not to arise fully armed from misery, does not arise at all in reality, it is born out of an *inadmissible frustration.* Sartre had already shown in the second part of his essay (*Cp,* 242ff.: *CP,* 124ff.) that the condition of the unskilled worker does not offer any solution other than that of a revolutionary conversion:

conversion envelops whatever it surpasses; here, it arises from a total lack, that is to say, precisely, from misery. As for freedom, says Sartre, when he speaks of masses: "They can't even imagine what it is" (*Cp*, 346; *CP*, 203).

How does Merleau-Ponty dare to uphold that the alternative "to die or obtain satisfaction" puts the proletarian face to face with a moral imperative in the Kantian sense of the word? How can he confuse a hungry man with the well-fed idealists who adhere to unions and sanctimonious leagues? The entire polemic which ensues is immediately discredited, since it is based on the confusion of a theory of need with a theory of freedom.

The reason for such a monumental error is obvious. What does not exist cannot have roots: Merleau-Ponty substitutes "the rape of freedom" [*Ad*, 146; *AD*, 107; above 364] for the entrenchment in need because he wants Sartre to deny any existence to the proletariat. His political thought would be a carbon copy of his ontology. The party "is a double of consciousness" (*Ad*, 143; *AD*, 105; above 363), asserts Merleau-Ponty. Pseudo-Sartre's ontology brings the sovereign consciousness and the opaque being together; his political thought only leaves "the brute will of the leaders face to face with the opaque necessity of things" (*Ad*, 227; *AD*, 168; above 410). The significant reality—here, the proletariat—would be dodged. "The proletariat of which Sartre is speaking is not verifiable, debatable or living. It is not a phenomenon but is rather a category delegated to represent humanity in Sartre's thought" (*Ad*, 227; *AD*, 169; above 411). "The proletariat is an idea of the leaders. The proletariat is suspended above history, it is caught in the fabric, it cannot be explained, it is cause of itself, as are all ideas" [*Ad*, 228; *AD*, 169; above 412]. "It is a definition and exists only in Sartre's mind" (*Ad*, 228–29; *AD*, 170). And Merleau-Ponty, far from being intimidated by Sartre's texts, declares: "It is not a historical reality" (*Ad*, 227; *AD*, 169; above 411), despite the fact that Sartre wrote in black and white: "The French proletariat is a historical reality" [*Cp*, 256; *CP*, 135].

Not only did he write it, but it is one of the major theses of his essay. In opposition to the Trotskyites, and in opposition to Claude Lefort, whom he accuses of treating the proletariat as an idea, Sartre keeps on insisting on the concrete, verifiable, and living characteristics which are given to each proletariat—in this case to the French proletariat—by its unique history. The upheavals through which the proletariat goes do not express an eternal essence. When Sartre speaks of workers' struggles, he refuses to see in them nothing more than the fatal repetition of an abstract outline: "I discover in these battles the action of precise factors; and in the sleep which followed, I see the effect of defeat and terror" (*Cp*, 253; *CP*, 132).

In disagreement with innumerable texts of Sartre in which he concretely describes history and the proletarian condition, Merleau-Ponty delivers one of his habitual dilemmas: the proletariat *is* or is *nothing*. To do so is to forget that in phenomenology—formerly held in esteem by Merleau-Ponty—the existent cannot be confined to such an alternative: it is made. Sartre, faithful to his doctrine, refuses to *reify* the proletariat; however, this certainly does not lead him to ignore its existence: "If the class exists, it will be something of a new proximity of each to all, something of a mode of presence which is achieved through and against the separative forces: it will create *unity* of the workers. . . . I wish only to show that class unity cannot be passively received or spontaneously produced" (*Cp*, 197; *CP*, 89–90). "The class makes and remakes itself continuously: it is movement, action." "The class, a *real* unity of crowds and historical masses, manifests itself by an operation that can be located in time and referred to an intention. The class is never separable from the concrete will which animates it nor from the ends it pursues. The proletariat forms itself by its day-to-day action" (*Cp*, 207; *CP*, 97). This thesis, Sartre notes, is closely akin to that of Marx, who also defines the class by *praxis*. Merleau-Ponty's bad faith consists here (knowing well that for Sartre, freedom, choice, and action never signified *decision*) in assimilating *praxis,* as Sartre understands it, to instantaneous and arbitrary decisions which would be motivated by nothing: "The proletariat begins to exist only by lightning-quick decisions and against all facts" (*Ad,* 156; *AD,* 114; above 370).

To the contrary, according to Sartre, the proletariat is born out of facts from the proletariat's misery, its need, and the industrial system. "For the worker, politics cannot be a luxury activity . . . politics is his need" (*Cp*, 242; *CP*, 124). Without *praxis,* the class does not exist; however, *praxis* implies certain very concrete conditions: "The system of production is for a class a necessary condition of its ability to exist. It is the total historical evolution, the development of capital and the role of the worker in the bourgeois society which will prevent the proletariat from being an arbitrary grouping of individuals" (*Cp*, 209; *CP*, 99).

Merleau-Ponty will say fine, but, nevertheless for Sartre, events take place as if the proletariat were nothing; it does not break off the abrupt encounter between consciousness and being, since the sole action it is allowed, is obedience to the party. "It exists immediately through obedience, and it ceases to exist immediately through disobedience" (*Ad,* 227; *AD,* 169; above 411). "There is no exchange between those who conceive the politics and those who execute it" (*Ad,* 202; *AD,* 150; above 395). The party arises *ex nihilo:* "If everything comes from freedom, if the workers were nothing, not even proletarians, before they create the

Party, the Party rests on nothing that has been established, not even on their common history" (*Ad,* 147; *AD,* 107–8; above 365). Once created, the party "exercises unjustifiable choice"; it decrees "without any previous motive and against all reason" (*Ad,* 188; *AD,* 140; above 387). Is this truly the way Sartre conceived the relationship of the masses to the party?

We have already stated it, and it will be necessary to repeat it as often as Merleau-Ponty keeps on repeating the contrary: nothing comes from freedom but from the situation. The living conditions of the semi-skilled worker, his exhaustion, the debasement of his knowledge, correlative with the mechanization of his work, prevent him from being both a worker and a militant; coming out of the mass, the militant—as Lenin himself said—must *leave it:* "The tandem of the technician and the semi-skilled worker must be complemented by that of the semi-skilled worker and the professional militant" (*Cp,* 360; *CP,* 213). "The new functionaries are legitimized by the need" (*Cp,* 360; *CP,* 213).

Born from a mass, which is not a nothing, but a mass which is concretely defined by the singular moment of the economy which exploits it; brought to power by the need the mass has for it, the party remains so inextricably bound to it that, without the mass, the party is literally nothing. "If the masses suddenly refused to follow it, it would lose everything; as powerful as it is, it resembles Antaeus, who had strength only when he was touching the earth" (*Cp,* 164; *CP,* 65). The party is "the perspective from which the proletariat can find a new role for itself in society and in turn take for object those who would make of it an object: it serves as both tradition and institution. But the content of these empty forms will grow through the very effort which the masses make to unify themselves" [*RL,* 60–61; *CP,* 273]. "The Party cannot be distinguished from the masses except insofar as it is their union" (*RL,* 60; *CP,* 273).

Against the Trotskyites and Lefort, Sartre denies that masses are endowed with spontaneous and organized intelligence, which allows them to produce a politics without the mediation of an apparatus: here again, he concurs with Marx. But he never thought that the masses were pure inertia, an opacity devoid of meaning. He says, to the contrary, that what triggers a great social movement is: "The origin of the current remains extra-union: it is hunger, anger or terror which sets things in motion, or sometimes, as in 1936, it is a hope that suddenly bolts from the blue" (*Cp,* 365–66; *CP,* 217). "Without the union organism, the movements would perhaps stop. . . . But the union organism by itself is incapable of producing movements; it gets them started only when it has caught up with their true cause" [*Cp,* 366; *CP,* 218]. Therefore, it is not the masses which obey the militant; on the contrary, it is the militant who must serve them. "The masses can be neither mobilized nor manipulated, they decide on action when they are transformed into an acting community by the play of external circumstances" (*Cp*, 383; *CP*, 229). The masses "indicate the goal to be attained; it is up to the militant to find the shortest path" (*Cp*, 376; *CP*, 225).

Thus, we are very far from a political conception which takes away from the control of the masses. Merleau-Ponty claims that, according to Sartre, "any idea of controlling the leaders is . . . out of the question" (*Ad*, 149; *AD*, 109; above 366). But Sartre writes: "The masses control the militant as the sea controls the helmsman . . . he will inspire confidence in them only if he agrees to lead them where they are going" (*Cp*, 363; *CP*, 215–16). "The officials steer the movement by successive approximations a turn of the helm to the left, a turn to the right" (*Cp*, 370; *CP*, 221). Merleau-Ponty claims that Sartre conceives the party's action "as a 'technique for the masses,' which 'churns' them like an emulsion. . . . It is just the opposite of an action in which the Party and the working class jointly live the same situation and thus make together the same history" (*Ad*, 163–64; *AD*, 120; above 375).

But if Sartre makes room for the *permanent agitation* through which the party fights against the forces of dissociation exerted on the masses, he is far from reducing the communist action to this exclusive technique, and to imply that he does is far from honest, since Sartre wrote that the party

> is a force of mediation between men . . . it [this mediation] is at certain times in the history of the working class, both natural and willed; this ambiguity . . . creates the possibility of a dialectic in which the people are sometimes contrasted to the Party and sometimes united with it. . . . Doubtless, its orders would be ineffective if they did not flow in the direction of *social currents,* but for the Party to guide itself upon the actual trends of the working movement, there must be such trends, and for them to exist and become manifest, a measure of unity is necessary. [*RL*, 8–9; *CP*, 236]

"Like every real relationship, the connection between a political party and the masses that it can gather is ambiguous: on the one hand, it is guided by them; on the other, it organizes them and attempts their education" (*Cp*, 155; *CP*, 58).

We are tickled to see Merleau-Ponty deny Sartre the right to resort to an ambiguous notion when Merleau-Ponty himself does not hesitate to put forward a *substantial action,* nor in every other breath oppose to the complexity of the real the simplistic assertions of the pseudo-Sartre. The same Merleau-Ponty becomes indignant when Sartre writes: "I do not think that one can interpret the present situation except as an inextricable mixture of action and passion in which passion temporarily dominates" (*RL*, 84; *CP*, 290). "But how one is to understand this mixture of fire and water?" Merleau-Ponty exclaims (*Ad*, 232 n.; *AD*, 172 n.; above 466, note 53). All Sartre's analyses seek precisely to call attention to this. The party's role is, according to him, to animate passivity. "To transform poverty into a factor of revolution, one must make such poverty, conscious of its nature and needs" (*RL*, 67; *CP*, 278). What the party represents in their eyes is "their aspirations, their inclinations, . . . but brought to a red heat, that is to say, to the highest degree of efficacy" (*Cp*, 155; *CP*, 58). Sartre says "The policy of the leaders and the mood of the masses would both . . . be functions of the external circumstances; ultimately one reacts on the other, they modify each other, adapt to each other and, finally, equilibrium is established, a reciprocal accommodation, the possibles go up in smoke like leaders, like mass; like mass, like leaders" (*Cp*, 230; *CP*, 114).

This description, as well as many others, show us the party and the working class living "together the same situation." We are far from the idea of an action imposed on the masses from the outside. However, Merleau-Ponty persists in his avowal, in spite of all these statements to the contrary, that for Sartre the party is *pure action;* it would be then perverse of us to burden pure action with the weight of reality. Action would no longer be pure. No doubt. But when did Sartre ever take the words of pure action in the meaning that Merleau-Ponty assigns them: an action without a root in fact and without a hold on what is given? Sartre has used the expression only twice, which Merleau-Ponty—employing the procedure of oversignification—makes one of the keys to his political thought. Opposing the party to the masses, Sartre writes "They will ultimately change the world, but, for the moment, the world is crushing them. . . . The Party is *pure action;* it must advance or disappear" (*Cp*, 156; *CP*, 58–59). This text means that the party can never slack off, fall asleep or wait: *pure action* is simply opposed here to *inaction.* A little bit further on Sartre explains that the man who would be a part of the mass is hindered and burdened with individual interests: "He must be wrenched away from them. The linking organism must be pure action. . . . The Party is the very moment which unites the workers by carrying them along towards the taking of power" (*Cp*, 249; *CP*, 129–30). Here purity is opposed to the weight of individual interests. But Sartre never assumed that the party's action would not be *applied.* The only evidence that Merleau-Ponty gives us in support of his interpretation is the following: "It is Sartre's ontology that determines that history as a common future be sustained by the pure action of a few, which is identical to the obedience of the others" (*Ad*, 219; *AD*, 163; above 406).

What we have just seen shows us what to think of Merleau-Ponty's interpretation of Sartre's ontology. Furthermore, let us point out that the manner in which he links Sartre's political thought to his ontology is, to say the least, arbitrary. Depending on expedience, Sartre's ontology can be either restrictive or, on the contrary, at liberty to rebel against all constraint. We are told here that his ontology only authorizes pure action, but I have already quoted excerpts which show that it does not admit acts which suddenly appear *ex nihilo;* therefore it does not admit pure action. Well? Isn't it Merleau-Ponty who proceeds here by pure assertion?

In light of the true Sartre, one is amused to read the dialogue that Merleau-Ponty pursues with the pseudo-Sartre. He argues: "The class is not placed before the militant like an object that his will molds or manipulates but that it is also behind him" (*Ad,* 167; *AD,* 123; above 376). "Ideas are neither received from the proletariat by the Party nor given by the Party to the proletariat; they are *elaborated* in the *Party*" (*Ad,* 157; *AD,* 116; above 371). Yet, Sartre writes "Since the masses cannot budge without shaking society, they are revolutionary by virtue of their *objective situation:* in order *to serve* them, the officials must elaborate a revolutionary policy" (*Cp,* 377; *CP,* 226). "If active experience begins in receptivity and uncertainty . . . the deciphering *can* be achieved by an intermediary. Still, a party can only try its keys; it cannot force them" (*RL,* 33; *CP,* 353). Merleau-Ponty reminds us that "Lenin gave consciousness the obligation of informing itself about everything the proletariat spontaneously does or says" (*Ad,* 175; *AD,* 129; above 381). But Sartre says "The essential task of the militants is to maintain contact with the masses" [*Cp,* 370; *CP,* 221]. "The militant must make conjectures on their frame of mind, on the effect his speeches have produced, on the *objective possibilities* of the situation" [*Cp,* 369; *CP,* 220]. And: "It must be able *to foresee* the worker's reactions. . . . How can the union decide, if it has not gathered information, conducted surveys and consulted statistics. The masses continuously give signs: it's up to the organizer to interpret them" (*Cp,* 367; *CP,* 218).

Placing itself beyond any criterion of truth "the Party cannot err," says Merleau-Ponty. But Sartre writes regarding the militant: "The synthesis which it carries out is itself only a reconstruction, the probability of which, in the best cases, cannot exceed that of scientific hypothesis before experimental verification. Naturally, it will be tested, but since the action itself takes the place of experimentation, error is expensive" (*Cp,* 370; *CP,* 221).

Merleau-Ponty criticizes Sartre for considering the relationship of the party with the masses as a relationship of end to means or means to end, whereas there is an open relationship between them. But Sartre writes regarding the masses: "Since they represent the very forces which can carry out the revolutionary undertaking, it will be said that they are the means of this policy insofar as they are its end" (*Cp*, 377–78; *CP*, 266). "And since it isn't a matter of changing them but of helping them to become what they are, the Party is at once their expression and their example" (*Cp*, 155; *CP*, 58).

Merleau-Ponty reminds us that "The Party has value for the militant only through the action to which it calls him, and this action is not *completely definable in advance*" (*Ad*, 172; *AD*, 127; above 379). But Sartre has explained that "the class *already united* can go beyond its leaders, steer them farther than they meant to go and can translate into the social sphere an initial decision which was perhaps only political" (*RL*, 64; *CP*, 275). To make a political theory spring from a series of pure actions without any reference to history or truth will obviously bring about the most absurd consequences. "The possibilities are all equally distant—in a sense at zero distance, since all there is to do is to will, in another sense infinitely distant" (*Ad*, 179; *AD*, 132; above 383). Sartre explains, however, that the role of the party is precisely its duty to organize all possibilities perceived by the mass as immediate, as being equally distant. This is the meaning [*sens*] of the use of the "double objective." "One discloses to the masses the remote consequences of their grievance actions, one teaches them under what general conditions their particular grievances will be redressed" (*Cp*, 378; *CP*, 227).

Merleau-Ponty claims, that, according to Sartre, *praxis* "is thus the vertiginous freedom, the magic power that is ours to act and to make ourselves whatever we want" (*Ad*, 179; *AD*, 132; above 383). Sartre writes: "The *praxis* was adumbrated by the movement of the economy" (*Cp*, 311; *CP*, 176). But Merleau-Ponty points out that "An immediate desire to change the world, resting on no historical buildup and including neither strategy nor tactics, is, in history, sentimentalism and vertigo of doing [*la loi du coeur et le vertige du faire*]" [*Ad*, 181 n.; *AD*, 134 n.; above 443, note 30]. And he wisely objects: "one cannot sanely attempt to recreate history by pure action alone, with no external complicity" [*Ad*, 193; *AD*, 143; above 390]. However, it is certainly not Sartre who thinks that one can "start from scratch," not the Sartre who wrote in his reply to Camus: "This first means accepting many things, if you hope to change a few of them" [*RC*, 110; *Sits.*, 90]. To tell the truth there is a certain madness in the words themselves as used by Merleau-Ponty: Where is point zero in history? Or if one situates it in the age of the pithecanthrope, how can one refer oneself to that?

"There is neither degree nor path between the actual society and the revolutionary society" (*Ad*, 204; *AD*, 151; above 396), says Merleau-

Ponty commenting on Sartre. Yet, Sartre writes: "In order that they (the masses) win one day, it is necessary to prepare for their triumph. To make alliances . . . to work out a strategy, to invent a tactic" (*Cp*, 357; *CP*, 211). The party's role, precisely its duty, is to mediate through its policies the demands of the masses; because "need is only a lack; it can be the foundation of a humanism but not of a strategy" [*Cp*, 376; *CP*, 225].

We can see now that in *Adventures of the Dialectic* the misrepresentation of Sartre's political thought is as radical as the falsification of his ontology. In the face of a proletariat as opaque and mute as things, the party would create history *ex nihilo* through instantaneous actions: the voluntarism of pure action is symmetrical to the imperialism of pure consciousness, giving its meaning to the world. They are both equally foreign to Sartre. According to him, the party's role is, on the contrary, to isolate the truth indicated in the world of probabilities by means of experience, which demands time and implies the possibility of error. It is on this truth, based on the needs of the masses, pushed and controlled by them, that the party is to elaborate a long term policy which would bring about the triumph of the demands of the masses.

IV

We would be tempted to think that the aberrations of pseudo-Sartreanism completely isolate it from reality. Nevertheless Merleau-Ponty admits a curious, preestablished harmony between the philosophical delirium which poses the subject as a sovereign demiurge and the madness of a politics of pure action: Sartre is thus an appropriate example of ultrabolshevism. His sole wrongdoing is to have adopted a favorable attitude toward this most recent avatar of communism. As a matter of fact, Sartre, says Merleau-Ponty, no longer believes in the immanent truth that according to Marx guarantees *praxis:* the revolution. His decision is, therefore, nothing more than a moral option betraying personal obsessions. If we confine ourselves to objectivity, we will necessarily side with this agnostic acommunism which Merleau-Ponty adopted ever since the Korean War convinced him of the need to support liberty.

We are now going to examine the different steps of this demonstration. For Sartre, revolution will no longer intervene except as myth and utopia. "The revolution of which Sartre speaks is absent in the sense which Marx said it was present, that is to say, as the 'internal mechanism' of the class struggle; and it is present in the sense in which Marxism believed it distant, that is to say, as 'the positing of ends' " (*Ad*, 183; *AD*, 136; above

385). But when Sartre says that today the proletariat has lost its grip on history, he is merely stating that workers no longer feel the revolution as their daily task; there is no longer an immediate coincidence between their specific claims and their will to change the world. This does not mean that their will has died out or that capitalism has ceased to be torn by contradictions which make its break-up necessary:

> Let us not go concluding that the proletariat has lost the memory of its infinite task: the truth of the matter is that the confluence of circumstances deprives it of any future by forcing it to stick to its immediate interests. . . . Never has the truth appeared so clearly, each class pursues the death of the other. . . . And in point of fact, if the crisis gets worse, it can lead to the revolution, that is to the blowup of an economy sapped by its internal contradictions. (*Cp*, 315; *CP*, 179).

Merleau-Ponty admits that "There is an ebb and flow of the proletariat living politically in the Party" (*Ad,* 163; *AD,* 120; above 374). Sartre sees in this day and age a period of ebb-tide: the proletariat nevertheless remains revolutionary in its objective situation, and if it needs the party to mediate its will into an effective praxis, one has no right to conclude that "the revolution itself will be the party's concern" [*Ad,* 183; *AD,* 136; above 384]. The revolution created by the party will not be *the same* as the one nurtured in the bosom of the proletariat; it will not be authentic, Merleau-Ponty says, for its authenticity would require the access of the proletarian to political power and management. Merleau-Ponty's entire reasoning relies on the dissociation he previously made between the apparatus and the masses. However, if the party is distinguished from the masses only insofar as it is their union, Merleau-Ponty's objections collapse by virtue of their own contradictions.

For lack of warranty, he adds, "revolution is defined only by its antagonism toward the class it eliminates" [*Ad,* 187; *AD,* 137; above 385]. "Sartre calls revolution 'outstripping the Other toward the unlimited task.' Marx thought: outstripping the Other and itself" [*Ad,* 185; *AD,* 137; above 385]. In fact, the idea of unlimited task implies for Sartre not that the revolution recedes to infinity, but that as soon as the bourgeoisie is eliminated as a class, the proletariat will necessarily have to surpass the moment of negation. If Sartre refuses to describe the exact shape that society will then take, it is because, for him as well as for Marx, revolution as a positing of ends is absent; one cannot positively imagine without lapsing into utopia. This does not mean that the future will then become a total obscurity that would be the case if the party were actually to recreate the future from the zero point of pure action; but the hypothesis is in itself mad. Incidentally, Merleau-Ponty recognizes that "one meets the C.P., not as pure action, but as applied action" [*Ad,* 235; *AD,* 175; above 415]. And it is as such that Sartre has always described it. It is a question of making a truth triumph historically, a truth which is inscribed in the structures of society; *praxis* is not invented *ex nihilo,* it is based on objective meanings indicated by the world. From this world to a revolutionary world, there is, thus, a perfectly intelligible passage. Certainly it does not follow that the future will be entirely foreseeable: it was not for Marx or Lenin either. Merleau-Ponty is the first one to recognize that *praxis,* because "it agrees to commit itself to more than what it knows of a party and of history, it allows more to be learned, and its motto could be *Clarum per obscurius*" (*Ad,* 264; *AD,* 196; above 433). Why, when this commitment is geared toward revolution, is it said all of a sudden and testily concluded that "the revolutionary choice is really a choice of 'something or other' " [*Ad,* 206; *AD,* 153; above 397], and that Sartre, contrary to *praxis,* practices the "*obscurius per clarum*"?

This is because Merleau-Ponty persists in reconstructing Sartre by using pure deduction, based on pseudo-Sartreanism. If Sartre denies history, dialectic, and finally revolution, his commitment can only be based on abstract principles. "A decisive reading into events depends, thus, upon a moral option." Merleau-Ponty acknowledges that political judgment "escapes morality as well as pure science. It is of the category of action, which makes for continual oscillation between morality and science" (*Ad,* 208; *AD,* 155; above 399). But since Sartre repudiates science, since in his philosophy "there is no truth of a society," decision is only a question of ethics. Feeling indicted by the look "of the least-favored," Sartre allegedly tries to defend himself through pure action, and since he himself cannot achieve it at every moment of his life, he delegates this task to the Communist Party with which he claims to feel affinity. " 'Pure action' is Sartre's response to this gaze. . . . We are in the magical or moral world" [*Ad,* 307; *AD,* 154; above 398].

Merleau-Ponty's interpretation here seems to betray his own personal obsessions, for Sartre never spoke of *indictment;* nor are the ideas of *redemption,* nor the concern of being *irreproachable* in the eyes of the proletariat, to be seen anywhere in his works. Nevertheless, Merleau-Ponty makes them the ultimate motivating forces for Sartre's decisions. Feigning to reckon with the other in the highest degree, Sartre, in reality, reckons only with himself. His attitude allegedly reveals the "madness of the *cogito* which has sworn to recapture its image in others" [*Ad,* 213; *AD,* 159; above 402]. Merleau-Ponty's emotional outburst makes him so distraught that he uses words side by side that clash with each other: the *cogito,* pure presence of the for-itself to itself, cannot have an image;

the image can appear only through this transcendent object that the Ego is. Elsewhere, in a more intelligible manner, Merleau-Ponty says that Sartre seeks "to put in agreement the determinations attributed by the other with what I am in my own eyes" [*Ad,* 209; *AD,* 156; above 399, a paraphrase]. Sartre has shown in *Saint Genet* that such an attempt is necessarily doomed to failure, and his book shows that there must be particular circumstances for an individual to base his life upon such an endeavor. It is clear, according to the manner Sartre uses to tell of Genet's experience, that he does not recognize himself in it. Nothing in his life or his work authorizes us to define him through this will of recuperation. Once again, Merleau-Ponty proceeds with the use of a purely unwarranted assertion. Moreover, he should ask himself why in this totality detotalized, which is referred to by an ambiguous word—the other—Sartre elects the look of the least-favored. If he is looking for a mirror, he can choose Aron's eyes, or Merleau-Ponty's, or that of the thinking elite. He wishes to be true to himself, answers Merleau-Ponty: But why is it that the rule is inscribed on this image and not on that other one? The rule is not provided from the beginning. Merleau-Ponty is true to form in renouncing the Marxist wait-and-see attitude, since an objective revelation would have brought him to contest his previous attitude: therefore, the rule depends on the manner in which we apprehend our situation, and consequently the truth of the world. The anticommunist is true to the world and to himself, and so is the communist. This formal explanation cannot give us an account of Sartre's concrete choice.

The fact is that it would be sufficient to read Sartre without bias; then one could grasp his objective reasons. When Sartre speaks of the look of the least-favored, he in no way comes into play himself. In describing the actual condition of the unskilled worker, he explains that in order to free the masses from their sense of inferiority, "it was necessary to make the masses understand that they were offering all men the chance to look at man and society in their truth, that is to say, with the eyes of the least favored" (*Cp,* 344; *CP,* 201). For, contrary to what Merleau-Ponty claims, Sartre does recognize a truth of society, a truth which is disguised by bourgeois myths and which is unveiled by the man of the masses. Sartre thinks that "the only human relationship is that of *real,* total man and that this relationship, travestied or passed over in silence, exists permanently within the masses and exists only there" [*Cp,* 344; *CP,* 201]. Obsessed with the Sartrean theory of the look, Merleau-Ponty wants to find in Sartre only this type of relationship; however, the look appears in the text to which he refers only as the unveiling of a total relationship. Sartre also says that the existence of the masses "introduces . . . the radical demand for the human in an inhuman society" [*Cp,* 346; *CP,* 203]. Here

Sartre is close to Marx, who also saw the proletarian as the only one capable of denouncing *the alienation* in which the entire society lives, because he feels annihilated by it, while the bourgeois is satisfied with the appearance of the human." Marx speaks of a categorical imperative of the revolution without Merleau-Ponty accusing him of deciphering history in the sole light of a moral option. There is in Sartre, as well as in Marx, this coming and going between truth and ethical decision which, according to Merleau-Ponty himself, characterizes the political judgment.

Yet, Merleau-Ponty persists in making Sartre's political attitude an utterly subjective one. Instead of pondering on the communist action, Sartre, allegedly, demiurgically decided to integrate it into the "Sartrean project." "It is not so much a question of knowing where communist action is going, so as either to associate oneself with it or not, as it is of finding a meaning for this action in the Sartrean project" (*Ad*, 261; *AD*, 194; above 432). And what is this project? If it is a matter of "redeeming itself through the future"—nothing in Sartre's work gives an inkling of this expression—why then prefer this future? Actions other than communist actions do exist. Moreover, if it is necessary to explain Sartre through the megalomania of the subject, what was the reason for his having waited such a long time before gluttonously devouring communism?

Merleau-Ponty finds the proof for Sartre's subjectivism in the fact that the latter started his new relationship with communism because of certain historical events; he forgets that he himself chose acommunism after a specific event—the Korean War—which was also a historical event. Conscious awareness by taking place in the present, at a precise moment, can thus unveil an objective reality and provoke an engagement which is not limited to the instant: this, it seems, is a truth of common sense. Besides, Sartre explains at length in *The Communists and Peace* that it is because he has found the true meaning of communist action and its necessity that he felt obliged to associate himself with it. His standpoint is clear to one who reads his essay without being blinded by pseudo-Sartreanism. He believes in certain contradictions in capitalism that, by making the situation of the exploited classes intolerable, turn the society in which we live into an inhuman society. He wants for himself and for the others, who are inextricably bound, the abolition of that alienation that all of us bear, but whose true brunt is fully borne only by the least favored in society. He knows that only the proletariat has the necessary force to change the world, and that it needs the party's mediation in order to apply it efficaciously. Therefore, he decided to become allied with those who want the same thing he does and who have the means to accomplish it: such is the meaning of his engagement.

However, Merleau-Ponty refuses to admit that Sartrean engagement has a positive definition and leads to a real action. A pure consciousness can only keep the world at a distance, it cannot concretely project itself onto it. Hence, for Sartre, to engage oneself will always be to disengage oneself; freedom appears only as a negation and when Sartre claims to act, he merely contemplates. Merleau-Ponty simply forgets that, in pure Sartreanism, there is never a pure consciousness: we have said it before and we need to repeat it again. Sartrean consciousness only *exists* in the world when it is *lost* in the world, committed, personified in a body and a situation. Man becomes a living being only when he has an effect on the world through positive projects, and these projects always have a temporal substantiality. Merleau-Ponty, in addition to his rejection of Sartre's theory of facticity, also dismisses his entire philosophy of time. He believes that time, for Sartre as well as for Descartes, is a continuous creation: freedom could only manifest itself through *ex nihilo* flashes, without any link between them, it would not allow any true action but only "sudden interventions into the world, for camera shots and flash bulbs" (*Ad,* 259; *AD,* 192–93; above 430–31). In this pseudo-Sartreanism, instead of a doing one finds only a *fiat* whose magical dimension is similar to that of the look. And Merleau-Ponty in a plausible way explains to the pseudo-Sartre that an authentic action bites on things, progresses in time, implies possibilities of failure, and is based on a choice which has roots in all aspects of our existence.

Meanwhile, Sartre in *Being and Nothingness* openly states his opposition to the *instantaneistic* concept of the consciousness that one encounters in Descartes and Husserl: the three temporal *ek-stases* for him are indissoluble, and the *cogito* itself, in its springing up, envelops both a past and a future. The choice, in particular, always retains in itself the past which it surpasses: "A converted atheist is not simply a believer: he is a believer who, on his own initiative, has negated atheism." And the choice always projects a future: "To choose is to effect the upsurge along with my engagement of a certain extension of concrete and continuous duration" [*EN,* 543; *BN,* 441]. In such a duration, the action organizes means in view of an end. Sartre carefully distinguishes the *fiat* of the emotional attitude which immediately poses the end in the imagination, from the *doing* which mediates the choice within the real substantiality of the world. "To act is to modify the shape of the world; it is to arrange means in view of an end" [*EN,* 508; *BN,* 409]. This is a long and exacting enterprise which also determines "a modification in the being of the transcendent." By biting into a reality which is *probability* and not certainty, it is evident that the enterprise entails a risk of failure. Thus, we are leagues away from the pseudo-engagement of the pseudo-Sartre which Merleau-Ponty defines as negativity, as an instantaneous, magic, and imaginary intervention. Incidentally, if Sartre were to practice such an engagement, it would be impossible for him to write a book or to engage in political action: he would be reduced to the radical ineffectiveness of Mr. Teste, who, as a matter of fact, remained silent.

Merleau-Ponty especially makes us want to smile when he sweetly asks Sartre: "How then shall I date my choices? They have innumerable precedents" (*Ad,* 265; *AD,* 197; above 435). We feel compelled to smile because one of the leitmotifs found throughout Sartre's work is precisely the totalitarian character of each human life. There is a transcendent signification—a type of intelligible character—which unites all our empirical choices; each one of our choices has its roots in our past. Freedom is not the contingency of the *clinamen:* "The freedom of the for-itself has always engaged; there is no question here of a freedom which could be undetermined and which would pre-exist its choice. We shall never apprehend ourselves except as a choice in the making" [*EN,* 558; *BN,* 455]. Sartre considers deliberation to be pure abstraction. "When I deliberate, the chips are down" [*EN,* 527; *BN,* 427]. According to him there is never a moment when choice begins. "I choose myself perpetually" [*EN,* 560; *BN,* 456]. One ought to read *Baudelaire, Saint Genet,* and *Henri Martin* to see that Sartre has no need to wait for Merleau-Ponty to suspect that one does not become either a poet or a communist in a lightning decision, without a precedent.

Communist action does not represent a train of convulsive bids for power; and to go back to Sartre's case, neither is his adhesion to communist action reduced to a string of realizations from afar. Sartre, says Merleau-Ponty, "knows that some people want to change the world," and he sympathizes with this intention, which is a way of not assuming it. The fact is that he belongs to those who want to change the world and he chooses the means which his concrete situation offers him—that of a bourgeois writer.

On this point, Merleau-Ponty aims his most contradictory reproaches at Sartre. He claims: "For him, to be committed is not to interpret and criticize oneself in contact with history; rather it is to recreate one's own relationship with history . . . it is to place oneself deliberately in the imaginary" (*Ad,* 262; *AD,* 195; above 432). At the time when Sartre, together with other intellectuals, Merleau-Ponty included, was attempting to create a rallying of the noncommunist left, such a reproach would have made sense; today, it only bewilders us. It is precisely because he has interpreted and criticized himself in contact with history that Sartre understood his powerlessness to change the world by his own force or by joining people who were as helpless as himself. He resolved to follow the type of action his objective situation indicated, that being the only really valid one: an alliance with real forces able to impose on history the meaning he wants to give.

Such an alliance, Merleau-Ponty argues, is only a spoken, imagined thought: it does not have the weight of an action. "There is perhaps not much sense in dealing with communism, which is an action, by means of pure thought" (*Ad,* 237; *AD,* 176; above 417). But hasn't Merleau-Ponty reproached the pseudo-Sartre for falsely creating a gulf between action and thought? What does such an arbitrary opposition signify? There is no pure thought since any unveiling is action; nor is there an action which does not imply an unveiling: one truly cannot see why "to think communism" is a contradictory enterprise. Moreover, Sartre's intervention does not limit itself only to that. Merleau-Ponty asserts—mistakenly believing that Sartre had said—that "all actions . . . are always symbolic actions and count as much upon the effect they will have as meaningful gesture and as the mark of an intention as upon the direct results of the event" (*Ad,* 270; *AD,* 200; above 437). Hence, Sartre's adherence, although it has no immediate results on the event, possesses at least the not inconsiderable reality of a meaningful manifestation: it can be an example or an appeal. Altering his stand, Merleau-Ponty nevertheless demands immediate results; the will to help the proletariat to free itself is discredited if we do not say "how our action will free it." Neither Marx nor Lenin nor any militant has drawn up in advance such a program of action. If Sartre were to risk doing so himself, then we could surely call him a utopian. But he modestly said in his "*Reply to Albert Camus*" that one must try to give history the meaning one sees as being the best "by not refusing our participation to any concrete action which may require it" [*RC,* 125; *Sits.,* 104]. This is a sensible answer and it is the opposite of the strange alternative proposed by Merleau-Ponty to have a plan for freeing the proletariat or to sit around doing nothing. By limiting ourselves to the accomplishment of these concrete actions, ordered by circumstances, we choose "a way of putting ourselves right with the world rather than entering it" (*Ad,* 259; *AD,* 193; above 431). But how can we enter a world we are already in? What date does Merleau-Ponty give for his own entering the world? He also reproaches Sartre for not taking "the world in charge," however, Merleau-Ponty does not indicate what this titanic operation would entail. Elsewhere, he says more sensibly: "No action assumes as its own all that happens" [*Ad,* 270; *AD,* 200; above 437].

Moreover, Merleau-Ponty will add that Sartre, in his desire to take charge of everything, fails to engage himself concretely in a real enterprise. Only in dreams can we accomplish anything we want. But once more Merleau-Ponty is misled by the erroneous idea that Sartre's philosophy is intuitive and claims to encompass everything. For Sartre, consciousness is always engaged, it is necessarily a finitude: and he intends to act only as a finite, limited, and situated individual.

"It is a solution for someone who lives in the capitalist world," Merleau-Ponty objects again [*Ad,* 240; *AD,* 178; above 419]. The fact is that Sartre lives in this world, so do the communists; the struggle to change society takes place in its bosom; it is in the world that one must seek a solution. However, Sartre's solution will not be accepted by the communists, says Merleau-Ponty. "He decrees coexistence between communism and the external opposition" [*Ad,* 240; *AD,* 178; above 419]. Here one is reminded of Zeno's sophisms in which he cleverly demonstrates why Achilles will never catch up with the turtle. It is a fact that there is a friendly coexistence between Sartre and the communists, and nothing authorizes Merleau-Ponty to assert that they do not *understand* him: comprehension does not imply identification but simply friendship. By associating himself with the communists, Sartre proves that he understands them; and because they ratify this alliance, they show in return that they understand him. It is futile to confine in formal contradictions an attitude which proves its viability in being alive.

Actually, in order to establish that the Sartrean choice only obeys subjective motives and that in reality nothing justifies it, Merleau-Ponty ought to succeed in proving that the weight of objectivity is on the side of acommunism. Let's examine his demonstration. The Korean War revealed to Merleau-Ponty what the Moscow trials, the Germano-Soviet pact, and the events in Prague had failed to make him discover, namely that revolutionary negativity is embodied in living men who exist positively. The result is that "Revolutionary society has its weight, its positivity, and it is no longer the absolute Other." Hurled down from the sublime point where he had been transported in thought in order to achieve a miraculous transubstantiation, Merleau-Ponty concluded then that "revolutions are true as movements and false as regimes" [*Ad,* 298; *AD,* 207]. It is thus, as in Prévert's poem, that the scientists displeased with the results of their experiments, came to the conclusion: "It is the rabbits that are wrong."

Merleau-Ponty will say no. It is not a matter of a subjective disappointment here, but a matter of a contradiction inherent in the revolutionary process. At best, the system it institutes is relatively justifiable; "the very nature of a revolution is to believe itself absolute" [*Ad,* 298; *AD,* 222]. "In fact," he says, "one does not kill for relative progress" [ibid.]. Who else would undertake to make a revolution without being convinced that he was creating a different society "because it is the good"? [ibid.]. The revolutionaries, of course. Merleau-Ponty, who answered the pseudo-Sartre with the statement that our intentions do not aim at closed meanings, nor do our wills aim at settled objectives, seems nevertheless to assume now that the revolutionary enterprise is preceded by a deliberation where the idea of absolute good wins the day. However, history shows Merleau-Ponty that revolutions spring up, little caring if they guarantee their justification in advance. What is found in their origins, is not the promise of a sun city, but the most modest of demands. When, in 1848, the national workshops closed, the workers took their protest onto the streets; they killed and were killed not for progress, whether absolute or relative, but for work and bread. One kills from hunger, anger, and despair. One kills to live. The stake is infinite for it represents life itself with its infinity of possibilities: but it never assumes the positive and utopian image of a paradisiacal society. If Merleau-Ponty assumes the contrary, it is because he ignores dire situations; neither the word nor the idea of need appear in his analyses. But an absolute of rebellion and insubordination erupts from dire needs, and that does not allow the revolutionary the opportunity of drawing up a balance sheet. In the quiet of his study, Merleau-Ponty may *tell* himself that if revolution does not achieve the absolute Good, the game is not worth the candle; but he is talking for himself; therefore, revolutions betray solely his dreams and not themselves.

In any case, he will say, for the one who is not involved in it, he sees no need for a revolution. The relative progress that it may accomplish could be achieved by other means. And here is when Merleau-Ponty, with surprising naïveté, discovers reformism. "The question arises whether there is not more of a *future* in a regime that does not intend to remake history from the ground up but only to change it" [*Ad,* 279; *AD,* 207]. Merleau-Ponty seems to believe that revolutionaries are people who ignore the question, whereas they solved it through a negative. They consider that a future freed from exploitation can only be created if one attacks exploitation at its roots, and such is the future they want. To pose the question in quantitative terms is nonsense. Here, one touches the deep viciousness of a thought, which feigning to believe in class struggle, resolutely neglects to take it into account. When Merleau-Ponty decides that the duty of acommunism must be to assess situations, he makes the mistake he ascribes to the pseudo-Sartre: in a trice he places himself outside history, he pretends to take an olympian view of the struggle between oppressors and oppressed, and then pretends to separate the combatants by casting the world into mathematical equations. But it is impossible to establish the criterion of the pluses and the minuses in a society which is torn apart: what is a gain in the eyes of the privileged is a loss for the oppressed, and vice-versa. The idea of a general interest is so hackneyed that one wonders how bourgeois economists dare to serve it to us again.

While waiting for the inventory to be accomplished, Merleau-Ponty limits himself to proposing an assessment of the Soviet regime: he repeats the indictment of the U.S.S.R. that floats around in all of Aron's books and in the columns of *L'Aurore*. He specifically repeats the Machiavellian slogan: revolution is nothing more than a change of elites. He concludes that what we know of the U.S.S.R. "is not sufficient to prove that the proletarians' interests lie in this system" [*Ad,* 245; *AD,* 182; above 422]. But is what we know of France sufficient to prove that the proletariat's interests lie in upholding its present regime? Merleau-Ponty will say it is not a question of upholding the present regime, but of settling oneself in it in order to change it. If this is the case, then what does the U.S.S.R. have to do in all of this? Let's rather confront the future of a France reshaped by the lucid action of the elite, with the France that would be born out of a revolution. The revolution necessarily institutes "an impure power," says Merleau-Ponty [*Ad,* 297; *AD,* 221]; but is it pure to prolong without clash or violence a state of affairs which Merleau-Ponty himself qualifies as unjustifiable? Merleau-Ponty is suspicious of the revolutionary action because "revolutionary action is secret, unverifiable" [*Ad,* 30f.; *AD,* 227]. Is the action he suggests verifiable?

It is here that his bad faith is so glaring. He wants to change history by working within the parliamentary regime, because the Parliament is the sole institution which guarantees a minimum of opposition and truth; he nevertheless admits that the democratic game puts the proletariat at an unfair disadvantage; but he hopes to offset this contradiction. He will do so by demanding that the working class, through its communist party, its strikes, and its popular movements, have the possibility of refusing the rules of the game. Thus, the new liberalism "lets even what contests it enter its universe" [*Ad,* 304; *AD,* 226]. Such a compromise is a revolting hypocrisy. It is not by chance that the parliamentary game is played to the detriment of the workers. Since Merleau-Ponty recognizes that class struggle does exist, he is aware that the democratic bourgeoisie necessarily exerts its power against the proletariat; the bourgeoisie might camouflage the injustice but it does not want to suppress it. Therefore, the concessions of the new liberalism would be nothing but mystifications. Tolerated because of their being a "useful menace" [*Ad,* 303; *AD,* 226], revolutionary movements will be stifled as soon as they appear to really have a chance of success. Merleau-Ponty must be quite a fool to expect that a class, which is the enemy of the proletariat, if entrusted with the task of remaking history, would do so *for* the proletariat.

Why does this regime inspire Merleau-Ponty with such confidence? Because it allows an opposition. But since Merleau-Ponty confuses opposition with the form it takes in Parliament, he, in effect, cannot recognize it anywhere outside a parliamentary regime. Meanwhile, the reproaches he levels at self-criticism, as practiced by the U.S.S.R. or the communist party, have as much significance as those that an alchemist, an astrologer, or some magus would level at scientific self-criticism. The scientific body of knowledge was built through discussions, passionate quarrels, the elimination of errors, and the invention of new truths. The only restriction on the critical process by which scientific knowledge is identified is that the process will never turn against the system as a whole. This does not signify that there were no interesting individual cases among the backward, the misled, the forerunners, the visionaries, and the illuminati who were fighting against the science of their time; but these people achieved no scientific posterity. Thus in a movement or a regime which seeks *to build* society according to a universal pattern, criticism can be carried extremely far; it can lead to drawbacks, to metamorphoses of error into truth, and vice-versa; it only needs to be integrated into the positive work that is being done. Whoever truly wants the structure to be successful will have to accept a rule that does not deprive him of his freedom any more than scientific discipline deprives the scientist of his. To choose a regime which works against the proletariat, hence a regime which we must disapprove on principle, under the pretext that it authorizes opposition, is to give preeminence of action when it should be only its guarantee. In other words, it is to place the abstract pleasure of expressing opinion ahead of the concrete will to rebuild the world. Furthermore, it is to dissociate oneself from the proletariat, whose cause one pretends to espouse knowing well that its opposition is not accepted by this Parliament which only concedes to the already privileged the right to quarrel among themselves.

In fact, the very idea of choosing *for* the proletariat implies that Merleau-Ponty, despite his statements, no longer believes in class struggle, that is to say, that he has opted for the bourgeoisie. If there is a struggle, one cannot want anything *for* the proletariat without wanting it *with* the proletariat. "The question is to know whether, for the proletariat, communism is worth what it costs," says Merleau-Ponty [*Ad,* 301; *AD,* 224]; he glimpses a stage beyond the communism-capitalism conflict. "One glimpses a generalized economy of which they are particular cases" [*Ad,* 303; *AD,* 225]. However, communism is not solely an economic system; it has a human dimension: it expresses the will of certain men who, first of all, demand to hold their lives in their own hands, instead of enduring the fate imposed on them by elites. To decide to bring them happiness in spite of themselves is to perpetuate oppression. Class struggle implies that one cannot include the will of both the exploiter and the exploited in any economy, however generalized it may be.

To be *for* the proletariat does not mean to acknowledge its misery from a distance and let it pass: it is to take its demands seriously. Merleau-Ponty decisively sides with the bourgeoisie guard dogs when he fails to take communism as a living reality, rooted in the situation of an exploited class, and instead calls it a figment of the imagination. For him, as for Aron and all the other bourgeois thinkers, communism becomes utopia. Therefore, the existing world, despite all the flaws that make it unjustifiable, leads to a favorable prejudice. What is revealing is that Merleau-Ponty repeats the charge against communism which was formerly set against Pascal's wager: "An eternity of imaginary happiness could not counterbalance an instant of life." This is to insinuate that the proletariat has to make a choice between a plenitude, perhaps minimal but real, and the emptiness of a barren dream; but what it has to do, in reality, is to tear itself away, at any price, from a condition which (as Merleau-Ponty acknowledges later) does not allow it to live. Here, Merleau-Ponty, when all is said and done, rediscovers the unimaginative wisdom of conservatives: "We know what we lose; we do not know what we will find." This signifies that he identifies with those who have something to lose, those for whom the *balance sheet* of this society is positive: in short, he identifies with the privileged. He has discovered, in fact, that unjustifiable societies do have, nevertheless, value. Or perhaps, he simply repeats here the idea of Marx and Engels, who start the *Communist Manifesto* by praising capitalism: the worth of a society is dialectically defined by the possibilities encompassed in it. Capitalist society exists only to be surpassed, and that is the aim of communism. Or perhaps, Merleau-Ponty, together with Malraux and other champions of Western civilization, decides that one can prefer values to men. The analytical thought of the bourgeois confines oppression to a single sector of society and recognizes that this singular wrong can compromise with other rights. Marx's synthetic thought, as well as Sartre's, considers that society in its totality is corrupted by exploitation: it measures values in the light of oppression. Such is the meaning of Sartre's appeal to the look of the least-favored, an appeal so poorly understood by Merleau-Ponty. For the least-favored, all values carry a minus sign. They exist only insofar as they negate the least-favored. The exploited, because it takes no part in any new human conquest, falls further behind and widens the chasm of its privation. When one has taken the proletariat's side, the values that are encompassed in unjustifiable societies make these societies only more unjustifiable. One feels sorry to have to remind Merleau-Ponty of these elementary truths, he who so justly wrote in *Humanism and Terror:* "The worth of a society is measured in terms of the worth attributed to the relationships of man with man." Today, he must decide whether to state with Aron that class struggle is an outdated notion; or holding out his hand to Mr. Jules Romain, whether to join openly our Western thinkers and the ethics of the elite in their contempt of the masses. But to write "a history in which the proletariat is nothing is not a human history" [*Ad,* 307; *AD,* 228] and to adhere to a regime which reduces the proletariat to nothing, is the most shameless of masquerades.

How shall we explain the enormous inconsistencies we find in Merleau-Ponty, both on the philosophical and political planes? What emerges from *Adventures of the Dialectic* is, first of all, that he fell victim to that old idealism traditional among French academics. One of them wrote about the 1914 War that it was "Descartes' battle against Kant." And thus, Merleau-Ponty sees in the Korean War a confrontation between Marxism and Stalinism: the Koreans in this matter were nonentities. He asks himself whether or not the proletariat is in itself the dialectic; as for the proletarians, he never pays them any heed. The revolution for him is "the critique in power" [*Ad,* 311; *AD,* 231]. He does not attach any importance to the changes that concrete revolutions bring about in the concrete condition of men. Reverting to the pre-Kantian ages of philosophy, he fabricates antinomies of concepts that he then uses for an excuse to negate the living truth of the world. In this way, concepts of critique and power exclude each other and are out of the question; thus, one must condemn revolutions as being deceptive. Or, on the contrary, he builds up ideal syntheses which he confuses with concrete solutions: if a generalized economy includes communism and capitalism, then communists and capitalists are reconciled! In defining a liberalism that envelops what it contests, he goes so far as to assert that the new liberals will indeed respect revolutionary movements: but it is with similar processes that Saint Anselm once proved God's existence.

It seems that this precedence given to the idea over a concrete man explains Merleau-Ponty's about-face. Revolution seduced him as long as he saw in it an already present truth whose revelation was immanent. In his book one feels the nostalgia of a golden age of revolution which is solely situated in Merleau-Ponty's inner life, but has nothing to do with the reality of things nor Marxism itself which closely adheres to reality. The proletariat was both "power and value," it had a mission, in the sacred meaning of the word. Merleau-Ponty says that now it is necessary "to secularize" communism which thus signifies that he had regarded it as sacred. If communism is no longer what anticommunists claim it is—a religion—a deceived Merleau-Ponty resolves to see in it only a utopia. He who defended the probable against the pseudo-Sartre is now driven by probabilism to agnosticism. If revolution entails a *perhaps* instead of a radiant certitude, if it presents itself as a *doing* and not as a truth already done, Merleau-Ponty then accuses those who want revolution of creating it *ex nihilo* and he does not see a middle ground between triumphant assertion and absolute doubt. Because he is no longer assured of an immediate apotheosis, he puts his wager on defeat. It is on this point that, politically, he is poles apart from Sartre. For Sartre, the truth of revolution is not an immediate or a distant triumph, before all else it is the class struggle as it exists today. This struggle aims at the future, but it is necessary right now to side with the exploited against exploitation, to refuse letting them bear the brunt of this adjusted capitalism that the class in power today takes pleasure in considering a universal panacea. If the fight is difficult and doubtful, Sartre does not think that sufficient reason for throwing oneself into the opposite camp; on the contrary, it is then that one's support is most needed.

Merleau-Ponty's mood regarding communism seems, therefore, to be the reflection of a religious soul's bitterness toward a world that is all too human. This partly explains his irritation with Sartre, who followed an opposite road. Merleau-Ponty's *a priori* construction of pseudo-Sartreanism remains nevertheless surprising. True, Merleau-Ponty has never understood Sartre. As early as *Phenomenology of Perception,* he coldly denied the entire Sartrean phenomenology of engaged freedom. Even if the conciliation of Sartre's ontology with his phenomenology raises difficulties,[7] one does not have the right to grab from his hands one "of the two ends of the chain," to use Merleau-Ponty's words. Such violence is even more scandalous today than ten years ago, because throughout the development of his work Sartre has insisted more and more on the engaged character of freedom, the facticity of the world, the embodiment of consciousness, the continuity of lived experience, the totalitarian character of the entire life. Yet, Merleau-Ponty does not ignore Sartre's books: when he answers the pseudo-Sartre, he usually employs Sartre's own ideas, and he uses terms which are reminiscent of those that Sartre had used himself: we have seen many examples of them. Perhaps the ideas Merleau-Ponty has in common with Sartre seem to him to be so exclusively his own that, in order to claim their originality, he is forced to invent a Sartre which would be a counter–Merleau-Pontyism. The method is a lazy one and not very honest. One could praise him for creating a philosophy that surpasses the difficulties of Sartreanism, but these difficulties do not permit Merleau-Ponty to mutilate Sartre's philosophy. Neither is it honest to make use of the pseudo-Sartre in order to write without compromising himself, a shoddy apology of the acommunist. Instead of clearly explaining how the acommunist "enters the world" and "takes charge of it," Merleau-Ponty suggests its flattering image to us by a negative. If the conscious and deliberate action is nothing more than thinking about oneself, if to side with the proletariat is the height of narcissism, then it will suffice to only dream to be a man of action, and abstention and selfishness will become the most effective ways to serve men: one can understand why these insinuations fill *Le Figaro* and Mr. Jacques Laurent with delight.

It appears that the periods of regression children go through are beneficial to their development; perhaps they may also be beneficial to an adult: let us hope that *Adventures of the Dialectic* has no more definitive significance. Distressed for having so long mistaken Kant for Marx, Merleau-Ponty thought that he could improve things by mistaking Sartre for Kant: doubtlessly in the end he will give back to each the place to which he is entitled. He fears that Sartre will forego the unveiling and still not succeed in acting. Nonetheless if Merleau-Ponty does not realize that pure assertion leads to the same madness as pure action, we shall have to deplore his renouncing acting without succeeding in unveiling.

Notes

Translated by Veronique Zaytzeff with the assistance of Frederick Morrison. Dedicated to Dr. Carol Keene, my former Dean and friend, who suggested the translation, read the final manuscript, and made useful comments on some philosophical fine points of the manuscript. I would also like to thank Southern Illinois University at Edwardsville for granting me a sabbatical to undertake this project. The references in brackets within the text itself represent passages quoted by Simone de Beauvoir without any reference to specific pagination. The references in parentheses are de Beauvoir's own notes. In the text as well as in the notes and the end of the translation, the French text is always quoted first. I have translated *sens* as "meaning," *signification* as "signification," *soi* as "self," *Moi* as "Ego," and *Je* as "the I."

List of Abbreviations:

Merleau-Ponty, *Aventures de la dialectique* (Paris: Gallimard, 1955). Abbreviated *Ad.*

Sartre, "Les Communistes et la paix," in *Situations,* VI (Paris: Gallimard, 1964). Abbreviated *Cp.*

Sartre, *L'Affaire Henri Martin,* Commentary by Jean-Paul Sartre (Paris: Gallimard, 1953). Abbreviated *HM.*

Sartre, *L'Être et le néant* (Paris: Gallimard, 1943). Abbreviated *EN.*

Sartre, "Réponse à Albert Camus," in *Situations,* IV (Paris: Gallimard, 1964). Abbreviated *RC.*

Sartre, "Réponse à Claude Lefort," in *Situations,* VII (Paris: Gallimard, 1965). Abbreviated *RL.*

Sartre, *Saint Genet: Comédien et martyr* (Paris: Gallimard, 1952). Abbreviated *SG.*
Sartre, *Situations, II* (Paris: Gallimard, 1948).
Merleau-Ponty, *Adventures of the Dialectic,* trans. Joseph Bien (Evanston: Northwestern University Press, 1973). Abbreviated *AD.*
Sartre, *Being and Nothingness,* trans. Hazel E. Barnes (New York: The Citadel Press, 1965). Abbreviated *BN.*
Sartre, "The Communists and Peace," trans. Martha H. Fletcher; and "A Reply to Claude Lefort," trans. Philip Berk. Both essays published in *The Communists and Peace* (New York: George Braziller, 1968). Abbreviated *CP.*
Sartre, *Existential Psychoanalysis,* trans. Hazel E. Barnes (Chicago: Henry Regnery Company, 1962). Abbreviated *EP.*
Sartre, *Saint Genet: Actor and Martyr,* trans. Bernard Frechtman (New York: George Braziller, 1963). Abbreviated *SGE.*
Sartre, *Situations,* contains "*Reply to Albert Camus,*" trans. Benita Eisler (New York: George Braziller, 1965). Abbreviated *Sits.*

1. "The purpose of this article is to declare my agreement with the communists on precise and limited subjects. I seek to understand what is happening in France, today, before our very eyes" [*Cp*, 168; *CP,* 68].

2. Jean-Paul Sartre, *L'Imaginaire* (Paris: Gallimard, 1948), 187–88; *The Psychology of Imagination,* trans. Bernard Frechtman (New York: Philosophical Library, 1948), 209–10.

3. What makes Merleau-Ponty's bad faith even more blatant is that Sartre wrote these lines in the last part of his essay, where, according to Merleau-Ponty himself, he does not adopt the point of view of immediacy. See *Cp*, 259ff.; *CP,* 137ff.

4. *RL,* 14; *CP,* 240. The context clearly shows that this dialectic is considered in this instance as being a valid one.

5. *Ad,* 267; *AD,* 198. How can Sartre return to a philosophy which, according to Merleau-Ponty, was never really his?

6. Fearing that one might use the process of the oversignificant here, one thing must be made clear: nothing is *nothing* only in relation with the bourgeois world of values and merit; but this absence is coupled with the very concrete presence of a need. Here, Sartre is very close to the Marxist formula: "The need of a thing is in itself a sufficient reason for its fulfillment."

7. Merleau-Ponty is perfectly aware that Sartre is in the process of preparing a philosophical work which attacks the question head-on.

24

The Philosophy of Existence

Maurice Merleau-Ponty

Translated by Allen S. Weiss

I would much rather speak to you of the philosophy of existence than of existentialism, for reasons that you probably already know. The term "existentialism" has come to designate almost exclusively the philosophical movement which arose in France after 1945, chiefly as a result of Sartre's instigation. In reality, this philosophical movement has its antecedents: it is tied to an entire philosophical tradition, a long and complicated tradition, since it actually begins with Kierkegaard's philosophy, and following this, is derived from philosophies such as Husserl's and Heidegger's in Germany, and in France, even before Sartre, from philosophies such as that of Gabriel Marcel. Thus, it is extremely difficult to isolate Sartre's attempt in relation to the other well-known efforts just mentioned. For me, Sartre's work was undeniably original. But since he was rebuilding an entire style of thought, it was truly impossible to grasp his philosophical efforts, his veritable philosophical politics, by separating it out from the rest. Bearing this in mind, I propose to discuss the beginnings of existentialist thought in France.

This beginning occurred in the years from 1930 to 1939 (the ten years which preceded the war). And since it is, as you know, especially in 1944 and 1945 that existentialism in the Sartrean sense appeared and established itself, I am talking about the period which immediately preceded its birth. However, it would be lengthy, difficult, and tedious to examine all of the writers who contributed to this period, so I propose a simpler manner of proceeding. I will examine a few of the ideas which formed the French philosophical landscape during the years—around 1930—when Sartre and I finished our studies. Following this, I will attempt to show how this landscape was disrupted or at least profoundly modified by the intervention of the authors who may be grouped under the heading of "philosophy of existence," which will then open up a perspective upon Sartre's attempt; and to see exactly how this attempt was related to the others, and how, conversely, it is tied to Sartre's more personal and more original talent.

Around 1930, when I finished my philosophical studies, how did things appear in France, from the philosophical point of view? It may be said that two influences, and only two, were dominant, and that the first of these was much more important: the key philosophical thought of the epoch in France had been that of Léon Brunschvicg. I do not know if Léon Brunschvicg is very well known today by philosophers outside of France. He was, among us students, absolutely and justly famous, perhaps not so much because of the philosophy he advocated and taught us, but because of his quite extraordinary personal qualities. He was a philosopher who had access to poetry and literature, who was an extraordinarily cultivated thinker, and his knowledge of the history of philosophy was as profound as possible. He was a man of the first order, not so much because of the conclusions of his doctrines, but because of his personal experience and talent, which were considerable. But then, exactly what doctrines did he propound, and, in short, how did he orient us? Without being philosophically technical, it can be explained in a few words: Brunschvicg transmitted to us the heritage of idealism, as Kant understood it. For him, this idealism was flexible, but it was nonetheless for the most part Kantian idealism. We became acquainted with Kant and Descartes through Brunschvicg, which is to say that this philosophy principally consisted of a reflexive endeavor, a return to the self. Whether pertaining to the perception of the objects that surround us or to scholarly activity, his philosophy in all cases sought to grasp both exterior perception and the constructions of science as creative and constructive activities of the mind. This was the truly constant theme of Brunschvicg's thought, for whom philosophy essentially consisted in the fact that the gaze—which scientists turn toward the object—is brought back to the mind which constructs the objects of science. Such was, in short, the allure of this philosophy, though it must be mentioned that its content is quite meager.

Brunschvicg had an admirable knowledge of the sciences, the history of the sciences, and the history of philosophy. But what he had to teach us as a philosopher nearly always consisted of a Cartesian reflection, by means of which he returned from the things to the subject which constructs the image of things. As regards pure philosophy, his essential contribution consisted precisely in informing us that we must turn toward the mind, toward the subject which constructs science and the perception of the world, but that lengthy philosophical descriptions or explications cannot be made of this mind, this subject. He said—and this was a formula that he readily employed—that human beings participate in the "one," that the "one" is the mind. He meant, by saying that this "one," this mind, is the same in everyone, that it is universal reason, but in describing it as such he wanted to oppose it to all other types of being. There is not your mind and my mind and the minds of others. No, there is a quality of thought in which we all participate, and philosophy begins and ends by returning to this unique principle of all thought. The entire history of philosophy, which Brunschvicg pursued, was the coming to consciousness of this spirituality. According to him, philosophies were worthwhile to the extent that they succeeded in being conscious projects, and he judged them according to this canon, this rule.

There was quite another philosophical influence at the same time as Brunschvicg, but it remained in the background for diverse reasons: this was the influence of Henri Bergson. Consider the fact that Bergson stopped teaching in 1930: he retired in order to devote himself entirely to his work. Also, he never taught in the university nor at the Sorbonne; since 1900 he had been a professor at the Collège de France. And it must be said that, for quite a long time—though this was about to disappear just as I began my studies—there was a certain hostility toward Bergson on the part of the Sorbonne, which was more rationalist in orientation—or so it was understood at the time. Did this hostility stem from the fact that for us Bergson was fully established when we began our philosophical studies? Was this why we tended—as is customary for students—to search for something else? The fact remains that Bergson's influence was not very important around 1930.

All the same, let us say a few words about this influence. If it had been exerted upon us, it would have been very different from the Kantianism and Cartesianism we received from Brunschvicg. Indeed, as you know quite well—nearly everyone knew Bergson, more or less—Bergson's philosophy is not at all an idealism. It by no means begins with a return to the *cogito,* to the subject of thought. It begins with a very different approach, one which involves a return to what Bergson called the immediate givens of consciousness. This is to say that I grasp myself, to begin with, as the first truth of philosophy; but I grasp myself not as pure thought, but as duration, as time. Bergson's analysis in *Matter and Memory,* for example, shows that if we consider time, we must necessarily center our consideration on the dimension of the present. For Bergson, the dimension of the present subsumes all consideration of the body and the exterior world. He defined the present as that upon which we act, and we clearly act with our bodies. So it is immediately apparent that this duration which Bergson calls to our attention implies a relation to our bodies: a completely carnal relation, as it were, to the world through the body.

Thus if we had been careful readers of Bergson, and if more thought had been given to him, we would have been drawn to a much more concrete philosophy, a philosophy much less reflexive than Brunschvicg's. But since Bergson was hardly read by my contemporaries, it is certain that we had to wait for the philosophies of existence in order to be able to learn much of what he would have been able to teach us. It is quite certain—as we realize more and more today—that Bergson, had we read him carefully, would have taught us things that ten or fifteen years later we believed to be discoveries made by the philosophy of existence itself.

But finally, since we are not really indebted to Bergson, let us come precisely to the period 1930–39, when we finished our studies, began to teach in the provincial *lycées* and to write doctoral theses. This period was the moment of our great initiation into the philosophy of existence, when we discovered Husserl, Jaspers, Heidegger, and Gabriel Marcel; and in particular, the review *Esprit*—a review which still exists and which you doubtlessly know—which at that time, under the impetus of Mounier (also a philosopher), was often oriented toward themes of philosophy of existence. I wish to briefly characterize these themes.

In reaction against philosophy of the idealist type—both Kantian and Cartesian—the philosophy of existence is primarily explicable by the importance of a completely different theme, that of *incarnation.* In the first writings of Gabriel Marcel, his *Metaphysical Journal,* for example, this theme was presented in a striking fashion. In philosophy, the body, my body, is usually considered to be an object, for the same reason that the bodies of others, animals, and, all told, even a table, are only exterior objects. I am mind, and opposite me there is, therefore, this body which is an object. What Gabriel Marcel maintained was precisely that this is not so, and that if I attentively regard my body, I cannot pretend that it is simply an object. In some respects it is me: "I am my body," he said. Yet it is not only the body that intervenes, for through it a general aspect of the sensible world was put under the scrutiny of our mind. Gabriel Marcel had quite long ago published an article entitled "Existence and Objectivity," in which he rightly opposed things which exist to objects, as in physical objects, objects construed by physicists. Sensible things, as they come under our scrutiny at the same time as the body, become the philosopher's themes for analysis. As Husserl said, through the perception we have of them, things are given to us in the flesh—carnally, *leibhaftig.* These philosophers set out to examine this sensible and carnal presence of the world, whereas previously, particularly under the influence of Kantian critique, scientific objects were what philosophers sought to analyze.

Undoubtedly, one has the feeling that in certain respects this position rejoins the Bergsonian one. But this is not yet something we could manage; we had to await the reading of these new writers in order to understand the significance of the theme of incarnation that we might have been able to learn from Bergson. In reality it is not only a theme, not merely a subject or an object of reflection that he proposed—it was a style of philosophizing. For example, Gabriel Marcel said that philosophy presents a particularity which differentiates it from all other sorts of disciplines: it deals with mysteries, not problems. This is the distinction which he made between the two. A problem is a question which I pose to myself and then resolve by considering different givens which are external to me. For example, if I wish to know how to construct a bridge or how to solve an equation, I consider the givens of the problem and then try to find the unknown. In philosophy it is an entirely different phenomenon, because, as Marcel said, in philosophy we must work out a very singular type of problem. In these problems, the one who poses them is also engaged. This person is not a spectator in relation to the problem, but is rather caught up in the matter, which for him defines the mystery.

If you think about this, you can see that, after all, what is expressed here in an abstract and general fashion was broached by my earlier examination of the sensible world. For it is precisely in the sensible world that we come to recognize such a strange sort of knowledge. I consider this sensible knowledge of the world completely paradoxical, in the sense that it always appears to me as already complete at the very instant that I pay attention to it. When I reflect, when I pay attention, my interior gaze bears upon my perception of things. This perception is already there. Thus, in the actual and concrete perception of the world, I am myself the subject, the one who speaks. I am already caught up in the game at the very moment that I attempt to understand what is happening. It is therefore the model of the sensible world that was used here. But finally, this philosophy far surpasses the simple emergence of a new theme of analysis: a new style of thinking was proposed to us at a time when it was necessary to consider philosophy as a mystery rather than as a problem.

A third theme which this philosophy presented to us for the first time—and which, moreover, still has great importance for all contemporary thought—is the theme of one's relations with the other. It is quite striking that this theme had not explicitly appeared in philosophy before the nineteenth century. Consider philosophers like Kant or Descartes: a philosopher reasons, and it goes without saying that his reasoning can be precisely reconstructed by another person, another reader. This can be accomplished so accurately that the philosopher and his readers parallel and reflect each other. There is no problem passing from one to the other. When Kant writes the *Critique of Pure Reason,* for example, he speaks of everyone's rationality and not only of his own. What the philosopher begins to understand, after Hegel in particular, is that in reality this is a much simpler matter than we had thought. For my relations with the other are not such that I can immediately affirm or postulate that what is true for me is also true for him. That is the problem. How is it that I know that there are other thinking beings entirely comparable to myself, since I know them only from the outside, while I know myself from the inside? Hence our third problem.

And with this problem of the other—to which we shall return—arises a theme which has increasing importance in French thought up through the present: this is the theme of history, which is essentially the same as the theme of the other. What simultaneously attracts and scandalizes philosophers about history is precisely man's given condition of not being alone, of always being considered in the presence of others, in an extraordinarily complex relation with them. The result is that we are no longer concerned simply with juxtaposed individuals, but with a sort of human tissue which is sometimes called "collectivity." History was not a subject often spoken of when I was a student. The history of thought was above all the history of philosophical systems. The moment that philosophy became interested in human and general history and joined the history of philosophy to human history in general, something had evidently changed. I simply wished to indicate how we were directed toward the explosion of 1945, and I now arrive at the main subject of this talk, which is an examination of Sartre's endeavor, what it had in common with its predecessors, and its originality.

Sartre knew all the philosophers of whom I just spoke; all of them are philosophers of existence in some respect. He discovered their works in the course of a stay at the Institut Français de Berlin during the years that preceded the war. I recall very well that upon his return he made us read Husserl, Scheler, and Heidegger, for example, all of whom were already slightly known in France but whose works were not widely read at that time. This philosophical education which he gave himself contributed to guiding us to these points of view in 1945.

But we must add that our time in occupied Paris during the war, the circumstances of the war and of those events resented by us all, also contributed to calling his attention to concrete problems and to orienting him toward a concrete philosophy, though they in no way altered his style of thought.

I recall quite well that in the years before the war, as we were talking one day, he offered an argument that seemed to have a paradoxical air to it, but which at bottom really didn't, at least not from the point of view of a certain philosophy. He said: "After all, there is not really any difference between a catastrophe in which 10 or 15 people die and a catastrophe in which 300 or 3000 people die. There is the difference in numbers, certainly, but for each dying individual, it is a world and a meaning that dies, and whether there be 300 or 3000 that die, the scandal is no greater. The scandal is exactly the same." This idea, to which he did not especially hold, struck me deeply. In retrospect, it struck me because I realized that such an idea reveals to what extent during the prewar years Sartre was removed from the political and historical point of view, from the perspective of heads of government. From the point of view of someone who has authority over other human beings, there is a great difference between an accident in which ten people die and an accident in which a thousand people die. From the statistical point of view, which is that of social and political life and history, there is an enormous difference. Only from the philosophical point of view, which considers each consciousness as a whole, there is no absolute difference between the death of one person and the death of a hundred people.

When one has lived through those years as we all had—I mean he, I, and all of our friends in Paris—with the presence of the Germans and all that it entailed, it can certainly be understood how it was natural for us to become increasingly oriented toward what happens, toward events, the exterior, toward political and social life. Consequently, the historical course of events played a role in orienting us toward the world, just as the philosophy of existence did, for its part, though by abstract philosophical means.

This combination of circumstances, plus the maturing of our own personal reflections, led Sartre to write his major work, *Being and Nothingness,* published before the end of the war. And all of our ideas formed in that period were to find their expression in the review *Les Temps modernes* founded in October 1945.

The themes dealt with by Sartre's philosophy are the same ones to which I just alluded, but they were transformed by his unique style of dealing with them. For example, the theme of incarnation, more generally spoken of as "situation": human beings, as Sartre presents them in *Being and Nothingness,* are situated beings. This theme existed before Sartre wrote of it, but he transformed it in the following manner: in *Being and Nothingness* he presents an extremely rigorous analysis, destined to show that what philosophers had called the "self," the "subject," "consciousness," or whatever else could not in reality be designated by a positive term. If I were to try to see what I really am, I would finally discover that nothing could be said of the self. Descartes already said something similar in his *Meditations,* when he said: I am not smoke, I am not subtle matter, I am thought, and a thought cannot be touched, cannot be seen, in a sense it is nothing, which is to say, it is not a visible thing. The "nothingness" in question in the famous book of which I speak is such that the subject, or what is usually called the subject, must be considered as nothing.

But naturally, nothing cannot rest upon itself. Nothing, that which is no thing, needs to be supported by positive and existing things. Thus we may say that the nothingness which we are drinks the being of the world, just as, in the legends of antiquity, the dead drink the blood of the living in order to come to life once again. Nothingness drinks being, and it thus assumes a place, a position, in the world. Why do I have a body? Because this self which I am and which is nothing needs a positive, existing apparatus to come to the world—it needs a body. This description of humanity as simultaneously "being and nothingness," as a nothingness which assumes a situation in the world and which comes to the world through this situation, is a uniquely Sartrean element which had nothing to do, I believe, with what authors such as Gabriel Marcel had previously presented through the same terms, "situation" or "incarnation. "

One may say that this self which is nothing is freedom. For what is it to be free if not to have the power to say "yes" or "no"; that is, not to be this thing or that beforehand, but to be what one wishes? Freedom—to repeat what we just said in other terms—consists not in living in nonbeing and indifferentiation but in opting for something, in choosing to do something. And this freedom—which is in itself an illusion, nonbeing—is only truly practiced when it sets itself a task and accomplishes something. We are free, Sartre said, to engage ourselves, meaning that even what is most free in us—our total independence with respect to all that is present—really can be spoken of only thanks to an act in which, on the contrary, we resolve ourselves, which we choose and through which we become something.

There is something equivalent in Sartre to what Gabriel Marcel called the mystery of being, but with an entirely different accent. The accent for Gabriel Marcel was, strictly speaking, religious. Yet it cannot be said that Sartre is, in the broad sense of the word, an irreligious philosopher, since to the contrary there is a domain where certain Christians have found themes in his work with which they agree. But for Sartre, all the same, what is called the mystery of being becomes in some respects a limpid mystery. There is a self which is nothing; there is the world which is made up of positive things; and the only task for the self which is nothing, for the self which is freedom, is to somehow make this world be. There are two entities face to face—if we indeed wish to separate them, for strictly speaking one cannot say face to face, since they are not separable; there are two entities, neither existing by itself, neither self-sufficient. Being needs humanity as witness, and humanity needs to enter into the world in order to be. The mystery which Gabriel Marcel calls the mystery of being becomes a sort of strangeness of fate that compels us to relate to a world that is profoundly alien to us. Since in the final analysis we are nothing, there will always be a distance between me and what I see, between me and what I do. Sartre called this distance a "channel of nothingness" [*manchon de néant*]. For example, what is there between me and this carafe I see? There is nothing; my gaze goes out to grasp it where it is. In a sense, therefore, it is as near to me as possible. Yet there exists this impalpable distance, which means that the carafe is an object and that I who perceive it am not an object, and I am not part of this object.

With this idea of nothingness, the problem of the other, for example, for which Sartre has provided an extraordinarily acute analysis, becomes yet more difficult, a problem which will naturally continue to concern us. For I obviously see the others, I see their bodies, but I do not see them from the inside. I do not see the center, since it is nothingness and is therefore not visible. According to Sartre, consequently, I no longer perceive them as others, and I can know that there are other people only when they gaze at me. For I find myself frozen by their gaze, transformed into an object by this exterior gaze. Hence I feel the other's presence within me in the form of a sort of loss of my substance, a loss of my freedom, hence I become an object under the other's gaze. This means that my relation with the other is by definition tragic, since I cannot grasp the other as he feels himself and as he exists as interior freedom. According to Sartre, I see a face, and it is frozen, a sort of destiny. Likewise, the other sees only my exterior, yet this entirely negative relation between us is fully effective and preoccupies us at every moment.

These two points of view provide the titles to the book's two parts, as well as the rubrics which have remained famous: the point of view of the *for-itself* and the point of view of the *for-others*. The *for-itself* is me just as I see myself, or you just as you see yourself. The *for-others* is me just as you see me, or you just as I see you. There is no possible coincidence between these two perspectives. I cannot be exactly in the eyes of the others as I am in my own eyes. This is impossible, even if I am as sincere, as frank as possible: by sheer position we could not coincide. Yet this image which you have of me bears upon my own regard, it strikes me, effects me, defines me, concerns me. This is precisely how the problem of the other—which certainly predates Sartre's philosophy—is revealed and becomes yet more urgent in his hands.

Finally there is the problem of history, to which we alluded earlier: this is a problem which poses the limit-case of the other. The problem of history is reinvested with an absolutely dramatic character, on account of the urgency of the questions themselves from the philosophical point of view, as well as on account of historical circumstances. For we must not forget that, in the France of 1945, we had a country which was governed by a political coalition, part of which was the French Communist Party, which is to say a lot. That signifies—political life itself being quite alien to a philosopher or a director of a journal as was Sartre—that it is not simply a matter of personal politics and French assemblies: it is a question of something quite different. It stemmed first of all from a camaraderie that existed during the period of the war and the resistance. And it also stemmed from the fact evident to all French people of the time, even to those who were politically far to the right—that nothing could be accomplished without the contribution, the participation of the Communist Party. This posed the problem of coexistence, as it were.

Sartre never was a Marxist. He was quite removed then, as now and always, from all types of materialism in the Marxist sense of this word. For Marx, there are causes which act upon consciousness, upon humans. For Sartre, there are no causes which can truly act upon consciousness. Consciousness is total, absolute freedom. The only point, which is not exactly a point of agreement, but which may be a point of convergence, is that for Sartre, if indeed I am nonbeing, absolute freedom—and therefore escape from all types of external determination—I bear responsibility for all that occurs outside of myself. For example, I bear responsibility for the image that others have of me. I abide by it, it matters to me, and I assume it. However, one finds a vast difference, you will note, between a philosophy which makes the subject, consciousness, humanity, depend upon exterior circumstances, and a philosophy which says that human beings, free subjects that they may be, cannot dissociate themselves from—and must take upon themselves—what occurs outside. This second attitude, which is Sartre's, is quite another matter. It is profoundly different from the Marxist philosophical point of view. This is the essence of the divergence expressed as far back as 1945 in *Les Temps modernes,* by Sartre's article on the question "Materialism and Revolution."

On the problem of history, Sartre's contribution consists in trying to lead the Marxist or communist readers of his journal to sway their thought, their philosophy, in his direction. It cannot be said that this attempt succeeded, an attempt which may retrospectively be considered very naive, but which was indispensable, considering the circumstances of the era. This attempt was still stressed during the most critical period of the Cold War, between 1952 and 1954, at the exact moment that I found it necessary to leave *Les Temps modernes,* despite the friendship which tied me to Sartre and which continues to bind us together. It was at that moment, in fact, that he most distanced himself from the communists. For this was the period when anticommunism appeared to some people as the alpha and omega of politics, when it seemed sufficient to be anticommunist in order to be political. Thereupon Sartre, who had never been a communist and who was not always well understood, considered it necessary to oppose such an attitude and thus to support the communists. Not that he thought the Russian regime could have done any better, but because he thought that the others were wrong in using Russia as a symbol of evil.

This period of extreme proximity to the communists ended with recent events, in particular the Hungarian uprising. At that time, Sartre completely broke with the communist party. And in his journal, what actually appeared (*Les Temps modernes* still existed) was somewhat derivative, a foreign literature of Marxist tendencies, principally from Polish publications or from publications which in a general manner reconsidered Stalinism and the entire system.

This was the adventure of 1945. Naturally, it may be asked: What remains of it? Apparently not much! Sartre himself renounced, so it would seem, dealing with political subjects, and devoted himself to several other works. In addition to purely philosophical works, he is writing an autobiography which will be an examination of his own life from the personal and historical point of view, which is ultimately a work quite distant from his politically engaged preoccupations of the times. As for so-called existentialism's public, this public seems to address its attention today at least partially to Heidegger's thought, for example, and consequently to a thought quite different from Sartre's own. In any case, it is different insofar as Heidegger was never in favor of engagement, which is to say, it is not a thought directly in contact with everyday events.

It may seem therefore that there are very few aspects of this heroic epoch of existentialism whose passing I regret. Far from it: it must be said that I owe a great deal to it, and in truth it can't quite be said—either in the matter of philosophy or in the matter of thought—that such an experience can be surpassed or that nothing remains of it. For philosophy and thought do not consist so much in reaching a certain place, goal, point, or conclusion, but rather in approaching this goal in a rigorous, fruitful manner. Consequently, if thought and philosophy are just that, it must be said that this experience must be attempted and that it continues to remain relevant. Especially when, as is the case with Sartre—while all the time changing, and producing a certain number of texts that may indeed refer to the events of the times—these works, like all great and good books, nevertheless offer readers a nearly perennial value.

Consequently, let us not speak too quickly of all this, of all that has passed. Sartre, in this endeavor, wrote prodigiously, and each of us gained much from this task. What was written in that period, all the same, represents a school of thought, even though we now consider the formal conclusions which were achieved at that time no longer our own.

25

Introduction to *Signs*

Maurice Merleau-Ponty

Translated by Richard C. McCleary

. . . Such in any case is the philosophy which has been essayed in parts of this volume.[1] If we are found to speak a little bit too loftily and sagely about politics, it is clear that our philosophy is not to blame. Perhaps the truth is that one would need many lives to enter each realm of experience with the total abandon it demands.

But is this sage and lofty tone really so false? Does it have so little to recommend it? Everything we believed to be thought through, and thought through correctly—freedom and authority, the citizen against authority, the heroism of the citizen, liberal humanism, formal democracy and the real democracy which suppresses it and realizes it, revolutionary heroism and humanism—has all fallen into ruin. We are filled with scruples about these matters; we reproach ourselves for speaking about them too dispassionately. But we should be careful. What we call disorder and ruin, others who are younger live as the natural order of things; and perhaps with ingenuity they are going to master it precisely because they no longer seek their bearings where we took ours. In the din of demolitions, many sullen passions, many hypocrisies or follies, and many false dilemmas also disappear. Who would have hoped it ten years ago? Perhaps we are at one of those moments when history moves on. We are stunned by French affairs or diplomacy's clamorous episodes. But underneath the clamor a silence is growing, an expectation. Why could it not be a hope?

One hesitates to write these words at the moment when Sartre, in a fine recollection of our youth, has for the first time adopted the tone of despair and rebellion.[2] But this rebellion is not a recrimination and an accusation brought against the world and others, nor is it a self-absolution. It does not revel in itself; it has a complete understanding of its own limits. It is like a reflective rebellion. Exactly. It is the regret at not having begun by rebelling. It is an "I ought to have" which it cannot be categorical, even in retrospect; for now as then Sartre knows perfectly well (and shows perfectly in his treatment of Nizan) that rebellion can neither remain the same nor be fulfilled in revolution. Thus he cherishes the idea of a rebellious youth, and it is a chimera; not just because there is no longer time, but because his precocious lucidity does not cut such a bad figure beside the violent delusions of others. One doubts that Sartre would have exchanged it (had he been at the age of illusions) for the illusions of wrath. It was not, as he insinuates, his natural indigence, but already the same acuteness, the same impatience with self-compromises and suspicious attitudes, the same modesty, and the same disinterestedness which have kept him from being shameless himself, and which are precisely the inspiration for the noble self-criticism we have just read. This preface to *Aden Arabie* is the mature Sartre lecturing the young Sartre, who like all young people pays no attention and persists there in our past; or more precisely, who is reborn at the turning of a page, forces his way into his judge, and speaks through his mouth; and speaks in such a decisive way that one finds it difficult to believe that he is so outmoded and blamable, and one comes to suspect what is after all likely, that there is only one Sartre.

We do not advise young readers to believe too hastily that Sartre's life is a failure because he failed to rebel, and that they can thus expect forty or fifty irreproachable years if they are only sufficiently rebellious. Sartre offers us a debate carried on between Sartre and Sartre across the past, the present, and others. In order to make the truth manifest, he sternly confronts the Sartre of twenty and the Sartre of the Liberation and more recent years; these characters with the Nizan of twenty, Nizan the communist, and the Nizan of September, 1939; and all those people with today's "angry young men." But we must not forget that the scenario is Sartre's. His continuing rule, since it is his freedom, is to refuse himself the excuses he gives so lavishly to others. His only fault, if it is one, is to set up this distinction between us and himself. In any case, it would be abusive of us to base our judgments upon it. Consequently, we must correct the perspective and recheck the balance sheet—on which, by the way, his cursed lucidity, in lighting up the labyrinths of rebellion and revolution, has recorded in spite of himself all we need to absolve him.

This text is no mirror dawdled down Sartre's way; it is an act of today's Sartre. We who read and recall cannot so easily separate the guilty man from his judge; we find a family likeness in them. No, the Sartre of twenty was not so unworthy of the one who now disowns him, and today's judge still resembles him in the strictness of his sentence. As an effort of an experience to understand itself; as a self-interpretation and, through that self, an interpretation of all things; this text is not written to be read passively like a report or an inventory, but to be deciphered, meditated upon, and reread. It surely has—and this is the lot of all good literature—a richer and perhaps a different meaning than the one the author put into it.

If this were the place to do it, we would have to analyze this extraordinary remembrance (after thirty years) of men past. We would have to show what is fanciful in it. Not, certainly, that Nizan was not beneath his external appearance of elegance and the greatest talents the man whom Sartre describes—righteous, full of courage, and faithful to his endowments—but because the Sartre of those same days has no less reality or weight in our memory.

I kept telling him, Sartre says, that we are free, and the thin smile at the corner of his mouth which was his only answer said more about it than all my speeches. I did not want to feel the physical weight of my chains, or know the external causes which hid my true being from me and bound me as a point of honor to freedom. I saw nothing which could touch or threaten that freedom. Foolishly, I thought I was immortal. I found nothing worth thinking about in either death or anguish. I was aware of nothing in me which was in danger of being lost. I was saved, elected. In fact, I was a thinking or a writing subject; I was living externally; and the realm of Spirit, where I had my dwelling, was no more than my abstract condition as a student nourished at the Prytaneum. Being ignorant of the needs and bonds in my own self, I was unaware of them in others; that is, I was unacquainted with the travail of their lives. When I saw suffering and anguish, I imputed them to complacency or even to affectation. Squabbling, panic, horror of amours and friendships, decisions to displease—in a word, the negative—could not really last; they were chosen attitudes. I believed that Nizan had decided to be the perfect communist. Because I was outside all struggles, particularly those of politics (and when I had engaged in politics it had been to bring my decency and my constructive, conciliatory humor to bear), I had no understanding of the effort Nizan had to make in order to emerge from childhood. Or of his loneliness. Or of his quest for salvation. His hatreds sprang from his life; they were solid gold. Mine came out of my head, counterfeit.

On one point we admit that Sartre is right. It is indeed astounding that he did not see in Nizan what hit one squarely in the eye: the meditation upon death and the fragility beneath the irony and mastery.

This means that there are two ways of being young, which are not easily comprehensible to one another. Some are fascinated by their childhood; it possesses them, holding them enchanted in a realm of privileged possibilities. Others, it casts out toward adult life; they believe that they have no past and are equally near to all possibilities. Sartre was one of the second type. Thus it was not easy to be his friend. The distance he put between himself and the conditions of his existence also separated him from what others have to live. No more than his own self did he allow other persons to "take hold"—to be their uneasiness or anguish before his eyes as they were secretly and shamefully in themselves. In himself and in others, he had to learn that nothing is without roots, and that the decision not to have any is another way of admitting them.

But must we say that the others, those who prolonged their childhood or wanted to preserve it in going beyond it (and who thus were seeking recipes for salvation), were right and Sartre was wrong? They had to learn that one does not go beyond what one preserves, that nothing could give them the wholeness they were nostalgic for, and that if they stubbornly persisted they would soon have no choice but to be simpletons or liars. Sartre did not join them in their quest. But could it have been public? From compromise to compromise, did it not require a chiaroscuro? And they were well aware that it did. That is why the intimate and distant relations between them and Sartre were humorous. Sartre reproaches himself for them now, but would they have put up with any other sort? The most we can say is that reserve and irony are contagious. Sartre did not understand Nizan because Nizan transformed his suffering into dandyism. His books, the sequel of his life, and (for Sartre) twenty years of experience after his death were necessary before Nizan was finally understood. But did Nizan want to be understood? Is not the suffering which Sartre is now talking about the kind of admission one would rather make to a reader than to a friend? Would Nizan have ever tolerated this confidential tone between Sartre and himself? Sartre knows the answer better than we do. But let us bring up a few minor facts.

One day while we were preparing for the École Normale, we saw entering our classroom with the aura of the chosen few a former student visiting for some reason unknown to us. He was admirably dressed in dark blue, and wore the tricolor cockade of Valois. They told me it was Nizan. Nothing in his dress or carriage advertised the labors of the Khagne or of the École Normale. And when our professor (who on the contrary still felt their effect) smilingly suggested that Nizan take his place with us again, he said "Why not?" in an icy voice and sat down quickly in an empty seat next to me where he buried himself impassibly in my Sophocles as if that had really been his only aim for the morning. When he came back from Aden, I found in my mail the card of Paul-Yves Nizan, who invited the conscript Merleau-Ponty, whose cousin he had known very well down there, to visit him one day soon in the pad he shared with Sartre. The meeting was according to protocol. Sartre's corner was empty and bare. Nizan in return had hung on the wall two foils crossed beneath a fencing mask, and it was against this background that the man whom I later knew had skirted suicide in Araby appeared to me. Much later, I ran into him on the back platform of bus S. He was married, a militant, and on this particular day loaded down with a heavy briefcase and untypically wearing a hat. He brought up Heidegger's name himself, and had a few words of praise for him in which I sensed a desire to show that he had not abandoned philosophy. But he spoke so coldly that I would not have dared to ask him openly.

I like to recall these little facts. They prove nothing, but they are vital. They make us feel that if Sartre did not follow too closely the travail which was going on in Nizan, Nizan for his part—by virtue of humor, reserve, and politeness—entered more than halfway into the game. I have said that Sartre would understand him only after thirty years, because Sartre was Sartre, but also because Nizan was Nizan. And above all because they both were young; that is, peremptory and timid. And perhaps after all for one final, deeper reason.

Did the Nizan Sartre reproaches himself for having misunderstood exist entirely in 1928—before his family, his books, his life as a militant, his break with the party, and above all his death at thirty-five? Because he perfected, enclosed, and immobilized himself in these thirty-five short years, they have slid twenty years behind us in a block, and now we would have it that everything he might have been is given at their inception and in each moment of them. Feverish like a beginning, his life is also solid like an ending. He is forever young. And because on the contrary we have been given time to be mistaken more than once, and to correct our mistakes, our comings and our goings cover up our tracks. Our own youth is worn out and insignificant for us, inaccessible to us as it really was. To another life which ends too soon, I apply the standard of hope. To mine, which is perpetuated, the severe rule of death. A young man has done a lot if he has been a "perhaps." It seems to us that a mature man who is still around has done nothing. As in the things of childhood, it is in the lost comrade that I find plenitude, *either because creative faith has dried up within me, or because reality takes shape only in my memory.*[3] Another retrospective illusion, which Bergson did not speak about: no longer that of preexistence, but that of fall from grace. Perhaps time does not flow from the future or the past. Perhaps it is distance which constitutes the reality another person has for us—above all another person who is lost.

But that distance would also rehabilitate us if we could only see ourselves from there. As a balance to what Sartre writes today about himself and Nizan at twenty, what the Nizan of fifty could have said about their youth will be forever missing. For us, they were two men starting out in life, and starting out opposite one another.

What makes Sartre's account melancholy is that in it one sees the two friends slowly learning from experience what they could have learned from one another at the outset. Nizan had been confiscated by his father's image. He was possessed by the drama (older than he was) of a worker who, having left his class, discovers that his life since then has been unreal and a failure, and ends his days hating himself. Consequently, Nizan knew from the start the weight of childhood, the body, and society, as well as the interwoven ties that bind us to our parents and to history in one single anguish. He would not have put an end to this fascination with his father's image, perhaps indeed he would have aggravated it, by simply choosing marriage and the family, taking up the father's role for his own. If he wanted to re-enter the life cycle his father's life had turned him out of, he had to purify its source, break with the society which had produced their solitude, and undo what his father had done, setting out upon his road again in the opposite direction.

In proportion to the passing years, the omens multiply, the evident truth approaches. The flight to Aden is the last attempt at a solution through adventure. It would have been no more than a diversion if Nizan had not found in the colonial regime (either by chance or because confusedly he was looking for this particular lesson) the clear image of our dependence in respect to the external world. So suffering has external causes; they are identifiable, have a name, can be abolished. So there is an external enemy, and we are helpless against him if we stay by ourselves. So life is war and social war.

Nizan already knew what Sartre said much later. In the beginning is not play but need. We do not keep the world, or situations, or others at the length of our gaze like a spectacle; we are intermingled with them, drinking them in through all our pores. We are what is lacking in everything else; and within us, with the nothingness which is the center of our being, a general principle of alienation is given. Before Sartre, Nizan lived this pantragism, this flood of anguish which is also the flux of history.

But for this very reason, and because he was not living in the tragic realm, Sartre understood much sooner the artifices of salvation and of the return to the positive. He was not exactly an optimist; he never equated the Good and Being. Nor was he saved, one of the elect. He was vigorous, gay, and enterprising; all things which lay before him were new and interesting. Precisely. He was *supralapsarian,* this side of tragedy and hope, and thus well equipped to tease out their secret knots. His premonitions find their factual demonstration in Nizan's experience during the ten years preceding the war; and when he tells about that experience today—when he takes it up again on his own account, profoundly and fraternally—he cannot help finding exactly what he has been telling us since then about conversions.

One day a man declares himself a Christian or a communist. Just what does he mean? We are not completely changed in an instant. What happens is simply that in recognizing an external cause of his destiny, man suddenly gets permission and even the mission (as I believe Maritain used to say) to *live in the bosom of the faith of his natural life.* It is neither necessary nor possible for his backslidings to stop; from then on they are "consecrated."[4] His torments are now stigmata whose stamp is an immense Truth. The sickness he was dying of helps him, and helps others, to live. He is not required to renounce his talents, if he has any. On the contrary, the loosening of the anguish which had clutched his throat releases them. To live, to be happy, to write meant to give in to slumber; it was suspect and base. Now it means recovering from sin what sin presumptuously had claimed, or, as Lenin used to say, stealing from the bourgeoisie what it had stolen.

Communism sees through a glass darkly in the perspective of a new man and a new society. But for the time being, and for a whole long period which is called negative, what it turns against the bourgeois state is the machinery of the state. The means it turns against evil are evil means. From now on, each thing has a double meaning, depending on whether it is judged according to its evil origin or in the perspective of the future it invokes. The Marxist is the wretch he was; he is also that wretchedness restored to its place in the total scheme of things and known in terms of its causes. As a writer in a period of "demoralization," he prolongs bourgeois decadence; but in the very process of doing so he bears witness to it and surpasses it toward a different future. Nizan the communist "saw the world and saw himself there."[5] He was subject and he was object. As object, lost along with his times; as subject, saved along with the future.

And yet this double-entried life is only one life. Marxist man is a product of history, and he also participates from within in history as the production of a new society and a new man. How is this possible? He would have to be reintegrated as a finite being into the infinite productivity. That is why many Marxists have been tempted by Spinozism, and Nizan was one of them. As Nizan did, Sartre liked Spinoza; but in opposition to the transcendent and the reconcilers, the equivalent of whose contrivances he was quick to find in Spinoza in the form of "the affirmative plenitude of the finite mode which at the same time bursts its bonds and returns to the infinite substance."[6] In the end, Spinoza does everything to hide the labor and the peculiar virtue of the negative; and Spinozist Marxism is simply a fraudulent way of assuring us in this life of the return of the positive. The adhesion to an infinite positivity is a pseudonym for naked anguish—the pretension to have crossed the negative and reached the other shore; to have exhausted, totaled up, internalized death. "We do not have even this, not even this unmediated communication with our nothingness."[7]

Sartre found this philosophical formulation later. But he sensed at twenty-five that there is trickery and falsification when the savior counts himself out of the reckoning. Nizan wanted to stop thinking about himself, and he succeeded; he had regard only for causal chains. But it was still he—the nay-sayer, the irreplaceable one—who annihilated himself in things.[8] True negativity cannot be made of two positivities joined together, my being as a product of capitalism and the affirmation of a new future through me. For there is a rivalry between them, and one or the other must win. Having become a means of edification and a professional theme, rebellion may be no longer felt, no longer lived. Marxist man is saved by the doctrine and the movement. He sets himself up in his job. According to the old criteria, he is lost. Or (and this is what happens to the best) he does not forget or lie to himself—his wisdom is reborn from his continual suffering, and his incredulity is his faith—but he cannot say so, and in that case he must lie to others. Hence the impression we get from so many conversations with communists: they possess the most objective thought there is, but the most anguished and, beneath its toughness, secretly slack and humid. Sartre has always known and said (and this is what has kept him from being a communist) that the communist negation, being positivity reversed, is not what it says it is, or that it doubletalks like a ventriloquist.

Since he understands the subterfuges of the "negative man" so well, it is astonishing that he should sometimes speak with such nostalgia of the wholly critical period prior to 1930, especially since the revolution already had its counterfeit coin in its "constructive" period. The explanation is that Sartre has resigned himself to the inevitable, later and upon reflection, as to a lesser evil. He never simply reoccupied the positions Nizan held thirty years ago. He justifies them at one remove from them, for reasons which remain his own, in the name of an experience which led him to involvement without modifying what he has always thought of salvation. But this experience, which begins in 1939, remains to be retraced.

In 1939, Nizan is going to discover abruptly that one is not so quickly saved, that adherence to communism does not free one from dilemmas and heart-rending anguish; while Sartre, who knew it, begins that apprenticeship in history and the positive which was to lead him later on to a sort of communism from without. Thus their paths cross. Nizan returns from communist politics to rebellion, and the apolitical Sartre becomes acquainted with the social. This fine account must be read. It must be read over Sartre's shoulder, as his pen sets it forth—all mixed in with his reflections, and mixing ours in too.

Nizan, he says, had admitted that the new man and the new society did not yet exist; that perhaps he would not see them himself; and that it was necessary to dedicate oneself to that unknown future without weighing the sacrifice or constantly haggling over and contesting the revolution's means. He said nothing about the purge trials. Comes another, clearer, test for him. Responsible for the foreign affairs section of a party journal, he has explained a hundred times that the Soviet alliance would avert both fascism and war. He repeats it in July, 1939, at Marseille, where Sartre accidentally runs into him.

Here I ask permission to add a word of my own: Nizan knew that perhaps we would not avoid both fascism and war, and within himself he had accepted war if it was the only means of containing fascism. It happens that I can bear witness to this. Maybe three weeks after meeting with Sartre, I in turn saw Nizan. It was in Corsica, at Porto, at Casanova's,[9] if I am not mistaken. He was gay and smiling, as Sartre had seen him. But (whether his friends were getting him ready for new line or whether they were themselves being worked on from higher up I do not know) he no longer said that fascism would be brought to its knees by fall. He says: "We will have war against Germany, but with the U.S.S.R. as an ally, and we shall win it in the end." He says firmly, serenely (I can still hear his voice), as if he were released from himself at last.

Fifteen days later came the Nazi-Soviet pact, and Nizan left the communist party. Not, he explained, because of the pact, which beat Hitler's Western friends at their own game. But the French party should have saved its dignity, pretending indignation and giving the appearance of declaring its independence. Nizan realized that to be a communist is not to play a role one has chosen but to be caught in a drama where without knowing it one receives a different role. It is a lifetime undertaking which one carries on in faith or ends up pulling out of, but which in any case exceeds agreed-upon limits and the promises of prudence. If it is like this, and if it is true that in the communist life as in the other nothing is ever irrevocably accomplished—if years of labor and of action can be stricken in a twinkling with derision—in that case, Nizan thinks, I cannot do it, and the answer is no.

What is Sartre thinking at the same moment? He would like to believe that Nizan has deceived him. But no, Nizan resigns. He is the one who has been deceived. They are two children in the world of politics. A harsh world where the risks cannot be calculated and where peace is perhaps given only to those who do not fear war. One acts in a show of force only if one is determined to make use of it. If one shows it fearfully, one has war and defeat. "I discovered . . . the monumental error of a whole generation . . . we were being pushed toward massacres across a fierce prelude to war, and we thought we were strolling on the lawns of peace."[10]

Thus Sartre and Nizan were deceived in different ways, and they learned a different lesson from their deception. Nizan had accepted force and war and death for a very clear cause; events made sport of his sacrifice, and he no longer had any sanctuary but himself. Sartre, who had believed in peace, discovered a nameless adversity which had to be clearly taken into account. A lesson he will not forget. It is the source of his pragmatism in politics. In a world bewitched, the question is not to know who is right, who follows the truest course, but who is the match for the Great Deceiver, and what action will be tough and supple enough to bring it to reason.

One can understand, then, the objections Sartre makes today to the Nizan of 1939, and why they are without weight against him. Nizan, he says, was angry. But is that anger a matter of mood? It is a mode of understanding which is not too inappropriate when fundamental meaning-structures are at stake. For anyone who has become a communist and has acted within the party day after day, things said and done have a weight, because he has said and done them too. In order to take the change in line of 1939 as he should, Nizan would have to have been a puppet. He would have to have been broken, and he had not become a communist to play the skeptic. Or, again, he would have to have been only a sympathizer. But the party is not at issue, Sartre also says. Death does not come to Nizan through the party. "The massacre was brought to birth by the Earth, and sprang forth on all sides."[11] All right. But this is justifying the party relatively as a fact in the earth's history. For Nizan, who is in it, it is all or nothing.

"An impulsive act," Sartre rejoins. "If he had lived, I tell myself that the Resistance would have brought him back into the ranks as it brought others."[12] In the ranks, certainly. But in the ranks of the party? That is another matter. It is almost the opposite: a function of authority, a mark of distinction. Even rallied to the cause, he would not have forgotten the episode. The communism he had abandoned was the sagacious doctrine for which the revolution is both family and fatherland. He would have found an adventurous communism which played the role of the revolution through the Resistance, after having played the role of defeatism, and in expecting to play, after the War, the role of reconstruction and compromise.

Even if he had wanted to, would Nizan have been able to follow this sequence—he who had believed in Marxism's truth? He would have been able to on the condition that he had not taken a position each time. It is one thing, from without or after the fact (which is the same thing), to justify with documents in hand the detours of communism. It is another thing to organize the deception and to be the deceiver. I recall having written from Lorraine, in October, 1939, some prophetic letters which divided the roles between us and the U.S.S.R. in a Machiavellian fashion. But I had not spent years preaching the Soviet alliance. Like Sartre, I had no party: a good position for serenely doing justice to the toughest of parties.

We were not wrong, but Nizan was right. Communism from without has no lessons to teach communists. Sometimes more cynical than they and sometimes less, rebellious where they give in, resigned where they refuse, it is a natural lack of comprehension of communist life. Nizan "unlearned," but that means learning, too. If his rebellion in 1939, which was based upon his reasons for being, and for being a communist, was a strategic withdrawal, then so was the Budapest uprising.

One starting out from anguish, the other from gaiety; one taking the road toward happiness, the other toward tragedy; both drawing near to communism, one from its classical and the other from its shadowy side; and both finally rejected by events; Nizan and Sartre have perhaps never been closer to one another than today, at the hour when their experiences mutually clarify one another in these profound pages. In order to say now what conclusions all this tends toward, we must draw out some of the sparkling words which this meditation strikes from Sartre.

What is unimpaired in Sartre is the sense of novelty and freedom: "Lost freedom will not be found except by being invented. It is forbidden to look back, even in order to determine the dimensions of our 'authentic' needs."[13] But where in the present are the arms and emblems of this true negativity, which cannot be satisfied with giving different names to the same things? Should we look to the new course of events or to new peoples for what the Russia of the October generation has not given to the world? Can we displace our radicalism? History gives no pure and simple answers. Shall we say to the young: "Be Cubans, be Russian or Chinese, according to your taste, be Africans? They will answer that it is pretty late to change extraction."[14] What perhaps is clear in China is at least implicit and confused here; the two histories do not mesh. Who would dare maintain that China, even if she has the power some day, will liberate, let us say, Hungary or France? And where in the France of

1960 is the sense of untamed freedom to be found? A few young people maintain it in their lives, a few Diogenes in their books. Where is it, let us not even say in public life but in the masses? Freedom and invention are in the minority, of the opposition. Man is hidden, well hidden, and this time we must make no mistake about it: this does not mean that he is there beneath a mask, ready to appear. Alienation is not simply privation of what was our own by natural right; and to bring it to an end, it will not suffice to steal what has been stolen, to give us back our due. The situation is far more serious: there are no faces underneath the masks, historical man has never been human, and yet no man is alone.

Thus we see by what right and in what sense Sartre can take up the young Nizan's claim again and offer it to the rebellious young men of today. "Nizan used to speak bitterly of the old guys who laid our women and intended to castrate us."[15] He wrote: "As long as men are not complete and free, they will dream at night."[16] He said "that love was true and they kept us from loving; that life could be true, that it could give birth to a true death, but they made us die before we were even born."[17] Thus our brother love is there, our sister life, and even our sister bodily death, as promising as childbirth. Being is there within reach; we only have to free it from the reign of the old men and the rich. Desire, be insatiable; "turn your rage upon those who have provoked it; do not try to escape your trouble; seek out its causes and smash them."[18] Alas! Nizan's story, which Sartre goes on to tell, shows clearly enough that it is not so easy to find the true causes—and *smash them* is precisely the language of a war in which the enemy is imperceptible. The complete man, the man who does not dream, who can die well because he lives well, and who can love his life because he envisages his death is, like the myth of the Androgynes, the symbol of what we lack.

It is just that since this truth would be too harsh, Sartre retranslates it into the language of the young, the language of the young Nizan. "In a society which reserves its women for the old and the rich. . . ."[19] This is the language of sons. It is the Oedipal word one hears in each generation. Sartre quite properly says that each child in becoming a father simultaneously kills his father and regenerates him. Let us add that the good father is an accessory to the immemorial childishness; he himself offers himself up to the murder which his childhood lives anew in, and which confirms him as a father. Better to be guilty than to have been impotent. Noble dodge for hiding life from children.

This bad world is the one "we have made for them."[20] These ruined lives are those "which have been made . . . which are being manufactured today for the young."[21] But that is not true. It is not true that we have at any moment been masters of things, nor that, having clear problems before us, we have botched everything by our futility. The young will learn precisely in reading this preface that their elders have not had such an easy life. Sartre is spoiling them. Or rather, exactly following the pattern he has always followed, he is hard on the children of his spirit, who are already in their forties, but grants everything to those who follow—and starts them out again in the eternal return of rivalry.

It is Nizan who was right; there is your man; read him. I would like to add: read Sartre too. This little sentence, for example, which weighs so heavily: "The same reasons take happiness from us and render us forever incapable of possessing it."[22] Does he mean the same causes, and that it is not this humanity but another which will be happy? That would be, like Pascal, staking everything on a beyond. However, he says the same *reasons*. The fall is thus not an accident; its causes count us as accomplices. There is equal weakness in blaming ourselves alone and in believing only in external causes. In one way or another we will always *miss the mark* if we do. Evil is not *created* by us or by others; it is born in this web that we have spun about us—and that is suffocating us. What sufficiently tough new men will be patient enough to really reweave it?

The remedy we seek does not lie in rebellion, but in unremitting *virtú*. A deception for whoever believed in salvation, and in a single means of salvation in all realms. Our history, where space reappears and China, Africa, Russia, and the West are not advancing at the same pace, is a fall for whoever believed that history, like a fan, is going to fold in upon itself. But if this philosophy of time was yet another reverie born of the age-old distress, why then should we judge the present from such a height in its name? There is no universal clock, but local histories take form beneath our eyes, and begin to regulate themselves, and haltingly are linked to one another and demand to live, and confirm the powerful in the wisdom which the immensity of the risks and the consciousness of their own disorder had given them. The world is more present to itself in all its parts than it ever was. In world capitalism and in world communism and between the two, more truth circulates today than twenty years ago. History never confesses, not even her lost illusions, but neither does she dream of them again.

Notes

1. Due to considerations of length, the first twenty pages of the Introduction have been omitted.—ED.

2. Preface to *Aden Arabie,* ed. F. Maspéro.

3. *Swann,* vol. 1, 265.
4. Preface to *Aden Arabie,* 51.
5. Ibid., 48.
6. Ibid., 55.
7. Ibid., 41.
8. Ibid., 55.
9. Laurent Casanova, French Resistance leader and (until he lost out to the Stalinist element) high-ranking communist official and deputy. His wife Danielle, killed by the Nazis, became one of the most popular martyrs of the Resistance.—TRANS.
10. Preface to *Aden Arabie,* 57.
11. Ibid., 60.
12. Ibid., 58.
13. Ibid., 44–45.
14. Ibid., 17.
15. Ibid., 29.
16. Ibid., 30.
17. Ibid., 45.
18. Ibid., 18.
19. Ibid., 29.
20. Ibid., 18.
21. Ibid., 61.
22. Ibid., 51.

Interrogation and Dialectic (from *The Visible and the Invisible*)

Maurice Merleau-Ponty

Translated by Alphonso Lingis

Perceptual Faith and Negativity

Philosophy believed it could overcome the contradictions of the perceptual faith by suspending it in order to disclose the motives that support it. The operation seems to be inevitable, and absolutely legitimate too, since in sum it consists in stating what our life takes as understood. Yet it reveals itself to be fallacious in that it transforms the perceptual faith, which is to be understood; it makes of it a belief among others, founded like any other on reasons—the reasons we have *to think that there is* a world. But it is clear that in the case of perception the conclusion comes before the reasons, which are there only to take its place or to back it up when it is shaken. If we search after the reasons, it is because we no longer succeed in seeing, or because other facts, like that of illusion, incite us to impugn the perceptual evidence itself. But to identify it with the reasons which we have to restore to it some value once it has been shaken is to postulate that the perceptual faith has always been a resistance to doubt, and the positive a negation of negation. The procedure of reflection, as an appeal to "the interior," retreats back from the world, consigns the faith in the world to the rank of things said or *statements*.[1] But then we have the feeling that this "explicitation" is a transformation without reconversion, that it rests upon itself, on the perceptual faith whose tenor it claims to give us and whose measure it claims to be: it is because first I believe in the world and in the things that I believe in the order and the connection of my thoughts. We are therefore led to seek, beneath the reflection itself, and as it were *in front of* the philosopher who reflects, the reasons for belief which he seeks within himself, in his thoughts, on the hither side of the world.

This critique of reflection does not only apply to its rudimentary forms, to a psychological reflection which turns away from the things in order to look back upon the "states of consciousness" through which the things are given to us, upon our "thoughts" taken in their formal reality as events situated in a stream of consciousness. Even a reiterated reflection, more self-conscious, which treats the states of consciousness in their turn as unities constituted before an absolute subject, liberates that absolute subject from all inherence in psychological events and defines our thoughts as pure relations to their "objective reality," their ideate, or their signification—even this purified reflection is not free from the reflective vice of transforming the openness upon the world into an assent of self with self, the institution of the world into an ideality of the world, the perceptual faith into acts or attitudes of a subject that does not participate in the world. If we wish to avoid this first, irretrievable, lie, it is therefore, with and through the reflection, the Being-subject and Being itself that we have to conceive anew, by concentrating our attention on the horizon of the world, at the confines of the universe of reflection. For it is the horizon of the world that secretly guides us in our constructions and harbors the truth of the procedures of reflection by which we pretend to reconstitute it—a first positivity of which no negation of our doubts could be the equivalent.

One will say, then, that before the reflection, and in order to make it possible, a naive frequenting of the world is necessary, and that the *Self* to which one returns is preceded by an alienated Self or a Self in ec-stasy in Being. The world, the things, what is, is (one will say) of itself, without common measure with our "thoughts." If we try to find out what "the thing" means for us, we find that it is what rests in itself, that it is exactly what it is, wholly in act, without any virtuality or potency, that it is by definition "transcendent," outside, absolutely foreign to all interiority. If it is perceived by someone, and in particular by me, this is not constitutive of its meaning as a thing, which on the contrary is to be there in indifference, in the night of identity, as pure in-itself. Such would be the description of Being to which we would be led if we really wished to rediscover the prereflective zone of the openness upon Being. And in order that this openness take place, in order that decidedly we get out of our thoughts, in order that nothing stand between us and it, it would be correlatively necessary to empty the Being-subject of all the phantoms with which philosophy has encumbered it. If I am to be in ec-stasy in the world and in the things, it is necessary that nothing detain me within myself far from them—no "representation," no "thought," no "image," and not even that epithet "subject," "mind," or "Ego," with which the philosopher wishes to distinguish me absolutely from the things, but which becomes misleading in its turn, since, like every designation, in the end it devolves into the positive, reintroduces a phantom of reality within me, and makes me think that I am a *res cogitans*—a very particular, elusive, invisible thing, but a thing all the same. The only way to ensure my access to the things themselves would be to purify my notion of the subjectivity completely: there is not even any "subjectivity" or "Ego"; the consciousness is without "inhabitant," I must extricate it completely from the secondary apperceptions that make of it the reverse of a body, the property of a "psychism," and I must discover it as the "nothing," the "void," which has the capacity for receiving the plenitude of the world, or rather which needs it to bear its own emptiness.

It is with this intuition of Being as absolute plenitude and absolute positivity, and with a view of nothingness purified of all the being we mix into it, that Sartre expects to account for our primordial access to the things, always tacitly understood in the philosophies of reflection, and always taken in realism as an action of the things upon us—which is unthinkable. From the moment that I conceive of myself as negativity and the world as positivity, there is no longer any interaction. I go with my whole self to meet a massive world; between it and myself there is neither any point of encounter nor point of reflection, since it is Being and I am nothing. We are and remain strictly opposed and strictly commingled precisely because we are not of the same order. Through the center of myself I remain absolutely foreign to the being of the things—and, precisely as such, destined for them, made for them. Here what one says of being and what one says of nothingness *are* but one and the same thing—they are the obverse and the reverse of the same thought; the clear vision of being such as it is under our eyes—as the being of the thing that is peaceably, obstinately itself, seated in itself, absolute non-me—is complementary or even synonymous with a conception of oneself as absence and elusion. The intuition of being is solidary with a sort of negintuition of nothingness (in the sense that we speak of negentropy), with the impossibility of our reducing ourselves to anything whatever—a state of consciousness, thought, an *ego,* or even a "subject."[2] Here everything depends on the strictness with which we will be able to think through the negative. We are not thinking it as negative if we treat it as an "object of thought" or try to say *what it is:* that is to make of it a more subtle or more rarefied species of being, it is to reintegrate it into being.[3] The only way to think of the negative is to think that it *is not,* and the only way to preserve its negative purity is (instead of juxtaposing it to being as a distinct substance, which is to immediately contaminate it with positivity) to see it out of the corner of one's eye as the sole *frontier* of being, implicated in being as what being would lack, if absolute fullness could lack anything—more precisely, as calling for being in order to not be nothing, and, as such, called forth by being as the sole supplement to being that would be conceivable, a lack of being, but at the same time a lack that constitutes itself into a lack, hence a fissure that deepens in the exact measure that it is filled. Take the *this* which is under my eyes and which seems to choke the void I am with its mass. In reality, this glass, this table, this room can be sensibly present to me only if nothing separates me from them, only if I am in them and not in myself, in my representations or my thoughts, only if I am nothing. Yet (one will say) inasmuch as I have *this* before myself I am not an absolute nothing, I am a determined nothing: not this glass, nor this table, nor this room; my emptiness is not indefinite, and to this extent at least my nothingness is filled or nullified. In reality, this pseudopositivity of my present is only a more profound or redoubled negation. It has its weight as an effective present; it occupies in full force the field of my life only because it is new, because it [breaks forth?] on the ground of the total world, but this also means that it is about to be reabsorbed into it: in another instant it will have disappeared, while I was speaking of it, and given place to another *this;* it will have fused into the rest of the world. It determines my emptiness only because it is ephemeral, constitutionally menaced by another *this.* What I call its force and its presence is the infinitesimal suspension of this menace, is the momentary retreat of the whole. Its "pressure" on me is only the unsure absence of the rest, the negation of those other negations which the past *thises* "have been" [*ont été*], which the future *thises* "will be," a negation that will soon rejoin them in the inactual and will have to be recommenced. Thus to fill up the fissure is in reality to deepen it, since the present one throws into it does not negate the negations that have been or will be in their own time, and displaces them only by exposing itself to the same imminent fate. The very plenitude of the present reveals itself upon examination to be our constitutive void carried to the second power. An effective or primordial negation must bear within itself what it negates, must be actively a negation of itself:

> In the measure . . . that the being that lacks—*is not* what it lacks, we apprehend a negation in it. But if this negation is not to vanish into pure

> exteriority—and along with it all possibility of negation in general its foundation lies in the necessity for the being that lacks—*to be* what it lacks. Thus the foundation of the negation is a negation of negation. But this negation-foundation is no more a *given* than is the lack of which it is an essential moment: it is as having to be. . . . It is only as a lack *to be suppressed* that the lack can be an internal lack for the for-itself.[4]

Finally it is with the same movement that nothingness hollows itself out and fills itself. A philosophy that really thinks the negation, that is, that thinks it as what is not through and through, is also a philosophy of Being.[5] We are beyond monism and dualism, because dualism has been pushed so far that the opposites, no longer in competition, are at rest the one against the other, coextensive with one another. Since nothingness is what is not,

> knowledge is reabsorbed into being: it is neither an attribute nor a function nor an accident of being; but *there is* only being. . . . At the end of this book we shall even be able to consider this articulation of the For-itself with respect to the In-itself as the perpetually moving outline of a quasi-totality which we can call *Being*. From the point of view of this totality, the upsurge of the For-itself is not only the absolute event of the For-itself, it is also *something that happens to the In-itself,* the sole adventure of the In-itself possible: for everything comes to pass as if the For-itself, by its very nihilation, constituted itself as "consciousness of—" that is, by its very transcendence escapes that law of the In-itself by which affirmation is choked up by the affirmed. The For-itself, through its self-negation, becomes affirmation of the In-itself. The intentional affirmation is like the reverse of the internal negation. . . . But then within the quasi-totality of Being, affirmation *happens* to the In-itself; it is the adventure of the In-itself *to be affirmed*. It happens to the In-itself that this affirmation, which could not be effected as the affirmation *of* self by the In-itself without destroying its being-in-itself, is realized by the For-itself; it is as a passive ec-stasy of the In-itself, which leaves it unaltered and which nonetheless is effected in it and on the basis of it. Everything comes to pass as if the For-itself had a Passion to lose itself in order that the affirmation "world" happen to the In-itself.[6]

From the point of view of a philosophy of the absolute negativity—which is at the same time a philosophy of the absolute positivity—all the problems of the classical philosophy volatilize, for they were problems about "compound" or "union," and compound and union are impossible between what is and what is not, but, for the same reason that makes the compound impossible, the one could not be thought without the other. Thus disappears the antinomy of idealism and realism: it is true that "knowledge" as nihilation is sustained only by the things themselves in which it is founded, that it could not affect being, that it "adds nothing" to it and "takes nothing" from it,[7] that it is a "shimmering of nothingness" at its surface[8]—and at the same time it is true that, again as nihilation, and inasmuch as nothingness is absolutely unknown to being, "knowledge" gives it this negative but original determination of being, "Being *such as it is,*" the being recognized or acknowledged, the sole being that *would have a meaning:* "this being which 'invests me' from all sides and from which *nothing* separates me, it is precisely *nothing* that separates me from it, and this nothing, because it is nothingness, is untraversable . . . the For-itself is immediate presence to being and, at the same time, there slips in as an infinite distance between itself and being."[9] Likewise it is true that the things are forever distinct from every "object of thought" or every "state of consciousness," transcendent, and at the same time that the consciousness that knows them is defined by its presence to itself, its immanence, the strict identity of appearing and being in it. The consciousness is immanence because it is nihilation, void, transparency; and it is open upon transcendent things because by itself this void would be *nothing,* because the existent consciousness is always gorged full of qualities, engulfed in the being it nihilates and over which it has, so to speak, no motor power, being of another order than it. My apprehension of myself is coextensive with my life, as its own possibility by principle—or, more exactly, it is this possibility that is me; I am this possibility, and, through it, all the others. But it is a possibility of nihilation, it leaves untouched the absolute actuality of my incarnate being as it does that of every being, it leaves intact the opacity of my life as long as I do not apply myself to it by reflection; and the *cogito* as an experience of my own being is a prereflective *cogito,* it does not pose my own being as an object before me. By position, and before all reflection, I touch myself through my situation; it is from it that I am referred back to myself; I am unaware of myself as nothingness, I believe only in the things. Precisely because, in what is most proper to me, I am nothing, nothing ever separates me from myself, but also nothing draws my attention to myself, and I am in ec-stasy in the things. If the negative is recognized for what it is,[10] if we practice negintuition in its regard, there is no longer a choice to be made between the unreflected and the reflection, between the perceptual faith and the immanence of my thoughts to myself who thinks: it is the same thing to be nothing and to inhabit the world; between the knowledge of self and the knowledge of the world there is no longer any debate over even ideal priority. In particular the world is no longer *founded on* the "I think," as the bound on the binding. What I "am" I am only at a distance, yonder, in this body, this personage, these thoughts, which I push before myself and which are only my least remote distances [*mes lointains mes moins éloignés*]; and conversely I adhere to this world which is not me as closely as to myself, in a sense it is only the prolongation of my body[11]—I am justified in saying that I am in the world. Idealism and the reflective cramp disappear because the relation of knowledge is based on a "relation of being," because for me to be is not to remain in identity, it is to bear before myself the identifiable, *what there is,* to which I add nothing but the tiny doublet "such as it is." And even this passage from the brute being to the acknowledged being or to its truth is required from the depths of the exterior being by its very quality of being exterior, while self-negation is required by the radical negation that I am.

If now we consider that other certitude of the perceptual faith, that of having access to the very world the others perceive, here is how it is translated in a truly negativist philosophy. *What* I see is not mine in the sense of being a private world. Henceforth the table is the table; even the perspective views which I have of it and which are bound to the position of my body are part of being and not of myself; even the aspects of the table that are bound to my psychophysical constitution—its singular color, if I am color-blind and the table is painted red—are still part of the system of the world. What is mine in my perception are its lacunae, and they would not be lacunae if the thing itself, behind them, did not betoken them to be such. Thus finally there remains, to constitute the "subjective" face of perception, only the secondary redoubling of the thing which is expressed in saying that we see it *such as it is.* Suppose now that there is another man before me who "looks at" what I call "the table." Between the table of my field (which is not one of my thoughts, but the table itself) and this body, this gaze, a relation is established which is neither of the two relations that a solipsist analysis furnishes: the gaze of the other man on the thing is neither a negation swept away by itself and opening upon the thing itself, nor is it the thing in the night of identity now installing itself in full light through the space I supply for it, or its plenitude now decompressing due to the void I provide about it. For the other's gaze on it is not a nothing for me, its exterior witness; whatever it may be in the last analysis, it is not nothing as I am nothing for myself, it does not have the power I have to push the things unto their truth or their meaning and to grasp them "such as they are." The perception others have of the world always leaves me with the impression that it is a blind palpation, and we are quite surprised when they say something about it that rejoins our perception, as we marvel when an infant begins to "understand." . . . And correlatively, the things, at the end of another's look, do not call for that look as a confirmation of their being, as that which makes them true or acknowledged things. It is always *my* things that the others look at, and the contact they have with those things does not incorporate them into a world that would be theirs. The perception of the world by the others cannot enter into competition with my own perception of it, for my position is not comparable to theirs; I live my perception from within, and, from within, it has an incomparable power of ontogenesis. This very power I have to reach the thing and hence to go beyond my private states of consciousness, because it is proper to the perception lived from within, that is, to my own perception, reduces me to a solipsism (this time transcendental) the very moment I thought myself delivered from it. This power of ontogenesis becomes my speciality and my difference. But for this very reason the intervention of the foreign spectator does not leave my relationship with the things untouched. Insinuating into the world "such as it is" the subuniverse of a behavior or of a private life, his intervention puts my devotion to being to the test; it calls into question the right I arrogated to myself to think it for all, it takes my generosity at its word, it summons me to keep the promises I made when I admitted that I was *nothing* and that I was surpassed by being. The gaze of the other men on the things is being which claims its due and which enjoins me to admit that my relationship with it passes through them. I remain the sole witness of the ontogenesis, the others can add nothing to the evidence of being for me. Before they intervene I already knew that being owes nothing to my states of consciousness; but the nothing I am and the being I see all the same formed a closed sphere. The other's gaze on the things is a second openness. Within this openness which I am, it is a question mark opposite the *solipsist* sphere, it is the possibility of a divergence between the nothing that I am and being. I remain the sole *ipse;* the other, as long as he does not speak, remains an inhabitant of my world, but he reminds me very imperiously that the *ipse* is a nothing, that this anonymity does not form the spectacle for itself, that it forms it for X, for all those presumptively who might wish to take part in it. One sole condition is laid down for their coming on the scene: that they could present themselves to me as other focuses of negativity. It is true that one does not see how they could fulfill that condition, since they are in front of me, on the side of being. But if one does not very well see how they could appear in the world, and if the privilege of my perspective seems to be absolute and my perception indeclinable, I have only provisionally acquired this privilege: it is not the privilege of a "subjective" series reserved for me; I, as it were, do everything that depends on me in order that the world lived by me be open to participation by others, since I am distinguishable only as a nothing which takes nothing from it, since I put into the arena of the world my body, my representations, my very thoughts *qua* mine, and since everything that one calls me is in principle open to a foreign gaze, should it but be willing to appear.

Will it appear? It cannot appear in the things. Whatever be the common opinion, it is not in their bodies, nor *anywhere,* that I see the others. It is not from a point of space that the other's gaze emanates. The other is born *from my side,* by a sort of propagation by cuttings or by subdivision, as the first other, says Genesis, was made from a part of Adam's body. But how is it conceivable that what is nothing be doubled? How would one discern one "nothing" from another? The question only shows that we have forgotten our principle on the way, that we have come to forget that nothingness is not, that we grasp it by negintuition and as the reverse of being. If there can be several beings, there will be as many nothingnesses. The question is not how one would discern one nothingness from another, for to say that I am nothing (in the sense of identity) is to say that I am (in the active sense) my body and *my* situation, and, reduced to its true terms, the question is whether there can be more than one body and more than one situation. But as soon as it is put in these terms, it is solved: to be sure, I will never find in my situation the proof that there actually are other situations (with their titular incumbents who also make being be—the same being as I do), but if my situation were to prove that, it would prove much more than it should, since then the existence of the other would result from my own existence. All one can ask is that my situation—that region of being that is the least distant from my constitutive nothingness—not be for me just one object among all those over which my look soars, that, as Descartes said, there be a certain particular right by which I call it my own, that it be a region of being which I assume first and foremost, through which I assume all the rest, that I have a certain particular bond with it, that it restrict the universality of my gaze in such a way that my view of being not be coextensive with being, and that beyond what I see the place be marked out for what the others see, if they come to be. But this is included in the very notion of situation and in the negintuition of nothingness: if I am nothing and if in order to come to the world I support myself particularly on one part of being, then, since that part does not thereby cease to be *outside* and to be subject to the actions that traverse the world, and since I am not informed about all those actions, there are some whose consequences I will have to assume as brute facts; my situation is opaque to my own eyes, it presents aspects that escape me and upon which an exterior look, if such were possible, would have more light. What I am all told overflows what I am for myself, my universality as nothingness is only presumption on my part, and since it is operative only through my situation, an exterior look that would encompass that situation would encompass my nothingness also. If I succeed in thinking the nonbeing of my nonbeing completely, I would agree that in order to be truly nonbeing, it renounces itself in favor of what I am as a whole or in fact. From then on everything is ready, not for an experience of the other (which we have seen is not positively possible), not for a proof of the other (which would proceed against its objective by rendering the other necessary on the basis of myself), but for an experience my passivity within being—not that being could by itself alone close in over my nothingness, but because it includes at least all the attributes which my nothingness is decked out with in fact. Since I inevitably identify myself with these attributes from the sole fact that they are my situation, since being is and nothingness is not, in this measure I am exposed, menaced. That this possibility is realized is in fact attested by the experience of shame, or my being reduced to what is visible in my situation. There is no positive experience of another, but there is an experience of my total being as compromised in the visible part of myself. For reflection, we—the others and myself—could not have in common a world that would be numerically the same, we could only rejoin one another in the common signification of our thoughts and in the indivision of ideality. If, on the contrary, we follow out the consequences of the negintuition all the way, we understand how our transcendental being and our empirical being are the obverse and the reverse of one another; we understand, through this expedient, that we are visible, we are not the adequate cause of all that we are, that the world is not only the term of our private ontogenesis but is what already sustains us while we traverse it with a look that, in its own way, is a part of it. I do not *know* the others, in the strong sense that I *know* myself; I therefore cannot flatter myself in supposing that I participate with them in a thought of the world which would be ideally the same thought. But my perception of the world feels it has an exterior; I feel at the surface of my visible being that my volubility dies away, that I become flesh, and that at the extremity of this inertia that was me there is something else, or rather an other who is not a thing. He then is seated nowhere, he is everywhere around me with the ubiquity of oneiric or mythical beings: for he is not entirely *ipse*—I alone am—but he is not caught up in the fabric of what I call being either. He encompasses it, he is a look come from nowhere and which therefore envelops me, me and my power for ontogenesis, from all sides. I knew very well that I was *nothing* and that this nothing swept itself away in favor of being. There remained for me to learn from the other that even this sacrifice does not suffice to equal the plenitude of being, that my fundamental negation is not complete as long as it has not itself been negated from without, and, by a foreign gaze, counted in with the beings. . . . But at the same time, since there are no degrees in nothingness, the other's intervention can teach me nothing about my nothingness of which I would have been absolutely ignorant. The solipsist being is already in himself the absolute other which he becomes for himself with the apparition of the other. I already have in the night of the In-itself all that is necessary in order to fabricate the other's private world, as the beyond inaccessible to me. The experience of the other's gaze upon me only prolongs my inward conviction of being nothing, of living only as a parasite on the world, of inhabiting a body and a situation. All told, therefore, a rigorous philosophy of negintuition accounts for the private worlds without shutting us up in them: strictly speaking there is no intermundane space; each one inhabits only his own, sees only according to his own point of view, enters into being only through his situation. But because he is nothing and because his relationship with his situation and with his body is a relation of being, his situation, his body, his thoughts do not form a screen between him and the world; on the contrary they are the vehicle of a relation to Being in which third parties, witnesses, can intervene. Their place is marked out in advance in the lacunae of my private world, which I know very well to be lacunae, since the "nothing" which I am would need the totality of being in order to be completely realized, and since it is evident that my situation, my body, my thoughts are only a part of it. While a philosophy of consciousness or of reflection can justify the perceptual faith in the unicity of the world only by reducing it to a consciousness of the identity of the world, and by making of illusion a simple privation, a philosophy of negativity entirely ratifies the pretension of the perceptual faith to open to us a world numerically one, common to all, through perspectives that are our own, because the *solus ipse,* as fundamental negation, is in advance open upon a background-world that exceeds all its perspectives, because the "incomparable monster" is in its heart convinced that its views are unequal to the whole, is all ready, if it encounters someone, to found a family, and because it has the momentum to go beyond itself. For the philosophy of reflection it is an inextricable difficulty to comprehend how a constitutive consciousness can pose another that would be its equal, and hence also constitutive—since the first must forthwith pass on to the rank of the constituted. The difficulty results from the fact that both are conceived as centrifugal acts, spiritual syntheses, in which case one does not see how they could ebb back toward their source. On the contrary it is for a philosophy of the negative the very definition of the *ipse* to adhere to a *de facto* situation or to sustain it as its bond with Being. This exterior at the same time confirms it in its particularity, renders it visible as a partial being to the others' look, and connects it back to the whole of Being. What was a stumbling block for the philosophy of reflection becomes, from the point of view of negativity, the principle of a solution. Everything really does come down to a matter of thinking the negative rigorously.

Finally the thought of the negative [*pensée du négatif*] satisfies the third exigency of the perceptual faith we spoke of at the start. We said that before all philosophy, perception is convinced that it has to do with a confused totality where all things, the bodies and the minds, are together, and which it calls the *world*. Here again the reflection attains its rigor only by destroying what we experience: it replaces the pell-mell of the world with a set of parallel consciousnesses, each observing its own law as if it had been regulated by the same clockmaker as the others, or each observing the laws of a universal thought that is immanent in all. From the point of view of a negativist philosophy, the synchronism of the consciousnesses is given by their common belongingness to a Being to which no one has the key and whose law they all observe—or rather, let us no longer say that there is synchronization: each experiences himself as involved with the others; there is a meeting ground which is Being itself inasmuch as each of us inheres in it through his situation. "There is only Being": each experiences himself given over to a body, to a situation, through them to being, and what he knows of himself passes entirely over to the other the very instant he experiences the other's medusan power. Hence each one knows that he himself and the others are *inscribed* in the world; what he feels, what he lives, what the others feel and live, even his dreams or their dreams, his illusions and theirs, are not islets, isolated fragments of being: all this, by reason of the fundamental exigency of our constitutive nothingnesses, is *of being*, has consistence, order, meaning, and there is a way to comprehend it. Even if what I live at present should reveal itself to be illusory, the critique of my illusion will not simply cast it out of the world, but on the contrary will show me its place, its relative legitimacy, its *truth*. If nothingness is destined for Being, my presence as a nothingness is an exigency for totality, for cohesion; it postulates that everywhere it is a matter of the same being. . . . All that is partial is to be reintegrated, every negation is in reality a determination, the being-self and the being-other and the being in itself are fragments of one sole being. The negativism, if it is rigorous, absolute, is a sort of positivism. The very movement by which a *this* is pronounced in my life, or this life in the world, is but the climax of negation, the negation that destroys itself. If a nothingness that is truly conceived as nothingness as such eludes all contamination with being and refuses to form a whole by juxtaposition with it, at the same time it demands to be all, it backs up being in its integral exigency, and, through a reversal of the pro and the con, is incorporated into being. When we have gone beyond the first steps, the radical distinction between being and nothingness, the analysis—which are abstract and superficial—we find at the center of things that the opposites are exclusionary to such an extent that the one without the other would be only an abstraction, that the force of being is supported by the frailty of the nothingness which is its accomplice, that the obscurity of the In Itself is for the clarity of the For Itself in general, if not for that of "my consciousness." The famous ontological problem, the "why is there something rather than nothing" disappears along with the alternative: there is not something *rather than nothing,* the nothing could not *take the place* of something or of being: nothingness inexists (in the negative sense) and being is, and the exact adjusting of the one upon the other no longer leaves room for a question. Everything is obscure when one has not thought out the negative; everything is clear when one has thought it as negative. For then what is called negation and what is called position appear as accomplices and even in a sort of equivalence. They confront one another "in a tumult like unto silence"; the world is like that band of foam on the ocean which appears immobile when seen from an airplane, but which suddenly, because it has extended itself by a line, is understood to be shimmering and living from close up. But one also understands that, seen from high enough, the amplitude of being will never exceed that of nothingness, nor the noise of the world its silence

In a sense the thought of the negative provides us with what we were searching for, terminates our research, brings philosophy to a standstill. We said that philosophy needs a contact with being prior to reflection, a contact which makes reflection itself possible. The "negintuition" of nothingness is the philosophical attitude that puts reflection and spontaneity in a sort of equivalence. If I really understand that nothingness is not, and that this is its own way of being, I understand that there can be no question of incorporating it into being, that it will always be this side of it, that I *qua* negativity am always behind all the things, cut off from them by virtue of my status as witness, always capable of suspending my adhesion to the world in order to make of it a thought of the world. And yet at the same time I understand that this thought of the world is *nothing,* that in this return to myself I do not discover a set of premises of which the world would be the consequence, that on the contrary it is the premise and my consciousness of it the consequence, that my intentions in themselves are empty, that they are only the flight of my emptiness after being, and that this flight owes its direction and its meaning to being, that our reconstructions or reconstitutions are suspended upon a primary evidence of the world which itself indicates its articulations to me. What I find "in myself," is always the reference to this originating presence, and to retire into oneself is identical to leaving oneself. For him who thinks the negative in its purity, there are not two movements—the abandonment to the world and the recovery by reflection; there are not two attitudes—the one, natural, of attention to the things, and the other, philosophical, of attention to the signification of the things, each retaining, as in reserve, the possibility of transforming itself into the other; there is a perception of being and an imperception of nothingness which are coextensive with one another, which are but one. An absolute negativism—that is, one that thinks the negative in its originality—and an absolute positivism—that is, one that thinks being in its plenitude and its self-sufficiency—are exactly synonymous; there is not the least divergence between them. To say that nothingness is not is the same as to say that there is only being—in other words, that one could not find nothingness among the things that are, as one of them, that *therefore* it must be backed up against them, that it must be no more than what makes them not be each for its own account, what makes them be together, what makes them be one sole Being. . . . The perspective in which Being and Nothingness are absolutely opposed, and the perspective in which Being itself, by definition given as identical with itself, eminently contains a contact—established, broken, and reestablished—with Nothingness, its being recognized, its negation negated—these two perspectives are but one; as absolutely opposed, Being and Nothingness are indiscernible. It is the absolute inexistence of Nothingness that makes it need Being and makes it hence be not visible except in the guise of "lakes of nonbeing," relative and localized nonbeings, reliefs or lacunae in the world. It is precisely because Being and Nothingness, the yes and the no, cannot be blended together like two ingredients that, when we see being, nothingness is immediately there, and not in the margin like the zone of nonvision around our field of vision, but over the whole expanse of what we see, as what installs it and disposes it before us as a spectacle. The strict thought of the negative is invulnerable, since it is also a thought of the absolute positivity and hence already contains everything one could oppose to it. It cannot be shown wanting nor be found shorthanded.

But is this not because it is ungraspable? It begins by opposing being and nothingness absolutely, and it ends by showing that the nothingness is in a way within being, which is the unique universe. When are we to believe it? At the beginning or at the end? The answer will be: it amounts to the same thing and there is no difference. Yet there is a difference between Being in the restricted sense with which one begins—which over its whole extension is absolutely exclusive of nothingness, and which nothingness needs if it is to be able to be named—and Being in the broad sense which one ends up with—which in a way contains nothingness, invokes it in order to become fully being, in order to become Being "such as it is." The two movements—that by which nothingness invokes being and that by which being invokes nothingness—do not merge into one: they cross. According to the first, being is negation of negation, it has an infrastructure of nothingness, it is an attribute of knowledge; according to the second, nothingness finally is reiterated position, position of position, it has an infrastructure of being, and knowledge is an attribute of being. In the first approach, being is considered from the point of view of nothingness. In the second, nothingness is considered from the point of view of being. Even if, in both cases, one ends up at an identification, it takes place in the first case for the profit of nothingness, in the second for the profit of being, and the two relationships are not identical. Let us examine each in turn.

One can first think starting from the pure negative. One shows that I, who question myself about being, am nothing. With this statement, one circumscribes an anti-nature which is me: I am what has no nature, I am a nothing. This conceptual or verbal fixation is only a first moment of analysis, but it is indispensable to introduce what follows, it commands it. It motivates the conclusions themselves, quite opposed to it, at which the thought of the negative will arrive; it codetermines their meaning by establishing them in advance in an order of univocal truth where the opposites can drive out one another but not pass into one another. In positing that nothingness is not, that nonbeing is its manner of being, that it is nonbeing through and through, the thought of the negative condemns itself to define being as absolute plenitude and proximity, it posits that being is. Because he who questions about being is a nothing, it is necessary that everything be absolutely outside of him, at a distance, and one could not conceive of a more or a less in this remoteness which is by principle. He who questions, having been once and for all defined as *nothing,* is installed at infinity; from there he apperceives all things in an absolute equidistance: before what is not, they are all, without any degree, of being, of the absolutely full and positive. Because the negative is the founding, the founded being is absolute positivity. One cannot even say that there is any *inference* here: the negintuition of nothingness is already the immediate presence to being. The power conceded to the philosopher to name this nothingness which he is, to coincide with this fissure in being, is already a variant of the principle of identity which defines being. In thinking on the basis of the pure negative we already decide to think according to identity; we are already in identity, since this negative which nothing can limit in its own order, having to go on to the limit of itself, will be also, and fundamentally, a negation of itself, and therefore will be pronounced in the form of an advent of pure being. There is a trap inherent in the thought of the negative: if we say that it is, we destroy its negativity; but if we maintain strictly that it is not, we still elevate it to a sort of positivity, we confer upon it a sort of being, since through and through and absolutely it is *nothing*. The negative becomes a sort of quality precisely because one fixes it in its power of refusal and evasion. A negativist thought is identical to a positivist thought, and in this reversal remains the same in that, whether considering the void of nothingness or the absolute fullness of being, it in every case ignores density, depth, the plurality of planes, the background worlds. When, starting from nothingness, it comes to pose being as absolute plenitude and positivity—more: to declare that there is only being and that being in a sense invokes and includes nothingness—it is not reintroducing elements that it would first methodically have excluded, it is not approaching the concrete, it is not following out the articulations of the whole: it is compensating for one abstraction with a counterabstraction. One must grant to it that the pure negative calls for pure being, but far from one having thus found for philosophy a position where self-consciousness would not be prejudicial to the transcendence of the thing, one compromises both of these, one accumulates the difficulties. For it is quite obvious that there is pure negation only in principle and that the existent For Itself is encumbered with a body, which is not outside if it is not inside, which intervenes between the For Itself and itself. Likewise pure being is nowhere to be found, for every alleged thing soon reveals itself to be an appearance, and these alternating and antagonistic images are not comprehensible as images of one sole being, for lack of degrees of being, for lack of organization in depth, and because this being, in order to be positive and full, must be flat, and hence remains *what it is* beyond the ambivalence to which we are confined. It is in appearance only that the immanent consciousness and the transcendence of being are reconciled by an analytic of Being and Nothingness: it is not being that is transcendent, it is I who hold it at arm's length by a sort of abnegation; it is not the world that is thick, it is I who am agile enough to make it be yonder. When here one moves from nothingness to being, and then to the ec-stasy of being in the nothingness that recognizes that being "such as it is," in fact there is neither progress nor synthesis, there is no transformation of the initial antithesis: one pushes unto its limits the initial analysis which remains valid to the letter, and which always animates the integral view of Being. Being's invoking of nothingness is *in truth* an invoking of Being by nothingness, an autonegation. Nothingness and being are always absolutely other than one another, it is precisely their isolation that unites them; they are not really united, they only more quickly succeed one another before thought.[12] Since the void of the For Itself fills up, since man is not immediately present to everything, but more especially to a body, to a situation, and only through them to the world, one admits the denseness of an unreflected being in the For Itself, and one admits that the reflective operation is second: one speaks of a *prereflective cogito.* But the ambivalence of the word conveys the ambivalence of a thought that can either remain itself, or negate itself in the night of the In Itself, but cannot find any inertia in itself: is the prereflective *cogito* something in us that is more ourselves than the *cogito* and the reflection that introduces it, or is it a *cogito* that from the depths of ourselves precedes itself, pronounces itself before we have pronounced it, because thought is what we are? The first hypothesis is precluded if I am a nothing; and the second restores to me my emptiness just when the question is to understand how my life can be opaque for itself. The very progress of the investigation cannot change the idea we form of *Being and Nothingness;* it can only disclose its unnoticed implications, so long as one thinks on the basis of the signification of being and the non-sense of nothingness. Even if the explanation apparently reverses the perspectives, the reversal is not effective; everything takes place between this entity and this negentity [*négatité*], and being, which is said to undergo a sort of assumption into nothingness, remains pure In Itself, absolute positivity; it is only as such that it knows this adventure—and this pure In Itself was from the beginning destined to be recognized, since it was as an autonegation of the negative that it had appeared. There is no first apprehension of ipseity and being which is transformed or surpassed; the reversal of the pro and the con is another formulation of the initial antithesis, which does not cease in it, which on the contrary is renewed in it. The thought of the pure negative or of the pure positive is therefore a high-altitude thought, which operates on the essence or on the pure negation of the essence, on terms whose signification has been fixed and which it holds in its possession. Sartre does indeed say that *at the end of his book* it will be permissible to move to a broader sense of Being, which contains Being and nothingness. But this is not because the initial opposition would have been overcome; it remains in all its rigor, it is that initial opposition that justifies its own reversal, that triumphs in this defeat; the passion of the For Itself, which sacrifices itself in order that being be, is still its own negation by itself. It is tacitly understood that from one end of the book to the other we are speaking of the same nothingness and of the same being, that one unique spectator is witness to the progress, that he is not himself caught up in the movement, and that inasmuch as that is so the movement is illusory. A negativist or positivist thought rediscovers that postulate of the philosophy of reflection that no result of the reflection can retroactively compromise him who operates the reflection nor change the idea we form of him for ourselves. And it cannot be otherwise if one starts with the pure negative: for it will never admit anything into itself, and even if one comes to recognize that it has need of Being, it will need Being only as a distant environment that does not adulterate it. It will dispose it about itself, as a pure spectacle or as what it has to be, it will elevate it to truth or to signification; but it will itself remain the nothingness it was, its devotion to Being will confirm it as nothingness.

The negativist (or positivist) thought establishes between nothingness and being a massive cohesion, both rigid and fragile at the same time: rigid since they are finally indiscernible, fragile since they remain unto the end absolute opposites. Their relation is, as the psychologists say, labile. This will be seen each time it is a question of comprehending how nothingness receives being into itself, and hence not only, as we said a moment ago, when it is a question of comprehending my incarnation, but also when it is a question of comprehending how I can assume the view another has of me, or finally our common belongingness to the world. It is as always by means of the negative purity of the For Itself that one seeks to comprehend the fact that it recognizes beings like unto itself: because I am no thing, and because all the same I have to be this emptiness, to make it be in the world, I take up again on my own account my body and my situation and the other's gaze which I see posed on this exterior that is me. For me there is no activity and presence of an other; there is on my part the experience of a passivity and of an alienation which I recognize concern me, because, being nothing, I have to be my situation. In the last analysis, therefore, the relationship remains one between me as nothingness and me as a man, and I do not deal with others, at most I deal with a neutral non-me, with a diffused negation of my nothingness. I am drawn out of myself by the other's gaze, but his power over me is exactly measured by the consent which I have given to my body, to my situation; he has alienating force only because I alienate myself. Philosophically speaking, there is no experience of the other. For the encounter with another to be thought, no transformation of the idea of myself that I form by myself is required. The encounter actualizes what was already possible on the basis of me alone. What the encounter brings is only the force of the fact: this consent to my body and to my situation which I prepared, whose principle I possessed, but only the principle, since a passivity that one poses oneself is not effective—here suddenly it is realized. The relation with another, says Sartre, is [evidently?] a fact, otherwise I should not be myself and he would not be other; the other exists in fact and for me exists only in fact. But just as "being is" *adds* nothing to "nothingness is not" and the recognition of Being as absolute plenitude and positivity changes nothing in the negintuition of nothingness, so also the other's gaze which suddenly congeals me adds to my universe no new dimension—it only confirms for me an inclusion in being which I knew from within; I only learn that there is about my universe an outside in general, as I learn by perception that the things it illuminates lived before it in the night of identity. The other is one of the empirical forms of the engulfment into Being. . . . And, to be sure, this analysis has its truth: to the whole extent that it is true that I am nothing, the other cannot appear to me otherwise than as the ultraworld from which emanates a gaze whose impact I feel on my body alone; to the whole extent that I am a thought, a consciousness, I am compelled to enter into the world only through it, and the other consciousnesses, the other thoughts, will be forever but the doubles or the younger sisters of my own. I will never live any but my own life and the others will never be but other myselves. But is this solipsism, this aspect of the phenomena, this structure of the relationship with another the whole or even the essential? It is but one empirical variant of it[13]—the ambivalent or labile relationship with the other—in which, moreover, analysis would rediscover the normal, canonical form, subjected in the particular case to a distortion that makes of the other an anonymous, faceless obsession, an other in general.

Let us even suppose that the other be the X titular of this look which I feel posed upon me and which congeals me: I do not advance one step into the elucidation of the phenomenon in saying that it is prepared for by me from within, that I, nothingness, have exposed myself to this look by taking up on my own account my body, my situation, my exterior, and that finally the other is the limiting case of my engulfment in Being. For as long as it is I who insert myself into Being, the one who inserts and the inserted keep their distances. Whereas the other's gaze—and it is here that it brings me something new—envelops me wholly, being and nothingness. This is what, in the relationship with another, depends on no interior possibility and what obliges us to say that it is a pure fact. But though this relationship be a part of my facticity, though it be an encounter that cannot be deduced from the For Itself, still it does present a sense for me; it is not a nameless catastrophe that leaves me petrified [*médusé*], it is the entry on the scene of someone else. I do not simply feel myself frozen, I am frozen by a look, and if it were for example an animal that looked at me, I would know only a feeble echo of this experience. Therefore, far from the sense of the other's look being exhausted in the burning it leaves at the point of my body he looks at, it is necessary that there be something in the other's look that designates it to me as a look of an other. It is necessary that something teach me that I am wholly implicated, being and nothingness, in this perception that takes possession of me and that the other perceive me soul and body. Hence, by making of the ambivalent relation the canonical form of the relationship with the other and by bringing to the foreground the objectification I suffer, one does not avoid having to recognize a positive perception of the ipseity by an exterior ipseity: the ambivalent relation refers to it as to its condition. In other words, the thought of the negative can very well found every position on a negation of negation, every centripetal relation on a centrifugal relation, but, whether in dealing with being in general or the being of the other, a moment comes when the negation of negation crystallizes into the simplicity of a *this:* there is a thing, here is someone. These events are more than the infrastructure of the For Itself—the For Itself's power for negation henceforth derives from their sovereign positivity. My knowledge only sanctions what being already was in itself, only rejoins it "such as it is"—and, likewise, instead of my shame constituting the whole sense of the other's existence, the other's existence is the truth of my shame. Finally, if we consider my relationship no longer with the solipsist Being and with the other, but now with Being inasmuch as it is aimed at by all of us, inasmuch as it is crammed full of others who perceive one another and perceive the same world—and the same one that I also perceive—the negativist thought is once again faced with the alternative: either remain faithful to the definition of myself as nothingness and Being as pure positivity—in which case we do not have before us a world as the whole of nature, humanity, and history, including me; the negations are only a shimmering on the surface of being, and the hard core of being is found only after one has effaced from it every possible, every past, all movement, all the imaginary or illusory attributes which are of me and not of it. Or if one does not mean to drive being back to this limit of pure positivity where there is nothing, and ascribe to the For Itself what makes up the whole content of our experience, then, in accordance with the very movement of the negativity when it goes all the way in its negation of itself, it is necessary to incorporate into being a whole quantity of negative attributes, the transitions, and the becoming, and the possible. As always the same negativist thought oscillates between these two images without being able to sacrifice one of them nor to unite them. It is ambivalence itself, that is, the absolute contradiction and the identity of being and nothingness, it is the "ventriloquial" thought that Plato speaks of, that which always affirms or denies in the hypothesis what it denies or affirms in the thesis, that which as high-altitude thinking belies the inherence of being in nothingness and of nothingness in being.

A philosophy of reflection, if it is not to be ignorant of itself, is led to question itself about what precedes itself, about our contact with being within ourselves and outside of ourselves, before all reflection. Yet by principle it can conceive of that contact with being only as a reflection before the reflection, because it develops under the domination of concepts such as "subject," "consciousness," "self-consciousness," "mind," all of which, even if in a refined form, involve the idea of a *res cogitans,* of a positive being of thought—whence there results the immanence in the unreflected of the results of reflection. We have therefore asked ourselves if a philosophy of the negative would not restore to us the brute being of the unreflected without compromising our power of reflection: a subjectivity that is nothing is in the immediate presence of being or in contact with the world, and at the same time as close to itself as one could like, since no opaqueness in it could separate it from itself. And yet, this analytic of being and nothingness leaves us with a difficulty. By principle it opposes them absolutely, it defines them as mutually exclusive—but if they are absolute opposites they are not defined by anything that would be proper to them. As soon as the one is negated the other is there, each of them is only the exclusion of the other, and nothing prevents them, in the end, from exchanging their roles: there subsists only the split between them. Reciprocally alternative as they may be, they together compose one sole universe of thought, since each of them is only its retreat before the other. To think the total being—what is totally, and hence also that to which nothing is lacking, what is the whole of being—it is necessary to be outside of it, a margin of nonbeing; but this margin excluded from the whole prevents it from being all—the true totality should contain it too, which, since it is a margin of nonbeing, is quite impossible. Thus, if being and nothingness are absolutely opposed, they are together founded in a sort of Hyper-being, which is mythical, since the force that requires it is their absolute repulsion. Such is the circle we have traversed, and which leads from absolute opposition to an identity which is only another figure of the opposition—either one thinks them in their opposition between what is and what is not, or on the contrary one identifies them by making of being either a redoubling of negation, or, inversely, a positivity so perfect that it contains eminently the recognition that the nothingness brings to it. But there is no progress, transformation, irreversible order from one of these relationships to the other; what leads us from the one to the other is not a movement of what is thought, it is the shifting of our attention or the choice we make of the one or other point of departure. But this reproach of ambivalence has no cogency against an analytic of Being and Nothingness that is a description in accordance with the fundamental structures of our contact with being: if this contact really is ambivalent, it is for us to accommodate ourselves to it, and logical difficulties cannot prevail against this description. In reality, the definitions of being as what is in all respects and without restriction, and of nothingness as what is not in any respect—this appropriation of an immediate being and of an immediate nothingness by thought, this intuition and this negintuition—are the abstract portrait of an experience, and it is on the terrain of experience that they must be discussed. Do they express well our contact with being, do they express it in full? They do assuredly express the experience of vision: the vision is a panorama; through the holes of the eyes and from the bottom of my invisible retreat, I survey the world and rejoin it where it is. There is a sort of madness in vision such that with it I go unto the world itself, and yet at the same time the parts of that world evidently do not coexist without me (the table in itself has nothing to do with the bed a yard away); the world is the vision of the world and could not be anything else. Being is bordered along its whole extension with a vision of being that is not a being, that is a nonbeing. For him who really coincides with the gaze and truly installs himself in the position of the seer, this is incontestable. But is this the whole truth, and can one then formulate it by saying that there is the In Itself as position, and that the For Itself inexists as negation? This formula is evidently abstract: taken literally it would make the experience of vision impossible, for if being is wholly in itself, it is itself only in the night of identity, and my look, which draws it therefrom, destroys it as being; and if the For Itself is pure negation, it is not even For Itself, it is unaware of itself for want of *there being* something in it to be known. I never have being as it is, I have it only as interiorized, reduced to its meaning as a spectacle. And, to top it all, I do not have nothingness either—which is entirely pledged to being, and which, it is true, always misses it: but this repeated failure does not render to non-being its purity. What then do I have? I have a nothingness filled with being, a being emptied by nothingness, and if this is not the destruction of each of the terms by the other, of me by the world and of the world by me, it is necessary that the annihilation of being and the sinking of the nothingness into it not be exterior relations and not be two distinct operations. This is what one tries to achieve by thinking vision as *nihilation*. Understood in this way, it makes the In Itself itself pass to the status of a world seen, and makes the For Itself pass to the status of a For Itself sunken into being, situated, incarnated. As an operative nothingness, my vision is a ubiquitous presence to the world itself, since it is without inertia and without opacity,[14] and at the same time irremediably distinct from what it sees, from which it is separated by the very emptiness that permits it to be vision.[15] But we find again here, in the analysis of experience, what we have found above in the dialectic of being and nothingness: if one really abides by their opposition—if to see is to not be, and if what is seen is being—one understands that vision would be an immediate presence to the world, but one does not see how the nothingness I am could at the same time separate me from being. If it does so, if being is transcendent to the vision, it is that then one has ceased to think of it as pure nonbeing, and moreover has ceased to think of being as pure In Itself. Either the analytic of being and nothingness is an idealism and does not give us the brute or prereflective being we seek, or, if it is something else, this is because it goes beyond and transforms the initial definitions. Then I am no longer the pure negative, to see is no longer simply to nihilate, the relation between what I see and I who see is not one of immediate or frontal contradiction; the things attract my look, my gaze caresses the things, it espouses their contours and their reliefs, between it and them we catch sight of a complicity. As for being, I can no longer define it as a hard core of positivity under the negative properties that would come to it from my vision: if one subtracts them all, there no longer remains anything to see; and nothing permits me to attribute them to the For Itself, which moreover is itself sunken into Being. The negations, the perspective deformations, the possibilities, which I have learned to consider as extrinsic denominations, I must now reintegrate into Being—which therefore is staggered out in depth, conceals itself at the same time that it discloses itself, is abyss and not plenitude. The analytic of Being and Nothingness spread over the things themselves an impalpable film: their *being for me,* which let us see them in themselves. Now, while on my side there has appeared the stratum of corporeal being into which my vision sinks, on the side of the things there is a profusion of perspectives which are not as nothing and which oblige me to say that the thing itself is always further on. Vision is not the immediate relationship of the For Itself with the In Itself, and we are invited to redefine the seer as well as the world seen. The analytic of Being and Nothingness is the seer who forgets that he has a body and that what he sees is always beneath what he sees, who tries to force the passage toward pure being and pure nothingness by installing himself in pure vision, who makes himself a visionary, but who is thrown back to his own opacity as a seer and to the depth of being. If we succeed in describing the access to the things themselves, it will only be through this opacity and this depth, which never cease: there is no thing fully observable, no inspection of the thing that would be without gaps and that would be total; we do not wait until we have observed it to say that the thing is there; on the contrary it is the appearance it has of being a thing that convinces us immediately that it would be possible to observe it. In the grain of the sensible we find the assurance for a series of cross-checkings, which do not constitute the ecceity of the thing but are derived from it. Conversely, the imaginary is not an absolute inobservable: it finds in the body analogues of itself that incarnate it. This distinction, like the others, has to be reconsidered and is not reducible to that between the full and the void.

For a philosophy that is installed in pure vision, in the aerial view of the panorama, there can be no encounter with another: for the look dominates; it can dominate only things, and if it falls upon men it transforms them into puppets which move only by springs. From the heights of the towers of Notre Dame, I cannot, when I like, feel myself to be on equal footing with those who, enclosed within those walls, there minutely pursue incomprehensible tasks. High places attract those who wish to look over the world with an eagle-eye view. Vision ceases to be solipsist only up close, when the other turns back upon me the luminous rays in which I had caught him, renders precise that corporeal adhesion of which I had a presentiment in the agile movements of his eyes, enlarges beyond measure that blind spot I divined at the center of my sovereign vision, and, invading my field through all its frontiers, attracts me into the prison I had prepared for him and, as long as he is there, makes me incapable of solitude. In every case, in the solipsism as in the alienation, how would we ever find a mind, an invisible, at the end of our look? Or, if the other also is pure vision, how would we see his vision? One would have to be him. The other can enter into the universe of the seer only by assault, as a pain and a catastrophe; he will rise up not before the seer, in the spectacle, but laterally, as a radical casting into question of the seer. Since he is only pure vision, the seer cannot encounter an other, who thereby would be a thing seen; if he leaves himself, it will only be by a turning back of the vision upon himself; if he finds an other, it will only be as his own being seen. There is no perception of the other by me; abruptly my ubiquity as a seer is belied, I feel myself seen—and the other is that X yonder which I do indeed have to think in order to account for the visible body that I suddenly feel myself to have. In appearance this manner of introducing the other as the unknown is the sole one that takes into account and accounts for his alterity. If there is an other, by definition I cannot install myself in him, coincide with him, live his very life: I live only my own. If there is an other, he is never in my eyes a For Itself, in the precise and given sense that I am, for myself. Even if our relationship leads me to admit or even to experience that "he too" thinks, that "he too" has a private landscape, I am not that thought as I am my own, I do not have that private landscape as I have my own. What I say of it is always derived from what I know of myself by myself: I concede that *if I inhabited* that body I should have another solitude, comparable to that which I have, and always divergent perspectively from it. But the "if I inhabited" is not a hypothesis; it is a fiction or a myth. The other's life, such as he lives it, is not for me who speaks an eventual experience or a possible: it is a prohibited experience, it is an impossible, and this is as it must be if the other is really the other. If the other is really the other, that is, a For Itself in the strong sense that I am for myself, *he must never be so before my eyes;* it is necessary that this other For Itself never fall under my look, it is necessary that there be no perception of an other, it is necessary that the other be my negation or my destruction. Every other interpretation, under the pretext of placing us, him and myself, in the same universe of thought, ruins the alterity of the other and hence marks the triumph of a disguised solipsism. Conversely, it is in making the other not only inaccessible but invisible for me that I guarantee his alterity and quit solipsism. Yet we are not at the end of our troubles, and the labyrinth is still more difficult than we thought. For if we formulate what we have just said into theses—that is: the other can be for me, and hence can be only my being seen, the other is the unknown incumbent of that zone of the not-mine which I am indeed obliged to mark out with dotted lines in being, since I feel myself seen—this agnosticism in regard to the other's being for himself, which appeared to guarantee his alterity, suddenly appears as the worst of infringements upon it. For he who states it implies that it is applicable to all those who hear him. He does not speak only of himself, of his own perspective, and for himself; he speaks for all. He says: *the For Itself* (in general) is alone . . . or: *the being for another* is the death of the For Itself, or things of this kind—without specifying whether this concerns the being for itself such as he lives it or the being for itself such as those who hear him live it, the being for another such as he experiences it or the being for another such as the others experience it. This singular that he permits himself—the For Itself, the For the Other—indicates that he means to speak in the name of all, that in his description he implies the power to speak for all, whereas the description contests this power. Hence I only apparently confine myself to my own experience—to my being for myself and to my being for another—and only apparently respect the radical originality of the for itself of another and his being for me. From the sole fact that I open in the wall of my solipsism the breach through which the gaze of another passes, it is no longer a dichotomy that I am dealing with—that of "the" For Itself and of "the" For the Other—it is a four-term system: my being for me, my being for the other, the for itself of another, and his being for me. The void that I wished to provide at the horizon of my universe, in order to lodge in it the author of my shame and the inconceivable image of me he forms, is not, whatever I may think, a void; it is not the simple or immediate negation of myself and of my universe. From the sole fact that I circumscribe it, be it with dotted lines, it is cut out in my universe; there is an intersection of my universe with that of another. We do not have *the* For Itself in general with *the* In Itself in general which it sustains, *the* For the Other in general, that is, the possibility for *every* For Itself to be incorporated into *the* In Itself in general by a foreign look; in other words we do not have my being for me and my being for the other virtually multiplied to *n* samples—we have face to face my being for myself, this same being for me offered as a spectacle to the other, the gaze of another as bearer of a being for itself which is a rejoinder of my own, but capable of petrifying [*méduser*] my own, and finally this same being for itself of the other aimed at and in some way reached, perceived, by my gaze upon him. There is, to be sure, no question of a reciprocal relationship between me and the other, since I am alone to be myself, since I am for myself the sole original of humanity, and the philosophy of vision is right in emphasizing the inevitable dissymmetry of the I-other relation. But, in spite of appearances, it is the philosophy of vision that installs itself dogmatically in all the situations at the same time, by declaring them impenetrable, by thinking each of them as the absolute negation of the others. I cannot even go the length of this absolute in negation; the negation here is a dogmatism; it secretly contains the absolute affirmation of the opposites. It is necessary that there be transition from the other to me and from me to the other precisely in order that I and the others not be posed dogmatically as universes equivalent by principle, and in order that the privilege of the For Itself for itself be recognized. In founding the experience of the other upon that of my objectification before him, the philosophy of vision believed it established between him and me a relationship that would be at the same time a relation of being—since it is in my very being that I am affected by the view the other gets of me—and a relation of pure negation, since this objectification which I undergo is literally incomprehensible to me. Here once again we find that one must choose: either[16] the relationship is really a relationship of being, in which case it is necessary that the other have in my eyes the status of a For Itself, that the outside of myself on which he has a hold also put me at his mercy as a pure For Itself, that my constitutive nothingness sink into my situation under my own eyes. And finally it is necessary that, instead of the other and me being two parallel For Itselfs each on his own stricken with the same mortal evil—the other's presence, which crushes us each in turn in the midst of our own universe of the In Itself—we be some for the others[17] a system of For Itselfs, sensitive to one another, such that the one knows the other not only in what he suffers from him, but more generally as a witness, who can be challenged because he is also himself accused, because he is not a pure gaze upon pure being any more than I am, because his views and my own are in advance inserted into a system of partial perspectives, referred to one same world in which we coexist and where our views intersect. For the other to be truly the other, it does not suffice and it is not necessary that he be a scourge, the continued threat of an absolute reversal of pro and con, a judge himself elevated above all contestation, without place, without relativities, faceless like an obsession, and capable of crushing me with a glance into the dust of my world. It is necessary and it suffices that he have the power to decenter me, to oppose his centering to my own, and he can do so only because we are not two nihilations installed in two universes of the In Itself, incomparable, but two entries to the same Being, each accessible to but one of us, but appearing to the other as *practicable by right,* because they both belong to the same Being. It is necessary and it suffices that the other's body which I see and his word which I hear, which are given to me as immediately present in my field, *do present to me in their own fashion what I will never be present to,* what will always be invisible to me, what I will never directly witness—an absence therefore, but not just any absence, a certain absence and a certain difference in terms of dimensions which are from the first common to us and which predestine the other to be a mirror of me as I am of him, which are responsible for the fact that we do not have two images side by side of someone and of ourselves, but one sole image in which we are both involved, which is responsible for the fact that my consciousness of myself and my myth of the other are not two contradictories, but rather each the reverse of the other. It is perhaps all that that is meant when it is said that the other is the X responsible for my being seen. But then it would be necessary to add that he can be this only because I see that he looks at me, and that he can look at me—me, the invisible—only because we belong to the same system of being for itself and being for another; we are moments of the same syntax, we count in the same world, we belong to the same Being. But this has no meaning for man taken as a pure vision: he does indeed have the conviction of going unto the things themselves, but, surprised in the act of seeing, suddenly he becomes one of them, and there is no passage from the one view to the other. Pure seer, he becomes a thing seen through an ontological catastrophe, through a pure event which is for him the impossible. Or, if he can comprehend it, it will be only by backing down on the alleged ubiquity of the vision, by foregoing the idea of being everything, that is, of being nothing, by learning to know, within the vision itself, a sort of palpation of the things, within the overhead survey itself, an inherence. To be sure, our world is principally and essentially visual; one would not make a world out of scents or sounds. But the privilege of vision is not to open *ex nihilo* upon a pure being *ad infinitum:* the vision too has a field, a range. Only at very great distances are the things it gives us pure things, identical to themselves and wholly positive, like the stars, and this horizon of the In Itself is visible only as the background of a zone of nearby things which, for their part, are open and inexhaustible.

Whether we are considering my relations with the things or my relations with the other (the two problems are but one, since the insularity of the For Itselfs is spanned only by their openness to the "same" things), the question is whether in the last analysis our life takes place between an absolutely individual and absolutely universal nothingness behind us and an absolutely individual and absolutely universal being before us—in which case we have the incomprehensible and impossible task of restoring to Being, in the form of thoughts and actions, everything we have taken from it, that is, everything that we are—or whether every relation between me and Being, even vision, even speech, is not a carnal relation, with the flesh of the world. In this case "pure" being only shows through at the horizon, at a distance which is not nothing, which is not spread out by me, which is something, which therefore itself belongs to being, which, between the "pure" being and myself, is the thickness of its being for me, of its being for the others—and which finally makes what merits the name of being be not the horizon of "pure" being but the system of perspectives that open into it, makes the integral being be not before me, but at the intersection of my views and at the intersection of my views with those of the others, at the intersection of my acts and at the intersection of my acts with those of the others, makes the sensible world and the historical world be always intermundane spaces, since they are what, beyond our views, renders them interdependent among themselves and interdependent with those of the others; they are the instances to which we address ourselves as soon as we live, the registers in which is inscribed what we see, what we do, to become there thing, world, history. Far from opening upon the blinding light of pure Being or of the Object, our life has, in the astronomical sense of the word, an atmosphere: it is constantly enshrouded by those mists we call the sensible world or history, the *one*[18] of the corporeal life and the *one* of the human life, the present and the past, as a pell-mell ensemble of bodies and minds, promiscuity of visages, words, actions, with, between them all, that cohesion which cannot be denied them since they are all differences, extreme divergencies of one same something. Before this inextricable involvement, there are two types of error; one is to deny it—under the pretext that it can be broken up by the accidents of my body, by death, or simply by my freedom. But this does not mean that when it does take place it would be only the sum of the partial processes without which it does not exist. The principle of principles here is that one cannot judge the powers of life by those of death, nor define without arbitrariness life as the sum of the forces that resist death, as if it were the necessary and sufficient definition of Being to be the suppression of nonbeing. The involvement of men in the world and of men in one another, even if it can be brought about only by means of *perceptions* and *acts,* is transversal with respect to the spatial and temporal multiplicity of the actual. But this must not lead us into the inverse error, which would be to treat this order of involvement as a transcendental, intemporal order, as a system of *a priori* conditions: that would be to postulate once again that life is only death nullified, since one thinks oneself obliged to explain by an outside principle everything in it that exceeds the simple summation of its necessary conditions. The openness upon a natural and historical world is not an illusion and is not an *a priori;* it is our involvement in Being. Sartre expressed this by saying that the For Itself is necessarily haunted by an imaginary In-Itself-for-itself. We only say that the In-Itself-for-itself is more than imaginary. The imaginary is without consistence, inobservable; it vanishes when one proceeds to vision. Thus the In-Itself-for-itself breaks up before the philosophical consciousness to give place to the Being which is and the Nothingness which is not, to the rigorous thought of a Nothingness which needs Being, which attains it by being a negation of itself, and which thus accomplishes the silent self-affirmation that was immanent in Being. The truth of the Sartrean In-Itself-for-itself is the intuition of pure Being and the negintuition of Nothingness. It seems to us that on the contrary it is necessary to recognize in it the solidity of myth, that is, of an operative imaginary, which is part of our institution, and which is indispensable for the definition of Being itself. With this difference, we are indeed speaking of the same thing; and Sartre has himself pointed out what intervenes between Being and Nothingness.

A philosophy of negativity, which lays down nothing *qua* nothing (and consequently being *qua* being) as the principle of its research, thinks these invisibles in their purity, and at the same time admits that the knowing of nothingness is a nothingness of knowing, that nothingness is accessible only in bastard forms, is incorporated into being. The philosophy of negativity is indissolubly logic and experience: in it the dialectic of being and nothingness is only a preparation for experience, and in return experience, such as it has described it, is sustained and elaborated by the pure entity of being, the pure negentity of nothingness. The pure negative, in negating itself, sacrifices itself to the positive; the pure positive, insofar as it affirms itself without restriction, sanctions this sacrifice—this movement of significations, which is only the being of being and the inexistence of nothingness followed into their consequences, the principle of noncontradiction put into application, gives the schema of a pure vision with which the philosopher coincides. If I identify myself with my view of the world, if I consider it in act and without any reflective withdrawal, it is indeed the concentration in a point of nothingness, where being itself, being such as it is in itself, becomes being-seen. What there is common to both the concrete descriptions and the logical analysis—even more: what in a philosophy of the negative identifies the absolute distinction between being and nothingness and the description of nothingness sunken into being—is that they are two forms of immediate thought. On the one hand, one seeks being and nothingness in the pure state, one wishes to approach them as closely as possible, one aims at being itself in its plenitude and nothingness itself in its vacuity, one presses the confused experience until one draws the entity and the negentity out of it, one squeezes it between them as between pincers; beyond the visible one trusts entirely in *what* we think under the terms of being and nothingness, one practices an "essentialist" thought which refers to significations beyond experience, and thus one constructs our relations with the world. And at the same time one installs oneself in our condition of being seers, one coincides with it, one oneself exercises the vision of which one speaks, one says nothing that does not come from the vision itself lived from within. The clarification of the significations is one with the exercise of life because it is tacitly understood that to live or to think is always (as one wants to say) to identify oneself, or to nihilate. If a philosophy of the negative is at the same time a determination of essences and a coinciding with lived experience, this is not due to accident, inconsistency, or eclecticism, but because spontaneity consists in being in the mode of not-being, the reflective critique in not being in the mode of being, and because these two relationships form a circuit which is us. In this universal ambivalence, the philosophy of the negative is, we said, ungraspable: and indeed everything one opposes to it, it accepts. That nothingness is not? That the idea of nothingness is a pseudo-idea? That being is transcendent or that the "human reality" is access to a being? That it is not man that has being, but being that has man? It is the first to agree; these are its own principles. The only thing is that in it they are identified with the opposite principles: precisely because the *nichtiges Nichts* is not, the "there is" is reserved to a being unalloyed, positive, full. Precisely because there is no idea of nothingness, nothingness nihilates freely while being is. Precisely because transcendence is access to a Being and flight from the Self, this centrifugal and impalpable force, which is us, presides over every apparition of Being, and it is in starting from the Self, by ec-stasy or alienation, that the "there is" is produced. Being has man, but because man gives himself to it. Whence comes that sort of sentiment of uneasiness that a philosophy of the negative leaves: it described our factual situation with more penetration than had ever before been done—and yet one retains the impression that this situation is one that is being surveyed from above, and indeed it is: the more one describes experience as a compound of being and nothingness, the more their absolute distinction is confirmed; the more the thought adheres to experience, the more it keeps it at a distance. Such is the sorcery of the thought of the negative. But this also means that it cannot be circumscribed or discerned by what it affirms—it affirms everything—but only by what it leaves aside, precisely in its will to be everything: that is to say, the situation of the philosopher who speaks as distinct from what he speaks of, insofar as that situation affects what he says with a certain latent content which is not its manifest content, insofar as it implies a divergence between the essences he fixes and the lived experience to which they are applied, between the operation of living the world and the entities and negentities in which he expresses it. If one takes this residue into account, there is no longer identity between the lived experience and the principle of noncontradiction; the thought, precisely as thought, can no longer flatter itself that it conveys all the lived experience: it retains everything, save its density and its weight. The lived experience can no longer recognize itself in the idealizations we draw from it. Between the thought or fixation of essences, which is the aerial view, and life, which is inherence in the world or vision, a divergence reappears, which forbids the thought to project itself in advance in the experience and invites it to recommence the description from closer up. For a philosophy conscious of itself as a cognition, as a second fixation of a preexisting experience, the formula *being is, nothingness is not* is an idealization, an approximation of the total situation, which involves, beyond *what* we say, the mute experience from which we draw what we say. And just as we are invited to rediscover behind the vision, as immediate presence to being, the flesh of being and the flesh of the seer, so also must we rediscover the common milieu where being and nothingness are only λεκτα laboring each against the other. Our point of departure shall not be *being is, nothingness is not* nor even *there is only being*—which are formulas of a totalizing thought, a high-altitude thought—but: there is being, there is a world, there is something; in the strong sense in which the Greek speaks of το λεγειν, there is cohesion, there is meaning. One does not arouse being from nothingness, *ex nihilo;* one starts with an ontological relief where one can never say that the ground be nothing. What is primary is not the full and positive being upon a ground of nothingness; it is a field of appearances, each of which, taken separately, will perhaps subsequently break up or be crossed out (this is the part of nothingness), but of which I only know that it will be replaced by another which will be the truth of the first, because there is a world, because there is something—a world, a something, which in order to be do not first have to nullify the nothing. It is still saying too much of nothingness to say that it *is not,* that it is pure negation: that is to fix it in its negativity, to treat it as a sort of essence, to introduce the positivity of words into it, whereas it can count only as what has neither name, nor repose, nor nature. By principle, a philosophy of the negative cannot start from "pure" negation, nor make of it the agent of its own negation. In reversing the positions of the philosophy of reflection, which put all the positive within and treated the outside as a simple negative, by on the contrary defining the mind as the pure negative which lives only from its contact with the exterior being, the philosophy of the negative bypasses the goal: once again, even though now for opposite reasons, it renders impossible that *openness upon being* which is the perceptual faith. The philosophy of reflection did not account for it, for lack of providing a distance between the idea and the idea of the idea, between the reflecting and the unreflected. It is again that distance that is lacking now, since he who thinks, being nothing, cannot be separated by anything from him who perceived naively, nor he who perceived naively from what he perceived. There is no openness upon being for a philosophy of thought and of our immanent thoughts—but there is none either for a philosophy of nothingness and being, for no more in this case than in the other is being far-off, at a distance, for good. Thought is too much closed in upon itself, but nothingness is too much outside of itself for one to be able to speak of openness upon being, and in this respect immanence and transcendence are indistinguishable. Let it be so, it will perhaps be said; let us start then with the openness upon being. Yet is it not necessary, in order for there really to be openness, that we leave the metaphysical plenum, that *he* who is open to being and who sees be an absolute lacuna in being, and finally that he be purely negative? Otherwise are we not driven from appearance to appearance, like the vulgar relativism, without the absolute appearance or consciousness, nor being in itself, ever coming to pass? Without the absolute negativity, are we not in a universe of physical or psychic images which float about without anyone being conscious of them? The objection postulates what is in question, that is, that one can think only beings (physical, physiological, "psychic") or "consciousnesses" absolutely foreign to existence as a thing. It announces the return to the reflective dichotomies of a thought that has less surmounted them than incorporated them in advance into the spontaneous life.

We do not think then that the dichotomy of Being and Nothingness continues to hold when one arrives at the descriptions of nothingness sunken into being; it seems to us therefore that it is an abstract introduction to those descriptions and that from the introduction to the descriptions there is movement, progress, surpassing. Could we not express this simply by saying that for the intuition of being and the negintuition of nothingness must be substituted a *dialectic*? From the most superficial level to the most profound, dialectical thought is that which admits reciprocal actions or interactions—which admits therefore that the total relation between a term A and a term B cannot be expressed in one sole proposition, that that relation covers over several others which cannot be superimposed, which are even opposed, which define so many points of view logically incompossible and yet really united within it—even more that each of these relations leads to its opposite or to its own reversal, and does so by its own movement. Thus Being, through the very exigency of each of the perspectives, and from the exclusive point of view that defines it, becomes a system with several entries. Hence it cannot be contemplated from without and in simultaneity, but must be effectively traversed. In this transition, the stages passed through are not simply passed, like the segment of the road I have traveled; they have called for or required the present stages and precisely what is new and disconcerting in them. The past stages continue therefore to be in the present stages—which also means that they are retroactively modified by them. Hence there is a question here not of a thought that follows a preestablished route but of a thought that itself traces its own course, that finds itself by advancing, that makes its own way, and thus proves that the way is practicable. This thought wholly subjugated to its content, from which it receives its incitement, could not express itself as a reflection or copy of an exterior process; it is the engendering of a relation starting from the other. Being neither an outside witness nor a pure agent, it is implicated in the movement and does not view it from above. In particular it does not formulate itself in successive statements which would have to be taken as they stand; each statement, in order to be true, must be referred, throughout the whole movement, to the stage from which it arises and has its full sense only if one takes into account not only what it says expressly but also its place within the whole which constitutes its latent content. Thus, he who speaks (and that which he understands tacitly) always codetermines the meaning of what he says, the philosopher is always implicated in the problems he poses, and there is no truth if one does not take into account, in the appraising of every statement, the presence of the philosopher who makes the statement. Between the manifest content and the latent content, there can be not only differences but also contradiction, and yet this double meaning belongs to the statement—as when we want to consider a thing in itself, and in doing so, concentrating ourselves on it, we come to determine it such as it is for us. Hence for the dialectical thought, the idea of the *in itself* and the idea of the *for us* have each its truth outside of itself, do not belong to the total or full thought, which would define itself throughout a limitless explicitation. In sum, therefore, whether in the relations within being or in the relations of being with me, dialectical thought is that which admits that each term is itself only by proceeding toward the opposed term, becomes what it is through the movement, that it is one and the same thing for each to pass into the other or to become itself, to leave itself or to retire into itself, that the centripetal movement and the centrifugal movement are one sole movement, because each term is its own mediation, the exigency for a becoming, and even for an autodestruction which gives the other. If such is the dialectical thought, is this not what we have tried to apply to the dichotomy of Being and Nothingness? Has not our discussion consisted in showing that the relationship between the two terms (whether one takes them in a relative sense, within the world, or in an absolute sense, as the index of the thinker and of what he thinks) covers a swarm of relations with double meaning, incompatible and yet necessary to one another (complementary, as the physicists say today), and that this complex totality is the truth of the abstract dichotomy from which we started? Is not the dialectic, through its avatars, in every case the reversal of relationships, their solidarity throughout the reversal, the intelligible movement which is not a sum of positions or of statements such as *being is, nothingness is not* but which distributes them over several planes, integrates them into a being in depth? Particularly in what concerns the relations between thought and Being, is not the dialectic the refusal of high-altitude thinking, of the wholly exterior being as well as the reflexivity? Is it not thought at work within Being, in contact with Being, for which it opens a space for manifestation, but in which all its own initiatives are inscribed, recorded, or sedimented, if only as errors surmounted, and take on the form of a history which has its sense, even if it turns in circles or marches in zigzags? In sum, is it not exactly the thought we are seeking, not ambivalent, "ventriloquial," but capable of differentiating and of integrating into one sole universe the double or even multiple meanings, as Heraclitus has already showed us opposite directions coinciding in the circular movement? This thought is capable of effecting this integration because the circular movement is neither the simple sum of the opposed movements nor a third movement added to them, but their *common meaning,* the two component movements visible as one sole movement, *having become* a totality, that is, a spectacle: thus because the dialectic is the thought of the Being-seen, of a Being that is not simple positivity, the In Itself, and not the Being-posed by a thought, but *Self-manifestation,* disclosure, in the process of forming itself. . . .

The dialectic is indeed all this, and it is, in this sense, what we are looking for. If nonetheless we have not hitherto said so, it is because, in the history of philosophy, it has never been all that unadulteratedly; it is because the dialectic is unstable (in the sense that the chemists give to the word), it is even essentially and by definition unstable, so that it has never been able to formulate itself into theses without denaturing itself, and because if one wishes to maintain its spirit it is perhaps necessary to not even name it. The sort of being to which it refers, and which we have been trying to indicate, is in fact not susceptible of being designated positively. It abounds in the sensible world, but on condition that the sensible world has been divested of all that the ontologies have added to it. One of the tasks of the dialectic, as a situational thought, a thought in contact with being, is to shake off the false evidences, to denounce the significations cut off from the experience of being, emptied—and to criticize itself in the measure that it itself becomes one of them. But this is what it is in danger of becoming as soon as it is stated in theses, in univocal significations, as soon as it is detached from its antepredicative context. It is essential to it that it be autocritical—and it is also essential to it to forget this as soon as it becomes what we call a *philosophy.* The very formulas by which it describes the movement of being are then liable to falsify that movement. Take the profound idea of self-mediation [*médiation par soi*], of a movement through which each term ceases to be itself in order to become itself, breaks up, opens up, negates itself, in order to realize itself. It can remain pure only if the mediating term and the mediated term—which are "the same"—are yet not the same in the sense of identity: for then, in the absence of all difference, there would be no mediation, movement, transformation; one would remain in full positivity. But there is no self-mediation either if the mediator is the simple or absolute negation of the mediated: the absolute negation would simply annihilate the mediated and, turning against itself, would annihilate itself also, so that there would still be no mediation, but a pure and simple retreat toward positivity. It is therefore ruled out that the mediation have its origin in the positive term, as though it were one of its *properties*—but it is likewise precluded that the mediation come to the positive term from an abyss of exterior negativity, which would have no hold on it and would leave it intact. Yet it is in this second manner that the dialectic is translated when it ceases to be a way of deciphering the being with which we are in contact, the being in the process of manifesting itself, the situational being, and when it wishes to formulate itself once and for all, without anything left over, state itself as a doctrine, sum itself up. Then, to get to the end, the negation is carried to the absolute, becomes negation of itself; at the same time being sinks back to the pure positive, the negation concentrates itself beyond it as absolute subjectivity—and the dialectical movement becomes pure identity of the opposites, ambivalence. It is thus that in Hegel, God, defined as abyss or absolute subjectivity, negates himself in order that the world be, that is, in order that there be a view upon himself that would not be his own and to which he would appear as posterior to being; in other words, God makes himself man—so that the philosophy of Hegel is an ambivalence of the theological and the anthropological. It is not otherwise that, for Sartre, the absolute opposition of Being and Nothingness gives place to a return to the positive, to a sacrifice of the For Itself—except that he rigorously maintains the consciousness of the negative as a margin about being, the negation of negation is not for him a speculative operation, an unfolding of God, and the In-Itself-for-itself consequently remains for him the natural illusion of the For Itself. But, with these reservations, the same metamorphosis of the dialectic, the same relapse into ambivalence occurs in both cases, and for the same reason: because the thought ceases to accompany or to be the dialectical movement, converts it into signification, thesis, or thing said, and thereby falls back into the ambivalent image of the Nothingness that sacrifices itself in order that Being be and of the Being that, from the depths of its primacy, tolerates being recognized by the Nothingness. There is a trap in the dialectic: whereas it is the very movement of the content, as it is realized by autoconstitution, or the art of retracing and following the relations between the appeal and the response, the problem and the solution, whereas the *dialectic* is by principle an epithet, as soon as one takes it as a motto, speaks of it instead of practicing it, it becomes a power of being, an explicative principle. What was Being's manner of being becomes an evil genius. Oh, Dialectic! says the philosopher, when he comes to recognize that perhaps the true philosophy flouts philosophy. Here the dialectic is almost someone; like the irony of things, it is a spell cast over the world that turns our expectations into derision, a sly power behind our back that confounds us, and, to top it all, has its own order and its rationality; it is not only a risk of non-sense, therefore, but much worse: the assurance that the things have *another sense* than that which we are in a position to recognize in them. Already we are on the way of the bad dialectic, that which, against its own principles, imposes an external law and framework upon the content and restores for its own uses the predialectical thought. Dialectical thought by principle excludes all *extrapolation,* since it teaches that there can always be a supplement of being in being, that quantitative differences veer into the qualitative, that the consciousness as consciousness of the exterior, being partial, abstract, is always deceived by the event. But this very slipping away of life and of history, which resolves the problems otherwise than the consciousness of the exterior would have done (sometimes better, sometimes not so well), is understood as a vector, a polarity of the dialectical movement, a preponderant force that always works in the same direction, that, in the name of the process, extends over the process, and therefore authorizes the determination of the ineluctable. And this is what happens as soon as the *meaning* of the dialectical movement is defined apart from the concrete constellation. The bad dialectic begins almost with the dialectic, and there is no good dialectic but that which criticizes itself and surpasses itself as a separate statement; the only good dialectic is the hyperdialectic. The bad dialectic is that which does not wish to lose its soul in order to save it, which wishes to be dialectical immediately, becomes autonomous, and ends up at cynicism, at formalism, for having eluded its own double meaning. What we call hyperdialectic is a thought that on the contrary is capable of reaching truth because it envisages without restriction the plurality of the relationships and what has been called ambiguity. The bad dialectic is that which thinks it recomposes being by a thetic thought, by an assemblage of statements, by thesis, antithesis, and synthesis; the good dialectic is that which is conscious of the fact that every *thesis* is an idealization, that Being is not made up of idealizations or of things said, as the old logic believed, but of bound wholes where signification never is except in tendency, where the inertia of the content never permits the defining of one term as positive, another term as negative, and still less a third term as absolute suppression of the negative by itself. The point to be noted is this: that the dialectic without synthesis of which we speak is not therefore skepticism, vulgar relativism, or the reign of the ineffable. What we reject or deny is not the idea of a surpassing that reassembles, it is the idea that it results in a new positive, a new position. In thought and in history as in life the only surpassings we know are concrete, partial, encumbered with survivals, saddled with deficits; there is no surpassing in all regards that would retain everything the preceding phases had acquired, mechanically add something more, and permit the ranking of the dialectical phases in a hierarchical order from the less to the more real, from the less to the more valid. But, on a defined part of the route, there can be progresses; especially there are solutions excluded in the long run. In other words, what we exclude from the dialectic is the idea of the pure negative, what we seek is a dialectical definition of being that can be neither the being for itself nor the being in itself—rapid, fragile, labile definitions, which, as Hegel rightly said, lead us back from the one to the other—nor the In-Itself-for-itself which is the height of ambivalence, [a definition][19] that must rediscover the being that lies before the cleavage operated by reflection, about it, on its horizon, not outside of us and not in us, but there where the two movements cross, there where "there is" something.

Perceptual Faith and Interrogation

These remarks concerning negativity permit us already to make more precise the meaning of our question before the world, for the most difficult part is to avoid mistaking what it is, what it can be, its exact and proper meaning, what it asks. We already know that it is not a question as to whether the world really is, or whether it is only a well-regulated dream: that question covers over others; it supposes that the dream, the image, be known, and be better known—it interrogates the world only in the name of an alleged positivity of the psychic. It casts over the world the shadow of a possible nonexistence—but it does not elucidate the mental existence it substitutes for it, which in fact it conceives as a weakened or degraded real existence. And if the doubt thus understood were lifted through some argument, the "real" existence which would be restored to our dreams would be the very same real existence, obscure and incomprehensible, with which we started, and everything would have to be begun over again. We are not asking ourselves if the world exists; we are asking what it is for it to exist. But even thus transformed, the question is not yet radical. For one can understand it still in a surface sense that hides its true mainspring. When we ask what it is for the things and for the world to exist, one might think that it is only a matter of defining a word. After all, the questions take place in language. Even if it seems to us that an affirmative thought can detach itself from words and rest on its internal adequation, negation and especially interrogation, which do not express any property intrinsic to the things, can be sustained only by the apparatus of language. One can therefore be tempted to count the philosophical question concerning the world among the facts of language, and it would seem that the response can be sought only in the meanings of words, since it is in words that the question will be answered. But our previous reflections have already taught us that this would be to evade it: the question concerning the meaning of the world's being is so little solvable by a definition of words—which would be drawn from the study of language, its powers, and the effective conditions for its functioning—that on the contrary it reappears within the study of language, which is but a particular form of it. One can reduce philosophy to a linguistic analysis only by supposing that language has its evidence within itself, that the signification of the word "world" or "thing" presents in principle no difficulty, that the rules for the legitimate use of the word can be clearly read in a univocal signification. But the linguists teach us that this is precisely not the case, that the univocal signification is but one part of the signification of the word, that beyond it there is always a halo of signification that manifests itself in new and unexpected modes of use, that there is an operation of language upon language which, even without other incitements, would launch language back into a new history, and makes of the word-meaning itself an enigma. Far from harboring the secret of the being of the world, language is itself a world, itself a being—a world and a being to the second power, since it does not speak in a vacuum, since it speaks *of* being and *of* the world and therefore redoubles their enigma instead of dissipating it. The philosophical interrogation concerning the world therefore does not consist in referring from the world itself to what we say of the world, since it is reiterated within language. To philosophize is not to cast the things into doubt in the name of the words, as if the universe of things said were clearer than that of the brute things, as if the effective world were a canton of language, perception a confused and mutilated speech, the signification of words a perfectly reassuring sphere of positivity. But this observation does not only argue against a positivism of language: it affects every attempt to seek the source of meaning in pure significations, even when no mention is made of language. The philosophical interrogation about the world cannot consist, for example, in casting into doubt the world in itself or the things in themselves for the profit of an order of "human phenomena," that is, of the coherent system of appearances such as we men can construct it, in the factual conditions that are ours, according to our psychophysical constitution and the types of connections that make the relation to an "object" possible for us. Whether this construction of the object be understood in terms of the method of the sciences and by the means of algorithm, or whether one confronts the *constructa* with the concrete because science after all wishes to be a *scientia intuitiva,* an understanding of the world itself, or whether finally one envisages more generally rendering explicit the acts and attitudes of all kinds—emotional, practical, axiological—by which a consciousness refers itself to objects or quasi-objects, refers them to one another, and effects the transition from one attitude to another—in all cases the question posed is not yet radical, ultimate. For over against the things and the world, which are obscure, one gives oneself the field of operations of consciousness and of the constructed significations whose terminal product one supposes the world and the things to be—and, before this field as before the field of language (which in fact it presupposes), the philosopher must ask himself if it is closed, if it suffices to itself, if, as an *artefact,*[20] it does not open upon an original perspective of natural being, if, even supposing it decisive in what concerns the being-verified, the being-averred, the being converted into an *object,* it does not have a horizon of brute being and of brute mind, from which the constructed objects and the significations emerge and which they do not account for.

Thus is specified the sense of our astonishment in face of the perceived world. It is not the Pyrrhonian doubt, it is not even the appeal to an immanent domain of positive thought of which the perceived world would be but the shadow: the shadow is in us rather than outside. In suspending the evidence of the world, in seeking recourse in our thought or our consciousness of the world, its operations and its theses, we would find nothing that surpasses or simply equals and explains the solidity of the world under our eyes and the cohesion of our life in it. By reversal of the pro and the con, we have come not only to rehabilitate negative thought as an original way of thinking, but also to formulate negatively—as that without which there is no representation—the principle of causality, and finally to conceive as negativity thought, which for Spinoza was the positive itself. Should it now be necessary to complete or rather to go beyond this reversal by saying that I am not capable of being for myself unless, at the center of myself, I am nothing at all, but that this central void must be borne by being, by a situation, a world, is never knowable except as the focus their perspectives indicate, and that in this sense there is a priority of being over thought? Thus would be brought to a close the cycle opened when Descartes showed that the thought of seeing is more certain than the thing seen or the vision—that the thought, precisely because it is nothing but absolute appearance, is absolutely indubitable and that, midway between being and nothingness, it stands more solid before the doubt than the positive and full things. To be sure, Descartes and Cartesianism had finally pushed this thinking thing which only half is over to the side of Being: since it is after all not nothing, and since nothingness has no properties, it became the sign and the trace of an infinite Being, of a spiritual positivity. But the withdrawal from the world, the return to the interior man, the *no* of reflection had all the same been installed in philosophy by the *cogito,* and had to produce in it all their consequences the day that the thought no longer believed it could grasp in itself the spontaneous genesis of a Being that is self-caused. Then negativity, which is not visible or has no properties, could no longer be borne by anything but by the world itself, could no longer be anything but a lacuna in Being. Between it and the world there would no longer even be room for the suspension of the doubt; the negativity in act would be existence itself, or at least the "there is" of the world, and philosophy would cease to be a question in order to be the consciousness of this double-faced act, of this no that is a yes, of this yes that is a no. The long evolution that had moved the positive from the world over to the side of the consciousness, which had become the correlative of the world and its connecting principle—but that at the same time prepared philosophy to install nonbeing as the pivot of being—would abruptly be concluded at the extremity of idealism by the rehabilitation and the primacy of the In Itself. . . .

This is what has finally appeared to us to be impossible. It seemed to us that this final avatar overcompensated for idealism rather than overcame it, that my immediate presence to the In Itself, established and undone at the same time by the infinite distance from what is nothing to what is, was, rather than a solution, a seesaw movement from realism to idealism. Philosophy is not a rupture with the world, nor a coinciding with it, but it is not the alternation of rupture and coincidence either. This double relation, which the philosophy of *Being and Nothingness* expresses so well, remains perhaps incomprehensible there because it is still a consciousness—a being that is wholly appearing—that is charged with bearing it. It has seemed to us that the task was to describe strictly our relation to the world not as an openness of nothingness upon being, but simply as openness: it is through openness that we will be able to understand being and nothingness, not through being and nothingness that we will be able to understand openness. From the point of view of *Being and Nothingness,* the openness upon being means that I visit it in itself: if it remains distant, this is because nothingness, the anonymous one in me that sees, pushes before itself a zone of void where being no longer only is, but *is seen.* It is therefore my constitutive nothingness that makes the distance from being as well as its proximity, the perspective as distinct from the thing itself, that constitutes the limits of my field into limits. It crosses these limits, this distance, by forming it; it makes perspectives arise only by first effectuating the flat projection; it goes to the *whole* because it is *nothing.* Then there is no longer any *something* and no longer openness, for there is no longer a labor of the look against its limits, there is no longer that inertia of the vision that makes us say that we have an openness upon the world. That sort of diaphragm of the vision, which through a compromise with the whole to be seen yields my point of view upon the world, is to be sure not fixed: nothing prevents us from crossing the limits with the movements of the look, but this freedom remains secretly bound; we can only displace our look, that is, transfer its limits elsewhere. But it is necessary that there be always a limit; what is won on one side must be lost from the other. An indirect and muted necessity weighs upon my vision. It is not the necessity of an objective frontier forever impassable, for the contours of my field are not lines. It is not cut out against an expanse of blackness; rather when I approach them, the things dissociate, my look loses its differentiation, and the vision ceases for lack of seer and of articulated things. Even without speaking of my motor power, I am therefore not shut up in one sector of the visible world. But I am curbed all the same, like those animals in zoological gardens without cages or bars, whose freedom gently comes to an end by some trench a little too broad for them to clear at one bound. The openness upon the world implies that the world be and remain a horizon, not because my vision would push the world back beyond itself, but because somehow he who sees is of it and is in it. Philosophy therefore does not seek to analyze our relationship with the world, to *undo* it as if it had been formed by assemblage; but it also does not terminate by an immediate and all-inclusive acknowledgment of Being, of which there would be nothing more to say. Philosophy cannot flatter itself that, by rendering explicit that relationship, it finds again in it what we would have put in it; it cannot reconstruct the thing and the world by condensing in them, in the form of implication, everything we have subsequently been able to think and say of them; rather, it remains a question, it interrogates the world and the thing, it revives, repeats, or imitates their crystallization before us. For this crystallization which is partly given to us ready-made is in other respects never terminated, and thereby we can see how the world comes about. It takes form under the domination of certain structural laws: events let rather general powers show through, powers such as the gaze or the word, which operate according to an identifiable style, according to "if . . . then . . ." relationships, according to a logic in action whose philosophical status must be defined if we wish to get out of the confusion in which the ready-made notions of thought, subject, and object throw us, and if we wish to know finally what the world is and what being is. Philosophy does not decompose our relationship with the world into real elements, or even into ideal references which would make of it an ideal object, but it discerns articulations in the world, it awakens in it regular relations of prepossession, of recapitulation, of overlapping, which are as dormant in our ontological landscape, subsist there only in the form of traces, and nevertheless continue to function there, continue to institute the new there.

The philosopher's manner of questioning is therefore not that of *cognition:* being and the world are not for the philosopher unknowns such as are to be determined through their relation with known terms, where both known and unknown terms belong in advance to the same order of *variables* which an active thought seeks to approximate as closely as possible. Nor is philosophy an *awakening of consciousness* [*prise de conscience*]: it is not a matter of philosophy rediscovering in a legislative consciousness the signification it would have given to the world and to being by nominal definition. Just as we do not speak for the sake of speaking but speak to someone *of* something or *of* someone, and in this initiative of speaking an aiming at the world and at the others is involved upon which is suspended all *that which* we say; so also the lexical signification and even the pure significations which are deliberately reconstructed, such as those of geometry, aim at a universe of brute being and of coexistence, toward which we were already thrown when we spoke and thought, and which, for its part, by principle does not admit the procedure of objectifying or reflective *approximation* since it is at a distance, by way of horizon, latent or dissimulated. It is that universe that philosophy aims at, that is, as we say, *the object* of philosophy—but here never will the lacuna be filled in, the unknown transformed into known; the "object" of philosophy will never come to fill in the philosophical question, since this obturation would take from it the depth and the distance that are essential to it. The effective, present, ultimate and primary being, the thing itself, are in principle apprehended in transparency through their perspectives, offer themselves therefore only to someone who wishes not to have them but to see them, not to hold them as with forceps, or to immobilize them as under the objective of a microscope, but to let them be and to witness their continued being—to someone who therefore limits himself to giving them the hollow, the free space they ask for in return, the resonance they require, who follows their own movement, who is therefore not a nothingness the full being would come to stop up, but a question consonant with the porous being which it questions and from which it obtains not an *answer,* but a confirmation of its astonishment. It is necessary to comprehend perception as this interrogative thought which lets the perceived world be rather than posits it, before which the things form and undo themselves in a sort of gliding, beneath the yes and the no.

Our discussion of the negative announces to us another paradox of philosophy, which distinguishes it from every problem of cognition and forbids us to speak in philosophy of a *solution:* as an approach to the far-off as far-off, it is also a question put to what does not speak. It asks of our experience of the world what the world is before it is a thing one speaks of and which is taken for granted, before it has been reduced to a set of manageable, disposable significations; it directs this question to our mute life, it addresses itself to that compound of the world and of ourselves that precedes reflection, because the examination of the significations in themselves would give us the world reduced to our idealizations and our syntax. But in addition, what it finds in thus returning to the sources, it says. It is itself a human construction, and the philosopher knows very well that, whatever be his effort, in the best of cases it will take its place among the *artefacts*[21] and products of culture, as an instance of them. If this paradox is not an impossibility, and if philosophy can speak, it is because language is not only the depository of fixed and acquired significations, because its cumulative power itself results from a power of anticipation or of prepossession, because one speaks not only of what one knows, so as to set out a display of it—but also of what one does not know, in order to know it—and because language in forming itself expresses, at least laterally, an ontogenesis of which it is a part. But from this it follows that the words most charged with philosophy are not necessarily those that contain what they say, but rather those that most energetically open upon Being, because they more closely convey the life of the whole and make our habitual evidences vibrate until they disjoin. Hence it is a question whether philosophy as reconquest of brute or wild being can be accomplished by the resources of the eloquent language, or whether it would not be necessary for philosophy to use language in a way that takes from it its power of immediate or direct signification in order to equal it with what it wishes all the same to say.

In sum, philosophy interrogates the perceptual faith—but neither expects nor receives an answer in the ordinary sense, because it is not the disclosing of a variable or of an unknown invariant that will satisfy this question, and because the existing world exists in the interrogative mode. Philosophy is the perceptual faith questioning itself about itself. One can say of it, as of every faith, that it is a faith *because* it is the possibility of doubt, and this indefatigable ranging over the things, which is our life, is also a continuous interrogation. It is not only philosophy, it is first the look that questions the things. We do not have a consciousness constitutive of the things, as idealism believes, nor a preordination of the things to the consciousness, as realism believes (they are indiscernible in what interests us here, because they both affirm the adequation of the thing and the mind)—we have with our body, our senses, our look, our power to understand speech and to speak, *measurants* [*mesurants*] for Being, dimensions to which we can refer it, but not a relation of adequation or of immanence. The perception of the world and of history is the practice of this measure, the reading off of their divergence or of their difference with respect to our norms. If we are ourselves in question in the very unfolding of our life, it is not because a central nonbeing threatens to revoke our consent to being at each instant; it is because we ourselves are one sole continued question, a perpetual enterprise of taking our bearings on the constellations of the world, and of taking the bearings of the things on our dimensions. The very questions of curiosity or those of science are interiorly animated by the fundamental interrogation which appears naked in philosophy. "From time to time, a man lifts his head, sniffs, listens, considers, recognizes his position: he thinks, he sighs, and, drawing his watch from the pocket lodged against his chest, looks at the time. *Where am I?* and, *What time is it?* such is the inexhaustible question turning from us to the world."[22] The watch and the map give here only a semblance of an answer: they indicate to us how what we are living is situated in relation to the course of the stars or to the course of a human day, or in relation to places that have a name. But where are these reference events and these landmarks themselves? They refer us to others, and the answer satisfies us only because we do not attend to it, because we think we are "at home." The question would arise again and indeed would be inexhaustible, almost insane, if we wished to situate our levels, measure our standards in their turn, if we were to ask: but where is the world itself? And why am I myself?[23] How old am I really? Am I really alone to be me? Have I not somewhere a double, a twin? These questions, which the sick man puts to himself in a moment of respite—or simply that glance at his watch, as if it were of great importance that the torment take place at a given inclination of the sun, at such or such hour in the life of the world—expose, at the moment that life is threatened, the underlying movement through which we have installed ourselves in the world and which recommences yet a little more time for itself. The ancients read in the heavens the hour to wage the battle. We no longer believe that it is written down anywhere. But we do and always will believe that what takes place here and now is one with the simultaneous; what takes place would not be entirely real for us if we did not know at what time. Its hour is no longer destined in advance for the event, but, whatever it be, the event appropriates it to itself; the event would not be entirely itself if we did not situate it in the immense simultaneity of the world and within its undivided thrust. Every question, even that of simple cognition, is part of the central question that is ourselves, of that appeal for totality to which no objective being answers, and which we now have to examine more precisely.

Notes

1. In English in the text.—Trans.

2. I am absolutely foreign to being and this is what makes me open to being *qua* "absolute plenitude and entire positivity" (Sartre, *L'Être et le néant* [Paris, 1943], 50. Hereafter *EN*). [English translation by Hazel E. Barnes, *Being and Nothingness* (New York, 1956), 15. Hereafter *BN*. The translations from this book have been slightly altered.—Trans.].

3. Sartre accepts all the arguments against the idea of nothingness one could offer: they prove that nothingness is not, which is precisely its sole manner of being.

4. *EN*, 248–49 [*BN*, 198].

5. The destiny of nothingness and that of being are the same if one thinks of nothingness properly.

6. *EN,* 268–69 [*BN,* 216–17].

7. *EN,* 232 [*BN,* 183].

8. *EN,* 268 [*BN,* 216].

9. *EN,* 269–70 [*BN,* 217–18].

10. One should say: for what it ~~is~~.

11. As Bergson said in *Les Deux sources:* my body extends unto the stars. [*Les Deux sources de la morale et de la religion* (Paris, 1932); "For if our body is the matter upon which our consciousness applies itself, it is coextensive with our consciousness. It includes everything that we perceive, it extends unto the stars" (277); English translation by R. Ashley Audra and Cloudesley Brereton, *The Two Sources of Morality and Religion* (New York, 1935), 246.—Ed.].

12. I said in turn that "nothingness is not" and "being is" are the same thought—and that nothingness and being are not united. Connect the two: they are not united precisely because they are the same thing in two contradictories = ambivalence.

13. The preceding sentence, to which the beginning of this one is linked, suffers from an apparently incomplete correction. The first version, which was rejected, was: "but the question is whether the negativist or positivist thought disclosing this aspect of the phenomena, this structure of the relationship with another, grasps the whole or even the essential. We say that, in principle, it can only grasp one empirical variant of it."—Ed.

14. The layer of the being-for-me of the world reveals: (1) a *depth* of being in itself; (2) an *opacity* of the being for itself.

15. These lines have been inserted here, in the course of the text itself:

"1) To say I am separated from being by a sheath of non-being—is true. But this sheath of non-being is not *me;* vision is not cognition, the I of vision is not nothingness.

2) The hard "core of being" Sartre speaks of. There is no core with, around the [no ?] that would be me (negations, shimmering at the surface of being). That being is transcendent means precisely: it is appearances crystallising, it is full and *empty,* it is *Gestalt* with horizon, it is duplicity of planes, it is, itself, *Verborgenheit*—it is it that perceives itself, as it is it that speaks in me."—Ed.

16. There is no *or* expressed in the continuation of the text. The reflection on the first term of the alternative decides the issue of the second. For, as will immediately become apparent, to say that the other does not crush me into my universe of the in itself is the same as to say that he is not the inexplicable negation of the For Itself I am. The author moreover returns to this latter idea in the note below.—Ed.

17. Some for the others and not only each for the other [*Les uns pour les autres et non pas seulement l'un pour l'autre*]. The problem of the other is always posed by the philosophies of the negative in the form of the problem of the other, as though the whole difficulty were to pass from the *one* to the *other.* This is significant: the other is not here *an other;* he is the non-I in general, the judge who condemns me or acquits me, and to whom I do not even think of opposing other judges. But, if one can show, as was done, for example, in Simone de Beauvoir's

She Came to Stay, that a trio decomposes into three couples, and—in supposing that there are, outside of all abstract reciprocity, successful couples—that there can be no trio that would be successful in the same sense, since it adds to the difficulties of the couple those of the concord between the three possible couples of which it is composed—still the fact remains that the problem of the other is not reducible to that of *the* other, and so much the less so in that the most strict couple always has its witnesses in third parties. Perhaps it even would be necessary to reverse the customary order of the philosophies of the negative, and say that the problem of *the* other is a particular case of the problem of others, since the relation with someone is always mediated by the relationship with third parties, that these have relationships among themselves that command those of *the* one and those of *the* other—and that this is so as far back as one goes toward the beginnings of life, since the Oedipus situation is still a triangular one. Now this is not only a matter of psychology, but also of philosophy—not only of the contents of the relationship with an other, but of its form and its essence as well: if the access to the other is an entry into a constellation of others (where there are of course stars of several magnitudes), it is difficult to maintain that the other be nothing but *the* absolute negation of myself. For when it is a matter of absolute negation there is but one of them; it absorbs into itself every rival negation. Even if we have one *principal other,* from whom are derived many secondary others in our life, the sole fact that he is not the unique other obliges us to comprehend him not as an absolute negation but as a negation-model, that is, in the last analysis, not as what contests my life but as what forms it, not as another universe in which I would be alienated but as the preferred variant of a life that has never been only my own. Even if each of us has his own archetype of the other, the very fact that he is open to participation, that he is a sort of cipher or symbol of the other, obliges us to pose the problem of the other, not as a problem of access to another nihilation, but as a problem of initiation to a symbolics and a typicality of the others of which the *being for itself* and the *being for the other* are reflective variants and not the essential forms.

18. The indefinite pronoun *on* used to name the anonymous, prepersonal subject. "We must conceive of a primordial [*One*] (*on*) that has its own authenticity and furthermore never ceases but continues to uphold the greatest passions of our adult life and to be experienced anew in each of our perceptions" (*Signes* [Paris, 1960], 221; English translation by Richard C. McCleary, *Signs* [Evanston: Northwestern University Press, 1960], 175).—TRANS.

19. We reintroduce this term between brackets to eliminate ambiguity.—ED.

20. In English in the text.—TRANS.

21. In English in the text.—TRANS.

22. Claudel, *Art poétique* (Paris, 1951), 9.

23. This is, says Alain, the question that, in *Manon Lescaut,* arises in the depths of woe. Strange caption: we have not located it in *Manon Lescaut.* One may wonder from what depth of reverie it came to Alain, and why disguised as a citation.

27

Merleau-Ponty *vivant*

Jean-Paul Sartre

Translated by Benita Eisher

I have lost so many friends who are still alive. No one was to blame. It was they. It was myself. Events made us, brought us together, separated us. And I know that Merleau-Ponty said the same thing when he thought of the people who haunted, and then left his life. But he never lost me, and he had to die for me to lose him. We were equals, friends, but not brothers. We understood this immediately, and at first, our differences amused us. And then, about 1950, the barometer fell: fair wind for Europe and the world, but as for us, a gale knocked our heads together, and a moment later, it tossed each of us at opposite poles of the other. Our ties, often strained, were never broken. If I were asked why, I would say that we had a great deal of luck, and sometimes even virtue, on our side. We each tried to remain true to ourselves and to one another, and we nearly succeeded. Merleau is still too much alive for anyone to be able to describe him. Perhaps he will be more easily approached—to my way of thinking, in any case—if I tell the story of that quarrel which never took place, our friendship.

At the École Normale, we knew each other without being friends. He was a day student, I was a boarder. Each of these states took itself for a chivalric order, in which the other was the foot soldier. When we were drafted, I was an enlisted man, and he became a second lieutenant. Thus he was a knight twice over.[1] We lost sight of each other. He had a teaching post in Beauvais, I think, while I taught in Le Havre. Each of us, nevertheless, was preparing himself, without knowing it, for an encounter with the other. Each of us was trying to understand the world insofar as he could, and with the means at his disposal. And we had the same means—then called Husserl and Heidegger—since we were similarly disposed.

One day in 1947, Merleau told me that he had never recovered from an incomparable childhood. He had known that private world of happiness from which only age drives us. Pascalian from adolescence, without even having read Pascal, he experienced his singular selfhood as the singularity of an adventure. To be someone, is something which happens and unhappens, but not without first tracing the ribs of a future, always new and always begun anew. What was he, if not this paradise lost, a wild and undeserved piece of luck, a gratuitous gift transformed, after the fall, into adversity, depopulating the world and disenchanting him in advance? This story is both extraordinary and commonplace. Our capacity for happiness is dependent upon a certain equilibrium between what we refuse and concede to our childhood. Completely deprived or completely endowed, we are lost. Thus, there are an infinite number of lots we can draw. His was to have won too soon. He had to live, nonetheless. To the end, it remained for him to make himself as the event had made him. That way and other ways. Seeking the golden age, and with that as his point of departure, he forged his myths and what he has since called his "style of life." It established his preferences—choosing, at the same time, the traditions which recalled the rituals of childhood, and the "spontaneity" which evoked childhood's superintended liberty. This naïveté, by starting from *what has happened,* also discovered the meaning of *what is happening,* and finally, it made a prophecy based on this inventory and its evaluation. This is what he felt as a young man, without as yet being able to express it. Through these detours, he finally arrived at philosophy. He wondered—nothing more. Everything is played out from the beginning, and we continue in spite of this. Why? Why do we lead a life which is disqualified by its absences? And what does it mean to live?

Futile and serious, our teachers were ignorant of history. They replied that these were questions which shouldn't be asked, or that they were badly expressed, or (and this was a tic of every teacher's at that time) that "the answers were to be found in the questions." To think is to weigh, said one of them, who did neither. And all of them said: man and nature form the object of universal concepts, which was precisely what Merleau-Ponty refused to accept. Tormented by the archaic secrets of his own prehistory, he was infuriated by these well-meaning souls who, taking themselves for small airplanes, indulged in "high-altitude" thinking, and forgot that we are grounded from birth. They pride themselves, he was to later say, on looking the world in the face. Don't they know that it envelops and produces us? The most subtle mind bears its stamp, and we cannot formulate a single thought which isn't conditioned in depth, from the outset, by the being to which it claims to allude. Since we are all ambiguous histories—luck and ill-luck, rational and irrational—whose origin is never knowledge, but the event, it is not even imaginable that we could translate our life, that unraveling mesh, in terms of cognition. And what can be the value of a human thought about man, since it is man himself who both makes the judgment and vouches for it? Thus did Merleau "ruminate" his life. But don't start thinking of Kierkegaard at this moment. It would be too soon. The Dane fled Hegelian knowledge. He invented opacities for himself from the dread of transparency. If daylight should penetrate him, Søren would be reduced to nothing. Merleau-Ponty is exactly the opposite. He wanted to understand, to understand *himself.* It wasn't his fault, if, through practice, he discovered the incompatibility between universalist idealism and what he would call his "primordial historicity." He never claimed to place unreason above rationalism. He only wanted to oppose history to the immobility of the Kantian subject. This is only, as Rouletabille said, "seizing reason by the right end," nothing more. In short, he was looking for his "anchorage." To begin at the beginning, we shall see what was missing for him: intentionality, situation, and twenty other tools which could be procured in Germany. About this time, but for other reasons, I needed the same instruments. I had come to phenomenology through Levinas, so I set off for Berlin where I remained for a year. When I returned, we had come to the same conclusion, without having any doubts of it. Until September, 1939, we each pursued our own reading and research at the same pace, but separately.

Philosophy, as we know, has no direct efficacity. It took the war to bring us close together. In 1941, intellectuals, more or less throughout the country, formed groups which claimed to be resisting the conquering enemy. I belonged to one of these groups, "Socialism and Liberty." Merleau joined us. This encounter was not the result of chance. Each of us had come from a *petit bourgeois* background. Our tastes, our tradition and our professional conscience moved both of us to defend freedom of the pen. Through this freedom, we discovered all the others. But aside from that, we were simpletons. Born of enthusiasm, our little group caught a fever and died a year later, of not knowing what to do. The other groups in the Occupied Zone met the same fate, and doubtless for the same reasons. In 1942, only one of them remained. A little later Gaullism and the Front National reclaimed these first-hour Resistants. As for the two of us, in spite of our failure, "Socialism and Liberty" had at least brought us into contact with one another. The era helped us. There was then, among Frenchmen, an unforgettable transparency of heart, which was the reverse of hatred. Through this national friendship, which approved of each man in advance, provided he hated the Nazis, we recognized each other. The key words were spoken: phenomenology, existence. We discovered our real concern. Too individualist to ever pool our research, we became reciprocal while remaining separate. Alone, each of us was too easily persuaded of having understood the idea of phenomenology. Together, we were, for each other, the incarnation of its ambiguity. Each of us viewed the work being done by the other as an unexpected, and sometimes hostile deviation from his own. Husserl became our bond and our division, at one and the same time. On this terrain, we were only, as Merleau so rightly said of language, "differences without terms, or rather, terms engendered by the differences which emerge between them." His recollections of our conversations varied. Basically, he was only interested in developing from within, and discussions distracted him. And then again, I made too many concessions to him, and with too much alacrity. Later, in his darker hours, he reproached me for this, as well as for having exposed *our* point of view to third parties without taking into account *his* reservations. He attributed this, he told me, to pride and some sort of blind disdain for others on my part. Nothing could be more unjust. I have always considered, and still consider, the truth to be a whole. On small issues, then, it seemed to me that I ought to relinquish my points of view if I hadn't been able to convince my interlocutor to relinquish his. Merleau-Ponty, on the contrary, found his security in a multiplicity of perspectives, seeing in them the different facets of being. And if I was silent on the subject of his reservations, it was in good faith. Or almost. Do we ever really know? My mistake was rather to have dropped the decimals, in order to achieve unanimity more quickly. In any case, he didn't hold this against me too much, since he continued in the affectionate idea of me as a conciliator. I don't really know whether he profited from these discussions. Sometimes, I doubt it. But I can't forget what I owe to them: ventilated thinking. To my mind, this was the purest moment in our friendship.

But he didn't tell me everything. We never talked politics except to discuss the BBC news. I had fallen into a state of disgust from which I emerged only when I could rally a solid organization. Merleau, at other times more reserved on the subject of our project, was less prone to ever forget about it. It offered to him the reflection of an event in miniature. It brought man back to himself, to the accident which he was, which he would continue to be and which he produced. What had they experienced, wanted, and finally, what had they done, these professors (including ourselves), these students, these engineers, so suddenly joined together, and just as suddenly separated by a whirlwind? Merleau-Ponty questioned perception. It was, he believed, one of the beginnings of the beginning. Through this ambiguous ordeal, our body is surrendered to the world and the world to our body. It is both the hinge and the anchorage. But the world is also history. Perhaps, before anything else, we are historical. In the margins of the book which he was slowly writing, he reflected upon that which ten years later would appear to him as the fundamental anchorage. The *Phenomenology of Perception* bears the traces of these ambiguous meditations, but I was unable to recognize them. He had needed these ten years in order to rejoin what he had sought since adolescence, this *being-event* of men, which can also be called existence. Perhaps I should say that phenomenology remained a "static" in his thesis, and that gradually, through a careful study, of which *Humanism and Terror* was the first stage, he was to transform it into a "dynamic." This would not be untrue: exaggerated, certainly, but clear. Let us say that this vulgarization at least allows us to penetrate the movement of his thought. Gently, carefully, inflexibly, it was turning back upon itself, in order to reach back to its primitive state. In those years which preceded the Liberation, he had not advanced very far. Nevertheless, he already knew that history could not look itself in the face, any more than nature, because it envelops us. How? How could this totality of future and past time enclose us? How can we discover the others within us as our profound truth? How can we perceive ourselves within them as the law of their truth? The question is already asked at the level of perceptive spontaneity and "intersubjectivity." It only becomes more urgent and more concrete when we replace the historical agent in the womb of universal flux. Work and anxiety, tools, governments, customs, culture—how can we "insert" the person into all of this? And inversely, how can he be extracted from that which he never tires of spinning, and which incessantly produces him?

Merleau had believed he would live in peace. A war had made him into a warrior, and he had made war. Suppose this strange merry-go-round were to define for us, both the limits and the scope of historical action? We had to examine it closely. Investigator, witness, defendant, and judge, he turned back and examined, in the light of our defeat, and the future German defeat (of which we were assured after Stalingrad), the false war which he had fought, the false peace in which he had thought he was going to live. And there he was, always, at the juncture of things, the briber bribed, the practical joker hoaxed, victim and accomplice, in spite of a good faith of which there could be no doubt, but which nevertheless had to be questioned.[2] Everything happened in silence. He had no need of a partner to make this new day dawn upon the singularity of his era, upon his own singularity. But we have the proof that he never ceased to reflect upon his era. Even in 1945 he wrote: "In sum, we have learned history and maintain that we must not forget it."[3]

This was the polite "we." In order to learn what he already knew, I still needed five years. Overwhelmed at birth and then frustrated, he was destined, by his experience, to discover the force of things, the inhuman powers which steal our acts and our thoughts. Invested, enveloped, predestined, yet free, his primitive intuition disposed him to understand the event—that adventure which issues from everywhere—devoid of consistence or significance as long as it hasn't filled us with its hazardous shadows, as long as it hasn't forced us to give to it, freely and in spite of ourselves, its iron necessity. Then, too he suffered in his relations with others. Everything had been too wonderful, too soon. The form of nature which first enveloped him was the Mother goddess, his own mother, whose eyes made him see what he saw. She was the *alter ego.* By her and through her, he lived this "intersubjectivity of immanence" which he has often described and which caused us to discover our "spontaneity" through another. With childhood dead, love remained, equally strong, but bereft. Certain that he would never again find this destroyed intimacy, he was only capable of demanding. All and nothing: sometimes too much, other times, not enough. He moved quickly from demands to disinterest, not without suffering from these failures which confirmed his exile. Misunderstandings, estrangements, separations due to mutual wrongs, his private life had already taught him that our acts become inscribed into our little world otherwise than we might have wished, and that they make us other than we were, by giving us, after the fact, intentions which we didn't have, but which we shall have from now on. After 1939, he lived within his miscalculations, within these incidental expenses which we have to accept because we weren't able to foresee them, and which are even peculiar to historical action. In 1945 he wrote: "We have been led to assume and to consider as our own, our intentions, the meaning which our acts have for us, but also the consequences which these acts have on the outside, the meaning which they take on within a certain historical context."[4] He saw his shadow "cast upon history as on a wall, this shape which found its actions on the outside, this objective mind which was himself."[5] Merleau felt sufficiently involved to have the constant awareness of restoring the world to the world, sufficiently free to objectify himself in history through this restitution. He freely compared himself to a wave, a crest among other crests, and the entire sea pulled upwards by a hemstitch of foam. A mixture of singular probabilities and generalities, the historical man would appear when his act, made and predicted from its farthest point to its most unknown objectivity, would introduce a beginning of reason into the primitive unreason. To his enemies, Merleau replied, in all certainly, that his interpretation of existence didn't oppose him to Marxism, and in proof of this, the well-known phrase: "Men make history on the foundations of past circumstances," could have passed, in his eyes, for a Marxist version of his own thinking.

The intellectual communists weren't wrong about us. As soon as the calm seas of 1945 were past, they attacked me. My political thinking was confused, my ideas were dangerous. Merleau, on the contrary, seemed close to them. A flirtation began. He often saw Courtade, Hervé, Desanti. His own traditionalism found company in theirs. After all, the communist party was a tradition. He preferred its rituals, its tough-mindedness, refired by twenty-five years of history, to the speculations of those without a party.

However, he was not a Marxist. It wasn't the idea which he rejected, but the fact that it was a dogma. He refused to acknowledge that historical materialism is the unique light of history, or that this light emanates from an eternal source, which principle extracts from the vicissitudes of the event. He reproached this intellectualism of objectivity, as he did classical rationalism, for looking the world in the face, and for forgetting that it envelops us. He would have accepted the doctrine if he could only have seen it as phosphorescence, a shawl upon the sea, billowed out, unfurled by the swells, and whose truth depended specifically upon its perpetual participation in the underwater surges. A system of references, yes: on condition that is it altered through the act of referring to it; an explanation, if you wish, but one which is deformed as it is explained. Should we speak here of a "Marxist relativism"? Yes and no. Whatever the doctrine might be, he distrusted it, fearing that it would only be another version of "high-altitude thinking." Thus, a relativism, but a relativism of precaution. He believed only in this one absolute: our anchorage, life. In essence, for what did he reproach the Marxist theory of history? Only this—which is capital, and nothing else—that it had not given contingency its rightful place:

> Every historical undertaking has something of an adventure about it, as it is never guaranteed by any *absolutely* rational structure of things. It always involves a utilization of chance, one must always be cunning with things (and with people), since we must bring forth an order not inherent to them. Thus, there still remains the possibility of an immense compromise, of a corruption of history, or of the class struggle, powerful enough to destroy, but not enough so to construct, and where the guiding lines of history, as they have been drawn in the *Communist Manifesto,* will be erased.

The contingency of each man and of all men, the contingency of the human venture, and within the womb of the latter, the contingency of the Marxist venture. Here we discover the fundamental experience of Merleau-Ponty. First he reflected upon the singularity of his life, then, turning back to his historical existence, he had discovered that the one and the other were made from the same cloth.

But given these reservations, he accepted historical materialism as a grid, as a regulating idea, or, if you prefer, as a heuristic scheme:

> For fifteen years now, there have been too many writers who have bypassed Marxism falsely for us to bother distinguishing among them. To go beyond a doctrine, one must first have reached its level, and be able to explain it better than the doctrine itself could. If, confronted by Marxism, we raise a few questions, it is not because we favor a more conservative philosophy of history which would only be still more abstract.

In short, Marxism *faute de mieux.*

Let us understand each other: fundamentally, Marxism is a practice whose origin is the class struggle. If you deny this struggle, there is nothing left of it. In 1945—and as long as the communist party shared power with the bourgeois parties—this struggle was not clearly distinguishable. The young intellectuals of the party believed in it faithfully. They weren't wrong. I say they *believed* in it, because they certainly couldn't see it under the phony mask of national unity. Merleau-Ponty often irritated them because he only half believed it. He had reflected upon the consequences of victory. No more allies, only two giants face to face. The latter, anxious to avoid friction, had redrawn the globe at Yalta. I'll take the East, you can have the West. But peace didn't interest them in the slightest. There would be a Third World War—there was no doubt of that—and each of them, anxious to win as quickly as possible, would come to terms with the other only to postpone the war until the best bases had been secured. In any case, the balance of power temporarily remained in favor of the West. Thus, in the moment of history, revolution in Europe was impossible. Neither Churchill, nor Roosevelt, nor finally even Stalin would have allowed it. We know what happened to the Greek resistance and how it was liquidated. Today everything is clear. History became one for the entire world. And the result was this contradiction, undecipherable at the time: the class struggle was transformed, place by place, into a conflict between nations—thus becoming separate wars. Today, *le Tiers Monde*[6] enlightens us. In 1945, we could neither understand, nor conceive of this metamorphosis. In short, we were blind. One-eyed, Merleau-Ponty came to conclusions which were shocking because they seemed self-evident. If the revolution could be stopped from the outside by the desire to maintain international balance, if exterior forces could crush it at birth, if the workers could no longer expect their emancipation to come from themselves, but from world conflict, then the revolutionary class had said its farewells. Only the bourgeoisie remained, surrounded by the immense mass of workers which it exploited and atomized. But the proletariat, that invincible force which brought sentence against capitalism, and whose mission was to overthrow it, the proletariat had simply left the stage. It was possible that it would return, perhaps tomorrow, perhaps in fifty years. It was equally possible that it would never return. Merleau-Ponty noted this absence, deploring it, as well he might, and suggested that we should organize ourselves without waiting, for as long as this absence might last. He went as far as to trace the guidelines of a program, in a text which I transcribe here from memory, but quite faithfully I'm sure: "While waiting, it is incumbent upon us that we do nothing which could prevent the rebirth of the proletariat, even better, that we do everything to help it re-constitute itself. In short, we must carry out the policy of the Communist Party." I vouch for the last words, in any case, as I was so struck by them. Born of the class struggle, the communist party determines its policy on the basis of this struggle. In capitalist countries, the party couldn't survive the disappearance of the proletariat. But Merleau-Ponty no longer believed in civil war, and by the same token, even challenged the legitimacy of the communist organization. The paradox remains that he proposed at this same moment, that we ally ourselves with the party.

There was still another paradox. Go find a bishop, and tell him, just to see what he will say: "God is dead. I doubt that he will be resurrected, but, in the meantime, I will go along with you." He will thank you for your gracious proposals, but he won't swallow them. But Merleau's communist friends took just the reverse attitude. They gave him hell, but nicely, and without driving him away. If we really think about it, this wasn't surprising. The party came out of the Resistance ahead. It was less strict in the choice of its fellow travelers. But, more than anything else, its intellectuals were in an uncomfortable position. Radical by the order of things, they would have wanted the proletariat to organize its conquests, continuing its march forward. The bourgeoisie, terrorized by the publicity given its betrayals, would have let them do anything. But, instead, the communists procrastinated. They said: "Let's seize power." And they were answered: "The Anglo-Saxons might intervene at any minute." A new contradiction appeared in the movement of a "flying wedge": in order to save peace and the socialist countries, a revolution required by the masses from within could be countermanded from without. These young men who had come to the party through the Resistance didn't retract their faith. Far from it. But there were doubts and disputes. After all, France was a bourgeois democracy. What was the C.P. doing in a tripartite government? Wasn't it the hostage of capitalism? They went on faithfully transmitting slogans which disturbed them: "We must know when to end a strike. . . . The revolutionary objective is the reconstruction of the country." But they couldn't prevent Merleau's conclusions from worrying them. At least at the edges. After all, he approved the party's policy of reform, this policy whose executors they made themselves through obedience. Could he be blamed for repeating out loud what they themselves occasionally whispered? Where is the proletariat? In point of fact, it was there, but bridled and muzzled. And by whom? Every day Merleau-Ponty, that Cassandra, irritated them a little more. And Merleau, in turn, was irritated by them. In both cases, unjustly.

What Merleau misunderstood was the fact that his friends had grown roots. He returned to this question fifteen years later in the preface to *Signs*. There, on the contrary, he insisted upon the status of a militant enveloped, involved, and who, nevertheless, would himself contribute through his fidelity and through his acts to making the party which had made him. This was ambiguous repentance, which led him, above all, to justify his denials. It is easy to laugh when you are serenely judging a policy from the outside. When those who create it from day to day, if only by their acquiescence, discover its meaning, and when they see their own shadow cast upon the wall, there is nothing left for them but to break with it. But the argument can be turned the other way, and I think that he knew it. For those young men who struggled between good faith and sworn faith, by means of acts which they daily assumed, and whose meaning they saw changed in their very hands, for them, more than once, the "high-altitude thinker" was Merleau-Ponty.

They, in turn, misunderstood him. They didn't know the road he had followed. From a few conversations which we had later, I was left with the feeling that before 1939, he had been closer to Marxism than he was ever to be subsequently. What made him withdraw from it? I imagine that it was the trials. He must have been very upset by them, for he spoke of them at great length, ten years later, in *Humanism and Terror.* After the trials, he could hardly even be disturbed by the German-Soviet Pact. He amused himself by writing rather "Machiavellian" letters to "distribute the blame." Through friends and through the writings of Rosa Luxemburg, he had been converted to the idea of the "spontaneity of the masses," which was close to the general movement of his particular movement. When he saw "reasons of state" smouldering behind the masses, he turned away.

A Christian at twenty, he ceased to be one because, as he said: "We believe that we believe, but we don't believe." More specifically, he asked that Catholicism reintegrate him in the unity of immanence, and this was precisely what it couldn't do. Christians love each other in God. I wouldn't go so far as to say that he moved from this idea to socialism: this would be too schematic. But the time came when he encountered Marxism and asked what it offered. He found this to be the future unity of a classless society and, in the meantime, the warm comradeship of battle. After 1936, there is no doubt. It was the communist party which disturbed him. One of his most constant characteristics was to seek everywhere for lost immanence, to be rejected by this immanence in favor of transcendence, and then, to vanish. Nevertheless, he didn't remain at this level of the original contradiction. From 1950 to 1962 he conceived gradually of a new link between being and intersubjectivity. But if, in 1945, he still dreamed of transcendence, he hadn't yet found it.

In short, he had come a long way, when, in spite of the disgusts he had endured, he proposed this hard-hitting, severe and disillusioned Marxism. And if it was true that he had "learned history" with no taste for it, from a sense of vocation and from obstinacy, it was equally true that he would never forget it. And this is what his communist friends, more sensitive to unreserved adherence than to specific and limited areas of agreement, didn't see at the time. Solely concerned, as he was, with probing his relation to history, I imagine that their criticisms would have affected him very little, causing him, at most, to persist in his ideas silently, if, by chance, we hadn't started *Les Temps modernes* just at that time. Now he had the instrument, and he was almost forced to express all the aspects of his thought.

We had dreamed of this review since 1943. If the truth is one, I thought, we must, as Gide said of God, seek it not elsewhere but everywhere. Each social product and each attitude—from the most private to the most public—are its allusive incarnations. An anecdote reflects an entire era as much as the substance of a political constitution. We would be hunters of meaning, we would speak the truth about the world and about our lives. Merleau found me optimistic. Was I so sure that there was meaning everywhere? To which I might have replied that there is meaning in nonmeaning and that it was up to us to find it. And I know what he would have replied in turn: explain barbarism all you want, you still won't dissipate its mystery. But the discussion never took place. I was the more dogmatic, he the more subtle, but this was a matter of temperament or, as we said, of character. We were both motivated by the same desire: to emerge from the tunnel and to see clearly. He wrote: "Our only recourse is in a reading of the present which is as complete and faithful as possible, which doesn't distort its meaning, which even acknowledges its chaos and inherent nonmeaning where they exist, but which doesn't refuse to discern there a direction and an idea."

This was our program. Today, after Merleau's death, it is still the program of the review. No, the real difference should be called our inequality. Since he had learned history, I was no longer his equal. While I still hung back, questioning the facts, he was already trying to make the events speak.

Facts *repeat* themselves. Of course, since they are always new—but what then? The annual play of a successful playwright is new. He had to invent the idea, and then reflect and work on it. Each word was a *trouvaille* and the actors, in turn, "struck" just the right note. For several days they had said, "I just don't feel the part," and then, suddenly, "I feel it." Then finally, on the day of the dress rehearsal, the unexpected happened. The play became what it was—which means—the same as all the others. The fact confirms and begins anew. It points to customs, old contradictions, sometimes, more profoundly, even to structures. The same adultery is committed every night, for fifty years, before the same bourgeois audience in the heart of Paris. By only seeking its permanencies, I hoped that we would unknowingly discover the ethnography of French society.

Merleau-Ponty didn't scorn permanencies. As a matter of fact, he loved the childish return of season and rituals. But for this same reason, hopelessly pining for his childhood, he knew that it would never return. If the adult, living in the world of adults, could be visited by the grace of his first years, it would be too wonderful. Life would be as round as the earth. Merleau, an exile, had very early *felt* what I could only *know*. We can't go backwards, the gesture cannot be reclaimed, the gentle contingency of birth is changed, by its very irreversibility, into destiny. I was not unaware that we proceed along the course of things and never retrace our steps. But for a long time, I cherished the illusion that each day we grow in value, trapped by the bourgeois myth of progress. Progress, that accumulation of capital and virtues. We keep everything. In short, I was approaching excellence. This was the mask of death. Today it is stripped away. But this mask repelled Merleau. Born to die, nothing could restore to him the immortality of his childhood. Such was his original experience of the event.

In the middle of the last century, he would have lived time in reverse, in vain, as did Baudelaire after the "break." The golden age over, there is only room for degradation. Merleau's virtue was to have avoided this reactionary myth. As much degradation as you like, but it is ours. We cannot be subjected to it, without bringing it about, which means without creating man and his works through it. The event falls upon us like a thief, it throws us into a ditch or perches us on top of a wall. We only hear his gunfire. But scarcely has he taken off, the police at his heels, then there we are so profoundly changed that we no longer even understand how we could formerly have loved, acted, lived. But who, in 1945, remembered the 30s? They were quietly preparing for retirement, the Occupation had killed them, and only their bones remained. A few of them dreamed of a return to prewar life. Merleau knew this couldn't happen, and that it was foolish and criminal to desire it. When he asked himself, in 1945, whether the human venture would founder in barbarism, or whether it would be vindicated in socialism, he was interrogating world history as though it were his own life. Time past, time recaptured? Digression, deviation, drifting; a hundred times rewritten, these words from his pen bear witness to the fact that we gain nothing without loss, that the future, even the closest, most docile future, betrays our hopes and our calculations. But, for the most part, it betrays them by fulfilling them. Our past acts return to us, from the depth of future years, unrecognizable, and yet ours. We must either despair, or find the changing reason for the change, and being unable to restore the old facts, we must institute new ones, at least in the heart of the event which disowns them. We should try to govern this strange drifting which we call history from the interior, by seeking the implicit objectives of men within the movement which carries us along, in order to propose them explicitly. This brought us back to questioning the event—and without distorting anything—in order to find within it a temporal logic. I would be tempted to call this logic a "dialectic," had not Merleau, from this time on, challenged the term, and if, ten years later, he hadn't more or less repudiated it.[7]

In sum, the prewar period denied the times. When our walls were blown down by a cyclone, we looked among the wreckage for the survivors, and we said to them: "It's nothing, really." The worst of it is that they believed us. Merleau-Ponty "learned history" more quickly than we did, because he took a painful and unqualified pleasure in time as it flowed by. This is what made him our political commentator without his even wanting to be, and without anyone being aware of him as such.

At that time, *Les Temps modernes* had an editorial staff which lacked any homogeneity whatsoever: Jean Paulhan, Raymond Aron, Albert Ollivier. Of course, they were our friends. But—unknown to everyone, and first of all, ourselves—we didn't share any of their ideas. In fact, only the day before, our inert coexistence had been a lively comradeship. Some of them had just come from London, others from hiding. But the Resistance soon dispersed. Each of them found his rightful place once again, whether it was *Le Figaro,* the *R.P.F.* [*Rassemblement du Peuple Français*], or the *Nouvelle nouvelle revue française.* The communists themselves, having participated in the first issue through the pen of Kanapa, took leave of us. It was a hard blow for those who remained. We lacked experience. Merleau saved the review by agreeing to direct it. He became editor-in-chief and political editor. This happened naturally. He didn't propose his services and I didn't allow myself to "choose" him. We simply announced jointly, after a certain time had elapsed, that he was going to assume this double job and that he couldn't resign them without the review folding. We only argued about one point: since the editorial staff had disappeared from the front cover, I suggested that Merleau's name appear there next to mine, as we were its two directors. He sharply refused. I repeated this request a hundred times during the years which followed, using only one argument. It would have been closer to the truth. A hundred times, smiling, relaxed, he repeated his refusal, explaining it by circumstantial reasons which were never the same. As his explanations changed constantly, and as his position remained unchanged, I concluded that he was hiding his real motives from me. I told him this, and he defended himself rather laconically. He didn't want to deceive me, he simply wanted to cut short any discussion of the subject. But then again whatever the subject happened to be, he never liked the debate to go to the heart of the issue. And here he won. I know no more about it today than I did in 1945. Was it modesty? I doubt it. It wasn't a matter of sharing honors, but responsibilities. I have been told the contrary. "You were the more well-known at the time. He was too proud to accept the benefit of this fame." It was true that I was better known, but I didn't boast of it. This was the time of the cellar rats, of existential suicides. The respectable papers covered me with dirt and the tabloids equally so. Notorious through misunderstanding. But, those who read, in *Samdei Soir,* the interesting account of a virgin whom I lured, so it would seem, to my room to show her my etchings, those people weren't reading *Les Temps modernes.* They wouldn't have even known of its existence. To the real readers of the review, on the contrary, we were both equally well-known. They read both our essays, preferring those of one, or the other, or politely dismissed both of us on equal terms. Merleau knew this as well as I. We showed each other the letters we received. In general, his public, mine, and that of *Les Temps modernes,* were one and the same, and the best we could have hoped for. They didn't shoot the piano player, but evaluated his work without concerning themselves with other matters. Merleau could neither suffer nor profit from my dubious renown. Should one say that he was afraid of being compromised? Nothing could have been more foreign to him. He proved this in the review itself, by publishing articles which created a scandal. Well, then? Why did he insist upon signing T.M. under editorials which he had conceived and edited from the first to the last word? All these writings which he didn't sign have been attributed, willy-nilly, to me. That goes without saying, since I seemed to be the only captain of that vessel. And last year, while glancing through some foreign bibliographies, I discovered that I was the author of his article on the Soviet camps—the very same one which he had acknowledged and legitimized in his last book. Why hadn't he signed it in 1950, since he was to use it again later if he hadn't been willing to sign it at first? Why did he leave all those bastards for the review, since it was entirely up to him to "regularize" them? That is the question. And I don't claim to answer it. I had to go on living, nonetheless, and I adopted the most convenient explanation. He insisted upon independence, and any chain would have weighed upon him, except this tacit agreement, renewed with each issue, which didn't commit anyone, and which either one of us could break within an hour. This is possible, and yet, today, I think that he distrusted me. He was aware of my incompetence, and he was afraid of my zeal. If I should ever start talking politics, where would we all end? I have no proof of this distrust, except the following: in 1947 I published in the review an essay, "What Is Literature?" He read the first proofs, and thought he had discovered a phrase which assimilated, as was the style then, fascism and "Stalinism" under the common heading of "totalitarianism." I was in Italy at the time, and on reading this, he wrote to me immediately. I received his letter in Naples, and I still recall my stupefaction. "If," he in substance said, "you really apply the same measuring rods to Communism and Nazism, I ask you to accept my resignation as of now." Happily, as I was able to prove to him, it only involved a typographical error. And the matter ended there, But when I think about it, this gives the measure of his distrust, First of all, in the state of proofs, the text was incomprehensible and visibly mutilated. Next, and Merleau knew this perfectly well, I had never indulged in this kind of foolishness. Finally, his resignation was tendered with a bit too much enthusiasm. In sum, everything indicates that he expected the worst. But what strikes me, above all, is the fact that he was afraid that I would bolt to the *right*. Why? Did he believe me to be right wing by temperament? Or did he simply fear that this hyena with a fountain pen, having been dismissed by the jackals, would apply for admission to the Pen Club? In any case, he was taking precautions against any blunders on my part. If any one of them proved inexcusable, he could retreat within twenty-four hours. This fire alarm was still in place five years later, when a political disagreement separated us. But then, Merleau didn't make use of it. As long as he could still hope that our conflicts would be resolved, he remained. His letter of 1947 proves that he would have left the review within the hour if I had fallen into the clutches of the right. When I moved further to the left, he accepted being compromised. He thought he already saw the ditch, the fall was imminent, and he nonetheless remained at my side, determined not to jump except as a last resort. For a long time, I believed that he had been wrong not to join me at the pillory. A public collaboration would have constrained us both, so I said to myself, to reciprocal concessions. We would have spared each other, to save the collective editorship. But for some time now, I am inclined to think that he was right. In 1952, our differences could neither be disguised nor destroyed. They didn't stem from our personalities, but from the situation. As long as the name of Merleau hadn't been pronounced, we could delay matters longer. The clandestine nature of our bond, planned to facilitate his retreat, gave us the means of remaining together until the very last minute. The separation was gentle. We felt no need to proclaim it, that is, to change it into a public dispute. That, perhaps, is what saved our friendship. In the circles close to both of us, these precautions gained him the reputation to an *éminence grise*. This was all the more untrue, as he was no one's advisor. Master of his party, as I was of mine, his role, like mine, was to decide and to write.

He made a great point, nevertheless, of insisting that I read his articles, both those signed T.M. and which involved the review as a whole, and those which bore his name and only committed him. Please understand me. This attitude *resembles* that of an employee, or a bureaucrat who sees to it that his actions are "covered" by his principal. In fact, it was just the reverse. Merleau had no other boss but himself. He was much better oriented than I in the ambiguous world of politics. I knew this. And it would be an understatement to say that I had faith in him. It seemed to me, reading him, that he revealed my own thoughts to me. But our "gentlemen's agreement" required that he consult me. Anonymous, he didn't want me to be saddled with his writings. He put all of his delicacy in them. I was still stammering in the new language he had already mastered. Aware of this, he had a horror of coercing or seducing me. Thus he brought me his manuscripts without any comment. In these first times, he took great pains just in order to be readable. I was lost in the political labyrinth. I approved everything he wrote in advance, and fled precipitously. He sought out my hiding place, trapping me there. I would suddenly find him before me smiling, holding out his manuscript. "I accept it, I agree with you," I stammered. "I'm delighted," he said without budging. And indicating with his left hand the sheets of papers which he proffered me with his right. "All the same, you should read them," he added patiently.

I read, I learned, I ended by becoming an avid reader. He was my guide. It was *Humanism and Terror* which caused me to make an important decision. This small dense book revealed to me the method and object. It gave me the push I had needed to release me from my immobility. We know what a scandal it created everywhere. Communists vomited on it, who today, don't see a thing wrong with it. But above all, it caused a fine commotion on our right. One sentence in particular, which assimilated the opponent to the traitor and inversely, the traitor to the opponent, set off the dynamite. In Merleau's mind, this applied to those disturbed and threatened societies which huddle together around a revolution. This was viewed as a sectarian condemnation of all opposition to Stalin. Within a few days, Merleau became the man with a knife between his teeth. When Simone de Beauvoir visited the editors of the *Partisan Review* in New York, they didn't bother to hide their dismay. We were being manipulated. The hand of Moscow held the pen of our father Joseph. Those poor people! One evening at Boris Vian's apartment, Camus took Merleau aside and reproached him for justifying the trials. It was most painful. I see them still. Camus, revolted, Merleau-Ponty courteous and firm, somewhat pale, the one indulging himself, the other refusing the delights of violence. Suddenly, Camus turned his back and left. I ran after him, accompanied by Jacques Bost. We found him in the deserted street. I tried as best I could to explain Merleau's ideas, which the latter hadn't deigned to do. With the sole result that we parted estranged. It took six months and a chance meeting to bring us together again. This memory is not a pleasant one for me. What a foolish idea it was to offer my services in this affair. It is true. I was to the right of Merleau, and to the left of Camus. What perverse humor prompted me to become the mediator between two friends, both of whom, a little later, were to reproach me for my friendship for the communists, and who are both dead, unreconciled?

In fact, by this little sentence which had everyone screaming, and which is now accepted by everyone as a basic truth, universally valid even beyond the limits intended by the author, Merleau did nothing but apply to other circumstances what the war had taught him. We will not be judged by our intentions alone. What reveals our worth as much and more than the intentional effects of our actions, are their involuntary results which we have guessed, exploited, or, in any case, assumed. "The man of action," he was to write later, quoting Hegel, "has the certainty that necessity, through his act, will become contingency, and contingency, necessity." And with that, he asked history the truly philosophic question: What is a detour? What is aimless drifting? We started out in foul weather, persevered stoically through strong winds, we grew old in grief, and now, here is the result. What is left of former objectives? What has gone overboard? A new society was born in midstream, created by the undertaking itself, gone astray through its deviation. What can this society permit? What must it reject at the risk of breaking its back? And whatever its heritages who is to tell us whether we have taken the shortest route, or whether we should attribute the meanderings to all of our deficiencies?

Through this rigorously unjust justice which preserves the wicked through their works, and which condemns men of good faith to hell for acts committed in all purity of heart, I finally discovered the reality of the event. In a word, it was Merleau who converted me. At heart, I was a throwback to anarchy, digging an abyss between the vague phantasmagoria of collectives and the precise ethic of my private life. He enlightened me. This reasonable, ambiguous, and insane undertaking, always unpredictable and always foreseen, which attains its objectives when it has forgotten what they were, which bypasses when it wants to remain faithful to them, which annihilates itself in the false purity of failure and degrades itself in victory, which sometimes abandons the enterprise midway, and other times denounces it when it no longer feels responsible—Merleau taught me that I would find it everywhere, in the most hidden aspect of my life as well as in the broad daylight of history, and that there is only one, which is the same for all of us: the event which makes us becoming action, action which unmakes us by becoming through us event, and which, since Marx and Hegel, we call *praxis*. In sum, he showed me that I was making history in the same way M. Jourdain was speaking prose. The course of things made the last rampart of my individualism crumble, carrying with it my private life. I found myself in the same places where I was beginning to escape. I recognized myself, more mysterious in the harsh light of day than I would ever have believed, and two million times richer. The time had come. Our era required that all men of letters write their dissertation on French politics. I prepared myself for this examination. Merleau instructed me without lecturing, from his experience and from the consequences of his writings. If, as he said, philosophy must be "spontaneity which teaches," I can say that, for me, he was the philosopher of his politics. And as for the latter, I maintain that we could have had no other, and that ours was the right one. One has to have a good start in order to survive. My start came from him and it was excellent. The proof of this is that our readers took all the curves with us. It will soon be seventeen years since the first issue of *Les Temps modernes* appeared. We have regularly gained subscribers, and we have lost a few dozen, at the very most.

In 1945 it was possible to choose between two positions. But no more than two. The first and better, was to talk to Marxists and to denounce, to them only, the fact that the revolution had been nipped in the bud, the Resistance murdered, the left shattered. Several periodicals took this position and disappeared, unheeded. This was a happy era when people had ears not to hear and eyes not to see. Far from believing that this failure condemned their effort, I maintain that we could have imitated them without foundering. The strength and the weakness of these reviews was to have restricted themselves to political ground. Our own published novels, literary essays, *témoignages,* documents—these rafts kept it afloat. But, to be able to denounce the betrayal of the revolution, one first had to be a revolutionary. Merleau was certainly not one, and I wasn't one yet. We didn't even have the right to call ourselves Marxists, in spite of our affinities for Marx. For revolution is not a state of soul. It is a daily practice illuminated by a theory. And even if it doesn't suffice to have read Marx in order to be a revolutionary, one joins him sooner or later as an agitator of revolution. The result is clear. Only men formed by this discipline could criticize the left with any efficacity. Thus, at the time, they would have had to belong, whether closely or loosely, to Trotskyite circles. But by the same token, and through no fault of their own, this allegiance disqualified them. In that bewildered left which dreamed of unity, they were considered "divisionists." Merleau-Ponty, as well, saw the threat clearly. He watched the working classes marking time, and he knew the reasons for it. But if this *petit bourgeois* intellectual had pointed to the gagged, chained, confused workers, defrauded of their victory (even had he burst into tears, even had he squeezed tears from his readers' eyes), he would simply have been practicing a higher form of demagoguery. But when, on the contrary, he concluded that the proletariat was on vacation, he was sincere and true to himself, and I was true to myself when I approved his conclusions. Us, revolutionaries? Go on! Revolution then seemed the most pleasant of myths, a sort of Kantian idea. I mouthed the word respectfully, knowing nothing about it. Moderate intellectuals, the Resistance had pulled us to the left, but not enough so. And then again, the left was dead. Left to our own devices, what were we, what could we be, if not reformers?

The other attitude remained. We had no choice, it was self-evident. Coming from middle-class backgrounds, we tried to be the connecting link between the *petit bourgeoisie* and the communist intellectuals. This bourgeoisie had engendered us. We had received its culture and values, as our heritage. But the Occupation had taught us that neither one nor the other should be taken for granted. We asked our friends in the communist party for the necessary tools to take humanism away from the bourgeois. We asked all our left wing friends to do this work with us. Merleau wrote: "We weren't wrong in 1939 to want liberty, truth, happiness, transparent relations among men, and we didn't renounce humanism. [But] the war . . . taught us that these values remain nominal . . . without a political and economic infrastructure which makes them part of existence." I can well see that this position, which one might call eclectic, wasn't viable in the long run, but I also see that both the French and international situations made it the only possible one. Why should we be more royalist than the king? We had forgotten the class struggle, this was a fact, but we were not the only ones to have done so. The event chose us to bear witness to what the *petit bourgeois* intelligentsia wanted in 1945, at that moment when the communists had lost the means and the intention of overthrowing the regime. This intelligentsia, so it seems to me, paradoxically wanted the communist party to make reformist concessions on the one hand, and on the other, they wanted the French proletariat to find its revolutionary aggression once more. The paradox is only one in appearance. This chauvinist class, exasperated by five years of occupation, was afraid of the Soviet Union, but would have been assuaged by a revolution which was "really our own kind." In any case, there are always degrees of being and thinking. Whatever the entreaties of this revolutionary and chauvinistic reformism, Merleau had no interest in being the mouthpiece of a flag-waving tricolor proletariat. For his part, he had begun—as had many others in other countries at this same moment—an immense labor of confrontation. He set about wearing down our abstract concepts into a Marxism which was transformed within him as soon as he had assimilated them.

Today the task is easier, and the Marxists—whether communist or not—have taken it up in turn. In 1948, it was thornier, inasmuch as the communist party intellectuals held no qualms about sending these two suspect bourgeois on their way, empty-handed, since they had announced themselves fellow travelers without anyone's having invited them on the trip. We had to defend Marxist ideology without hiding our reservations and our hesitancies. We had to go a part of the way with people who, in turn, treated us like police-intellectuals. We had to thrust and parry without being insulting or severing relations; criticize freely but with moderation these cadavers, who didn't tolerate a single disagreement; affirm, in spite of our solitude, that we were marching along at their side, at the side of the working class (reading us, the bourgeois laughed derisively) but without forbidding ourselves, when necessary, to take sides hastily with the communist party, as we did at the beginning of the war in Indochina, or to fight for peace and the lessening of tension, within the confines of our confidential review, as though we were publishing a popular daily. They didn't forbid us to refrain from every virtuous passion, particularly self-importance and anger, to speak in the desert as though before a gathering of the nation, but without losing sight of the fact that we were utterly inconsequential, and finally, they didn't forbid us to remember at each moment, that one doesn't need success in order to persevere, but that nevertheless, perseverance has success as its goal. In spite of these jeers and low blows, Merleau-Ponty did the work properly, unfalteringly and with taste. It was his job. He didn't unveil—and who did?—the reality of the years around 1945, but he profited from the illusory French unity to remain as close to the communists as possible in order to broach impossible but necessary subjects of discussion, and to lay the foundations, beyond Marx, for what he sometimes called "left-wing thought." In one sense, he failed. Left-wing thought is Marxism, nothing more, nothing less. But, history recuperates from everything but death. If Marxism is today in the process of becoming *all of left-wing thought,* we owe this, in the first place, to a handful of men, of which he was one. The *petits bourgeoisie,* as I have said, were moving toward the left. The stop signal was heard everywhere, but this movement had already achieved advanced positions. Merleau gave the most basic expression to the common desire for democratic union and for reform.

Two years of clear sailing and then came the declaration of the Cold War. Merleau could see through Marshall's homilies, and denounced them as the generosity of an ogre. This was the time of shifting alliances. The communist party got tough, the right took off toward the center, and at the same moment, we began to hear the death rattle of the R.P.F. The bourgeoisie lifted its head, christened itself the third force and enunciated the doctrine of the *cordon sanitaire.* We were pressed to take sides, but Merleau refused. Sometimes he needed to stand his ground: "the blow from Prague," one strike following another, the fall of the tripartite government, the Gaullist tidal wave in the municipal elections. He had written: "The class struggle is masked," and he unmasked it. Nevertheless, we persisted with our offers of mediation which no one took seriously, all the more certain that we could, in our two persons, effect the unity of the left since, at this time, it had no other representative. The R.D.R. [*Rassemblement Démocratique Révolutionaire*] was born, a mediating neutrality between two power blocs, between the advanced segment of the reformist *petite bourgeoisie* and the revolutionary workers. They asked me to join them, and allowing myself to be persuaded that it shared our goals, I accepted. Merleau, solicited elsewhere, nevertheless joined in order not to disavow me. I wasn't long in discovering that I had made a mistake. In order to live as closely as possible to the Communist Party, to force it to accept certain criticisms, we had, first of all, to be politically ineffective, so that they could envision another use for us. Merleau-Ponty was just their man. Solitary, without partisans or zealous disciples, his thinking, always new and renewed, had faith only in itself. The *Rassemblement,* on the contrary, however small it was and admitted itself to be, was counting on force of numbers. And thus it opened hostilities, even though it hoped to stop them at once. Where else could it have recruited advocates of revolution except in communist or near-communist circles? The party, bristling, treated this group as an enemy from the very first day, to their great shock. The ambiguity of this situation was at the origin of our internal divisions. Some of them, disgusted, turned toward the right. In general these were the "organizers." The others, the majority, claiming to be unshakable, aligned themselves with the social action of the French Communist Party. The latter, which included us, reproached the others for having abandoned the initial program. "Where is your neutralism?" we asked them. They in turn retorted with, "And where is yours?"

Did Merleau discover before I did that political thought is not easily integrated unless carried to its extreme, when it is taken up elsewhere by those who need it? Or, rather, isn't it that he was as little able in 1948 as in 1941 to restrain himself from showing a certain scorn for these groups which he found too young, which lacked roots and tradition? The fact is that he never attended the meetings of the governing board, of which he was, nevertheless, a founding member. At least, this is what I was told, as I didn't go very often myself. He may also have rightly feared that we would pervert the meaning of his undertaking, and that *Les Temps modernes* would become the monthly organ of the R.D.R. He said nothing to me about all this—perhaps because he shared my imprudence, perhaps because he did not want to reproach me for it, counting on the event to open my eyes. In short, he directed the review as usual leaving me to wage war alone, intermittently, under the banner of neutrality.

In any case, by the spring of 1949, we were in agreement: the R.D.R. wasn't viable. The Movement for Peace, then headed by Yves Farge, was scheduled to hold a congress in Paris. As soon as the *Rassemblement* was informed of this, they hastily invited some well-known Americans, and decided to devote a few days after the congress as "study days" for peace. We had evidence that the right-wing press could be counted upon to spread the news. In brief, these days devoted to pacifism were only a ploy, encouraged, if not inspired by the Americans. Richard Wright came to see me. He was worried. He had been too openly solicited by the American Embassy for him to want to speak. "Where are we going?" he asked. Merleau joined us. The three of us decided not to appear at any of the meetings, and we wrote a joint letter explaining our abstention. The war of the two peaces was waged without us. At the Vel d'Hiv, they heard an American brag about the atom bomb, but they didn't see us there. The militants were outraged. In June, 1949, they went to the leaders and told them what they thought of them. I joined my voice to theirs. We assassinated the R.D.R. and I left for Mexico, disillusioned but reassured. Merleau hadn't appeared at the congress, but there was no doubting his opinion. I told myself that I needed this unpleasant experience in order to share his beliefs entirely. And from this, it had taken nothing but the perfectly reasonable irrationality of politics to make us fall into an anticommunism which we vomited, but which we nevertheless had to adopt.

When I saw him again in the fall, I told him that I had finally understood him. No more active politics. The review and the review only. I submitted various projects to him. Why not devote an issue to the Soviet Union? Our accord, it seemed to me, was total. We became interchangeable. So I was all the more astonished when my suggestions found so little echo. It would have been one thing if he had simply pointed out their absurdity to me. But, no, he just let them drop, silent and grim. It was because he had had wind of the Soviet camps. We had been told of the documents at the same time as Rousset, but through another source. Merleau's editorial appeared in the issue of January, 1950. You can also read it in *Signs*. This time I allowed my zeal to go as far as asking him to let me read it, even before he offered it to me. I didn't skip a word approving everything, and first of all, the faithfulness of the author to himself. He exposed the facts and concluded his first paragraph with this sentence:

> If the concentration camps number ten million, while, at the same time at the other end of the Soviet hierarchy, salaries and standards of living are fifteen to twenty times higher than those of free workers, then the entire system is changing its course and its meaning; in spite of the nationalization of production, and although private exploitation of man by man and unemployment don't exist, we ask what reason we still have to speak of socialism in connection with that country?

How could the Soviet workers tolerate this offensive return of slavery on their own soil? The explanation, he answered, is that it happened gradually, "without deliberate planning, from crisis to crisis, from expediency to expediency." The Soviet citizens know the code, they know that the camps exist. What they don't know, perhaps, is the extent of the repression. When they discover it, it's too late. They have become accustomed to it through gradual doses.

> A great many young heroes . . . gifted bureaucrats, who had never known, in the sense of 1917, a critical mind and open discussion, will continue to believe that these prisoners are mad men, asocial beings, men of ill will. . . . Communists throughout the world expect that through a kind of magical emanation so many factories and so much wealth must one day produce the whole man, even if, in order to create him, ten million Russians must be reduced to slavery.

The existence of the camps, he said, make it possible to measure the illusions of today's communists. But he immediately added:

> It is just this illusion which forbids us to confuse Communism with Fascism. If our Communists accept slave labor camps and oppression, it is because they are waiting for the classless society. . . . A Nazi was never encumbered with ideas such as the recognition of man by man, or internationalism, or a classless society. And while it is true that these ideas only find an unfaithful transmitter in Communism today they are still inherent in it.

And he added more explicitly,

> We have the same values as a Communist. . . . We may think that he compromises them by incorporating them into today's Communism, but they still remain ours, while, on the contrary, we have nothing in common with the majority of Communism's enemies. . . . The U.S.S.R. is, *grosso modo,* on the side of those forces which are fighting against the forms of exploitation familiar to us. . . . We must not be indulgent towards Communism but neither must we, in any case, make pacts with its adversaries. The only healthy criticism is that which aims, both within and without the Soviet Union, at destroying exploitation and oppression.

Nothing could be clearer. Whatever its crimes, the Soviet Union has this enormous advantage over bourgeois democracies: revolutionary aims. An Englishman had observed: "The camps are their colonies." To which Merleau answered: "In that case, our colonies are—*mutatis mutandis*—our slave labor camps." But our camps have no other goal than to further enrich the privileged classes. Those of the Russians are perhaps still more criminal since they betray the revolution. The fact remains that they began with the idea of serving it. It may be that Marxism has been bastardized, that interior problems and external pressure have warped the government, distorted institutions, and deflected socialism from its course. Russia is not comparable to other countries. It is only permissible to judge it when one has accepted its undertaking, and then only in the name of that undertaking.

In brief, five years after his first article, in a moment of extreme danger, he returned to the principle of his politics: on the side of the party, right next to it, but never within. The party was our only pole, outside opposition our only attitude toward it. To attack only the U.S.S.R. was to absolve the West. You may well find an echo of Trotsky in this unyielding statement. If, said Trotsky, the Soviet Union is attacked, we must defend the foundations of socialism. As for the Stalinist bureaucracy, it is not for capitalism to settle its count, the Russian proletariat will take care of that.

But Merleau's voice had grown somber. He spoke coldly, even his anger lacked passion, almost lacking life, as though he had already begun to feel the first symptoms of that lassitude of the soul which is our common disease. Go back to the texts of 1945, make the comparison. You will gauge his disappointments, the wearing down of his hopes. In 1949: "We will carry out, without illusions, the policy of the C.P." In his article of 1950: "We have the same values as a Communist," and, as though he were pointing out the weakness of this purely moral bond: "People will tell me that the Communists have no values. . . . They have them *in spite of themselves.*" To be in accord with them, we had to credit them with our maxims, knowing all the while that they rejected them. As for political agreement, it wasn't even a question of that anymore. In 1945 he forbade himself any thought, any action which might be harmful to the resurrection of the proletariat. In 1950, he simply refused to attack oppression in Russia alone. Either it must be denounced everywhere or nowhere. The fact was that the U.S.S.R. of 1945 had seemed "ambiguous" to him. He found in it "signs of progress and symptoms of regression." This nation was emerging from a dreadful ordeal, it was possible to hope. In 1950, after the revelation of the concentration camp system: "We ask what reason we still have to talk of socialism." A single concession: the U.S.S.R. is, *grosso modo* on the right side of the barrier, with forces which are fighting against oppression. Nothing more. The revolutionary objective "to produce the whole man" is reduced, in the context of 1950, to being only an illusion of the communist parties. One could say that, about this time, Merleau found himself at the crossroads and that he was still loath to choose. Would he continue to favor the U.S.S.R. in order to remain true to himself and to the underprivileged classes? Or would he detach himself from this society of concentration camps? If it should be proved to him that both are made from the same clay, why should one ask more of him than of the opposing powers of prey? A final scruple restrained him: "The decadence of Russian Communism doesn't make the class struggle a myth, nor more generally, does it make Marxist criticism null and void."

Were we so sure that we could reject the Stalinist regime without rejecting Marxism? I received an indignant letter from Bloch-Michel, which said, in substance: "How can you not understand that the Soviet economy needs manual slave labor, and that it systematically recruits millions of underfed and overexploited workers every year?" If he was right, Marx had thrown us from one barbarism into another. I showed the letter to Merleau, who didn't find it convincing. We found legitimate rage in it, and reasons of the heart, but not of the head. No matter. Better thought out, substantiated by proven facts, by arguments, how did we know that it wouldn't have dissolved our loyalty? The problems of industrialization, a period of socialist accumulation, being surrounded on all sides, the resistance of the peasants, the necessity of assuring adequate food production, demographic problems, suspicion, police terror and dictatorship—this combination of facts and consequences amply sufficed to overpower us. But what could we have said, what could we have done, even had it been proven to us that the concentration camp system had been required by the infrastructure? We would have had to know much more about the USSR and its production quotas. Several years later, I was able to acquire this knowledge, and I was liberated from my fears at the very hour when the camps opened their gates. But throughout the winter of 1950 we lived in grim uncertainty. The fact was that we couldn't be disturbed by the power of the communists without being disturbed about ourselves. However inadmissible may have been their policies, we couldn't disavow them, at least not in the old capitalist countries, without resigning ourselves to a kind of betrayal. And it is the same thing to ask, "Just how far can they go?" as "How far can I follow them?" There is a morality of politics—a difficult subject, and never clearly treated—and when politics must betray its morality, to choose morality is to betray politics. Now, find your way out of that one! Particularly when the politics has taken as its goal bringing about the reign of the human. At the same moment as Europe discovered the camps, Merleau finally came upon the class struggle unmasked: strikes and repression, the massacres in Madagascar, the war in Vietnam, McCarthyism and the American Terror, the reawakening of Nazism, the Church in power everywhere, sanctimoniously protecting the rebirth of fascism with her cloak. How could we not smell the stench of the bourgeois cadaver? And how could we publicly condemn slavery in the East without abandoning, on our side, the exploited to their exploitation? But could we allow ourselves to work with the party, if this would mean putting France into chains and covering it with barbed wire? What should we do? Should we mercilessly strike those giants to the left and the right who wouldn't even feel our blows? This was the solution of despair. Merleau suggested this, for lack of a better one. I saw no other solution either, but I was worried. We hadn't budged an inch, the yes had simply changed to no. In 1945 we said, "Gentlemen, we are everybody's friend, and above all, the friend of our dear C.P." And five years later, "We are the enemies of all, the only privilege of the Party is that it still deserves our severity." Without even speaking of it, we both had the feeling that this "high-altitude" objectivity wouldn't take us very far. We hadn't chosen when choice had been imposed upon everyone, and we had been right. Perhaps now, our universal surliness could delay the choice for a few more months. But whether publishers of a daily paper, or a weekly magazine, it was high time that we take the plunge or simply fold. The somewhat confidential character of our review gave us some respite, but our position, at first political, was in danger of gradually becoming moralistic. We never descended to the level of beautiful souls, but fine sentiments were flowering in our vicinity, at the same time that manuscripts were becoming scarcer. We were slowing down, people no longer wanted to write for us.

Once in China, I was shown the statues of two traitors in the bottom of a ditch. People had spat on them for centuries. They were all shiny, eroded by human saliva. We weren't shiny yet, but erosion had started. We wouldn't be forgiven for refusing Manicheism. On the right, they hired butchers' boys to insult us. Everything was permitted them. They showed their behinds to the critics, who discovered that this was the "new generation." All of the fairies had been present at their cradle, but one. They disappeared for lack of talent. They lacked a certain zest, nothing more, but it had been denied them at birth. They would be dying of starvation today if they weren't fed by the Algerian War. Crime pays. They made a lot of noise, but did little damage. On the left, things were more serious. Our friends in the party hadn't been able to digest the article on the camps. Right was on our side, and this was our feast. Their insults didn't bother me in the least: rat, hyena, viper, polecat—I rather liked this bestiary. It took me out of myself. Merleau was more upset by it, still recalling the comradeship of 1945. There were two times of day to be abused: first he was insulted in the early morning news sheets; then, by the end of the evening, he received the clandestine apologies of his communist friends. This lasted until it was found simpler for these same people to take on more work. They wrote the articles at dawn and apologized at twilight. Merleau suffered less from being insulted by those close to him than from the fact of being no longer able to respect them. Today, I would say that they were possessed by a violence which was literally mad, born of an exhausting war which wore them out, which took place elsewhere, but whose effects made themselves felt even in the depths of our province. They tried to believe they were others, and they couldn't quite succeed. Merleau, I think, saw their faults and not their disease, this provincialism. This is conceivable as he knew them in their day-to-day life. In short, he kept his distance since this was what they wanted. The communist party had tolerated these fringes of critical sympathy on its edges without liking them. Beginning in 1949, it decided to annihilate them. Outside friends were kindly requested to keep their mouths shut. Should one of them make public his reservation, they would disgust him into becoming an enemy. Thus the party proved to every militant (and each militant thought he proved to himself) that free examination of dogma is the beginning of treason. What Merleau's friends hated in him was *themselves*. What anguish there was in all that, and how it exploded after the electric shock of the Twentieth Congress! Merleau knew the music. Communist tantrums didn't reduce him to anticommunism. He took the blows without giving them. He did the right thing and let them talk. In short, he went on with his undertaking. No matter. They cut off his oxygen, exiling him once more to the combustible gas of solitary life. Born of historic upheaval, the Communist Party, with its traditions and restraints, had formerly seemed to him, even from afar, as a possible society. Now he had lost it. To be sure, he had numerous friends who weren't communists, and who remained loyal to him. But what could he find in them except the affectionate indifference of the prewar period? They sat around a common table, eating together, in order to pretend for a moment that they had a common task. These completely diverse men, still in a state of shock from the intrusion of history into their private lives, had nothing in common but a bottle of Scotch and a leg of lamb. And of course these reunions came to the same thing as death certificates. The Resistance had crumbled, he finally realized that. But these aperceptions have no profound truth unless we feel them as a creeping form of our own death. I saw Merleau often during the winter and spring. He showed hardly any sign of nerves, but he was extremely hypersensitive. I felt that, little by little, he was dying. Five years later he was to write: "The writer knows full well that there is no common denominator between the rumination of his life and what this life might have given his work, making it clearer and more precise." This is true. Everyone ruminates. We mull over insults suffered, disgust swallowed, accusations, recriminations, pleading; and then we try to piece everything together, end to end, fragmented material with neither head nor tail. Merleau, like each of us, was familiar with these tedious repetitions, occasionally pierced by a flash of lightning. But that year, there was neither thunder nor light. He tried to take his bearings, to go back to that crossroads where his own history intersected the history of France and of the world, where the course of his thinking had been born from the course of things. This was what he had tried and succeeded in doing between 1939 and 1945. But in 1950, it was too late and too soon. "I would like," he said to me one day, "to write a novel about myself." I replied: "Why not write an autobiography?" "There are too many unanswered questions. In a novel, I could give them imaginary resolutions." Don't be deceived by this recourse to imagination. Let me remind you here of the role assigned to imagination in phenomenology, within this complex movement which realizes itself through the intuition of an essence. It was nonetheless true that this life was running out, but through meditation, it was discovering shores of shadow, solutions of continuity. In order then, to have launched, in spite of himself, into this conflict with old friends, wouldn't he have to have made a mistake at the very beginning? Or else, wasn't he forced to assume, at the risk of destroying himself, the deviations and digressions of an immense movement which had produced him and yet whose inner mechanism remained out of his reach? Or else—and as he himself had indicated in 1945, as a simple conjecture—hadn't we all fallen, for a time at least, into nonmeaning? Perhaps there was nothing else for us to do but endure, by holding fast to a few rare values. He kept his office at *Les Temps modernes* and refused to change any of his activities. But, while it brought him closer to his origins, the "rumination of his life" slowly turned him away from day-to-day politics. This was his good fortune. When someone leaves the marginal zone of the Communist Party, they have to go somewhere. They walk for a while, and suddenly find themselves on the right. Merleau never committed this treason. When he was dismissed, he took refuge in his inner life.

Summer came. The Koreans had begun fighting among themselves. We were separated from one another when the news reached us, and each of us, by himself, made his own comments on the situation. We met again for a day, in August, in Saint-Raphael. Too late. We were overjoyed to rediscover our respective gestures, voices, all those familiar singularities which all friends throughout the world love in their friends. A single flaw: our thoughts, already formed, were incommunicable. From morning to night, we only talked of war, lying by the water's edge, immobile, then at a table, then at the terrace of a café, surrounded by naked vacationers. We argued while walking, we were still arguing at the station as I waited for my train. Two deaf men—we needn't have bothered. I talked more than he did, I'm afraid, and not without vehemence. He replied calmly, briefly. His flickering, thin smile with its childlike malice, made me hope that he still hesitated. But no. He had never trumpeted his decisions. I was forced to recognize that he had made up his mind. He repeated quietly: "The only thing left for us is silence."

"Who is 'us'," I said, pretending not to understand.

"Well, us. *Les Temps modernes.*"

"You mean, you want us to put the key under the door?"

"No, not that. But I don't want us to breathe another word of politics."

"But why not?"

"They're fighting."

"Well, all right, in Korea."

"Tomorrow they'll be fighting everywhere."

"And even if they were fighting here, why should we be quiet?"

"Because brute force will decide the outcome. Why speak to what has no ears?"

I leaned out of the window and waved, as one should. I saw that he waved back, but I remained in a state of shock until the journey's end.

Very unjustly, I reproached him for wanting to muffle criticism just at the moment went the cannons were beginning to rumble. This was the farthest thing from his mind. He had simply come across an overwhelming piece of evidence. The Soviet Union, he believed, had wanted to compensate for its inferior position in the arms race by assuring itself of strategic superiority. This meant, first of all, that Stalin considered war inevitable. It was no longer a question of preventing it, but of winning. And it merely sufficed that things should appear fatal to one of the powers, for things to become so in effect. This would be one matter if the capitalist forces were the first to attack. The world would be blown to pieces but the human venture, even shattered, would still have meaning. Something would die, which at least, would have tried to be born. But since preventative aggression was coming from the socialist countries, history would only be the shroud of mankind. The end of the game. For Merleau-Ponty, as for many others, 1950 was the crucial year. Then he believed he had seen the Stalinist doctrine without its mask, and it was nothing more than Bonapartism. Either the U.S.S.R. was not the country of socialism, in which case socialism didn't exist anywhere and doubtless, wasn't even possible; or else, socialism was *that,* this abominable monster, this police state, the power of beasts of prey. In short, Bloch-Michel hadn't been able to convince Merleau-Ponty that socialist society was based upon slavery, but Merleau had convinced himself that it had engendered—whether by chance or necessity, or the two combined—imperialism. This didn't mean, of course, that he took sides with the other monster, capitalist imperialism. "But what difference is there," he said to himself, "one equals the other." Such was the metamorphosis. He refused to be outraged by the Soviet Union. "Outraged in the name of what? Throughout the world they exploit, they pillage, they slaughter. So let's not blame any one party." The Soviet Union had simply lost, in his eyes, any privileged status. It was nothing more nor less than the other powers of prey. At this period he believed that the internal reactions of history had definitely perverted its course. It would continue paralyzed, deflected by its own wastes, until the final fall. Thus, any reasonable words could only lie. Silence, the refusal of complicity was all that remained. At first he had hoped to salvage what he considered to be of value in the two systems. To the better of the two, he wanted to make a gift of what the other had acquired. Disappointed, he next resolved to denounce exploitation everywhere. But after a new disappointment, he calmly decided not to denounce anything, anywhere, until a bomb from the East or West would put an end to our brief histories. Affirmative, then negative, then silent, he hadn't moved an inch. In any case, we shall misunderstand this moderation completely if we only see it as exterior positions held together by a suicide. I have said before that his worst rages were like underwater torpedoes which only damaged him. Hope remains in the wildest fury, but in this calm funereal refusal, no hope remained.

My reflections didn't go as far as his, which is what saved me from melancholy. Merleau made light of the Koreans, whereas I saw nothing but them. He moved too quickly on to world strategy, whereas I gazed hypnotized at the blood. The fault lies, I thought, with those horse traders at Yalta, who had sliced Korea in two. We were both wrong, through ignorance, but not without good reason. Where, at that time, could we have found our knowledge? Who could have revealed to us that a military cancer was consuming the United States and that, already in the Truman era, the civilians were fighting with their backs to the walls? How, in August 1950, could we have guessed MacArthur's plan, and his intention to profit from a conflict in order to return China to the Nationalist Chinese lobby? Did we know anything about Syngman Rhee? This feudal prince of a state reduced to poverty, or about the designs of the agricultural South upon Northern industry? The communist press hardly mentioned any of that. It knew nothing more about it than we did and was satisfied with denouncing the crimes of the imperialist powers, that is, the Americans, without carrying the analysis any further. And then again, it discredited itself with a lie, before going any further. The only established fact was that the Northern troops had been the first to cross the dividing parallel. But the communist press persisted in claiming the opposite. Today we know the truth, which is that the American troops, in conjunction with the feudal warriors of Seoul, set a trap for the communists which the latter fell into. There were daily frontier incidents and the South Koreans profited from them, making such provocative moves that the North Koreans, outwitted, made the enormous mistake of attacking first, to forestall a blow which the others had no desire to strike. But the fault of the communist party everywhere was to think it would reveal the people's opinion, the only profound and true one, by offering them doctored truths. No, I have no further doubts about it. In this whole miserable business, the real warmongers were the feudalists of the South and the American imperialists. But neither do I doubt that the North attacked first. The task of the C.P. was not an easy one. If it acknowledged the facts, even for the purpose of interpreting their real meaning, its enemies everywhere would cry that it had been reduced to confessions. If denied these facts, its friends would discover the lie and withdraw. It had been less than a year since the existence of the Soviet camps had been revealed to us. We were still suspicious, ready to believe the worst. But in fact, the Soviet Union deplored this conflict, which threatened to drag it into a war which it was not the least prepared to win. Nevertheless, it had to support North Korea under pain of losing its influence in Asia. But, on the contrary, young China entered the fray, knowing itself to be the object of American covetousness. Then, too, communist China's revolutionary sense of brotherhood, its permanent interests, its international policy, all these demanded its intervention. But our information, in the summer of 1950, was too meager to permit us to distribute the blame. Merleau believed in Stalin's guilt because he had to believe in it. I didn't believe anything. I was swimming in uncertainty. This was my good luck. I wasn't even tempted to think that midnight had struck for our century, nor that we were living in the year 1000, nor that the curtain was about to rise on the Apocalypse. I viewed this scene of vast conflagration from afar, and saw only some fire.

In Paris, I saw Merleau once again. He was colder, more somber. Certain of our friends, his wife informed me, devoutly hoped that I would blow my brains out the day the Cossacks crossed our borders. It went without saying that they were also howling for Merleau's brains. Suicide didn't tempt me. I laughed. Merleau-Ponty watched me without laughing. He was imagining war and exile. He seemed lighthearted, with that boyish air which I always knew him to assume when matters threatened to turn serious. He would be an elevator man in New York. A disturbing joke. This was another version of suicide. If war broke out, it wouldn't suffice that he cease to write, he would have to refuse to teach. Imprisoned in a cage, he would only press buttons and would mortify himself through silence. This gravity is so rare that it takes one by surprise. However, it was his, ours, it is mine still. On one point, we were in agreement with those decent people who wanted our death. In politics, one must pay. We weren't men of action, but wrong ideas are crimes as much as wrong acts. How did he judge himself? He didn't tell me, but he seemed disturbed and disturbing. If ever, I said to myself, he should come to pass sentence upon himself, his hidden virulence will make him proceed immediately to execution. Later, I often wondered how his icy anger toward the U.S.S.R. could have turned into this morose attitude toward himself. If we had fallen into barbarism, we couldn't say a word, or even be silent without conducting ourselves as barbarians. Why did he reproach himself for these sincere and judicious articles? The absurdity of the world had stolen his thought from him, nothing more. He replied to that in *Signs*, with an explanation of Nizan, which is also valid for him:

> Today we understand the objections which Sartre makes to the Nizan of 1939, and why they do not hold up against him. Nizan, he said, was angry. But is this anger a circumstance of mood? It is a mode of knowledge which is not inappropriate to fundamental issues. For someone who became a Communist and who acted within the Party, day after day, there is a burden to be borne of things said and done, since he, too, said and did them. To have taken the events of 1939 as he should, Nizan would have had to be a wooden dummy, to be broken. . . . I remember having written prophetic letters in October, 1939, which, redistributed in Machiavellian fashion, the blame between the Soviet Union and us. But I hadn't spent those years in preaching Soviet alliance. Like Sartre, I was without a party—a good position from which to dispense justice serenely to the toughest side.

Merleau-Ponty, far from being a communist, had never even tried to be. It was not even a question for him of "acting within the Party," but he lived its life daily through the friends he had chosen. He didn't reproach himself for "things said and done," but for the commentaries which he had written about these things, for his decision never to propose a criticism without having tried to understand and to justify. Still, he had been right, for one does not know unless one gives. But the consequence was that he suffered because he gave for nothing. He had said: "Historic man has only one way of submitting to barbarism, and that is to create it." He was the victim of those whom he had so patiently defended, because he had made himself into their accomplice. In short, he abandoned politics at that moment when he decided that it had misled him: with dignity and guilt. He had tried to live, now he walled himself up. To be sure, he was to change his mind later about all of this, and come to other conclusions, but that was in 1955. For five years, this stone of sorrow weighed upon his heart.

There was no lack of people to explain this turnabout by his class: he was a *petit bourgeois* with liberal ideas, he went as far as he could and then stopped. How simple it all is! And those who said this were themselves *petits bourgeois,* raised in liberalism and who, notwithstanding, opted for the Manicheism which Merleau refused. In fact, it was the fault of history that the thread was broken. She wears out the men she uses, riding them to death, like horses. She chooses the actors, transforming them to the marrow by the roles she imposes upon them, and then, at the slightest change, she casts them aside for brand new ones, whom she then hurls into the fray with no preparation. Merleau began work in the milieu which the Resistance had produced. When it died, he thought that this union would eminently survive through some sort of future humanism which the classes, by their struggle itself, could construct together. He "carried out the policy of the Communist Party," but refused, nevertheless, to condemn *en bloc* the cultural heritage of the bourgeoisie. Thanks to this effort to hold on to both ends of the chain, the circulation of ideas in France never stopped entirely. Here as everywhere, people detest intelligence, but before 1958, intellectual McCarthyism was unknown. Moreover, the official thinkers of the Communist Party condemned his ideas, but their betters always knew that they would have to be revived, and that Marxist anthropology had the duty to assimilate them. Without Merleau-Ponty, do you think for a minute that Tran Duc Tao would have written his thesis, which tried to annex Husserl to Marx? In many archaic religions, there are holy persons who exercise the function of *lieur*.[8] Everything must be attached and tied by them. Merleau-Ponty played their part politically. Born of union, he refused to break it and his function was to bind. The ambiguity of his heuristic Marxism, of which he said, at the same time, that it couldn't suffice and that we had nothing else, was, I think, that it made possible meetings and discussions which will be continuous. Thus did he, for his part, make the history of this postwar period as much as it can be made by an intellectual. But, inversely, history made him while being made by him. Refusing to ratify the ruptures, hanging on with each hand to continents which were moving apart, he finally found, but without illusions, his old idea of catholicity. On both sides of the barricade, there are only men. Thus the human invention is born everywhere, We shall not judge it in terms of its origin, but on its content. It sufficed that the *lieur* use all his strength to keep the two terms of the contradiction together, to delay the explosion for as long as he could. The creations, daughters of chance and of reason, will witness that the reign of man is possible. I can't decide whether this idea was late or early in October, 1950. One thing only is certain. It was not on time. The entire world was being shattered.

Every thought translated a prejudice, or tried to be a weapon; not a tie was formed without others being broken. To aid his friends, each man had to spill the blood of his enemies. Others besides the *lieur* condemned Manicheism and violence, but they condemned it precisely because they were Manicheistic and violent: in a word, to serve the bourgeoisie. Merleau-Ponty was the only one not to hail the triumph of discord, the only one who did not agree—in the name of our "catholic" vocation—that love everywhere was to become the other side of hatred. History had given him to us; but, well before his death, it took him away.

In *Les Temps modernes,* we underplayed politics. It must be confessed that our readers weren't aware of this immediately. Sometimes we just procrastinated for so long that when we finally got around to discussing an issue everyone had forgotten it. But in the long run, people got angry. Uncertain, they asked for enlightenment. It was our bounden duty to provide them with explanations, or to admit that we were as stymied as they. We received angry letters; the critics became involved. I recently found in an old issue of *L'Observateur* a "Review of Reviews" which severely took us to task. We were aware, one and the other, one through the other, of these reproaches, but never said a word about them. This would have started the argument all over again. I was quite irritated. Did Merleau realize that he was *imposing* his silence on us? But then, as I reasoned to myself, the review belonged to him. He had defined its political orientation, and I had followed him. Even if our mutism was the ultimate consequence of this orientation, I still had to go along with him. It was harder for me to bear his smiling gloominess. He seemed to reproach us for having accompanied him in this wretched business and sometimes for having embarked on it. The truth was that he felt our growing discord and it hurt him.

We emerged from this stalemate without having decided anything, without speaking. Dzélépy and Stone sent us good, well-informed articles which revealed the war from day to day under a new light. These articles confirmed my opinions, and Merleau felt that they didn't disprove his. Thus, we didn't go back to the origins of our conflict. He didn't care much for the articles in any case, but he was too honest to reject them, and I didn't dare insist that we print them. I won't claim that we published them: they were published. We next saw them in the review. Others followed, finding the way to the printers by themselves. This was the beginning of an astonishing transformation. Although it had lost its political editor, *Les Temps modernes* persisted in obeying him in spite of himself. In other words, the review indicated its radicalism all alone. Our colleagues there had been with the review for a long time. Most of them didn't see us very often. They had changed in order to remain as close as possible to the Communist Party, believing that they were following, when, in fact, they were leading us. Young men had joined the review because of the reputation Merleau had given it. It was, so they believed, the only publication in this iron age which held, at the same time, both to its preferences and its lucidity. Of these newcomers, none were communists, but none wanted to draw away from the party. Thus, in more brutal circumstances, they restored to *Les Temps modernes* the position which Merleau had given it in 1945. But now, this came to the same as turning everything upside down. In order to remain so close to the communists, we were forced, in 1951, to break with the remains of what still called itself the left. Merleau kept silent. Or rather, with a certain degree of sadism, he gagged himself, and for the sake of our friendship and our professional conscience, forced himself to let pass a stream of tendentious articles which talked above the readers' heads and revealed, even through the mailing wrapper, through everything, even a film review, a vague, confused, impersonal point of view neither his nor entirely mine. Thus, in the course of those six years, we each discovered that the review had acquired a kind of independence, directing us as much as we directed it. In short, during the interregnum, between 1950 and 1952, a vessel without a captain recruited, by itself, the officers who saved it from perdition. If Merleau, upon contemplating this sardine rushing in the wake of a whale could still say to himself, "This is my work," he must have swallowed several fine draughts of gall. For he was deeply attached to the review, that life born of himself, and which, day after day, he kept alive. I think he suddenly viewed himself as a father who, having just the day before treated his son as a child, suddenly discovers a sullen almost hostile adolescent "warped by bad influences." Sometimes I tell myself that our common error was to have kept silent, *even then,* when we were uncertain and undecided. But no. The dice were cast.

The world had a war psychosis and I had a bad conscience. Everywhere in the West, people, nonchalant in tone but wild-eyed with fear, asked what the Russians would do with Europe when they took over. "It's inevitable," said the parlor strategists. The same people smugly evoked the "corner of Brittany" which the United States would maintain in Finistere to facilitate future debarkations. Fine. If the fighting was on our soil, there would be no problem. But other prophets believed that the U.S. would seek its real battlefields on other continents. What would we do in that case?

One answer was given by bourgeois young virgins. An entire class of a girls' *lycée* in Paris made a vow of collective suicide. The black heroism of these poor children said a great deal about the terror of their parents. I heard very dear friends, former members of the Resistance, coldly declare that they would take to the woods and wage guerrilla warfare. This time, I told them, you will be more likely to be shooting Frenchmen. I saw from their eyes that this didn't perturb them in the least, or rather, that hysteria had made them fixate on this unrealistic resolve. Others chose realism. They would take a plane for the New World. In those years, I was a little less insane than the others. I didn't believe in the Apocalypse, if for no other reason than a lazy imagination. But I became more depressed. In the subway a man cried, "*Vivement les Russes!*" I stared at him. An entire life was written on his face. Perhaps in his place, I would have said the same. I told myself: "And suppose this war really does take place?" People repeated to me: "You must go. If you stay, you will either make speeches on the Soviet radio or be silenced for good in a camp." These predictions hardly frightened me as I didn't believe in the invasion. Nevertheless, they did impress me. I saw them as intellectual games which, by pushing things to extremes, revealed to each man the necessity to choose, and the consequences of his choice. To stay, I was told, was to collaborate or die. And what about leaving? Living in Buenos Aires among rich Frenchmen, while abandoning my poorer countrymen to their fate—wasn't that collaborating? And with the enemy class? It *was* your class, people will say. So what? Does that prove it wasn't the enemy of men?

If we must betray, let it be, as Nizan said in *Les Chiens de garde,* the smallest number for the greatest good. In these morose fantasies, I felt my back to the wall. Everyone had chosen. When my turn came, I tried to hang back with neutrality. Several of us supported Rivet's candidacy, but the Communist Party had frightened away those to his right. He was beaten.

Some communists came to see me about the affair concerning Henri Martin.[9] They were trying to unite intellectuals of every variety, polished slimy or slippery, to bring the matter to the public's attention. As soon as I had even a whiff of the story, it struck me as so stupid that I unreservedly joined my name to those protesting. We decided to write a book about it, and I left for Italy. It was spring. I learned from the Italian newspapers of Duclos's arrest, the theft of his diaries, the farce of the carrier pigeons. These sordid childish tricks turned my stomach. There may have been more ignoble ones, but none more revelatory. An anticommunist is a rat. I couldn't see any way out of that one, and I never will. People may find me very naive, and for that matter, I had seen other examples of this kind of thing, which hadn't affected me. But after ten years of ruminating, I had come to the breaking point, and only needed that one straw. In the language of the Church, this was my conversion. In 1950, Merleau too, was converted. Each of us was conditioned, but in opposite directions. Our slowly accumulated disgust made the one discover, in an instant, the horror of Stalinism, and the other, that of his own class. In the name of those principles which it had inculcated into me, in the name of its humanism and its "humanities," in the name of liberty, equality, fraternity, I swore to the bourgeoisie a hatred which would only die with me. When I precipitously returned to Paris, I had to write or suffocate. Day and night, I wrote the first part of *The Communists and Peace.*

Merleau was not one to harbor any indulgence for the police methods of a dying regime. He seemed surprised by my zeal, but he strongly encouraged me to publish this essay, which, at first, was to have been only an article. When he read it, one glance was enough for him. "The U.S.S.R. wants peace," I said. "It has to have peace. The only threat of war comes from the West." I didn't say a word about the Korean conflict, but in spite of my precautions, it seemed as though I had planned a systematic refutation of our political editor, opposing point by point, my views to his. In fact, I had simply written at top speed, with rage in my heart, gaily, tactlessly. When even the best prepared conversions explode, the joy of the storm is unleashed where before there had been only total darkness, without a glimmer of light. I had never thought for a moment of sparing his feelings. But because of his affection for me, he chose to be amused by my wrath, instead of angered. However, a little while later, he pointed out that certain of our readers didn't agree with me. They shared my feelings about the tactics of our government—that went without saying—but to their mind, I made too many allowances to the communists. "How will you reply?" I asked. It so happened that "to be continued" was printed at the end of the first study. "I'll answer them," he said, "after the next issue." Around 1948, in fact, the noncommunist left elaborated the outline for a dissertation which became classic.

(1) Thesis: They demonstrated the degradation of the government, its wrongs against the working classes, showing that here the Communist Party was right. (2) Antithesis: They revealed the vileness of the Politburo and its mistakes, showing how it, too, had injured the masses. (3) Conclusion: They dismissed each of them on equal terms, indicating a middle course, without failing to cite the Scandinavian countries in their support. In Merleau's view, I had only developed the thesis. He was still hoping—without too many illusions—that the antithesis was yet to come.

It never came. Nor did the continuation of the article appear in the following issue. The truth was that I was out of breath. I realized that I didn't know anything. Giving a Chief of Police hell wasn't enough to acquire insight into the whole century. I had read everything, but I had to reread it all. I only had Ariadne's thread, but it sufficed, as it was the inexhaustible and difficult class struggle. I reread. I still had a few cells left in my brain, and I racked them to exhaustion. I met Farge, I joined the Movement for Peace. I went to Vienna. One day I brought my second article to the printer which was, in fact, only a rough draft. The outline for the dissertation entitled, "The Third Force," was definitely cast aside. Far from attacking the communists, I declared myself a fellow traveler. At the end of the article, I once again noted "To be continued," but there was no further doubt permissible. Merleau only saw the article in the final proofs. The fact that I didn't give them to him myself was an aggravating circumstance. He read them at just that moment when he had to make up the issue. Why hadn't I submitted my manuscript to him, since he had never failed to submit his to me? Was I taking myself seriously for good now? I don't think that was it. Nor do I think I was fleeing from his remonstrances or objections. Rather would I blame that heedlessness of rage which, refusing all caution, heads straight for its object. I believed, I knew, I was disenchanted. Consequently, I would not go through all that again. In our all but confidential review, one had to shout to be heard. I would shout. I would stand on the side of the communists, and I would proclaim it. I am not going to give the objective reasons for my attitude. They aren't important here. I will only say that they alone counted, that I considered them urgent ones and that I still do. As for the heart's reasons, I find two. I felt that I was being prodded by our new staff, which was waiting for us to take the step. I knew that I could count on their approval, and again, I realize now that I rather resented Merleau for having imposed his silence upon me in 1950. The review had been floating for two years. I wasn't going to stand for it any more. Let each one judge. I have no excuse, I don't want any. What may be of interest in this adventure—which each of us lived painfully—is that it shows the sources from which discord may spring in the heart of the most loyal friendship and closest agreement. New circumstances and a disintegrating institution—our conflict had no other causes. The institution was our unspoken contract. Valid when Merleau talked and I was silent, this accord had never precisely defined our respective areas of specialization. Each of us, without even admitting it to himself, had appropriated the review. On one side, as in "The Caucasian Chalk Circle," there was my official and nominal paternity (for in everything concerning politics, mine was only that) and, on the other side, Merleau's paternity by adoption, five years of jealous care. Everything came to a head abruptly, in exasperation. We learned that each of us, by mutism as well as speech, had compromised the other. We only survived when we had but one thought, which was the case as long as I didn't think for myself. When two heads are under the same hat, how is the right one to be chosen? Seen from the outside, one could say that things had determined their own course. This is true, but it is too easy an explanation. It is true in general that empires crumble and parties die when they are no longer moving in the direction of history. And we must still further acknowledge that this idea, perhaps the most difficult of all, is carelessly handled by most writers. But how can someone who, even cautiously, applies the great social forces to himself, make use of them to explain the growth, life, and death of micro-organisms like *Les Temps modernes*? Would he say that a collective movement doesn't proceed without partial disasters? And then, whatever may have been the case, we had to live out this adventure by ourselves, hear the sentence pronounced upon us, execute it, and, as Merleau later said, institute it. And in all of this, there were wrongs on both sides, and in both our hearts, a futile good will.

Merleau could have ended things then and there. He could have provoked a quarrel or written against me. Eloquently, he abstained from either of these. For a time we remained this strange couple: two friends who still loved one another, each persisting in his opposition to the other, with but one voice between them. I admired his moderation all the more since, at this same time, we had some loudly announced defections. One of our oldest collaborators left us in haste for the *Nouvelle nouvelle revue française* where he immediately began putting "the Hitlero-Stalinists" on trial, plaiting a martyr's wreath for Lucien Rebatet. I wonder what is left of that one—possibly a dust speck of boredom off in the provinces, nothing more.

During the following years, I had the delight of witnessing several similar disintegrations. In order to fill the gaps and to solicit some articles, I held a meeting of our associates on alternate Sundays at my apartment. Merleau-Ponty came assiduously, the last to arrive, the first to leave, conversing in a low voice with everyone about everything except the review. He nevertheless had allies there, such as Claude Lefort, who disapproved of my position; Lefevre-Pontalis, who wasn't interested in politics; Colette Audry, who feared my excesses; and Erval. Merleau would not have had any trouble becoming the head of a strong opposition. He refused on grounds of principle—a review isn't a parliamentary assembly—and friendship. He refused to influence the group, while observing without pleasure that the group was influencing me. The majority was orienting itself toward this critical comradeship which he was just abandoning. Even in the face of virulent anticommunism, it proposed to put a damper on the critics by insisting upon this quality of association. Above all, I think that Merleau found these meetings ridiculous and wholly unproductive. So they were after awhile, not without his mutism making its contribution. But what should he have said? I never failed to ask for his opinions. He never gave them. It was as though he wanted to make it clear to me that I had no business asking his views on details, since I hadn't deigned to consult him on the essentials. He probably felt that I was appeasing my conscience cheaply and had no desire to come to my aid. My conscience, in fact, was clear, and I reproached Merleau for refusing his help. This complaint will seem unfair. All considered, it was asking him to collaborate in an enterprise which he openly disavowed. I realized this. But, after all, he was still one of ours, and from time to time, he still couldn't help taking the initiative—in general, a happy one. If, beginning in 1950, he had resigned his post as political editor, he was still editor-in-chief. In all ambiguous situations—prolonged to avoid a rupture—everything we do, in one direction or the other, makes matters worse.

But our misunderstanding had more serious causes, of an altogether different order. I thought that while I was being faithful to his thought of 1945, he was abandoning it. He thought he was remaining true to himself and I betraying him. I claimed to be carrying on his work, he accused me of spoiling it. This conflict didn't stem from us, but from the world, and both of us were right. His political thought was born of the Resistance, which means from a united left. Within this union, it would have slid toward the most extreme radicalism, but it needed this atmosphere of triple entente. The Communist Party guaranteed him the practical efficacity of common action. The allied parties of the left assured him that they would preserve humanism and certain traditional values by giving them real content. When, about 1950, everything exploded, he saw only debris. In his eyes, my madness was to hang on to a piece of flotsam while waiting for the rest to reconstruct the vessel automatically. For my part, I took sides when the left crumbled because I believed its reconstruction was up to us. And certainly not from the top, but from the bottom. To be sure, we had no contact whatever with the masses, and we were, consequently, without any power. But our job was no less clear. Faced with the unholy alliance of the bourgeoisie and the socialist leaders, we had no other alternative but to stay as close to the communist party as possible, and implore the others to join us. We had to attack the bourgeoisie without letup, laying bare its politics, tearing its pitiful arguments to shreds. We certainly wouldn't refrain from criticizing the communist party or the Soviet Union, but without it being a question—impossible task—of changing them. In the eyes of our readers, we hoped to prefigure future agreements by setting this minuscule example: an accord with the communists which took nothing away from our freedom of judgment. Thus was I able to imagine, without bad faith, that I was continuing Merleau-Ponty's attitude.

In fact, however, the contradiction was not in us, but, beginning with 1945, in our position. To be for the whole is to refuse to choose among its parts. The privileged status which Merleau accorded the communists was not an option: he considered their regime barely preferable. When the moment to choose came, he remained true to himself, and jumped ship so as not to survive the unity which had gone under. I, a newcomer, chose the party precisely in the name of that unity. I believed that this unity couldn't be recreated, unless in proximity to the party. Thus the same idea of union, at a few years' remove, had led one of us to reject the very choice which it had imposed upon the other. Everything comes from structure and from event at the same time. France is so constituted that the party couldn't take power by itself. So, first of all, we had to think in terms of alliances. In the tripartite government, Merleau could still see the successor to the Popular Front. But in 1952, without any change in the demographic structure of the country, I could no longer confuse the Third Force—a simple right-wing front—with the union of the masses. We would never be able to seize power from the right, however, without first bringing together all the forces of the left. The Popular Front remained the necessary means of conquest at just the moment when the Cold War made it an impossibility. While waiting for a regrouping which seemed very far away, we still had to keep its possibility alive from day to day by concluding alliances with the party on a local basis. To choose or not to choose. After only five years, these attitudes aimed at the same objective. Two attitudes? A single one, rather, opposing us like two adversaries, by forcing each of us to insist upon choosing one of his two contradictory components. In order to remain true to his refusals, Merleau forgot his desire for union. And to give future unity a chance, I forgot my universalism and chose to begin by accumulating disunity.

These words may seem abstract, but in fact we had to live these historical determinants, which means that we lent them our life, our passions, our skin. I made fun of Merleau's "spontaneity." Indeed, in 1945 union did seem complete. He had a good headstart to carry him along. He, in turn, made fun of my naïveté and *voluntarism.*[10] But by 1952, union was over. And banking on false hopes didn't suffice to bring it back. The truth was that we were each recruited according to our aptitudes: Merleau when it was the time of subtleties, and I, when the time of the assassins had come. Lefort and I had some lively discussions. I proposed that he criticize me in the review itself. He accepted and submitted quite a nasty article. Angered, I replied in kind. Merleau, as a mutual friend, witnessed his becoming, despite himself, burdened with a new job. He had to volunteer as a mediator. Lefort had the courtesy to submit his article to Merleau. I did the same with mine. It was my article which exasperated him. He informed me, with his usual gentle manner, that he would resign for good if I didn't cut a certain paragraph, which, as I think about it now, was unnecessarily violent. I seem to recall that Lefort made some sacrifices on his part. This didn't prevent both articles from exuding ill will. Merleau was devoted to both of us. All the blows which we dealt each other fell upon him. Without entirely agreeing with Lefort, he was closer to his point of view than to mine. Suddenly his tongue loosened. And so did mine. We launched into a long and futile explanation which bounced from one subject to another and from one discussion to another. Is there a spontaneity of the masses? Can groups find their cohesion from within? Ambiguous questions which at times took us back to politics, to the role of the Communist Party, to Rosa Luxemburg, to Lenin, and at other times, back to sociology, to existence itself, which means, to philosophy, to our "style of life," to our "anchorage," and to ourselves. Each word brought us back to the way of the world and to our own temperaments, and vice-versa. Beneath our intellectual divergences of 1941, so calmly accepted when Husserl alone was the cause, we discovered, astounded, that our conflicts had, at times, stemmed from our childhood, or went back to the elementary differences of our two organisms; and that, at other times, they were between the flesh and the skin; in one of us, hypocrisies, complicities, a passion for activism hiding his defeats, and in the other, retractile emotions and a desperate quietism. Of course, none of these were completely true or completely false. We quarrelled because we put the same ardor into convincing, understanding, and accusing ourselves. This passionate dialogue which started in my office, midway between good and bad faith, continued in Saint Tropez, was resumed again in Paris, on the benches of the Café Procope, and continued still in my apartment. I went on a trip and he wrote me a long letter. I answered it when the temperature was 95 degrees in the shade, which didn't help matters. What were we hoping for? At heart, nothing. We were carrying out the "labor of rupture" in the sense in which Freud has so aptly shown that mourning is labor. I think that the object of this dismal rumination *à deux,* this reassessment which made us lose our way, was to break our ties, one by one, with small jolts of anger, to cloud the transparency of our friendship until it had made us strangers. This undertaking, had it completed its course, would have ended in complete estrangement. One incident, however, intervened.

A Marxist whom I met by chance proposed writing on "the contradictions of capitalism" for the review. As he said, it was a familiar subject, but one which was poorly understood and upon which he could throw some new light. He didn't belong to the party, but was a party in himself, and one of the most rigid. He was so filled with the awareness of doing me a favor, that I was convinced. I warned Merleau, who knew the man, but he didn't say a word. As I was obliged to leave Paris, the article was submitted in my absence. It was a complete zero. As editor-in-chief, Merleau couldn't bring himself to let it appear without prefacing it by a "heading" which he wrote, and which presented in so many words, our apologies to the readers. He also took this occasion to reproach the writer in two lines for not having even mentioned the contradictions of socialism; that would have to wait for another time, wouldn't it? On my return, Merleau said nothing about any of this. Warned by a colleague, I had a look at the proofs and read the article under his heading, all the more irritated by the former as I found the latter still less defensible. Merleau, having "locked up" the issue, had in turn gone away and couldn't be reached. Alone, in a state of joyous rage, I deleted the heading and the article appeared bareheaded. You can guess the rest. A few days later Merleau received the final proofs of the review, and realizing that his text had been omitted, took it all as badly as possible. He rushed to the telephone and gave me his resignation, this time for good. We were on the telephone for more than two hours. Jean Cao, grimly listening to half of this conversation, perched on an armchair near the window, thought he was witnessing the last moments of the review. We accused each other mutually of abusing power. I suggested an immediate meeting. I tried in every way possible to make him change his mind. He was unshakable. For several months I didn't see him. He never again appeared at the offices of *Les Temps modernes,* and never had anything to do with it again.

If I tell this idiotic story at all, it is, first of all, because of its very futility. I think it over and say to myself, "It's heartbreaking," and at the same time, "It had to end that way." Just that way, badly, stupidly, inevitably. The canvas was ready, the end established in advance, like the *commedia dell' arte.* The only thing left for us to do was to improvise the rupture. We did it badly, but good or bad, we played the scene out, and others took our place on stage. I don't know which of us was the more to blame, and I have no consuming interest in that aspect of it. For in fact, the final guilt was written into our two roles. It had long been established that we would separate because of mutual wrongs, on a childish pretext. Because our collaboration couldn't continue, we had to break with each other, or the review dissolve.

Without *Les Temps modernes,* the events of 1950 would not have had that much influence on our friendship. We would simply have fought over politics more often, or taken greater care never to discuss them. The fact is that the event generally touches people on one side, and they feel nothing except a dull shock, an unfathomable anguish. Unless, on the other hand, the event leaps at their throat and bowls them over in passing. In either case, they don't know what hit them. But scarcely has chance placed in our hands the most infinitesimal means of influencing or expressing historical movement, than the forces leading us are immediately stripped bare, causing us to discover "our cast shadow" on the blinding wall of objectivity. The review was nothing: just a sign of the times, like a hundred thousand others. But no matter. It belonged to history. Through it, both of us experienced our substance as historical objects. It was our objectivization, Through it, the course of things gave us our map and our double function; at first more united than we would ever have been without it, and then more divided. That goes without saying. Once we are caught in the gears, we are dragged in all the way. The little freedom left us is resumed in the instant where we decide whether or not to put our finger in. In a word, our beginning belongs to us. Afterwards we can only will our destiny.

The beginning wasn't bad—for this one reason, still mysterious to me. Contrary to the desire of all our colleagues, Merleau had, from the very first day, claimed the weakest position on the review. Doing everything, with no names mentioned, refusing any status which might defend him against my vagaries or my shifts of gear, it was as though he only wanted to receive his power from a living accord, as though his most useful weapon would be its fragility, and as though his moral authority alone must guarantee his functions. Nothing protected him, and because of that he was not bound by anything or anyone. Present among us, as much in command as I was, and yet light and free as air. Had he agreed to having his name on the cover, he would have had to combat me, perhaps overthrow me. But he had envisaged this possibility from the first day, and refused on principle to wage a battle which would have demeaned us both and for no good reason. When the day came, a telephone call sufficed. He had made his decision, informed me of it, and disappeared. There was a sacrifice, nonetheless: the sacrifice was himself, *Les Temps modernes,* and me. We were all victims of this purifying murder. Merleau mutilated himself, leaving me in the clutches of these fearful allies who, so I thought, would gnaw me to the bone, or reject me as they had rejected him. He abandoned his review to my incompetence. This aggressive expiation must have absorbed the greater part of his resentment. In any case, it allowed us to interrupt the labor of rupture and to save our friendship.

At first, he avoided me. Did he fear that the sight of me would awaken his pain? Perhaps. But it seems to me more likely that he wanted to give our common future a chance. I would run into him on occasion. We always stopped to talk for a minute. When we were on the point of going our separate ways, I would suggest that he come and see us tomorrow, next week. He would reply with a firmly courteous, "I'll call you," and he never called. But another labor had begun—the liquidation of grudges, *rapprochement*—all that was ended by grief. In 1952 Merleau lost his mother.

He was as devoted to her as to his own life. More exactly, she *was* his life. He owed his infant happiness to the care which she lavished upon him. She was the lucid witness of his childhood, and because of that, when exile came, she remained its guardian. Without her, the past would have been swallowed up in the sands. Through her, it was preserved—out of reach, but alive. Until his mother's death, Merleau-Ponty lived that golden age by mourning it, like a paradise each day a little more distant, and in the carnal and daily presence of she who had given it to him. All the connivance of mother and son aimed at taking them back to old memories. Thus, for as long as she lived Merleau's banishment retained its gentle quality, and occasionally, was just reduced to the naked difference which separates two inseparable lives. As long as they were two to reconstruct, and sometimes to revive the long prehistory of his gestures, his passions, his tastes, he still had the hope of reconquering this immediate accord with all those things which are the good fortune of children who are loved. But when his mother died, the wind slammed all the doors shut, and he knew that they were closed forever. Memories *à deux* are rituals. The survivor finds only dead leaves, only words. When, a short time later, Merleau-Ponty met Simone de Beauvoir, he said to her casually, with that sad gaiety which masked his most sincere moments: "But I am more than half dead." His childhood had died, and for the second time. As a young man, he had dreamed of finding his salvation through the Christian community, as an adult, through political comradeship. Twice disappointed, he suddenly discovered the reason for these defeats: "to be saved," on all levels, on all orders would be to begin our first years anew. We repeat ourselves incessantly, we never start again. Seeing his childhood founder he understood himself. His only yearning had been to find it again, and this impossible desire was his particular vocation, his destiny. What was left of it? Nothing. For some time now, he had been silent. Silence wasn't enough, he became a recluse, only leaving his office for the Collège de France. I saw no more of him until 1956, and even his best friends saw him less.

I should at least indicate what was going on in his mind in the course of the three years which separated us. But, as I have warned my readers, my only object here is to tell the story of a friendship. For this reason I am more interested in the development of his ideas, than in the ideas themselves. Others will analyze the latter in detail, and much better than I could do. It is the man whom I want to reestablish, not as he was to himself, but as he lived in my life and I lived in his. I don't know to what degree this can be truthful. People will find me a questionable character, painting me negatively because of the way that I paint Merleau. Very well. In any case, I am sincere. I am describing things as I understood them.

Pain is emptiness. Other people would have remained hollow simulacra of hermits. But his pain, at the same time as it severed him from us, led Merleau back to his first meditation, to that good fortune which made him so unfortunate. I am struck by the unity of this life. Well before the war, this young Oedipus turned back upon his origins, trying to understand the rational unreason which had produced him. At just the moment when he was approaching it and writing the *Phenomenology of Perception,* history was at our throats, but he struggled against it without interrupting his research. Let us call that the first period of his reflection. The second period begins with the Occupation and continues until 1950. His thesis finished, he seemed to have abandoned his investigation in order to interrogate the history and politics of our time. But his concerns had changed in appearance only. Everything coalesced since history is a form of envelopment, since we are "anchored" in it, since we have to be placed historically, not *a priori,* nor by some sort of "all-surveying system of thought," but by the concrete experience of the movement which carries us along. If we really read them, Merleau's commentaries on politics are only a political experience in the process of becoming by itself and in every sense of the word, the *subject* of meditation. If writings are acts, we can say that he acted in order to appropriate his action and to find himself in depth. Viewed in the general prospective of history, Merleau is an intellectual of middle-class background, made radical by the Resistance and carried away by the breakdown of the left.[11] Trapped from within, his life turned back upon itself to seize the advent of the human in all its singularity. And however cruel, it is also obvious that his disappointment of 1950 must have been of help to him. It removed him from our grim fields of battle, but, by the same token, it presented him with an enigma—*the self*—neither quite the same nor quite another. Unlike Stendhal, he was not trying to understand the individual he was, but rather, in the manner of Montaigne, to understand the person, that incomparable mixture of the particular and the universal. It didn't suffice, however. Knots still remained to be untied. And he was still trying when his mother's death intervened to cut them. One can only admire how, through his grief, he appropriated this stroke of bad luck, converting it into his most rigorous necessity. Although signs of it had appeared for several years before, the third period of his meditation began in 1953.

Initially, this period was one of renewed inquiry and of mourning, at the same time. Thrown back upon himself for the third time by this death, he wanted it to enlighten his birth. *Something must happen* to the newborn infant, this seer-made-visible, who appears in the visible work: something, anything, even if it is only dying. He called this first tension between appearance and disappearance "primordial historicity." It is in it and through it that everything happens. From our first moment, we are precipitated into irreversible inflexibility. To survive birth, even for an instant, is an adventure, as it is an adventure not to survive. We do not escape this unreason which he calls our contingency. It is not enough to say that we are born to die, we are born at the moment of death. But at the same moment, the fact of his being alive prevented his mother from disappearing entirely. Not that he believed in our survival. His refusal to be considered an atheist in the last years wasn't out of consideration to his brief surge of Christianity in the past, but was simply to give the dead a chance. This precaution wasn't enough. What was he really doing by reviving a dead woman through ritual? Did this revive her by a dream or was it *instituting* her?

Life, death, existence, being: he had to stand at their crossroads in order to carry on his dual investigation. In one sense, none of the ideas which he had advanced in his thesis had changed. But in another sense, they were all changed beyond recognition. He buried himself in the night of nonknowledge, in search of what he then called "the fundamental." For example, we read in *Signs:* "What is of interest to the philosopher (in anthropology) is precisely that it takes man as he is, in his effective situation in life and knowledge. The philosopher interested in anthropology is not one who wants to explain or construct the world, but he who aims at inserting us more deeply into being."[12]

At the level of presence and absence, the philosopher appears, blind and clairvoyant. If *knowledge* claims to explain or construct, he doesn't even want *to know.* He lives within this mixture of oxygen and combustible gases which we call the True, but he doesn't deign to package truths, not even for distribution in the schools or textbooks. He does nothing but dig deeper, nothing but allow himself to flow, alive, without interrupting his endeavors, into the ludicrous abyss, the only one accessible to him in order to seek within himself the door opening onto the night of what is not yet the self. This is to define philosophy as meditation in the Cartesian sense of the word, which means as endlessly sustained tension between existence and being. That ambiguous rib is the origin. In order to think, he must be. The slightest thought transcends being by instituting him for others. This happens in a twinkling. It is the absurd and definitive birth, an indestructible event which changes into advent and defines the singularity of a life by its vocation for death. Savage and opaque, it is the work which retains being within its recesses. This unreason is the undertaking which will subsist in the community as its future *raison d'être.* And above all, it is language, that "fundamental," for the Word is only Being in the heart of man thrown out to exhaust itself within *meaning.* In short, it is man, burst forth in a single spurt, transcending his presence in being, to reach toward his presence in the other, transcending the past to reach toward the future, transcending each thing and his selfness to reach toward the sign. For this reason, Merleau, toward the end of his life, was inclined to give an ever more important place to the unconscious. He must have agreed with Lacan's formula: "The unconscious is structured like a language." But, as a philosopher, he stood at the opposite pole from psychoanalysis. The unconscious fascinated him, as being at once the chain and the hinge of being and existence.

One day Merleau-Ponty became furious with dialectic and maltreated it. Not, as he explains in *Signs,* that he would have agreed to its omission. The positive always has its negative corollary and vice-versa. Consequently, the one will flow eternally through the other in a circular motion. As it turns, the philosopher turns as well. He must follow the circuitous route of his object scrupulously, and in a spirit of discovery, must penetrate his night as a spiral. Thus, Merleau-Ponty developed the habit of following each No until he saw it transformed into Yes, and each Yes until it changed into No. He became so skillful at this *jeu de furet*[13] that he virtually developed it into a method which I would call reversal. Through it, he jumps from one point of view to another, denying and affirming, changing more to less and less to more. Everything is contradictory and also true. I shall give only one example of this: "At least as much as Freud explains adult behavior by an inherited fatality of childhood, he also points out a *premature* adult life within childhood, as exemplified by . . . a first choice in relating to others in terms of generosity and avarice."[14] *At least as much:* for him, contradictory truths never fight one another. There is no danger of their blocking movement or provoking an explosion. Moreover, are they, strictly speaking, contradictory? Even if we accept this, we must recognize that contradiction, weakened by circular motion, loses its function as a "mobile of history," appearing in Merleau's view as the indication of a paradox, the living sign of fundamental ambiguity. In short, Merleau-Ponty accepts thesis and antithesis. It is synthesis which he rejects, reproaching it for changing dialectic into a building game. Spirals, on the contrary, are never allowed to conclude. Instead, each one manifests in its own way, the merry-go-round of being and existence. Children of the primordial slime, we shall be reduced to impressions in clay, if we don't begin with its denial. Let us turn things around. We, whose very existence is the negation of that which is, what do we do from the first to the last instant, if not presage being, institute and restore it by means of and on behalf of others, within the milieu of intersubjectivity? Instituting and presaging being is all very well, but as for seeing it face to face—we cannot count on that. We only know it through signs. Thus, the philosopher never stops going around in circles, nor stops the treadmill from turning:

> This being, perceived through the stirrings of time, always sighted by our perception, by our carnal being, but towards which there can be no question of traveling, because the distance covered would remove his consciousness of "being, this fleeing of far-off distances," as Heidegger says, always proposed for our transcendence, is the dialectical idea of being, as defined by Parmenides, beyond the multiplicity of things which are, and by this principle, sighted through them, since separated from them—this being would be only a flash of lightning and night sky.[15]

Merleau was still flirting. In this text he again speaks of dialectic, but he is not referring to Hegel, but to Parmenides and Plato. The role of meditation is to trace a line of circumference around its *subject* passing incessantly through the same points. But just what does this line perceive? An absence? A presence? The two together? Refracted through a prism, exterior being is broken down, multiplied, placed out of reach. But by the same movement, it interiorizes itself, becoming being from within, present entirely, forever, without losing its intangibility. And naturally, the inverse is also true. Interior being, this dangerous and miserly coil within us, does not cease to manifest its assimilation to nature, the indefinite unfolding of exterior being. Thus, turning and meditating, Merleau remained true to his spontaneous thought, to slow rumination pierced by rays of light. This is what he was discreetly erecting by means of a method which takes the form of a decapitated dialectic.

This descent into Hell at last allowed him to find the most profound merry-go-round of all—a discovery of the heart. And its proof is that it strikes with a somber density. I shall now tell how he informed me of it, almost two years ago today. Merleau painted himself in his subject matter, subtle and laconic, tackling problems head on when he seems to touch them only obliquely. I asked him whether he was working. He hesitated. "I may possibly write on nature," and then to lead me on, he added, "I read a sentence in Whitehead which struck me: 'Nature is in tatters.' " As you may have already guessed, he didn't add another word. I left him without having understood this. I was studying "dialectical materialism" at the time, and the word "nature" evoked for me our psychochemical perceptions. Still another misunderstanding. I had forgotten that, in his view, nature was the sensory world, this "decidedly universal" world where we encounter things and creatures, our own bodies and those of others. To understand him, I had to await the publication of his last article: "Eye and Mind." I imagine that this long essay must have formed part of the book he was writing. It was, in any case, related to it, and constantly refers to an idea which is going to be expressed, but which remains unformulated.

More hostile than ever to intellectualism, Merleau interrogated the painter and his savage, manual thinking. Through his paintings, he tries to seize the meaning of painting. At these times, nature reveals her tatters to him. That far off mountain, he asks us in so many words, how does it manifest itself? By discontinuous, at times intermittent signals, slivers of scattered phantasmagoria, reflections of light, plays of shadow. This dust surprises us by its inconsistency. But our eye is precisely a "computer of being." With these airborne signs it will produce an accumulated heap of the heaviest terrestrial mass. Our gaze is no longer content "to perceive being through the motion of time." We could say that its present mission was to erect from this motion the ever-absent unity starting from multiplicity. "Doesn't this unity exist?" we will ask. It is and it is not, like the dead clothes which haunt the tatters, like Mallarmé's rose, "absent from each bouquet." Being is through us who are through it. All of this, to be sure, does not work without the other. This is how Merleau explains Husserl's difficult affirmation. "The transcendental conscience is intersubjectivity." Nothing, he thinks, can see without its being at the same time visible. How could we grasp what is if we were not? Here it is not a question of simple "noesis" producing its noetic correlative through these apparitions. Once again, to think we must be. The thing which is constituted through everyone, by means of each one, always an endlessly beveled whole, returns us, each through all, to our ontological status. We are the sea. Having floated to the surface, every piece of flotsam is as innumerable as the waves, through them and like them absolute. The painter is the privileged artisan, the best witness of this mediated reciprocity. "The body is caught in the fabric of the world, but the world is made of the stuff of my body." A new spiral, but more profound than the others because it touches upon the "labyrinth of incarnation." Through my flesh, nature is made flesh. But, inversely, if painting is possible, then the ribs of being which the painter perceives within the thing, and which he fixes on canvas must designate within himself the "flexions" of his being. "The painting . . . doesn't relate to anything among empirical things, save on condition of being autofigurative: it is only a show of things by being a show of nothing, demonstrating how things become things and the world, the world." This is precisely what gives "the occupation of painter an urgency which surpasses every other urgency." Through its figuration of being from the outside, it presents being to others from the inside, *his* flesh and theirs. It is not even enough to say that it presents. For, as Merleau says, "Culture is advent." Thus the artist has the sacred function of instituting being within the milieu of men, which means going beyond "the layers of brute being of which the activist is unaware," toward this eminent being which is *meaning*. And this is not only true of the artist, but of each one of us as well. "Expression," he says, "is the fundamental of the body." And what is there to express if not *being*. We do not make a move without restoring, instituting and bringing about its presence. Primordial historicity, our birth at the moment of death, is that surge from the depths through which the event becomes man, who, by naming things, declines his being. Such is also the history of the group, in its most basic sense. "How should we define this milieu where a form burdened with contingency suddenly opens a cycle of the future and governs it with the authority of the established, if not as history?"

This was the point of departure for his final thoughts. I have told how his last philosophy, "weighed down by contingency," patiently gnawing at chance and by chance interrupted, began with a discovery of the heart. Against grief and absence, it is he, in turn, who discovers himself. Merleau was the real "computer of being." He was left with a handful of relics and memories, but our gaze doesn't have far to go before it brings forth being from the mountain. With the rags and tatters of memory, the heart tears being from the dead. With the event which killed them, it brings about their advent. It is not only a question of restoring their eternity to the smiles and words which have disappeared. To live is to deepen them, to transform them, by our smiles and words into themselves, a little more each day, endlessly. There is a progress of the dead, and this is our history. Thus Merleau made himself into his mother's guardian as she had been the guardian of his childhood. Born of her at the moment of death, he wanted death to be her rebirth. For this reason, he found more real flowers in absence than in presence. "Eye and Mind" contains a strange quotation. In *Marianne,* Marivaux, reflecting upon the force and dignity of the passions, sings the praises of men who remove themselves from life rather than deny their being. What appealed to Merleau in these few lines was their revelation of an indestructible slab beneath the transparency of the shallow stream which is life. But don't think that he was returning to Cartesian substance. Hardly had he closed the quotation marks and taken up his pen again on his own account, than the slab crumbled into discontinuous sparks, again becoming that ragged being we must continue to be, perhaps only a disorderly imperative, and one which, at times, may be better ordered by suicide than by a living victory. But, by the same movement, since that is our rule, we shall institute within the human community, the being of the dead through our death, our being through that of the dead.

How far did he go in those somber years which changed him into himself? Reading him, at times, it would seem that being invents man in order to make itself manifest through him. Didn't Merleau, from time to time, think he perceived some sort of transcendent mandate "hidden in immanence" within us? In one of his articles, he congratulates a mystic for having written that God is below us, and Merleau added, in so many words, "Why not?" He dreamed of this Almighty who would need men, who would still be called into question in each one's heart, and yet would remain total being, unceasingly, infinitely instituted by intersubjectivity, the only one who we shall lead to the fount of our being, and who will share with us all the insecurity of the human adventure. Here we are obviously dealing only with a metaphorical indication. But the fact that he chose this metaphor is not without significance. Everything is there:

the discovery and the risk of being is below us, a gigantic beggar-woman clad in rags, we need only an imperceptible change for her to become *our task*. God, the task of man? Merleau never wrote this, and forbade himself even to think it. Nothing says that he may not, at times, have dreamed it, but his method of inquiry was much too rigorous to allow him to advance anything as which he hadn't established. He worked without haste. He was waiting.

People have claimed that he came closer to Heidegger. This is doubtless true, but it must be qualified. As long as his childhood was assured him Merleau felt no need to go back to the roots of his research. When his mother died, and childhood was abolished with her, absence and presence, being and nonbeing, flowed into one another. Through phenomenology, and without ever departing from it, Merleau hoped to rejoin the imperatives of ontology. That which is no more, is not yet, and never will be.

It is for man to give being to beings. These tasks evolved from his life and from his bereavement. Through them, he found occasion to reread Heidegger and to understand him better, but not to be influenced by him. Their paths crossed, that was all. Being is the only concern of the German philosopher. And in spite of a philosophy which they at times share, Merleau's principal concern remained man. When the former speaks of "the opening towards being," I feel a sense of alienation. I am certainly not denying that disturbing words come from Merleau's pen as well, for example: "Henceforth, the irrelative is not nature itself, nor is it the system of seizure of absolute conscience, nor is it even man, but rather, this 'teleology' which is written and thought between quotation marks—the joints and framework of a being which effects itself by means of man." The quotation marks have nothing to do with the problem. But it doesn't matter. This was said in passing. It is unfortunate that a man can still write today that the absolute is not man; but what he denies our domain, he accords to no other. His irrelative is really a reciprocal relationship closed in upon itself. Man is designated by his fundamental vocation which is to institute being, but equally so, being is designated by its destiny which is to effect itself through man. I have told how, at least twice—in the Christian community and in the brotherhood of political struggle—Merleau had sought envelopment within immanence, and had collided against the transcendent. More than ever avoiding any recourse to Hegelian synthesis, his lost thoughts attempt to resolve the contradiction which he had lived. He lets transcendence flow into immanence, there to be dissolved at the same time as it is protected against annihilation by its very impalpability. It will be only absence and supplication, deriving its all-encompassing power from its infinite weakness. And, in a certain sense, isn't this the fundamental contradiction of humanism? Can dialectical materialism—in whose name many will try to criticize this meditation—do without an ontology? Looking at this more closely, however, and brushing aside the absurd theory of a reflection, don't we see, discreetly implicit, the idea of a layer of brute being which produces and sustains action and thought?

No. For the man who wrote this a few months before his death never stopped being a humanist: "In that instant where *l'homme-éclair* is kindled, everything is explained." And then what? To effect being is to consecrate it, which to be sure means to humanize it. Merleau doesn't maintain that we must perish in order for being to be, but just the contrary, that we shall institute being by that same act which causes us to be born human. Pascalian more than ever before, he repeats to us again: "Man is absolutely distinct from the animal species precisely in that he has no original equipment whatever, and is the dwelling-place of the contingent, sometimes taking the form of a kind of miracle and other times, the form of an adversity without motive." That suffices for man never to be the animal of a species, or the object of a universal concept, but rather, as soon as he appears, he is the explosion of event. But he finds the same lesson in the humanist Montaigne. "The explanations which define man as metaphysics or physics are those which Montaigne rejects in advance, since it is still man who 'proves' philosophies and science, and they are explained by him, rather than he by them." Man will never think man. He makes him at every instant. And isn't this real humanism? Man will never be the total object of knowledge, for he is the subject of history.

The philosopher had grown somber, but it is still not hard to find a certain optimism in his last works. Nothing comes to an end, nothing is lost. An endeavor is born, instituting with one stroke *its* man—all man is a flash—and dies with him, or insanely survives him, only to end, in any case, in disaster, and at this same instant of disaster, it opens a door to the future. Spartacus fighting and dying is all of man. Who can say it better? A word is all words gathered up in a few sounds: a picture is all of painting. "In this sense," he says, "progress both is and is not." History constantly moves into our prehistoric environment. With each flash of light, the whole is illuminated, instituted, unravels and vanishes, immortal. Apelles, Rembrandt, Klee have each, in turn, *revealed being* within a defined civilization, with the means at hand. And well before the first of these was born, all of painting was already manifest in the caves of Lascaux.

Precisely because he is ceaselessly resumed in this ever-renewed flash of light, there will be a future for man. And there will also be the contingency of good and of evil. Merleau no longer favored or condemned anyone. Adversity had placed us within a hairsbreadth of barbarism. The miracle, always and everywhere possible, could make us emerge from it. Since each gesture of our body and our language, each act of political life "spontaneously" takes into account others, transcending the singular within itself to reach toward the universal, so, although it is in no sense inevitable or promised, and although we ask less that it improve us in our being than that it clean up the wastes of our life, a *relative progress* has to be the most likely conjecture. "Very probably, experience will end by eliminating the wrong solutions." It was, I think, in this hope that Merleau agreed to write a few political commentaries for *L'Express.* The East and West, two growing economies, two industrial societies, each of them torn by contradictions. He would have hoped, above and beyond their regimes, to extricate their common needs at the level of their infrastructure, or, at least, their lines of convergence. This was his way of remaining true to himself. Again, it was a matter of refusing the Manichean option. There had been unity once. Before the loss of this minor paradise, he had wanted to denounce exploitation everywhere. Then he had shut himself away in silence. He emerged from this silence to seek everywhere for reasons to hope. Without any illusions; *la virtú,*[16] nothing more. We are entangled. The ties uniting us to others are false ones. There is no regime which, by itself, would suffice to disentangle them, but perhaps the men who come after us, all men together, will have the power and the patience to take up this work where we left it.

The directions of our thinking separated us from one another a little more each day. His grief and voluntary seclusion made any reconciliation more difficult. In 1955 we all but lost each other through abstractions. He wrote a book on dialectic, where he strongly took me to task. Simone de Beauvoir replied to him in *Les Temps modernes* in terms no less strong. This was the first and last time that we fought in writing. By publishing our dissensions, we almost made them irremediable. But, on the contrary, at just the moment when our friendship seemed dead, it imperceptibly began to flower once more. Undoubtedly, he had taken too many pains to avoid violence. He needed some of it to liquidate his remaining grudges, to tell me once and for all what was in his heart. In short, the matter ended there, and we saw each other again soon afterwards.

This was in Venice, in the first months of 1956. La Société Européenne de Culture had organized a meeting there of writers from the East and West. I was present. As I sat down, I leaned over and read Merleau-Ponty's name on the place-card. They thought we would be pleased to be seated next to one another. The discussion began but I was only half-listening. I was waiting for Merleau, not without dread. He came in, late as usual. Someone was speaking, he came in behind me, on tiptoe, lightly touched my shoulder and when I turned around, he smiled at me. The talks continued for several days. We didn't entirely agree, he and I, except to both be irritated when an Italian spoke who was too eloquent, or an Englishman who was too naive, both of whom had as their mission to make the whole project fail. But in the presence of many diverse men, some older, others younger than ourselves, from the four corners of Europe, we two felt united by one culture, and one experience which was only valid for us. We spent several evenings together, with a certain awkwardness, never alone. It was better that way. Our friends who were present ensured us against ourselves, against the temptation to reestablish our intimacy prematurely. As a consequence of this security, we only spoke to one another. Each of us were without any illusions about the significance of the meetings, but we each still hoped—he because he was a *lieur;* I, to "favor" the left—that they would resume the following year. When it came time to edit the final minutes, we discovered that we were of the same opinion. It was nothing, yet it proved that a common labor could reunite us.

We met again in Paris, in Rome and again in Paris. Alone: this was the second step. The awkwardness remained, then seemed to disappear. Another emotion was born, tenderness. This gentle funereal affection brings exhausted friends together again, friends so torn by strife that they have nothing left in common but their quarrel, and even that had ceased, one fine day, for lack of an object. The object had been the review. It had united, then divided us. Now it didn't even divide us any more. Our precautions had just missed estranging us. Forewarned, we took care never to spare each other again. Too late. Whatever we might do, each of us now only committed himself. When we took our bearings, I felt rather as though we had come to the point of exchanging family gossip: Aunt Marie is going to have an operation, nephew Charles has received his *bachot* . . . and that we were seated side by side on a park bench, with rugs over our knees, tracing figures in the dust with the tips of our canes. What was missing? It was not affection or esteem, but the undertaking. Buried, having been unable to separate us, our past activity took its revenge by making us pensioners of friendship.

We had to wait for the third step without forcing things. I waited, sure that we would find our friendship again. We were agreed in condemning the Algerian war unreservedly. He had returned his red ribbon [of the *Légion d'Honneur*] to Guy Mollet. Each of us were opposed to the rough draft of dictatorship which was Gaullism. We may not have shared the same point of view as to the means of fighting it. That would come. When fascism returns, it finds its old friends again. I saw Merleau again in March of that same year. I gave a lecture at the École Normale and he came. This touched me. For years it had always been me who urged that we get together, who suggested our meetings. Now, for the first time, he went out of his way spontaneously. Not in order to hear me elaborate ideas which he knew by heart, but to see me. At the end of the lecture, we gathered with Hyppolite and Canguilhem. This was a happy moment for me. But later I learned that Merleau still felt an awkwardness which persisted between us. There wasn't the shadow of it on my part, but unfortunately I was groggy with a case of grippe. When we parted he hadn't said a word about feeling disappointed, but for a split second, it crossed my mind that his face had saddened. And then I forgot about it. "Everything is just as it was," I told myself. "Everything will begin anew." A few days later I learned of his death. Our friendship had ended upon this final misunderstanding. Alive we would have dissipated it, starting with my return. Maybe. Absent, we shall always be for one another what we have always been. Strangers.

There is no doubt about it. His readers may know him. He "met them in his works." Each time I become his reader, I shall get to know him—and myself—better. One hundred fifty pages of his future book are saved from oblivion, and then there is also "Eye and Mind," which says it all, providing one can decipher it. For all of us, we who shall "institute" this system of thought in tatters, it will remain one of the prisms of our "intersubjectivity." At this moment, when M. Papon, the Chief of Police, sums up public opinion by declaring that nothing surprises him, Merleau provides the antidote—being surprised by everything. He is a child scandalized by our futile grown-up certitudes, who asks shocking questions which the adults never answer. Why do we live? Why do we die? Nothing seems natural to him—neither that there should be a history or a nature. He does not understand how it can happen that necessity turns into contingency and that all contingency terminates in necessity. He says this, and we, in reading him, are sucked into this spiral from which we shall never again escape. But he is not interrogating us. He is too afraid that we will hang on to dogmatisms which reassure us. He will be this interrogation of himself because the "writer has chosen insecurity": our fundamental situation as well as the difficult attitude which unveils this situation to us. It is not fitting that we ask him the answers. What he teaches us is the method of a preliminary inquiry. He recalls, after Plato, that the philosopher is he who is never astonished, but more rigorous than his Greek master, he adds that the philosophic attitude disappears as soon as astonishment ceases. The inverse of all those who predicate the "becoming-world" of philosophy, he replies that man, even were he to be one day happy, free and transparent to his fellow man, would be astonished by his suspect happiness inasmuch as we are engaged for the present, in creating our own happiness. If he hadn't felt that this word had been debased by overuse, I would freely say that he was able to discover the internal dialectic of the questioner and the questioned, and that he applied it to the fundamental question which, for all our pretense of answers, we avoid. To follow him we must renounce these two contradictory securities between which we incessantly oscillate. For we generally reassure ourselves through the use of two opposing but parallel universal concepts, each of which we take for objects. The first tells each of us that he is a man among men, and the second that he is *other* among others. But the latter is worthless since man makes himself unceasingly, but can never quite think himself. And the former deceives us since we are precisely alike in that each differs from all. Leaping from one of these ideas to the other, like monkeys from branch to branch, we avoid singularity, which is not so much a fact as a perpetual postulation. Severing our ties with our contemporaries, the bourgeoisie imprisons us within the cocoon of private life and defines us, with snips of the scissors, as *individuals,* which means, as molecules without history who drag themselves from one instant to the next. In Merleau, we discover ourselves through the contingency of our anchorage in nature and history, that is, through the temporal adventure which we are in the womb of the human adventure. Thus history makes us universal in the exact measure which we make it particular. This is the important gift which Merleau offers us, through his desperate struggle to keep digging in the same place. Setting out from the well-known universality of the singular, he arrives at the singularity of the universal. It is he who unearthed the capital contradiction: Every history is all history, when *l'homme-éclair* is kindled, all is said. Every life, every moment, every era—contingent miracles or contingent failures—are *incarnations.* The word becomes flesh, the universal is only established by the living singularity which deforms it by singularizing it. Do not read this simply as a new chopped-up form of "tragic consciousness." It is just the opposite. Hegel is describing the tragic opposition of two abstract notions, those same ones which I have said were the poles of our security. But for Merleau, universality is never universal, except in high-altitude thinking. It is born along with the flesh, flesh of our flesh. It retains in its most subtle degree our singularity. Such is the warning that anthropology—psychoanalysis or Marxism—should never forget; nor, as do the Freudians too often, that each man is everyman, and that in all men, we must take into account the *flash of light,* the singular universalization of universality. Nor, should we forget, as novice dialecticians, that the Soviet Union is not the simple beginning of universal revolution, but its incarnation as well, and that 1917 gives future socialism its indelible characteristics. This problem is a difficult one. Neither ordinary anthropology nor historical materialism will deliver us from it. Merleau didn't pretend to supply the solutions—quite the contrary. Had he lived, he would have buried himself, always turning, always deeper, until he had gone to the root of the givens of the question, as we can see from what he says of primordial historicity in "Eye and Mind." He hadn't come to the end of his philosophy, or at least, he hadn't the time to express it completely. Is this a failure? No, it is simply a continuation of the contingency of birth by the contingency of death. Singularized by this double absurdity, and meditating upon singularity from the beginning of his thought until his death, this life assumes an inimitable "style," and justifies the monitions of the work. As for the latter, which is inseparable from his life, a flash of light between two risks, illuminating the middle of our night, we could apply to him word for word the statement which he wrote at the beginning of this year [1961]:

> If we cannot establish a painting, nor even elsewhere, a hierarchy, nor even speak of progress, it is not some sort of destiny which keeps us back. It is rather that, in one sense the first painting went straight to the heart of the future. If no painting completes painting, if no work of art completes itself absolutely, each creation changes, alters, enlightens, deepens, confirms, exalts, recreates or creates all the others in advance. If creations are not previous knowledge, it is not only that they pass away like everything else, but also that they have almost their whole life ahead of them.

Question without an answer, *virtú* without illusion, the creation enters universal culture in the singular, but lodges there as a universal in the singularity of history. Changing, as Hegel has said, the contingent into the necessary and the necessary into the contingent, it has as its function to incarnate the problem of incarnation. For you, the rendezvous is in his work.

But I had other rendezvous with him, and I don't want to lie about our relationship, nor end on a note of lofty optimism. I still see his last melancholy expression—as we parted, at the rue Claude Bernard—disappointed, suddenly closed. He remains inside me, a painful sore, infected by sorrow, remorse, and some bitterness. Changed from within, our friendship is there summed up forever. I neither accord any privilege to its last moments, nor do I believe that these moments contain the truth about a lifetime. Yet in that life, everything had been gathered up: all the silences with which, starting in 1950, he opposed me, are frozen in that silent expression, and reciprocally. I still feel to this day the eternity of his absence as a deliberate mutism. It is clear to me that our final misunderstanding—which would have been nothing, had I seen him alive again—was made of the same fabric as all the others. It compromised nothing, revealing our mutual affection, our common desire not to spoil anything between us, but it also showed our lives were out-of-phase, causing our initiatives to be out-of-step; and then joined later by adversity, which suspended our dealings without violence, but forever. Death is an incarnation like birth. His death was nonmeaning, full of a meaning which remained obscure, but fulfilled in all that concerned us, the contingency and necessity of a friendship without joy. Nevertheless, there had been something for which to strive. With our good qualities and our failings, the public violence of the one and the secret outrage of the other, we weren't so badly suited after all. And what did we do with it? Nothing, except avoid total estrangement. Each of you may blame who he will. In any case, we weren't really very guilty, so little, in fact, that sometimes all I can see in our adventure was its necessity. That is the way men live in our time. That is the way they love. Badly. This is true, but it is also true that it was us, we two, who loved each other badly. There is nothing to be concluded from this except that this long friendship, neither done nor undone, obliterated when it was about to be reborn, or broken, remains inside me, an ever-open wound.

Notes

1. I don't know whether he regretted, in 1939, when he came into contact with what his chiefs referred to curiously as "the men," that he hadn't enlisted as a simple soldier. But I know that when I saw my officiers, those incompetents, I regretted for my part, my prewar anarchy. Since we had to fight, we were wrong to have left leadership in the hands of these conceited imbeciles. In any case, we know that Merleau remained an officier after the brief period of Resistance, which accounts for some of the difficulties between us.

2. Not as I did, in 1942, by the eidetic imagery of bad faith, but by the empirical study of our historical fidelities, and of the inhuman forces which pervert them.

3. Maurice Merleau-Ponty, "La guerre a eu lieu," in *Les Temps modernes* (October 1945).

4. Ibid.

5. Ibid.

6. *Le Tiers Monde:* literally "the Third World," designating the politically nonaligned, underdeveloped countries.—Trans.

7. In 1945 he didn't declare himself: he found the word too ambitious to be applied to the modest activity of *Les Temps modernes.*

8. *Lieur:* literally, *binder* or *trusser.*—TRANS.

9. *L'Affaire Henri Martin* (Paris, 1953). Commentary by Jean-Paul Sartre, with texts by Hervé Bazin, et al., a *cause célèbre* which involved the court martial of Henri Martin, a naval officier, during the war in Indochina.—TRANS.

10. Voluntarism: Sartre's term for the belief in the will.—TRANS.

11. It goes without saying that we could all define ourselves in the same way, save that our drifting varies, taking us sometimes in opposite directions.

12. "De Mauss à Lévi-Strauss."

13. *Jeu de furet:* Children's game in which the players, standing in a circle, hold a string around which a ring is passed from one to another. The game is played to a song which refers to the *furet,* the ferret, who runs around in a circle.—TRANS.

14. Maurice Merleau-Ponty, *Signes* (Paris, 1960), 270.

15. Ibid., 197. The problem there was one of characterizing the *present moment* of philosophical research. Merleau gave it these two characteristics: "existence and dialectic." But some months earlier, he had given a lecture at the Recontres Internationales de Genève on philosophy in our time, and it is remarkable that he never mentioned dialectic there to describe our problems. On the contrary, he avoided the word *contradiction* and wrote: "Incarnation and the other are the *labyrinth* of reflection and sensibility for our contemporaries."

16. *Virtú:* besides the concept of virtue, the Italian word also implies courage and manliness.—TRANS.

Bibliography: Works on the Debate between Sartre and Merleau-Ponty

Archard, David. *Marxism and Existentialism: The Political Philosophy of Sartre and Merleau-Ponty.* Belfast: Blackstaff Press, 1980.

Arntz, J. "L'athéisme au nom de l'homme? L'athéisme de Jean-Paul Sartre et de Maurice Merleau-Ponty." *Concilium* 16 (1966), 59–64.

Aron, Raymond. "Of Passions and Polemics." *Encounter* 34 (1970), 49–55.

Bannan, John F. "Merleau-Ponty and Sartre." In his *The Philosophy of Merleau-Ponty,* 229–243. New York: Harcourt, Brace and World, 1967.

Bello Reguera, Eduardo. "Estudio sobre la relación Sartre y Merleau-Ponty." *Arbor* 93 (1976), 7–25.

———. *De Sartre a Merleau-Ponty: Dialéctica de la libertad y el sentido.* Murcia: Publicaciones Universidad de Murcia, 1979.

Bonomi, Andrea. "La polemica contra Sartre." *Aut Aut* 66 (1961), 562–67.

Burnier, Michel-Antoine. *Les Existentialistes et la politique.* Paris: Gallimard, 1966. In English as *Choice of Action: The French Existentialists on the Political Front Line.* Translated by Bernard Murchland. New York: Random House, 1968.

Capizzi, Antonio. "Su una divergenza fra Sartre e Merleau-Ponty." *La Cultura* 8 (1968), 147–50.

De Waelhens, Alphonse. "Merleau-Ponty en Sartre." *Tijdschrift voor Filosofie* 12 (1950), 447–503.

———. "Note sur l'évolution de la notion d'inconscient chez Sartre et Merleau-Ponty." In *Les Philosophies de l'existence et les limites de l'homme,* 73–87. Edited by Jeanne Parain-Vial. Paris: J. Vrin, 1981.

Dufrenne, Mikel. "Les Aventures de la dialectique ou les avatars d'une amitié philosophique." In his *Jalons,* 169–73. The Hague: Martinus Nijhoff.

Elliot, Gregory. "Further Adventures of the Dialectic: Merleau-Ponty, Sartre, Althusser." *Philosophy* 21 (1987), supplement, 195–214.

Florival, Ghislaine. "Sartre et Merleau-Ponty." In *Philosophy and Culture.* Volume 4, 170–74. Edited by Venany Cauchy. Montreal: Editions Montmorency, 1988.

Flynn, Bernard. "The Question of Ontology: Sartre and Merleau-Ponty." In *The Horizons of the Flesh: Critical Perspectives on the Thought of Merleau-Ponty,* 114–26. Edited by Garth Gillian. Carbondale: Southern Illinois University Press, 1973.

Journal of the British Society for Phenomenology 15 (1984), 107–213. Special issue: *Sartre on Merleau-Ponty.*

Kaelin, Eugene. *An Existentialist Aesthetic: The Theories of Sartre and Merleau-Ponty.* Madison: University of Wisconsin Press, 1962.

Kwant, Rémy C. "Merleau-Ponty and Sartre." In his *The Phenomenological Philosophy of Merleau-Ponty,* 203–23. Pittsburgh: Duquesne University Press, 1963.

Lapointe, François H. "The Phenomenological Psychology of Sartre and Merleau-Ponty. A Bibliographical Essay." *Dialogos* 8 (1972), 161–82.

———. "The Phenomenology of Desire and Love in Sartre and Merleau-Ponty." *Journal of Phenomenological Psychology* 4 (1974), 445–59.

Lessing, Arthur. "Sartre and Merleau-Ponty." *Barat Review* 5 (1970), 55–59.

———. "Walking in the World: Sartre and Merleau-Ponty." *Human Inquiries* 11 (1971), 43–55.

Lingis, Alphonso. "Intuition of Freedom, Intuition of Law." *Journal of Philosophy* 79 (1982), 588–96.

Maier, Willi. *Das Problem der Leiblichkeit bei Sartre und Merleau-Ponty.* Tübingen: Niemeyer Verlag, 1964.

McLure, Roger. "Sartre and Merleau-Ponty." In *European Philosophy and the Human and Social Sciences,* 170–211. Edited by Simon Glynn. Hampshire: Gower, 1986.

Merleau-Ponty, Maurice. "Il n'y a pas de bonne façon d'être homme: La rencontre de Sartre et de Merleau-Ponty. Entretien entre C. Charbonnier et M. Merleau-Ponty, Mai 1959." *Esprit* 7–8 (1980), 39–41.

Patock, Jan. "Die Kritik des psychologischen Objektivismus und das Problem der phänomenologischen Psychologie bei Sartre und Merleau-Ponty." In *Proceedings of the 14th International Congress of Philosophy,* 175–84. Vienna: Herder, 1968.

Patri, Aimé. "Journal des idées: Sartre et Merleau-Ponty." *Preuves,* no. 135 (1962), 84–86.

Pingaud, Bernard. "Merleau-Ponty, Sartre et la littérature." *L'Arc* 46 (1971), 80–87.

Piorkowski, Henry. "The Path of Phenomenology: Husserl, Heidegger, Sartre, Merleau-Ponty." *Annual Report of the Duns Scotus Philosophical Association* 30 (1966), 177–221.

Podleck, A. *Der Leib als Weise des in-der-Welt-Seins.* Bonn: Bouvier, 1956.

Quilliot, R. "De *Nekrassov* à Merleau-Ponty: misères de la philosophie et du journalisme." *Revue Socialiste* 92 (1955), 551–55.

Rabil, Albert. "Merleau-Ponty and Sartrian Existentialism." In his *Merleau-Ponty: Existentialist of the Social World,* 116–40. New York: Columbia University Press, 1967.

Revue Internationale de Philosophie 39, nos. 152–153 (1985). Special issue: *Sartre: Avec un inédit sur Merleau-Ponty.*

Roman, Joël. "Une amitié existentialiste. Sartre et Merleau-Ponty." *Revue Internationale de Philosophie* 39 (1985), 30–55.

Ross, Howard. "Merleau-Ponty and Jean-Paul Sartre on the Nature of Consciousness." *Cogito* (Philippines) 3 (1985), 115–21.

Schmidt, James. "Lordship and Bondage in Merleau-Ponty and Sartre." *Political Theory* 7 (1979), 201–27.

Senofore, Ciro. *Sartre e Merleau-Ponty.* Napoli: Libreria Scientifica Editrice, 1972.

Sorel, Jean-Jacques. "Merleau-Ponty contre Sartre." *France Observateur* 6, no. 263 (1955), 16–18.

Truc, Gonzague. "J.-P. Sartre, M. Merleau-Ponty et l'athéisme radical." *Écrits de Paris* 131 (1955), 27–31.

Weightman, J. G. "The French Debate." *The New Statesman and Nation* 53, no. 1329 (1956), 245–46.

Whitford, Margaret. *Merleau-Ponty's Critique of Sartre's Philosophy.* Lexington: French Forum Publishers, 1982.

Notes on Contributors

Leo Rauch was the author of *The Political Animal: Studies in Political Theory from Machiavelli to Marx* (1981), *Hegel and the Human Spirit* (1983), as well as numerous translations, articles, and monographs. A native of Berlin, Rauch taught at New York University, the University of Texas at Austin, Ohio State University, and Babson College, among other institutions. He was also an accomplished musician and painter. Leo Rauch passed away in August 1997.

John M. Moreland has taught and lectured in philosophy, in the areas of epistemology, philosophy of science, mathematical logic, and probability theory, as well as in management science and marketing at a variety of colleges and universities in the United States, including Pitzer College, University of California, Irvine (1971–72), California State University at Sonoma (1972–73), Augusta College (1973–78), University of San Diego (1986–87), and Oregon Graduate Institute (1993–94). His articles and reviews on French phenomenology, the riddle of induction, and epistemology have appeared in *Philosophy of Science* and *Philosophy Today,* while his articles in computer science and management have appeared in such journals as *Computer Graphics World, Computer Design,* and *Computer-Aided Engineering.* Dr. Moreland left teaching in 1978 for a position in the computer graphics industry, where he has served in various senior management positions. He continues to lecture on management and on selected philosophical topics as his other duties permit.

Before his death, **Colin Smith** was reader in French at University College, London. Later he became professor of French at Reading University. He is best known for his now standard translation of Merleau-Ponty's *Phenomenology of Perception* (1962). He is the author of *Contemporary French Philosophy* (1964).

James F. Sheridan is professor emeritus of philosophy at Allegheny College in Meadville, Pennsylvania. His books are *Sartre: The Radical Conversion* (1969), *Once More—From the Middle* (1972), *Psyche-Lectures on Philosophy and Psychology* (1979), and *Mystery Delight—A Philosophy of Nature* (1981).

Margaret Whitford is professor of modern French thought at Queen Mary and Westfield College at the University of London. She is the author of *Merleau-Ponty's*

Critique of Sartre's Philosophy (1982) and *Luce Irigaray: Philosophy of the Feminine* (1991). She is the co-editor of *The Irigaray Reader: Feminist Perspectives in Philosophy* (1988), *Engaging with Irigaray: Feminist Philosophy and Modern European Thought* (1994), and *Knowing the Difference: Feminist Perspectives in Epistemology* (1994).

C. M. T. Hanly is professor emeritus of philosophy at the University of Toronto. He is a training and supervising analyst in the Toronto Institute of Psychoanalysis and is in full-time private psychoanalytic practice. He is currently vice-president of the International Psychoanalytic Association. He is the author of The *Problem of Truth in Applied Psychoanalysis, Existentialism and Psychoanalysis* (1992) and other books as well as articles on theoretical, clinical, and applied psychoanalysis in the major English-language psychoanalytic journals.

Before his retirement **François H. Lapointe** was professor of psychology and philosophy. He has published many works on Sartre, Merleau-Ponty, and French existentialism. He is the author of, among other titles, *Jean-Paul Sartre and His Critics: An International Bibliography* (1975, 1981), *Maurice Merleau-Ponty and His Critics: An International Bibliography* (1976), *Gabriel Marcel and His Critics: An International Bibliography* (1977), *Claude Levi-Strauss and His Critics: An International Bibliography* (1977), and *Edmund Husserl and His Critics: An International Bibliography* (1980).

Monika Langer is associate professor of philosophy at the University of Victoria in British Columbia. She has taught at the University of Toronto, Yale University, the University of Alberta, and Dalhousie University. Her principal areas of interest include continental philosophy, feminist philosophy, social-political philosophy, and philosophy in literature. She is the author of *Merleau-Ponty's Phenomenology of Perception: A Guide and Commentary* (1989). Her articles have appeared in such journals as *Philosophy Today, Canadian Journal of Political and Social Theory, Teaching Philosophy, Thesis Eleven, The Trumpeter,* and in the Library of the Living Philosophers volume *The Philosophy of Jean-Paul Sartre.* She is a co-editor of *The New Reality: The Politics of Restraint in British Columbia* (1984).

Martin C. Dillon is Distinguished Teaching Professor of Philosophy at Binghamton University. His publications include *Merleau-Ponty's Ontology* (1988, 1997), *Merleau-Ponty Vivant* (1991), *Semiological Reductionism: A Critique of the Deconstructivist Movement in Postmodern Thought* (1995), *Écart & Différance: Merleau-Ponty and Derrida on Seeing and Writing* (1997), and over fifty journal articles, many of which are devoted to Merleau-Ponty scholarship. Dillon is now completing work on two books, *Art, Truth, and Illusion: Nietzsche's Ontology* and *Beyond Romance: The Philosophy of Sexlove.*

Glen A. Mazis is associate professor of philosophy and humanities at Penn State Harrisburg in the interdisciplinary School of Humanities. He has published numerous essays in philosophical journals, such as *The British Journal of Phenomenology, Soundings, Philosophy Today,* and *The Semiotic Web,* and has contributed essays to many anthologies, especially on the work of Merleau-Ponty. He is author of *Emotion and Embodiment: Fragile Ontology* (1993), a phenomenology of the emotions, and of *The Trickster, Magician, and Grieving Man: Reconnecting Men with Earth* (1994), a critique of the tradition of heroic masculinity. Professor Mazis is currently working on another book entitled *Earthbodies: Rediscovering our Planetary Senses.*

Joseph S. Catalano is professor emeritus at Kean College of New Jersey. He has published many works on French existentialism. He is the author of *A Commentary on Jean-Paul Sartre's "Being and Nothingness"* (1974, 1980), *A Commentary on Jean-Paul Sartre's Critique of Dialectical Reason* (1986), *Good Faith and Other Essays* (1996), *Thinking Matter* (forthcoming 1998), and *The Anthropocentric Universe* (forthcoming 1998).

John J. Compton is professor of philosophy at Vanderbilt University. He has published numerous articles on phenomenology, philosophy of science, metaphysics, philosophy of nature, and philosophy of mind, including many on Sartre and Merleau-Ponty.

Ronald L. Hall is professor of philosophy and religious studies at Francis Marion University, where he has taught since 1973. He is the author of *Word and Spirit: A Kierkegaardian Critique of the Modern Age* (1993).

Jon Stewart is associate professor at the Søren Kierkegaard Research Centre at the University of Copenhagen, Denmark. He has held posts at the Westfälische Wilhelms-Universität in Münster, the Université Libre in Brussels, and the Humboldt-Universität in Berlin. He has done work in the areas of German Idealism, French phenomenology and existentialism, and Kierkegaard studies. He is the editor of *The Hegel Myths and Legends* (1996), *The Phenomenology of Spirit Reader: Critical and Interpretive Essays* (1998), and the co-editor of *Kierkegaard Revisited* (1997).

Before his retirement in 1982, **Graham Daniels** was lecturer in the Department of French Studies at Manchester University. He is the author of a number of articles and reviews on various aspects of modern French literature.

Ronald Aronson is professor in the Interdisciplinary Studies Progam at Wayne State University. He is the author of several works on Sartre and most recently *After Marxism* (1995). He is co-editor of the journal *Sartre Studies International.*

Thomas R. Flynn is Samuel Candler Dobbs Professor of Philosophy at Emory University. He is the author of *Sartre, Foucault and Historical Reason,* vol. 1, *Toward an Existentialist Theory of History* (1997) and *Sartre and Marxist Existentialism: The Test Case of Collective Responsibility* (1984) as well as co-editor of *Dialectic and Narrative* (1993).

Mikel Dufrenne was professor of philosophy at the University of Poitiers and later at the University of Paris, Nanterre. For many years he edited the journal

Revue d'Esthétique. He was the author of numerous works including *Karls Jaspers et la philosophie de l'existence* (1947), *La personnalité de base: un concept sociologique* (1953), *Phénoménologie de l'expérience esthétique* (1953), translated as *The Phenomenology of Aesthetic Experience* (1973), *La notion d'a priori* (1959), *Le poetique* (1963), *Jalons* (1966), *Esthétique et philosophie* (1967), and *Art et politique* (1974). Mikel Dufrenne passed away in 1995.

Marjorie Grene is professor emeritus of philosophy at the University of California, Davis, and adjunct professor of philosophy and honorary distinguished professor at Virginia Tech. She has published in a number of areas in the history of philosophy. These works include *A Portrait of Aristotle* (1963, 1998), *Sartre* (1973), and *Descartes* (1985, 1998). Her most recent book is *A Philosophical Testament* (1995).

John O'Neill is distinguished research professor of sociology at York University, Toronto, an affiliate of the Centre for Comparative Literature at the University of Toronto, and a fellow of the Royal Society of Canada. He was senior scholar at the Laidlaw Foundation in 1993–94, working on the Children at Risk Program. He is the author of *Sociology as Skin Trade* (1972), *Making Sense Together* (1974), *Essaying Montaigne* (1982), and *Five Bodies: The Human Shape of Modern Society* (1985). His more recent books are *The Communicative Body: Studies in Communicative Philosophy, Politics and Psychology* (1989), *Plato's Cave: Desire, Power and the Specular Functions of the Media* (1991), *The Missing Child in Liberal Theory* (1994), and *The Poverty of Postmodernism* (1995). He is co-editor of the international quarterly, *Philosophy of the Social Sciences.* Currently he is working on the political economy of child suffering, welfare state theory, and civic practice.